Multimedia: Making It Work

Seventh Edition

Tay Vaughan

New York Chicago San Francisco Lisbon London
Madrid Mexico City Milan New Delhi San Juan
Seoul Singapore Sydney Toronto

Sponsoring Editor
Tim Green

Project Editor
Jody McKenzie

Acquisitions Coordinator
Jennifer Housh

Technical Editor
Joseph Silverthorn

Copy Editor
Julie Smith

Proofreader
Stefany Otis

Indexer
Jack Lewis

Production Supervisor
Jim Kussow

Composition
Tolman Creek Design

Illustration
Tolman Creek Design

Art Director, Cover
Jeff Weeks

Cover Designer
Jeff Weeks

The **McGraw·Hill** Companies

McGraw-Hill books are available at special quantity discounts to use as premiums and sales promotions or for use in corporate training programs. For more information, please write to the Director of Special Sales, Professional Publishing, McGraw-Hill, Two Penn Plaza, New York, NY 10121-2298. Or contact your local bookstore.

Multimedia: Making It Work, Seventh Edition

1234567890 QPD QPD 019876

ISBN-13: 978-0-07-226451-7
ISBN-10:   0-07-226451-9

International Edition ISBN-13: 978-0-07-128682-4, ISBN-10: 0-07-128682-9
Copyright © 2008. Exclusive rights by The McGraw-Hill Companies, Inc., for manufacture and export. This book cannot be reexported from the country to which it is consigned by McGraw-Hill. The International Edition is not available in North America.

Dedication

For Elizabeth Hunter Vaughan and Gerta Karola Streuli

About the Author

Tay Vaughan is a widely known multimedia authority. He has developed and produced award-winning projects for clients such as Apple, Microsoft, Lotus, Novell, and Sun. He is president of Timestream®, a multiformat CD-ROM and Internet design and publishing company.

About the Technical Editor

Joseph Silverthorn B.A., M.F.A. is a U.C.L.A. graduate. He is currently a tenured professor at Olympic College in Bremerton, Washington, and creator of the Integrated Multimedia Program there. He and his wife own Thistleberry Productions, Inc., a marketing and production company. He and his crews, while working for Walt Disney Studios (KCAL-TV9), have won several Emmys and the Edgar R. Murrow Award, among other awards.

Contents

Acknowledgments

This seventh edition of *Multimedia: Making It Work* includes the cumulated input and advice of many colleagues and friends over a 15-year period. Each time I revise and update this book, I am pleased to see that the acknowledgments section grows. Indeed, it is difficult to delete people from this (huge) list because, like the stones of a medieval castle still occupied, new and revised material relies upon the older foundation. I will continue accumulating the names of the good people who have helped me build this edifice and list them here, at least until my publisher cries "Enough!" and provides substantial reason to press the DELETE key.

At McGraw-Hill, Tim Green, Jennifer Housh, Jody McKenzie, and Julie Smith were instrumental in producing this seventh edition. Jimmie Young from Tolman Creek Design did the layout. As technical editor for the seventh edition, Joe Silverthorn updated references and helped to bring current the detailed descriptions of the many elements of multimedia that are discussed in the book.

In past editions, Brad Borch, Chris Johnson, Jennie Yates, John and Kathryn Ross, Madhu Prasher, Frank Zurbano, Judith Brown, Athena Honore, Roger Stewart, Alissa Larson, Cindy Wathen, Eileen Corcoran, Megg Bonar, Robin Small, Lyssa Wald, Scott Rogers, Stephane Thomas, Bob Myren, Heidi Poulin, Mark Karmendy, Joanne Cuthbertson, Bill Pollock, Jeff Pepper, Kathy Hashimoto, Marla Shelasky, Linda Medoff, Valerie Robbins, Cindy Brown, Larry Levitsky, Frances Stack, Jill Pisoni, Carol Henry, and Linda Beatty went out of their way to keep me on track. Chip Harris, Donna Booher, Takis Metaxas, Dan Hilgert, Helayne Waldman, Hank Duderstadt, Dina Medina, Joyce Edwards, Theo Posselt, Ann Stewart, Graham Arlen, Kathy Gardner, Steve Goeckler, Steve Peha, Christine Perey, Pam Sansbury, Terry Schussler, Alden Trull, Eric Butler, and Michael Allen have contributed to making the work more complete since its first edition.

Since the fifth edition, peer reviewers Sandi Watkins, Dana Bass, David Williams, Joseph Parente, Elaine Winston, Wes Baker, Celina Byers, Nancy Doubleday, Tom Duff, Chris Hand, Scott Herd, Kenneth Hoffman, Sherry Hutson, Judith Junger, Ari Kissiloff, Peter Korovessis, Sallie Kravetz, Jeff Kushner, Theresa McHugh, Ken Messersmith, Marianne Nilsson, Lyn Pemberton, Samuel Shiffman, and Dennis Woytek have added significant structure to the book's foundation.

I would also like to acknowledge many friends in the computer and publishing industries who continue to make this book possible. They send me quotes and multimedia anecdotes to enliven the book; many arranged for me to review and test software and hardware; many have been there when I needed them. Some from editions past have changed companies or left the industry; my friend Dana Atchley, the well-known digital storyteller, has died. Whole companies in the list below have died, too, since the first edition of this book, but their discorporation is mourned differently from the heartfelt loss of the real people and real creators who launched the information age. I would like to thank them all for the time and courtesy they have afforded me on this long-legged project:

Grace Abbett, Adobe Systems
Jennifer Ackman, Edelman Worldwide
Eric Alderman, HyperMedia Group
Heather Alexander, Waggener/Edstrom
Laura Ames, Elgin/Syferd PR
Kurt Andersen, Andersen Design
Ines Anderson, Claris
Travis Anton, BoxTop Software
David Antoniuk, Live Oak Multimedia
Yasemin Argun, Corel Systems
Cornelia Atchley, Comprehensive Technologies
Dana Atchley, Network Productions
Pamela Atkinson, Pioneer Software
Paul Babb, Maxon Computer

Ann Bagley, Asymetrix
Patricia Baird, Hypermedia Journal
Gary Baker, Technology Solutions
Richard Bangs, Mountain Travel-Sobek
Sean Barger, Equilibrium
Jon Barrett, Dycam
Kathryn Barrett, O'Reilly
Heinz Bartesch, The Search Firm
Bob Bauld, Bob Bauld Productions
Thomas Beinar, Add-On America/Rohm
Bob Bell, SFSU Multimedia Studies Program
George Bell, Ocron
Mike Bellefeuille, Corel Systems
Andrew Bergstein, Altec Lansing

Kathy Berlan, Borland International
Camarero Bernard, mFactory
Brian Berson, Diamondsoft
Bren Besser, Unlimited Access
Time Bigoness, Equilibrium
Ken Birge, Weber Shandwick
Nancy Blachman, Variable Symbols
Dana Blankenhorn, Have Modem Will Travel
Brian Blum, The Software Toolworks
Sharon Bodenschatz, International Typeface
Michele Boeding, ICOM Simulations
Donna Booher, Timestream
Gail Bower, TMS
Kellie Bowman, Adobe
Susan Boyer, Blue Sky Software
Deborah Brown, Technology Solutions
Eric Brown, NewMedia Magazine
Russell Brown, Adobe Systems
Tiffany Brown, Network Associates
Stephanie Bryan, SuperMac
Ann Marie Buddrus, Digital Media Design
David Bunnell, NewMedia Magazine
Jeff Burger, Creative Technologies
Steven Burger, Ricoh
Bridget Burke, Gryphon Software
Dominique Busso, OpenMind
Ben Calica, Tools for the Mind
Doug Campbell, Spinnaker Software
Teri Campbell, MetaCreations
Doug Camplejohn, Apple Computer
Norman Cardella, Best-Seller
Tim Carrigan, Multimedia Magazine
Mike Childs, Global Mapper Software
Herman Chin, Computer Associates International
Curtis Christiansen, Deneba Software
Jane Chuey, Macromedia
Angie Ciarloni, Hayes
Kevin Clark, Strata
Cathy Clarke, DXM Productions
Regina Coffman, Smith Micro
Frank Colin, Equilibrium
David Collier, decode communications
David Conti, AimTech
Freda Cook, Aldus
Renee Cooper, Miramar Systems
Wendy Cornish, Vividus
Patrick Crisp, Caere
Michelle Cunningham, Symantec
Lee Curtis, CE Software
Eric Dahlinger, Newer Technology
Kirsten Davidson, Autodesk
John deLorimier, Kallisto Productions
John Derryberry, A&R Partners/Adobe
Jeff Dewey, Luminaria
Jennifer Doettling, Delta Point
Sarah Duckett, Sonic Solutions

Hank Duderstadt, Timestream
Mike Duffy, The Software Toolworks
Eileen Ebner, McLean Public Relations
Dawn Echols, Oracle
Dorothy Eckel, Specular International
Joyce Edwards, Timestream
Kevin Edwards, c|net
Mark Edwards, Independent Multimedia Developer
Dan Elenbaas, Amaze!
Ellen Elias, O'Reilly & Associates
Shelly Ellison, Tektronix
Heidi Elmer, Sonic Foundry
Kathy Englar, RayDream
Jonathan Epstein, MPC World
Jeff Essex, Audio Synchrosy
Sharron Evans, Graphic Directions
Kiko Fagan, Attorney at Law
Joe Fantuzzi, Macromedia
Lee Feldman, Voxware
Laura Finkelman, S & S Communications
Holly Fisher, MetaTools
Sean Flaherty, Nemetschek/VectorWorks
Terry Fleming, Timeworks
Patrick Ford, Microsoft
Marty Fortier, Prosonus
Robin Galipeau, Mutual/Hadwen Imaging
Kathy Gardner, Gardner Associates
Peter Gariepy, Zedcor
Bill Gates, Microsoft
Petra Gerwin, Mathematica
John Geyer, Terran Interactive
Jonathan Gibson, Form and Function
Karen Giles, Borland
Amanda Goodenough, AmandaStories
Danny Goodman, Concentrics Technology
Howard Gordon, Xing Technology
Jessica Gould, Corel
Jonathan Graham, Iomega
Catherine Greene, LightSource
Fred Greguras, Fenwick & West
Maralyn Guarino, Blue Sky Software
Cari Gushiken, Copithorne & Bellows
Kim Haas, McLean Public Relations
Marc Hall, Deneba Software
Johan Hamberg, Timestream
Lynda Hardman, CWI - Netherlands
Tom Hargadon, Conference Communications
Chip Harris, InHouse Productions
Scott Harris, Chief Architect
Sue Hart, FileMaker
Trip Hawkins, 3DO/Electronic Arts
Randy Haykin, Apple Computer
Jodi Hazzan, SoftQuad
Ray Heizer, Heizer Software
Dave Heller, Salient Software
Josh Hendrix, CoSA

Maria Hermanussen, Gold Disk
Allan Hessenflow, HandMade Software
Lars Hidde, The HyperMedia Group
Erica Hill, Nuance
Dave Hobbs, LickThis
Petra Hodges, Mathematica
Kerry Hodgins, Corel
John Holder, John V. Holder Software
Elena Holland, Traveling Software
Mike Holm, Apple Computer
Robert Hone, Red Hill Studios
Kevin Howat, MacMillan Digital
Joy Hsu, Sonnet Technologies
Tom Hughes, PhotoDisc
Claudia Husemann, Cunningham Communications
Les Inanchy, Sony CD-ROM Division
Tom Inglesby, Manufacturing Systems
Carl Jaffe, Yale University School of Medicine
Farrah Jinha, Vertigo 3D
Cynthia Johnson, BoxTop Software
Scott Johnson, NTERGAID
JoAnn Johnston, Regis McKenna
Neele Johnston, Autodesk
Jedidah Karanja, Genealogy.com
Dave Kaufer, Waggener/Edstrom
David Kazanjian, AFTRA Actor
Jenna Keller, Alexander Communications
Helen Kendrick, Software Publishing
Benita Kenn, Creative Labs
Duncan Kennedy, Tribeworks
Trudy Kerr, Alexander Communications
Gary Kevorkian, ULead Systems
Deirdre Kidd, Nemetschek
David Kleinberg, NetObjects
Jeff Kleindinst, Turtle Beach Systems
Kevin Klingler, Sonic Desktop Software
Sharon Klocek, Visual In-Seitz
Christina Knighton, Play Incorporated
Lewis Kraus, InfoUse
Katrina Krebs, Micrografx
Kevin Krejci, Pop Rocket
Larry Kubo, Ocron
Jennifer Kuhl, Peppercom
Howard Kwak, Multimedia SourceBook
Irving Kwong, Waggener/Edstrom
Craig LaGrow, Morph's Outpost
Kimberly Larkin, Alexander Communications
Kevin LaRue, Allegiant Technologies
Mark Law, Extensis
Nicole Lazzaro, ONYX Productions
Alan Levine, Maricopa Community Colleges
Bob LeVitus, LeVitus Productions
Steven Levy, MacWorld
Kitten Linderman, LaserSoft Imaging
Leigh-Ann Lindsey, Mathematica
Rob Lippincott, Lotus

Mark Lissick, C-Star Technology
Jason Lockhart, G3 Systems
Elliot Luber, Technology Solutions
David Ludwig, Interactive Learning Designs
Kirk Lyford, Vivid Details
Jennifer Lyng, Aladdin Systems
John MacLeod, FastForward
Philip Malkin, Passport Designs
Kevin Mallon, FileMaker
Basil Maloney, Winalysis
Kathy Mandle, Adobe
Audrey Mann, Technology Solutions
Lisa Mann, O'Reilly
Brent Marcus, Bender/Helper Impact
Nicole Martin, Netopia/Farallon Division
Jim Matthews, Fetch Software
Michael Pilmer, Alien Skin
Robert May, Ikonic
Georgia McCabe, Applied Graphics Technologies
Rod McCall, Runtime Revolution
Russ McCann, Ares Software
Kevin McCarthy, Medius IV
Charles McConathy, MicroNet Technology
Carol McGarry, Schwartz Communications
Laurie McLean, McLean Public Relations
Amy McManus, Delta Point
Bert Medley, "The NBC Today Show"
Art Metz, Metz
Steve Michel, Author
Aline Mikaelian, Screenplay Systems
Nancy Miller, Canto Software
Doug Millison, Morph's Outpost
Karen Milne, Insignia Solutions
Brian Molyneaux, Heizer Software
Molly Morelock, Macromedia
Jeff Morgan, Radmedia
Rob Morris, VGraph
Glenn Morrisey, Asymetrix
Terry Morse, Terry Morse Software
Brendan Mullin, Peppercom
Rachel Muñoz, Caere
Philip Murray, Knowledge Management Associates
Heather Nagey, Runtime
Chuck Nakell, Inspiration Software
Kee Nethery, Kagi Engineering
Chris Newell, Musitek
Mark Newman, Photographer
Wendy Woods Newman, Newsbytes
Terry Nizko, AimTech
Glenn Ochsenreiter, MPC Marketing Council
Maureen O'Conell, Apple Computer
Jim O'Gara, Altsys
Eric Olson, Virtus
Karen Oppenheim, Cunningham Communications
Kim Osborne, Symantec
Nicole DeMeo Overson, GoLive Systems

Andy Parng, PixoArts
David Pawlan, Timestream
Naomi Pearce, Barebones Software
Susan Pearson, Waggener/Edstrom
Lorena Peer, Chroma Graphics
Steve Peha, Music Technology Associates
Sylvester Pesek, Optical Media International
Christiane Petite, Symantec
Paul Phelan, INESC (Portugal)
Scott Pink, Bronson
Audrey Pobre, Quarterdeck
Dave Pola, Equilibrium
JB Popplewell, Alien Skin Software
Melissa Rabin, Miramar
Shirley Rafieetary, Medius IV
Tom Randolph, FM Towns/Fujitsu
Steven Rappaport, Interactive Records
Ronelle Reed, Switzer Communications
David Reid, Author
Diane Reynolds, Graphsoft
Laurie Robinson, Gold Disk
Chuck Rogers, MacSpeech
Connie Roloff, Software Products International
John Rootenberg, Paceworks
Amedeo Rosa, Alien Skin Software
Steve Rubenstein, San Francisco Chronicle
Jill Ryan, McLean Public Relations
Marie Salerno, AFTRA/SAG
John Sammis, DataDescription
Jay Sandom, Einstein & Sandom
Pam Sansbury, Disc Manufacturing
Richard Santalesa, R&D Technologies
Anne Sauer, Fast Electronic U.S.
Joe Scarano, DS Design
Sonya Schaefer, Adobe
Rochelle Schiffman, Electronics for Imaging
Rachel Schindler, Macromedia
Melissa Scott, Window Painters
Sandy Scott, Soft-Kat
Brigid Sealy, INESC (Portugal)
Karl Seppala, Gold Disk
Chip Shabazian, Ocron
Ashley Sharp, Virtus
Philip Shaw, CodeStyle
Elizabeth Siedow, Macromedia
Adam Silver, Videologic
Stephanie Simpson, Adaptec
Marlene Sinicki, Designer
Chris Smith, VideoLabs
Brian Snook, Visual In-Seitz
Kent Sokoloff, Timestream
Simone Souza, Roxio
David Spitzer, Hewlett-Packard
Chris Sprigman, King & Spalding
Domenic Stansberry, Author
Ann Stewart, Interactive Dimensions

Polina Sukonik, Xaos Tools
Lisa Sunaki, Autodesk
Lee Swearingen, DXM Productions
Joe Taglia, Insignia Solutions
Meredith Taitz, Bare Bones Software
Marty Taucher, Microsoft
Bill Tchakirides, U-Design Type Foundry
Toni Teator, NetObjects
Amy Tenderich, Norton-Lambert
Lori Ternacole, SoftQuad
Dave Terran, WordPerfect
Leo Thomas, Eastman Kodak
Terry Thompson, Timestream
Bill Thursby, Thursby Software Systems
Alexandrea Todd, McLean Public Relations
Kim Tompkins, Micrografx
Tom Toperczer, Imspace Systems
Cara Ucci, Autodesk
Ross Uchimura, GC3
Jane Van Saun, Scansoft
David Vasquez, SFSU Multimedia Studies Program
Sally von Bargen, 21st Century Media
Dan Wagner, Miramar Systems
Helayne Waldman, SFSU Multimedia Studies Program
James J. Waldron, Visage
Arnold Waldstein, Creative Labs
Keri Walker, Apple Computer
Brad Walter, Leister Productions
Jon Ward, Tribeworks
Stefan Wennik, Bitstream
Chris Wheeler, TechSmith
Tom White, Roland
John Wilczak, HSC Software
Darby Williams, Microsoft
Laura Williams, Waggener/Edstrom
Mark Williams, Microsoft
Shelly Williams, Prosonus
Hal Wine, Programmer
Sara Winge, O'Reilly & Associates
Warren Witt, Thursby Software Systems
Marcus Woehrmann, Handmade Software
Sandy Wong, Fenwick & West
Greg Wood, Corel
Chris Yalonis, Passport Designs
Alexandra Yessios, auto*des*sys
Karl-Heinz Zahorsky, LaserSoft Imaging
Barbara Zediker, Pioneer
Frank Zellis, KyZen

Introduction

Since the first edition of this book in 1992, it has been necessary to update its content every two years or so. In writing this seventh edition, however, it has become clear that changes in multimedia tools, technologies, and delivery platforms are occurring at an increasingly rapid pace. Indeed, the rate of change itself seems logarithmic as new ideas and new applications of multimedia are born, gain traction, and then bear yet newer ideas in often unpredictable and immediate follow-ons. Overnight, words like "podcast" and "mashup" enter the lexicon and explode through the Internet into common usage.

In a 2006 presentation, Lee Rainie, Director of the Pew Internet & American Life Project, described the transformation of media ecology by comparing the home media and communications tools of 1975 and 2006. We can but hope that smart programmers will soon reduce the complicated multimedia interfaces of everyday life to a simpler, easily learned human interface:

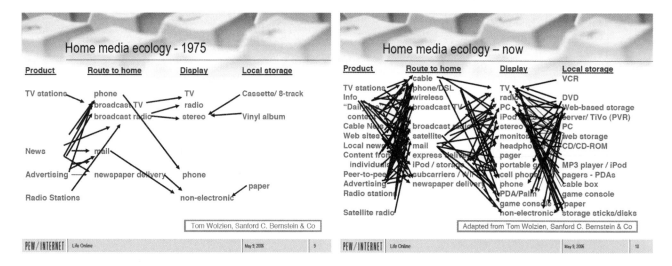

Happily for the longevity of this book, the fundamental concepts and techniques required to work with the elements of multimedia remain unchanged, and there are serious learning curves to climb before you can make your multimedia-capable computer stand up and dance!

This is a book about the basic parts of multimedia as much as about how to sew these parts together with current technology and tools. It is a book that shows you how to use text, images, sound, and video to deliver your messages and content in meaningful ways. It is about designing, organizing, and producing multimedia projects of all kinds and avoiding technical and legal pitfalls along the way. Above all, it is a practical guide to making multimedia, complete with keywords, quizzes, exercises, tips, pointers, and answers.

The first part deals with the basic elements of multimedia and the skills required to work with them. Hardware and software tools are described in detail. You will learn about the importance of text and how to make characters look pretty, about making graphic art on your computer and how to choose colors, and about how to digitize sound and video segments. You will learn about human interaction and how to design a user-friendly computer interface. Then you will be introduced to the step-by-step creative and organizing process that results in a finished multimedia project. You will even learn how to deliver your multimedia projects on the Web.

I have written this book for people who make or want to make multimedia, for people who gladly take up new challenges and are unafraid of intensely creative work. The words and ideas of this book are the harvest of many years in the computer industry and of hands-on experience deep in the factory where multimedia is being made. The book is intended to be, above all, useful.

For focus, I chose two well-known computer environments to discuss in detail throughout the book: Microsoft's Windows and Apple's Macintosh—the most widely used platforms for making and delivering multimedia. But multimedia is by no means limited to these platforms, and most of the ideas discussed in the book are translatable to other operating systems. Today, the fastest moving wavefront in multimedia may be seen on the Internet, so I have updated and enlarged the chapters about designing, creating, and delivering multimedia for the Web.

I have made a great effort to include in this book references to as much multimedia software and hardware as I could, trying not to miss any players. But because the industry is fast paced and rapidly evolving, and because, while writing this book, I have rediscovered the finite limits of my own time, I am sure some have fallen into the bit bucket anyway. Immutable physical laws have prevented me from including the fine details of 40 or 50 hardware and software manuals and technical resources into the pages allowed for this book. The distillation presented here should, however, point you toward further information and study. I have also made a great effort to double-check my words and statements for accuracy; if errors have slipped past, they are mine alone.

A decade ago, people's experience on the information highway was a smooth ride paved with behavioral etiquette and with many kindnesses evolved from properly socialized dot-EDU users. Commerce was prohibited. Discourse and idea exchange through e-mail and newsgroups was encouraged. Language shortcuts such as IMHO (In My Humble Opinion) and smiley faces were de jure. RTFM was reserved for only the most surly.

Who could have predicted the impact of commerce, when the dot-com top-level-domain was opened for business? Well, Adam Smith's free hand of capitalism is at work, straining First Amendment rights to free speech and inciting road rage on the information highway. Now you can buy a million e-mail addresses delivered to you on a CD-ROM in a plain manila envelope, and if only half a percent of recipients respond to your body part enhancement, vitamin, or mortgage rate spam, you can make a fortune. Not only are computer platforms and multimedia implements changing, so is our notion of etiquette. With the tools described in this book, you will be able to shape the very nature of information and how it is accessed and presented, and you will invent the future. Remember to be polite: some people suggest that if you go flying back through time and you see somebody else flying forward into the future, it's probably best to avoid eye contact.

Some years ago, after completing a book about HyperCard, I swore never to write another. Writing a book is much like childbirth, I believe. In the beginning, it gestates slowly, usually over a few months. Then it ramps up inexorably and quickly toward deadline, until all attention is focused upon the delivery itself, and the pain and workload are great. Editors cry, "Push." Afterwards, you remember it was rough, but memories of the pain itself become diffused, and one is only too easily persuaded to do it again. I am glad to share my multimedia experiences with you, and hope that in reading this book you will become better at what you do.

Tay Vaughan
Appleton, Maine
November 2006

Resources for Teachers

Resources for teachers are provided via an Online Learning Center. For access to the site, if you are an instructor who has adopted this textbook, please contact your McGraw-Hill sales representative. The Online Learning Center includes:

- Answer keys to the end-of-chapter Key Term Quiz and Multiple Choice Quiz in the textbook
- An Instructor's Manual that maps to the organization of the textbook
- PowerPoint slides on the lecture topics
- A test bank featuring questions written by experienced IT instructors

CHAPTER 1

What Is Multimedia?

In this chapter, you will learn how to:

- Define common multimedia terms such as multimedia, integration, interactive, HTML, and authoring

- Describe the two primary multimedia delivery media—CD-ROM and DVD versus the World Wide Web—and their primary differences

- Describe several different environments in which multimedia might be used, and several different aspects of multimedia that provide a benefit over other forms of information presentation

- Qualify various characteristics of multimedia: nonlinear versus linear content

- Cite the history of multimedia and note important projected changes in the future of multimedia

ULTIMEDIA is an eerie wail as two cat's eyes appear on a dark screen. It's the red rose that dissolves into a little girl's face when you press "Valentine's Day." It's a small window of video laid onto a map of India, showing an old man recalling his dusty journey to meet a rajah there. It's a catalog of hybrid cars with a guide to help you buy one. It's a real-time video conference with colleagues in Paris, London, and Hong Kong, using whiteboards, microphones, and question techniques (www.webtrain.com) on your office computer. At home, it's an algebra or geography lesson for a fifth-grader. At the arcade, it's goggle-faced kids flying fighter planes in sweaty, virtual reality. On a DVD, it's the interactive video sequence (or screen hot spots) that explain how the Harry Potter movie was made—all using your remote control.

Multimedia is any combination of text, art, sound, animation, and video delivered to you by computer or other electronic or digitally manipulated means. It is richly presented sensation. When you weave together the sensual elements of multimedia—dazzling pictures and animations, engaging sounds, compelling video clips, and raw textual information—you can electrify the thought and action centers of people's minds. When you give them interactive control of the process, they can be enchanted.

This book is about creating each of the elements of multimedia and about how you can weave them together for maximum effect. This book is for computer beginners and computer experts. It is for serious multimedia producers—and for their clients as well. It is for desktop publishers and video producers who may need a leg-up as they watch traditional methods for delivery of information and ideas evolve into new, technology-driven formats. This book is also for hobbyists, who want to make albums and family histories on the World Wide Web; for mainstream businesses, where word-processed documents and spreadsheets are illustrated with audio, video, and graphic animations; for public speakers, who use animation and sound on large monitors and auditorium projection systems to present ideas and information to an audience; for information managers, who organize and distribute digital images, sound, video, and text; and for educators and trainers, who design and present information for learning.

If you are new to multimedia and are facing a major investment in hardware, software, and the time you will need to learn each new tool, take a gradual approach to these challenges. Begin by studying each element of multimedia and learning one or more tools for creating and editing that element. Get to know how to use text and **fonts**, how to make and edit colorful graphic images and animate them into movies, and how to record and edit digital sound. Browse the computer trade periodicals that contain the most up-to-date information. Your skills will be most valuable if you develop a broad foundation of knowledge about each of the basic elements of multimedia.

Producing a multimedia project or a **web site** requires more than creative skill and high technology. You need organizing and business talent as well. For example, issues of ownership and copyright will be attached to some elements that you wish to use, such as text from books, scanned images from magazines, or audio and video clips. The use of these resources often requires permission, and even payment of a fee to the owner. Indeed, the management and production infrastructure of a multimedia project may be as intense and complicated as the technology and creative skills you bring to bear in rendering it. Keys to successful development of a multimedia project are management of digital tools and skill sets, teamwork, general project management, documenting and archiving the process, and delivering the completed product on time and within budget.

Definitions

Multimedia is, as described previously, a woven combination of **digitally manipulated** text, photographs, graphic art, sound, animation, and video elements. When you allow an end user—also known as the viewer of a multimedia project—to control what and when the elements are delivered, it is called **interactive multimedia**. When you provide a structure of linked elements through which the user can navigate, interactive multimedia becomes **hypermedia**.

Although the definition of multimedia is a simple one, making it work can be complicated. Not only do you need to understand how to make each multimedia element stand up and dance, but you also need to know how to use multimedia computer tools and technologies to weave them together. The people who weave multimedia into meaningful tapestries are called **multimedia developers**.

The software vehicle, the messages, and the content presented on a computer, television screen, PDA (personal digital assistant) or cell phone together constitute a **multimedia project**. If the project is to be shipped

> The implementation of multimedia capabilities in computers is just the latest episode in a long series: cave painting, hand-crafted manuscripts, the printing press, radio, and television... These advances reflect the innate desire of man to create outlets for creative expression, to use technology and imagination to gain empowerment and freedom for ideas.
>
> Glenn Ochsenreiter, Director, Multimedia PC Council

or sold to consumers or end users, typically in a box or sleeve or delivered on the Internet, with or without instructions, it is a **multimedia title**. Your project may also be a page or site on the World Wide Web, where you can weave the elements of multimedia into documents with **HTML** (Hypertext Markup Language) or **DHTML** (Dynamic Hypertext Markup Language) or **XML** (eXtensible Markup Language) and play rich media files created in such programs as Adobe's Flash, LiveMotion, or Apple's QuickTime by installing plug-ins into a **browser** application such as Internet Explorer or Firefox. Browsers are software programs or tools for viewing content on the Web. See Chapter 13 for more about plug-ins, multimedia, and the Web.

A multimedia project need not be interactive to be called multimedia: users can sit back and watch it just as they do a movie or the television. In such cases a project is **linear**, or starting at the beginning and running through to the end. When users are given navigational control and can wander through the content at will, multimedia becomes **nonlinear** and user interactive, and is a powerful personal gateway to information.

Determining how a user will interact with and navigate through the **content** of a project requires great attention to the message, the **scripting** or **storyboarding**, the artwork, and the programming. You can break an entire project with a badly designed interface. You can also lose the message in a project with inadequate or inaccurate content.

Multimedia elements are typically sewn together into a project using **authoring tools**. These software tools are designed to manage individual multimedia elements and provide user interaction. **Integrated multimedia** is the "weaving" part of the multimedia definition, where source documents such as montages, graphics, video cuts, and sounds merge into a final presentation. In addition to providing a method for users to interact with the project, most authoring tools also offer facilities for creating and editing text and images and controls for playing back separate audio and video files that have been created with editing tools designed for these media. The sum of what gets played back and how it is presented to the viewer on a monitor is the **graphical user interface**, or GUI (pronounced "gooey"). The GUI is more than just the actual graphics on the screen—it also often provides the rules or structure for the user's input. The hardware and software that govern the limits of what can happen here are the multimedia **platform** or **environment**.

CD-ROM, DVD, and the Multimedia Highway

Multimedia requires large amounts of digital memory when stored in an end user's library, or large amounts of **bandwidth** when distributed over wires, glass fiber, or airwaves on a network. The greater the bandwidth, the bigger the pipeline, so more content can be delivered to end users quickly.

CD-ROM, DVD, Flash Drives, and Multimedia

CD-ROM (compact disc read-only memory, see Chapter 18) discs can be mass-produced for pennies and can contain up to 80 minutes of full-screen video, images, or sound. The disc can also contain unique mixes of images, sounds, text, video, and animations controlled by an authoring system to provide unlimited user interaction.

Discs can be stamped out of polycarbonate plastic as fast as cookies on a baker's production line and just as cheaply. Virtually all personal computers sold today include at least a CD-ROM player, and the software that drives these computers is commonly delivered on a CD-ROM disc. Many systems also come with a DVD player combination that can read and burn CD-ROMs as well. Multilayered Digital Versatile Disc (**DVD**) technology increases the capacity and multimedia capability of CDs to as much as 18GB of storage on a single disc. CD and DVD **burners** are used for reading discs and for making them, too, in audio, video, and data formats. DVD authoring and integration software allows the creation of interactive front-end menus for both films and games.

In the very long term, however, CD-ROM and DVD discs are but interim memory technologies that will be replaced by new devices such as Flash Drives and Thumb Drives that do not require moving parts. As the data highway described next becomes more and more pervasive and users become better connected, copper wire, glass fiber, and radio/cellular technologies may prevail as the most common delivery means for interactive multimedia files, served across the broadband Internet or from dedicated computer farms and storage facilities.

The Multimedia Highway

These days telecommunications networks are global, so when information providers and content owners determine the worth of their products and how to charge money for them, information elements will ultimately link up online as **distributed resources** on a data highway (actually more like a toll road), where you will pay to acquire and use multimedia-based information.

Curiously, the actual glass fiber cables that make up much of the physical backbone of the data highway are, in many cases, owned by railroads and pipeline companies who simply buried the cable on existing rights of way, where no special permits and environmental studies are necessary. One railroad in the United States invested more than a million dollars in a special cable-laying trenching car; in the United Kingdom, there is talk of placing a fiber-optic cable backbone along the decaying 19th-century canal and barge system. Bandwidth on these fiber-optic lines is leased to others, so competing retailers such as AT&T, MCI, and Sprint may even share the same cable.

Full-text content from books and magazines is downloadable on the data highway; feature movies are played at home; real-time news feeds from anywhere on earth are available; lectures from participating universities are monitored for education credits; street maps of cities are viewable—with recommendations for restaurants, in any language—and online travelogues include testimonials and video tracks. Just think—each of these interfaces or gateways to information is a multimedia project waiting to be developed!

. . . .

http://www.moviefone.com

http://www.travelocity.com

http://www.nytimes.com

http://www.5pm.co.uk

Show times for many major cities, restaurants, vacation trips, and current news items are quickly available on the Web

. . . .

Interactive multimedia is delivered to many homes throughout the world. Interest from a confluence of entertainment mega-corps, information publishers and providers, cable and telephone companies, and hardware and software manufacturers is driving this inevitable evolution, and profound changes in global communications strategy are on the drawing boards. What will be piped through this new system for entertainment, reference, and lifelong learning experiences are the very **multimedia elements** discussed in the chapters of this book, including text, graphics, animation, sound, and video. (The software tools for making and editing these elements are discussed in Chapters 4–8, while the methods for delivering these elements on the Internet are described in Chapter 14.)

The actual content provided, let us hope, will be excellent fare, generated by thinking and caring creative people using ideas that will propel all of us into a better world. Entertainment companies that own content easily converted to multimedia projects are teaming up with cable TV companies. Film studios are creating new divisions to produce interactive multimedia and wealthy talents have formed new companies to join in on the action. Even without a clear business model with known profits, large media corporations are uniting to create huge conglomerates to control the content and delivery of tomorrow's information.

Some companies will own the routes for carrying data, other companies will own the hardware and software interfaces at the end of the line, at offices and homes. Some will knit it all together and provide supply-on-demand and billing services. Regardless of who owns the roadways and the hardware boxes, multimedia producers will create the new literature and the rich content sent along them. This is a fresh and exciting industry that is coming of age, but one that is still faced with many growing pains.

Where to Use Multimedia

Multimedia is appropriate whenever a human interface connects a human user to electronic information of any kind. Multimedia enhances minimalist, text-only computer interfaces and yields measurable benefit by gaining and holding attention and interest; in short, multimedia improves information retention. When it's properly constructed, multimedia can also be profoundly entertaining as well as useful.

Multimedia in Business

Business applications for multimedia include presentations, training, marketing, advertising, product demos, simulations, databases, catalogs, instant messaging, and networked communications. Voice mail and video conferencing are provided on many local and wide area networks (LANs and WANs) using distributed networks and Internet protocols.

After a morning of mind-numbing overhead presentations delivered from the podium of a national sales conference, a multimedia presentation can make an audience come alive. Most presentation software packages let you add audio and video clips to the usual slide show of graphics and text material.

Multimedia is enjoying widespread use in training programs. Flight attendants learn to manage international terrorism and security through simulation. Drug enforcement agencies of the UN are trained using interactive videos and photographs to recognize likely hiding places on airplanes and ships. Medical doctors and veterinarians can practice surgery methods via simulation prior to actual surgery. Mechanics learn to repair engines. Salespeople learn about product lines and leave behind software to train their customers. Fighter pilots practice full-terrain sorties before spooling up for the real thing. Increasingly easy-to-use authoring programs and media production tools even let workers on assembly lines create their own training programs for use by their peers. Figure 1-1 is from an animated project made with Adobe GoLive CS2 that describes the process of making such a product.

> Multimedia is a very effective presentation and sales tool. If you're being driven somewhere in the back seat of a car, you may not remember how you got to your destination. If you had been driving the car yourself, chances are you could get there again. Studies indicate that if you're stimulated with audio, you will have about a 20 percent retention rate. With audio-visual, retention is up to 30 percent and in interactive multimedia presentations, where you are really involved, the retention rate is as high as 60 percent.
>
> Jay Sandom,
> Einstein & Sandom

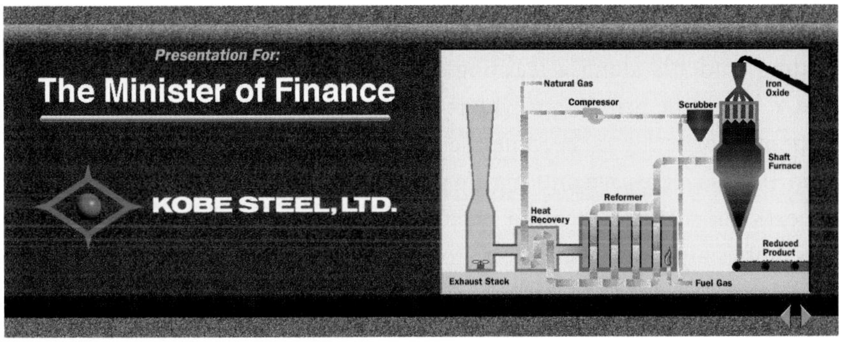

Figure 1-1 Animated instructional and training multimedia can simulate the real thing, allowing trainees to actually turn valves and flip switches.

> History has proven that advances in the way we communicate can give rise to entirely new communication cultures. Much like the transition from radio to TV, the evolution from text messaging to multimedia messaging (MMS) marks a whole new era of mobile communications, combining images with sound and text.
>
> ....
>
> Jorma Ollila, Chairman and CEO of Nokia

> Technological literacy must become the standard in our country. Preparing children for a lifetime of computer use is just as essential today as teaching them the basics of reading, writing, and arithmetic.
>
> ....
>
> Bill Clinton, former president of the United States

Multimedia around the office has also become more commonplace. Image capture hardware is used for building employee ID and badging databases, for video annotation, and for real-time teleconferencing. Presentation documents attached to e-mail and video conferencing is widely available. Laptop computers and high-resolution projectors are commonplace for multimedia presentations on the road. Cell phones and personal digital assistants (PDAs) utilizing Bluetooth and Wi-Fi communications technology make communication and the pursuit of business more efficient.

As companies and businesses catch on to the power of multimedia, the cost of installing multimedia capability decreases, meaning that more applications can be developed both in-house and by third parties, which allow businesses to run more smoothly and effectively. These advances will change the very way business is transacted by affirming the use of multimedia that offers a significant contribution to the bottom line while also advertising the public image of the business as an investor in technology.

Multimedia in Schools

Schools are perhaps the destination most in need of multimedia. Many schools in the United States today are chronically under funded and occasionally slow to adopt new technologies, and it is here that the power of multimedia can be maximized for the greatest long-term benefit to all.

In the 1990s, the U.S. government challenged the telecommunications industry to connect every classroom, library, clinic, and hospital in America to the information superhighway. Funded by telephone surcharges (eRate), most schools and libraries in America are now connected. Steps have also been taken to provide governmental support for state-of-the-art technology in low-income rural and urban school districts. The National Grid for Learning (NGfL) has established similar aims for schools in the United Kingdom.

Multimedia will provoke radical changes in the teaching process during the coming decades, particularly as smart students discover they can go beyond the limits of traditional teaching methods. There is, indeed, a move away from the transmission or passive-learner model of learning to the experiential learning or active-learner model. In some instances, teachers may become more like guides and mentors, or facilitators of learning, leading students along a learning path, rather than the more traditional role of being the primary providers of information and understanding. The students, not teachers, become the core of the teaching and learning process. This is a sensitive and highly politicized subject among educators, so educational software is often positioned as "enriching" the learning process, not as a potential substitute for traditional teacher-based methods.

Figure 1-2 shows the title screen from an advanced electronic teaching tool prepared by Yale University School of Medicine. It provides physicians with over 100 case presentations and gives cardiologists, radiologists,

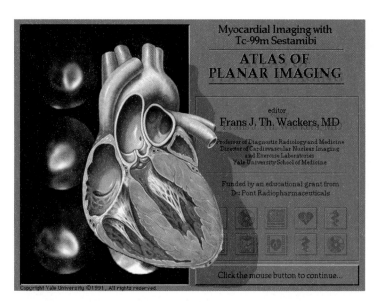

Figure 1-2 This multimedia project from Yale University School of Medicine lets physicians and radiology professionals learn new technologies at their own pace.

medical students, and fellows an opportunity for in-depth learning of new clinical techniques in nuclear cardiac perfusion imaging.

An interesting use of multimedia in schools involves the students themselves. Students can put together interactive magazines and newsletters, make original art using image manipulation software tools (see Chapter 10), interview students, townspeople, coaches, and teachers, and they can even make QuickTime movies (see Chapter 5). They can also design and run web sites.

At one time, laserdiscs brought the greatest amount of multimedia to the classroom—in 1994, there were more than 2,500 educational titles available on laserdisc for grades K–12, the majority aimed at science and social science curricula. Use of laserdiscs has been supplanted as schools have purchased more computers with CD-ROM and DVD players. And as schools become part of the Internet, multimedia arrives by glass fiber and over a network

ITV (Interactive TV) is widely used among campuses to join students from different locations into one class with one teacher. Remote trucks containing computers, generators, and a satellite dish can be dispatched to areas where people want to learn but have no computers or schools near them. In the online version of school, students can enroll at schools all over the world and interact with particular teachers and other students— classes can be accessed at the convenience of the student's lifestyle while the teacher may be relaxing on a beach and communicating via a wireless system. Washington On Line (www.waol.org), for example, offers classes to students who do not wish to spend gas money, fight traffic, and compete for parking space; they even provide training to professors so they can learn how best to present their classes online.

An interactive episode of *Wild Kingdom* might start out with normal narration. "We're here in the Serengeti to learn about the animals." I see a lion on the screen and think, "I want to learn about the lion." So I point at the lion, and it zooms up on the screen. The narration is now just about the lion. I say, "Well that's really interesting, but I wonder how the lion hunts." I point at a hunt icon. Now the lion is hunting, and the narrator tells me about how it hunts. I dream about being the lion. I select another icon and now see the world from the lion's point of view, making the same kinds of decisions the lion has to make—with some hints as I go along. I'm told how I'm doing and how well I'm surviving. Kids could get very motivated from experiencing what it's like to be a lion and from wanting to be a competent lion. Pretty soon they'd be digging deeper into the information resource, finding out about animals in different parts of the world, studying geography from maps displayed on the screen, learning which animals are endangered species...

Trip Hawkins, Chairman & CEO, 3DO Company

First Person

From time to time during my childhood I would hear bits and pieces of family lore about my great-grandfather, Victor C. Vaughan, who had been, at least it seemed from snatches of occasional conversation, a Famous Person many years ago. Not until adulthood, though, did I come across his autobiography and have a chance to meet him as a real person. Today he comes to mind when we discuss "radical changes in the teaching process." He was educated the old-fashioned way on a small farm in Missouri; I'll let him tell you what it was like:

> …I received the better part of my education at home. My wise mother did not pretend to dictate my instruction. She simply placed the books she desired me to read within my reach and supplied no others. I sat many a night into the wee small hours and absorbed, by the light of a sycamore ball floating in a cup of grease, the wonderful stories of Walter Scott. I knew every one of his characters in detail and sought their prototypes among those about me. I clothed the farm and the neighboring hills and dales with romance. Rob Roy's cave was a certainty. I discovered it in a high bluff on the creek. I read the works of Dickens and Thackeray with like avidity and recited the *Prisoner of Chillon* and the *Corsair*. These and books of like character filled my library shelves. There were also volumes of ancient history and I remember with what eagerness and enthusiasm I read the *Decline and Fall of the Roman Empire*. "Poor training," a present-day educator would say, for one whose adult life was to be devoted to science. This may be true, but I am reciting facts. I cannot deny that my scientific work might have been more productive had my early training been different. However, I am not making a plea for a handicap, and I remain grateful to my mother for the books I read in childhood. They continue to be associated with her hallowed memory. I never open one of these now ancient volumes without seeing her face, as with lighted candle she came to my room and gently urged me to go to bed.

Victor C. Vaughan continued to learn and apply eagerness and enthusiasm to every subject. Among his accomplishments, he became Dean of the Medical School at the University of Michigan and President of the American Medical Association. He was Surgeon General during the great Spanish Flu pandemic of 1918 and, it is said, he remained bitter to his last days that science, his great love, was unable to unravel the causes of that disaster.

It may be that today's multimedia and interactive distance learning using video and audio delivered across broadband connections may not be sufficient to compete with the light of a sycamore ball floating in a cup of grease. It may be that the fundamental driver towards the success of any person's education remains, simply and plainly, eagerness and enthusiasm.

Multimedia at Home

From gardening, cooking, home design, remodeling, and repair to genealogy software (see Figure 1-3), multimedia has entered the home. Eventually, most multimedia projects will reach the home via television sets or monitors with built-in interactive user inputs—either on old-fashioned

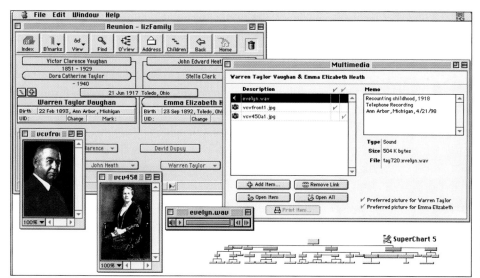

Figure 1-3 Genealogy software such as Reunion from Leister Productions lets families add text, images, sounds, and video clips as they build their family trees.

color TVs or on new high-definition sets. The multimedia viewed on these sets will likely arrive on a pay-for-use basis along the data highway.

Today, home consumers of multimedia either own a computer with an attached CD-ROM or DVD drive or a set-top player that hooks up to the television, such as a Nintendo, X-box, or Sony PlayStation machine. There is increasing **convergence** or melding of computer-based multimedia with entertainment and games-based media traditionally described as "shoot-em-up." Nintendo alone has sold over 100 million game players worldwide along with more than 750 million games. Users with TiVo technology (www.tivo.com) can store 80 hours of television viewing and gaming on a stand-alone hard disk.

Live Internet pay-for-play gaming with multiple players has also become popular, bringing multimedia to homes on the data highway, often in combination with CD-ROMs inserted into the user's machine. Microsoft's Internet Gaming Zone and Sony's Station web site boast more than a million registered users each—Microsoft claims to be the most successful, with tens of thousands of people logged on and playing every evening.

Multimedia in Public Places

In hotels, train stations, shopping malls, museums, libraries, and grocery stores, multimedia is already available at stand-alone terminals or kiosks, providing information and help for customers. Multimedia is piped to wireless devices such as cell phones and PDAs. Such installations reduce demand on traditional information booths and personnel, add value, and are available around the clock, even in the middle of the night, when live help is off duty. The way we live is changing as multimedia penetrates

My wife, the keeper of remotes, has rigged an entertainment system in our house that includes a remote controlled, ceiling mounted 96" × 96" drop-down screen, a 27" 16 × 9 format LCD screen, and an 1100 lumin Dell LCD projector connected to Wavecable, our Internet provider. We can watch our own CDs or Internet or Wavecable's TV/HDTV on our big screen while we track a sports show on the smaller screen off another Wavecable box. We have three cable boxes in our house.

Joe Silverthorn,
Interactive Media Professor,
Olympic College

our day-to-day experience and our culture. Imagine a friend's bout of maudlin drunk dialing (DD) on a new Nokia phone, with the camera accidentally enabled.

Figure 1-4 shows a menu screen from a supermarket kiosk that provides services ranging from meal planning to coupons. Hotel kiosks list nearby restaurants, maps of the city, airline schedules, and provide guest services such as automated checkout. Printers are often attached so that users can walk away with a printed copy of the information. Museum kiosks are not only used to guide patrons through the exhibits, but when installed at each exhibit, provide great added depth, allowing visitors to browse through richly detailed information specific to that display.

The power of multimedia has been part of the human experience for many thousands of years, and the mystical chants of monks, cantors, and shamans accompanied by potent visual cues, raised icons, and persuasive text has long been known to produce effective responses in public places. Scriabin, the 19th-century Russian composer, used an orchestra, a piano, a chorus, and a special color organ to synthesize music and color in his Fifth Symphony, *Prometheus*. Probably suffering from synesthesia (a strange condition where a sensory stimulus, such as a color, evokes a false response, such as a smell), Scriabin talked of tactile symphonies with burning incense scored into the work. He also claimed that colors could be heard; Table 1-1 lists the colors of his color organ.

Figure 1-4 Kiosks in public places can make everyday life simpler.

Frequency (Hz)	Note	Scriabin's Color
256	C	Red
277	C#	Violet
298	D	Yellow
319	D#	Glint of steel
341	E	Pearly white shimmer of moonlight
362	F	Deep red
383	F#	Bright blue
405	G	Rosy orange
426	G#	Purple
447	A	Green
469	A#	Glint of steel
490	B	Pearly blue

Table 1-1 Scriabin's Color Organ

Prometheus premiered before a live audience in Moscow in 1911, but the color organ had proved technologically too complicated and was eliminated from the program. Then Scriabin died suddenly of blood poisoning from a boil on his lip, so his ultimate multimedia vision, the Mysterium, remained unwritten. He would have reveled in today's world of MIDI synthesizers (see Chapter 5), rich computer colors, and video digitizers, and, though smell is not yet part of any multimedia standard, he would surely have researched that concept, too. The platforms for multimedia presentation have much improved since Scriabin's time. Today, multimedia is found in churches and places of worship as live video with attached song lyrics shown on large screens using elaborate sound systems with special effects lighting and recording facilities. Scriabin would have loved this.

Virtual Reality

At the convergence of technology and creative invention in multimedia is virtual reality, or VR. Goggles, helmets, special gloves, and bizarre human interfaces attempt to place you "inside" a lifelike experience. Take a step forward, and the view gets closer; turn your head, and the view rotates. Reach out and grab an object; your hand moves in front of you. Maybe the object explodes in a 90-decibel crescendo as you wrap your fingers around it. Or it slips out from your grip, falls to the floor, and hurriedly escapes through a mouse hole at the bottom of the wall.

VR requires terrific computing horsepower to be realistic. In VR, your cyberspace is made up of many thousands of geometric objects plotted in three-dimensional space: the more objects and the more points that describe the objects, the higher the resolution and the more realistic your view. As you move about, each motion or action requires the computer to recalculate the position, angle, size, and shape of *all* the objects that make up your view, and many thousands of computations must occur as fast as 30 times per second to seem smooth.

On the World Wide Web, standards for transmitting virtual reality worlds or scenes in VRML (Virtual Reality Modeling Language) documents (with the file name extension .wrl) have been developed. Intel and software makers such as Adobe have announced support for new 3-D technologies.

Using high-speed dedicated computers, multi-million-dollar flight simulators built by Singer, RediFusion, and others have led the way in commercial application of VR. Pilots of F-16s, Boeing 777s, and Rockwell space shuttles have made many simulated dry runs before doing the real thing. At the Maine Maritime Academy and other merchant marine officer training schools, computer-controlled simulators teach the intricate loading and unloading of oil tankers and container ships.

> BattleTech is pretty cool. I've played the one in Chicago. The key to winning is getting a unit where the controls work smoothly; otherwise you wind up running in circles until someone puts you out of your misery.
>
> Rich Santalesa, Editor, *NetGuide* Magazine

People who work in VR do not see themselves as part of "multimedia." VR deals with goggles and gloves and is still a research field where no authoring products are available, and you need a hell of a computer to develop the real-time 3-D graphics. Although there is a middle ground covered by such things as QuickTime VR and VRML that gives multimedia developers a "window" into VR, people often confuse multimedia and VR and want to create futuristic environments using multimedia-authoring tools not designed for that purpose.

....

Takis Metaxis, Assistant Professor of Computer Science, Wellesley College

Specialized public game arcades have been built recently to offer VR combat and flying experiences for a price. For example, BattleTech is a ten-minute interactive video encounter with hostile robots, created by Virtual World Entertainment, and located in both California and Illinois. In this game, you compete against others, perhaps your friends, who share couches in the same area called a Containment Bay. The computer keeps score in a fast and sweaty firefight. Similar "attractions" will bring VR to the public, particularly a youthful public, with increasing presence in the marketplace.

Virtual reality (VR) is an extension of multimedia—and it uses the basic multimedia elements of imagery, sound, and animation. Because it requires instrumented feedback from a wired-up person, VR is perhaps interactive multimedia at its fullest extension.

Chapter 1 Review

■ Chapter Summary

For your review, here's a summary of the important concepts discussed in this chapter.

Define common multimedia terms such as multimedia, integration, interactive, HTML, and authoring

- Multimedia is any combination of text, graphic art, sound, animation, and video delivered by computer or other electronic means.

- Multimedia production requires creative, technical, organizing, and business ability.

Describe the two primary multimedia delivery media—CD-ROM and DVD versus the World Wide Web—and their primary differences

- Multimedia projects often require a large amount of digital memory; hence they are often stored on CD-ROM or DVDs.

- Multimedia also includes web pages in HTML or DHTML (XML) on the World Wide Web, and can include rich media created by various tools using plug-ins.

- Web sites with rich media require large amounts of bandwidth.

Describe several different environments in which multimedia might be used and several different aspects of multimedia that provide a benefit over other forms of information

- Multimedia is appropriate wherever a human interacts with electronic information.

- Areas in which multimedia presentations are suitable include education, training, marketing, advertising, product demos, databases, catalogs, entertainment, and networked communications.

Qualify various characteristics of multimedia: non-linear versus linear content

- Multimedia presentations can be nonlinear (interactive) or linear (passive).

- Multimedia can contain structured linking called hypermedia.

- Multimedia developers produce multimedia titles using authoring tools.

- Multimedia projects, when published, are multimedia titles.

Cite the history of multimedia and note important projected changes in the future of multimedia

- The promise of multimedia has spawned numerous mergers, expansions, and other ventures. These include hardware, software, content, and delivery services.

- The future of multimedia will include high-bandwidth access to a wide array of multimedia resources and learning materials.

■ Key Terms

authoring tools *(2)*
bandwidth *(2)*
browser *(2)*
burners *(3)*
CD-ROM *(3)*
content *(2)*
convergence *(9)*
DHTML *(2)*
digitally manipulated *(1)*
distributed resources *(3)*
DVD *(3)*

environment *(2)*
font *(1)*
graphical user interface (GUI) *(2)*
HTML *(2)*
hypermedia *(1)*
integrated multimedia *(2)*
interactive multimedia *(1)*
ITV *(7)*
linear *(2)*
multimedia *(0)*
multimedia developers *(1)*

multimedia elements *(4)*
multimedia project *(1)*
multimedia title *(2)*
nonlinear *(2)*
platform *(2)*
scripting *(2)*
storyboarding *(2)*
web site *(1)*
XML *(2)*

Key Term Quiz

1. _____ is any combination of text, graphic art, sound, animation, and video delivered to you by computer or other electronic means.

2. _____ allows an end user to control what and when the elements are delivered.

3. _____ is a structure of linked elements through which the user can navigate.

4. A _____ multimedia project allows users to sit back and watch it just as they do a movie or the television.

5. _____ tools are software tools designed to manage individual multimedia elements and provide user interaction.

6. The sum of what gets played back and how it is presented to the viewer on a monitor is the _____.

7. The hardware and software that govern the limits of what can happen are the multimedia _____.

8. The information that makes up a multimedia presentation is referred to as _____.

9. CD and DVD _____ are used for reading and making discs.

10. HTML and DHTML web pages or sites are generally viewed using a _____.

Multiple Choice Quiz

1. LAN stands for:
   a. logical access node
   b. link/asset navigator
   c. local area network
   d. list authoring number
   e. low-angle noise

2. A browser is used to view:
   a. program code
   b. storyboards
   c. fonts
   d. Web-based pages and documents
   e. videodiscs

3. The "ROM" in "CD-ROM" stands for:
   a. random-order memory
   b. real-object memory
   c. read-only memory
   d. raster-output memory
   e. red-orange memory

4. The software vehicle, the messages, and the content presented on a computer or television screen together make up:
   a. a multimedia project
   b. a CD-ROM
   c. a web site
   d. a multimedia title
   e. an authoring tool

5. A project that is shipped or sold to consumers or end users, typically in a box or sleeve or on the Internet, with or without instructions, is:
   a. a CD-ROM
   b. an authoring tool
   c. a multimedia project
   d. a multimedia title

6. The 19th-century Russian composer who used an orchestra, a piano, a chorus, and a special color organ to synthesize music and color in his Fifth Symphony, *Prometheus* was:
   a. Rachmaninoff
   b. Tchaikovsky
   c. Scriabin
   d. Rimsky-Korsakoff
   e. Shostakovitch

7. Which one of the following *is not/are not* typically part of a multimedia specification?
   a. text
   b. odors
   c. sound
   d. video
   e. pictures

8. VR stands for:
   a. virtual reality
   b. visual response

c. video raster

d. variable rate

e. valid registry

9. According to one source, in interactive multimedia presentations where you are really involved, the retention rate is as high as:
   a. 20 percent
   b. 40 percent
   c. 80 percent
   d. 60 percent
   e. 100 percent

10. Which of the following is displayable on a web page after installation of a browser plug-in?
    a. Windows 98
    b. Adobe Flash
    c. Mozilla
    d. Internet Explorer
    e. Netscape Navigator

11. PDA stands for:
    a. primary digital asset
    b. processor digital application
    c. personal digital assistant
    d. practical digital accessory
    e. portable digital armor

12. The glass fiber cables that make up much of the physical backbone of the data highway are, in many cases, owned by:
    a. local governments
    b. Howard Johnson

c. television networks

d. railroads and pipeline companies

e. book publishers

13. DVD stands for:
    a. Digital Versatile Disc
    b. Digital Video Disc
    c. Duplicated Virtual Disc
    d. Density-Variable Disc
    e. Double-View Disc

14. At one time, the technology that brought the greatest amount of multimedia to the classroom was the:
    a. beta videotape
    b. DVD
    c. SmartMedia card
    d. broadband connection
    e. laserdisc

15. Which of the following is *not* a technology likely to prevail as a delivery means for interactive multimedia files?
    a. copper wire
    b. glass fiber
    c. radio/cellular
    d. floppy disk
    e. CD-ROM

■ Essay Quiz

1. Briefly discuss the history and future of multimedia. How might multimedia be used to improve the lives of its users? How might it influence users in negative ways? What might be its shortcomings?

2. You are a marketing director for a small telecommunications company. You are considering using multimedia to market your company's product. Put together an outline detailing the benefits and drawbacks of using a CD-ROM presentation, a multimedia web site, or a television advertisement.

3. Multimedia is shifting from being localized (contained on a CD-ROM) to being distributed (available on the Word Wide Web). What are some of the implications of this? Who will have access to the presentation? How will you keep it secure? How will you distribute it?

Lab Projects

■ Project 1.1

You have been given the task of creating an interactive Web presentation for marketing a new bicycle. Visit four different bicycle web sites using a suitable search tool. For each web site you visit, write in the table below the name of the site, its URL, and:

1. Describe each site in terms of its multimedia incorporation.

2. Discuss whether its multimedia content is appropriate and where and how additional media content might improve the site.

3. Describe what multimedia presentation formats it uses. Video? Virtual reality (or QuickTime VR)? 3-D animations?

Site 1	
URL (address):	
Describe the GUI. What navigational elements does it have? What colors does it use? Is it cluttered?	
Describe any multimedia presentations of specific products. What formats did they use?	
Site 2	
URL (address):	
Describe the GUI. What navigational elements does it have? What colors does it use? Is it cluttered?	
Describe any multimedia presentations of specific products. What formats did they use?	

Site 3	
URL (address):	
Describe the GUI. What navigational elements does it have? What colors does it use? Is it cluttered?	
Describe any multimedia presentations of specific products. What formats did they use?	
Site 4	
URL (address):	
Describe the GUI. What navigational elements does it have? What colors does it use? Is it cluttered?	
Describe any multimedia presentations of specific products. What formats did they use?	

■ Project 1.2

Review an educational multimedia CD-ROM title, and then fill out the table below.

Title of CD	
Describe the GUI. What navigational elements does it have? What color scheme(s) does it use? Is it cluttered?	
Describe the educational content. Is it well organized? Would you be able to easily learn the subject matter using this package?	
Describe the product in terms of its multimedia incorporation.	
Discuss whether its multimedia content is appropriate and where and how additional media content might improve the site.	

■ Project 1.3

Contact a local multimedia development company. Ask them what kinds of products they develop and whether they would describe two projects they have recently completed. Be sure that they provide you with enough information to answer each of the following questions.

Multimedia Project 1

1. Name of project.
2. Kind of product created.
3. What authoring tool(s) were used to create the project?
4. Who made up the development team for the project?
5. How did the production of the project develop?
6. How long did the project take to complete?
7. What problems were encountered?

Multimedia Project 2

1. Name of project.
2. Kind of product created.
3. What authoring tool(s) were used to create the project?
4. Who made up the development team for the project?
5. How did the production of the project develop?
6. How long did the project take to complete?
7. What problems were encountered?

■ Project 1.4

Visit a large public area such as a shopping mall, the downtown area of a city, or a museum. Locate a kiosk or other public multimedia installation. Spend 15 minutes observing who uses it and for how long.

1. Describe the installation. Where was it located? Is there a lot of foot traffic going past it? Is it conveniently located? Is it accessible to a wide range of users (tall, short, disabled, wheelchair, or vision impaired)?

2. Describe the usage pattern. Characterize the users. Were children attracted to it? Did users "play" with it?

CHAPTER 2

Introduction to Making Multimedia

IN CHAPTER 1, you learned what multimedia is, what it may become, and where you can experience it. In this chapter, you will be introduced to the workshop where it's made. This chapter provides guidance and suggestions for getting started. In later chapters you will learn more details about planning a project and the tools required; producing, managing; and designing a project; getting material and content for your project; testing your work; and, ultimately, shipping it to end users or posting it to the Web.

The Stages of a Project

Most multimedia and web projects must be undertaken in stages. Some stages should be completed before other stages begin, and some stages may be skipped or combined. Here are the four basic stages in a multimedia project:

1. **Planning and costing:** A project always begins with an idea or a need that you then refine by outlining its messages and objectives. Identify how you will make each message and objective work within your authoring system. Before you begin developing, plan out the writing skills, graphic art, music, video, and other multimedia expertise that you will require. Develop a creative, graphic **look and feel**, as well as a structure and a navigational system that will allow the viewer to visit the messages and content. Estimate the time you'll need to do all the elements, and then prepare a budget. Work up a short **prototype** or **proof of concept**, a simple, working example to demonstrate whether or not your idea is feasible. The ease with which you can create materials with today's production and authoring tools tempts new developers to immediately move into production—jumping in before planning. This often results in false starts and wasted time and, in the long run, higher development cost. The more time you spend getting a handle on your project by defining its content and structure in the beginning, the faster you can later build it, and the less reworking and rearranging will be required midstream. Think it through before you start! Your creative ideas and trials will grow into screens and buttons (or the look

and feel), and your proof of concept will help you test whether your ideas will work. You may discover that by breaking the rules, you can invent something terrific!

2. **Designing and producing:** Perform each of the planned tasks to create a finished product. During this stage, there may be many feedback cycles with a client until the client is happy.

3. **Testing:** Test your programs to make sure that they meet the objectives of your project, work properly on the intended delivery platforms, and meet the needs of your client or end user.

4. **Delivering:** Package and deliver the project to the end user.

What You Need

You need hardware, software, and good ideas to make multimedia. To make *good* multimedia, you need talent and skill. You also need to stay organized, because as the construction work gets under way, all the little bits and pieces of multimedia content—the six audio recordings of Alaskan Eskimos, the Christmas-two-years-ago snapshot of your niece, the 41 articles still to scan with your optical character recognition (OCR) program—will get lost under growing piles of paper, CDs, videotapes, phone messages, permissions and releases, cookie crumbs, Xerox copies, and yesterday's mail. Even in serious offices, where people sweep all flat surfaces of paperwork and rubber bands at five o'clock, there will be a mess.

You will need time and money (for consumable resources such as CD-R blanks and other memory or digital storage, for telephoning and postage, and possibly for paying for special services and time, yours included), and you will need to budget these precious commodities (see Chapter 15).

You may also need the help of other people. Multimedia development of any scale greater than the most basic level is inherently a team effort: artwork is performed by graphic artists, video shoots by video producers, sound editing by audio producers, and programming by programmers (see Chapter 3). You will certainly wish to provide plenty of coffee and snacks, whether working alone or as a team. Late nights are often involved in the making of multimedia.

Hardware

This book will help you understand the two most significant platforms for producing and delivering multimedia projects: the **Apple Macintosh** operating system (**OS**) and the **Microsoft Windows** OS, found running on most Intel-based PCs (including Intel-based Macintoshes). These computers, with their graphical user interfaces and huge installed base of many millions of users throughout the world, are the most commonly used platforms for the development and delivery of today's multimedia.

> You have to have a real yearning to communicate because multimedia is creating, essentially, an entirely new syntax for communication. You must have an interest in human psychology because you need to anticipate the brainwaves of all the potential end users. What will they expect from the program now? What will they want to do with the program now? How can you integrate all the multimedia elements in a really elegant and powerful way? You should adopt a strategy that allows you to prototype and test your interactive design assumptions.
>
> Ann Marie Buddrus, President, Digital Media Design

Certainly, detailed and animated multimedia is also created on specialized workstations from Silicon Graphics, Sun Microsystems, and even on mainframes, but the Macintosh and the Windows PC offer a compelling combination of affordability, software availability, and worldwide obtainability. Regardless of the delivery vehicle for your multimedia—whether it's destined to play on a computer, on a game box from Sega, Nintendo, or Sony, or as bits moving down the data highway—most multimedia will probably be made on a Macintosh or on a PC.

While it is difficult to conceive of a million of anything (pennies in a drawer, people in a city, bytes on a hard drive), there are tens of millions of copies of Windows now in use around the world. Though the Macintosh platform does not boast the market share of Windows, its operating system is in many ways more friendly for multimedia production, in part because the hardware platforms provided by Apple are better equipped to manage both sound and video editing. Hardware and **peripherals**, such as monitors, disk drives, scanners, and network gear are described in Chapter 9. Audio hardware is discussed in Chapter 5, and video hardware is discussed in Chapter 8. The workings and requisite tools of the Internet are discussed in Chapters 12, 13, and 14.

The basic principles for creating and editing multimedia elements are the same for Macintoshes and PCs. A graphic image is still a graphic image, and a digitized sound is still a digitized sound, regardless of the methods or tools used to make and display it or to play it back. Indeed, many software tools readily convert picture, sound, and other multimedia files (and even whole functioning projects) from Macintosh to Windows format, and vice versa, using known file formats or even **binary compatible** files that require no conversion at all. While there is a lot of talk about **platform-independent** delivery of multimedia on the Internet, with every new version of a browser there are still annoying failures on both platforms. These failures in **cross-platform** compatibility can consume great amounts of time as you prepare for delivery by testing and developing workarounds and tweaks so your project performs properly in various target environments. In this book, the icon shown to the left will flag complicated or difficult cross-platform issues that may warrant your special attention.

Software

Multimedia software tells the hardware what to do. Display the color red. Move that tiger three leaps to the left. Slide in the words "Now You've Done It!" from the right and blink them on and off. Play the sound of cymbals crashing. Run the digitized movie of Captain Hook. Turn down the volume on that MP3 file!

In this book, the discussion of software tools is divided into three parts to cover different types of tools: tools like word processors and image and sound editors used for creating multimedia elements, multimedia authoring tools, and tools for developing multimedia on the Internet.

Chapter 10 teaches you about the basic production tools used to work with text, images, sounds, and video. In that chapter you will also learn about handy tools for capturing screen images, translating among file formats, and editing your resources. These tools are used whether you are preparing multimedia for local delivery (CD-ROM, interactive DVD, or hard drive) or distant delivery via the Web.

In Chapter 11, you'll encounter the increasingly wide selection of specialized tools for authoring multimedia.

Chapters 13 and 14 discuss techniques and methods for designing and delivering multimedia on the Web.

You don't have to be a programmer or a computer scientist to make multimedia work for you, but you do need some familiarity with terms and building blocks; as even the simplest multimedia tools require a modicum of knowledge to operate. If someone asks to borrow a metric 13mm wrench, you should know they are probably working with a nut or a bolt (and if you are an expert, you might know that a ½-inch wrench can usually be substituted). If someone sends you a file in Macintosh AIF format, you should know that you're getting **digitized** sound. Don't be afraid of the little things that so easily depress the uninformed. From plumbing to nuclear physics, learning is a matter of time and practice. You will be frustrated as you work your way up the learning curves of multimedia. There will be things you want to do, but you will not know how to work the tools. Take the time to learn the fundamentals of computers and multimedia taught in this book. Then, load up your tools and open the help files; your learning curve will be easier to manage because you have the bigger picture.

As you explore the workings of multimedia, you should know that Web addresses are not guaranteed to be permanent, but can abruptly disappear, just like the addresses for physical locations when the house burns down or floats away in a flood.

Microsoft.com, walmart.com, mcdonalds.com, and visa.com, however, represent such monoliths of business that it seems unlikely that they will float away, at least soon, in the river of time. If, when trying to connect to a URL, you receive a "404 – Not Found" error message, try stripping away the directories and subdirectories and file names from the URL and then connect to the domain name itself. If you can connect to the domain name, you may find a menu that will then take you to the relocated document from another direction. If, for example, you are looking for a list of tools useful to Web service providers at http://www.w3.org/hypertext/ WWW/Tools/ and the document is not there, try to connect to http:// www.w3.org/, and then follow the hypertext menus provided. If none of these efforts brings you to your destination, you can try one of the search engines listed in Chapter 12.

First Person

After getting my pilot's license for flying small, single-engine airplanes, I traveled from San Francisco to New York on a Boeing 747. Looking out the window at those perfectly circular irrigated farms in Nebraska and Iowa, my lazy thoughts drifted from corn to water to Chevys on levies to girls to football to rope swings splashing into sun-drenched rivers.

There was a small airport below. Would that make a good emergency field for a dead-stick Cessna? Mmmmm, I drifted. What if *this* plane had an emergency?

Mmmmm. What if the crew had been poisoned and we were on autopilot, and a flight attendant had just interrupted the movie to ask if there were a pilot on board? Mmmmm. I knew that if I had to sit in the pilot's seat of that 747 I wouldn't have a clue, and the plane would go down. Thousands of switches, glass screens, levers, pedals, blinking lights, and somewhere a radio, all waiting for me to do something with them. Hollywood's version of this scenario, with the "tower" talking us down, would never work because I couldn't even turn on the radio.

It's like that when you learn multimedia. The same sinking feeling, frustration and not knowing. But, because you have this book in hand, you're already in the pilot's seat and are on the way towards a successful landing. Relax. Step-by-step it will get easier. Manuals, online help systems, and instructors are your tower, and you have plenty of fuel. In the same way tens of thousands of pilots have learned to fly, you will learn to make multimedia!

Creativity

Before beginning a multimedia project, you must first develop a sense of its scope and content. Let the project take shape in your head as you think through the various methods available to get your message across to your viewers.

The most precious asset you can bring to the multimedia workshop is your creativity. It's what separates run-of-the-mill or underwhelming multimedia from compelling, engaging, and award-winning products, whether we're talking about a short sales presentation viewed solely by colleagues within your firm or provided for a full-blown CD-ROM title.

You have a lot of room for creative risk taking, because the rules for what works and what doesn't work are still being empirically discovered, and there are few known formulas for multimedia success. Indeed, companies that produce a terrific multimedia title are usually rewarded in the marketplace, but their success can be fleeting. This is because competitors often reverse-engineer the product, and then produce knockoffs using similar approaches and techniques, which appear on the market six months later. Good web site ideas and programming are easily cloned.

The evolution of multimedia is evident when you look at some of the first multimedia projects done on computers and compare them to today's titles. Taking inspiration from earlier experiments, developers modify and add their own creative touches for designing their own unique multimedia projects.

It is very difficult to learn creativity. Some people might say it's impossible—and that you have to be born with it. But, like traditional artists who work in paint, marble, or bronze, the better you know your medium, the better able you are to express your creativity. In the case of multimedia, this means you need to know your hardware and software first. Once you're proficient with the hardware and software tools, you might ask yourself, "What can I build that will look great, sound great, and knock the socks off the viewer?" This is a rhetorical question, and its answer is actually another question—which is simply, "How creative are you?"

WARNING   *If you are managing a multimedia project, remember that creative talent is priceless, so be certain to reward it well. If you don't, you may find that your talent takes a job elsewhere, even at lower pay!*

Organization

It's essential that you develop an organized outline and a plan that rationally details the skills, time, budget, tools, and resources you will need for a project. These should be in place before you start to render graphics, sounds, and other components, and a protocol should be established for naming the files so you can organize them for quick retrieval when you need them. These files—called **assets**—should continue to be monitored throughout the project's execution. Chapter 15 provides planning and costing models for a multimedia project, while Chapter 16 discusses the details of multimedia project and asset management.

First Person

The Credit Alligator usually appears late in a multimedia project and has nothing to do with MasterCard or Visa. This gnarly animal typically lives unseen in the delicate fringes of workgroup politics, but can appear very suddenly, causing great distraction during beta testing, adding moments of personal tension, and occasionally destroying friendships and business relationships.

After hard cash, the most satisfying remuneration for your sweaty effort and creative, late-night contributions to a multimedia project is to see your name listed in the credits for a particular project. Indeed, getting visible credit is a special, high-value currency, in part because it can be added to your portfolio to help you land the next job. The more of this currency you have, the higher your potential wage and the more likely you will remain employed doing what you like to do.

Start building defenses against this alligator up front. When you negotiate the original contract with whoever pays the multimedia bill, be sure to include wording such as: "We shall be allowed to include a production credit display on the closing screen or in another mutually agreeable position in the finished work." If you are an individual who is contracting to a producer, be sure it is understood that *if* there is a credit page, your name will be on it.

Not all clients will stand for a credit page. Large companies, for example, use many outside contractors to produce multimedia, but as a policy rarely allow contributors to be credited by name. Some contractors and frustrated employees develop ingenious workarounds for burying these important intellectual credits within their work.

The Credit Alligator raises its bumpy head over the little things, too, and there are often no appropriate defenses for it. For example, if your name begins with a letter that is toward the end of the alphabet, you may never appear first on the list of contributors, even if your contribution was major. Of course, if your name is Walsh or Young, you have endured this ordering system since first-grade lineups. Warning: reversing an alphabetic credit list from last to first will only create or heighten tension; to propose such a list is, in itself, ego-driven and self-serving. Learn to work around it.

The most treacherous place for the Credit Alligator to lurk is in the busy stretch of time during the finalizing of a CD-based project and the "going gold" process of producing a final master. If you are not participating in the final mastering but have contributed a piece or pieces to the project, you must trust the person doing the mastering to do it the right way. But, unfortunately it doesn't always happen the way you want it to.

One company recently consulted on a job where their work represented the second-greatest contribution from a group of about 15 contributors, all of whom had credit screens. Their contract required credit, but in the final version of the storyboard, they discovered their screen buried at the end of a four-minute linear sequence of all the other credits and advertisements. They asked the producer to move it up. "Sorry," said the producer, "it was an oversight." Then in the last-minute process of re-sequencing, the producer also switched the contracted company's custom music to his own company's credit screen, leaving our friend's screen attached to a pretty ugly leftover sound byte. Because the company was not included in the final feedback and approval loop, they discovered this "little mistake" only after mass replication. It's tough to change 50,000 shrink-wrapped CD-ROMs, so at that point there was nothing to say.

Crediting creative talent is sensitive stuff. Avoid recurring bouts with the Credit Alligator by publicizing your policy about credit screens. Talk about intellectual credit openly, not as a last-minute thing. Negotiate hard for inclusion of credit in all the projects you undertake for clients. Remember, multimedia doesn't spring from the bankrolls of investors and publishers—it's the result of the hard work of talented, real people.

Chapter 2 Review

Chapter Summary

For your review, here's a summary of the important concepts discussed in this chapter.

Describe the four primary stages of a project

- Most multimedia and Web projects must be undertaken in stages. These four stages include planning and costing, designing and producing, testing, and delivering.

Describe the skills and talents needed for a multimedia project

- Successful multimedia requires a combination of talents and skills, not only on the artistic side but in organization, time, and money.

- Above all, you must have a desire to communicate.

Identify the most common hardware platforms for multimedia production and delivery

- Multimedia developers have claimed that Apple's Macintosh is better equipped to manage sound and video editing, despite the huge installed base of Windows-based PCs.

- While there are tools that allow for cross-platform and platform-independent media development, frustrating incompatibilities remain.

Discuss some of the common pitfalls of multimedia production, including the difficulty of appropriately crediting the production team

- Trying to do it all, rather than building a good crew with appropriate skills, is tempting—but usually fatal.

- The most precious asset you can apply to a multimedia project is creativity. Creativity is a concept that is very difficult to learn.

- Credit for a project is a valuable commodity. Negotiate or make allowances for project credits early on.

Key Terms

Apple Macintosh *(19)*	**designing** *(19)*	**planning** *(18)*
assets *(23)*	**digitized** *(21)*	**platform-independent** *(20)*
binary compatible *(20)*	**look and feel** *(18)*	**producing** *(19)*
costing *(18)*	**Microsoft Windows** *(19)*	**proof of concept** *(18)*
cross-platform *(20)*	**OS** *(19)*	**prototype** *(18)*
delivering *(19)*	**peripherals** *(20)*	**testing** *(19)*

Key Term Quiz

1. Files containing images, text, and other content used to develop a multimedia project are called _____.

2. _____ is an operating system.

3. Sounds that are converted from tape recordings for use on a computer have been _____.

4. A _____ is a simple, working example that demonstrates whether or not an idea is feasible.

5. A _____ file requires no cross-platform conversion.

■ Multiple Choice Quiz

1. Which of the following is *not* a stage of multimedia production?
    a. testing
    b. planning and costing
    c. designing and producing
    d. marketing
    e. delivering

2. Which of these is *not* a common platform for producing and delivering multimedia projects?
    a. Macintosh OSX
    b. Windows 98
    c. Macintosh Classic
    d. Windows XP
    e. IBM VMS

3. Which hardware platform is considered by many multimedia developers to be better equipped for managing both sound and video editing?
    a. Dell
    b. Sun
    c. Apple
    d. IBM
    e. Silicon Graphics

4. The most precious asset you can bring to the multimedia workshop is your:
    a. creativity
    b. programming skill
    c. musical ability
    d. film and video production talent
    e. checking account

5. According to one quotation, "Multimedia is creating, essentially, an entirely new syntax for":
    a. communication
    b. marketing
    c. publishing

d. creativity
e. technology

6. If, when trying to connect to a URL, you receive a "404 – Not Found" error message, you should:
    a. contact the Web host to notify them of a core meltdown
    b. try the same URL with a(n) ftp:// or smtp:// prefix
    c. strip away directories, subdirectories, and file names from the URL and connect to the domain name itself
    d. restart the computer and try again
    e. update your browser to a newer, more compatible version

7. Which of the following is *not* a danger to multimedia production?
    a. breaking well-established rules of multimedia
    b. the Credit Alligator
    c. platform incompatibilities
    d. copying success of competitors
    e. cost overruns

8. For multimedia production, mastering your medium means knowing:
    a. instructional design
    b. video production
    c. hardware and software
    d. screenwriting
    e. marketing and communications

■ Essay Quiz

1. You are a team leader who has been given six months to produce a multimedia title that will demonstrate your company's capabilities. Write a brief outline describing the timeline and the possible costs associated with the four stages of the project (you do not have to estimate actual amounts, just estimate percentage of budget). Justify your estimates.

2. You are a team leader given the task of developing a web site for an automotive dealership. Discuss the thought process you might go through to determine what that site should do.

3. You are a team leader given the task of developing a CD-ROM for training on a new kind of heart/lung machine. Discuss the thought process you might go through to determine what that CD-ROM should do.

4. You are a team leader given the task of developing a CD-ROM to promote a nonprofit. Discuss the thought process you might go through to determine what that CD-ROM should do and how it should look.

5. Consider your own skills, abilities, and goals. Where do you see yourself fitting into a multimedia production team? What abilities would you bring to a team now? What abilities do you need to work to develop? What are your creative abilities? What is your level of mastery of multimedia tools (software and hard-

Lab Projects

■ Project 2.1

Contact a multimedia development company. Ask them about their creative process. How often do they hold staff meetings? Do they hold frequent brainstorming sessions? Do they use different teams for different projects? What are the backgrounds of the various team members?

■ Project 2.2

Review two CD-ROMs (ideally, the same title, released for both Macintosh and PC platforms). Try to view them on both an Apple Macintosh and on a PC running Windows, preferably side by side. What similarities exist between the two in terms of structure, navigation, and so on? What differences do you see?

■ Project 2.3

Create the credits for an imaginary multimedia production. Include several outside organizations, such as video production companies and audio mixing/post-production facilities. Don't forget to include copywriters and other content providers. It may be helpful to look at the credits for an actual production.

Multimedia Skills

COMPUTER scientists, physicians, and firemen share highest honors as the most respected professions in the United States, according to a recent study of occupations. Are multimedia developers computer scientists? Or are they programmers, graphic artists, musicians, animators, storyboard craftspeople, information specialists, instructional designers, and/or Renaissance authors? However you define them, they come from all corners of the computer, art, literary, film, and audio worlds. Video producers become experts with computer-generated animations and MIDI controls for their edit suites. Architects become bored with two-dimensional drafting and create three-dimensional animated walkthroughs. Oil field engineers get tired of FORTRAN and design mouse-driven human interfaces. Classical painters learn the electronic elements of red, green, and blue and create fantastic, computer-based artwork. A multimedia developer might be any or all of these and typically doesn't fit a traditional management information system (MIS) or computer science mold; many have never seen a line of C++ code or booted up a Linux server. Perhaps, in the broadest definition, multimedia developers might simply be called information technology workers.

Consider Leonardo da Vinci, the Renaissance man who was scientist, architect, builder, creative designer, craftsman, and poet folded into one. To produce good multimedia, you will need a similar diverse range of skills—detailed knowledge of computers, text, graphic arts, sound, and video. These skills, the **multimedia skill set**, may be available in a single individual or, more likely, in a composite of individuals working as a team. Complex multimedia projects are, indeed, often assembled by teams of artists and computer craftspeople, where tasks can be delegated to those most skilled in a particular discipline or craft. Many job titles and collaborative team roles for multimedia development are being adapted to pull from a mix of motion picture industry, radio and television broadcasting, and computer software industry experiences.

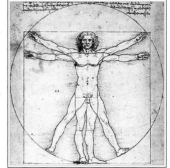

> ***WARNING*** *A multimedia expert working alone will be hard-pressed to compete with a team of experts and may be overwhelmed by the sheer amount of effort required to build a complex project single-handedly.*

The Team

A typical team for developing multimedia for CD-ROM, DVD, or the Web consists of people who bring various abilities to the table. Often, individual members of multimedia production teams wear several hats: graphic designers may also do interface design, scanning, and image processing. A project manager or producer may also be the video producer or scriptwriter. Depending upon the scope and content of your project and the mix of people required, according to Wes Baker, a professor at Cedarville University in Cedarville, Ohio, a multimedia production team may require as many as 18 discrete roles, including:

Executive Producer
Producer/Project Manager
Creative Director/Multimedia Designer
Art Director/Visual Designer
Artist
Interface Designer
Game Designer
Subject Matter Expert
Instructional Designer/Training Specialist
Scriptwriter
Animator (2-D/3-D)
Sound Producer
Music Composer
Video Producer
Multimedia Programmer
HTML Coder
Lawyer/Media Acquisition
Marketing Director

> Mere possession of the equipment does not make one into a videographer, film editor, set designer, scriptwriter, audio engineer, animator, and programmer. Some people do possess all of the innate talents required to produce decent multimedia, but few have mastered all the skills required to bring a major project to fruition. More typically, world-class productions are realized through the teamwork of a variety of talented people with specialized experience.
>
> Jeff Burger,
> Contributing Editor,
> *NewMedia* magazine

Project Manager

A project manager's role is at the center of the action. He or she is responsible for the overall development and implementation of a project as well as for day-to-day operations. Budgets, schedules, creative sessions, time sheets, illness, invoices, and team dynamics—the **project manager** is the glue that holds it together.

Mark Williams

Production of a CD-ROM reference guide at Microsoft involved a core team headed by project manager Mark Williams, along with additional specialists, technicians, and assistants, who were brought on board as needed.

At Microsoft, project managers are called program managers, but it means exactly the same thing. The program manager has two major areas of responsibility: design and management. Design consists of devising a vision for the product, working out the complete functionality with the design team, and then putting it into a complete functional spec and adjusting it as necessary throughout the development of the product. The management side consists of scheduling and assigning tasks, running meetings, and managing milestones—essentially overseeing all aspects of product development from beginning to end.

Our core team consisted of a project manager (me), a **subject matter expert** (who is called an editor at Microsoft), a graphic designer, and a programmer (also called a software development engineer). Another important team member was the product manager—a marketing person who is responsible for representing the product to the outside world. We also found that it was very valuable to get early design input from the person who creates the online and printed help for the product and from the person who eventually manages the testing of the product.

In the production phase we brought in additional talent for scanning images, digitizing sound, proofreading, and other production tasks. We also worked with numerous specialists along the way, such as an audio producer for securing sound track material and, crucially, acquisitions specialists. The acquisitions folks were vital to the effort because we were trying to get a variety of media from people who really didn't understand what we were doing.

Speccing the right content and being able to acquire it was critical. Our pictures and content are all of the highest quality, and the design is clear and easy to use. Keeping a vision of the product in mind—and making sure that the design really meets the needs of the end user—is very important. Constant usability testing gives us a way to keep the end user involved in the design process.

A good project manager must completely understand the strengths and limitations of hardware and software so that he or she can make good decisions about what to do and what not to do. Aside from that I'd say the most important skills are people skills (keeping your team happy and motivated), organizational skills, and attention to all the myriad details of a project. At the same time, it's critical to keep the big picture, the vision, in mind, so that everything that needs to get done does in fact *get* done.

Project Manager/Interface Expert

Multimedia company looking to immediately fill position working on interactive television project for major telecommunications company. Project manager needed to manage production and design efforts on large-scale, interactive television project for air in United States.

- Must be adept and experienced at managing complex projects, preferably with large corporate accounts.

- Must have solid understanding of interactivity and experience with interactive media in the broadcast television world.

- Must have several years of experience with interface design or have worked in management of an interface design group.

- Must have good design sensibilities.

- Communication skills a must; candidate must be an articulate and effective communicator, an excellent listener, and should be able to act as a conduit for the information passing between our team and the client's teams.

- Superior attention to detail and ability to coordinate large amounts of information a must.

- Prefer entertainment experience—ideally, television or video production.

- Solid computer or digital media experience and knowledge a must.

- Travel required for visiting focus groups and gathering consumer information.

- Must function well in fast-paced, team-oriented environment.

- Position must be filled immediately.

Multimedia Designer

The look and feel of a multimedia project should be pleasing and aesthetic, as well as inviting and engaging. Screens should present an appealing mix of color, shape, and type. The project should maintain visual consistency, using only those elements that support the overall message of the program. Navigation clues should be clear and consistent, icons should be meaningful, and screen elements should be simple and straightforward. If the project is instructional, its design should be sensitive to the needs and styles of its learner population, demonstrate sound instructional principles, and promote mastery of subject matter. But who puts it all together?

Graphic designers, illustrators, animators, and image processing specialists deal with the visuals. **Instructional designers** are specialists in education or training and make sure that the subject matter is clear and properly presented for the intended audience. **Interface designers** devise the navigation pathways and content maps. **Information designers** structure content, determine user pathways and feedback, and select presentation media based on an awareness of the strengths of the many separate media that make up multimedia.

Kurt Andersen

Kurt Andersen is an instructional designer and was a senior designer at the George Lucas Educational Foundation, where he designed multimedia prototypes for middle school math and science curricula.

 A **multimedia designer** often wears many hats, but most importantly he or she looks at the overall content of a project, creates a structure for the content, determines the design elements required to support that structure, and then decides which media are appropriate for presenting which pieces of content. In essence, the multimedia designer (sometimes called an information designer) prepares the blueprint for the entire project: content, media, and interaction.

From an interactive standpoint, many multimedia projects are too passive—you click and watch. The challenge is to get beyond what is appealing visually and design products that are activity-based. A multimedia project needs to be truly interactive, and this means that as a designer you have to have a clear picture of what goes on whenever the user interacts with the program.

Advances in technology are bringing us closer to this point. For example, one of the most interesting things going on is the development of *adaptive systems*, which accept user input and modify themselves based on this input. In training projects, they're called intelligent tutors. Right now, we're working on a medical application that will analyze a patient's history and background in order to present information that is personalized to that particular patient.

I was recently a member of two different teams that developed multimedia prototypes for middle school science and mathematics at the George Lucas Educational Foundation. Our approach was to develop prototypes that might be distributed as exemplars of rigorous, engaging, effective multimedia design using leading-edge technology. The real challenge was to create a program that presented mathematics so that users could play, explore, and develop their own conceptual schema around the concepts we were developing. We were also challenged to implement our ideas from a technological standpoint. For example, we wound up hooking up a high-end rendering machine so that we could do 3-D graphics on the fly.

Multimedia designers need a variety of skills. You need to be able to analyze content structurally and match it up with effective presentation methods. You need to be an expert on different media types, and a capable media integrator, in order to create an overall vision. The ability to look at information from different points of view and a willingness to shift your own point of view to be empathetic with end users are absolutely essential. So are interpersonal skills, because you spend so much of your time interacting with other team members, with clients, and extracting information from subject matter experts. You must be able to "talk the talk" with all of them. Finally, you must understand the capabilities of your resources, both technological and human, and know when to push ahead and when to stop.

Multimedia Designer/Producer

Seeking an experienced, new-media professional who loves inventing the future and enjoys the challenge of integrating complex information and media systems.

Our ideal candidate has solid experience in interface design, product prototyping, and marketing communication. Knowledge of image manipulation is critical, as well as proven skills in Lingo scripting and the use of digital time-based authoring tools. We seek a team player with excellent communication skills and grace under pressure.

- Must have experience designing large information and/or entertainment systems.
- Must have experience creating system flows and program architectures.
- Must have solid organizational skills and attention to detail.

Interface Designer

Like a good film editor, an interface designer's best work is never seen by the viewer—it's "transparent." In its simplest form, an interface provides control to the people who use it. It also provides access to the "media" part of multimedia, meaning the text, graphics, animation, audio, and video—without calling attention to itself. The elegant simplicity of a multimedia title screen, the ease with which a user can move about within a project, effective use of windows, backgrounds, icons, and control panels—these are the result of an interface designer's work.

Nicole Lazzaro

Nicole Lazzaro is an award-winning interface designer with XEODesign in Oakland, California, and teaches interface design at San Francisco State University's Multimedia Studies Program. She spends her days thinking of new ways to design multimedia interfaces that feel more like real life.

The role of an interface designer is to create a software device that organizes the multimedia content, lets the user access or modify that content, and presents the content on screen. These three areas—information design, interactive design, and media design—are central to the creation of any interface, and of course they overlap.

In the real world, design responsibilities are often assigned differently depending on the project. An interface designer may also be the multimedia designer or the graphic designer. Sometimes all of the design is given to one person; sometimes it is divided among group members; and sometimes the interface springs from the group as a whole. In the best of all worlds, everyone has input into the final vision, but realistically, everyone also has other responsibilities outside of interface design. The advantage of dedicating one team member experienced in a number of interface solutions to this particular task is to make sure the end user does not get left out of the equation. A good interface designer will create a product that rewards exploration and encourages use. You have to design the interface from the ground up, not just slap on some graphics and fancy icons after most of the programming is done.

A crucial skill is being familiar with a lot of multimedia interfaces so that you are able to visualize ideas as they are discussed. What is the best way to represent this function? Will this program look better using a hierarchical menu or a book metaphor? What will be the user's experience? Being familiar with film or video editing can be helpful, because telling a story with sounds and images is what most multimedia experiences are all about. From a visual perspective, cinematography and film editing are, I think, the closest parallels to what we would call interface design. These techniques can seamlessly change a point of view or tell a story more effectively, and they are being used by interface designers today. Knowing an authoring system is also crucial, so that you can develop your ideas in some interactive fashion and be able to present them to your design group. Having basic drawing skills also helps, because then you can describe how a screen looks using pencil and paper. Also, learn how to do user testing, and do lots of it!

> **Artist/Designer** needed to create graphics for interactive multimedia titles aimed at children. Solid experience in graphic design, including knowledge of Adobe Photoshop and Adobe Premiere. Must have superior illustration ability. Must have experience in animation. Experience in video graphics and editing (Premiere, Avid, Media100, etc.) a plus.

Writer

Multimedia writers do everything writers of linear media do, and more. They create character, action, and point of view—a traditional **scriptwriter's** tools of the trade—and they also create interactivity. They write proposals, they script voice-overs and actors' narrations, they write text screens to deliver messages, and they develop characters designed for an interactive environment.

Writers of text screens are sometimes referred to as content writers. They glean information from content experts, synthesize it, and then communicate it in a clear and concise manner. Scriptwriters write dialog, narration, and voice-overs. Both often get involved in overall design.

Domenic Stansberry

Domenic Stansberry is a writer/designer who has worked on interactive multimedia dramas for commercial products. He has also written for documentary film and published two books of fiction.

The role of the writer changes with each different project, depending on the people you're working with. But multimedia writing is always different from writing a film or video script. In a film or video, you're plotting a story the way a dramatist or novelist would. With multimedia, it can be more difficult: you're still thinking dramatically, but in smaller, more discrete units that have to inter-relate to each other, and that have to be compiled into a puzzle of sorts.

In traditional drama there are characters and an inevitability about what happens to those characters. You build circumstances that have certain significance for your characters as they go on to meet their destiny. In multimedia, we plot out stories that can go many different ways. This is inherently contradictory to the way we've thought about dramatic structure. Intelligent writers are still working hard to invent interactive dramatic structures: we see some attempts in games, which are obstacle driven. The user needs to perform a task and is presented with an obstacle—and then a need to overcome the obstacle and move on. This is not unlike the position a character takes in a story or movie where characters are presented with physical or psychological obstacles and must find a way to get beyond them. It's really too bad that writers are not brought in on more game projects…the quality of the interaction would be much higher if they were.

I work best when I am involved at the conceptual level of a project, but in many projects, the flowcharts are generated first. Then as the writing process unfolds, you find that the flowchart doesn't work because the material isn't what the flowchart wants it to be. When you're working on a dramatic script, you have to make the characters and the drama work first, before you start doing flowcharts. So if the writer is invited into the process at Step 7 and handed a flowchart, you're going to run into a problem. Another problem lies in working with people who are mainly from computer backgrounds. They are used to the writer as a writer of documentation—someone who comes in at the end of a project and writes a manual about how the product works. Computer people are often very uncomfortable with media people playing a role at the heart of the creative process. You need to develop a sense about where other team members are coming from when you are brought on to a project, and try to educate them if necessary.

But in the final analysis, the producer or project manager has to be the person to handle conflict in differing team members' visions. A good producer will get the most out of team members by getting them to work not against each other, but together toward their strengths. There are bound to be competing visions on a project, and in the best-case scenario, the team members will work out their differences through a consensus process. But if they can't, the producer has to have a guiding vision.

> **Multimedia Writer** needed for multimedia kiosk in retail outlet.
> Must be familiar with interactive design and user interface issues.
> Background in marketing or copywriting a plus. Ability to work
> under tight deadlines in a team environment essential. Candidates
> will be asked to provide writing samples.

Video Specialist

Prior to the 2000s, producing video was extremely expensive, requiring a large crew and expensive equipment. Recently, however, the cost of the equipment and the size of the crew needed have dropped dramatically, and digital video presentation methods such as Apple's QuickTime or Microsoft's Windows Media Player have combined increasingly capable hardware and software. The result is that video images delivered in a multimedia production have improved from postage-stamp-sized windows playing at low frame rates to full-screen (or nearly full-screen) windows playing at 30 frames per second. As shooting, editing, and preparing video has migrated to an all-digital format and become increasingly affordable to multimedia developers, video elements have become more and more part of the multimedia mix.

For high-quality productions, it may still be necessary for a **video specialist** to be responsible for an entire team of videographers, sound technicians, lighting designers, set designers, script supervisors, gaffers, grips, production assistants, and actors. However, for many modest projects, a video specialist may shoot and edit all of the footage without outside help.

Whether working individually or managing a large crew, a video specialist needs to understand how to shoot quality video, how to transfer the video footage to a computer, how to edit the footage down to the final product using a digital nonlinear editing system (NLE), and how to prepare the completed video files for the most efficient delivery on CD, DVD, or the Web.

Oliver Streuli

Oliver Streuli has worked as a post-production editor on several Hollywood productions (*Silence of the Lambs*, *Family Man*, and *Rush Hour 2*). He currently works in Switzerland where he specializes in post-production of commercials, corporate marketing and educational videos, and broadcast programming.

 Editing images into a creative and understandable flow is a rewarding career, although the actual work is generally done behind-the-scenes. Most people never notice good video editing, but practically everyone notices lousy work with sync problems and poor color correction. Post production includes mixing, adding titles, creating graphics and special effects, and tweaking audio. A working knowledge of tools like Adobe Photoshop, AfterEffects, and ProTools is immensely helpful, while extensive knowledge of nonlinear editing programs like Final Cut Pro or Avid is mandatory.

The workflow of a successful video project starts with good video and sound material—if the raw material is bad, there is only so much an editor can do to improve it. Editing a project can take anywhere from a few hours to a few months. For a 30-second commercial, you might have hours and hours of raw footage (also called dailies or rushes). The first edit is considered an "offline edit" and is done with compressed video and with titles and effects roughed in to save disk space. An Edit Decision List (EDL) is created during the offline editing process. This list of selected scenes becomes the "online edit," which incorporates only footage specified in the EDL. Special effects, titles, graphics, and color corrections are then added. A sound studio will likely make an audio track of voiceovers, background music, and jingles that need to be mixed in, so a misstep during the offline editing process can trickle down and create plenty of problems later during online or audio sessions. Attention to detail and a willingness to ask questions goes a very long way towards a smooth project.

> **Video Specialist** wanted for multimedia production. Must have strong background in video direction, nonlinear editing, and preparing digital video for efficient delivery. Good understanding of shooting for interactive programming required. A background working with Ultimatte green screens for compositing live video with computer-generated backgrounds a plus.

Audio Specialist

The quality of audio elements can make or break a multimedia project. **Audio specialists** are the wizards who make a multimedia program come alive, by designing and producing music, voice-over narrations, and sound effects. They perform a variety of functions on the multimedia team and may enlist help from one or many others, including composers, audio engineers, or recording technicians. Audio specialists may be responsible for locating and selecting suitable music and talent, scheduling recording sessions, and digitizing and editing recorded material into computer files (see Chapter 5).

Chip Harris

Chip Harris studied trumpet and electronic music composition at the Peabody Conservatory of Music, and he has worked with the noted composer Jean Eichelberger Ivy. He has recorded releases on major and independent labels, including Atlantic, RCA, and Warner Brothers, has composed music for CD-ROM titles for Virgin Games, Accolade, and E-greetings, and has created soundtracks for Clio and Joey award-winning spots.

An audio specialist working in multimedia should have a thorough understanding of the requirements involved in producing a successful sound track. Most often this person will be either an engineer, technician, composer, sound designer, or any combination of the above. On the rare occasion where all of these skills are requisite for employment, the position would most likely be for an audio department manager for a good-sized and well-funded multimedia company with in-house production facilities. However, even though positions such as these aren't plentiful, the skills and talents necessary for quality multimedia audio production are needed every day by companies who have opted to outsource their audio to independent contractors.

Whether it's recording voice-over talent for a business application, composing a musical score for a shoot-'em up game, or designing sound effects that reflect the particular feel of a product, the end result will rely on knowing the medium going in. By this I mean, for example, at what sampling rate will the audio be delivered? How much space is available for *all* audio combined? Can different sampling rates be applied to voice-over and music to save space and enhance overall quality? In composition will looping be required of individual pieces to provide a seamless score and to save valuable space? And who will do the looping, the composer or the engineer? Will some voice-over talents sound presentable at higher sampling rates but not at lower? Will the producer understand the difference?

Of course, these are only a few examples of the questions and problems to be dealt with in multimedia audio production. But attention to detail, listening for a cohesive presentation, and quality recording techniques are the strong glue that successfully binds the diverse audio components together.

Multimedia Audio Specialist

Audio specialist needed for multimedia project.

Must have strong background in studio recording techniques—preferably with time spent in the trenches as an engineer in a commercial studio working on a wide range of projects. Must be comfortable working with computers and be open and able to learn new technology and make it work, with high-quality results. Familiarity with standard recording practices, knowledge of music production, and the ability to work with artists a definite plus. Requires fluency in MIDI; experience with sequencing software, patch librarians, and synth programming; and knowledge of sampling/samplers, hard disk recording, and editing. In addition to having a solid technical foundation, you must be able to survive long hours in the studio riding faders and pushing buttons.

Multimedia Programmer

A **multimedia programmer** or software engineer integrates all the multimedia elements of a project into a seamless whole using an authoring system or programming language (see Chapter 11). Multimedia programming functions range from coding simple displays of multimedia elements to controlling peripheral devices such as CD or DVD players and managing complex timing, transitions, and record keeping. Creative multimedia programmers can coax extra (and sometimes unexpected) performance from multimedia-authoring and programming systems. Without programming talent, there can be no multimedia. Code, whether written in JavaScript, OpenScript, Lingo, HyperTalk, Authorware, Java, or C++, is the sheet music played by a well-orchestrated multimedia project.

Hal Wine

Hal Wine is a programmer familiar with both the Windows and Macintosh environments. In his many years of experience, he has worked in most of the important areas of computing and for many of the leading computing companies.

 The programmer on a multimedia team is called on to perform a number of tasks, from assisting producers in organizing their code more effectively to enhancing the production and playback tools. The most important skill a multimedia programmer can bring to a team is the ability to quickly learn and understand systems—and not just understand the various calls, but know *why* those calls are needed. In other words, you should be able to read between the lines of the technical manuals, so that your solutions are harmonious with the philosophy and intent of the system designers.

Multimedia products are displayed on a large variety of display systems, and the enhancement needed often requires going behind the normal system safeguards to meet the objective. Such programming requires a thorough understanding of the target operating system and the device capabilities needed to produce a robust solution.

While multimedia authoring tools are continually improving, they are also still evolving. Many times a producer will want to do something slightly beyond the built-in capabilities of the tools, and the programmer will build extensions to the authoring and presentation suite in order to add the desired capability or effect.

Many of the workers on a multimedia team have come to computing from a background in another discipline such as graphic art or journalism, and while they may have strong creative skills, most can benefit from learning more about computing techniques. Often, a multimedia programmer acts as a teacher and technical coach to the team. This implies having better than average communication and comprehension skills, both verbal and written, and the ability to listen!

I often come in to handle "emergencies" in multimedia projects, rather than participate in the whole project's life cycle. This provides me with maximum variety in my own work, which really keeps me on my toes. Sometimes, I'll be working for several clients simultaneously. The downside is that I miss out on a lot of the creative synergy; but even so, coming in on the spur of the moment, trying to understand the parameters of the problem, and producing robust solutions quickly leads to quite a bit of creativity, too. Knowing how to make your own latte is also useful.

Interactive Programmer (HTML, JavaScript, Flash, PHP, and C/C++) needed to work on multimedia prototyping and authoring tools for CD-ROM and interactive web-based projects.

- Thorough knowledge of ActionScript, JavaScript, Flash, PHP, and C/C++, Macintosh and Windows environments required.
- Must have working familiarity with digital media, particularly digital video.
- Must have a demonstrated track record of delivering quality programming on tight schedules.
- Must function well in fast-paced, team-oriented environment.
- Knowledge of AJAX methodologies desired.

Producer of Multimedia for the Web

Web site **producer** is a new occupation, but putting together a coordinated set of pages for the World Wide Web requires the same creative process, skill sets, and (often) teamwork as any kind of multimedia does. With a little effort, many of us could put up a simple web page with a few links, but this differs greatly from designing, implementing, and maintaining a complex site with many areas of content and many distinct messages. With the advent of Shockwave for Director and Flash, a web site can now be a full-fledged multimedia offering. A web site should never be finished, but should remain dynamic, fluid, and alive. Unlike a CD-ROM multimedia product replicated many times in permanent plastic, the work product at a web site is available for tweaking at any time.

Kevin Edwards

Kevin Edwards is Senior Multimedia Producer for CNET, a publicly traded media company that integrates television programming with a network of sites on the World Wide Web. In both types of media, CNET provides information about computers, the Internet, and future technology using engaging content and design. CNET has about 2 million members on the Internet, and its television programming—which airs on the USA Network, the Sci-Fi Channel, and in national syndication—reaches an estimated weekly audience of more than 8 million viewers.

 Years ago I headed out to San Francisco to join CNET. I wore a lot of different hats at CNET, but my primary responsibility was with the company's online foray into multimedia. For example, early on we did a year-long project with Intel, where I was involved from original concept through implementation. The project merged hot media properties with cutting-edge technology to create a brand-new experience in web-based browsing, allowing users to become participants in the experience rather than just observers.

What helped me keep this project in focus was my well-rounded knowledge and ability to perform in all of the different roles required to produce the site—

whether graphics, HTML, editorial, support, audio/video, or some other task. While it's a lot of fun to change hats and do many different tasks, it can be a lot of responsibility and pretty stressful. For me, building the original site meant that for a year and a half I was totally plugged into the Net, checking on our site, looking at stats, and analyzing what was going on in the entertainment/technology industries. This meant keeping Web profession hours rather than banker's hours, which meant it was pretty rare for me to take a day off, even on weekends, and my office became more of my living space than my apartment. To keep from burning out, you have to have a sense of ownership and a passion for what you're doing.

The best situation is when your team is composed of people who also turn into close friends. During this project we worked incredibly well together: each knew his or her particular field 100 percent and respected the other team members. We worked hard, played hard, and were able to really rock when put to the test. In fact, there were a couple of people who started the project with very little experience, but their eagerness and ability to learn, and the group's willingness to teach, made it happen.

> **Web Site Producer** Excellent full-time opportunity with a large manufacturing firm. Responsible for developing Web projects from concept through implementation for internal and external clients. Interact with all levels of management, network teams, and development teams to provide efficient project solutions. Knowledge of HTML coding of tables, frames, and forms, knowledge of CGI scripting, and knowledge of Photoshop and Flash required. Exciting opportunity for a self-motivated individual looking for a career in new media. This new entry-level position in the firm's national marketing department requires a team player with creative ideas who is interested in gaining experience and knowledge in every aspect of web site development. Job responsibilities include maintaining/updating site content, managing documents, and developing new site features.

The Sum of Parts

Successful multimedia projects begin with selecting "team players." But selection is only the beginning of a team-building process that must continue through a project's duration. **Team building** refers to activities that help a group and its members function at optimum levels of performance by creating a work culture that incorporates the styles of its members. You should encourage communication styles that are fluid and inclusive, and you should develop models for decision making that respect individual talents, expertise, and personalities. This isn't easy, but repeated studies have shown that workgroup managers with well-developed team skills are more successful than managers who dive headlong into projects without attention to team dynamics. Although it's usually a project manager who initiates team building, all team members should recognize their role; gentle collaboration is a key element of successful projects.

Currently, the Bureau of Labor Statistics does not have a category for jobs specific to multimedia. Some related areas listed by the bureau include

- Artists and related workers
- Designers
- Motion picture production and distribution
- Television, video, and motion picture camera operators and editors
- Writers and editors

You can also check out career information sites such as SkillsNet.net, Vault.com, and WetFeet.com for current information on careers in new media.

Computer Programmers

Computer programmers write, test, and maintain the detailed instructions, called programs or software; computers must follow to perform their functions. Programmers also conceive, design, and test logical structures for solving problems by computer. Many technical innovations in programming—advanced computing technologies and sophisticated new languages and programming tools—have redefined the role of a programmer and elevated much of the programming work done today. As a result, it is becoming more difficult to distinguish different computer specialists—including programmers—since job titles shift so rapidly in order to reflect new areas of specialization or changes in technology. Job titles and descriptions also may vary, depending on the organization. In this occupational statement, "computer programmer" refers to individuals whose main job function is programming; but keep in mind that this group has a wide range of responsibilities and educational backgrounds.

Employment of programmers is expected to grow faster than the average for all occupations through 2008. Jobs for both systems and applications programmers should be plentiful in data processing service firms, software houses, and computer consulting businesses. These types of establishments are part of computer and data processing services, which is projected to be the fastest growing industry in the economy.

Programmers generally work in offices in comfortable surroundings. Many programmers may work long hours or weekends to meet deadlines or fix critical problems that occur during off hours. Given the technology available, telecommuting is becoming common for a wide range of computer professionals—including computer programmers. Programmers can access a system from remote locations, to make it easier to make corrections or fix problems. Like other workers who spend long periods of time in front of a computer terminal typing at a keyboard, programmers are susceptible to eyestrain, back discomfort, and hand and wrist problems, such as carpal tunnel syndrome.

A growing number of computer programmers are employed on a temporary or contract basis or work as independent consultants, as companies demand expertise with new programming languages or specialized areas of application. Rather than hiring programmers as permanent employees and then laying them off after a job is completed, employers can contract with temporary help agencies, consulting firms, or directly with programmers themselves.

When hiring programmers, employers look for people with the necessary programming skills who can think logically and pay close attention to detail. The job calls for patience, persistence, and the ability to work on exacting analytical work, especially under pressure. Ingenuity and imagination are also particularly important, when programmers design solutions and test their work for potential failures. Since programmers are expected to work in teams and interact directly with users, employers want programmers who are able to communicate with nontechnical personnel.

From *The Occupational Outlook Handbook*, U.S. Department of Labor, Bureau of Labor Statistics (http://stats.bls.gov/oco/ocos110.htm)

Chapter 3 Review

Chapter Summary

For your review, here's a summary of the important concepts discussed in this chapter.

Understand the multimedia skill set and discuss how it applies to multimedia projects

- Identify the typical members of a multimedia project team and describe the skills that they need for their work.

- The multimedia skill set includes detailed knowledge of computers, text, graphic arts, sound, and video.

- This skill set is most likely found in a composite of individuals working as a team.

Define the skills needed to successfully manage a project team

- A project manager is responsible for the overall development and implementation of a project as well as for the day-to-day operations.

- In any project, including multimedia, team-building activities improve productivity by fostering communication and a work culture that helps its members work together.

List the multimedia skill categories related to the information and interface of a project

- Instructional designers make sure that the subject matter is clear and properly presented.

- Interface designers devise the navigation pathways and content maps on screen that let the user access or modify that content.

- Information designers structure content, determine user pathways and feedback, and select presentation media.

- Multimedia writers, sometimes called content writers, create characters, action, and point of view—and they also create interactivity.

Identify the multimedia skill categories related to the media used in a project

- Multimedia video specialists must know the basics about shooting good video, and be thoroughly familiar with the tools and techniques used for digital editing on computers.

- Multimedia video specialists must understand the potentials and limitations of the medium, including interactivity, how it will affect the video, and how these limitations affect the video production itself.

- Audio specialists design and produce music, voice-over narrations, and sound effects.

- Audio specialists may be responsible for locating and selecting suitable music and talent, scheduling recording sessions, and digitizing and editing recorded material into computer files.

Define the multimedia skill categories related to computer programming aspects of a project

- A multimedia programmer or software engineer uses an authoring system or programming language to integrate the multimedia elements of a project into a seamless whole.

- Sometimes programmers need to build extensions to the authoring and presentation suite in order to extend the system's capabilities.

Describe the special skills required for a web-delivered multimedia project

- Web site producers not only put together a coordinated set of pages for the World Wide Web but also constantly coordinate updates and changes.

Key Terms

audio specialist (37)
information designer (31)
instructional designer (31)
interface designer (31)
multimedia designer (32)

multimedia programmer (38)
multimedia skill set (28)
producer (40)
project manager (29)
scriptwriter (34)

subject matter expert (30)
team building (41)
video specialist (36)

Key Term Quiz

1. The diverse range of abilities needed to produce a new-media project is called the _____ (three words).

2. The person responsible for overall development and implementation of a project, as well as for day-to-day operations, is the _____ (two words).

3. The most appropriate title for the people whose job it is to look at the overall content of a project, create a structure, determine the design elements, and assign media to the content is the _____ (two words).

4. The work of a(n) _____ (two words) is best when it is "transparent"— as in never noticed by the user.

5. The most appropriate title for the person whose job it is to devise the navigation pathways and content maps is the _____ (two words).

6. The most appropriate title for the person whose job it is to structure content, determine user pathways and feedback, and select presentation media based on an awareness of the strengths of the many separate media that make up the total multimedia is the _____ (two words).

7. The most appropriate title for the person whose job it is to create characters, action, point of view, and interactivity, as well as write proposals, script voice-overs, actors' narrations, and text screens is the _____.

8. The most appropriate title for the person whose job it is to integrate all the multimedia elements of a project into a seamless whole using an authoring system or programming language is the _____ (two words).

9. Activities that help a group and its members function at optimum levels of performance by creating a work culture that incorporates the styles of its members is called _____ (two words).

Multiple Choice Quiz

1. According to a recent study of occupations, which of these professions is *not* among the most respected professions in the United States?
   a. computer scientists
   b. physicians
   c. lawyers
   d. dentists
   e. all are among those listed

2. At Microsoft Corporation, the product manager:
   a. coordinates the project's internal resources
   b. represents the product to the outside world
   c. oversees the entire team
   d. acquires the assets used in the project
   e. ensures the project does not go over budget

3. Which of these is *not* likely to be the responsibility of a project manager?
   a. managing the overall development and implementation of a project
   b. overseeing budgets, schedules, creative sessions, and team dynamics

   c. acting as the "glue" that holds the project together
   d. understanding the strengths and limitations of hardware and software
   e. developing extensions to the authoring system

4. Which of these is *not* likely to be the responsibility of a multimedia designer?
   a. creating interfaces
   b. creating budgets and timelines for the project
   c. ensuring the visual consistency of the project
   d. structuring content
   e. selecting media types for content

5. According to one quote, the multimedia designer is sometimes called:
   a. a digital media engineer
   b. a pixologist
   c. an information designer

d. a meta-data designer

e. a media integrator

6. According to one quote, from an interactive standpoint, many multimedia projects are too:

   a. interactive

   b. fast-paced

   c. game-like

   d. passive

   e. complex

7. An interface should:

   a. be "transparent" to the user

   b. provide control to the people who use it

   c. allow the user to move about within the project

   d. provide access to the "media" in the project

   e. all of the above

8. According to one quote, from a visual perspective, interface design most closely parallels:

   a. mapmaking

   b. cinematography and film editing

   c. technical writing

   d. fine art

   e. technical drawing and illustration

9. According to one quote, interface designers should:

   a. be familiar with film editing

   b. know an authoring system

   c. have basic drawing skills

   d. know how to do user testing

   e. all of the above

10. Multimedia writers are typically involved in writing all of the following *except:*

   a. proposals

   b. script voice-overs

   c. actors' narrations

   d. authoring-language scripts

   e. text screens to deliver messages

11. Writing for multimedia can be more difficult than writing for other media because:

   a. character development is much more critical

   b. the dramatic structures of multimedia are much more confined

   c. multimedia development cycles are much shorter

   d. writers must think in smaller, more discrete and interconnected units

   e. all of the above

12. Which of these is *not* a necessary capability for a multimedia video specialist?

   a. skill in managing all phases of video production

   b. familiarity with the tools and techniques used for digital video editing on computers

   c. ability to incorporate all the sophisticated video effects into a multimedia production

   d. ability to make a video look larger than it really is

   e. familiarity with interactivity and how it will affect the video

13. Which of the following is probably *not* a consideration of the multimedia audio specialist?

   a. the sampling rate at which the audio will be delivered

   b. how much space is available for all audio

   c. which authoring system or programming language to use

   d. locating and selecting suitable music and talent

   e. digitizing and editing recorded material into computer files

14. According to one quote, the most important skill a multimedia programmer can bring to a team is the ability to:

   a. quickly learn and understand systems

   b. control peripheral devices such as laserdisc players

   c. manage complex timing, transitions, and record keeping

   d. coax extra performance from multimedia authoring and programming systems

   e. act as a teacher and technical coach to the team

15. Producing multimedia for the Web is different from producing for CD-ROM because:

   a. the Web development industry is much more focused on sales and marketing

   b. Web development is much better adapted to larger, longer media

   c. Web design is much closer to print design; multimedia is more like film

   d. Web interface design is much more complex than CD-ROM interface design

   e. a web site is never finished, but is always available for changes

■ Essay Quiz

1. Discuss why the multimedia skill set is different from other project skill sets.

2. List and define the skills in the multimedia skill set. Describe several ways of categorizing the skills; for example, how each skill is related to project management, to design, to media, and to programming.

3. Describe the skills related to organizing, structuring, and editing the information in a multimedia project. What are the various titles within this category, and what are the distinctions among these skills?

4. Define multimedia computer programming. How does the programmer fit into the team? Is he or she at the end of the process, simply putting all the parts together after everyone else is finished? How can the other skill sets benefit from understanding what the programmer does, and the authoring tools he or she uses?

5. Why are multimedia projects most frequently performed by teams? Whose responsibility is it to ensure that the team operates effectively? What can be done to promote team effectiveness?

Lab Projects

■ Project 3.1

Locate three CD-ROMs and review the credits. How many members were on the team? What were their titles? How many team members performed more than one role? What tasks were "outsourced" (performed by outside companies)? Make a table that compares the titles for similar roles among the three CDs. For each one, discuss how the team related to the product. (For example, if the product included original video footage, how large was the video production team?)

■ Project 3.2

Locate three web sites and locate the credits (sites should be large enough to have a professional web development team). How many members were on the team? What were their titles? How many team members performed more than one role? What tasks were "outsourced" (performed by outside companies)? Make a table that compares the titles for similar roles among the sites. For each one, discuss how the team related to the site.

■ Project 3.3

Compare and contrast the credits between the teams for the CD-ROMs and the web sites. How did the titles differ? Were there more artists or programmers? Were there any unique job titles? What can you infer from the differences you found between the CD-ROM and web site teams?

■ Project 3.4

"Easter eggs" are small features hidden in web sites, games, and CD-ROMs. They often include personal information about the development team that produced the project. Do a search for Easter eggs on the Web, and try to locate several. Describe what you find there. What do these hidden features say about the team that worked on the project?

CHAPTER 4

Text

USING text and symbols for communication is a very recent human development that began about 6,000 years ago in the Mediterranean Fertile Crescent—Mesopotamia, Egypt, Sumeria, and Babylonia—when the first meaningful marks were scraped onto mud tablets and left to harden in the sun. Only members of the ruling classes and the priesthood were allowed to read and write the pictographic signs and cuneiforms.

The earliest messages delivered in written words typically contained information vital to the management of people, politics, and taxes. Because this new medium did not require rote memorization by frail human gray matter, written messages became popular among the elite. Unlike their human counterparts, these new messages were less likely to perish due to dysentery or acts of God, or suffer from amnesia. Even if a message were intercepted by foes or competitors, it would still be indecipherable—except by those few who had acquired reading skills.

In fact, because those who could read probably attended the same private school or shared the same tutors, in those days reading, writing, and power politics were naturally intertwined. In some former eras it was a capital offense to read unless you belonged to the proper social class or possessed a patent granted to you by your rulers.

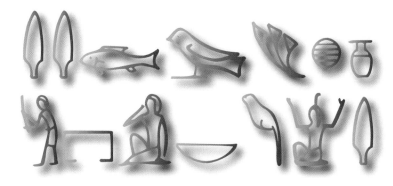

Today, text and the ability to read it are doorways to power and knowledge. Reading and writing are expected and necessary skills within most modern cultures. Now, depending upon your proficiency with words, you may be awarded a doctorate instead of the death penalty. And, as has been the case throughout history, text still delivers information that can have potent meaning.

With the recent explosion of the Internet and the World Wide Web, text has become more important than ever. Indeed, the native language of the Web is HTML (Hypertext Markup Language), originally designed to display simple text documents on computer screens, with occasional graphic images thrown in as illustrations (see Chapter 12 for more history of the Internet). Academic papers, magazine articles, complex instruction manuals, and even the contents of entire books are now available for reading with a web browser. Add a built-in function that links, with a click of the mouse, selected words and phrases to other related and perhaps more-detailed material (the "hypertext" part of HTML, discussed later in this chapter), and you can surf the Net in a medium much richer than the paper pages of a book.

First Person

In the 15th century, when the Church was a strong power throughout Europe, Johann Gensfleisch zum Gutenberg, a trained goldsmith from Mainz, Germany, invented moveable type for printing presses. He used this new invention for the task of producing religious literature, indulgence slips, and the Holy Bible. In the case of the Bible, he sold his copies to people who could read Latin and pay the equivalent of three years of a clerk's wage to own a personal copy of this Great Work. Other printers, including the Estienne family in France and Aldus Manutius in Italy, soon entered the publishing marketplace to compete, and they changed the fabric of society. The mass production of identical copies of text enabled an information-based paradigm shift that changed the human universe in a substantial way. Lots of scribes and illuminators were put out of business.

By way of pointing out that some elements of the human equation may be constant throughout history, I would remark that like many adventurers surfing the waves of today's revolution, Gutenberg took on a financial investor, Johann Fust. Gutenberg, who was a visionary craftsman perhaps better suited to lab and shop work, defaulted on a payment to Fust in 1455, was sued, and lost his press and all its profits. Toward the end of his life, it is said that he was granted a place as courtier to the archbishop of Mainz. This position had perhaps better remuneration than the diminishing social security plan rewarding today's surfer who wipes out while hanging ten at the leading edge of the business world.

(From a speech by Tay Vaughan to the jointly held World Conference on Educational Multimedia and Hypermedia and World Conference on Educational Telecommunications, Freiburg, Germany, June 1998)

The social impact of this text-biased medium on the way people access and use information will be profound as the Web matures. In contrast to today's television medium, which consists of sound and images with a few text headlines "dumbed down" to the level of a perceived lowest common denominator of passive audience, the Web offers an active experience laden with enough choices to challenge even bright people who can read. More than television, with its 5 or 50 or even 400 channels, the Web offers an explorer's paradise of billions of HTML documents. Yahoo! Search has

> With its penchant for interactivity, multimedia too often ignores the power of narrative, of stories. There's really something to be said for documents with a beginning, middle, and end.
>
> Steven Levy, author of Hackers, Artificial Life, Insanely Great, Unicorn's Secret, and Crypto; Senior Editor and chief technology writer for *Newsweek*

> I'd like to write something that comes from things the way wine comes from grapes.
>
> Walter Benjamin, Philosopher/Writer

claimed "Our index now provides access to over 20 billion items. For those who are curious, this update includes just over 19.2 billion web documents, 1.6 billion images, and over 50 million audio and video files." As bandwidth improves and more multimedia elements are successfully embedded within these documents, developers of content will not escape the difficult design issues discussed in Chapter 16. Who is the audience? What words should I use?

The Power of Meaning

Even a single word may be cloaked in many meanings, so as you begin working with text it is important to cultivate accuracy and conciseness in the specific words you choose. In multimedia, these are the words that will appear in your titles, menus, and navigation aids as well as in your narrative or content.

Today's poets and songwriters concentrate text by distilling lengthy prose into few words heavy with meaning. Advertising wordsmiths render the meaning of entire product lines into an evocative single word, logo, or tag line. Multimedia authors weave words, symbols, sounds, and images, and then blend text into the mix to create integrated tools and interfaces for acquiring, displaying, and disseminating messages and data.

The words "Barbie," "green," and "lite" may each easily trigger a rush of different meanings. A piercing cry in the night, the sight of fire engines leaving your street as you steer your car into your neighborhood, the scent of drying kelp along the seashore, the feel of rough pine bark against your chest as you climb, fingernails on a chalkboard—all these raw sensory messages are important only because of what they mean to you. Indeed, you alone know the words that will stop you dead in your tracks with anger, or, better, soothe you seductively over a quiet dinner for two. These words have meaning.

All of these examples demonstrate the following multimedia principle: it's important to design labels for title screens, menus, and buttons or "tabs" using words that have the most precise and powerful meanings to express what you need to say. Understand the subtle shadings. GO BACK! is more powerful than Previous; Quit is more powerful than Close. TERRIFIC! may work better than That Answer Was Correct.

Experiment with the words you plan to use by letting others try them. If you have the budget, set up a focus group to have potential users experience your words. Watch them work. See if users flinch, balk, or click the Help button in confusion. See if they can even find the Help button.

Words and symbols in any form, spoken or written, are the most common system of communication. They deliver the most widely understood meaning to the greatest number of people—accurately and in detail. Because of this, they are vital elements of multimedia menus, navigation systems, keyword lists, and content. You will reward yourself and your users if you take the time to use excellent words. Let your poet loose!

TIP *Browse through a thesaurus. You will be surprised at the number of synonyms and related words that are closely associated to the word you start with, and you will certainly find the one word that most perfectly fits your need. The majority of today's popular word processors ship with a bundled electronic thesaurus.*

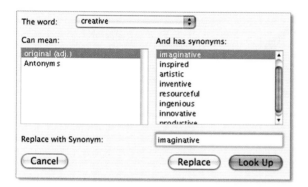

If you are reading this book in English, you might consider yourself lucky. A study by the British Council projected that 1 billion people will speak English by the beginning of the second millennium as a first, second, or "foreign" language. English is the official or joint official language of more than 75 countries, and Algeria, when it dumped French in favor of English as the second language in schools, irritated a great many Parisian intellectuals. More than two-thirds of the world's scientists read English, and three-quarters of the world's mail is written in English. It is estimated that 80 percent of the world's information that is stored on computers is written in English.

About Fonts and Faces

A **typeface** is a family of graphic characters that usually includes many type sizes and styles. A **font** is a collection of characters of a single size and style belonging to a particular typeface family. Typical font **styles** are boldface and italic. Your computer software may add other style **attributes**, such as underlining and outlining of characters. Type sizes are usually expressed in points; one **point** is .0138 inch, or about ¹⁄₇₂ of an inch. The font's size is the distance from the top of the capital letters to the bottom of the descenders in letters such as *g* and *y*. Helvetica, Times, and Courier are typefaces; Times 12-point italic is a font. In the computer world, the term font is commonly used when typeface or face would be more correct.

When we have a technical meeting with engineers coming from Germany, France, Spain, Sweden, Japan, and other countries, people say "Hello!" when they walk into the room; English is clearly the international common language of business and commerce and science. Sometimes the etiquette of polite speech is even more fascinating: when you have a room with a group of Germans talking to each other in German and suddenly a foreign visitor comes in, from one sentence to the other, they seamlessly switch to English.

Dipl.-Ing. Roland Cuny, Karlsruhe, Germany

A font's size does not exactly describe the height or width of its characters. This is because the **x-height** (the height of the lowercase letter *x*) of two fonts may vary, while the height of the capital letters of those fonts may be the same (see Figure 4-1). Computer fonts automatically add space below the descender (and sometimes above) to provide appropriate line spacing, or **leading** (pronounced "ledding," named for the thin strips of lead inserted between the lines by traditional typesetters).

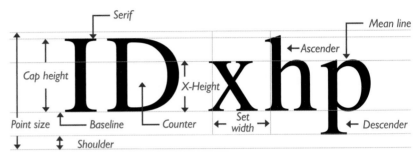

Figure 4-1 The measurement of type

Leading can be adjusted in most programs on both the Macintosh and the PC. Typically you will find this fine-tuning adjustment in the Text menu of image-editing programs or the Paragraph menu of word processing programs, though this is not an official standard. No matter where your application has placed the controls for leading, you will need to experiment with them to achieve the best result for your font. With a font editing program like Fontographer from Fontlab, Ltd. at www.fontlab.com (you'll see an example of it later in the chapter), adjustments can also be made along the horizontal axis of text. In this program the character metrics of each character and the kerning of character pairs can be altered. **Character metrics** are the general measurements applied to individual characters; **kerning** is the spacing between character pairs. When working with PostScript, TrueType, and Master fonts—but not bitmapped fonts—(see "Computers and Text" later in this chapter), the metrics of a font can be altered to create interesting effects. For example, you can adjust the body width of each character from regular to **condensed** to **expanded**, as displayed in this example using the Sabon font:

Regular
Condensed
Expanded

Or you can adjust the spacing between characters (**tracking**) and the kerning between pairs of characters:

Tighter Track   Av   Av

Looser Track   Kerned   Unkerned

When it converts the letter *A* from a mathematical representation to a recognizable symbol displayed on the screen or in printed output (a process called **rasterizing**), the computer must know how to represent the letter using tiny square **pixels** (picture elements), or dots. It does this according to the hardware available and your specification, from a choice of available typefaces and fonts. High-resolution monitors and printers can make more attractive-looking and varied characters because there are more fine little squares or **dots per inch (dpi)**. And today's broad selection of software fonts makes it easier to find the right typeface and font for your needs. The same letter can look very different when you use different fonts and faces:

A A *A* A A A A *A* **A**

Cases

In centuries when type was set by hand, the type for a single font was always stored in two trays, or *cases;* the upper tray held capital letters, and the lower tray held the small letters. Today, a capital letter is called **uppercase**, and a small letter is called **lowercase**.

TIP   *Studies have shown that words and sentences with mixed upper- and lowercase letters are easier to read than words or sentences in all caps (uppercase).*

In some situations, such as for passwords, a computer is **case sensitive**, meaning that the text's upper- and lowercase letters must match exactly to be recognized. But nowadays, in most situations requiring keyboard input, all computers recognize both the upper- and lowercase forms of a character to be the same. In that manner, the computer is said to be **case insensitive**.

WARNING   *The directory and file names used in Uniform Resource Locator (URL) addresses on the Internet are case sensitive! Thus, http://www.timestream .com/info/people/biotay/biotay1.html points to a different directory and file than http://www.timestream.com/info/people/bioTay/biotay1.html. On the other hand, the record type (HTTP) and the domain name (www.timestream.com), and e-mail addresses (tay@timestream.com) as well, are usually case insensitive. Read more about addresses on the Internet in Chapter 12.*

Recently, company and product names such as EveryWare, AirWorks, PhotoDisc, FileMaker, and WebStar have become popular. Placing an uppercase letter in the middle of a word, called an **intercap**, is a trend that emerged from the computer programming community, where coders discovered they could better recognize the words they used for variables and commands when the words were intercapped.

Serif Versus Sans Serif

Typefaces can be described in many ways, just as a home advertised by a realtor, a wine described by a food critic, or a political candidate's platform can all be described in many ways. Type has been characterized as feminine, masculine, delicate, formal, capricious, witty, comic, happy, technical, newsy—you name it. But one approach for categorizing typefaces is universally understood, and it has less to do with the reader's response to the type than it does with the type's mechanical and historical properties. This approach uses the terms **serif** and **sans serif**.

Serif versus sans serif is the simplest way to categorize a typeface; the type either has a serif or it doesn't (*sans* is French for "without"). The serif is the little decoration at the end of a letter stroke. Times, New Century Schoolbook, Bookman, and Palatino are examples of serif fonts. Helvetica, Verdana, Arial, Optima, and Avant Garde are sans serif. Notice the difference between serif and sans serif:

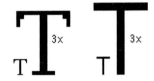

On the printed page, serif fonts are traditionally used for body text because the serifs are said to help guide the reader's eye along the line of text. Sans serif fonts, on the other hand, are used for headlines and bold statements. But the computer world of standard, 72 dpi monitor resolution is not the same as the print world, and it can be argued that sans serif fonts are far more legible and attractive when used in the small sizes of a text field on a screen. Indeed, careful selection of a sans serif font designed to be legible in the small sizes (such as Geneva on the Macintosh or Small Fonts in Windows) makes more sense when you are presenting a substantial amount of text on the screen. The Times font at 9-point size may look too busy and actually be difficult and tiring to read. And a large, bold serif font for a title or headline can deliver a message of elegance and character in your graphic layout. Use what is right for your delivery system, which may not necessarily be the same as what is right when you're printing the material to paper. This is because when you're printing out what you create on a computer monitor, **WYSIWYG** (What You See Is What You Get) is more of a goal than absolute fact.

Using Text in Multimedia

Imagine designing a project that used no text at all. Its content could not be at all complex, and you would need to use many pictures and symbols to train your audience how to navigate through the project. Certainly voice and sound could guide the audience, but users would quickly tire of this because greater effort is required to pay attention to spoken words than to browse text with the eye.

A single item of menu text accompanied by a single action (a mouse click, keystroke, or finger pressed to the monitor) requires little training and is clean and immediate. Use text for titles and headlines (what it's all about), for menus (where to go), for navigation (how to get there), and for content (what you see when you get there).

TIP   *In designing your navigation system, bring the user to a particular destination with as few actions and as short a wait as possible. If the user never needs the Help button to get there or never has to click the Back button when at a dead end, you're doing everything right!*

Designing with Text

Computer screens provide a very small workspace for developing complex ideas. At some time or another, you will need to deliver high-impact or concise text messages on the computer screen in as condensed a form as possible. From a design perspective, your choice of font size and the number of headlines you place on a particular screen must be related both to the complexity of your message and to its venue.

If your messages are part of an interactive project or web site where you know the user is seeking information, you can pack a great deal of text information onto the screen before it becomes overwhelmingly busy. Seekers want dense material, and while they travel along your navigational pathways, they will scroll through relevant text and study the details. Here is where you must strike a balance, however. Too little text on a screen requires annoying page turns and unnecessary mouse clicks and waits; too much text can make the screen seem overcrowded and unpleasant.

On the other hand, if you are creating presentation slides for public-speaking support, the text will be keyed to a live presentation where the text accents the main message. In this case, use bulleted points in large fonts and few words with lots of white space. Let the audience focus on the speaker at the podium, rather than spend its time reading fine points and subpoints projected on a screen.

TIP *A lengthy text document read by a web browser may scroll for hundreds of lines without annoying the user because it's expected. As a rule of thumb, however, try to make your web pages no longer than one-and-a-half to two screenfuls of text. On a common 1024x768-pixel monitor, you have about 600 pixels in height to work with before scrolling is necessary while viewing web content in a browser. For printing text documents, provide a separate link to a complete document in either plain text (.txt), word processor (.doc or .wpd), or Adobe PDF format (.pdf) instead of relying on a browser's print facilities. It is often more convenient to print and read a document than to scroll through many pages of text on a monitor.*

Choosing Text Fonts

Picking the fonts to use in your multimedia presentation may be somewhat difficult from a design standpoint. Here again, you must be a poet, an advertising psychologist, and also a graphic designer. Try to intuit the potential reaction of the user to what is on the screen. Here are a few design suggestions that may help:

Can you read me?

Can you read me?

- For small type, use the most legible font available. Decorative fonts that cannot be read are useless, as shown here.

- Use as few different faces as possible in the same work, but vary the weight and size of your typeface using italic and bold styles where they look good. Using too many fonts on the same page is called ransom-note typography.

- In text blocks, adjust the leading for the most pleasing line spacing. Lines too tightly packed are difficult to read.

- Vary the size of a font in proportion to the importance of the message you are delivering.

- In large-size headlines, adjust the spacing between letters (kerning) so that the spacing feels right. Big gaps between large letters can turn your title into a toothless waif. You may need to kern by hand, using a bitmapped version of your text.

- To make your type stand out or be more legible, explore the effects of different colors and of placing the text on various backgrounds. Try reverse type for a stark, white-on-black message.

- Use anti-aliased text where you want a gentle and blended look for titles and headlines. This can give a more professional appearance. **Anti-aliasing** blends the colors along the edges of the letters (called **dithering**) to create a soft transition between the letter and its background. (Figure 4-4, later in the chapter, shows an example of anti-aliased type.)

■ Try drop caps (like the T to the left) and initial caps to accent your words. Most word processors and text editors will let you create drop caps and SMALL CAPS in your text. Adobe and others make initial caps (such as the one shown to the right from Adobe, called Gothic). The letters are actually carefully drawn artwork and are available in special libraries as encapsulated PostScript files (EPSF).

■ Coding an initial cap for a web page is simple. Use HTML 3.0's <font> tag's size attribute:

```
<font face="Verdana" size="-1"          <!-- Set to your desired font and size -->

<font size="+2">T</font>ry drop caps</font> <!-- Increase the size of the initial letter -->
```

■ If you are using centered type in a text block, keep the number of lines and their width to a minimum.

■ For attention-grabbing results with single words or short phrases, try graphically altering and distorting your text and delivering the result as an image. Wrap your word onto a sphere, bend it into a wave, or splash it with rainbow colors.

■ Experiment with drop shadows. Place a copy of the word on top of the original, and offset the original up and over a few pixels. Then color the original gray (or any other color). The word may become more legible and provide much greater impact. With web sites, shadowed text and graphics on a plain white background add depth to a page. Surround headlines with plenty of white space. **White space** is a designer's term for roomy blank areas, while programmers call the invisible character made by a space (ASCII 32) or a tab (ASCII 9) white space. Web designers use a nonbreaking space entity ( ) to force spaces into lines of text in HTML documents.

■ Pick the fonts that seem right to you for getting your message across, then double-check your choice against other opinions. Learn to accept criticism.

■ Use meaningful words or phrases for links and menu items.

■ Text links (**anchors**) on web pages can accent your message: they normally stand out by color and underlining. Use link colors consistently throughout a site, and avoid iridescent green on red or purple on puce.

■ Bold or emphasize text to highlight ideas or concepts, but do not make text look like a link or a button when it is not. Text on a web page is easily colored using the color attribute of the HTML 3.0 <font> tag, for example, <font color="red">. Note that in HTML 4.0, the <font> tag has been deprecated in favor of cascading style sheet (CSS) rules. See Chapter 14 for more about CSS.

■ On a web page, put vital text elements and menus in the top 320 pixels. Studies of surfer habits have discovered that only 10 to 15 percent of surfers *ever* scroll *any* page.

. . . .

http://www.webstyleguide.com/type/index.html

http://www.sun.com/980713/webwriting/

http://www.webgrammar.com/typography.html

Useful web sites describing type and how to use it

. . . .

CROSS PLATFORM *Characters identified in a particular font (say, Garamond 10-point) do not always look the same on a Macintosh as they do on Windows display monitors. Typically, what is called 12-point on a Macintosh will be a 10- or 9-point size in Windows. And the actual shape of the characters may be different (see Figure 4-2). Take care to visually test the flow of your text on all platforms.*

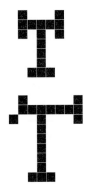

Uppercase 10 pt Garamond T on a Macintosh

Uppercase 10 pt Garamond T in Windows

Figure 4-2 Examples of "Garamond" typeface displayed on a Macintosh (top) and in Windows.

Menus for Navigation

An interactive multimedia project or web site typically consists of a body of information, or content, through which a user navigates by pressing a key, clicking a mouse, or pressing a touch screen. The simplest menus consist of text lists of topics. Users choose a topic, click it, and go there. As multimedia and graphical user interfaces become pervasive in the computer community, certain intuitive actions are being widely learned.

For example, if there are three words on a computer screen, the typical response from the user, without prompting, is to click one of these words to evoke activity. Sometimes menu items are surrounded by boxes or made to look like push buttons. Or, to conserve space, text such as Throw Tomatoes, Play Video, and Press to Quit is often shortened to Tomatoes, Video, and Quit. Regardless, the user deduces the function.

My parents offered my brother and sister $50 to teach me the alphabet, but that didn't work. So I flunked second grade. I had the same nun again, and she was mean. She paddled me for two years, but I still didn't learn the alphabet or how to read. By the time I was 15 or 16, I could get by in class with reading. But I could never spell. I was a woodshop major in high school, and my typical report card was two Cs, three Ds, and an F. I just got used to it. Though reading is still difficult for me, I do like readers. I like the written language because I like photocopying. I believe in double-spacing, since it helps my business!

Paul Orfalea, founder of Kinko's, discussing his reading disability

Text is helpful to users to provide perpetual cues about their location within the body of content. When users must click up and down through many layers of menus to reach their goal, they may not get lost, but they may feel transported to the winding and narrow streets of a medieval city where only the locals know the way. This is especially true if the user moves slowly from screen to screen en route to that goal. If Throw Tomatoes leads to Red or Green, then to California or Massachusetts, then to President or Vice President, then to Forehead or Chest, then to Arrested or Got Away, and so on, the user can end up tangled in the branches of a navigation tree without cues or a map. However, if an interactive textual or symbolic list of the branches taken (all the way from the beginning) is continuously displayed, the user can at any time skip intervening steps in a nonlinear manner or easily return to one of the previous locations in the list.

Tomatoes

Red

Massachusetts

President

Chest

Arrested

The more locations included in the menu list, the more options available for navigation. On the Web, designers typically place on every page at least a Main Menu of links that offers the user a handhold and mechanism for returning to the beginning. Often they will also place a list, such as

Home > Store > Home & Garden > Patio & Grilling > Gas Grills & Accessories > Gas Grills > Burners

along the tops of storefronts to let shoppers know where they are currently located within the store.

Navigation methodologies and navigation maps are discussed in greater detail in Chapter 16 and, in the case of surfing the Web, in Chapter 14.

TIP   *Avoid using more than a few levels of GO BACKs or RETURNs if you do not provide a map. Too much tunneling in and out with repetitive mouse clicks will frustrate users and discourage exploration. Display a perpetual menu of interactive text or symbolic cues so users can always extricate themselves from any place in the tunnel. In a web browser, this can be handled by a Back button containing a history of pages visited.*

Buttons for Interaction

In most modern cultures a doorbell is recognized by its context (next to the door itself, possibly lit); but if you grew up in a high-rise apartment, you may have seen 50 or more buttons at the entrance. Unless you knew that yours was the third from the top on the left, you could find your button only by reading the printed or scrawled name beside it. And certainly your Aunt Barbara needed this text cue to avoid having to push the Help button, which in this case rang in the building superintendent's apartment.

In multimedia, **buttons** are the objects, such as blocks of text, a pretty blue triangle, or a photograph, that make things happen when they are clicked. They were invented for the sole purpose of being pushed or prodded with cursor, mouse, key, or finger—and to manifest properties such as highlighting or other visual or sound effects to indicate that you hit the target. On the Web, text and graphic art may be buttons. Buttons and the art of button design and human interaction are discussed in detail in Chapter 16. For now, remember that the rules for proper selection of text and fonts in your projects apply to buttons as well as headlines, bulleted items, and blocks of text.

The automatic button-making tools supplied with multimedia and HTML page authoring systems are useful, but in creating the text for you, they offer little opportunity to fine-tune the look of the text. Character- and word-wrap, highlighting, and inverting are automatically applied to your buttons, as needed, by the authoring system. These default buttons and styles may seem overused or trite, but by using common button styles, shapes, borders, and highlights, you increase the probability that users will know what to do with them—especially when they are also labeled.

> When I was four years old, a button was the little plastic knob mounted in brass next to the front door. When I pushed it, a muffled ringing sound worked its way through the house from the kitchen. Sometimes I would push the button a lot and somebody would always come to the door. As an adult, I'm still pushing buttons to make things happen.
>
> Ann Stewart, Multimedia Developer, Smyrna, Tennessee

WARNING *In multimedia authoring software, the text that labels your predesigned buttons is typically generated by the same routines that draw text into fields. So make sure that the fonts you select for your buttons are available in the environments in which you will run your software. Your button fonts will need to travel with your project. See Table 4-1 for a list of fonts typical in Windows and Macintosh installations. These are perhaps safest for button labeling and for page design on the Web; you can expect them to be available on most personal computers. Note that fonts are considered intellectual property and may only be used when properly licensed. See "Managing Your Fonts" later in this chapter.*

Philip Shaw at http://www.codestyle.org maintains a useful list of the most commonly installed fonts for both Mac and Windows, shown in Table 4-1. The most common reported fonts on the Windows platform are the heavy sans serif Arial Black at 93 percent frequency, Comic Sans MS, display style Impact, and regular sans serif Verdana. The most common font reported for the Mac platform is the typewriter style monospace Monaco at 97 percent frequency, closely followed by the classic sans serif Helvetica and Microsoft's Verdana.

Windows Font	Installed (%)	Macintosh Font	Installed (%)
Arial Black	95.40%	Monaco	96.08%
Verdana	94.16%	Arial	95.77%
Comic Sans MS	93.87%	Arial Black	95.75%
Arial	93.79%	Helvetica	95.45%
Courier New	93.58%	Courier	95.30%
Impact	93.45%	Verdana	93.10%
Lucida Console	93.16%	Comic Sans MS	92.01%
Tahoma	93.12%	Courier New	91.69%
Trebuchet MS	90.80%	Trebuchet MS	91.38%
Lucida Sans Unicode	86.12%	Geneva	91.07%
Arial Narrow	84.76%	Georgia	90.91%
Georgia	83.93%	Times New Roman	88.87%
Bookman Old Style	81.15%	Skia	86.52%
Century Gothic	80.78%	Times	86.21%
Book Antiqua	79.29%	Apple Chancery	86.05%
Times New Roman	78.13%	Arial Narrow	85.89%
Garamond	72.74%	Impact	85.89%
Haettenschweiler	72.08%	Hoefler Text	83.70%
Lucida Sans	63.29%	Andale Mono	81.97%
Marlett	60.98%	Futura	79.94%
Terminal	56.43%	Palatino	79.78%
Copperplate Gothic Bold	47.85%	Optima	78.68%
Century Schoolbook	43.21%	New York	78.06%
Arial Unicode MS	43.12%	Arial Rounded MT Bold	77.90%
Lucida Sans Typewriter	42.16%	Chicago	77.43%
Lucida Handwriting	41.71%	Brush Script MT	77.12%
Arial Rounded MT Bold	41.34%	Lucida Grande	76.80%
OCR A Extended	40.18%	Charcoal	75.71%
MS Outlook	39.71%	Copperplate	75.39%
Lucida Bright	39.29%	Gadget	71.32%
Calisto MT	38.73%	Tahoma	71.16%

Table 4-1 The Most Commonly Installed Fonts on Windows and Macintosh Computers (May 2006)

Windows Font	Installed (%)	Macintosh Font	Installed (%)
Brush Script MT	33.80%	Capitals	70.06%
Britannic Bold	32.06%	Techno	69.91%
Algerian	32.02%	Sand	69.75%
Playbill	30.86%	Textile	69.12%
Wide Latin	30.78%	Lucida Bright	61.59%
Matura MT Script Capitals	30.28%	Lucida Sans	60.32%
Footlight MT Light	29.87%	Lucida Sans Typewriter	58.41%
Colonna MT	26.88%	Avant Garde	50.62%
Andale Mono	23.36%	VT 100	36.73%

Table 4-1 The Most Commonly Installed Fonts on Windows and Macintosh Computers (May 2006) *(continued)*

Before you can use a font, it must be recognized by the computer's operating system. If you want to use fonts other than those installed with your basic operating system, you will need to install them. When you install applications, fonts are often added to your collection.

Pick a font for buttons that is, above all, legible; then adjust the text size of the labels to provide adequate space between the button's rim and the text. You can choose from many styles of buttons and several standard methodologies for highlighting. You will want to experiment to get the right combinations of font, spacing, and colors for just the right look.

In HTML 3.0, the <font> tag can be used to specify a font to be displayed (if the font is present on the system). Use of a **cascading style sheet (CSS)**, preferred over the <font> tag, allows you to be quite precise about font faces, sizes, and other attributes.

WARNING *Although in HTML 4 you can specify a base font size, color, and face for displaying text on a web page, you still have no guarantee that the font is installed in the user's system. If it is missing, a browser will attempt to substitute a similar font, but the look is not guaranteed to be the same as the one you have designed. In the font-family property you can add a generic catch-all such as "serif" or "sans serif" to cover an instance when your specified fonts are unavailable. If the right look is important to you, provide a way to download the font to the end user's computer. If the look is crucial, use a bitmap image of the text drawn in the selected font.*

In a list of choices, you can include the names of both Windows and Macintosh fonts; if the font is not found on the local computer, the browser's default font will be displayed:

<font face="Helvetica, Arial, Verdana">

or using CSS,

<h1 {font-family: Helvetica, Arial, Verdana, sans-serif;}

To address copyright and cross-platform font issues, Microsoft hired type designer Matthew Carter of Carter & Cone Type, Inc. (http://www .myfonts.com/foundry/cartercone/) to design a serif font and a sans serif font that display well on a computer monitor. The two fonts Carter designed are Georgia (the serif font) and Verdana (the sans serif font), both of which Microsoft makes available for free. Since they are freely available and designed specifically for screen display, many designers recommend them as a "first choice" when specifying font faces for web pages.

In most authoring platforms, it is easy to make your own buttons from bitmaps or drawn objects. In a message-passing authoring system, where you can script activity when the mouse button is up or down over an object, you can quickly replace one bitmap with another highlighted or colored version of the bitmap to show that the button has been "pushed" or that the mouse is hovering over it. Making your own buttons from bitmaps or drawn objects gives you greater design power and creative freedom and also insures against the missing font problem. On the other hand, this custom work may require a good deal more time. You can also implement these graphic image **rollovers** on web pages, using JavaScript to replace the image when there is a MouseOver or hover event; when a MouseUp event occurs on the image, the user can be directed to another page (see "Clickable Buttons" in Chapter 14). Typically the destination address (URL) is displayed in the status window of the browser when the mouse is over a linked image or text element. So users know first if the mouse is over an active button and second, where that button will take them if they click.

Whether default or custom, treat the design and labeling of your buttons as an industrial art project: buttons are the part of your project the user touches.

Fields for Reading

You are already working uphill when you design text to be read on the screen. Experiments have shown that reading text on a computer screen is slower and more difficult than reading the same text in hard-copy or book form. Indeed, many users, it seems, would rather print out their reports and e-mail messages and read them on paper than page through screens of text. Reading hard copy is still more comfortable.

WARNING *Research has shown that when people read text on a computer screen they blink only 3 to 5 times per minute, but they blink 20 to 25 times per minute when reading text on paper. This reduced eye movement may cause dryness, fatigue, and possibly damage to the eyes. Research also suggests that monitors should be placed lower than eye level.*

Unless the very purpose of your multimedia project or web site is to display large blocks of text, try to present to the user only a few paragraphs of text per page. Use a font that is easy to read rather than a prettier font that is illegible. Try to display whole paragraphs on the screen, and avoid breaks where users must go back and forth between pages to read an entire paragraph.

Portrait Versus Landscape

Traditional hard-copy and printed documents in the taller-than-wide orientation are simply not readable on a typical monitor with a wider-than-tall aspect ratio. The taller-than-wide orientation used for printed documents is called **portrait**; this is the 8.5-by-11-inch size unique to the United States or the internationally designated standard A4 size, 8.27 by 11.69 inches. The wider-than-tall orientation normal to monitors is called **landscape**. Shrinking an 11-inch-tall portrait page of text into your available monitor height usually yields illegible chicken tracks. There are four possible solutions if you are working with a block of text that is taller than what will fit:

■ Put the text into a scrolling field. This is the solution used by web browsers.

■ Put the text into a single field or graphic image in a project window, and let the user move the whole window up or down upon command. This is most appropriate when you need to present text with page breaks and formatting identical to the printed document. This is used by Adobe's popular Acrobat Reader for displaying PDF files.

■ Break the text into fields that fit on monitor-sized pages, and design control buttons to flip through these pages.

■ Design your multimedia project for a special monitor that is taller than it is wide (portrait) or a normal monitor rotated onto its side. Dedicated "page view" monitors are expensive; they are used for commercial print-based typesetting and layout. Video controllers in Windows and Mac OS can rotate the text display for you:

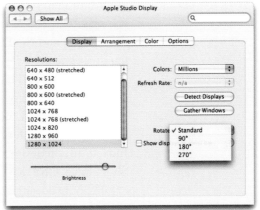

HTML Documents

The standard document format used for displaying text pages on the Web is called Hypertext Markup Language (HTML). In an HTML document you can specify typefaces, sizes, colors, and other properties by "marking up" the text in the document with **tags**. The process of marking up documents is simple: Where you want text to be bold, surround it with the tags <B> and </B> or <STRONG> and </STRONG>; the text between the tags will then be displayed by your browser application in bold type. Where you have a header, surround it with <H1> and </H1>; for an ordered list of things (1, 2, 3, ... or a, b, c, ..., etc.), surround your list with <OL> and </OL>. There are many tags you can use to lay out a page. How HTML works is discussed in greater detail in Chapters 13 and 14. There are also many good HTML learning guides and references available on the Web.

· ·

http://www.w3.org/TR/html4/

http://www.w3.org/MarkUp/Guide/

htttp://www.w3schools.com/html/default.asp

http://www.htmlcodetutorial.com

Check out these web sites for more information about HTML

· ·

The remarkable growth of the Web is straining the "old" designs for displaying text on computers. Indeed, while marked-up text files (HTML documents) remain at the foundation of Web activity, when you visit a well-designed web site, you often discover graphic images, animations, and interactive work-arounds contrived to *avoid* displaying text. The neat paragraphs, indented lists, and formats for text documents for which HTML was originally intended are evolving into multimedia documents, not text documents, and the HTML method and standard is consequently suffering great stress.

As features and tags and plug-ins and special scripts are tacked onto or embedded into HTML to satisfy the demand for multimedia interfaces, at some point HTML will need to be redesigned and stretched into a multimedia delivery tool, not just a text display tool with assorted attachments. Indeed, this redesign and stretching is under way in the form of Flash, Shockwave, CSS, XML, QuickTime, PDF, and AJAX.

HTML doesn't provide you with much flexibility to make pretty text elements, but you may be able to lay out pleasing documents using blockquote indents, tables, frames, and horizontal rules. Pretty text in HTML documents is typically done as graphical bitmaps that are placed within the HTML document's layout with image tags, <IMG>. Indeed, using plain HTML, you do not know what font a reader will use to view your document—the default display font is a preference that can be set in the viewer's browser, which knows it's available on that viewer's machine. So some viewers may read your words in serif Times Roman, others in sans serif Helvetica or Arial. **Dynamic HTML**, however, uses cascading style sheets to define choices ranging from line height to margin width to font face. A font face, if not found, is degraded to the next best match. Indeed, using CSS, you can define the following text properties: font-weight, font-family, font-size, font-size-adjust, font-variant, font-style, font-stretch, text-decoration, text-transform, text-shadow, letter-spacing, word-spacing, line-height, vertical-align, text-indent, text-align, and direction. Designing documents for the Web is discussed in Chapter 14.

Symbols and Icons

Symbols are concentrated text in the form of stand-alone graphic constructs. Symbols convey meaningful messages. The Macintosh trash can symbol, for instance, tells you where to throw away old files; the Windows hourglass cursor tells you to wait while the computer is processing. Though you may think of symbols as belonging strictly to the realm of graphic art, in multimedia you should treat them as text—or visual words—because they carry meaning. Symbols such as the familiar trash can and hourglass are more properly called **icons**: these are symbolic representations of objects and processes common to the graphical user interfaces of many computer operating systems.

Certainly text is more efficient than imagery and pictures for delivering a precise message to users. On the other hand, pictures, icons, moving images, and sounds are most easily recalled and remembered by viewers.

With multimedia, you have the power to blend both text and icons (as well as colors, sounds, images, and motion video) to enhance the overall impact and value of your message.

Word meanings are shared by millions of people, but the special symbols you design for a multimedia project are not; these symbols must be learned before they can be useful message carriers. Some symbols are more widely used and understood than others, but readers of even these common symbols had to grow accustomed to their meanings. Learning a system of symbols can be as difficult as lessons in any foreign language.

WARNING   *Do not be seduced into creating your own language of symbols and icons.*

Here are some symbols you may already know:

And here are some astronomer's symbols from the days of Kepler and Galileo that you may not have learned. Still in heavy use by astrologers, they represent the 12 constellations of the zodiac:

♀ ♈ ♉ ♊ ♋ ♌ ♍ ♎ ♏ ♐ ♑ ♒ ♓

But why are there 13 icons in the illustration above? Or did you notice? Find the sign for the planet Venus among the constellations. Not easy if you are unfamiliar with the meaning of these symbols.

When HyperCard was first introduced in 1987, there was a flurry of creative attempts by graphic artists to create interesting navigational symbols to alleviate the need for text. The screens were pure graphic art and power—all lines and angles and stunning shadows. But many users were frustrated because they could not get to the data right away and had to first wade through help and guidance material to learn the symbols. In this context it is clearly safer, from a product design point of view, to combine symbols with text cues. This ensures the graphic impact of the symbols but allows prompting the user on their meaning. The Macintosh trash can icon, incidentally, also has a text label, "Trash," just in case people don't get the idea from the symbol.

Nonetheless, a few symbols have emerged in the interactive multimedia world as an accepted lexicon of navigation cues that do not need text.

These symbols are by no means universal, but Figure 4-3 shows some that have roots from the days of teletypewriters, others from early HyperCard and videodisc development, and yet others from the consumer electronics world. Even for these common symbols, text labels are often added to the graphic icons to avoid uncertainty.

Figure 4-3 Some symbols are easily recognized but may still require text titles. "Smiley" symbols, or emoticons, used in Internet conversation to express mood, are made up entirely of text and punctuation characters.

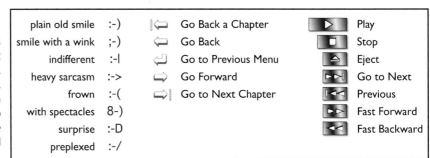

plain old smile	:-)		Go Back a Chapter		Play
smile with a wink	;-)		Go Back		Stop
indifferent	:-l		Go to Previous Menu		Eject
heavy sarcasm	:->		Go Forward		Go to Next
frown	:-(		Go to Next Chapter		Previous
with spectacles	8-)				Fast Forward
surprise	:-D				Fast Backward
preplexed	:-/				

Animating Text

There are plenty of ways to retain a viewer's attention when displaying text. For example, you can animate bulleted text and have it "fly" onto the screen. You can "grow" a headline a character at a time. For speakers, simply highlighting the important text works well as a pointing device. When there are several points to be made, you can stack keywords and flash them past the viewer in a timed automated sequence (as in the roadside Burma Shave ads—signs placed every half mile or so along the highway, each offering the motorist just a few more words toward a complete slogan). You might fly in some keywords, dissolve others, rotate or spin others, and so forth, until you have a dynamic bulleted list of words that is interesting to watch. But be careful—don't overdo the special effects, or they will become boring.

Powerful but inexpensive applications such as Xaos Tools' TypeCaster (see "Making Pretty Text") let you create 3-D text using both TrueType and Type 1 Adobe fonts. You can also use Illustrator or FreeHand EPS (Encapsulated PostScript) outline files to create still images in 3-D and then animate the results to create QuickTime movies with broadcast-quality rendering.

Computers and Text

Very early in the development of the Macintosh computer's monitor hardware, Apple chose to use a resolution of 72 pixels per inch. This matches the standard measurement of the printing industry (72 points per inch) and allows desktop publishers and designers to see on the monitor what their printed output will look like (WYSIWYG). In addition, Apple made each pixel square-shaped, providing even measurements in all directions.

Until the Macintosh was invented, and the VGA video standard set for the PC (at 96 pixels per inch), pixels were typically taller than they were wide. The aspect ratio for older EGA monitors, for example, is 1.33:1, taller than it is wide. VGA and SVGA monitor resolutions for both Macintosh and Windows display pixels at an aspect ratio of 1:1 (square).

The Font Wars

In 1985, the desktop publishing revolution was spearheaded by Apple and the Macintosh computer, in combination with word processing and page layout software products that enabled a high-resolution 300 dpi laser printer using special software to "draw" the shapes of characters as a cluster of square pixels computed from the geometry of the character. This special software was **Adobe's PostScript** page description and outline font language. It was licensed by Apple and included in the firmware of Apple's LaserWriter laser printer.

PostScript is really a method of describing an image in terms of mathematical constructs (Bezier curves), so it is used not only to describe the individual characters of a font but also to describe entire illustrations and whole pages of text. Because each PostScript character is a mathematical formula, it can be easily scaled bigger or smaller so it looks right whether drawn at 24 points or 96 points, whether the printer is a 300 dpi Laser-Writer or a high-resolution 1200, 2400, or even 3600 dpi image setter suitable for the finest print jobs. And the PostScript characters can be drawn much faster than in the old-fashioned way. Before PostScript, the printing software looked up the character's shape in a bitmap table containing a representation of the pixels of every character in every size. PostScript quickly became the de facto industry font and printing standard for desktop publishing and played a significant role in the early success of Apple's Macintosh computer.

There are two kinds of PostScript fonts: Type 3 and Type 1. Type 3 font technology is *older* than Type 1 and was developed for output to printers; it is rarely used by multimedia developers. There are currently over 6,000 different Type 1 typefaces available. Type 1 fonts also contain **hints**, which are special instructions for grid-fitting to help improve resolution. Hints can apply to a font in general or to specific characters at a particular resolution.

Other companies followed Adobe into the desktop publishing arena with their own proprietary and competitive systems for scalable outline fonts. In May 1989, Apple and Microsoft announced a joint effort to develop a "better and faster" quadratic curves outline font methodology, called **TrueType**. In addition to printing smooth characters on printers, TrueType would draw characters to a low-resolution (72 dpi or 96 dpi) monitor. Furthermore, Apple and Microsoft would no longer need to license the PostScript technology from Adobe for their operating systems. Today, TrueType fonts ship with the Windows and Macintosh computers. Microsoft licensed a set of fonts from Monotype, a font "foundry" company, which became the fonts that ship with Windows.

Though the PostScript-versus-TrueType war continues to reverberate through the computer and publishing industries, multimedia developers really only need to be concerned about how these scaled fonts look on monitors, not about how they are printed to paper—unless, of course, you are printing perfect proposals, bids, storyboards, reports, and above all, invoices :-). TrueType and PostScript outline fonts allow text to be drawn at any size on your computer screen without **jaggies**:

The Jaggies

Jaggies are avoided by anti-aliasing the edges of the text characters, making them seem smoother to the eye. Note the improved look of the anti-aliased letters in the bottom row of letters in Figure 4-4. Pasting an image that was anti-aliased against a light background onto a darker-colored background using transparency (so the new, dark background is seen, instead of the old, light one) can be problematic: the blending pixels along the edge will show as a halo and may have to be edited one by one.

Small Typefaces

In the early days of both Macintosh and Windows, a bitmap for the font and size was always required in the system in order to display text without jaggies. A collection of special, memory-hungry bitmaps was required to display fonts outside the normal range installed on the computer. True-Type and PostScript/ATM, using mathematical formulas, allowed you to display smooth-edged type of any size and style on your monitor without requiring a collection of bitmap files.

Unfortunately, this helpful innovation does not come without a penalty. The smaller fonts (12 points and less) are not as legible on your monitor when drawn by mathematical formula as they are when drawn from bitmaps. TrueType and PostScript/ATM do their best to render the small sizes, but they are hard pressed to compete with the clarity of font bitmaps. These were carefully hand-tweaked by type designers to provide optimum legibility at monitor resolutions. Moving a single pixel in a small letter can make a subtle but critical difference.

To provide the quality of hand-crafted bitmapped fonts for smaller sizes, TrueType font foundries often provide hints to control which pixels in a character are turned on or off at low resolution and size. These are called Enhanced Screen Quality (ESQ) TrueType fonts.

Figure 4-4 Anti-aliasing text and graphics creates "smooth" boundaries between colors. The top row of letters is not anti-aliased; the bottom row is

....

http://www.fonts.com

More detail about TrueType ESQ fonts
....

WARNING *Bitmapped, TrueType, and PostScript fonts do not display (or print) exactly the same, even though they may share the same name and size. The three technologies use different formulas. This means that word-wrapping in a text field may change. So if you build a field or a button that precisely fits text displayed with PostScript, be aware that if you then display it with the same font in TrueType, the text may be truncated or wrapped, wrecking your layout.*

Font Foundries

Collections of fonts are available through retail channels or directly from their manufacturers. Typefaces are created in a **foundry**, a term much like case, that has carried over from times when lead was poured into molds to make letter faces. There is also a special interest group (SIG) at America Online (go to Computing:Software Libraries:Desktop & Web Publishing Forum:Fonts) where people who enjoy designing and making interesting fonts post them for others to download—hundreds and hundreds of them with names like Evil of Frankenstein, CocaCola, Kerouac, LED, Poncho-Via (sic), Spaghetti, TreeFrog, and Sassy. When you purchase some applications, such as CorelDraw or Adobe Illustrator, many extra fonts are included for free.

....

http://www.typequarry.com/

http://www.oldfonts.com/

http://www.myfonts.com/foundry/

http://www.bitstream.com

http://www.fonts.com/-

http://www.will-harris.com/type.htm

Commercial type foundries and font sites. These gateways lead to a discussion of fonts and where to find them. With *Esperfonto*, Will Harris provides an interesting tool for making font decisions: Casual or Formal, Body or Display, Friendly or Serious, Cool or Warm, Modern or Traditional
....

WARNING *It is easy to spend hours and hours downloading neat and interesting fonts; they are like the midnight snack table on a Caribbean cruise liner—ice carvings and delectable goodies laid out as far as the eye can see.*

Managing Your Fonts

Never assume that the fonts you have installed on your computer will also be installed on another person's computer. Pay attention to the way you include fonts in a project so that you never face the nightmare of your carefully picked fonts being replaced by an ill-suited default font like Courier (see the next "First Person"). If your work is being distributed to sites that may not have the fonts you are using, or if you do not license these fonts for distribution with your work, be sure to bitmap the special font text you use for titles, headlines, buttons, and so forth. For text to be entered by users, it is safest to stay with the installed Windows or Macintosh fonts, because you know they are universally available on that platform. In Windows, use the TrueType fonts installed during the Setup procedure.

First Person

We had a short break between sessions to install the software for a panel discussion about multimedia. Four of us brought media with discussion material. Our moderator installed her presentation first, and we heard her wail, "Something's wrong with my fonts!" We all looked at her ugly 48-point Geneva and felt sorry for her; we knew her mistake. The beautiful fonts she had installed on her home system were not installed in the system of the Macintosh being used for the big-screen projector, and she had failed to bring the fonts along, separately or in the resource fork of her project. By then, it was too late anyway.

 You won't be able to print with Helvetica or stroke its characters because the font's outline file is missing or ATM is turned off.

OK

TIP *Always be sure your fonts travel with your application when you are delivering software to run on a hardware platform other than the one you used to create the application. To avoid many font display problems, particularly for menus and headlines, you may wish to snap a picture of your text with a screen capture utility and use this image, or bitmap, instead of text that you type into a text field. (Chapter 6 describes bitmaps and how to capture and edit images.) This will ensure that the screen always looks right, regardless of what hardware platform you use or what fonts are installed.*

Character Sets and Alphabets

Knowing that there is a wide selection of characters available to you on your computer and understanding how you can create and use special and custom-made characters will broaden your creative range when you design and build multimedia projects.

The ASCII Character Set

The **American Standard Code for Information Interchange (ASCII)** is the 7-bit character coding system most commonly used by computer systems in the United States and abroad. ASCII assigns a number or value to 128 characters, including both lower- and uppercase letters, punctuation marks, Arabic numbers, and math symbols. Also included are 32 control characters used for device control messages, such as carriage return, line feed, tab, and form feed.

ASCII code numbers always represent a letter or symbol of the English alphabet, so that a computer or printer can work with the number that represents the letter, regardless of what the letter might actually look like on the screen or printout. To a computer working with the ASCII character set, the number 65, for example, always represents an uppercase letter A. Later, when displayed on a monitor or printed, the number is turned into the letter.

ASCII was invented and standardized for analog teletype communication early in the age of bits and bytes. The capabilities of the technology have now moved far beyond the original intent of the standard, but because millions of installed computers and printers use ASCII, it is difficult to set any new standards for text without the expense and effort of replacing existing hardware. At least, for these 128 characters, most computers and printers share the same values.

On the Macintosh, use KeyCaps, a desk accessory delivered with the system and found in the Apple menu, to examine the fonts and characters available to your Macintosh system. In Windows, use the Character Map accessory (Charmap.exe) to view and access characters, especially those "un-Roman" fonts not on the keyboard, such as Carta or Symbol, as illustrated in Figure 4-5.

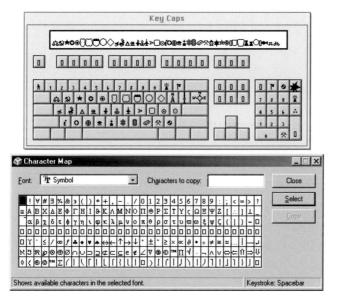

Figure 4-5 KeyCaps on the Macintosh and Charmap.exe in Windows let you see which key to press on the keyboard to print a character in a font face.

TIP   *The Charmap application (Charmap.exe) is part of Windows, but is not always automatically installed with the system software. Look in Start | Programs | Accessories | System Tools; if it's not there, look in your Windows folder for Charmap.exe. To install Charmap.exe from your Windows CD, go to Start | Settings | Control Panel. Select Add/Remove Programs. Then click on the Windows Setup tab. Double-click on Accessories, and check the box next to Character Map. Click OK, and Windows will install Charmap.exe from the installer CD into your Windows folder. To launch it, go to Start | Programs | Accessories | System Tools | Character Map.*

The Extended Character Set

A byte, which consists of 8 bits, is the most commonly used building block for computer processing. ASCII uses only 7 bits to code its 128 characters; the 8th bit of the byte is unused. This extra bit allows another 128 characters to be encoded before the byte is used up, and computer systems today use these extra 128 values for an extended character set. The extended character set is most commonly filled with ANSI (American National Standards Institute) standard characters, including often-used symbols, such as ¢ or ∞, and international diacritics or alphabet characters, such as ä or ñ. This fuller set of 255 characters is also known as the ISO-Latin-1 character set; it is used when programming the text of HTML web pages.

 CROSS PLATFORM   *The rules for encoding extended characters are not standardized. Thus ASCII value 165, for example, may be a bullet (•) character on the Macintosh; the character for Japanese yen (¥) in Windows (ANSI); or a capital N with tilde (Ñ) in DOS.*

Unicode

As the computer market has become more international, one of the resulting problems has been handling the various international language alphabets. It was at best difficult, and at times impossible, to translate the text portions of programs from one script to another. For example, the differences between the Roman script used by western European writers and the kanji script used by Japanese writers made it particularly challenging to transfer innovative programs from one market to another.

· ·

http://www.unicode.org

The Unicode organization supports standards for managing the characters of all known languages in the world

· ·

Since 1989, a concerted effort on the part of linguists, engineers, and information professionals from many well-known computer companies has been focused on a 16-bit architecture for multilingual text and character encoding. Called **Unicode**, the original standard accommodated up to about 65,000 characters to include the characters from all known languages and alphabets in the world.

Where several languages share a set of symbols that have a historically related derivation, the shared symbols of each language are unified into collections of symbols (called **scripts**). A single script can work for tens or even hundreds of languages (for example, the Latin script used for English and most European languages). Sometimes, however, only one script will work for a language (such as the Korean Hangul). Here are the 25 supported scripts of Version 2.0 of the Unicode standard:

Arabic	Gujarati	Latin
Armenian	Gurmkhi	Lao
Bengali	Han	Malayalam
Bopomofo	Hangul	Oriya
Cyrillic	Hebrew	Phonetic
Devanagari	Hiragana	Tamil
Georgian	Kannada	Telugu
Greek	Katakana	Thai
		Tibetan

Unicode also contains collections of symbols and special characters in secondary scripts:

Numbers	General diacritics	General punctuation
General symbols	Mathematical symbols	Technical symbols
Dingbats	Arrows, blocks, box drawing forms, and geometric shapes	Miscellaneous symbols
		Presentation forms

The Unicode standard includes more than 18,000 Han characters (ideographs for Japanese, Chinese, and Korean), and future releases will include obsolete alphabets such as cuneiform, hieroglyphs, and ancient Han characters. In addition, character space will be reserved for users and publishers to create their own scripts, designed especially for their own applications. For example, a carpenter might develop a script that included a character meaning "half-inch Sheetrock," another character meaning "three-quarter-inch plywood," and so forth. HTML 4.0 allows access to the Unicode characters by numeric reference. Thus 水 (in hexadecimal) represents the Chinese character for water.

While 65,000 characters are sufficient for encoding most of the many thousands of characters used in major languages of the world, the Unicode standard and ISO/IEC 10646 now support three encoding forms that use a common repertoire of characters but allow for encoding as many as a million more characters. This is sufficient for all known character encoding requirements, including full coverage of all historic scripts of the world, as well as common notational systems.

The Unicode® Standard: A Technical Introduction *(http://www.unicode.org/ unicode/standard/principles.html)*

Mapping Text Across Platforms

If you build your multimedia project on a Windows platform and play it back on a Macintosh platform (or vice versa), there will be subtle (and sometimes not-so-subtle) differences. Fonts are perhaps the greatest cross-platform concern, because they must be mapped to the other machine. If a specified font doesn't exist on the target machine, a substitute must be provided that does exist on the target. This is **font substitution**. Windows and Macintosh provide default fonts for this substitution.

In many cross-platform-savvy applications, you can explicitly define the mapping of your fonts. In Adobe Director MX, for example, you can control **font mapping** behavior by altering the FONTMAP.TXT file; Director remaps those fonts that the target system cannot provide. Table 4-2 shows some typical mappings used by Director when crossing platforms.

Mac→Win	Win→Mac
Mac:Chicago→Win:System	Win:Arial→Mac:Helvetica
Mac:Courier→Win:Courier New	Win:Courier→Mac:Courier
Mac:Geneva→Win:MS Sans Serif	Win:Courier New→Mac:Courier
Mac:Helvetica→Win:Arial	Win:MS Serif→Mac:New York
Mac:Monaco→Win:Terminal	Win:MS Sans Serif→Mac:Geneva
Mac:New York→Win:MS Serif	Win:Symbol→Mac:Symbol Map None
Mac:Symbol→Win:Symbol Map None	Win:System→Mac:Chicago
Mac:Times→Win:Times New Roman (sizes: 14→12, 18→14, 24→18, 30→24)	Win:Terminal→Mac:Monaco
Mac:Palatino→Win:Times New Roman	Win:Times New Roman→Mac:Times (sizes: 12→14, 14→18, 18→24, 24→30)

Table 4-2 Typical Mappings for Standard Macintosh and Windows Fonts Used by Adobe DirectorMX

It is not just fonts that are problematic; characters, too, must be mapped across platforms. Character mapping allows bullets, accented characters, and other curious characters that are part of the extended character set on one platform to appear correctly when text is moved to the other platform. Curly quotation marks, for example, rarely, if ever, map successfully across platforms.

To solve font and character uncertainties when working across platforms, many multimedia developers convert the text of their projects into bitmaps. These bitmaps may also be converted to 1-bit images that do not require great memory for storage in a project. Once converted to a bitmap, however, text cannot be edited or reworked without editing the bitmap in an image-editing program or creating a new bitmap.

First Person

While we were in the early phases of producing my CD-ROM, Multimedia: Working It Out!, I sold the rights to distribute it into Korea and Mainland China. Nobody on the production team had ever seen a computer that typed short-form Mandarin, and we knew that even when the English was localized, we would be hard pressed to recognize any of the text, much less edit or alter it in its new form.

So we devised a structured system of labels and names for Multimedia: Working It Out! and converted all the text in the project (about 600 "pages" of about a paragraph each) into 1-bit bitmaps in a Director movie. Donna Booher edited and formatted the text in Microsoft Word, Dan Hilgert bitmapped and screen-captured each page with Capture and Photoshop, and Peter Wolf imported the PICT files into Director (by the hundreds) as cast members. Each cast member had a unique (but systematic) name associated with a Director movie, a heading, and various icons. It took a while.

The localizers across the Pacific, then, would simply translate a page or a series of pages using their own native-language word processor, capture their own bitmaps, and we would substitute the new bitmaps

for the old using the unique identification labels. No language skills required!

When we started, Terry Thompson devised a color-coded master filing system and database so that all the word-processed text and the screen-captured bitmaps would remain neatly side by side and concurrent. This is called *version control*. By the time this project shipped, Donna's computer was crashing four or five times a day and we had lost files, Dan had gone back to school, Peter and I were slapping miscellaneous text elements into the project without tracking where they came from, and we were changing labels and moving cast members around as we streamlined performance, debugged, and staggered toward a golden master and the Federal Express drop-off. We had converted Terry's neatly organized system into chaos.

After the CD-ROMs were pressed, and there wasn't anything anybody could change anymore anyway, we did a tricky thing with Lingo programming, DeBabelizer, and OmniPage Pro to convert the final project's bitmapped text back into word processor text.

First we collected all the bitmapped text into a single Director movie (we weren't interested in pretty pictures, QuickTime, sounds, or other types

of cast members, just text). Then we placed each page of bitmapped text into a movie frame (Cast to Time), neatly labeled that frame at the top with the identifying code of the image using a Lingo handler, and saved all of the frames as PICT images (an automatic command in Director's Export menu). With DeBabelizer, we batch-converted these hundreds of PICT images from 72 dpi (screen capture resolution) to 300 dpi (printer resolution) and saved each as a 1-bit TIFF image. The process was automatic.

OmniPage Pro is a powerful optical character recognition (OCR) program that usually reads documents on a flatbed scanner and turns them into nicely formatted word processing documents. OmniPage (ah ha!) allows batch processing of TIFF (and more recently, PICT) images at 300 dpi, so we ran all of these TIFFs (automatically) through OmniPage, and bingo!, they came out as archival word processing files. Then we sent the word files to Guido Mozzi in Italy so his team of translators could begin localizing there.

Some efforts are cyclical, we have discovered. The trick is to learn something and improve the process each time the task comes around!

The written Japanese language consists of three different types of character sets, namely: kanji, katakana, and hiragana. Kanji was originally taken from the Chinese language and is essentially a pictographic representation of the spoken word. Each kanji has two different readings, "on-yomi" and "kun-yomi," respectively, the "Chinese rendering" and the "Japanese rendering." Both are used depending on the conjugation of the kanji with other kanji.

Due to certain incompatibilities between the Japanese spoken word and kanji, two sets of kana or phonetic syllabary (alphabet) were developed. Katakana is the "square" kana and is used today for writing only foreign words or onomatopoeic expressions. Hiragana is the "cursive" kana and can be used alone to represent a certain word or combined with kanji to form other words and sentences. Romaji, a more recent addition to the alphabets of Japan, allows for the phonetic spelling of the Japanese language using the Roman characters familiar to the Western world.

....

Ross Uchimura, Executive Vice-President, GC3 Ltd., a cross-cultural expert

Languages in the World of Computers

In modern Western languages, words are made up of symbols or letters strung together, representing as a whole the sounds of a spoken word. This is not so for Eastern languages such as Chinese, Japanese, and Korean (and the ancient languages of Sumeria, Egypt, and Mesopotamia). In these languages, an entire concept might be represented by a single word symbol that is unrelated to a specific phonetic sound.

The letters or symbols of a language are its alphabet. In English, the alphabet consists of 26 Roman or Latin letters; in Japanese, the kanji alphabet comprises more than 3,000 kanas, or whole words. The Russian alphabet, made up of Cyrillic characters based on the ancient Greek alphabet, has about the same number of letters as a Roman alphabet. All languages, from Navajo to Hebrew, have their own unique alphabets.

Most modern alphabets share one very important attribute: the graphic shapes and method for writing the Arabic numbers 0 1 2 3 4 5 6 7 8 9. This is a simple system for representing decimal numbers, which lends itself to easy reading, writing, manipulation, and calculation. Expressing and performing

$$16 + 32 = 48$$

is much easier in Arabic numbers than in Roman or Greek numerals:

$$XVI + XXXII = XLVIII$$

$$\iota\varsigma + \lambda\beta = \mu\eta$$

Use of Arabic notation has gradually spread across the world to supplant other systems, although Roman numerals are still used today in Western languages in certain forms and contexts.

Translating or designing multimedia (or any computer-based material) into a language other than the one in which it was originally written is called **localization**. This process deals with everything from the month/day/year order for expressing dates to providing special alphabetical characters on keyboards and printers. Even the many Western languages that share the Roman alphabet have their own peculiarities and often require special characters to represent special sounds. For example, German has its umlaut (¨); French its various accents (é), the cedilla (ç), and other diacritics; and Spanish its tilde (ñ). These characters are typically available in the extended character set of a font.

Special Characters in HTML   In HTML, **character entities** based upon the ISO-Latin-1 standard make up the alphabet that is recognized by browser software on the World Wide Web. All of the usual characters of an English keyboard are included (the 7-bit ASCII set is built in), but for the extended character set that includes tildes, umlauts, accents, and special symbols, you must use an escape sequence to represent them in an

First Person

When I was in Germany some years ago, I read a curious report in the *Frankfurter Allgemeine* about a fellow who was suing the local electric utility for not correcting the spelling of his name to its proper form in the German alphabet. His name had an umlaut in it (Wörm), but his bill always read Woerm. In German, the letter ö sounds different from the letter o, so I can't say I blamed him. At first he didn't pay his bill, claiming that he wasn't that person; then the courts told him to pay anyway. So he initiated a civil suit to protect his name.

It seems the utility was using a legacy IBM system with a high-speed chain printer to produce the monthly bills, and none of the umlaut characters were available on the ASCII-based chain. By long-standing convention, when you are limited to the English alphabet, the letter *e* immediately follows any umlautless vowel, to indicate that the umlaut should be there but isn't. Today, with high-speed laser printers and special fonts, the problem has probably gone away.

More recently, there are reports that the California Department of Motor Vehicles cannot handle blank spaces in the name fields of its massive database, so Rip Van Winkle's name was changed to Rip VanWinkle without his permission. Expect a lawsuit.

ISO-Latin-1 HTML document. A character entity is represented either by a number or by a word and is always prefixed by an ampersand (escape) and followed by a semicolon. For example, the name for the copyright symbol is "copy" and its number is 169. The symbol may be inserted into a document either as © or as ©—either way, the character © is generated by the browser. The list of character entities allowed in standard HTML is growing and will soon include mathematical symbols and even icons to represent things like trash cans, clocks, and disk drives. Word processors for languages other than English automatically insert the necessary character entities when a document is saved in HTML format or specify the character set to use.

. . . .

http://www.w3.org/TR/REC-html40/sgml/entities.html

An encyclopedic discussion and reference for HTML character entity references

. . . .

Multilanguage Web Pages When building a project in more than one language for the Web, consider translating the languages that use Roman fonts and displaying them as text in the browser in the normal way. Languages other than English may have many escaped characters, as you can see in Figure 4-6. If Chinese or Japanese or Arabic is desired, translate the Roman text onto a computer running an operating system using that native language. For the web page, the translator can then capture a screen image of the translated text, and you can embed that image into your web page. This process takes precise coordination among the designers, the content providers, and the translators, but it can be done smoothly with careful labeling of the bits and pieces.

```
<p>
What can this integrated network solution offer your business?
Lower costs, increased flexibility, and greater reliability by support-
ing all voice and data requirments, including:</p>
<p>
O que esta solu&ccedil;&atilde;o de rede integrada pode oferecer
a sua empresa? Menores custos, elevada flexibilidade, e maior con-
fiabilidade, pelo suporte a todos os requisitos de voz e dados, inclu-
indo:</p>
<p>
Qu&eacute; puede ofrecerle a su negocio esta soluci&oacute;n in-
tegrada de redes? Menores costos, mayor flexibilidad y mayor fiabil-
idad mediante la compatibilidad con todos los requisitos para voz y
datos, incluso:</p>
<p>
<img src="images/chinese/story 1-1.gif">
```

這種綜合性的網路產品能為您的公司企業帶來哪些好處呢？它能降低成本，提昇
服務的靈活性，以及具有更大的可靠性，因為它能支持各種話音與數據傳輸的要
求，包括：

```
</p>
<p>
<img src="images/japanese/story 1-1.gif">
```

この統合的ネットワークソリューションは、以下を含む音声・データ要件のすべてに対応し、費用
節減、フレキシビリティや信頼性の向上を実現させます。

求，包括：

```
</p>
```

Figure 4-6 Portion of a five-language web site using normal HTML code for the Roman languages and screen-captured graphic images to display the Chinese and Japanese translations.

Font Editing and Design Tools

Special font editing tools can be used to make your own type, so you can communicate an idea or graphic feeling exactly. With these tools, professional typographers create distinct text and display faces. Graphic designers, publishers, and ad agencies can design instant variations of existing typefaces.

Typeface designs fall into the category of industrial design and have been determined by the courts in some cases to be protected by patent. For example, design patents have been issued for Bigelow & Holmes' Lucida, ITC Stone, and for Adobe's Minion.

___

WARNING   *If your commercial project includes special fonts, be sure that your license agreement with the font supplier allows you to distribute them with your project.*

Occasionally in your projects you may require special characters. With the tools described in the paragraphs that follow, you can easily substitute characters of your own design for any unused characters in the extended character set. You can even include several custom versions of your client's company logo or other special symbols relevant to your content or subject right in your text font.

• •

http://www.fontfoundry.com

http://www.larabiefonts.com

There are hundreds of sites for downloading free and shareware fonts drawn by others. For starters, try these two.

• •

Fontographer

Fontographer, supplied by Fontlab, Ltd. located at www.fontlab.com, is a specialized graphics editor for both Macintosh and Windows platforms. You can use it to develop PostScript, TrueType, and bitmapped fonts for Macintosh, Windows, DOS, NeXT, and Sun workstations. Designers can also modify existing typefaces, incorporate PostScript artwork, automatically trace scanned images, and create designs from scratch. A sample of the Fontographer screen is shown in Figure 4-7.

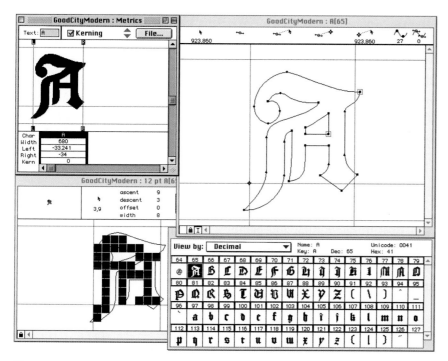

Figure 4-7 Fontographer is a powerful font editor for Macintosh and Windows.

Fontographer's features include a freehand drawing tool to create professional and precise inline and outline drawings of calligraphic and script characters, using either the mouse or alternative input methods (such as Wacom pressure-sensitive pen systems and CalComp DrawingBoard). Fontographer allows the creation of multiple font designs from two existing typefaces, and you can design lighter or heavier fonts by modifying the weight of an entire typeface.

Fontographer for Windows opens any PostScript Type 1 or TrueType font for the PC and lets you create condensed, expanded, and oblique versions of the same font or modify any of those fonts to suit your design needs. One character, several characters, or entire fonts can be scaled, rotated, and skewed to create new and unique typefaces. A metric window provides complete control over character width, spacing, offset, and kerning. The current Windows version of Fontographer does not make Multiple Master fonts (PostScript fonts that allow you to adjust a range of certain characteristics for a set of characters, such as serif to sans serif or condensed to extended) or Type 3 PostScript fonts, and it does not have an Option-Copy, Paste feature for bringing drawings through the clipboard from FreeHand MX or Illustrator CS2. Nor can the current version read a Macintosh Fontographer database; font transfer is accomplished through Type 1 PostScript.

Making Pretty Text

To make your text look pretty, you need a toolbox full of fonts and special graphics applications that can stretch, shade, shadow, color, and anti-alias your words into real artwork. Pretty text is typically found in bitmapped drawings where characters have been tweaked, manipulated, and blended into a graphic image. Simply choosing the font is the first step. Most designers find it easier to make pretty type starting with ready-made fonts, but some will create their own custom fonts using font editing and design tools such as Fontographer, previously described.

With the proper tools and a creative mind, you can create endless variations on plain-old type, and you not only choose but also customize the styles that will fit with your design needs.

Most image-editing and painting applications let you make text using the fonts available in your system. You can colorize the text, stretch, squeeze, and rotate it, and you can filter it through various plug-ins to generate wild graphic results.

Figure 4-8 is an image with text created in Photoshop. The rose was scanned from a photograph, separated from its background (1), and placed onto black (2). A 200-point word, "Rose," was typed in bold black Peignot Light onto a white background without anti-aliasing (3). Then a rainbow of hues was "stolen" from the little strip on Photoshop's color wheel by screen-capturing, and the strip was duplicated horizontally until it would

When they first invented typesetting there were variants cut of each character so text would look as if it had been handwritten by a monk! Desktop designers have been fighting so hard to get their setting to look like it's come from a Berthold system, that most of the new potential of desktop typography has been overlooked.

....

David Collier, Author of
Collier's Rules for Desktop Design and Typography

be large enough to cover the entire word (4). Selecting and dragging the rainbow of colors on top of the word, the rainbow was laid onto the black letters by removing white from the underlying image using Photoshop's Composite Controls—note the lower slider is moved one value to the left, from 255 to 254 (5). The characters of the word were then selected along their edges by selecting all the white background with the Magic Wand tool, then inverting that selection (Invert in the Select menu). The rainbow word was dragged on top of the red rose (6), and a two-pixel border around it was selected (Border in the Select menu). Then the word was finally anti-aliased onto the background using the Blur filter, blurring just the border of the word (7).

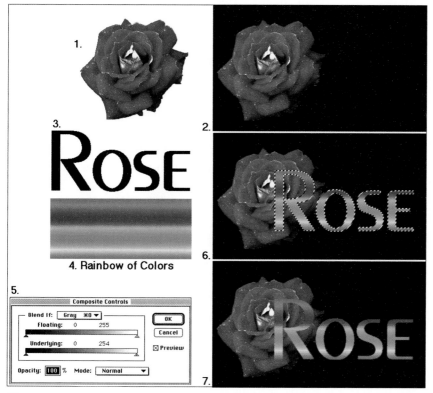

Figure 4-8 Image-editing applications let you make pretty text.

Three-dimensional modeling programs allow you to create a character, add depth to it or extrude it, shade and light it, and manipulate it into other shapes. The character here was generated in just this way and, when animated using Adobe's Director MX, spins in place:

Inexpensive applications such as Strider's TypeStyler (http://typest1 .fatcow.com), COOL 3D from U-Lead, and plug-ins for Photoshop from Xaos Tools (TypeCaster) and Vertigo (HotTEXT) are designed to manipulate typefaces in a graphical way. Custom-tortured characters can be captured as a bitmap and incorporated into your project. These 3-D programs let you put together interesting still and animated titles and headlines for web pages, documents, presentations, reports, videos, and multimedia titles. You can rotate the text, adjust style, color, texture, camera angle, and background, and even map images onto the surface. There are many sources of support for GIF animations with transparency and interlacing. Working in 3-D space takes some practice until you become intuitively comfortable with the notion of roll, pitch, and yaw and familiar with the application's controls for adjusting lights, textures, and views.

Hypermedia and Hypertext

Multimedia—the combination of text, graphic, and audio elements into a single collection or presentation—becomes interactive multimedia when you give the user some control over what information is viewed and when it is viewed. Interactive multimedia becomes hypermedia when its designer provides a structure of linked elements through which a user can navigate and interact.

When a hypermedia project includes large amounts of text or symbolic content, this content can be indexed and its elements then linked together to afford rapid electronic retrieval of the associated information. When words are keyed or indexed to other words, you have a **hypertext system**; the "text" part of this term represents the project's content and meaning, rather than the graphical presentation of the text. Hypertext is what the World Wide Web is all about.

When text is stored in a computer instead of on printed pages, the computer's powerful processing capabilities can be applied to make the text more accessible and meaningful. The text can then be called **hypertext**; because the words, sections, and thoughts are linked, the user can navigate through text in a nonlinear way, quickly and intuitively.

Using hypertext systems, you can electronically search through all the text of a computer-resident book, locate references to a certain word, and then immediately view the page where the word was found. Or you can create complicated Boolean searches (using terms such as AND, OR, NOT, and BOTH) to locate the occurrences of several related words, such as "Elwood," "Gloria," "mortgage," and "happiness," in a paragraph or on a page. Whole documents can be linked to other documents.

A word can be made hot, as can a button, thus leading the user from one reference to another. Click on the word "Elwood," and you may find yourself reading a biography or resume; click on "mortgage," and a calculator pops up. Some authoring systems (see Chapter 7) incorporate a hypertext facility that allows you to identify words in a text field using a bold or colored style, then link them to other words, pages, or activities, such as playing a sound or video clip related to that hot word. You cannot do this kind of nonlinear and associative navigation in a sequentially organized book. But on a CD-ROM, where you might have more than 100,000 pages of text to investigate, search, and browse, hypertext is invaluable.

Because hypertext is the organized cross-linking of words not only to other words but also to associated images, video clips, sounds, and other exhibits, hypertext often becomes simply an additional feature within an overall multimedia design. The term "hyper" (from the Greek word "over" (υπερ) has come to imply that user interaction is a critical part of the design, whether for text browsing or for the multimedia project as a whole. When interaction and cross-linking is then added to multimedia, and the navigation system is nonlinear, multimedia becomes hypermedia.

In 1945, Vannevar Bush wrote a seminal eight-page article, "As We May Think," for the *Atlantic Monthly* (http://www.theatlantic.com/unbound/flashbks/computer/bushf.htm). This short treatise, in which he discusses the need for new methodologies for accessing information, has become the historic cornerstone of hypertext experimentation. Doug Englebart (inventor of the mouse) and Ted Nelson (who coined the term "hypertext" in 1965) have actively championed the research and innovations required of computer technology for implementing useful hypertext systems, and they have worked to combat the historic inertia of linear thought. Nelson would claim that the very structure of thought is neither sequential nor linear and that computer-based hypertext systems will fundamentally alter the way humans approach literature and the expression of ideas during the coming decades.

The argument against this theory of associative thought is that people are, indeed, more comfortable with linear thinking and are easily overwhelmed by too much freedom, becoming quickly lost in the chaos of nonlinear gigabytes. As a practical reminder, it is important always to provide location markers, either text-and-symbol menus or illustrative maps, for users who travel the threads of nonlinear systems.

The Power of Hypertext

In a fully indexed hypertext system, all words can be found immediately. Suppose you search a large database for "boats," and you come up with a whopping 1,623 references, or hits—among them, Noah's Ark (open boat in water), television situation comedies (*The Love Boat*), political criticisms of cabinet members who challenged the status quo (rocked the boat), cabinet members who were stupid (missed the boat), and Christmas dinner trimmings (Grandmother's gravy boat). So you narrow your search and look for

[Vannevar] Bush identified the problem—and the need to provide new ways to access information—but was he right about how the mind works? I suspect a purely associative model of human memory and mental processes is too simplistic.

Philip Murray, *From Ventura to Hypertext*, Knowledge Management Associates, Danvers, MA

"boats" and "water" when both words are mentioned on the same page; this time you get 286 hits. "Boats," "water," and "storms" gets you 37; "boats," "water," "storms," and "San Francisco," a single hit. With over a thousand hits, you are lost. With one hit, you have something! But you still may not find what you are looking for, as you can see in this fictional example:

The *storm* had come and gone quickly across the Colorado plains, but *water* was still puddled at the foot of the house-high bank of mud that had slid into town when the dam burst. In front of the general store, which had remained standing, four strong men carefully lifted a tiny *boat* onto the large dray wagon borrowed from the woodcutters. On a layer of blankets in the bilge of the *boat*, the undertaker had carefully laid out the remains of both the mayor and his paramour. The mayor had not drowned in the flood, but died of a heart attack in the midst of the panic. Children covered the *boat* with freshly cut pine boughs while horses were quickly harnessed to the wagon, and a strange procession began to move slowly down *San Francisco* Street toward the new cemetery. …

The power of such search-and-retrieval systems provided by a computer for large volumes of data is immense, but clearly this power must be channeled in meaningful ways. Links among words or clusters of information need to be designed so that they make sense. Judgments must be made about relationships and the way information content is organized and made available to users. The lenses through which vast amounts of data are viewed must necessarily be ground and shaped by those who design the access system.

The issue of who designs the lenses and how the designers maintain impartial focus is troubling to many scientists, archivists, and students of cognitive thinking. The scientists would remain "hermeneutically" neutral, they would balance freedom against authority and warn against the epistemological unknowns of this new intellectual technology. They are aware of the forces that allow advertising and marketing craftspeople to intuitively twist meanings and spin events to their own purposes, with actions that can affect the knowledge and views of many millions of people and thus history itself. But these forces remain poorly understood, are not easily controlled by authority, and will express themselves with immeasurably far-reaching, long-term impact on the shape of human culture.

The multimedia designer controls the filtering mechanisms and places the lenses within the multimedia project. A manufacturer, for instance, that presents its products using interactive multimedia can bring abundant information and selling power within reach of the user, including background information, collateral marketing material, pricing statistics, and technical data. The project design will be, of course, biased—to sell more of the manufacturer's products and generate more profit; but this bias is assumed and understood in these circumstances. When the assumptions

The hype about hypertext may be justified. It can provide a computer-supported information environment which can add to our appreciation of the text, can go some way towards aping the mental agility of the human mind, can allow navigation along patterns of association, can provide a nonlinear information environment. But the problems of constructing nonlinear documents are not few and can prove to be very complex.

Patricia Baird, Editor of *Hypermedia*, a scientific journal published in the United Kingdom

Hypermedia on its own simply functions as a reference tool. But when it is integrated within a goal-based activity, it becomes a powerful learning resource.

Brigid Sealy & Paul Phelan, INESC, Porto, Portugal (conclusions from research funded by the European Commission's Human Capital and Mobility Program)

and understandings of inherent bias in any information base break down, when fiction or incomplete data is presented as full fact, these are the times when the powerful forces of multimedia and hypermedia can have their greatest deleterious effect.

WARNING   *Bad multimedia projects will not alter the collective view of history; really bad projects might.*

Using Hypertext

Special programs for information management and hypertext have been designed to present electronic text, images, and other elements in a database fashion. Commercial systems have been used for large and complicated mixtures of text and images—for example, a detailed repair manual for a Boeing 747 aircraft, a parts catalog for Pratt & Whitney jet turbine engines, an instant reference to hazardous chemicals, and electronic reference libraries used in legal and library environments. Such searchable database engines are widely used on the Web, where **software robots** visit millions of web pages and index entire web sites. Hypertext databases rely upon proprietary indexing systems that carefully scan the entire body of text and create very fast cross-referencing indexes that point to the location of specific words, documents, and images. Indeed, a hypertext index by itself can be as large as 50 percent to 100 percent the size of the original document. Indexes are essential for speedy performance. Google's search engine produces about 1,220,000,000 hits in less than a quarter of a second!

Commercial hypertext systems were developed historically to retrofit gigantic bodies of information. Licenses for use and distribution of these commercial systems

are expensive, and the hypertext-based projects typically require the large mass-storage capability of one or many CD-ROMs and/or dedicated gigabyte hard disks. Simpler but effective hypertext indexing tools are available for both Macintosh and Windows, and they offer fairly elaborate features designed to work in concert with many multimedia authoring systems. Server-based hypertext and database engines designed for the Web are now widely available and competitively priced.

TIP   *Rather than designing an elaborate, fully cross-referenced hypertext system for your multimedia project, you can "hardwire" the links between the most salient words (highlight them in your text) so that a mouse click leads to a topic menu specific to the chosen word. Though this constrains the user's movement through the text, the user will not perceive it as such, and you can thus maintain strict control over your navigation pathways and design.*

Searching for Words

Although the designer of a hypermedia database makes assumptions, he or she also presents users with tools and a meaningful interface to exercise the assumptions. Employing this interface, users can tailor word searches to find very specific combinations. Following are typical methods for word searching in hypermedia systems:

- Categories: Selecting or limiting the documents, pages, or fields of text within which to search for a word or words.

- Word relationships: Searching for words according to their general proximity and order. For example, you might search for "party" and "beer" only when they occur on the same page or in the same paragraph.

- Adjacency: Searching for words occurring next to one another, usually in phrases and proper names. For instance, find "widow" only when "black" is the preceding adjacent word.

- Alternates: Applying an OR criterion to search for two or more words, such as "bacon" or "eggs."

- Association: Applying an AND criterion to search for two or more words, such as "skiff," "tender," "dinghy," and "rowboat."

- Negation: Applying a NOT criterion to search exclusively for references to a word that are not associated with the word. For example, find all occurrences of "paste" when "library" is not present in the same sentence.

- Truncation: Searching for a word with any of its possible suffixes. For example, to find all occurrences of "girl" and "girls," you may need to specify something like **girl#**. Multiple character suffixes can be managed with another specifier, so **geo*** might yield "geo," "geology," and "geometry," as well as "George."

- Intermediate words: Searching for words that occur between what might normally be adjacent words, such as a middle name or initial in a proper name.

- Frequency: Searching for words based on how often they appear: the more times a term is mentioned in a document, the more relevant the document is to this term.

Hypermedia Structures

Two buzzwords used often in hypertext systems are link and node. **Links** are connections between the conceptual elements, that is, the **nodes** that may consist of text, graphics, sounds, or related information in the knowledge base. Links connect Caesar Augustus with Rome, for example, and grapes with wine, and love with hate. The art of hypermedia design lies in the visualization of these nodes and their links so that they make sense, not nonsense, and can form the backbone of a knowledge access system. Along with the use of HTML for the World Wide Web, the term **anchor** is used for the reference from one document to another document, image, sound, or file on the Web (see Chapter 14).

Links are the navigation pathways and menus; nodes are accessible topics, documents, messages, and content elements. A **link anchor** is where you come from; a **link end** is the destination node linked to the anchor. Some hypertext systems provide unidirectional navigation and offer no return pathway; others are bidirectional.

The simplest way to navigate hypermedia structures is via buttons that let you access linked information (text, graphics, and sounds) that is contained at the nodes. When you've finished examining the information, you return to your starting location. A typical navigation structure might look like the following:

Pages of text with hot words linked to InfoBites only

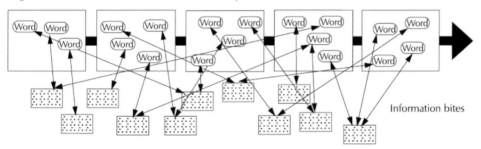

Information bites

Navigation becomes more complicated when you add associative links that connect elements not directly in the hierarchy or sequence. These are the paths where users can begin to get lost if you do not provide location markers. A link can lead to a node that provides further links, as shown here:

Pages of text with hot words linked to InfoBites linked to pages and to other InfoBites

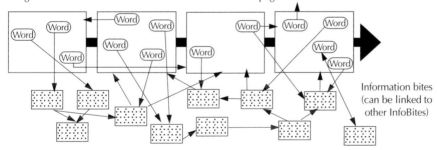

Information bites (can be linked to other InfoBites)

When you offer full-text search through an information base, there may be links between any number of items at your current node and any number of other nodes with items that meet your relationship criteria. When users are browsing freely through this system, and one page does not follow the next (as expected in the linear metaphor of books and literature), users can get lost in the associative maze of the designer's content:

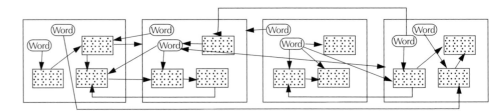

One publisher of hypermedia products claims that becoming lost in "hyperspace" may not be all that bad. The struggle to find your way back can be valuable in itself, and certainly a learning experience.

Hypertext Tools

Two functions are common to most hypermedia text management systems, and they are often provided as separate applications: building (or authoring) and reading. The builder creates the links, identifies nodes, and generates the all-important index of words. The index methodology and the search algorithms used to find and group words according to user search criteria are typically proprietary, and they represent an area where computers are carefully optimized for performance—finding search words among a list of many tens of thousands of words requires speed-demon programming.

Hypertext systems are currently used for electronic publishing and reference works, technical documentation, educational courseware, interactive kiosks, electronic catalogs, interactive fiction, and text and image databases. Today these tools are used extensively with information organized in a linear fashion; it still may be many years before the majority of multimedia project users become comfortable with fully nonlinear hypertext and hypermedia systems. When (and perhaps if) they do, the methodology of human thought and conceptual management—indeed, the way we think—will be forever changed.

Hypermedia can take advantage of powerful capabilities that are becoming clearer as the new multimedia medium matures, giving us a greater choice in exploration, if not in outright plot definition, for example. From my experiences with "Playa Sirenas," the real challenge facing storytellers in this new medium is allowing readers appropriate choices (some authorship of the story, really) while they navigate through the hypermedia experience, without destroying the successful and basic patterns that have been part of storytelling since people first gathered around campfires.

There is something organic about these time-proven storytelling patterns. As an author in the new medium, you must first design the DNA or template of your story, then allow (and promote) mutation along evolutionary lines that you, as the author, have created as part of the template…

Hermann Steffen, hypermedia novelist, San Jose, Costa Rica

Chapter 4 Review

■ Chapter Summary

For your review, here's a summary of the important concepts discussed in this chapter.

Discuss the importance of text in a multimedia presentation

■ With the recent explosion of the Internet and the World Wide Web, text has become more important than ever. Words and symbols in any form, spoken or written, are the most common system of communication. It's important to design labels for title screens, menus, and buttons using words that have the most precise and powerful meanings to express what you need to say. Experiment with the words you plan to use by letting others try them.

List some attributes of a block of text

■ Typical font styles are bold, italic, and underlined.

■ Type sizes are usually expressed in points (about 72 per inch).

■ Leading is the space between lines.

■ Kerning is the space between individual characters.

■ Alignment can be left, right, centered, or justified.

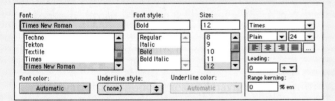

List at least three styles for a font

■ Three common styles are bold, italic, and underline, but there are several others; some, such as superscript, emboss, or strikethrough, have specialized uses.

☐ Strikethrough   ☐ Shadow   ☑ Small caps
☐ Double strikethrough   ☐ Outline   ☐ All caps
☐ Superscript   ☐ Emboss   ☐ Hidden
☐ Subscript   ☐ Engrave

Describe the difference between a typeface and a font

■ A typeface is a family of graphic characters that usually includes many type sizes and styles.

■ A font is a collection of characters of a single size and style belonging to a particular typeface family.

List at least three factors that affect the legibility of text

■ Size, color, background color, style, and leading.

■ Serif versus sans serif is the simplest way to categorize a typeface. The serif is the little decoration at the end of a letter stroke. On the printed page, serif fonts are traditionally used for body text because the serifs are said to help guide the reader's eye along the line of text. Sans serif fonts, on the other hand, are used for headlines and bold statements. But sans serif fonts are far more legible and attractive when used in the small sizes of a text field on a screen.

Discuss font encoding systems and HTML character encoding standards

■ The standard document format used for pages on the Web is called Hypertext Markup Language

HTML Entities		
Dec	**Entity**	**Char**
8595	&darr;	↓
8596	&harr;	↔
8629	&crarr;	↵
8656	&lArr;	⇐
8657	&uArr;	⇑
8658	&rArr;	⇒
8659	&dArr;	⇓
8660	&hArr;	⇔
8704	&forall;	∀
8706	&part;	∂
8707	&exist;	∃
8709	&empty;	∅
8711	&nabla;	∇
8712	&isin;	∈
8713	&notin;	∉
8715	&ni;	∋
8719	&prod;	∏
8721	&sum;	∑
8722	&minus;	−
8727	&lowast;	∗
8730	&radic;	√
8733	&prop;	∝
8734	&infin;	∞
8736	&ang;	∠
8743	&and;	∧
8744	&or;	∨
8745	&cap;	∩
8746	&cup;	∪
8747	&int;	∫
8756	&there4;	∴
8764	&sim;	∼
8773	&cong;	≅
8776	&asymp;	≈
8800	&ne;	≠
8801	&equiv;	≡
8804	&le;	≤
8805	&ge;	≥
8834	&sub;	⊂
8835	&sup;	⊃
8836	&nsub;	⊄
8838	&sube;	⊆
8839	&supe;	⊇
8853	&oplus;	⊕

(HTML). In an HTML document you can specify typefaces, sizes, colors, and other properties by "marking up" the text in the document with tags. The remarkable growth of the Web is straining the "old" designs for displaying text on computers. Dynamic HTML uses cascading style sheets (CSSs) to define choices ranging from line height to margin width to font face.

Define multimedia, interactive multimedia, hypermedia, hypertext, links, anchors, and nodes

- Multimedia—the combination of text, graphic, and audio elements into a single collection or presentation—becomes interactive multimedia when you give the user some control over what information is viewed and when it is viewed. Interactive multimedia becomes hypermedia when its designer provides a structure of linked elements through which a user can navigate and interact.

- When a hypermedia project includes large amounts of text or symbolic content, this content can be indexed and its elements then linked together to afford rapid electronic retrieval of the associated information. When words are keyed or indexed to other words, you have a hypertext system; the "text" part of this term represents the project's content and meaning, rather than the graphical presentation of the text. Hypertext is what the World Wide Web is all about.

- When text lives in a computer instead of on printed pages, the computer's powerful processing capabilities can be applied to make the text more accessible and meaningful. The text can then be called hypertext; because the words, sections, and thoughts are linked, the user can navigate through text in a nonlinear way, quickly and intuitively. Because hypertext is the organized cross-linking of words not only to other words but also to associated images, video clips, sounds, and other exhibits, hypertext often becomes simply an additional feature within an overall multimedia design.

- Links are connections between the conceptual elements, that is, the nodes containing text, graphics, sounds, or related information in the knowledge base. The term anchor is formally used in HTML as the reference from one document to another document, image, sound, or file. Links are the navigation pathways and menus; nodes are accessible topics, documents, messages, and content elements. A link anchor is where you come from; a link end is the destination node linked to the anchor.

Discuss the potential and limitations of hypertext and hyperlinking systems

- You can search and view potentially billions of documents and files (information), but you can also become "lost in hyperspace."

■ Key Terms

■ Key Term Quiz

1. Type sizes are usually expressed in _____.
2. When a password must be entered in upper- or lowercase in order to match the original password, it is said to be _____.
3. Symbolic representations of objects and processes common to the graphical user interfaces of many computer operating systems are called _____.
4. Special HTML characters, always prefixed by an ampersand (escape) and followed by a semicolon, are called _____.
5. "What you see is what you get" is spoken as _____.
6. Translating or designing multimedia (or any computer-based material) into a language other than the one in which it was originally written is called _____.
7. The little decoration at the end of a letter stroke is a _____.
8. Designers call roomy blank areas _____.
9. _____ blends the colors along the edges of the letters (called dithering) to create a soft transition between the letter and its background.
10. Conceptual elements consisting of text, graphics, sounds, or related information in the knowledge base, are called _____.

■ Multiple Choice Quiz

1. A family of graphic characters that usually includes many type sizes and styles is called a:
    a. typeface
    b. font
    c. point
    d. link
    e. node

2. Which of the following is a term that applies to the spacing between characters of text?
    a. leading
    b. kerning
    c. tracking
    d. points
    e. dithering

3. Intercapping, the practice of placing a capital in the middle of a word, is a trend that emerged from the computer programming community because:
    a. it looks cool
    b. they wanted to copy marketing practices in the electronics industry
    c. they found they could see the words used for variables and commands better
    d. one of the first computer programmers had a faulty SHIFT key on his keyboard
    e. it increases security in case-sensitive passwords

4. Dynamic HTML uses _____ to define choices ranging from line height to margin width to font face.
    a. cascading style sheets
    b. font mapping
    c. font substitution
    d. software robots
    e. encapsulated PostScript

5. If a DHTML document includes a font face that is not installed on the user's computer, a browser will:
    a. automatically download the correct font
    b. refuse to load the page
    c. leave a blank space where that text is
    d. crash
    e. try to substitute the font with a similar looking font

6. In the URL http://www.timestream.com/info/people/biotay/biotay1.html, which part is case sensitive?
    a. the record type: "http://"
    b. the domain name: "timestream.com"
    c. the subdomain "www"
    d. the document path: "info/people/biotay/biotay1.html"
    e. all are case sensitive

7. Multimedia becomes interactive multimedia when:
    a. the user has some control over what information is viewed and when it is viewed
    b. the information is displayed by a computer with a touchscreen or other input device
    c. the information is available on the Web—either the Internet or a local area network
    d. quizzes and tests with evaluations and scoring are included
    e. the user can change such attributes as volume and type size

8. Interactive multimedia becomes hypermedia when:
    a. the information is available on the Web—either the Internet or a local area network
    b. quizzes and tests with evaluations and scoring are included
    c. it includes a structure of linked elements through which a user can navigate and interact
    d. the user can change such attributes as volume and type size
    e. the content formatting complies with the American Standard Code for Information Interchange

9. Web pages are coded using:
    a. Unicode
    b. American Standard Code for Information Interchange
    c. File Transfer Protocol
    d. Hypertext Markup Language
    e. encapsulated PostScript

10. Which of the following provides a system for dynamically displaying a font?
    a. Apache
    b. PostScript
    c. HTTPD
    d. serif
    e. WYSIWYG

11. A printed page might be presented in which of these orientations?
    a. newsscape
    b. portrait
    c. flat-file
    d. x-height
    e. node

12. Which of the following is a character encoding system?
    a. FontTab
    b. HTML
    c. CSS
    d. WYSIWYG
    e. Unicode

13. The reference from one document to another document, image, sound, or file on the Web is a(n):
    a. sweetspot
    b. anchor
    c. node
    d. tag
    e. button

14. Which of the following is a problem that might apply to hypermedia?
    a. Users' eye movements affect their ability to link.
    b. Users will be turned off by excessive animation.
    c. Hypermedia software might create inappropriate links.
    d. Current hyperlinking technology far exceeds what today's desktop computers can handle.
    e. Search results generally are too granular to be useful.

15. Which of the following is a typical method for word searching in a hypermedia system?
    a. best fit
    b. adjacency
    c. popularity
    d. tracking
    e. localization

■ Essay Quiz

1. Describe what characteristics a block of text might have.

2. Describe what characteristics a typeface might have.

3. Discuss the problems encountered using text across computer platforms and in different languages.

4. Discuss the differences among multimedia, interactive multimedia, hypertext, and hypermedia.

5. Your boss wants you to create a hypermedia system for Web visitors to find technical support information about your company. What are some of the implications in creating this system? Should you hand-build the links or use an automatic indexing system? Why?

Lab Projects

■ Project 4.1

Visit a web site and print out a page. Visit the same page on another computer (preferably on another operating system), and print out the same page.

Compare the pages. Are the printouts different? Why?

■ Project 4.2

From three different publications, select a printed page. Circle the different blocks of text. Characterize the types of text used in each block by providing for each page:

- Publication name and page number.
- Which blocks are headlines? What type of font is used? Is it bold? serif? Characterize the text. How is it spaced?
- Which blocks are body text? What type of font is used? Is it bold? serif? Characterize the text. How is it spaced?

■ Project 4.3

Access a computer. Identify two programs that allow you to manipulate text. Write some text in varied styles and fonts. Print the results. For each, list:

- The program's name.
- The ways in which that program allows you to change text. Can you easily change the font? the color? the style? the spacing?

■ Project 4.4

Create a new document in a word processing application. Next, type in a line of text and copy the line five times. Now change each line into a different font. Recopy the entire set of lines three times. Finally, change the size of the first set to 10-point text, the second to 18-point text, and the third set to 36-point text.

- Which of the smallest lines of text is most readable?
- Which line of text stands out the most?

■ Project 4.5

Review two different games or educational programs delivered on CD-ROM. Create a diagram that shows how the information in each is structured. For each, describe:

- How are the navigational structures similar in the two programs?
- What words are common to both programs (for example, "Quit," "Home," "Help," etc.)?

Sound

SOUND is perhaps the most sensuous element of multimedia. It is meaningful "speech" in any language, from a whisper to a scream. It can provide the listening pleasure of music, the startling accent of special effects, or the ambience of a mood-setting background. Some feel-good music powerfully fills the heart, generating emotions of love or otherwise elevating listeners closer to Heaven. How you use the power of sound can make the difference between an ordinary multimedia presentation and a professionally spectacular one. Misuse of sound, however, can wreck your project.

The Power of Sound

When something vibrates in the air by moving back and forth (such as the cone of a loudspeaker), it creates waves of pressure. These waves spread like the ripples from a pebble tossed into a still pool, and when they reach your eardrums, you experience the changes of pressure, or vibrations, as sound. In air, the ripples propagate at about 750 miles per hour, or Mach 1 at sea level. Sound waves vary in sound pressure level (amplitude) and in frequency or pitch. Many sound waves mixed together form an audio sea of symphonic music, speech, or just plain noise.

Acoustics is the branch of physics that studies sound. Sound pressure levels (loudness or volume) are measured in **decibels (dB)**; a decibel measurement is actually the ratio between a chosen reference point on a logarithmic scale and the level that is actually experienced. When you quadruple the sound output power, there is only a 6 dB increase; when you make the sound 100 times more intense, the increase in dB is not hundredfold, but only 20 dB. This scale makes sense because humans perceive sound pressure levels over an extraordinarily broad dynamic range. The decibel scale, with some examples, is shown in Table 5-1; notice the relationship between power (measured in watts) and dB.

Sound is energy, just like the waves breaking on a sandy beach, and too much volume can permanently damage the delicate receiving mechanisms behind your eardrums, typically dulling your hearing in the 6 kHz range. In terms of volume, what you hear subjectively is not what you hear objectively. The perception of loudness is dependent upon the frequency or pitch of the sound: at low frequencies, more power is required to de-

dB	Watts	Example
195	25–40 million	Saturn rocket
170	100,000	Jet engine with afterburner
160	10,000	Turbojet engine at 7,000-pounds thrust
150	1,000	ALSETEX splinterless stun grenade
140	100	2 JBL2226 speakers pulling 2,400 watts inside an automobile
130	10	75-piece orchestra, at *fortissimo*
120	1	Large chipping hammer
110	0.1	Riveting machine
100	0.01	Automobile on highway
90	0.001	Subway train; a shouting voice
80	0.0001	Inside a 1952 Corvette at 60 mph
70	0.00001	Voice conversation; freight train 100 feet away
60	0.000001	Large department store
50	0.0000001	Average residence or small business office
40	0.00000001	Residential areas of Chicago at night
30	0.000000001	Very soft whisper
20	0.0000000001	Sound studio

Table 5-1   Typical Sound Levels in Decibels (dB) and Watts

liver the same perceived loudness as for a sound at the middle or higher frequency ranges. You may feel the sound more than hear it. For instance, when the ambient noise level is above 90 dB in the workplace, people are likely to make increased numbers of errors in susceptible tasks—especially when there is a high-frequency component to the noise. When the level is above 80 dB, it is quite impossible to use a telephone. Experiments by researchers in residential areas have shown that a sound generator at 45 dB produces no reaction from neighbors; at 45 to 55 dB, sporadic complaints; at 50 to 60 dB, widespread complaints; at 55 to 65 dB, threats of community action; and at more than 65 dB, vigorous community action. This research from the 1950s continues to provide helpful guidelines for practicing rock musicians and multimedia developers today.

There is a great deal more to acoustics than just volume and pitch. If you are interested, there are many texts that discuss why middle C on a cello does not sound like middle C on a bassoon; or why a five-year-old can hear a 1,000 Hz tone played at 20 dB, while an older adult with presbycusis (loss of hearing sensitivity due to age) cannot. Your use of sound in multimedia projects will not likely require highly specialized knowledge of harmonics, intervals, sine waves, notation, octaves, or the physics of acoustics and vibration, but you do need to know the following:

- How to make sounds
- How to record and edit sounds on your computer
- How to incorporate sounds into your multimedia work

Multimedia System Sounds

You can use sound right off the bat on both the Macintosh and on a multimedia PC running Windows, because beeps and warning sounds are available as soon as you install the operating system. Open the Sound Control Panel to listen to your system sounds, change them, or make a new, custom sound (see Figure 5-1).

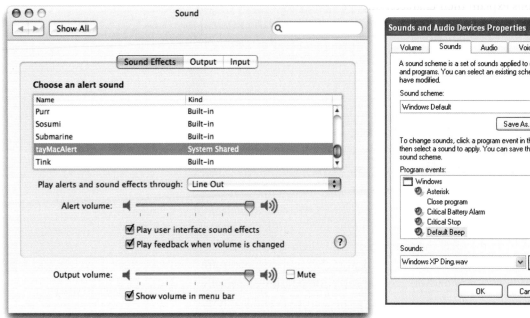

Figure 5-1 Sound Control Panels for Windows and Macintosh

In Windows, system sounds are WAV files, and they reside in the Windows\Media subdirectory. Available system event sounds include start.wav, chimes.wav, chord.wav, ding.wav, logoff.wav, notify.wav, recycle.wav, tada .wav, and the Microsoft sound.wav that typically plays when Windows starts up. If you have installed Microsoft Office, you will have more choices, such as applause.wav, camera.wav, carbrake.wav, cashreg.wav, chimes .wav, clap.wav, driveby.wav, drumroll.wav, explode.wav, glass.wav, gunshot .wav, laser.wav, projctor.wav, ricochet.wav, type.wav, and whoosh.wav.

which equals 1,764,000 bytes. A 40-second mono recording at 11 kHz, 8-bit resolution would be

$$11000 * 40 * 8 / 8 * 1$$

which equals 440,000 bytes.

Consumer-grade audio compact discs are recorded in stereo at a sampling rate of 44.1 kHz and a 16-bit resolution. Fortunately, for hard disk storage requirements at least, user expectations of audio quality are somewhat lower for computer-based multimedia presentations than they are for Grammy Award–winning recordings. (See Vaughan's Law of Multimedia Minimums in the "Production Tips" section of this chapter.)

TIP *The only reason to digitize audio at a higher specification than can be used by the target playback device is for archiving it. As playback technologies and bandwidth improve over time, you may wish (someday) for higher-quality original files when you upgrade a product. Save the originals!*

I have a 20-second sample of a song which I play to my class at 8K, 22K, 44K, and 48K, and I have the students listen and compare quality. They comment that 8K does not sound all that bad *until* they hear the 44K and 48K. They also see (hear) very little difference between 44K and 48K.

Dennis Woytek,
Assistant Professor
of Multimedia Technology,
Duquesne University

Setting Proper Recording Levels

A distorted recording sounds terrible. If the signal you feed into your computer is too "hot" to handle, the result will be an unpleasant crackling or background ripping noise. Conversely, recordings that are made at too low a level are often unusable because the amount of sound recorded does not sufficiently exceed the residual noise levels of the recording process itself. The trick is to set the right levels when you record.

Any good piece of digital audio recording and editing software will display digital meters to let you know how loud your sound is. Watch the meters closely during recording, and you'll never have a problem. Unlike analog meters that usually have a 0 setting somewhere in the middle and extend up into ranges like +5, +8, or even higher, digital meters peak out. To avoid distortion, do not cross over this limit. If this happens, lower your volume (either by lowering the input level of the recording device or the output level of your source) and try again. Try to keep peak levels between −3 and −10. Any time you go over the peak, whether you can hear it or not, you introduce distortion into the recording.

Editing Digital Recordings

Once a recording has been made, it will almost certainly need to be edited. Shown in Figure 5-4 with its special effects menu, Audacity is a free open-source sound editing application for Windows, Macintosh, and Linux operating systems (http://audacity.sourceforge.net). With such a tool you can create sound tracks and digital mixes. The basic sound editing operations that most multimedia producers need are described in the paragraphs that follow.

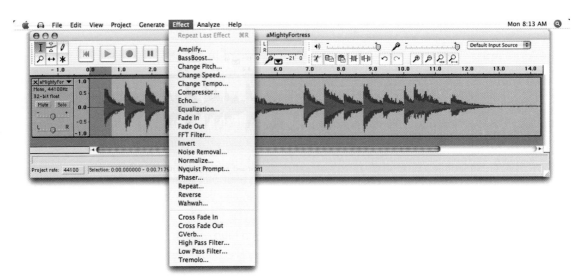

Figure 5-4 Audacity is free, open-source software for recording and editing sounds.

Multiple Tracks Being able to edit and combine multiple tracks (for sound effects, voice-overs, music, etc.) and then merge the tracks and export them in a "final mix" to a single audio file is important.

Trimming Removing "dead air" or blank space from the front of a recording and any unnecessary extra time off the end is your first sound editing task. Trimming even a few seconds here and there might make a big difference in your file size. Trimming is typically accomplished by dragging the mouse cursor over a graphic representation of your recording and choosing a menu command such as Cut, Clear, Erase, or Silence.

Splicing and Assembly Using the same tools mentioned for trimming, you will probably want to remove the extraneous noises that inevitably creep into a recording. Even the most controlled studio voice-overs require touch-up. Also, you may need to assemble longer recordings by cutting and pasting together many shorter ones. In the old days, this was done by splicing and assembling actual pieces of magnetic tape.

Volume Adjustments If you are trying to assemble ten different recordings into a single sound track, there is little chance that all the segments will have the same volume. To provide a consistent volume level, select all the data in the file, and raise or lower the overall volume by a certain amount. Don't increase the volume too much, or you may distort the file. It is best to use a sound editor to **normalize** the assembled audio file to a particular level, say 80 percent to 90 percent of maximum (without clipping), or about −16 dB. Without normalizing to this rule-of-thumb level, your final sound track might play too softly or too loudly. Even pros can leave out this important step. Sometimes an audio CD just doesn't seem to have the same loudness as the last one you played, or it is too loud and you can hear clipping. Figure 5-5 shows the normalizing process at work in Sound Forge.

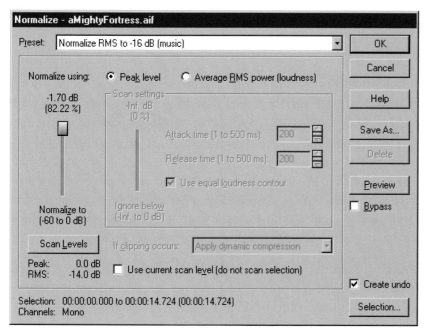

Figure 5-5 Normalizing evens out the sound level in an audio file.

Format Conversion   In some cases, your digital audio editing software might read a format different from that read by your presentation or authoring program. Most sound editing software will save files in your choice of many formats, most of which can be read and imported by multimedia authoring systems.

Resampling or Downsampling   If you have recorded and edited your sounds at 16-bit sampling rates but are using lower rates and resolutions in your project, you must **resample** or **downsample** the file. Your software will examine the existing digital recording, and work through it to reduce the number of samples. This process may save considerable disk space.

Fade-ins and Fade-outs   Most programs offer enveloping capability, useful for long sections that you wish to fade in or fade out gradually. This enveloping helps to smooth out the very beginning and the very end of a sound file.

Equalization   Some programs offer **digital equalization (EQ)** capabilities that allow you to modify a recording's frequency content so that it sounds brighter or darker.

Time Stretching   Advanced programs let you alter the length (in time) of a sound file without changing its pitch. This feature can be very useful, but watch out: most **time-stretching** algorithms will severely degrade the audio quality of the file if the length is altered more than a few percent in either direction.

Digital Signal Processing (DSP)   Some programs allow you to process the signal with reverberation, multitap delay, chorus, flange, and other special effects using **digital signal processing (DSP)** routines.

Being able to process a sound source with effects can greatly add to a project. To create an environment by placing the sound inside a room, hall, or even a cathedral can bring depth and dimension to a project. But a little can go a long way—do not overdo the sound effects! Once a sound effect is processed and mixed onto a track, it cannot be further edited; so always save the original so you can tweak it again if you are not happy.

Reversing Sounds   Another simple manipulation is to reverse all or a portion of a digital audio recording. Sounds, particularly spoken dialog, can produce a surreal, otherworldly effect when played backward.

Making MIDI Audio

Composing your own original score can be one of the most creative and rewarding aspects of building a multimedia project, and **MIDI (Musical Instrument Digital Interface)** is the quickest, easiest, and most flexible tool for this task. Yet creating an original MIDI score is hard work. Knowing something about music, being able to play the piano, and having a lot of good ideas are just the prerequisites to building a good score; beyond that, it takes time and musical skill to work with MIDI.

Happily, you can always hire someone to do the job for you. In addition to the talented MIDI composers who charge substantial rates for their services, many young composers are also available who want to get into multimedia. With a little research, you can often find a MIDI musician to work for limited compensation. Remember, however, that you often get what you pay for.

The process of creating MIDI music is quite different from digitizing existing audio. If you think of digitized audio as analogous to a bitmapped graphic image (both use sampling of the original analog medium to create a digital copy), then MIDI is analogous to structured or vector graphics (both involve instructions provided to software to be able to re-create the original on the fly). For digitized audio you simply play the audio through a computer or device that can digitally record the sound. To make MIDI scores, however, you will need **sequencer software** (as illustrated in Figure 5-6) and a **sound synthesizer** (typically built into the sound board on PCs, but an add-on board or peripheral for the Macintosh). A **MIDI keyboard** is also useful for simplifying the creation of musical scores. The MIDI keyboard is not, however, necessary for playback unless the keyboard has its own built-in synthesizer (most do) that you wish to specify for playback. Note that you could only provide that kind of specification for a special production, not software headed for general consumer release where you have no control over playback hardware.

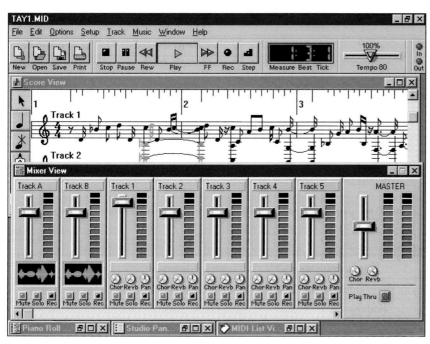

Figure 5-6 Sequencing software allows you to record, edit, and save music generated from a MIDI keyboard or instrument.

The sequencer software lets you record and edit MIDI data. Rather than recording a note, the software creates data about each note as it is played on a MIDI keyboard (or another MIDI device)—which note it is, how much pressure was used on the keyboard to play the note, how long it was sustained, and how long it takes for the note to decay or fade away, for example. This information, when played back through a MIDI device, allows the note to be reproduced exactly. Because the quality of the playback depends upon the end user's MIDI device rather than the recording, MIDI is **device dependent**. The sequencer software quantizes your score to adjust for timing inconsistencies (a great feature for those who can't keep the beat), and it may also print a neatly penned copy of your score to paper. SmartScore software from Musitek is not only a sequencer, it can be used to go the other way, too: using a scanner, it will recognize notation and convert sheet music to multitrack MIDI files in your computer (see Figure 5-7).

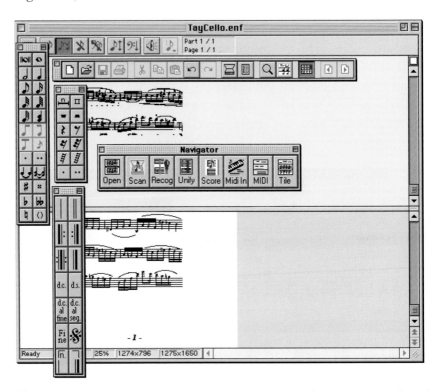

Figure 5-7 SmartScore from Musitek scans sheet music and converts it to multitrack MIDI files.

. . . .

http://www.musitek.com

For converting sheet music to MIDI

. . . .

An advantage of structured data such as MIDI is the ease with which you can edit the data. Let's say you have a piece of music being played on a honky-tonk piano, but your client decides he wants the sound of a soprano saxophone instead. If you had the music in digitized audio, you would have to re-record and redigitize the music. When it is in MIDI data, however, there is a value that designates the instrument to be used for playing back the music. To change instruments, you just change that value. Instruments that you can synthesize are identified by a **General MIDI** numbering system that ranges from 0 to 127 (see Table 5-3). Note that some MIDI devices offset the numbers by one, using 1 to 128. Most software has a switch to accommodate these devices. Until this system came along, there was always a risk that a MIDI file originally composed with, say, piano, electric guitar, and bass, might be played back with piccolo, tambourine, and glockenspiel if the ID numbers were not precisely mapped to match your original hardware setup. This was usually the case when you played a MIDI file on a MIDI configuration different from the one that recorded the file.

ID	Sound	ID	Sound	ID	Sound	ID	Sound
0	Acoustic grand piano	29	Overdriven guitar	58	Tuba	87	Lead 8 (Bass + lead)
1	Bright acoustic piano	30	Distortion guitar	59	Muted trumpet	88	Pad 1 (New Age)
2	Electric grand piano	31	Guitar harmonics	60	French horn	89	Pad 2 (Warm)
3	Honky-tonk piano	32	Acoustic bass	61	Brass section	90	Pad 3 (Polysynth)
4	Rhodes piano	33	Electric bass (finger)	62	Synth brass 1	91	Pad 4 (Choir)
5	Chorused piano	34	Electric bass (pick)	63	Synth brass 2	92	Pad 5 (Bowed)
6	Harpsichord	35	Fretless bass	64	Soprano saxophone	93	Pad 6 (Metallic)
7	Clarinet	36	Slap bass 1	65	Alto saxophone	94	Pad 7 (Halo)
8	Celesta	37	Slap bass 2	66	Tenor saxophone	95	Pad 8 (Sweep)
9	Glockenspiel	38	Synth bass 1	67	Baritone saxophone	96	FX 1 (Rain)
10	Music box	39	Synth bass 2	68	Oboe	97	FX 2 (Soundtrack)
11	Vibraphone	40	Violin	69	English horn	98	FX 3 (Crystal)
12	Marimba	41	Viola	70	Bassoon	99	FX 4 (Atmosphere)
13	Xylophone	42	Cello	71	Clarinet	100	FX 5 (Brightness)
14	Tubular bells	43	Contrabass	72	Piccolo	101	FX 6 (Goblins)
15	Dulcimer	44	Tremolo strings	73	Flute	102	FX 7 (Echoes)
16	Hammond organ	45	Pizzicato strings	74	Recorder	103	FX 8 (Sci-Fi)
17	Percussive organ	46	Orchestral harp	75	Pan flute	104	Sitar
18	Rock organ	47	Timpani	76	Bottle blow	105	Banjo
19	Church organ	48	String ensemble 1	77	Shakuhachi	106	Shamisen
20	Reed organ	49	String ensemble 2	78	Whistle	107	Koto
21	Accordion	50	SynthStrings 1	79	Ocarina	108	Kalimba
22	Harmonica	51	SynthStrings 2	80	Lead 1 (Square)	109	Bagpipe
23	Tango accordion	52	Choir aahs	81	Lead 2 (Sawtooth)	110	Fiddle
24	Acoustic guitar (nylon)	53	Voice oohs	82	Lead 3 (Calliope lead)	111	Shanai
25	Acoustic guitar (steel)	54	Synth voice	83	Lead 4 (Chiff lead)	112	Tinkle bell
26	Electric guitar (jazz)	55	Orchestra hit	84	Lead 5 (Charang)	113	Agogo
27	Electric guitar (clean)	56	Trumpet	85	Lead 6 (Voice)	114	Steel drums
28	Electric guitar (muted)	57	Trombone	86	Lead 7 (Fifths)	115	Wood block

Table 5-3 General MIDI Instrument Sounds

ID	Sound	ID	Sound	ID	Sound	ID	Sound
116	Taiko drum	37	Side stick	52	Chinese cymbal	67	High agogo
117	Melodic tom	38	Acoustic snare	53	Ride bell	68	Low agogo
118	Synth drum	39	Hand clap	54	Tambourine	69	Cabasa
119	Reverse cymbal	40	Electric snare	55	Splash cymbal	70	Maracas
120	Guitar fret noise	41	Low-floor tom	56	Cowbell	71	Short whistle
121	Breath noise	42	Closed high-hat	57	Crash cymbal 2	72	Long whistle
122	Seashore	43	High-floor tom	58	Vibraslap	73	Short guiro
123	Bird tweet	44	Pedal high-hat	59	Ride cymbal 2	74	Long guiro
124	Telephone ring	45	Low tom	60	High bongo	75	Claves
125	Helicopter	46	Open high-hat	61	Low bongo	76	High wood block
126	Applause	47	Low-mid tom	62	Mute high conga	77	Low wood block
127	Gunshot	48	High-mid tom	63	Open high conga	78	Mute cuica
Percussion Keys		49	Crash cymbal 1	64	Low conga	79	Open cuica
35	Acoustic bass drum	50	High tom	65	High timbale	80	Mute triangle
36	Bass drum 1	51	Ride cymbal 1	66	Low timbale	81	Open triangle

Table 5-3   General MIDI Instrument Sounds *(continued)*

TIP   *Making MIDI files is as complex as recording good sampled files; so it often pays to find someone already set up with the equipment and skills to create your score, rather than investing in both the hardware and the learning curve.*

Once you have gathered your audio material, you will need to edit it to precisely fit your multimedia project. As you edit, you will continue to make creative decisions. Because it is so easy to edit MIDI data, you can make many fine adjustments to your music.

Since MIDI is device dependent and the quality of consumer MIDI playback hardware varies greatly, MIDI's true place in multimedia work may be as a production tool rather than a delivery medium. MIDI is by far the best way to create original music for multimedia projects, so use MIDI to get the flexibility and creative control you want. Then, once the music is completed and fits your project, lock it down for delivery by turning it into digital audio data.

TIP   *Test your MIDI files thoroughly by playing them back on a variety of hardware devices before you incorporate them into your multimedia project.*

Audio File Formats

When you create multimedia, it is likely that you will deal with file formats and translators for text, sounds, images, animations, or digital video clips. A sound file's format is simply a recognized methodology for organizing the digitized sound's data bits and bytes into a data file. The structure of the file must be known, of course, before the data can be saved or later loaded into a computer to be edited and/or played as sound. Table 5-4 shows some of the common sound formats used for multimedia.

Purpose	Extension	MIME-Type	Purpose	Extension	MIME-Type
669 MOD Music	.669		MIDI	.mid	audio/mid
AIFF Audio	.aifc	audio/aiff	MIDI	.mid	audio/midi
AIFF Audio	.aiff	audio/aiff	MIDI	.mid	audio/x-midi
AIFF Sound	.aiff	audio/x-aiff	MIDI	.midi	audio/mid
AIFF Sound Compressed	.aife	audio/x-aiff	MIDI	.midi	audio/midi
AIFF Sound	.aif	audio/x-aiff	MIDI	.midi	audio/x-midi
aLAW Sound	.al		MIDI	.smf	audio/mid
Amiga 8-bit sound	.8svx		MIDI	.smf	audio/midi
Amiga IFF Sound	.svx		MIDI	.smf	audio/x-midi
Amiga MED Sound	.med		MP3 Audio	.mp3	audio/mpeg
Amiga OctaMed music	.8med		MP3 Audio	.mp3	audio/x-mpeg
AU Audio	.snd	audio/basic	MPEG audio stream	.m1a	audio/mpeg
AU Audio	.ulw	audio/basic	MPEG audio stream	.m1s	audio/mpeg
Beatnik	.rmf	audio/rmf	MPEG audio stream	.m1s	audio/x-mpeg
Beatnik	.rmf	audio/x-rmf	MPEG audio stream	.mp2	audio/x-mpeg
µLaw Sound	.au	audio/basic	MPEG audio stream	.mpa	audio/mpeg
µLaw Sound	.ul	audio/basic	MPEG audio stream	.mpeg	audio/x-mpeg
MIDI	.kar	audio/mid	MPEG audio stream	.mpg	audio/mpeg
MIDI	.kar	audio/midi	MPEG audio stream	.mpg	audio/x-mpeg
MIDI	.kar	audio/x-midi	MPEG audio stream	.mpm	audio/mpeg

Table 5-4   Common File Types Used for Digitized Sounds (Internet MIME-Types)

Purpose	Extension	MIME-Type	Purpose	Extension	MIME-Type
MPEG audio stream	.mpm	audio/x-mpeg	RealAudio	.ra	audio/x-pn-realaudio
MPEG audio stream	.mpv	video/mpeg	RealAudio	.ra	audio/vnd.rn-realaudio
MPEG-1 Audio Movie	.mp2	audio/x-mpeg	RealAudio	.ram	audio/x-pn-realaudio
MPEG-1 Audio Movie	.mpa	audio/x-mpeg	RealAudio	.rm	audio/x-pn-realaudio
MPEG-1 Audio Movie	.m15		Sound Designer 2 File	.sd2	
MPEG-1 Audio Movie	.m1a	audio/x-mpeg	Sound of various types	.snd	
MPEG-1 Audio Movie	.m75		SoundEdit Sound ex SOX	.hcom	
MPEG-1 Layer 3	.mp3		VOC Sound	.voc	
Ogg-Vorbis	.ogg	audio/x-ogg	WAV Audio	.wav	audio/wav
QCP Audio	.qcp	audio/vnd.qcelp	Windows Media	.wma	audio/x-ms-wma
Real Time Streaming Protocol	.rtsp	application/x-rtsp			

Table 5-4 Common File Types Used for Digitized Sounds (Internet MIME-Types) *(continued)*

On the Macintosh, digitized sounds may be stored as data files (for example, AIF or **SDII**), or they may be stored as resources in the resource fork of the system or application as **SNDs**. The Macintosh uses a unique, dual-fork file structure, and you will need to know whether the file resides in a resource fork or as a stand-alone file.

In Windows, digitized sounds are most commonly stored as WAV files. For the Internet, new formats are emerging as companies develop solutions for streaming and playing sound on the Web. These solutions are discussed in detail in Chapter 13.

There are many ways to store the bits and bytes that describe a sampled waveform sound. The method used for Red Book Audio data files on consumer-grade music CDs is **Linear Pulse Code Modulation**. An audio CD can provide up to 80 minutes of playing time, which is enough for a slow-tempo rendition of Beethoven's Ninth Symphony. Incidentally, being able to contain Beethoven's Ninth is reported to have been Philips's and Sony's actual size criterion during early research and development for determining the length of the sectors and ultimately the physical size of the compact disc format itself. The **CD-ROM/XA (extended architecture)** format for reading and writing CDs was developed later so you could put several recording sessions onto a single CD-R (recordable) disc.

The **AIFF** sound format (or **AIFC** when supporting **MACE compression** schemes of 3:1 and 6:1) is preferred for Macintosh sound files, where all the sound data resides in the data fork. The **wave format (WAV)** was introduced by Microsoft and IBM with the introduction of Windows.

Both Macintosh and Windows can make use of MIDI files. A MIDI interface is built into many sound boards on the PC. On the Macintosh, a MIDI adapter is required for MIDI instrument input and output. On both platforms, MIDI sounds are typically stored in files with the .mid extension.

MIDI Versus Digital Audio

MIDI (Musical Instrument Digital Interface) is a communications standard developed in the early 1980s for electronic musical instruments and computers. It allows music and sound synthesizers from different manufacturers to communicate with each other by sending messages along cables connected to the devices. MIDI provides a protocol for passing detailed descriptions of a musical score, such as the notes, sequences of notes, and the instrument that will play these notes. But MIDI data is not digitized sound; it is a shorthand representation of music stored in numeric form. Digital audio is a recording, MIDI is a score—the first depends on the capabilities of your sound system, the other on the quality of your musical instruments *and* the capabilities of your sound system.

A MIDI file is a list of time-stamped commands that are recordings of musical actions (the pressing down of a piano key or a sustain pedal, for example, or the movement of a control wheel or slider). When sent to a MIDI playback device, this results in sound. A concise MIDI message can cause a complex sound or sequence of sounds to play on an instrument or synthesizer; so MIDI files tend to be significantly smaller (per second of sound delivered to the user) than equivalent digitized waveform files.

In contrast to MIDI data, digital audio data is the actual representation of a sound, stored in the form of thousands of individual numbers (called *samples*). The digital data represents the instantaneous amplitude (or loudness) of a sound at discrete slices of time. Because it is not device dependent, digital audio sounds the same every time it is played. But that consistency comes at a price: large data storage files. Digital sound is used for music CDs and **MP3** files (a music compression scheme to reduce file size developed by the Motion Picture Experts Group).

MIDI data is to digital audio data what vector or drawn graphics are to bitmapped graphics. That is, MIDI data is device dependent; digital data is not. Just as the appearance of vector graphics differs depending on the printer device or display screen, the sounds produced by MIDI music files depend on the particular MIDI device used for playback. Similarly, a roll of perforated player-piano score played on a concert grand would sound different than if played on a honky-tonk piano. Digital data, on the other hand, produces sounds that are more or less identical regardless of the playback system. The MIDI standard is like PostScript, letting instruments communicate in a well-understood language.

MIDI has several advantages over digital audio and two huge disadvantages. First, the advantages:

■ MIDI files are much more compact than digital audio files, and the size of a MIDI file is completely independent of playback quality. In general, MIDI files will be 200 to 1,000 times smaller than CD-quality digital audio files. Because MIDI files are small, they don't take up as much RAM, disk space, and CPU resources.

■ Because they are small, MIDI files embedded in web pages load and play more quickly than their digital equivalents.

■ In some cases, if the MIDI sound source you are using is of high quality, MIDI files may sound better than digital audio files.

■ You can change the length of a MIDI file (by varying its tempo) without changing the pitch of the music or degrading the audio quality. MIDI data is completely editable—right down to the level of an individual note. You can manipulate the smallest detail of a MIDI composition (often with submillisecond accuracy) in ways that are impossible with digital audio.

Now for MIDI's disadvantages:

■ Because MIDI data does not represent sound but musical instruments, you can be certain that playback will be accurate only if the MIDI playback device is identical to the device used for production. Imagine the emotional humming chorus from *Madame Butterfly* sung by a chorus of Budweiser frogs—same score, wrong instrument. Even with the General MIDI standard (see the General MIDI table of instrument sounds in Table 5-3), the sound of a MIDI instrument varies according to the electronics of the playback device and the sound generation method it uses.

■ Also, MIDI cannot easily be used to play back spoken dialog, although expensive and technically tricky digital samplers are available.

In general, the most important advantage of digital audio is its consistent playback quality, but this is where MIDI is the least reliable! With digital audio you can be more confident that the audio track for your multimedia project will sound as good in the end as it did in the beginning when you created it. For this reason, it's no surprise that digital audio is used far more frequently than MIDI data for multimedia sound tracks.

There are two additional and often more compelling reasons to work with digital audio:

■ A wider selection of application software and system support for digital audio is available for both the Macintosh and Windows platforms.

- The preparation and programming required for creating digital audio do not demand knowledge of music theory, while working with MIDI data usually does require a modicum of familiarity with musical scores, keyboards, and notation, as well as audio production.

Choosing Between MIDI and Digital Audio

In general, use MIDI data in the following circumstances:

- Digital audio won't work because you don't have enough RAM, hard disk space, CPU processing power, or bandwidth.
- You have a high-quality MIDI sound source.
- You have complete control over the machines on which your program will be delivered, so you know that your users will have high-quality MIDI playback hardware.
- You don't need spoken dialog.

In general, use digital audio in the following circumstances:

- You don't have control over the playback hardware.
- You have the computing resources and bandwidth to handle digital files.
- You need spoken dialog.

Sound for the World Wide Web

In the early days of the Internet, when connected machines typically ran in a Unix environment, the common file format for sounds (**.au**) was the international telephone format (CCITT G711) of **µLaw** (also known as *Mu-law* or *µ-law,* nicknamed the "TalkRadio" or "Geek of the Week" format and pronounced "mew-law"). It provided meager 8 kHz sampling rates at 8-bit mono, but produced very small file sizes. Today, the µLaw format supports 8 kHz at 16 bits in 2:1 compression. **aLaw** is the European equivalent of µLaw. Many more sound file types are now commonly found on the Web (see Table 5-4).

There are two methods for playing either digital or MIDI sound on the Web. First, you can wait for the entire sound file to download to your computer, then play it back with a helper application. Second, you can begin to play the sound file being downloaded as soon as enough of the sound is cached in your computer's **buffer** (a place where data is stored temporarily). The downloading continues to fill the buffer faster than you empty it by playing the sound file, allowing the sound file to stream into your computer in the background, keeping ahead of what has already been played so the playback doesn't pause or break up. **Streaming** files are dependent upon connection speed: you must wait longer (**streaming latency**) before the streamed sound begins to play when using a 28.8 Kbps modem (low band-width) than when using a high-speed T1 connection (high bandwidth). Watch out for jitter: streaming files may begin to play just fine, but then skip or momentarily stop due to insufficient bandwidth.

Adobe's Flash allows you to integrate the sound tracks that you have made using a sound editor into a web-based multimedia presentation, including both event sounds like button clicks and streaming sounds like background music. Because it can read and save MP3 files, Flash offers web designers serious and powerful options for solving the quality co-nundrum of high-quality (big) files and slow downloads versus low-qual-ity (small) files and speedy delivery—with nice results. Figure 5-8 shows Flash being used to assemble a music and graphic project. Check out Chapter 13, which discusses techniques used to deliver sound and motion video for the Web.

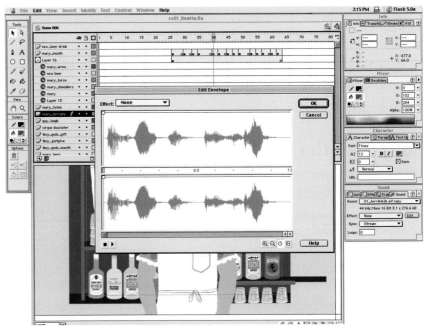

Figure 5-8 Flash can be used to integrate many audio files and deliver them to the Web.

Adding Sound to Your Multimedia Project

The original 128K Macintosh, released in January 1984, was technically a multimedia-capable machine. It displayed bitmapped graphics (albeit in black and white) and, more significantly, boasted 8-bit digital audio capa-bility right on the motherboard. In fact, the very first Macintosh actually introduced itself by voice when it was unveiled by Steve Jobs.

Here's a little history: In order to use the Apple moniker, the original founders of Apple Computer, Inc., worked out an arrangement with the Beatles (yes, *those* Beatles). One part of that agreement stipulated that Apple Computer, Inc., would never venture into the music business. To Steve Jobs and Steve Wozniak, working out of their garage in the late 1970s on a machine that could barely manage a convincing system beep, that clause probably seemed a harmless one. Little did they know that less than ten years later their computer would become the most popular music computer in the world.

Over the years, many people have speculated that the agreement with the Beatles has kept Apple out of the music business and delayed development of system software for audio applications. Although Apple would doubtless deny this, the company did finally pay representatives of the Beatles about $30 million to settle the issue once and for all.

Apple then broke new ground, outpacing Microsoft's **Audio Video Interleaved (.avi)** technology, with the release of QuickTime. **QuickTime movie (.mov)** files became a standard file format for displaying digitized motion video from hard disk or CD-ROM without special hardware. This was especially true once Apple released a PC version of the QuickTime software, making it (unlike .avi files) a cross-platform file format. Digital audio data is interleaved with video information in the file, and when it is played back, the audio stays synchronized to the motion picture. You can use QuickTime just to play stereo sounds and MIDI; the video part of QuickTime is not required. QuickTime will display many graphic image formats as well.

Breaking ground again, Apple now offers 200,000 songs at the iTunes Music Store (http://www.apple.com/music/store/) using Advanced Audio Coding (ACC, part of the MPEG-4 standard) as well as MP3 formats, and successfully sells music at a flat rate of 99 cents per song.

Whether you're working on a Macintosh or in Windows, you will need to follow certain steps to bring an audio recording into your multimedia project. Here is a brief overview of the process:

1. Determine the file formats that are compatible with your multimedia authoring software and the delivery medium(s) you will be using (for file storage and bandwith capacity).

2. Determine the sound playback capabilities (codecs and plug-ins) that the end user's system offers.

3. Decide what kind of sound is needed (such as background music, special sound effects, and spoken dialog). Decide where these audio events will occur in the flow of your project. Fit the sound cues into your storyboard, or make up a cue sheet.

4. Decide where and when you want to use either digital audio or MIDI data.

5. Acquire source material by creating it from scratch or purchasing it.

6. Edit the sounds to fit your project.

7. Test the sounds to be sure they are timed properly with the project's images. This may involve repeating steps 1 through 4 until everything is in sync.

First Person

In April 1992, Microsoft rolled out its new version of Windows 3.1 with speeches and a live MIDI performance at the Spring COMDEX/Windows World Trade Show in Chicago. Tracy Hurst played the piano and Steve Peha worked the electronic interface. As Tracy played "Striving for Glory: The Windows 3.1 Theme" on his Roland HP-5700, the music was instantaneously transcribed by Midisoft Studio, and the notes ran real-time across the 50-foot big screen, like sing-along bouncing balls. The show worked perfectly, and *Windows* magazine later called it a tour de force for Windows multimedia. It was slick.

But I knew these people who looked so professional and confident. I knew about the late nights, the crashed disk drives, the long drive from Boston, and the hurried runs to the nearest Radio Shack. This performance was not just about MIDI; it was about multimedia development in general. Hard work and technology are the substantial, invisible part of the iceberg supporting multimedia's visible leading edge.

When it's time to import your compiled and edited sounds into your project, you'll need to know how your particular multimedia software environment handles sound data. Each authoring program handles sound a bit differently, but the process is usually fairly straightforward: just tell your software which file you want to play and when to play it. This is usually handled by an importing or "linking" process during which you identify the files. Multimedia authoring tools and environments are discussed in Chapter 11.

Scripting languages such as Lingo (Director), and ActionScript (Flash) provide a greater level of control over audio playback, but you'll need to know about the programming language and environment. In authoring environments, it is usually a simple matter to play a sound when the user clicks a button, but this may not be enough. If the user changes screens while a long file is playing, for example, you may need to program the sound to stop before leaving the current screen. If the file to be played cannot be found on the hard disk, you may need to code an entire section for error handling and file location. Sample code is generally provided in both printed and online documentation for software that includes sound playback.

Music CDs

The method for digitally encoding the high-quality stereo of the consumer CD music market is an international standard, called ISO 10149. This is also known as the **Red Book** standard (derived simply from the color of the standard's book jacket). Developers of this standard claim that the digital audio sample size and sampling rate of Red Book Audio (16 bits at 44.1 kHz) allow accurate reproduction of all the sounds that humans can hear. Until recently, dedicated professional sound-studio equipment was used for this high-fidelity recording; today most off-the-shelf computers will record and play 16-bit sampled sound at 44.1 kHz and at 48 kHz. Burning software such as Toast and CD-Creator from Roxio can translate the digital files of Red Book Audio found on consumer compact discs directly into a digital sound file format such as MP3 or WAV, or decompress these files into CD-Audio format.

Unlike DVDs, audio CDs do not contain information about artists, titles, or tracklists of songs. But player software such as Apple iTunes, Yahoo Music Engine, AOL Winamp, Real Rhapsody, and Napster will automatically link to a database on the Internet when you insert a music CD. The precise length of your CD's Table of Contents (TOC) is then matched against the known TOC length for more than 5 million CDs containing more than 60 million songs. When it finds a match, the database service sends back what it knows about the CD you inserted. The database, formerly known as the Compact Disc Database or CDDB, was built up over the years by fans from all over the world submitting information about their favorite CDs. The database is currently maintained by Gracenote Media Recognition Service (www.gracenote.com/music/index_old.html).

Space Considerations

The substantial amount of digital sound information required for high-quality sound takes up a lot of disk storage space, especially when the quantity is doubled for two-channel stereo. It takes about 1.94MB to store 11 seconds of uncompressed Red Book stereo sound.

If monaural sound is adequate for your project, you can cut your storage space requirement in half or get double the playing time in the same memory space. With compression techniques, you might be able to store the sound in one-eighth the space, but you will lose some fidelity due to the rounding-off effects of quantization. Further, to conserve space you can try downsampling, or reducing the number of sample slices you take in a second. Many multimedia developers use 8-bit sample sizes at 22.05 kHz sampling rates because they consider the sound to be good enough (about the quality of AM radio), and they save immense amounts of digital real estate by not using the Red Book standard.

The following formula will help you estimate your storage needs. If you are using two channels for stereo, double the result.

(sampling rate * bits per sample) / 8 = bytes per second

If you prefer to solve for kilobytes (KB), not bytes, then try:

sample rate * sample size / 8 * # seconds * 2 (if stereo) = file size in KB

For example, 60 seconds of stereo in Red Book Audio:

$$44.1 * 16 / 8 * 60 * 2 = 10{,}584\text{KB} \cong 10.59\text{MB}$$

This is an approximate result using 1000 instead of 1024 bytes per KB, but yielding the quick handy answer "...about ten and a half megabytes."

You face important trade-offs when deciding how to manage digitized sound in your multimedia project. How much sound quality can you sacrifice in order to reduce storage? What compression techniques make sense? Will compressed sound work in your authoring platform? What is good enough but not amateurish? Can you get away with 8 bits at 11.025 kHz for voice mail, product testimonials, and voice-overs and then switch to higher sampling rates for music?

Production Tips

A classic physical anthropology law (Liebig's Law of the Minimum) proposes that the evolution of eyesight, locomotor speed, sense of smell, or any other species trait will cease when that trait becomes sufficiently adequate to meet the survival requirements of the competitive environment. If the trait is good enough, the organism expends no more effort improving it. Thus, if consumer-grade electronics and a handheld microphone are good enough for making your sound, and if you, your client, and your audience are all satisfied with the results, conserve your energy and money and avoid any more expenditure. And keep this Law of Minimums in mind when you make all your trade-off decisions involving other areas of high technology and multimedia, too.

Vaughan's Law of Multimedia Minimums

There is an acceptable minimum level of adequacy that will satisfy the audience, even when that level may not be the best that technology, money, or time and effort can buy.

Audio Recording

You can record your sound material to cassette tapes as the first step in the digitizing process. With tape, you can do many takes of the same sound or voice, listen to all the takes, and pick the best one to digitize. By recording on inexpensive media rather than directly to disk, you avoid filling up

With the collaboration of composer Dave Soldier, Komar & Melamid's Most Wanted Painting project (http://www.diacenter.org/km/index.html) was extended into the realm of music. A poll, written by Dave Soldier, was conducted on Dia's web site (http://www.diacenter.org) in spring 1996. Approximately 500 visitors took the survey. Dave Soldier and Nina Mankin used the survey results to write music and lyrics for the Most Wanted and Most Unwanted songs.

A Note from the Composer

This survey confirms the hypothesis that today's popular music indeed provides an accurate estimate of the wishes of the vox populi. The most favored ensemble, determined from a rating by participants of their favorite instruments in combination, comprises a moderately sized group (three to ten instruments) consisting of guitar, piano, saxophone, bass, drums, violin, cello, synthesizer, with low male and female vocals singing in rock/r&b style. The favorite lyrics narrate a love story, and the favorite listening circumstance is at home. The only feature in lyric subjects that occurs in both most wanted and unwanted categories is "intellectual stimulation." Most participants desire music of moderate duration (approximately 5 minutes), moderate pitch range, moderate tempo, and moderate to loud volume, and display a profound dislike of the alternatives. If the survey provides an accurate analysis of these factors for the population, and assuming that the preference for each factor follows a Gaussian (bell-curve) distribution, the combination of these qualities, even to the point of sensory overload and stylistic discohesion, will result in a musical work that will be unavoidably and uncontrollably "liked" by 72 plus or minus 12 percent (standard deviation; Kolmogorov-Smirnov statistic) of listeners. The most unwanted music is over 25 minutes long, veers wildly between loud and quiet sections, between fast and slow tempos, and features timbres of extremely high and low pitch, with each dichotomy presented in abrupt transition. The most unwanted orchestra was determined to be large and features the accordion and bagpipe (which tie at 13 percent as the most unwanted instrument), banjo, flute, tuba, harp, organ, synthesizer (the only instrument that appears in both the most wanted and most unwanted ensembles). An operatic soprano raps and sings atonal music, advertising jingles, political slogans, and "elevator" music, and a children's choir sings jingles and holiday songs. The most unwanted subjects for lyrics are cowboys and holidays, and the most unwanted listening circumstances are involuntary exposure to commercials and elevator music. Therefore, it can be shown that if there is no covariance—someone who dislikes bagpipes is as likely to hate elevator music as someone who despises the organ, for example— fewer than 200 individuals of the world's total population would enjoy this piece.

Dave Soldier, composer and musician, who provides the Most Wanted Song and the Most Unwanted Song on a CD at http://www.diacenter.org/km/musiccd.html

your hard disk with throw-away stuff. If your project requires CD-quality digitized sound at 44.1 kHz and 16 bits, you should hire a sound studio. High-fidelity sound recording is a specialized craft, a skill learned in great part by trial and error, much like photography. If you do decide to do it yourself at CD-quality levels, be prepared to invest in an acoustically treated room, high-end amplifiers and recording equipment, and expensive microphones.

As already stated, there are many trade-offs involved in making multimedia. For example, if you are satisfied with 22.05 kHz in your project or are constrained to this rate by storage considerations, any consumer-grade tape recorder of reasonable quality will do fine. This, of course, also applies to conversations recorded from the telephone, where a sampling rate of 11.025 kHz is adequate. Noise reduction circuits and metal tapes are helpful to remove hiss, but at a sampling rate of 22.05 kHz you are only going to be digitizing audio frequencies as high as about 11 kHz, anyway. Both the high and low ends of the audio hearing spectrum are therefore less important to you, and that is OK, because those areas are precisely the add-value focus of very elaborate and expensive consumer equipment.

Video cassette recorders (VCRs) usually have excellent stereo audio circuits, and many good multimedia sounds were first recorded and digitized using the audio tracks of videotape.

Digital audio tape (DAT) systems are available in the consumer marketplace. They provide a tape-based 44.1 kHz, 16-bit record and playback capability. You may, however, find that DAT is high-fidelity overkill for your needs, because the recordings are too accurate, precisely recording glitches, background noises, microphone pops, and coughs from the next room. A good editor can help reduce the impact of these noises, but at the cost of your time and money.

Keeping Track of Your Sounds

If you use a tape deck or recorder, be sure it has a good counter built into it, so that you can mark and log the locations of various takes and events on the tape and quickly find them later. Get into the habit of jotting down the counter position and tape content whenever you record sounds.

In an elaborate project with many sounds, it is important to maintain a good database, keeping a physical track of your original material—just in case you need to revert to it when your disk drive crashes. This database is particularly important because you may need to give your sound files such unhelpful names as SND0094A.WAV or CHAPT1-3.WAV; these names won't contain many cues about the files' actual content, and you will need a more descriptive cross-reference at hand. You don't want to have to load and play all the sound files from SND0080.WAV through SND0097 .WAV just to find the one you need.

See Chapter 16 for suggestions about the management of such multimedia project resources.

Testing and Evaluation

Putting everything together can be tough, but testing and evaluating what you've done can be even tougher—especially if your project involves a complicated live presentation, or if you're shipping a commercial multimedia application. Unless you plan ahead, problems will not emerge until you begin testing.

Both digital audio and MIDI are time-based events, but most animation and computer-based video will play only as fast as the CPU can handle it. A 60-second digital audio or MIDI file will play for the same length of time on both slow and fast computers. On the other hand, an animation on a fast machine may run five to ten times faster than on a slow one. If you time your music to animations running on a slow machine, and then play your project back on a faster machine, you may find that the music plays on after the speedier animation sequences are done. Since you can't make a slow machine run faster, the usual solution is to make a fast machine run slower. Chapter 15 discusses the need for determining minimum platform specifications early in the development of any project.

TIP   *During editing and authoring, regularly test the sound-and-image synchronization of your project on the slowest platform as well as the fastest. If you are delivering your sound on the Web, test it with different browsers and different connection speeds.*

Don't forget to evaluate your sound storage medium. How much RAM does your project need to run effectively? Some authoring and delivery packages will stream sound directly off the hard disk or CD-ROM; others require the sound to be loaded into memory from the hard disk before they play. Sometimes you will need to break a sound or a music file into smaller parts. Some 8-bit audio cards may choke on a 16-bit file. And MIDI files that sound terrific on an expensive General MIDI sound card during development will not have the same quality on a low-end FM-synthesis device at the end user's site.

In the world of professional film and video production, sound is incorporated during **post-production**, or a **post-session**, after all the film and video footage has been assembled. Just so with multimedia—and don't give it short shrift because of time or budget constraints. The sound track can make or break your project!

Copyright Issues

Ownership rights are significant issues for multimedia producers who would love to use a few bars of Madonna's latest hit or a nostalgic background of Bach suites played by Pablo Casals. Producers may rightfully fret about copyrights and permissions. Most developers play it safe by always making their own custom music from scratch in a sound studio, or with synthesizers, or by using sounds that have a clear and paid-for ownership and permission trail. Others simply take a risk and break the law.

WARNING *You are breaking the law if you record and use copyrighted material without first securing the appropriate rights from the owner or publisher of the material.*

As more and more multimedia is produced by more and more developers who are hungry for sound content, the copyright of sounds and images has become a major issue—not so much about who owns something, but how much of it they own. Because it is so easy to manipulate and edit a sound, just how much of someone's original work do you have to change before it then becomes your own? There are separate licensing issues for use of a musical composition (even if you create a MIDI performance of it yourself) and for use of a particular recording of a musical composition (as when you make a copy from a tape, record, or CD). There are special licensing arrangements for use of music in different types of multimedia programs—from a presentation you create for a client for a presentation to a stockholders meeting to a music bed under a commercial program. As this suggests, music licensing is a specialized and complicated area, so you should make sure you have cleared all the necessary rights before using any music in a product. Copyright issues and methods of securing permission for use (equally relevant for sounds, still images, and motion video) are discussed in more detail in Chapter 17.

• •

http://www.harryfox.com

The Harry Fox Agency represents more than 27,000 music publishers and is the premier licensing resource for the mechanical use of music reproduced in all formats and media.

• •

A number of software vendors have entered the multimedia marketplace by selling digitized clip sounds with an unlimited-use, royalty-free license. Some of these products include musical clips, and some just include sound effects (doors closing, dogs barking, and water dripping). Other products have a mixture of both. But beware of sources claiming to be public domain that offer "Phaser" and "Beam-Me-Up" clips from such favorites as *Star Trek*, or one-liners from Humphrey Bogart movies, because these sounds have likely been used without permission. Also, carefully read the licensing terms that come with any collection you purchase. Although the box may claim that the sounds are "unlimited-use, royalty free," the fine print inside most likely limits their use to your personal machine and does not include the right to use them in any commercial use or republication in a form that would allow others to obtain them (such as using them on a web site).

WARNING *Taking a camera or tape or video recorder to some public events may be illegal without proper permission.*

> We needed some digital sound effects for the Dr. J and Larry Bird basketball game we were making. So we bought some Warriors tickets and took a tape recorder to the Oakland Coliseum and just recorded the sounds while we watched the game. It was a great tax deduction, and we got to go to the game for nothing!
>
> Trip Hawkins, Chairman, Electronics Arts

Chapter 5 Review

■ Chapter Summary

For your review, here's a summary of the important concepts discussed in this chapter.

Discuss the general principles of sound and how it can be used in a multimedia project

■ How you use the power of sound can make the difference between an ordinary multimedia presentation and a professionally spectacular one. Misuse of sound, however, can wreck your project.

■ When something vibrates in the air by moving back and forth, it creates waves of pressure. These waves spread, and when they reach your eardrums, you experience the vibrations as sound.

■ Acoustics is the branch of physics that studies sound.

■ Sound pressure levels (loudness or volume) are measured in decibels (dB).

Define MIDI and list its attributes

■ MIDI data is not digitized sound; it is a shorthand representation of music stored in numeric form.

■ MIDI files tend to be significantly smaller than equivalent digitized waveform files.

■ MIDI data is device dependent; its playback depends on the capabilities of the end user's system.

■ Because they are small, MIDI files embedded in web pages load and play more quickly than their digital equivalents.

■ You can change the length of a MIDI file (by varying its tempo) without changing the pitch of the music or degrading the audio quality. MIDI data is completely editable.

■ MIDI cannot easily be used to play back spoken dialog.

■ Working with MIDI requires familiarity with musical scores, keyboards, and notation as well as audio production.

Define digital audio and discuss its attributes, including how sound is sampled and sampling parameters

■ Digital audio data is the actual representation of a sound, stored in the form of thousands of individual samples that represent the amplitude (or loudness) of a sound at a discrete point in time.

■ How often the samples are taken is the sampling rate.

■ The three sampling frequencies most often used in multimedia are CD-quality 44.1 kHz (kilohertz), 22.05 kHz, and 11.025 kHz.

■ Digital audio is not device dependent, and sounds the same every time it is played. For this reason digital audio is used far more frequently than MIDI data for multimedia sound tracks.

■ You can digitize sounds from any source, live or prerecorded.

■ The amount of information stored about each sample is the sample size and is determined by the number of bits used to describe the amplitude of the sound wave when the sample is taken.

■ Sample sizes are either 8 bits or 16 bits.

■ The value of each sample is rounded off to the nearest integer (quantization).

■ The preparation and programming required for creating digital audio do not demand knowledge of music theory.

Compare and contrast the use of MIDI and digitized audio in a multimedia production

■ MIDI is analogous to structured or vector graphics, while digitized audio is analogous to bit-mapped images.

■ MIDI is device dependent, meaning the quality of the playback is dependent upon the hardware installed on the user's machine, while digitized audio is device independent.

- Use MIDI only when you have control over the playback hardware and know your users will be using a high-quality MIDI device for playback.

- MIDI files are much smaller than digitized audio, so they may be used for delivery of music under the right circumstances.

- Use digitized audio for spoken dialog.

List the important steps and considerations in recording and editing digital audio

- The file size (in bytes) of a digital recording is sampling rate * duration of recording in seconds * (bit resolution / 8) * number of tracks (1 for mono, 2 for stereo).

- Consumer-grade audio compact discs are recorded in stereo at a sampling rate of 44.1 kHz and a 16-bit resolution. Other sampling rates include 22.05 and 11 kHz, at either 16 or 8 bits.

- When recording (digitizing) audio, it's important to keep the recording level near the maximum without going over it.

- Important steps in digital sound editing include removing blank space from the start and end of a recording and normalizing the sound to bring all clips to approximately the same level.

- The native sound file formats for most Macintosh sound editing software are the SND and AIF formats, and most authoring systems will read these formats. In Windows, the native sound file format for most editing software is a WAV file.

- Many audio editors provide tools such as resampling, fade-ins and -outs, equalization, time stretching, various digital signal processing effects, and reversing sounds.

Discuss audio file formats used in multimedia projects and how they are used

- MIDI scores require sequencer software and a sound synthesizer.

- The General MIDI format standardizes a set of MIDI instruments, ensuring that the MIDI sequence is played correctly.

- Streaming files begin playing when part of the file has been buffered into the computer's memory and are dependent upon connection speed.

- Adobe's Flash provides powerful tools for integrating and streaming sounds, including the MP3 format.

- Apple's QuickTime is a file format that, among other capabilities, enables digital audio to be interleaved with video information.

Cite the considerations involved in managing audio files and integrating them into multimedia projects

- Because sounds are time based, you may need to consider what happens to sounds that are playing in your project when the user goes to a different location.

- Appropriate use of sound requires technical considerations of disk space or bandwidth as well as the abilities of the authoring system to use various file formats and compression algorithms.

- Do not use equipment and standards that exceed what your project requires.

- Keep track of your audio files, and be sure to back them up.

- Regularly test the sound-and-image synchronization of your project.

- Evaluate your sound's RAM requirements as well as your users' playback setup.

- Be sure you understand the implications of using copyrighted material. You are breaking the law if you record and use copyrighted material without first securing the appropriate rights from the owner or publisher.

- You can purchase and use digitized clip sounds with an unlimited-use, royalty-free license.

■ Key Terms

acoustics *(96)*
AIF format *(99)*
AIFC *(112)*
AIFF *(112)*
aLaw *(115)*
.au *(115)*
audio resolution *(101)*
Audio Video Interleaved
  (.avi) *(117)*
bitdepth *(99)*
buffer *(115)*
CD-quality *(99)*
CD-ROM/XA (extended
  architecture) *(112)*
decibels (dB) *(96)*
device dependent *(107)*
device independent *(99)*

digital audio *(99)*
digital audio tape (DAT) *(122)*
digital equalization (EQ) *(106)*
digital signal processing
  (DSP) *(106)*
downsample *(105)*
General MIDI *(108)*
Linear Pulse Code
  Modulation *(112)*
MACE compression *(112)*
MIDI *(106)*
MIDI keyboard *(107)*
MP3 *(113)*
normalize *(104)*
post-production,
  post-session *(123)*
quantization *(100)*

QuickTime movie (.mov) *(117)*
Red Book Audio *(119)*
resample *(105)*
sample *(99)*
sample size *(99)*
sampling rate *(99)*
SDII *(112)*
sequencer software *(107)*
SND *(112)*
sound synthesizer *(107)*
streaming *(115)*
streaming latency *(116)*
time stretching *(106)*
μLaw *(115)*
wave format (WAV) *(112)*

■ Key Term Quiz

1. The branch of physics that studies sound is _____.

2. Sound pressure levels (loudness or volume) are measured in _____.

3. The process of adjusting the level of a number of tracks to bring them all up to about the same level is called _____.

4. When audio is measured in order to be digitally stored, the value of each measurement is rounded off to the nearest integer in a process called _____.

5. Reducing the number of separate measurements of an audio file is called _____.

6. The standard file format for displaying digitized motion video on the Macintosh is _____.

7. The most common file format for editing sound on the Macintosh is _____.

8. The audio file format introduced by Microsoft and IBM with the introduction of Windows is the _____.

9. The process of playing a sound file while part of the file is still downloading is called _____.

10. Some software allows you to begin playing a downloading sound file as soon as enough of the sound is cached in your computer's _____.

■ Multiple Choice Quiz

1. The file format that uses a shorthand representation of musical notes and durations stored in numeric form is:
   a. AIFF
   b. CD-ROM/XA
   c. DSP
   d. MIDI
   e. QuickTime

2. Which of these statements regarding the MIDI audio format is *not* true?
   a. The sound can easily be changed by changing instruments.
   b. Spoken audio can easily be included.
   c. Sound tracks can be created using sequencing software.
   d. Files are generally smaller than the same digital audio sound.
   e. Sounds can be stretched and timing changed with no distortion of the quality.

3. The primary benefit of the General MIDI over the previous MIDI specification is that:
   a. the file sizes are much smaller due to the compression scheme
   b. users can easily edit and adjust the data structures
   c. it can be easily converted into the CD-ROM/XA format
   d. MIDI files can be easily integrated into the computer's operating system as system sounds
   e. the instruments are the same regardless of the playback source

4. What happens when an audio signal exceeds the recording device's maximum recording level?
   a. The signal is compressed to an appropriate level.
   b. "Clipping" of the signal occurs, introducing distortion.
   c. The audio clip is extended to accommodate the extra data.
   d. The entire clip's volume is reduced correspondingly.
   e. The extra bits go into a buffer for later use.

5. As one story goes, the criterion used to set the length of the sectors and ultimately the physical size of the compact disc format was based on the length of:
   a. the Beatles' "White Album"
   b. Handel's *Messiah*
   c. Beethoven's Ninth Symphony
   d. Bach's *St. John's Passion*
   e. Iron Butterfly's live rendition of "Innagaddadavida"

6. The process of recording a sound, stored in the form of thousands of individual measurements, each at a discrete point in time, is called:
   a. sampling
   b. synthesizing
   c. sizing
   d. quantizing
   e. streaming

7. The file size of a 5-second recording sampled at 22 kHz, 16-bit stereo (two tracks) would be about:
   a. 110,000 bytes
   b. 220,000 bytes
   c. 440,000 bytes
   d. 550,000 bytes
   e. 880,000 bytes

8. Which of the following sound file characteristics does *not* directly affect the size of a digital audio file?
   a. sample rate
   b. sample size
   c. tracks (stereo vs. mono)
   d. volume
   e. compression

9. Each individual measurement of a sound that is stored as digital information is called a:
   a. buffer
   b. stream
   c. sample
   d. capture
   e. byte

10. Audio recorded at 44.1 kHz (kilohertz), 16-bit stereo is considered:
    a. phone-quality
    b. voice-quality
    c. FM-quality
    d. CD-quality
    e. AM-quality

11. Removing blank space or "dead air" at the beginning or end of a recording is sometimes called:
    a. quieting
    b. pre-rolling
    c. quantizing
    d. trimming
    e. flashing

12. DSP stands for:
    a. dynamic sound programming
    b. data structuring parameters
    c. direct splicing and partitioning
    d. delayed streaming playback
    e. digital signal processing

13. Sequencing software:
    a. places audio clips in order in a soundtrack
    b. records and edits MIDI data
    c. applies filters to digital audio clips in a predetermined order
    d. manages a project by creating a timeline of events
    e. helps synchronize images with a sound track

14. The slower a user's connection, the longer he must wait for enough of the sound to download so that the entire file will have downloaded by the time the sound reaches the end. This effect is called:
    a. streaming latency
    b. post-processing
    c. compression
    d. digital signal processing
    e. multitap delay

15. The Red Book standard was so named because:
    a. the standard was pioneered in the former Soviet Union
    b. red is an acronym for "Registered Electronic Data"
    c. the standard's book jacket was red
    d. it was so expensive to produce CDs early on that most producers were "in the red"
    e. the dye in the first recordable CDs had a reddish tint

■ Essay Quiz

1. Discuss the implications of using audio in a production, focusing on the purpose of the audio, how to manage audio files, and copyright issues.

2. List the four main sampling rates and the two sampling depths. Briefly describe what each is most useful for. How does mono versus stereo come into the equation?

3. You have been assigned to design and produce the audio portions of a multimedia project. The program will be delivered on a CD-ROM, and video clips will take up most of the CD. You have only 50MB of storage space to store 20 one-minute clips of speech, 10 songs averaging three minutes long, and a background sound loop. What sampling rates and depths should you use for the speech, for the music, and for the background sound? Why? Roughly calculate the file size totals for these specifications, and be sure that you end up with less than the 50MB of storage space allotted. Discuss your reasoning.

4. Describe what MIDI is, what its benefits are, and how it is best used in a multimedia project.

5. List the steps you would go through to record, edit, and process a set of sound files for inclusion on a web site. How would you digitally process the files to ensure they are consistent, have minimum file size, and sound their best?

Lab Projects

■ Project 5.1

Go online and locate three sound editors (either from a shareware site or demo versions of commercial software). Document their capabilities. What file formats can they import from and export to? How many tracks can they handle? What DSP effects do they provide?

■ Project 5.2

Record two sounds using a simple recording device—a cassette recorder will work. One sound should be of speech, and one should be music. Connect the output from the recorder to a computer's audio input. Using a sound capture and editing tool, capture both clips in 44 kHz, 16-bit stereo (if you can't record in stereo, ignore the applicable directions). Capture the clips three times—once at a very low level, once at the correct level (just below peaking), and once at levels that are well over the maximum. Listen to the six clips. Note your observations regarding noise and distortion. Run all three clips through the editor's Normalize effect. Again, listen to the clips and note your observations.

■ Project 5.3

Down-convert the two normalized samples recorded at the correct level to 22.05, 11, and 5 kHz. Convert each of these eight (four sampling rates × two files) to mono. You should now have 16 different files; 8 of the speech and 8 of music. Document the file size of each, and make a note of how each sounds (even better, enlist the aid of someone else who can listen while you play the sounds back, without telling them which you are playing). Which are acceptable? At what point does the lowered quality become unacceptable?

■ Project 5.4

Visit three web sites that use sound (you may need to find Flash-based web sites). Where, when, and how is sound used? Does the sound fit the mood of the site? Is there background sound? Can the sounds be turned on and off? Document your findings.

■ Project 5.5

Locate three web sites that offer "royalty-free" or "buyout" music. Such sites almost always allow visitors to listen to low-quality samples. What formats are the samples provided in? Listen to some of the samples. Try to identify which are synthesized and which are actual instruments playing the music. What are the license arrangements for using the music? Document your findings, noting the various lengths and formats the music is provided in.

■ Project 5.6

Visit the web site for the Harry Fox Agency and check the licensing terms for different uses of musical compositions and recordings of music. Briefly describe the terms for using music for which you have created a performance, for using a recording of a piece of music in a multimedia program, and for selling a product that contains music. Identify differences in rates for use of music in different types of media (for example, using as part of a one-time presentation to a limited audience, using in a multimedia product for commercial release,

Images

WHAT you see on a multimedia computer screen at any given time is a composite of elements: text, symbols, photograph-like bitmaps, vector-drawn graphics, three-dimensional renderings, distinctive buttons to click, and windows of motion video. Some parts of this image may even twitch or move so that the screen never seems still and tempts your eye. It may be a very colorful screen with gentle pastel washes of mauve and puce, or it may be brutally primary with splashes of Crayola red and blue and yellow and green. It might be stark black and white, full of sharp angles, or softened with gray-scale blends and anti-aliasing. It may be elegant or, by design, not. The computer screen is where the action is, and it contains much more than your message; it is also the viewer's primary connection to all of your project's content.

This chapter will help you understand the visual elements that make up a multimedia screen. Graphic elements can usually be scaled to different sizes, colorized or patterned or made transparent, placed in front of or behind other objects, or be made visible or invisible on command. How you blend these elements, how you choose your colors and fonts, the tricks that you use that catch the eye, how adept you are at using your tools—these are the hallmarks of your skill, talent, knowledge, and creativity coalesced into the all-important visual connection to your viewers.

Before You Start to Create

At the beginning of a project, the screen is a blank canvas, ready for you, the multimedia designer, to express your craft. The screen will change again and again during the course of your project as you experiment, as you stretch and reshape elements, draw new objects and throw out old ones, and test various colors and effects—creating the vehicle for your message. Indeed, many multimedia designers are known to experience a mild shiver when they pull down the New... menu and draw their first colors onto a fresh screen. Just so; this screen represents a powerful and seductive avenue for channeling creativity.

WARNING *Multimedia designers are regularly lured into agonizingly steep learning curves, long nights of cerebral problem solving, and the pursuit of performance perfection. If you are fundamentally creative, multimedia may become a calling, not a profession.*

Plan Your Approach

Whether you use templates and ready-made screens provided by your authoring system; clip art or objects crafted by others; or even if you simply clone the look and feel of another project—there will always be a starting point where your page is "clean." But even before reaching this starting point, be sure you have given your project a good deal of thought and planning. Work out your graphic approach, either in your head or during creative sessions with your client or colleagues. There are strong arguments against drawing on a fresh screen without such foresight and preparation. To get a handle on any multimedia project, you start with pencil, eraser, and paper. Outline your project and your graphic ideas first: make a flow-chart; storyboard the project using stick figures; use three-by-five index cards and shuffle them until you get it right.

Organize Your Tools

Most authoring systems provide the tools with which you can create the graphic objects of multimedia (text, interactive buttons, vector-drawn objects, and bitmaps) directly on your screen. If one of these tools is not included, the authoring system usually offers a mechanism for importing the object you need from another application. When you are working with animated objects or motion video, most authoring systems include a feature for activating these elements, such as a programming language or special functions for embedding them. Likely, too, your tools will offer a library of special effects—including zooms, wipes, and dissolves. Many multimedia designers do not limit their toolkits to the features of a single authoring platform, but employ a variety of applications and tools to accomplish many specialized tasks.

Multiple Monitors

When developing multimedia, it is helpful to have more than one monitor, or a single high-resolution monitor with lots of screen **real estate** (viewing area), hooked up to your computer. In this way, you can display the full-screen working area of your project or presentation and still have space to put your tools and other menus. This is particularly important in an authoring system such as Flash or Director, where the edits and changes you make in one window are immediately visible in the presentation window—provided the presentation window is not obscured by your editing tool! During development there is a lot of cutting and pasting among

The organizing and creative process begins with drawings in pen or pencil on paper. Too many times we are enthused about the color and the computer graphics tools, but they can overwhelm the creative design process.

Dennis Woytek, Assistant Professor, Duquesne University

I like "do-overs," where you make quick and dirty buttons now, or live text now, but go back later and replace those placeholders with more refined images or pretty bitmapped text. This do-over approach lets you work two ends against the middle—you can get right into designing navigation and animation, but know that you will put in the "good" images later.

Sherry Hutson, Lecturer, University of Illinois at Springfield

windows and among various applications, and with an extra monitor, you can open many windows at once and spread them out. Both Macintosh and Windows operating systems support this extra hardware.

A few weeks of having to repeatedly bring windows to the front, and then hide them again to see the results of your editing, will probably convince you to invest in a second or larger monitor.

Making Still Images

Still images may be small or large, or even full screen. They may be colored, placed at random on the screen, evenly geometric, or oddly shaped. Still images may be a single tree on a wintry hillside; stacked boxes of text against a gray, tartan, or Italian marble background; an engineering drawing; a snapshot of your department manager's new BMW. Whatever their form, still images are generated by the computer in two ways: as **bitmaps** (or paint graphics) and as **vector-drawn** (or just plain "drawn") graphics.

Bitmaps are used for photo-realistic images and for complex drawings requiring fine detail. Vector-drawn objects are used for lines, boxes, circles, polygons, and other graphic shapes that can be mathematically expressed in angles, coordinates, and distances. A drawn object can be filled with color and patterns, and you can select it as a single object. The appearance of both types of images depends on the display resolution and capabilities of your computer's graphics hardware and monitor. Both types of images are stored in various file formats and can be translated from one application to another or from one computer platform to another. Typically, image files are compressed to save memory and disk space; many bitmap image file formats already use compression within the file itself—for example, **GIF**, **JPEG**, and PNG.

Still images may be the most important element of your multimedia project or web site. If you are designing multimedia by yourself, put yourself in the role of graphic artist and layout designer. Take the time necessary to discover all the tricks you can learn about your drawing software. Competent, computer-literate skills in graphic art and design are vital to the success of your project. Remember—more than anything else, the user's judgment of your work will be heavily influenced by the work's visual impact.

Bitmaps

A **bit** is the simplest element in the digital world, an electronic digit that is either on or off, black or white, or true (1) or false (0). This is referred to as **binary**, since only two states (on or off) are available. A **map** is a two-dimensional matrix of these bits. A bitmap, then, is a simple matrix of the tiny dots that form an image and are displayed on a computer screen or printed.

A one-dimensional matrix (1-bit depth) is used to display monochrome images—a bitmap where each bit is most commonly set to black or white. Depending upon your software, any two colors that represent the on and off (1 or 0) states may be used. More information is required to describe shades of gray or the more than 16 million colors that each picture element can have in a color image, as illustrated in Figure 6-1. These picture elements (known as **pels** or, more commonly, pixels) can be either on or off, as in the 1-bit bitmap, or, by using more bits to describe them, can represent varying shades of color (4 bits for 16 colors; 8 bits for 256 colors; 15 bits for 32,768 colors; 16 bits for 65,536 colors; 24 bits for 16,772,216 colors). Thus, with 2 bits, for example, the available zeros and ones can be combined in only four possible ways and can, then, describe only four possible colors:

Bit Depth	Number of Colors Possible	Available Binary Combinations for Describing a Color
1-bit	2	0, 1
2-bit	4	00, 01, 10, 11
4-bit	16	0000, 0001, 0011, 0111, 1111, 0010, 0100, 1000, 0110, 1100, 1010, 0101, 1110, 1101, 1001, 1011

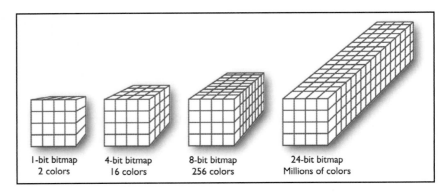

Figure 6-1 A bitmap is a data matrix that describes the characteristics of all the pixels making up an image. Here, each cube represents the data required to display a 4x4-pixel image (the face of the cube) at various color depths (with each cube extending behind the face indicating the number of bits—zeros or ones—used to represent the color for that pixel).

Together, the state of all the pixels on a computer screen make up the image seen by the viewer, whether in combinations of black and white or colored pixels in a line of text, a photograph-like picture, or a simple background pattern. Figure 6-2 demonstrates various color depths and compression formats. Image 1 is 24 bits deep (millions of colors); Image 2 is dithered to 8 bits using an adaptive palette (the best 256 colors to represent the image); Image 3 is also dithered to 8 bits, but uses the Macintosh system palette (an optimized standard mix of 256 colors). Image 4 is dithered to 4 bits (any 16 colors); Image 5 is dithered to 8-bit gray-scale (256 shades of gray); Image 6 is dithered to 4-bit gray-scale (16 shades of gray); and Image 7 is dithered to 1 bit (two colors—in this case, black and white).

Where do bitmaps come from? How are they made? You can do the following:

- Make a bitmap from scratch with a paint or drawing program.

- Grab a bitmap from an active computer screen with a screen capture program, and then paste it into a paint program or your application.

- Capture a bitmap from a photo, artwork, or a television image using a scanner or video capture device that digitizes the image.

Once made, a bitmap can be copied, altered, e-mailed, and otherwise used in many creative ways.

Clip Art

If you do not want to make your own, you can get bitmaps from suppliers of clip art, and from photograph suppliers who have already digitized the images for you. Clip art is available on CD-ROMs and through online services. Many graphics applications are shipped with clip art and useful

Is there a colour scheme that will appear coloured or at least solid black for the colour-impaired?

If you're gathering empirical evidence, I have something called red-green colour blindness (it is quite common in males). It doesn't mean that you don't know which traffic light is showing! What it means mainly is that the *tone* of red-type colours doesn't seem so different to the tone of greens—the obvious case is a poppy field. I can see the poppies as red OK if I look carefully or they are pointed out to me, but other people see them kind of exploding out of the green...

For people like me, a vibrant yellow always works. I read somewhere that black on yellow is a reliable "strong" combination. Certainly it is used by one of the motoring organisations in the UK for special diversion notices and the like.

....

Graham Samuel, Educational Software Developer, The Living Fossil Co., London

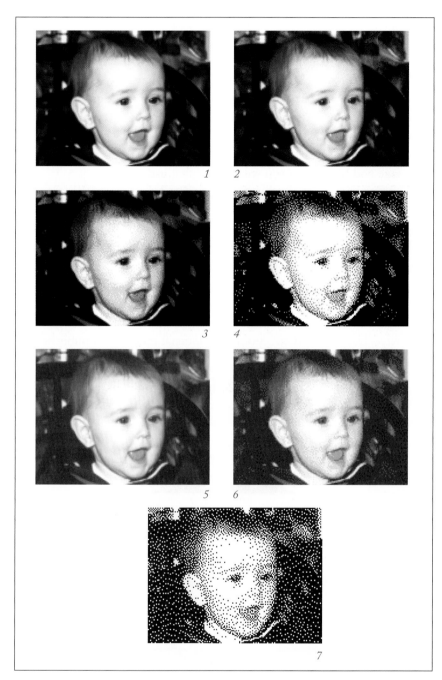

Figure 6-2 These images show the color depth of bitmaps as described in Figure 6-1. Note that Images 4 and 6 require the same memory (same file size), but the gray-scale image is superior. Because file size (download time) is important for images that are displayed on the Web, designers often dither GIF bitmap files to the lowest color depth that will still provide an acceptable image.

graphics, or the company will send you a collection when you register the product. A clip art collection may contain a random assortment of images, or it may contain a series of graphics, photographs, sound, and video related to a single topic. For example, many software tool suppliers bundle extensive clip art collections with their image-editing software. Some 3-D modeling programs incorporate libraries of pre-made 3-D models into the application, allowing you to drag and drop common objects into a scene.

Legal rights protecting use of images from clip libraries fall into three basic groupings. Public domain images were either never protected by a copyright or their copyright protection has ended. Generally these can be freely used without obtaining permission or paying a license fee, though there still may be an ownership issue for a particular work of art (such as a painting owned by an art gallery). Royalty free images are purchased and then used without paying additional license fees. Rights-managed images require that you negotiate with the rights holder regarding terms for using the image and how much you will pay for that use.

Figure 6-3 shows a page of thumbnails describing a commercially available resource called PhotoDisc, now a part of Getty Images http:// creative.gettyimages.com/source/home/home.aspx. Each of these CD-ROMs contains about 400 full-color, high-resolution bitmaps with a license for their "unlimited use." But you should note that "unlimited use" often contains caveats: in many cases there is an upper limit to the number of "units" of your own product that you may distribute without paying more, so you need to read the fine print. These additional fees are usually reasonable, however, and affect only commercial multimedia publishers.

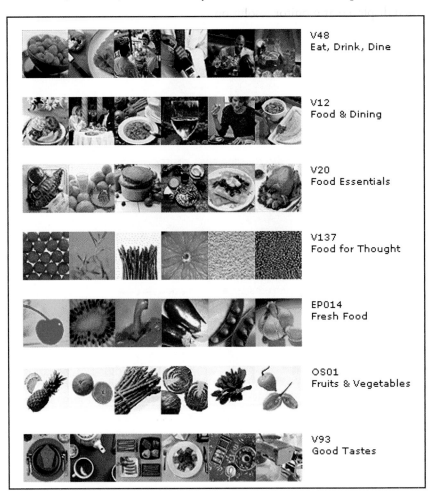

Figure 6-3 A page of thumbnails showing the content of various Photodisc CD-ROMs from Getty Images

You can also download a bitmap from a web site: on a Macintosh, click and hold on the image to see a menu of options; in Windows, right-click on an image to see a menu. Choose "Download image to disk" or "Save picture as…"

WARNING *To avoid legal problems, always assume that an image on the Web is protected by copyright, even if there is no copyright notice shown. Just because you can easily download an image from a web site, doesn't mean that you can reuse that image in your own work without permission or paying a license fee. See Chapter 17 for more about copyright protection.*

Once you have a clip art bitmap, you can manipulate and adjust many of its properties (such as brightness, contrast, color depth, hue, and size). You can also cut and paste among many bitmaps using specialized image-editing or "darkroom" programs. If the clip art image is high resolution (aimed at 300 or 600 dpi printers, not 72 dpi monitors), you may discover that you can grab just a tiny portion of the high-res image—say, a sheep in the far corner of a farmyard or a car in a parking lot—and it will look great when displayed at monitor resolution.

Bitmap Software

The abilities and features of painting and image-editing programs for both the Macintosh and Windows range from simple to complex. The best programs are available in versions that run and look the same on both platforms, and the graphics files you make can be saved in many formats, readable across platforms.

The Macintosh does not ship with a painting tool, and Windows provides only the rudimentary Paint (see Figure 6-4), so you will need to acquire this very important software separately—often bitmap editing or painting programs come as part of a bundle when you purchase your computer, monitor, or scanner. Most multimedia authoring tools offer bitmap editing features. Director (see Figure 6-5) includes a powerful image editor that provides advanced tools such as "onion-skinning" and image filtering using common plug-ins from Photoshop CS2 and other third-party designers.

Buying and learning to use a high-powered paint program and image editor is a necessary investment in your multimedia future.

For photorealism, scan a photograph or use a digital camera, and then edit the image in an image-editing program. It is virtually impossible to create a realistic-looking photo from scratch using an image-editing program.

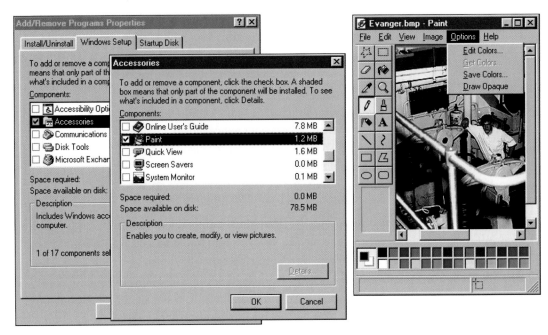

Figure 6-4 The Windows Paint accessory provides rudimentary bitmap editing.

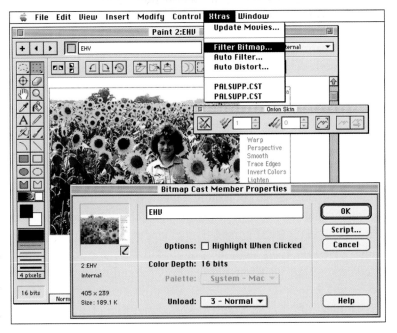

Figure 6-5 Director, like most serious multimedia authoring packages, includes powerful image-editing tools.

Artistic painting tools are offered by Corel's Painter IX.5, which provides hundreds of brushes, sprays, watercolors, inks, and textures to mimic the output of these natural media in a bitmap (see Figure 6-6).

You can use your image-editing software to create original images, such as cartoons, symbols, buttons, bitmapped text, and abstract images that have a refined "graphic" look. Many designers create curvy and

Figure 6-6 Painter is used for creating original artwork; for book, medical, and architectural illustration; to transform photographs into realistic-looking paintings; to build seamless patterns for fabrics; and for storyboarding scene concepts and costumes for movies and theater.

complicated looks using a vector-based drawing program such as Adobe's Illustrator, CorelDraw, or InDesign and then convert the resulting drawn image to a bitmap.

Capturing and Editing Images

The image you see on your monitor is a digital bitmap stored in video memory, updated about every 1/60 of a second or faster, depending upon your monitor's **scan rate** (see Chapter 9). As you assemble images for your multimedia project, you may often need to capture and store an image directly from your screen. The simplest way to capture what you see on the screen at any given moment is to press the proper keys on your computer keyboard. This causes a conversion from the screen buffer to a format that you can use.

- Both the Macintosh and Windows environments have a **clipboard**—an area of memory where data such as text and images is temporarily stored when you cut or copy them within an application. In Windows, when you press PRINT SCREEN, a copy of your screen's image goes to the clipboard. From the clipboard, you can then paste the captured bitmap into an application (such as Paint, which comes with Windows).

- On the Macintosh, the keystroke combination COMMAND-SHIFT-3 creates a readable PNG-format file named Picture and places it in your active disk drive's root directory. You can then import this file's image into your multimedia authoring system or paint program. You can also press COMMAND-CONTROL-SHIFT-4 to drag a rectangle on your screen, capture what is inside the rectangle and place it on the clipboard, ready for pasting.

■ **Screen capture** utilities for Macintosh and Windows go a step further and are indispensable to multimedia artists. With a keystroke, they let you select an area of the screen and save the selection in various formats.

The way to get more creative power when manipulating bitmaps is to use an image-editing program. These are the king-of-the-mountain programs that let you not only retouch the blemishes and details of photo images, but also do tricks like placing an image of your own face at the helm of a square-rigger or right at the sideline at last year's Super Bowl. Figure 6-7 shows just such a composite image, made from two photographs. It was created by graphic artist Frank Zurbano and shows his fiancée, Brandy Rowell, chasing after wedding gifts on the lawn where they will be married.

In addition to letting you enhance and make composite images, image-editing tools allow you to alter and distort images. A color photograph of a red rose can be changed into a purple rose, or blue if you prefer. A small child standing next to her older brother can be "stretched" to tower over him. **Morphing** is another effect that can be used to manipulate still images or to create interesting and often bizarre animated transformations. Morphing (see Figure 6-8) allows you to smoothly blend two images so that one image seems to melt into the next, often producing some amusing results.

Image-editing programs may, indeed, represent the single most significant advance in computer image processing during the late 1980s, bringing truly amazing power to PC desktops. Such tools are indispensable for excellent multimedia production.

Figure 6-7 Image-editing programs let you add and delete elements.

CROSS PLATFORM *When you import a color or gray-scale bitmap from the Macintosh to Windows, the colors will seem darker and richer, even though they have precisely the same red, green, and blue (RGB) values. In some cases, this may improve the look of your image, but in other cases you will want to first lighten (increase the brightness and possibly lower the contrast) of the Macintosh bitmap before bringing it into Windows.*

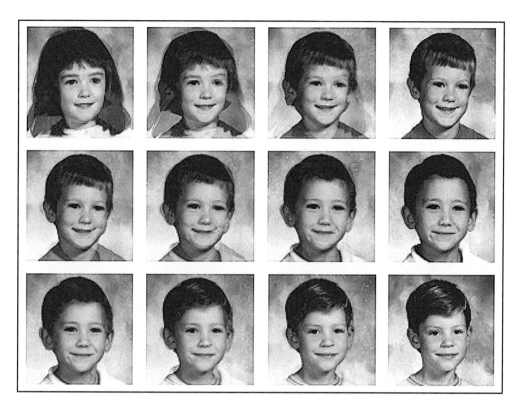

Figure 6-8 Morphing software was used to seamlessly transform the images of 16 kindergartners. When a sound track of music and voices was added to the four-minute piece, it made a compelling QuickTime video about how similar children are to each other.

Scanning Images

After poring through countless clip art collections, you still haven't found the unusual background you want for a screen about gardening. Sometimes when you search for something too hard, you don't realize that it's right in front of you. Everyday objects can be scanned and manipulated using image-editing tools, such as those described in the previous section, to create unusual, attention-getting effects. For example, to enliven a screen with a gardening motif, scan a mixture of seeds, some fall foliage, or grass-stained garden gloves. Open the scan in an image-editing program and experiment with different filters, the contrast, and various special effects. Be creative, and don't be afraid to try strange combinations—sometimes mistakes yield the most intriguing results.

Another alternative to computer-generated graphics is to create artwork using traditional methods: watercolors, pastels, and even crayons. You can then scan the image, make necessary alterations, and tweak pixels on the computer. Too many designers have fallen into the trap of trying to draw detailed sketches using a mouse or drawing tablet, when a pencil or pen on paper would have produced better results quicker. In Chapter 16, Figure 16-7 shows a web page that uses a large image map of a seacoast

We have to keep saturation in mind *all* the time when doing our web pages... viewing the graphics on both Macs and PCs before actually using them. For instance, when doing our Halloween pages, we used a very cool pumpkin background that was beautifully saturated on the Mac side. On Windows, though, it was way too dark, and you couldn't read the overlying text. We had to lighten the GIF on the Mac side a few times before using it cross platform.

Rich Santalesa, Editor,
NetGuide Magazine

village for navigation. The picture of the village was drawn on a large sheet of paper by artist Carolyn Brown using a fine pen. Then it was digitized in sections because the original drawing was too large for the scanner top. Four scans were stitched together into a single image using Photoshop layers, and the image was resized to fit the web page. Finally, it was colorized to look "old" and reduced in color depth to 4 bits so that it would load quickly on the Internet as a GIF.

Vector Drawing

Most multimedia authoring systems provide for use of vector-drawn objects such as lines, rectangles, ovals, polygons, complex drawings created from those objects, and text.

■ Computer-aided design (CAD) programs have traditionally used vector-drawn object systems for creating the highly complex and geometric renderings needed by architects and engineers.

■ Graphic artists designing for print media use vector-drawn objects because the same mathematics that put a rectangle on your screen can also place that rectangle (or the fancy curves of a good line-art illustration) on paper without jaggies. This requires the higher resolution of the printer, using a page description language such as PostScript.

■ Programs for 3-D animation also use vector-drawn graphics. For example, the various changes of position, rotation, and shading of light required to spin an extruded corporate logo must be calculated mathematically. (Animation is discussed in Chapter 7.)

How Vector Drawing Works

A **vector** is a line that is described by the location of its two endpoints. A simple rectangle, for example, might be defined as follows:

RECT 0,0, 200,200

Using Cartesian coordinates, your software will draw a rectangle (RECT) starting at the upper-left corner of your screen (0,0) and going 200 pixels horizontally to the right and 200 pixels downward (200,200) to mark the opposite corner. This rectangle would be a square, as all sides are identical lengths. For this description

RECT 0,0,200,200,RED,BLUE

your software will draw the same square with a red boundary line and fill the square with the color blue. You can, of course, add other parameters to describe a fill pattern or the width of the boundary line.

Cartesian coordinates are a pair of numbers that describe a point in two-dimensional space as the intersection of horizontal and vertical lines (the x and y axes). They are always listed in the order x,y. In three-dimensional space, a third dimension—depth—is described by the z axis (x,y,z). This coordinate system is named for the French philosopher and mathematician, René Descartes.

Vector-Drawn Objects Versus Bitmaps

Vector-drawn objects are described and drawn to the computer screen using a fraction of the memory space required to describe and store the same object in bitmap form. The concise description of the vector-drawn colored square described in the previous section contains less than 30 bytes of alphanumeric data (even less when the description is tokenized or compressed). On the other hand, the same square as an uncompressed bitmap image, in black and white (which requires the least memory, at 1-bit color depth per pixel) would take 5,000 bytes to describe (200 × 200 / 8). Remember that you need to divide by 8 because there are 8 bits in each byte of data. Furthermore, a 200-pixel square image made in 256 colors (8-bit color depth per pixel) would require a whopping 40,000 bytes as a bitmap (200 × 200).

Because of this file size advantage, web pages that use vector graphics in plug-ins such as Flash download faster and, when used for animation, draw faster than pages displaying bitmaps. It is only when you draw many hundreds of objects on your screen that you may experience a slowdown while you wait for the screen to be refreshed—the size, location, and other properties for each of the objects must be computed. Thus, a single image made up of 500 individual line and rectangle objects, for example, may take longer for the computer to process and place on the screen than an image consisting of just a few drawn circle objects.

A vector-drawn object is created "on the fly," that is, the computer draws the image from the instructions it has been given, rather than displaying a pre-created image. This means that vector objects are easily scalable without loss of resolution or image quality. A large drawn image can be shrunk to the size of a postage stamp, and while it may not look good on a computer monitor at 72 dpi, it may look great when printed at 300 dpi to a color printer. Resizing a bitmapped image requires either duplicating pixels (creating a blocky, jagged look) or throwing pixels away (eliminating details). Because vector images are drawn from instructions on the fly, a rescaled image retains the quality of the original.

TIP   *Using a single bitmap for a complicated image may give you faster screen-refresh performance than using a large number of vector-drawn objects to make that same screen.*

Converting Between Bitmaps and Drawn Images

Most drawing programs offer several file formats for saving your work, and, if you wish, you can convert a drawing that consists of several vector-drawn objects into a bitmap when you save the drawing. You can also grab a bit-mapped screen image of your drawn objects with a capture program.

Converting bitmaps to drawn objects is more difficult. There are, how-ever, programs and utilities that will compute the bounds of a bitmapped image or the shapes of colors within an image and then derive the poly-gon object that describes the image. This procedure is called **autotracing** and is available in vector drawing applications such as Illustrator or Free-hand. Flash has a Trace Bitmap menu option that converts a bitmapped image into a vector image. Be cautious: the size of your Flash file may actually balloon because the bitmapped image is replaced by hundreds or even thousands of tiny vector-drawn objects, leading to slow processing and display.

3-D Drawing and Rendering

Drawing in perspective or in 3-D on a two-dimensional surface takes spe-cial skill and talent. Creating objects in three dimensions on a computer screen can be difficult for designers comfortable with squares, circles, and other x (width) and y (height) geometries on a two-dimensional screen. Dedicated software is available to help you render three-dimensional scenes, complete with directional lighting and special effects, but be pre-pared for late nights and steep learning curves as you become familiar with nurbs, deformations, mesh generations, and skinning! From making 3-D text to creating detailed walkthroughs of 3-D space, each application will demand study and practice before you are efficient and comfortable with its feature set and power.

The production values of multimedia projects have increased dramati-cally since the late 1980s, and as the production bar has risen, end users' expectations have also ratcheted upward. The multimedia production bar moves like a high jump or pole vault contest—as each new project im-proves on the last, competitors must jump to meet the new, higher stan-dard. Flat and colorless 2-D screens are no longer sufficient for a successful commercial multimedia project. 3-D-rendered graphic art and animation has become commonplace, providing more lifelike substance and feel to projects. Luckily, in an arena where only high-powered workstations could supply the raw computing horsepower for effective 3-D designing, inex-pensive desktop PCs and excellent software have made 3-D modeling at-tainable by most multimedia developers.

Today many products—including Carrera and form•Z—are touted as essential tools for illustration, animation, and multimedia production. New-Tek's Lightwave and Autodesk's Maya are industry-standard, high-end ani-mation programs used for everything from multimedia programs and game designs to special effects in films and even feature-length movies.

Form•Z is a state-of-the-art 3-D solid and surface modeler with drafting and rendering, Boolean opera-tions, 3-D form editing and sculpting, terrain modeling, curved splines, and meshes including NURBS, 3-D text, object rounding, symbol in-stances and libraries, helixes, deformations, metaformz, image-based mesh genera-tion and displacements, skin-ning, numerous file format translators, and more. Ren-derZone adds photo-realistic rendering, and RadioZity provides the most accurate simulation of light effects.

....

Marketing literature from
auto•des•sys, Inc.
(*www.formz.com*)

For 3-D, the depth (**z dimension**) of cubes and spheres must be cal-culated and displayed so that the perspective of the rendered object seems correct to the eye. As illustrated in Figure 6-9, most 3-D software packages provide adjustable views so you can see your work from the top, bottom, or sides.

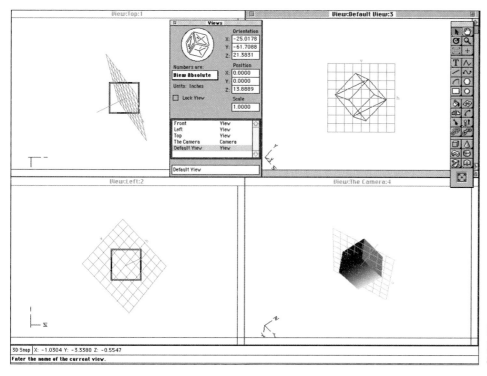

Figure 6-9 3-D applications provide x, y, and z axes and adjustable perspective views.

A great deal of information is needed to display a 3-D scene. **Scenes** consist of **objects** that in turn contain many small elements such as blocks, cylinders, spheres, or cones (described using mathematical constructs or formulas). The more elements contained in an object, the more complicated its structure will be and, usually, the finer its resolution and smoothness.

Objects and elements in 3-D space carry with them **properties** such as shape, color, texture, shading, and location. A scene contains many dif-ferent objects. Imagine a scene with a table, chairs, and a background. Zoom into one of the objects—the chair, for example, in Figure 6-10. It has 11 objects made up of various blocks and rectangles. Objects are cre-ated by **modeling** them using a 3-D application.

To model an object that you want to place into your scene, you must start with a **shape**. You can create a shape from scratch, or you can import a previously made shape from a library of geometric shapes called **primitives**, typically blocks, cylinders, spheres, and cones. In most 3-D applications, you can create any 2-D shape with a drawing tool or place the outline of a letter, then extrude or lathe it into the third dimension along the z axis (see

Figure 6-10 A chair modeled in Carrara is made up of various blocks and rectangles.

Figure 6-11). When you **extrude** a plane surface, its shape extends some distance, either perpendicular to the shape's outline or along a defined path. When you **lathe** a shape, a profile of the shape is **rotated** around a defined axis (you can set the direction) to create the 3-D object. Other methods for creating 3-D objects differ among the various software packages.

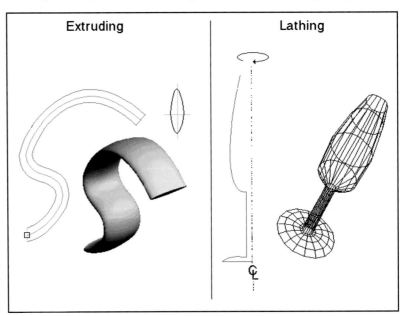

Figure 6-11 A free-form object created by extrusion and a wine flute created by lathing

Once you have created a 3-D object, you can apply **textures** and colors to it to make it seem more realistic, whether rough and coarse or shiny and smooth. You can also apply a color or pattern, or even a bitmapped picture, to texture your object. Thus you can build a table, apply an oak finish, and then stain it purple or blue or iridescent yellow. You can add coffee cup rings and spilled cheese dip with appropriate coloring and texturing.

To model a scene, you place all of your objects into 3-D space. Some complex scenes may contain hundreds (if not thousands) of elements. In modeling your scene, you can also set up one or more lights that will create diffuse or sharp shades and shadows on your objects and will also reflect, or **flare**, where the light is most intense. Then you can add a background and set a camera view, the location and angle from which you will view the final rendered scene.

Shading can usually be applied in several ways. As illustrated in Figure 6-12, flat shading (*b*) is the fastest for the computer to render and is most often used in preview mode. Gouraud shading (*a*), Phong shading (*d*), and ray tracing (*c*) take longer to render but provide photorealistic images.

When you have completed the modeling of your scene or an object in it, you then must render it for final output. **Rendering** is when the computer finally uses intricate algorithms to apply the effects you have specified on the objects you have created. Figure 6-13 shows a background, an object, and the rendered composite.

Rendering an image requires great computing muscle and often takes many hours for a single image, and you will feel the strength (or weakness) of your hardware. Indeed, some multimedia and animation companies dedicate certain computers solely for rendering. The final images for the classic animated movie *Toy Story* were rendered on a "farm" of 87 dual-processor and 30 quad-processor 100 MHz SPARCstation 20s. It took 46 days of continuous processing to render that film's 110,000 frames at a rate of about one frame every one to three hours.

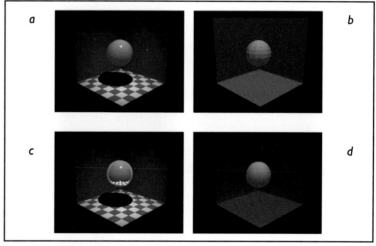

Figure 6-12   A scene rendered with four different methods of shading

---

NOTE   *Farms of many computers hooked together may also be called "clusters of workstations," or COWs. There is occasionally humorous contention regarding proper nomenclature: it seems that developers who live and work in cities tend to prefer the notion of computer farms; developers in rural communities already familiar with farms prefer to call these beasts COWs.*

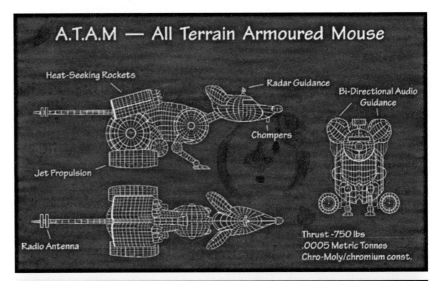

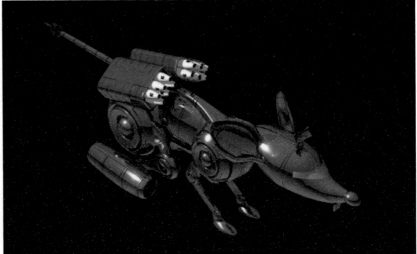

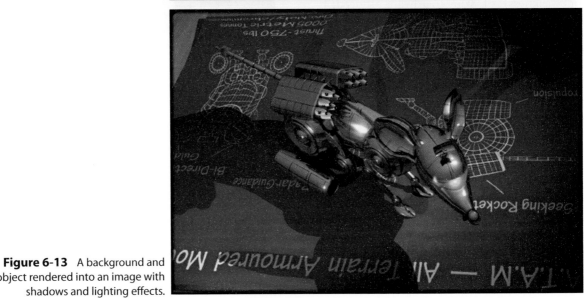

Figure 6-13 A background and object rendered into an image with shadows and lighting effects.

Panoramas

QuickTime VR (QTVR) provides a method for viewing a single surrounding image as if you were "inside" the picture and able to look up or down, turn, or zoom in on features. To make this work, you need to stitch together many images taken from different angles around a circle. Software such as ULead COOL 360 or Panorama Factory works by importing a sequence of photos and letting you adjust them precisely into a single seamless bitmap, where the right edge attaches to the left edge. You should allow some overlap when you take each photo in your 360-degree panorama, and you may need to adjust each photo's contrast, brightness, hue, and saturation while stitching. Most software also allows you to adjust perspective to compensate for different focal lengths or camera heights. When done, you can save this panoramic image to QTVR format or as a flat image.

Color

Color is a vital component of multimedia. The next few sections explain where color comes from and how colors are displayed on a computer monitor. Management of color is both a subjective and a technical exercise. Picking the right colors and combinations of colors for your project can involve many tries until you feel the result is right. But the technical description of a color may be expressed in known physical values (humans, for example, perceive colors with wavelengths ranging from 400 to 600 nanometers on the electromagnetic spectrum), and several methods and models describe color space using mathematics and values (see Figure 6-14).

Understanding Natural Light and Color

Light comes from an atom when an electron passes from a higher to a lower energy level; thus each atom produces uniquely specific colors. This explanation of light, known as the **quantum theory**, was developed by physicist Max Planck in the late 19th century. Niels Bohr, another physicist, later showed that an excited atom that has absorbed energy and whose electrons have moved into higher orbits will throw off that energy in the form of quanta, or photons, when it reverts to a stable state. This is where light comes from.

Color is the frequency of a light wave within the narrow band of the electromagnetic spectrum to which the human eye responds. The letters of the mnemonic ROY G. BIV, learned by many of us to remember the colors of the rainbow, are the ascending frequencies of the visible light spectrum: red, orange, yellow, green, blue, indigo, and violet. Light that is infrared, or below the frequency of red light and not perceivable by the human eye, can be created and viewed by electronic diodes and sensors, and it is used for TV and VCR remote controls, for wireless communications among computers, and for night goggles used in the military. Infrared light is radiated heat. Ultraviolet light, on the other hand, is beyond the higher end of the visible spectrum and can be damaging to humans.

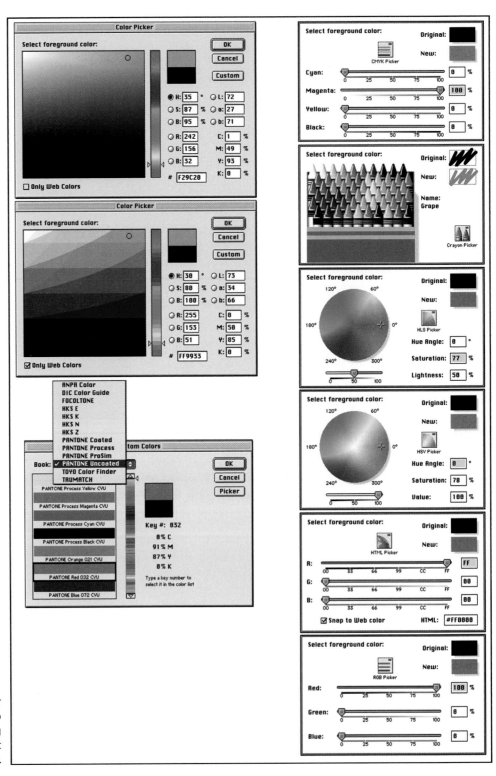

Figure 6-14 Color pickers allow you to select a color using one or more different models of color space.

The color white is a noisy mixture of all the color frequencies in the visible spectrum. Sunlight and fluorescent tubes produce white light (though, technically, even they vary in color temperature—sunlight is affected by the angle at which the light is coming through the atmosphere, and fluorescent tubes provide spikes in the blue-green parts of the color spectrum); tungsten lamp filaments produce light with a yellowish cast; sodium vapor lamps, typically used for low-cost outdoor street lighting, produce an orange light characteristic of the sodium atom. These are the most common sources of light in the everyday (or every night) world. The light these sources produce typically reaches your eye as a reflection of that light into the lens of your eye.

The cornea of the eye acts as a lens to focus light rays onto the retina. The light rays stimulate many thousands of specialized nerves, called rods, which cover the surface of the retina. Receptors in the cones are sensitive to red, green, and blue light, and all the nerves together transmit the pattern of color information to the brain. The eye can differentiate among about 80,000 colors, or **hues**, consisting of combinations of red, green, and blue.

As color information is sent to the brain, other parts of the mind massage the data en route to its point of cognitive recognition. Human response to color is complicated by cultural and experiential filters that cause otherwise straightforward color frequencies to carry pleasant, unpleasant, soothing, depressing, and many other special meanings. In Western cultures, for example, red is the color of anger and danger; in Eastern cultures, red is the color of happiness. Red is the traditional color for Chinese restaurant motifs, to make them attractive and happy places; Western restaurants are often decorated in quieter pastels and earth tones. White, not black, is the color of funerals in Chinese culture.

Green, blue, yellow, orange, purple, pink, brown, black, gray, and white are the ten most common color-describing words used in all human languages and cultures. Komar and Melamid's interesting tongue-in-cheek Internet study (http://www.diacenter.org/km/index.html) has determined that the favorite color in the world is blue.

· ·

See what an image looks like to someone with glaucoma, cataracts, macular degeneration, or a color deficit:

http://www.webaim.org

http://www.vischeck.com/examples/

· ·

Computerized Color

Because the eye's receptors are sensitive to red, green, and blue light, by adjusting combinations of these three colors, the eye and brain will interpolate the combinations of colors in between. This is the psychology, not the physics, of color: what you perceive as orange on a computer monitor is a combination of two frequencies of green and red light, not the actual spectral frequency you see when you look at that namesake fruit, an orange, in sunlight. Various color models are illustrated in Figure 6-14. Although the eye perceives colors based upon red, green, and blue, there are actually two basic methods of making color: additive and subtractive.

Additive Color

In the **additive color** method, a color is created by combining colored light sources in three primary colors: red, green, and blue (**RGB**). This is the process used for a TV or computer monitor. On the back of the glass face of a monitor are thousands of phosphorescing chemical dots. These dots are each about .30mm or less in diameter (the **dot pitch**), and are positioned very carefully and very close together, arranged in triads of red, green, and blue. These dots are bombarded by electrons that "paint" the screen at high speeds (about 30 times a second for a TV set and about 60 times a second for a computer monitor). The red, green, and blue dots light up when hit by the electron beam. The eye sees the combination of red, green, and blue light and interpolates it to create all other colors.

Subtractive Color

In the **subtractive color** method, color is created by combining colored media such as paints or ink that absorb (or subtract) some parts of the color spectrum of light and reflect the others back to the eye. Subtractive color is the process used to create color in printing. The printed page is made up of tiny halftone dots of three primary colors: cyan, magenta, and yellow (designated as CMY). Four-color printing includes black (which is technically not a color but, rather, the absence of color). Since the letter B is already used for blue, black is designated with a K (so four-color printing is designated as **CMYK**). The color remaining in the reflected part of the light that reaches your eye from the printed page is the color you perceive.

All these factors make computerized color pretty tricky to manage. The fact that a paint program uses RGB to create the colors on your monitor, while your printer uses CMYK to print out your image explains the problem of matching what you see on the screen with your printout. High-end image-editing programs such as Photoshop deal with this problem by allowing you to calibrate your monitor with your printer.

The following chart shows the three primary additive colors and how, when one of the primary colors is subtracted from this RGB mix, the subtractive primary color is perceived. The numbers in parentheses indicate the amount of red, green, and blue (in that order) used to create each of the colors in 24-bit color, which is described in the next section. A zero indicates a lack of that primary color, while 255 is the maximum amount of that color.

RGB Combination (R,G,B)	Perceived Color
Red only (255,0,0)	Red
Green only (0,255,0)	Green
Blue only (0,0,255)	Blue
Red and green (blue subtracted) (255,255,0)	Yellow
Red and blue (green subtracted) (255,0,255)	Magenta
Green and blue (red subtracted) (0,255,255)	Cyan
Red, green, and blue (255,255,255)	White
None (0,0,0)	Black

Monitors and Color

Whether you are able to design for a higher resolution with many colors depends upon the target audience for your production. Ideally, you will know the specification for your target audience's monitors, and you can design for that. That design luxury only occurs when you are designing a production for a client with a common set of hardware platforms. Designing for a more general audience, you must consider the current distribution of display hardware—check some "tracker" web sites that gather display setting information from visitors. The following chart reports the results from one such site, www.w3schools.com/browsers/, in June 2006:

Resolution:

Higher	1024x768	800x600	640x480	Unknown
17%	57%	20%	0%	6%

Color depth:

16,777,216	65,536	256
81%	16%	3%

Computer Color Models

The color of a pixel on your computer monitor is typically expressed as an amount of red, green, and blue. It takes more computer memory and processing speed to digitally manage and display the greater combinations of red, green, and blue values that make more shades of color visible to the eye.

Models or methodologies used to specify colors in computer terms are RGB, HSB, HSL, CMYK, CIE, and others. Using the 24-bit RGB (red, green, blue) model, you specify a color by setting each amount of red, green, and blue to a value in a range of 256 choices, from zero to 255. Eight bits of memory are required to define those 256 possible choices, and that has to be done for each of the three primary colors; a total of 24 bits of memory (8 + 8 + 8 = 24) are therefore needed to describe the exact color, which is one of "millions" (256 × 256 × 256 = 16,777,216). When web browsers were first developed, the software engineers chose to represent the color amounts for each color channel in a hexadecimal pair. Rather than using one number between 0 and 255, two **hexadecimal** numbers, written in a scale of 16 numbers and letters in the range "0123456789ABCDEF" represent the required 8 bits (16 × 16 = 256) needed to specify the intensity of red, green, and blue. Thus, in HTML, you can specify pure green as #00FF00, where there is no red (first pair is #00), there is maximum green (second pair is #FF), and there is no blue (last pair is #00). The number sign (#) specifies the value as hexadecimal.

Red	Green	Blue	Color
255 (#FF)	255 (#FF)	255 (#FF)	White (#FFFFFF)
255 (#FF)	255 (#FF)	0 (#00)	Yellow (#FFFF00)
255 (#FF)	0 (#00)	255 (#FF)	Magenta (#FF00FF)
0 (#00)	255 (#FF)	255 (#FF)	Cyan (#00FFFF)
255 (#FF)	0 (#00)	0 (#00)	Red (#FF0000)
0 (#00)	255 (#FF)	0 (#00)	Green (#00FF00)
0 (#00)	0 (#00)	255 (#FF)	Blue (#0000FF)
0 (#00)	0 (#00)	0 (#00)	Black (#000000)

In the HSB (hue, saturation, brightness) and HSL (hue, saturation, lightness) models, you specify hue or color as an angle from 0 to 360 degrees on a color wheel, and saturation, brightness, and lightness as percentages. Saturation is the intensity of a color. At 100 percent saturation a color is pure; at 0 percent saturation, the color is white, black, or gray. Lightness or brightness is the percentage of black or white that is mixed with a color. A lightness of 100 percent will yield a white color; 0 percent is black; the pure color has a 50 percent lightness.

The CMYK color model is less applicable to multimedia production. It is used primarily in the printing trade where cyan, magenta, yellow, and black are used to print process color separations.

Other color models include CIE, YIQ, YUV, and YCC. CIE describes color value in terms of frequency, saturation, and illuminance (blue/yellow or red/green, which in turn corresponds to the color receptors in the cones

Color	Degrees
Red	0°
Yellow	60°
Green	120°
Cyan	180°
Blue	240°
Magenta	300°

of the eye). CIE more closely resembles how human beings perceive color, but certain devices such as scanners are unable to replicate the process.

YIQ and YUV were developed for broadcast TV (composite NTSC). They are based on luminance and chrominance expressed as the amplitude of a wave and the phase of the wave relative to some reference. Detail is carried by luminance (black and white), so reduction in color does not result in the loss of image definition detail. This analog process can be translated to a number value so that the computer can use a palette or CLUT (color lookup table) to assign a color to a pixel.

The Photo YCC model has been developed by Kodak to provide a definition that enables consistent representation of digital color images from negatives, slides, and other high-quality input. YCC is used for PhotoCD images.

Color Palettes

Palettes are mathematical tables that define the color of a pixel displayed on the screen. On the Macintosh, these tables are called **color lookup tables (CLUTs)**. In Windows, the term palette is used. The most common palettes are 1, 4, 8, 16, and 24 bits deep:

Color Depth	Colors Available
1-bit	Black and white (or any two colors)
4-bit	16 colors
8-bit	256 colors (good enough for color images)
16-bit	Thousands of colors (65,536; excellent for color images)
24-bit	More than 16 million colors (16,777,216; totally photorealistic)

For 256-color, 8-bit **VGA** systems, the computer uses a color lookup table or palette to determine which 256 colors out of the millions possible are available to you at any one time. Figure 6-15 shows the default Macintosh and Windows system palettes as well as other combinations of 256 colors. The default system colors were statistically selected by Apple and Microsoft engineers (working independently) to be the colors and shades that are most "popular" in photographic images; the two palettes are, of course, different.

Paint programs provide a palette tool for displaying available colors. Most color pickers and selectors (see Figure 6-14) also provide a mechanism for specifying a palette color numerically when precision is required. Palette display and color picking tools, however, are not uniform among applications or across platforms.

To generate a palette which is best for representing a particular image, we support Heckbert's median cut algorithm. This algorithm first builds a three-dimensional table (a histogram cube) indicating how popular any given colour in the RGB cube is in the image being converted. It then proceeds to subdivide this histogram cube (by dividing boxes in half) until it has created as many boxes as there are palette entries. The decision as to where to divide a box is based on the distribution of colours within the box. This algorithm attempts to create boxes which have approximately equal popularity in the image. Palette entries are then assigned to represent each box. There are other methods of generating a palette from an image, but Heckbert's algorithm is generally regarded as the best trade-off between speed and quality.

....

Allan Hessenflow of HandMade Software, makers of Image Alchemy, describing how an 8-bit palette is made

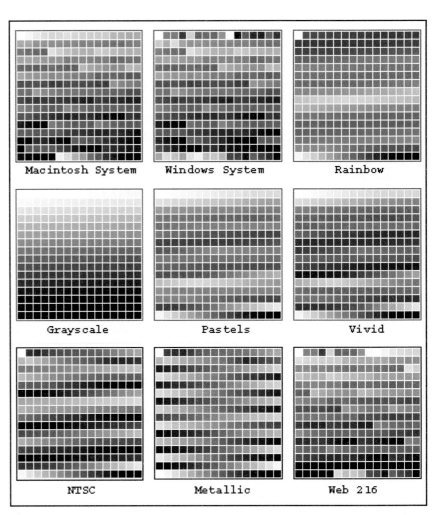

Figure 6-15 These palettes of 256 colors (8-bit color depth) are provided in Adobe's Director. Images saved in the popular GIF format for use on the Web cannot contain more than 256 colors.

In 24-bit color systems, your graphics adapter works with three channels of 256 discrete shades of each color (red, green, and blue) represented as the three axes of a cube. This allows a total of 16,777,216 colors (256 × 256 × 256). Just as the 44.1 kHz sampled-sound standard for CD music on compact discs that is discussed in Chapter 5 covers the range of human hearing, the color range offered by 24-bit systems covers what the human eye can sense. Even though millions of colors can be painted on a computer screen in 24-bit mode, only 307,200 (640 × 480) actual pixels will be available at any one time on a typical Macintosh or Windows display monitor set to 640 × 480. This is, however, more than sufficient for excellent gradients and photorealism. A 16-bit system provides a total of 32,768 different colors (32 × 32 × 32) that are quite realistic and smooth.

NOTE *Macintosh terminology is different from Windows terminology in describing color depth. On the Macintosh, display choices are typically "256, Thousands, or Millions." In Windows, you may choose from "256, High-color, or True-color." Both descriptions represent 8-bit, 16-bit, and 24-bit color depth, respectively.*

And here are some color techniques to avoid when the destination of your work is a videotape or TV monitor:

- Avoid using a pattern or mosaic.

- Avoid thin horizontal lines.

- Avoid extremely bright or intense colors that may flare up on a television screen; stick to pastels and earth colors.

- Avoid some reds that may turn brown on television.

Dithering

If you start out with a 24-bit scanned image that contains millions of colors and need to reduce it to an 8-bit, 256 color image, you get the best replication of the original image by dithering the colors in the image. **Dithering** is a process whereby the color value of each pixel is changed to the closest matching color value in the target palette, using a mathematical algorithm. Often the adjacent pixels are also examined, and patterns of different colors are created in the more limited palette to best represent the original colors. Since there are now only 256 colors available to represent the thousands or even millions of colors in the original image, pixels using the 256 remaining colors are intermixed and the eye perceives a color not in the palette, created by blending the colors mixed together. Thus any given pixel might not be mapped to its closest palette entry, but instead to the average over some area of the image; this average will be closer to the correct color than a substitute color would be. How well the dithered image renders a good approximation of the original depends upon the algorithm used and whether you allow the image-editing program to select the best set of 256 colors from the original image (called an adaptive palette) or force it to use a predetermined set of 256 colors (as, for example, with a System palette or the browser-safe web palette). Figure 6-16 compares the same scanned image dithered from millions of colors to 256 colors, 16 colors, 16 grays, and black and white.

TIP *To improve performance on the Web, a common trick is to make two files: a very compact black-and-white dithered image and the full-color image. In HTML, use the lowsrc attribute for the <IMG> graphic tag, so that the black-and-white picture displays fast. Then later, the browser will draw the full-color graphic over the black-and-white one.*

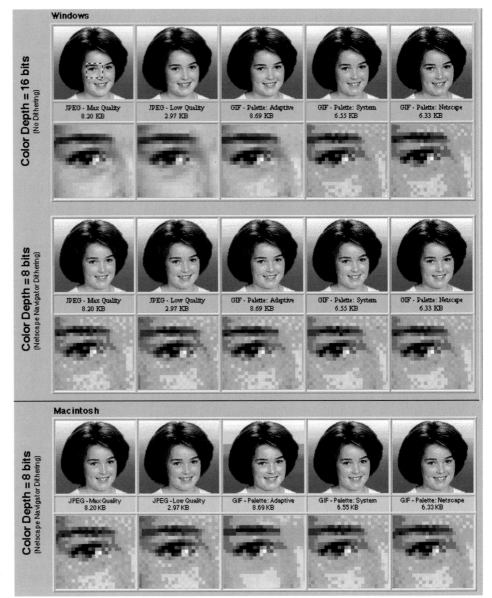

Figure 6-16 These images were dithered in Photoshop to best fit the 8-bit palettes of GIF files (Adaptive, System, or Custom 216 Netscape). Also shown are JPEG files compressed with highest and lowest quality and their actual file sizes. The files were then displayed using a browser at 16-bit and then 8-bit color depth. Note the subtle differences among palettes and systems, especially in the gradient blue background. Gradients do not usually dither well into 8-bit palettes.

Dithering concepts are important to understand when you are working with bitmaps derived from RGB information or based upon different palettes or CLUTs. The palette for the image of a rose, for example, may contain mostly shades of red with a number of greens thrown in for the stem and leaves. The image of your pretty Delft vase, into which you want to electronically place the rose, may be mostly blues and grays. Your software will use a dithering algorithm to find the 256 color shades that best represent both images, generating a new palette in the process.

Dithering software is usually built into image-editing programs and is also available in many multimedia authoring systems as part of the application's palette management suite of tools.

TIP   *Instead of trying to display a photorealistic image using 16 colors, or if you are not satisfied with the colors of your image, consider dithering your photo to a gray-scale image. It will show extraordinary detail.*

WARNING   *It is very difficult to create outstanding graphics with just 16 colors. Using various two-color dithers will certainly improve your range of perceived colors, but you will need to double your graphics budget—optimizing the look of drawn and painted objects at this color depth is painstaking and time consuming.*

Image File Formats

As mentioned earlier in this chapter, there are many file formats used to store bitmaps and drawings. Developers of paint and draw applications continually create native file formats that allow their programs to load and save files more quickly or more efficiently. Most of these applications, however, offer a Save As option that lets you write files in other common formats. And third-party translators are now widely available, for files generated on the same platform as well as for going cross platform between Macintosh and PC/Windows (and others).

If you are using a specialized application to make bitmaps or drawings, make sure your multimedia authoring package can import the image files you produce, and that your application can export such a file. You need a common format. Most applications on any operating system can manage JPEG, GIF, PNG, and TIFF image formats.

Macintosh Formats

On the Macintosh, just about every image application can import or export PICT files. **PICT** is a complicated but versatile format developed by Apple as a common format always available to Macintosh users. In a PICT file, both bitmaps and vector-drawn objects can live side by side, and programs such as Revolution or Canvas make use of this feature, providing editors for both drawn and bitmapped graphics. Many drawing programs for the Macintosh, such as Illustrator or Freehand, will allow you to import a bitmap but offer no facility for editing it. Multimedia authoring programs that can import PICT images may not utilize the drawn objects that are part of the file, but will usually convert them to bitmaps for you.

> Multimedia is just another way to transform ambiguity. There were so many ambiguous colors in this scan, I decided to make them unambiguous. How do you like the purple?
>
> Lars Hidde, explaining why he dithered a perfectly fine 256-color image into a 16-color default palette

I needed to get about 40 bitmap files from the Macintosh to the Sun SPARCstation. "Piece of cake," I said. "Give me a few minutes." The network hadn't gone down in three days, and we were connected at Ethernet speeds. Well, the files had been saved in native Photoshop format on the Macintosh. So I launched Photoshop, opened each file, and then saved it in PICT format. The translator program I wanted to use to convert Macintosh PICT files to Sun raster files was an MS-DOS application, so I renamed all the Macintosh files to fit the DOS eight-plus-three-character file name convention. Then I cranked up the PC, launched the translator, and batch-processed all of the files into RAS files using the network. The 40 new files were now on the Macintosh, mixed in with the original PICTs. I collected the needed raster files into a single folder on the Macintosh and then sent the whole thing over to the Sun.

A few minutes? The process kept three chairs warm for about two hours.

Windows Formats

The **device-independent bitmap (DIB)** is Windows' common image file format, usually written as BMP files. DIBs can stand alone, or they can be buried within a **Resource Interchange File Format (RIFF)** file. A RIFF is actually the preferred file type for all multimedia development in Windows, because this format was designed to contain many types of files, including bitmaps, MIDI scores, and formatted text.

The bitmap formats used most often by Windows developers are DIB, BMP, PCX, and TIFF. A **BMP** file is a Windows bitmap file. **PCX** files were originally developed for use in Z-Soft MS-DOS paint packages; these files can be opened and saved by almost all MS-DOS paint software and desktop publishing software. **TIFF**, or Tagged Interchange File Format, was designed to be a universal bitmapped iage format and is also used extensively in desktop publishing packages. Often, applications use a proprietary file format to store their images. Adobe creates a PSD file for Photoshop and an AIX file for Illustrator; Corel creates a CDR file; Micrografx Designer and Picture Publisher applications use DSF and PPF files. If you import your artwork into other programs, such as multimedia authoring systems, be sure you save your bitmaps in a format that can be imported by that application.

The list to the right contains image file formats you might find in the Windows environment.

Cross-Platform Formats

For handling drawn objects across many platforms, there are two common formats: DXF and IGS. **DXF** was developed by AutoDesk as an ASCII-based drawing interchange file for AutoCAD, but the format is used today by many computer-aided design applications. **IGS** (or IGES, for Initial Graphics Exchange Standard) was developed by an industry committee as a broader standard for transferring CAD drawings. These formats are also used in 3-D rendering and animation programs.

JPEG and GIF images are the most common bitmap formats used on the Web and may be considered cross platform, as all browsers will display them. Adobe's popular PDF (Portable Document File) file manages both bitmaps and drawn art (as well as text and other multimedia content), and is commonly used to deliver a "finished product" that contains multiple assets.

Format	Extension
Microsoft Windows DIB	.bmp, .dib, .rle
Microsoft RLE DIB	.dib
Microsoft Palette	.pal
Microsoft RIFF DIB	.rdi
Computer Graphics Metafile	.cgm
Micrografx Designer/Draw	.drw
AutoCAD Format 2-D	.dxf
Encapsulated PostScript	.eps
CompuServe GIF	.gif
HP Graphic Language	.hgl
JPEG	.jpg
PC Paintbrush	.pcx
Apple Macintosh PICT	.pic or .pct
Lotus 1-2-3 Graphics	.pic
AutoCAD Import	.plt
Portable Network Graphic	.png
Truevision TGA	.tga
TIFF	.tif
Windows Metafile	.wmf
DrawPerfect	.wpg

Chapter 6 Review

■ Chapter Summary

For your review, here's a summary of the important concepts discussed in this chapter.

Discuss the various factors that apply to the use of images in multimedia

■ What you see on a multimedia computer screen is the viewer's primary connection to all of your project's content.

■ Work out your graphic approach before you begin, either in your head or during creative sessions with your client or colleagues.

■ To get a handle on any multimedia project, start with pencil, eraser, and paper. Outline your project and your graphic ideas first: make a flowchart; storyboard the project using stick figures; use three-by-five index cards and shuffle them until you get it right.

■ Most authoring systems provide simple tools for creating the graphic objects directly on your screen. Most can also import objects from other applications.

■ Multimedia designers employ a variety of applications and tools to accomplish many specialized tasks.

Describe the capabilities and limitations of bitmap images

■ Bitmaps are an image type most appropriate for photorealistic images and complex drawings requiring fine detail.

■ Limitations of bitmapped images include large files sizes and the inability to scale or resize the image easily while maintaining quality.

■ A bitmap is a simple information matrix describing the individual dots of an image, called pixels.

■ The image's bit-depth determines the number of colors that can be displayed by an individual pixel.

■ You can grab a bitmap image from a screen, scan it with a scanner, download it from a web site, or capture it from a video capture device.

■ You can then manipulate and adjust many of its properties, and cut and paste among many bitmaps using specialized image-editing or "darkroom" programs.

■ When you import a color or gray-scale bitmap from the Macintosh to Windows, the colors will seem darker and richer.

Describe the capabilities and limitations of vector images

■ Vector images are most appropriate for lines, boxes, circles, polygons, and other graphic shapes that can be mathematically expressed in angles, coordinates, and distances.

■ A vector object can be filled with color and patterns, and you can select it as a single object.

■ Vector-drawn objects use a fraction of the memory space required to describe and store the same object in bitmap form.

■ For the Web, pages that use vector graphics in plug-ins such as Flash download faster and, when used for animation, draw faster than bitmaps.

■ Most drawing programs can export a vector drawing as a bitmap.

■ Converting bitmaps to vector-drawn objects is difficult; however, auto-tracing programs can compute the boundaries of shapes and colors in bitmapped images and then derive the polygon object that describes those bounds.

■ Vector images require a plug-in (such as a Flash player) for display on a web page.

■ Vector images cannot be used for photo-realistic images.

Define various aspects of 3-D modeling

■ For 3-D, the depth (z dimension) of cubes and spheres must be calculated and displayed so that the perspective of the rendered object seems correct to the eye.

- Objects and elements in 3-D space carry with them properties such as shape, color, texture, shading, and location.

- Objects are created by modeling them using a 3-D application.

- To model an object that you want to place into your scene, you must start with a shape.

- When you extrude a plane surface, it extends its shape some distance, either perpendicular to the shape's outline or along a defined path.

- When you lathe a shape, a profile of the shape is rotated around a defined axis (you can set the direction) to create the 3-D object.

- Rendering is when the computer finally uses intricate algorithms to apply the effects you have specified on the objects you have created.

Describe the use of colors and palettes in multimedia

- Color is the frequency of a light wave within the narrow band of the electromagnetic spectrum to which the human eye responds.

- Different cultures associate certain colors with different meanings.

- The lowest common denominator for a multimedia display is a color monitor that displays 8 bits of color information per pixel in a matrix of 640 pixels across and 480 pixels down (640 × 480). Whether or not you move to a higher-resolution display with a greater color depth requires you to identify the types of hardware on which your program will be viewed.

- For 256-color, 8-bit VGA systems, the computer uses a color lookup table or palette to determine which 256 colors out of the millions possible are available to you at any one time.

- Dithering is a process whereby the color value of each pixel is changed to the closest matching color value in the target palette, using a mathematical algorithm.

- If you are using a specialized application to make bitmaps or drawings, make sure your multimedia authoring package can import the image files you produce, and that your application can export such a file.

Cite the various file types used in multimedia

- On the Macintosh, PICT is a complicated but versatile format developed by Apple as a common format that is always available to Macintosh users.

- Windows uses device-independent bitmaps (DIBs) as its common image file format, usually written as BMP files.

- TIFF, or Tagged Interchange File Format, was designed to be a universal bitmapped image format and is also used extensively in desktop publishing packages.

- For handling drawn objects across many platforms, there are two common formats: DXF and IGS. JPEG and GIF images are the most common bitmap formats used on the Web and may be considered cross platform, as all browsers will display them.

■ Key Terms

additive color *(154)*
autotracing *(146)*
binary *(134)*
bit *(134)*
bitmap *(134)*
BMP *(162)*
Cartesian coordinates *(144)*
clipboard *(141)*
CMYK *(154)*
color lookup table (CLUT) *(157)*
device-independent
bitmap (DIB) *(162)*

dithering *(159)*
dot pitch *(154)*
DXF *(163)*
extrude *(148)*
flare *(149)*
GIF *(134)*
hexadecimal *(156)*
hues *(153)*
IGS *(163)*
JPEG *(134)*
lathe *(148)*

map *(134)*
modeling *(147)*
morphing *(142)*
objects *(147)*
palettes *(157)*
PCX *(162)*
pels *(135)*
PICT *(161)*
primitives *(147)*
properties *(147)*
quantum theory *(151)*

▪ Key Term Quiz

1. The working area of a computer monitor is sometimes called _____.

2. The type of image used for photo-realistic images and for complex drawings requiring fine detail is the _____.

3. The type of image used for lines, boxes, circles, polygons, and other graphic shapes that can be mathematically expressed in angles, coordinates, and distances is the _____.

4. The picture elements that make up a bitmap are called _____.

5. _____ allows you to smoothly blend two images so that one image seems to melt into the next.

6. The process that computes the bounds of the shapes of colors within a bitmap image and then derives the polygon object that describes that image is called _____.

7. _____ is when the computer uses intricate algorithms to apply the effects you have specified on the objects you have created for a final 3-D image.

8. _____ provides a method for viewing a single surrounding image as if you were "inside" the picture and able to look up or down, turn, or zoom in on features.

9. The collection of color values held in a color lookup table is called a _____.

10. _____ is a process whereby the color value of each pixel is changed to the closest matching color value in the target palette, using a mathematical algorithm.

▪ Multiple Choice Quiz

1. What is the best way to start creating your project's interface?
   a. Start with pencil, eraser, and paper.
   b. Outline your project and graphic ideas.
   c. Storyboard using stick figures.
   d. Use three-by-five index cards and shuffle them.
   e. all of the above

2. Which image file type is best for photographs?
   a. vector
   b. encapsulated PostScript
   c. bitmap
   d. Shockwave
   e. laser

3. A 16-bit image is capable of representing how many different colors?
   a. 2
   b. 16
   c. 256
   d. 65,536
   e. 16,772,216

4. Vector-drawn objects are used for all of the following *except*:
   a. lines
   b. circles
   c. polygons
   d. photographs
   e. boxes

5. "Unlimited use" of stock photography may actually impose a limitation on:
   a. the number of units you can distribute without paying more.
   b. the number of changes you can make to the image.
   c. converting the image to another file format.
   d. the filters you may use to alter the image.
   e. the price you can charge for your product.

6. Name the area of memory where data such as text and images is temporarily stored when you cut or copy within an application.
   a. scrapbook
   b. notepad
   c. junkyard
   d. filedump
   e. clipboard

7. Perhaps the single most significant advance in computer image processing during the late 1980s was the development of:
   a. digital cameras
   b. 3-D modeling programs
   c. image-editing programs
   d. scanners
   e. electronic crayons

8. When an image created on a Macintosh is viewed on a PC:
   a. it appears darker and richer because the values have changed
   b. it appears lighter and less saturated because the values have changed
   c. it appears darker and richer even though the values have not changed
   d. it appears lighter and less saturated even though the values have not changed
   e. it appears exactly the same

9. Graphic artists designing for print media use vector-drawn objects because:
   a. they can contain more subtle variations in shading than bitmap graphics
   b. printing inks respond better to them
   c. they can be converted across platforms more easily
   d. they can be printed at any size
   e. they can be viewed directly in Web browsers

10. The 3-D process of extending a plane surface some distance, either perpendicular to the shape's outline or along a defined path, is called:
    a. lathing
    b. rendering
    c. modeling
    d. extruding
    e. skinning

11. The VGA standard is:
    a. 8 bits of color information per pixel in a matrix of 640 pixels across and 480 pixels down
    b. 16 bits of color information per pixel in a matrix of 640 pixels across and 480 pixels down
    c. 16 bits of color information per pixel in a matrix of 800 pixels across and 600 pixels down
    d. 24 bits of color information per pixel in a matrix of 800 pixels across and 600 pixels down
    e. 24 bits of color information per pixel in a matrix of 1024 pixels across and 768 pixels down

12. Which of these is the correct HTML representation of magenta (red + blue)?
    a. 00GGHH
    b. #FF00FF
    c. 255,0,255
    d. %R100-%G0-%B100
    e. <color = "magenta">

13. Which of the following is *not* a color specification format?
  a. RGB
  b. HSB
  c. GIF
  d. CMYK
  e. CIE

14. Which of the following is *not* a native Windows graphics file format?
  a. BMP
  b. RIFF
  c. TIFF
  d. PCX
  e. PICT

15. TIFF stands for:
  a. Transitional Image File Format
  b. Total Inclusion File Format
  c. Tagged Interchange File Format
  d. Temporary Instruction File Format
  e. Table Index File Format

■ Essay Quiz

1. Discuss the difference between bitmap and vector graphics. Describe five different graphic elements you might use in a project, for example, the background, buttons, icons, or text. Would you use a vector tool or a bitmap tool for each element? Why?

2. You are assigned to create an interface that will look good across platforms. What is the difference between images as shown on a Macintosh and PC? How would you deal with this problem?

3. List several simple geometric shapes. If you have a 3-D modeling program available, using these shapes, extrude or lathe them to create various objects, such as a teapot, a tree, a car, a table, or a lamp. Think of some other objects. How would you use the simple geometric shapes (called "primitives") to create the 3-D object?

4. You are a designer given the task of creating a web site for a new division of your company. Start by defining the characteristics of the customers of the company and the kind of image the company wishes to present to its customers. Then specify a color palette to be used for the design of the site. Defend your color choices by discussing the associations people have with the colors and how they relate to your customers and the company's image.

Lab Projects

■ Project 6.1

Select five different web pages, each from a different web site. Select pages that contain lots of colors and images, both photographs and graphics. View the five different pages on both a Macintosh and PC screen, preferably side by side, as well as on more than one computer on the same platform (for example, one Mac, two Windows computers). Note the differences in how each page appears across platforms and across screens. For each page, write a paragraph describing how they differ in terms of color tone, saturation, and any other characteristics that you notice.

■ Project 6.2

Using the capture tool built into the operating system or another dedicated tool, capture and save five different screens. Use the tools to save the entire screen, areas of the screen, the front most window, an image with a menu pulled down, and an image with the cursor (some capture programs may not be able to capture all these different types of images). Save the files and print them out.

■ Project 6.3

Download three different images from a web site. One should be photographic, one should be a graphic (solid colors or gradients), and one should be a mix. Convert the images to 256 colors. Use the tools available to use different dithering patterns and palettes. Print out the files before and after reducing to 256 colors. Write the file sizes on each one. If you have Photoshop 5.5 or later or Fireworks available, use one of those programs to compare the effects of applying different palettes and compression methods to the original images.

■ Project 6.4

Visit three different web sites. Describe the palette of color chosen. Describe it in subjective terms. Is it vibrant? childish? muted? subtle? Why? What cultural or other factors determined the color selection? Print out a page from each site, and write a paragraph describing the colors and images used in each one.

■ Project 6.5

Open an image in an image-editing program capable of identifying colors. Select three different pixels in the image. Sample the color and write down its value in RGB, HSB, CMYK, and web (hexadecimal) color.

Point	RGB	HSB	CMYK	Hexadecimal
1				
2				
3				

■ Project 6.6

Go to a web tracking site such as www.thecounter.com (or find another site by searching on such key words as "screen resolution" and "statistics"), and find its breakdown of current statistics on the hardware configurations of the visitors to its site. Compare those most recent figures with those reported in this chapter. How have the screen resolution and color depth percentages changed since May 2003? How might these figures help you design a site? What are the limitations of these tracking figures?

Animation

BY definition, **animation** makes static presentations come alive. It is visual change over time and can add great power to your multimedia projects and web pages. Many multimedia applications for both Macintosh and Windows provide animation tools.

The Power of Motion

You can animate your whole project, or you can animate here and there, accenting and adding spice. For a brief product demonstration with little user interaction, it might make sense to design the entire project as a movie and keep the presentation always in motion. For speaker support, you can animate bulleted text or fly it onto the screen, or you can use charts with quantities that grow or dwindle; then, give the speaker control of these eye-catchers. In a parts-assembly training manual, you might show components exploding into an expanded view.

Visual effects such as wipes, fades, zooms, and dissolves are available in most authoring packages, and some of these can be used for primitive animation. For example, you can slide images onto the screen with a wipe, or you can make an object implode with an iris/close effect. Figure 7-1 shows the many transition effects available in Adobe's Director and Premiere.

But animation is more than wipes, fades, and zooms. Animation is an object actually moving across or *into* or *out of* the screen; a spinning globe of our earth; a car driving along a line-art highway; a bug crawling out from under a stack of papers, with a screaming voice from the speaker telling you to "Shoot it, now!" Until QuickTime and AVI motion video became more commonplace, animations were the primary source of dynamic action in multimedia presentations.

WARNING *Overuse of animation and annoying visual effects can ruin a multimedia project. (Check out http://www.dack.com/web/flash_evil.html for a discussion of gratuitous use.)*

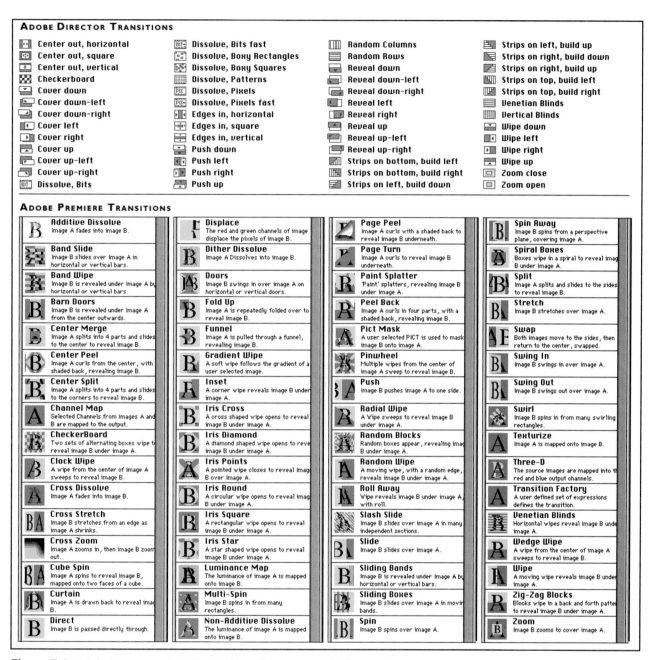

Figure 7-1 Adobe Director and Adobe Primiere offer many visual effects and transitions.

Principles of Animation

Animation is possible because of a biological phenomenon known as **persistence of vision** and a psychological phenomenon called **phi**. An object seen by the human eye remains chemically mapped on the eye's retina for a brief time after viewing. Combined with the human mind's need to conceptually complete a perceived action, this makes it possible for a series of images that are changed very slightly and very rapidly, one after the other, to seemingly blend together into a visual illusion of movement. The illustration shows a few cels, or frames, of a rotating logo. When the images are progressively and rapidly changed, the arrow of the compass is perceived to be spinning.

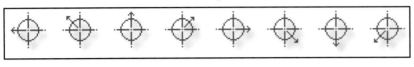

Television video builds 30 entire frames or pictures every second; the speed with which each frame is replaced by the next one makes the images appear to blend smoothly into movement. Movies on film are typically shot at a shutter rate of 24 frames per second, but using projection tricks (the projector's shutter flashes light through each image twice), the flicker rate is increased to 48 times per second, and the human eye thus sees a motion picture. On some projectors, each frame is shown three times before the pull-down claw moves to the next frame, for a total of 72 flickers per second, which helps to eliminate the flicker effect: the more interruptions per second, the more continuous the beam of light appears. Quickly changing the viewed image is the principle of an animatic, a flip-book, or a zoetrope. To make an object travel across the screen while it changes its shape, just change the shape and also move, or **translate**, it a few pixels for each frame. Then, when you play the frames back at a faster speed, the changes blend together and you have motion and animation. It's the same magic as when the hand is quicker than the eye, and you don't see the pea moving in the blur of the gypsy's cups.

Animation by Computer

Using appropriate software and techniques, you can animate visual images in many ways. The simplest animations occur in two-dimensional (2-D) space; more complicated animations occur in an intermediate "2½-D" space (where shadowing, highlights, and forced perspective provide an illusion of depth, the third dimension); and the most realistic animations occur in three-dimensional (3-D) space.

In 2-D space, the visual changes that bring an image alive occur on the flat Cartesian x and y axes of the screen. A blinking word, a **color-cycling** logo (where the colors of an image are rapidly altered according to a formula), a cel animation (described more fully later on in this chapter), or a button or tab that changes state on mouse rollover to let a user know it is active are all examples of **2-D animations**. These are simple and static, not changing their position on the screen. **Path animation** in 2-D space increases the complexity of an animation and provides motion, changing the location of an image along a predetermined path (position) during a specified amount of time (speed). Authoring and presentation software such as Flash or PowerPoint provide user-friendly tools to compute position changes and redraw an image in a new location, allowing you to generate a bouncing ball or slide a corporate mascot onto the screen. Combining changes in an image with changes in its position allows you to "walk" your corporate mascot onto the stage.

In **2½-D animation,** an illusion of depth (the z axis) is added to an image through shadowing and highlighting, but the image itself still rests on the flat x and y axes in two dimensions. Embossing, shadowing, beveling, and highlighting provide a sense of depth by raising an image or cutting it into a background. Zaxwerks' 3D Invigorator (http://www .zaxwerks.com), for example, provides 3-D effects for text and images and, while calling itself "3D," works within the 2-D space of image editors and drawing programs such as Adobe Illustrator, Photoshop, Fireworks, and After Effects.

In **3-D animation,** software creates a virtual realm in three dimensions, and changes (motion) are calculated along all three axes (x, y, and z), allowing an image or object that itself is created with a front, back, sides, top, and bottom to move towards or away from the viewer, or, in this virtual space of light sources and points of view, allowing the viewer to wander around and get a look at all the object's parts from all angles. Such animations are typically rendered frame by frame by high-end 3-D animation programs such as NewTek's Lightwave or AutoDesk's Maya.

Today, computers have taken the handwork out of the animation and rendering process, and commercial films such as *Jurassic Park*, *Beauty and the Beast*, *Toy Story*, and *Open Season* have utilized the power of computers. (See Chapter 6 for an account of the historic "computer wall" of 117 Sun SPARCstations used to render the animated feature *Toy Story*.)

Animation Techniques

When you create an animation, organize its execution into a series of logical steps. First, gather up in your mind all the activities you wish to provide in the animation. If it is complicated, you may wish to create a written script with a list of activities and required objects and then create a storyboard to visualize the animation. Choose the animation tool best suited for the job, and then build and tweak your sequences. This may include creating objects, planning their movements, texturing their surfaces, adding lights, experimenting with lighting effects, and positioning the camera or point of view. Allow plenty of time for this phase when you are experimenting and testing. Finally, post-process your animation, doing any special renderings and adding sound effects.

> I grew up using cel techniques and a huge animation crane to photograph with. I can tell you the static electricity caused hell with dust on the cels. Do you know why most 2-D animated characters in the past, like Mickey Mouse, wore white gloves? It was an inside joke…We all wore white gloves to protect the cels! And the reason most animated characters had only three fingers and a thumb inside their gloves was because it saved us time and money to drop that extra finger.
>
> Joe Silverthorn, Integrated Multimedia Instructor,

Cel Animation

The animation techniques made famous by Disney use a series of progressively different graphics or cels on each frame of movie film (which plays at 24 frames per second). A minute of animation may thus require as many as 1,440 separate frames, and each frame may be composed of many layers of cels. The term **cel** derives from the clear celluloid sheets that were used for drawing each frame, which have been replaced today by layers of digital imagery. Cels of famous animated cartoons have become sought-after, suitable-for-framing collector's items.

Cel animation artwork begins with **keyframes** (the first and last frame of an action). For example, when an animated figure of a woman walks across the screen, she balances the weight of her entire body on one foot and then the other in a series of falls and recoveries, with the opposite foot and leg catching up to support the body. Thus the first keyframe to portray a single step might be the woman pitching her body weight forward off the left foot and leg, while her center of gravity shifts forward; the feet are close together, and she appears to be falling. The last keyframe might be the right foot and leg catching the body's fall, with the center of gravity now centered between the outstretched stride and the left and right feet positioned far apart.

The series of frames in between the keyframes are drawn in a process called tweening. **Tweening** is an action that requires calculating the number of frames between keyframes and the path the action takes, and then actually sketching with pencil the series of progressively different outlines. As tweening progresses, the action sequence is checked by flipping through the frames. The penciled frames are assembled and then actually filmed as a **pencil test** to check smoothness, continuity, and timing.

When the pencil frames are satisfactory, they are permanently inked, photocopied onto cels, and given to artists who use acrylic colors to paint the details for each cel. Women were often preferred for this painstaking inking and painting work as they were deemed patient, neat, and had great eyes for detail. In the hands of a master, cel paint applied to the back of acetate can be simply flat and perfectly even, or it can produce beautiful and subtle effects, with feathered edges or smudges.

The cels for each frame of our example of a walking woman—which may consist of a text title, a background, foreground, characters (with perhaps separate cels for a left arm, a right arm, legs, shoes, a body, and facial features)—are carefully registered and stacked. It is this composite that becomes the final photographed single frame in an animated movie. For experimenting with frame editing and timing, Lunch Box DV from Animation Toolworks (http://www.animationtoolworks.com) requires only a video camera and a monitor to get started.

Computer Animation

Computer animation programs typically employ the same logic and procedural concepts as cel animation and use the vocabulary of classic cel animation—terms such as layer, keyframe, and tweening. The primary difference among animation software programs is in how much must be drawn by the animator and how much is automatically generated by the software (see Figure 7-2). In path-based 2-D and 2½-D animation, an animator simply creates an object (or imports an object as clip art) and describes a path for the object to follow. The computer software then takes over, actually creating the animation on the fly as the program is being viewed by your user. In cel-based 2-D animation, each frame of an animation is provided by the animator, and the frames are then composited (usually with some tweening help available from the software) into a single file of images to be played in sequence. ULead's GIF Animator and Alchemy's GIF Construction Set Pro simply string together your collection of frames. Other 2-D animation programs may use digital video schemes, such as AVI or QuickTime, for playing back an animation.

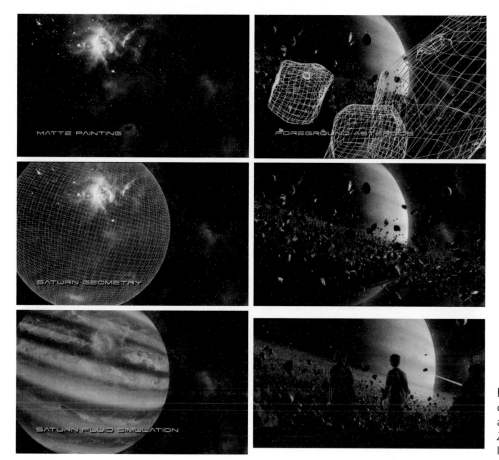

Figure 7-2 Several cels or digital image layers in a frame from the movie *Zathura* (Columbia Pictures/ Imageworks, 2005)

For 3-D animation, most of your effort may be spent in creating the models of individual objects and designing the characteristics of their shapes and surfaces. It is the software that then computes the movement of the objects within the 3-D space and renders each frame, in the end stitching them together in a digital output file as an AVI or QuickTime movie.

On the computer, paint is most often filled or drawn with tools using features such as gradients and anti-aliasing. The word **inks**, in computer animation terminology, usually means special methods for computing color values, providing edge detection, and layering so that images can blend or otherwise mix their colors to produce special transparencies, inversions, and effects.

You can usually set your own frame rates on the computer. 2-D cel-based animated GIFs, for example, allow you to specify how long each frame is to be displayed and how many times the animation should loop before stopping. 3-D animations output as digital video files can be set to run at 15 or 24 or 30 frames per second. However, the rate at which changes are computed and screens are actually refreshed will depend on the speed and power of your user's display platform and hardware, especially for animations such as path animations that are being generated by the computer on the fly. Although your animations will probably never push the limits of a monitor's scan rate (about 60 to 70 frames per second), animation does put raw computing horsepower to task. If you cannot compute all your changes and display them as a new frame on your monitor within, say, $\frac{1}{15}$th of a second, then the animation may appear jerky and slow. Underpowered computers may have trouble displaying digital video files specified to run at a set frame rate. Luckily, when the files include audio, the software maintains the continuity of the audio at all cost, preferring to drop visual frames or hold a single frame for several seconds while the audio plays.

TIP   *The smaller the object in path-based 2-D animation, the faster it can move. Bouncing a 10-pixel-diameter tennis ball on your screen provides far snappier motion than bouncing a 150-pixel-diameter beach ball.*

Kinematics   **Kinematics** is the study of the movement and motion of structures that have joints, such as a walking man. Animating a walking step is tricky: you need to calculate the position, rotation, velocity, and acceleration of all the joints and articulated parts involved—knees bend, hips flex, shoulders swing, and the head bobs. e-frontier's Poser, a 3-D modeling program, provides pre-assembled adjustable human models (male, female, infant, teenage, and superhero) in many poses, such as "walking" or "thinking." As you can see in Figure 7-3, you can pose figures in 3-D and then scale and manipulate individual body parts. Surface textures can then be applied to create muscle-bound hulks or smooth chrome androids. **Inverse kinematics**, available in high-end 3-D programs such as Lightwave and Maya, is the process by which you link objects such as hands to arms and define their relationships and limits (for example, elbows cannot bend backwards). Once those relationships and parameters have been set, you can then drag these parts around and let the computer calculate the result.

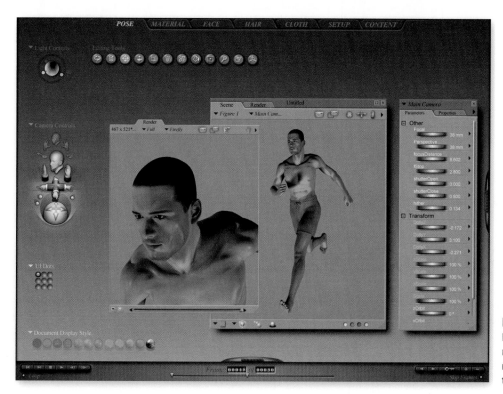

Figure 7-3 e-frontier's Poser understands human motion and inverse kinematics: move an arm, and the shoulders follow.

Morphing   **Morphing** is a popular (if not overused) effect in which one image transforms into another. Morphing applications and other modeling tools that offer this effect can transition not only between still images but often between moving images as well. Some products that offer morphing features are Black Belt's Easy Morph and WinImages, Human Software's Squizz, and Valis Group's Flo', MetaFlo', and MovieFlo'. Figure 7-4 illustrates part of a morph in which 16 kindergarten children are dissolved one into the other in a continuous, compelling motion video.

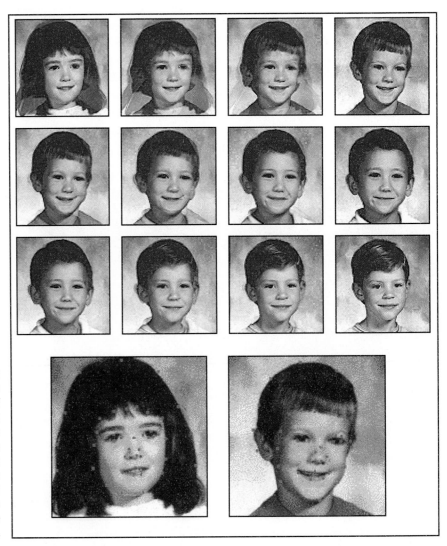

Figure 7-4 Morphing software was used to seamlessly transform the images of 16 kindergartners. When a sound track of music and voices was added to the four-minute piece, it made a compelling QuickTime video about how similar children are to each other. Matching key points (red) in the start and end image guide the morphing transition.

The morphed images were built at a rate of eight frames per second, with each transition taking a total of four seconds (32 separate images for each transition), and the number of key points was held to a minimum to shorten rendering time. Setting key points is crucial for smooth transition between two images. The point you set in the start image will move to the corresponding point in the end image—this is important for things like eyes and noses, which you want to end up in about the same place (even if they look different) after the transition. The more key points, the smoother the morph. In Figure 7-4, the red dot on each child's temple is a matching key point.

Animation File Formats

Some file formats are designed specifically to contain animations, so they can be ported among applications and platforms with the proper translators. Those formats include Director (.dir and .dcr), AnimatorPro (.fli using 320 × 200-pixel images and .flc), 3D Studio Max (.max), SuperCard and Director (.pics), CompuServe GIF89a (.gif), and Flash (.fla and .swf). Because file size is a critical factor when downloading animations to play on web pages, file compression is an essential part of preparing animation files for the Web. A Director's native movie file (.dir), for example, must be preprocessed and compressed into a proprietary Shockwave animation file (.dcr) for the Web. Compression for Director movies is as much as 75 percent or more with this tool, turning 100K files into 25K files and significantly speeding up download/display times on the Internet. Flash, widely used for web-based animation, makes extensive use of vector graphics (see Chapter 6) to keep the post-compression file size at absolute minimums. As with Director, its native .fla files must be converted to Shockwave Flash files (.swf) in order to play on the Web. To view these animations within a web page, special plug-ins or players are required (see Chapter 13).

In some cases, especially with 3-D animations, the individual rendered frames of an animation are put together into one of the standard digital video file formats, such as the Windows Audio Video Interleaved format (.avi), QuickTime (.qt, .mov), or Motion Picture Experts Group video (.mpeg or .mpg). These can be played using the media players shipped with computer operating systems.

Making Animations That Work

Animation catches the eye and makes things noticeable. But, like sound, animation quickly becomes trite if it is improperly applied. Unless your project has a backbone of movie-like, animated imagery, use animation carefully (and sparingly) to achieve the greatest impact. Your screens will otherwise become busy and "noisy."

Multimedia authoring systems typically provide tools to simplify creating animations within that authoring system, and they often have a mechanism for playing the special animation files created by dedicated animation software. Today, the most widely used tool for creating multimedia animations for Macintosh and Windows environments is Adobe's Flash.

The following sections provide examples to demonstrate that computer-generated animations actually consist of many bits and pieces carefully orchestrated to appear as one image, in motion—just like the many layers in classical cel animation.

A Rolling Ball

First, create a new, blank image file that is 100×100 pixels, and fill it with a sphere.

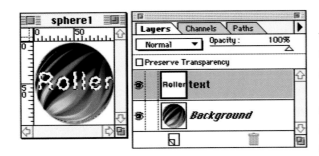

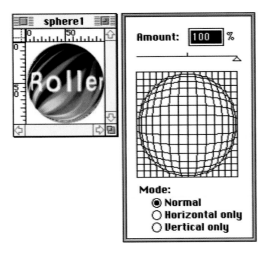

Create a new layer in Photoshop, and place some white text on this layer at the center of the image. Make the text spherical using Photoshop's distortion filter, and save the result (see the illustrations to the left).

To animate the sphere by rolling it across the screen, you first need to make a number of rotated images of the sphere. Rotate the image in 45-degree increments to create a total of eight images, rotating a full circle of 360 degrees. When displayed sequentially at the same location, the sphere spins:

For a realistic rolling effect, the circumference (calculated at pi times 100, or about 314 pixels) is divided by 8 (yielding about 40 pixels). As each image is successively displayed, the ball is moved 40 pixels along a line. Being where the rubber meets the road, this math applies when you roll any round object in a straight line perpendicular to your line of sight.

A Bouncing Ball

With the simplest tools, you can make a bouncing ball to animate your web site using GIF89a. This is a version of the GIF image format that allows multiple images to be put into a single file and then displayed as an animation in a web browser or presentation program that recognizes the format. The individual frames that make up the **animated GIF** can be created in any paint or image-processing program, but it takes a specialized program to put the frames together into a GIF89a file format. (Animating with GIF89a files is discussed in Chapter 14.) Like the rolling ball example, you simply need to flash a ball on the computer screen rapidly and in a different place each time to make it bounce up and down. And like the rolling ball, where you should compute the circumference of the ball and divide by the number of images to determine how far it rolls each time it flashes, there are some commonsense computations to consider with a bouncing ball, too. In the formula, s equals distance, a equals acceleration due to gravity, and t equals time:

$$s = \tfrac{1}{2}at^2$$

Gravity makes your bouncing ball accelerate on its downward course and decelerate on its upward course (when it moves slower and slower until it actually stops and then accelerates downward again). As Galileo discovered while dropping feathers and rocks from the leaning tower of Pisa, a beach ball and a golf ball accelerate downward at the same rate until they hit the ground. But the real world of Italy is full of air, so the feather falls gently while the rock pounds dirt. It is in this real world that you should compose your animations, tempering them always with commonsense physics to give them the ring of truth.

Unless your animation requires precision, ignore the hard numbers you learned in high school (like 32 feet per second per second), and simply figure that your ball will uniformly accelerate and decelerate up and down the pixels of your screen by the squares: 1, 4, 9, 16, 25, 36, 49, 64, 81, 100 are the squares of 1, 2, 3, 4, 5, 6, 7, 8, 9, and 10. This is illustrated in Figure 7-5. In the case of a perpetual-motion bouncing ball (even better than silly putty), it goes up the same way it comes down, forever, and this makes the job easy, because the up and down movements are symmetrical. You can use the same images for downward motion as you use for upward—as in frames 11 through 18 in Figure 7-5—by *reversing* them. You might also add a squash frame (not shown in Figure 7-5) when the ball hits the floor. The amount of squash would be determined by the type of ball—a steel ball or a balloon or a very soft rubber ball. The ball would squash when it hit and un-squash as it bounced up again. With a bit of programming, you might allow the user to choose the elasticity of the object, the amount of gravity, and the length of fall.

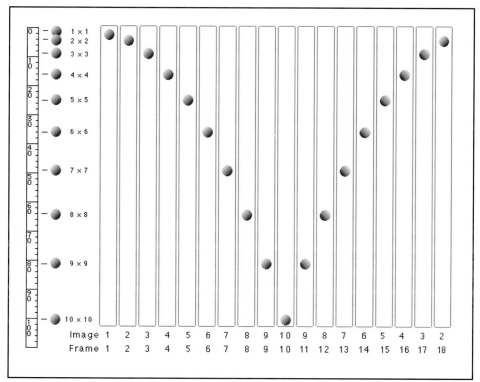

Figure 7-5 To make a bouncing ball seem natural, don't forget the effects of gravity. If you loop the 18 images shown here, the ball will bounce forever.

Open a graphics program and paint a ball about 15 pixels in diameter (if you have an odd-number diameter, there is a middle pixel that can be your center alignment point). If you wish to be fancy, make the ball with a 3-D graphics tool that will shade it as a sphere. Then duplicate the ball, placing each copy of it in a vertical line at the ten locations 1, 4, 9, 16, 25, 36, 49, 64, 81, and 100. The goal is to create a separate image file for each location of the ball, like the pages of a flip-book. With Photoshop, you can create a single file with ten layers to contain each ball at its proper location, and you can add an eleventh background layer, too. Then save each layer showing against the background as a separate file. (Use numbers in your file names like ball01, ball02, and so on, to keep them organized.)

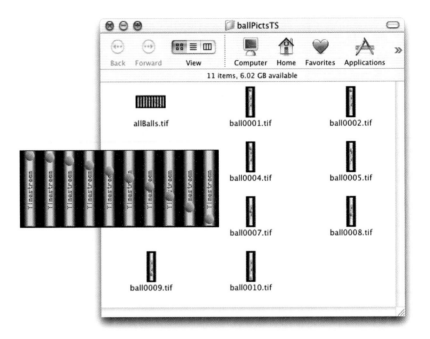

This is a construction process also easily managed with Director or Flash, in which you can place the same cast member or object (the ball) where you wish on the presentation stage. In Director, use the score's extended view, because the precise vertical location of your object is reported along the bottom line:

Frame																		
	1				5					10					15			
➔ 1	B ▪ 0 0 0 2 BKGND I ◆+ 0 1	-◆ 0 0 0 2 BKGND I ◆+ 0 4	-◆ 0 0 0 2 MATTE ◆+ 0 9	-◆ 0 0 0 2 MATTE ◆+ 0 16	-◆ 0 0 0 2 MATTE ◆+ 0 25	-◆ 0 0 0 2 MATTE ◆+ 0 36	-◆ 0 0 0 2 MATTE ◆+ 0 49	-◆ 0 0 0 2 MATTE ◆+ 0 64	-◆ 0 0 0 2 MATTE ◆+ 0 81	-◆ 0 0 0 2 MATTE ◆+ 0 100	-◆ 0 0 0 2 MATTE ◆+ 0 81	-◆ 0 0 0 2 MATTE ◆+ 0 64	-◆ 0 0 0 2 MATTE ◆+ 0 49	-◆ 0 0 0 2 MATTE ◆+ 0 36	-◆ 0 0 0 2 MATTE ◆+ 0 25	-◆ 0 0 0 2 MATTE ◆+ 0 16	-◆ 0 0 0 2 MATTE ◆+ 0 9	-◆ 0 0 0 2 MATTE ◆+ 0 4

You can also add a background and other art elements, and when you are done, you can export each frame as a graphics file using the export function. You will probably also wish to set the size of your stage to a small area just sufficient for your animation, say 32×120 pixels. The smaller the better if users will be downloading this animated GIF file into their web browsers.

To turn your collection of images into a GIF89a animation, you need an application like BoxTop Software's GIFmation (for Macintosh; see Figure 7-6) or ULead's GIF Animator (for Windows). These tools organize the sequence of images to be shown, set timing and transparency, and (most importantly) let you save the final GIF file in the proper format. See Chapter 14 for more details about animated GIF files and where to use them.

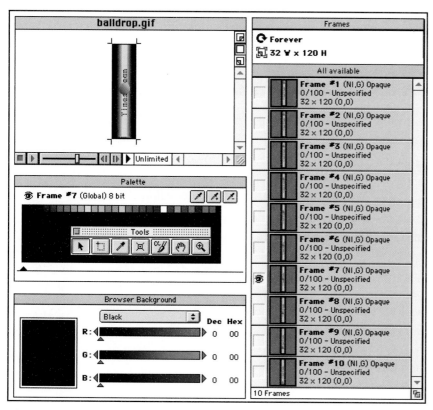

Figure 7-6 GIFmation from BoxTop Software lets you organize images into animated GIF files playable by web browsers.

Creating an Animated Scene

A creative committee organized a brief storyboard of a gorilla chasing a man. From a CD-ROM containing many images licensed for unlimited use, a photograph was chosen of Manhattan's Central Park where a bridge crossed a small river and high-rise apartments lined the horizon.

The chase scene would occur across the bridge. To produce frames of the running man, a real actor was videotaped running in place against an Ultimatte chroma-keyed blue background in a studio; a few frames of this were grabbed, and the blue background was removed from each image. The gorilla was difficult to find, so a toy model dinosaur about 25 centimeters tall was used; again, a few frames were captured and the background made transparent to form a composite. That was all that was required for image resources.

As illustrated in Figure 7-7*a*, the background was carefully cut in half along the edge of the bridge, so that the bridge railing could be placed in front of the runners. The running man was organized in a series of six frames that could be repeated many times across the screen to provide the pumping motions of running. The same was done for the dinosaur, to give him a lumbering, bulky look as he chased the little man across the bridge (see Figure 7-7*b*). The result, in Figure 7-7*c*, was simple and quickly achieved.

First Person

The animation storyboard called for a photorealistic monster chasing a running man through a city park amid screams of terror. The man was already in Director, running in great strides across an arched footbridge in a woodsy scene with high-rises in the background; he even looked over his shoulder a few times in panic. We were scouting around for an effective Godzilla when a friend dropped by with a motorized, 12-inch Tyrannosaurus Rex from Toys'R'Us. It was perfect—opening a toothy, gaping mouth every few steps as it lumbered along on C batteries.

I took the dinosaur and a video camera home to the delight and fascination of my three-year-old daughter, who helped rig a white sheet in front of the living room fireplace and a cardboard-box runway where Mr. TRex could strut his stuff before the camera. A couple of lamps gave him a sweaty sheen. We recorded about five minutes of video as my daughter happily retrieved Mr. TRex each time he nosed off the "cliff" at the end of the stage.

I grabbed a still image about every fourth frame of the recording and imported the resulting files into Director as cast members. They needed a little cleanup and scaling, but the fellow looked really convincing when he was finally scored to run across the bridge. Next day, I mixed a bunch of sounds—singing birds, running footsteps, screams, roars, sirens, and gunshots—and it was done.

(a)

(b)

(c)

Figure 7-7 The upper portion of the photo was placed behind the runners (*b*) and the lower portion in front of them, to make them appear to run behind the bridge railing (*c*).

Chapter 7 Review

■ Chapter Summary

For your review, here's a summary of the important concepts discussed in this chapter.

Define animation and describe how it can be used in multimedia

- By definition, animation is the act of making something come alive.

- Depending on the size of the project, you can animate the whole thing or you can just animate parts of it.

- Visual effects such as wipes, fades, zooms, and dissolves, available in most authoring packages, are a simple form of animation.

- Animation is an object actually moving across, into, or out of the screen.

- Animation is possible because of a biological phenomenon known as persistence of vision and a psychological phenomenon called phi.

- With animation, a series of images are changed very slightly and very rapidly, one after the other, seemingly blending together into a visual illusion of movement.

- Television video builds 30 entire frames or pictures every second. Movies on film are typically shot at a shutter rate of 24 frames per second.

Discuss the origins of cel animation and define the words that originate from this technique

- Cel animation, an animation technique made famous by Disney, uses a series of progressively different graphics on each frame of movie film.

- Cel animation artwork begins with keyframes; these are the first and last frames of an action.

- Tweening is an action that involves creating the frames to depict the action that happens between keyframes.

- Computer animation programs typically employ the same logic and procedural concepts as cel animation.

Define the capabilities of computer animation and the mathematical techniques that differ from traditional cel animation

- You can usually set your own frame rates on the computer, but the rate at which changes are computed and screens are actually refreshed will depend on the speed and power of your display platform and hardware.

- Kinematics is the study of the movement and motion of structures that have joints.

- Inverse kinematics is the process in which you link objects such as hands to arms and define their relationships and limits, then drag these parts around and let the computer calculate the result.

- Morphing is an effect in which one image transforms into another.

Discuss some of the general principles and factors that apply to creating computer animations for multimedia presentations

- Some file formats are designed specifically to contain animations, and they can be ported among applications and platforms with the proper translators.

- Multimedia authoring systems typically provide tools to simplify creating animations within that authoring system.

- The most widely used tool for creating multimedia animations for Macintosh and Windows environments is Adobe's Director.

- With the simplest tools, you can make a bouncing ball to animate your web site using GIF89a.

- Making animations appear natural requires a basic understanding of the principles of physics. You should compose your animations using these principles, tempering them always with commonsense physics to give them the ring of truth.

■ Key Terms

animated GIF *(180)*
animation *(170)*
cel *(174)*
cel animation *(174)*
color cycling *(172)*
inks *(176)*
inverse kinematics *(177)*

keyframes *(174)*
kinematics *(176)*
morphing *(177)*
path animation *(172)*
pencil test *(174)*
persistence of vision *(171)*
phi *(171)*

3-D animation *(173)*
translate *(172)*
tweening *(174)*
2-D animation *(172)*
2½-D animation *(173)*

■ Key Term Quiz

1. An object seen by the human eye remains chemically mapped on the retina for a brief time after viewing. This phenomenon is called _____.

2. The human mind needs to conceptually complete a perceived action. This phenomenon is called _____.

3. To make an object travel across the screen while it changes its shape, just change the shape and also move or _____ it a few pixels for each frame.

4. The animation technique made famous by Disney involves showing a different image for each frame. This technique is called _____ animation.

5. The first and last frames of an action are called _____.

6. The series of frames in between the first and last frames in an action are drawn in a process called _____.

7. In computer animation terminology, _____ usually refers to special methods that allow images to blend or otherwise mix their colors to produce special transparencies, inversions, and effects.

8. The study of the movement and motion of structures that have joints is called _____.

9. The effect in which one image transforms into another is known as _____.

Multiple Choice Quiz

1. Most authoring packages include visual effects such as:
   a. panning, zooming, and tilting
   b. wipes, fades, zooms, and dissolves
   c. morphing
   d. tweening
   e. inverse kinematics

2. The term cel derives from:
   a. the concept of each action in a sequence being a separate element or "cell"
   b. the fact that the inks used in early animations were based on extracts from celery plants
   c. an abbreviation of the phrase "composite element"
   d. the fact that the first animations were the work of communist dissidents who were organized into cells
   e. the clear celluloid sheets that were used for drawing each frame

3. Which of these is *not* a reason why animation is perceived as motion?
   a. An image remains in the eye chemically for a brief time after viewing.
   b. Our mind tries to "connect the dots" by completing perceived actions.
   c. The use of darker colors for moving objects is interpreted by the mind as motion.
   d. A sequence of images is read as continuous motion.
   e. All of the above are valid reasons.

4. Movies on film are typically shot at a shutter rate of:
   a. 15 frames per second
   b. 24 frames per second
   c. 29.97 frames per second
   d. 30 frames per second
   e. 48 frames per second

5. The clear sheets that were used for drawing each frame of animation have been replaced today by:
   a. acetate or plastic
   b. titanium
   c. fiberglass
   d. epoxy resin
   e. digital paper

6. Today's computer animation programs most closely resemble:
   a. film "rotoscoping" techniques
   b. the "phi" phenomenon described by Carl Jung
   c. neuro-kinetics techniques pioneered by NASA
   d. traditional cel animation
   e. none of the above

7. The technical limitation you are likely to encounter in creating animations is:
   a. the monitor's refresh rate
   b. the computer's processing capability
   c. the ability to accurately calculate physical actions
   d. the "persistence of vision" phenomenon
   e. the monitor's color gamut

8. In general, the animation may appear jerky and slow if each frame is displayed for more than about:
   a. ⅟30 of a second
   b. ⅟15 of a second
   c. ¼ of a second
   d. ½ of a second
   e. 1 second

9. The process in which you link objects such as hands to arms and define their relationships and limits (for example, elbows cannot bend backwards), then drag these parts around and let the computer calculate the result is called:
   a. rotoscoping
   b. de-morphing

c. meta-articulation

d. cyber-motion

e. inverse kinematics

10. To create a smooth transition between two images when morphing, it's important to set numerous:

    a. layers

    b. keyframes

    c. key points

    d. anchor tags

    e. splines

11. The standard frame rate of computer animations is:

    a. 10 frames per second

    b. 15 frames per second

    c. 24 frames per second

    d. 30 frames per second

    e. There is no standard; it depends on the file's settings.

12. Today, the most widely used tool for creating vector-based animations is:

    a. Adobe's Flash

    b. Adobe's GoLive

    c. Corel's CorelDraw

d. Microsoft's KineMatix

e. Activa's InterStudio

13. The Director file format has which extension?

    a. .dir and .dcr

    b. .fli and .flc

    c. .avi

    d. .qt, .mov

    e. .mpeg or .mpg

14. The file format that is most widely supported for web animations is:

    a. PICT

    b. .DCR

    c. GIF89a

    d. JPEG

    e. AIFF

15. To keep the post-compression file size at absolute minimums, Flash makes extensive use of:

    a. inverse kinematics

    b. cel-type animation

    c. vector graphics

    d. inks

    e. NURBS

■ Essay Quiz

1. Discuss the physical and psychological principles as to why animation works, as well as how it is usually presented.

2. Briefly discuss the origins of cel animation and the concepts that go into creating these animations. Be sure to include keyframes, tweening, and inks.

3. You need to create a simple animation of an animated logo. The logo depicts a planet orbiting the sun. Describe the motion in a storyboard. List the points in the action that would make good keyframes, and explain why. How would you need to manipulate the planet to make its motion look natural?

4. You need to create a simple animation of a man bowling, with the ball rolling down the alley, and striking the pins. Describe the sequence of motions in a storyboard. Discuss the various techniques and principles you might employ to accurately represent the motion of the man moving, the ball rolling, and the pins falling.

5. Discuss where and how you might use animation in one of the following projects. Be creative. Where would animation be appropriate? Where would it be distracting? How could it best be used to visually illustrate a concept?

    a. a web site for sports car enthusiasts

    b. a presentation to shareholders of a financial report

    c. a training CD on a printing press

    d. a CD that depicts the history of a railroad

Lab Projects

■ Project 7.1

Use a search engine to search on the words "animation" and "definition." Create a document that provides many different definitions of the term animation. Describe the differences among definitions. Which elements make the most difference among them—type of motion, process used for creation, method of playback, or something else? What do all (or, at least, most) of the definitions have in common?

■ Project 7.2

Locate a GIF animation at any web site. (Go to Google and do an image search using the term "animated GIF." You may get as many as 229,000 hits!) Save the file of your choice to your computer's hard drive. (On the Mac you can generally drag the image onto your desktop. On Windows, right-click and select "Save Picture (or Image) As".) Using one of the shareware or freeware GIF animators available, open the file. Save the individual frames as separate files and print them out. Note how the GIF89a specification enables files to be saved so that only the differences between keyframes are saved.

■ Project 7.3

Pick an animation software package available for either the Macintosh or Windows that offers at least one form of animation (for example, 2-D cel animation, animated GIF, or 3-D animation). List its name and discuss its capabilities. Is the software capable of layers? Keyframes? Tweening? Morphing? Will it allow you to create cross-platform files for playback? Does it require a plug-in for viewing in a web browser?

■ Project 7.4

Conceptualize a brief animated sequence. Include a number of moving elements that move into and out of the frame. Consider where the keyframes should be. How do the elements move? Do they get bigger or smaller? Do they rotate? Do they "deform" (change shape)?

Create a storyboard with sketches showing at least ten of the keyframes.

Video

SINCE the first silent film movie flickered to life, people have been fascinated with "motion" pictures. To this day, motion video is the element of multimedia that can draw gasps from a crowd at a trade show or firmly hold a student's interest in a computer-based learning project. Digital video is the most engaging of multimedia venues, and it is a powerful tool for bringing computer users closer to the real world. It is also an excellent method for delivering multimedia to an audience raised on television. With video elements in your project, you can effectively present your messages and reinforce your story, and viewers tend to retain more of what they see. But take care! Video that is not thought out or well produced can degrade your presentation.

Of all the multimedia elements, video places the highest performance demand on your computer—and its memory and storage. Consider that a high-quality color still image on a computer screen could require as much as a megabyte or more of storage memory. Multiply this by 30—the number of times per second that the picture is replaced to provide the appearance of motion—and you would need at least 30 megabytes of storage to play your video for one second, more than 1.8 gigabytes of storage for a minute, and 108 gigabytes or more for an hour. Just moving all this picture data from computer memory to the screen at that rate would challenge the processing capability of a supercomputer. These massive memory storage demands would make the Library of Congress look like a tiny magazine rack at your local grocery store. Some of the hottest and most arcane multimedia technologies and research efforts today deal with compressing digital video image data into manageable streams of information. This allows a massive amount of imagery to be squeezed into a comparatively small data file, which can still deliver a good viewing experience on the intended viewing platform during playback.

If you control the delivery platform for your multimedia project, you can specify special hardware and software enhancements that will allow you to work with full-screen, full-motion video, and sophisticated audio for high-quality surround sound. Or you can design a project to meet a specific compression standard, such as MPEG-2 for DVD (Digital Versatile Disc) playback or MPEG-4 for home video. You can install a superfast **RAID (Redundant Array of Independent Disks)** system that

In this chapter, you will learn how to:

- Consider the implications of using digital video in multimedia

- Discuss video recording and how it relates to multimedia production

- Prepare digital video and images for conversion to television

- Shoot and edit video for use in multimedia

- Select the best video recording formats for your multimedia project

- Begin preparing video for the Web, DVD, and CD-ROM

will support high-speed data transfer rates. You can include instructions in your authoring system (for example, in Flash or Adobe Acrobat Connect) that will spool video clips into RAM, ready for high-speed playback *before* they need to play. Having control of the playback platform is always good, but it is seldom available in the real world, so as you develop your video elements, you will need to make many choices and compromises based upon your assessment of the "lowest common denominator" playback platform where your project will be used.

Using Video

Carefully planned, well-executed video clips can make a dramatic difference in a multimedia project. A clip of John F. Kennedy proclaiming, "Ich bin ein Berliner" in video and sound is more compelling than a scrolling text field containing that same speech. Before deciding whether to add video to your project, however, it is essential to have an understanding of the medium, its limitations, and its costs. This chapter provides a foundation to help you understand how video works, the different formats and standards for recording and playing video, and the differences between computer and television video. The equipment needed to shoot and edit video, as well as tips for adding video to your project, are also covered.

Video standards and formats are still being refined as transport, storage, compression, and display technologies take shape in laboratories and in the marketplace and while equipment and post-processing evolves from its analog beginnings to become fully digital, from capture to display. Working with multimedia video today can be like a Mojave Desert camping trip: you may pitch your tent on comfortable high ground and find that overnight the shifting sands have buried both your approach and your investment. Firm ground tends to shift rapidly in the 100 mph back draft of the many silicon engineers, computer scientists, and start-up company salespeople driving in the fast lane of competition with compression schemes, RAID hard disk towers, and interleaving software. This is especially true today while broadcast television moves from the analog **National Television Standards Committee (NTSC)** standard to the new (and evolving) **Digital Television (DTV)** standard. According to the Federal Communications Commission's schedule, by 2006 all television broadcast stations will be switched over to the digital standard, and many consumers will have purchased digital television sets or display monitors. The environment in which you will deliver your multimedia content is always changing.

Digital video has supplanted analog video as the method of choice for making and delivering video for multimedia use. While broadcast stations and professional production and post-production houses remain invested in older analog video hardware, procurement of newer, digital video gear

Full-motion video on personal computers changes everything. It is like turning a ten-speed bicycle into a Harley-Davidson.

....

David Bunnell

Since multimedia gives you the ability to present information in a variety of ways, let the content drive the selection of media for each chunk of information to be presented. Use traditional text and graphics where appropriate; add animation when "still life" won't get your message across; add audio when further explanation is required; resort to video only when all other methods pale by comparison.

....

David A. Ludwig,
Interactive Learning Designs

produces excellent finished products at a fraction of the cost of analog gear. As pressured demand for digital output rises, the analog video hardware will fade away. A digital camcorder directly connected to a computer workstation using **FireWire (IEEE 1394)** cables eliminates the image-degrading analog-to-digital conversion step typically performed by video capture cards bringing the power of nonlinear video editing and production to everyday users.

Obtaining Video Clips

If your project will include video, consider whether you should shoot new "footage" (a legacy term from the film and analog world) or acquire preexisting content for your video clips. There are many sources for film and video clips: a friend's home movies may suffice, or you can go to a "stock" footage house or a television station or movie studio. But acquiring footage that you do not own outright can be a nightmare—it is expensive, and licensing rights and permissions may be difficult, if not impossible, to obtain. Each second of video could cost $50 to $100 or more to license. Even a "public domain clip" from the National Archives will cost a minimum of $125 to copy the footage, and the turnaround time can take up to six weeks. Many companies sell royalty-free stock CDs specifically for multimedia productions—these are lower resolution than broadcast quality and typically less than full-frame video.

On some projects, you will have no choice but to pay the price for required footage. If it is absolutely essential that your project include a clip of Elvis Presley crooning "You Ain't Nothing But a Hound Dog," and an Elvis impersonator just won't do, you will have to negotiate for rights to use the real thing. If your budget can't cover the cost of licensing a particular video clip, you may want to consider using other alternatives. You could try locating a less expensive archival video source, using a series of still images rather than video, or shooting your own video. If you shoot your own video for a project, make sure you have talent releases from all persons who appear or speak and permission to use the audio effects and music you weave into it. Licensing, permissions, and legal issues are discussed more fully in Chapter 17.

Before you head out to the field with your camcorder in hand, it is important to understand at least the basics of video recording and editing, as well as the constraints of using video in a multimedia project. The remainder of this chapter will help you to understand how video works and will provide practical guidelines for shooting your own videos.

How Video Works

When light reflected from an object passes through a video camera lens, that light is converted into an electronic signal by a special sensor called a

charge-coupled device (CCD). Top-quality broadcast cameras and even camcorders may have as many as three CCDs (one for each color of red, green, and blue) to enhance the resolution of the camera. The output of the CCD is processed by the camera into a signal containing three channels of color information and synchronization pulses (sync). There are several video standards for managing CCD output, each dealing with the amount of separation between the components of the signal. The more separation of the color information found in the signal, the higher the quality of the image (and the more expensive the equipment). If each channel of color information is transmitted as a separate signal on its own conductor, the signal output is called **RGB** (red, green, and blue), which is the preferred method for higher-quality and professional video work. Output can also be split into two separate chroma (color) channels, Cb/Cr (blue and red chroma components) and a luma component channel (Y), which makes the dark and light part of the video picture. These components are often confused with the YUV color space in which time = Y, x-axis = U and y-axis = V.

Further confusing things, the non-RGB component cables usually have red, green, and blue plugs and jacks, even though the two methods of signal transfer are not compatible. Lower in quality is the Y/C signal that makes up Separate Video (S-Video), an analog video signal, used in Super VHS and Hi-8 video. As with component video, the Y indicates the brightness (or luminance) information, but in S-Video color (or chrominance), information is combined and designated by C. The least separation (and thus the lowest quality for a video signal) occurs when all the signals are mixed together and carried on a single cable as a composite of the three color channels and the sync signal; this system yields less-precise color definition, which cannot be manipulated or color corrected as much as an RGB or component signal.

In analog systems, the video signal from the camera is delivered to the Video In connector(s) of a VCR, where it is recorded on magnetic videotape. A camcorder combines both camera and tape recorder in a single device. One or two channels of sound may also be recorded on the videotape (mono or stereo). The video signal is written to tape by a spinning recording head that changes the local magnetic properties of the tape's surface in a series of long diagonal stripes. Because the head is canted or tilted at a slight angle compared with the path of the tape, it follows a helical (spiral) path, which is called **helical scan** recording. As illustrated in Figure 8-1, each stripe represents information for one field of a video frame. A single video frame is made up of two fields that are interlaced (described in detail under "NTSC" later in the chapter). Audio is recorded on a separate straight-line track at the top of the videotape, although with some recording systems (notably for ¾-inch tape and for ½-inch tape with high-fidelity audio), sound is recorded helically between the video tracks.

At the bottom of the tape is a control track containing the pulses used to regulate speed. **Tracking** is fine adjustment of the tape so that the tracks are properly aligned as the tape moves across the playback head. This is how your VCR works when you rent *Singing in the Rain* (on video tape) for the weekend. DVDs do this quite differently.

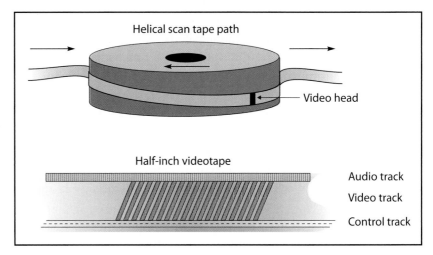

Figure 8-1   Diagram of tape path across the video head for analog recording

In digital systems, the video signal from the camera is first digitized as a single frame, and the data is compressed before it is written to the tape in one of several proprietary and competing formats: DV, DVCPRO, or DVCAM (see Figure 8-2). There are other configurations of video tapes that only would be used with high-end video production in conjunction with high-end video equipment, in a professional situation.

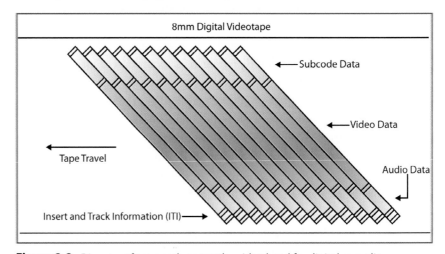

Figure 8-2   Diagram of tape path across the video head for digital recording

First Person

Surf Alligators live within the cusps of breaking technology waves. They can be snuffed with good knowledge, tools, and a network of colleagues willing to answer arcane questions. Catching these alligators requires the patience of Costa Rican beach children who cast unbaited three-barbed hooks into the incoming waves to yank out their surprised and luckless silver prey.

Years ago, my 19-inch RGB monitor, a Hitachi rebranded by both SuperMac and Silicon Graphics, had BNC inputs for red, green, and blue and required that horizontal sync be superimposed on the green channel. This was supported by SuperMacs and other NuBus video cards at 8-bit color depth. I wanted the Quadra 840AV's internal video support for 19-inch monitors at 16 bits, extolled in Apple's literature. But no way would my monitor work, and it took four days of calling around to discover why. Sorry, no sync on green from that Quadra, they said. Throw the monitor away. Get one with more BNC inputs.

Apple's User Assistance Center (usually busy and not open at 1:00 a.m.) was of no help. My arcane questions were not in the annoying hierarchy of voice message help, and it took two days to get hold of a real person to tell me the answer wasn't in her data bank. I felt like trolling with those Costa Rican fish hooks across the many rows of phone-answering cubicles at the Assistance Center, and yanking real hard.

Real information was finally forthcoming when I contacted two guys on Apple's Quadra hardware team through e-mail. They had docs that explained all and included the peculiar sensing codes (pins 4, 7, and 10 of the 15-pin monitor connector) used by the Quadra's built-in video to automatically adjust to most monitors. I felt 100 percent better when I knew the *why* of it, even though I did have to buy a new monitor.

Every time you upgrade your computer hardware, and occasionally when you upgrade your software, you are likely to attract Surf Alligators. These perils aren't like the steep learning curves, where with effort you can incrementally improve your skill; they are brutally mechanical and test you in other ways: either you know it or you don't. If you don't know it, it won't work. Period.

By 2001, small and inexpensive cable adapters were widely available with lots of little dip switches to set the TTL signals Apple uses to declare monitor size and frequency, and for mixing sync onto the green channel.

Not so long ago a video cassette recorder would also add the video and sound signals to a sub-carrier and modulate them into a radio frequency (RF) in the FM broadcast band. This is the NTSC, PAL, or SECAM signal that was available at the Antenna Out connector of a VCR. (These signal standards are explained in the next section.) Usually you would choose to have the signal modulated on either Channel 3 or Channel 4, and the resulting signal or picture was then demodulated by the TV receiver and displayed on the selected channel. Many television sets provided a separate composite signal connector, and some models included component connectors to avoid the unnecessary step of modulating and demodulating the signal into the broadcast frequency bands. Video monitors only have component connections, as there was no built-in receiver for RF signals.

Colored phosphors on the CRT (cathode ray tube) screen glowed red, green, or blue when they were energized by the electron beam. Because the intensity of the beam varied as it moved across the screen, some colors glowed brighter than others. Finely tuned magnets around the picture tube aimed the electrons precisely onto the phosphor screen while the intensity of the beam was varied according to the video signal. This is why you needed to keep speakers (which had strong magnets in them) away from the television screen. A strong external magnetic field would skew the electron beam to one area of the screen and sometimes caused a permanent blotch that could not be fixed by **degaussing**—an electronic process that readjusts the magnets that guide the electrons. If you had the misfortune to forget and wear a watch, the degausser might stop it permanently for you and then erase the magnetic strips on your credit cards in your wallet as well.

All of these electronic activities work in concert to yield a television picture on a CRT. Flat screen displays that are all-digital, using either liquid crystal display (LCD) or plasma technologies are becoming increasingly popular and supplanting CRTs.

Analog Display Standards

Three analog broadcast video standards are commonly in use around the world: NTSC, PAL, and SECAM. In the United States, the NTSC standard is being phased out, replaced by the ATSC Digital Television Standard. Because these standards and formats are not easily interchangeable, it is important to know where your multimedia project will be used. A video cassette recorded in the United States (which uses NTSC) will not play on a television set in any European country (which uses either PAL or SECAM), even though the recording method and style of the cassette is "VHS." Likewise, tapes recorded in European PAL or SECAM formats will not play back on an NTSC video cassette recorder. Each system is based on a different standard that defines the way information is encoded to produce the electronic signal that ultimately creates a television picture. Multiformat VCRs can play back all three standards but typically cannot dub from one standard to another. **Dubbing** between standards still requires high-end, specialized equipment.

NTSC

The United States, Canada, Mexico, Japan, and many other countries used a system for broadcasting and displaying video that is based upon the specifications set forth by the 1952 National Television Standards Committee. These standards defined a method for encoding information into the electronic signal that ultimately created a television picture. As specified by the NTSC standard, a single frame of video was made up of 525 horizontal scan lines drawn onto the inside face of a phosphor-coated picture tube every ⅓₀th of a second by a fast-moving electron beam. The drawing occurred so fast that your eye would perceive the image as stable. The electron beam actually made two passes as it drew a single video frame—first it laid down all the odd-numbered lines, and then all the even-numbered lines. Each of these passes (which happen at a rate of 60 per second, or 60 Hz) painted a field, and the two fields were then combined to create a single frame at a rate of 30 frames per second (fps). (Technically, the speed is actually 29.97 Hz.) This process of building a single frame from two fields was called **interlacing**, a technique that helps to prevent flicker on television screens. Computer monitors used a different **progressive-scan** technology, and drew the lines of an entire frame in a single pass, without interlacing them and without flicker.

> Sometimes we define "NTSC" as "Never The Same Color."
>
> Richard Santalesa,
> R&D Technologies

PAL

The **Phase Alternate Line (PAL)** system was used in the United Kingdom, Western Europe, Australia, South Africa, China, and South America. PAL increased the screen resolution to 625 horizontal lines, but slowed the scan rate to 25 frames per second. As with NTSC, the even and odd lines were interlaced, each field taking ¹⁄₅₀ of a second to draw (50 Hz).

SECAM

The **Sequential Color and Memory (SECAM)** (taken from the French name, reported variously as Système Électronic pour Couleur Avec Mémoire or Séquentiel Couleur Avec Mémoire) system was used in France, Eastern Europe, the former USSR, and a few other countries. Although SECAM is a 625-line, 50 Hz system, it differed greatly from both the NTSC and the PAL color systems in its basic technology and broadcast method. Often, however, TV sets sold in Europe utilized dual components and could handle both PAL and SECAM systems.

ATSC DTV

What started as the High Definition Television (HDTV) initiative of the Federal Communications Commission in the 1980s, changed first to the Advanced Television (ATV) initiative and then finished as the Digital Television (DTV) initiative by the time the FCC announced the change in 1996. This standard, which was slightly modified from both the Digital Television Standard (ATSC Doc. A/53) and the Digital Audio Compression Standard (ATSC Doc. A/52), moved U.S. television from an analog to digital standard. It also provided TV stations with sufficient bandwidth to present four or five Standard Television (STV, providing the NTSC's resolution of 525 lines with a 3:4 aspect ratio, but in a digital signal) signals or one HDTV signal (providing 1,080 lines of resolution with a movie screen's 16:9 aspect ratio). More significantly for multimedia producers,

With digital television, broadcasters will be able to offer free television of higher resolution and better picture quality than now exists under the current mode of TV transmission. If broadcasters so choose, they can offer what has been called "High Definition Television," or HDTV, with theater-quality pictures and CD-quality sound.

Alternatively, a broadcaster can offer several different TV programs at the same time, with picture and sound quality better than is generally available today. In addition, a broadcaster will be able to simultaneously transmit a variety of other information through a data bit-stream to both enhance its TV programs and to provide entirely new services. For example, TV programs can be broadcast with a variety of languages and captions, and sports programs can be broadcast so that the individual viewer might select his or her favorite camera angle or call up player statistics, game scores, or other information. Broadcasters also will be able to transmit to your television an entire edition of a newspaper, sports information, computer software, telephone directories, stock market updates, interactive educational material, and any other information that can be translated into digital bits.

....

From the FCC's Digital Television FAQ (http://www.fcc.gov/mb/policy/dtv/)

this emerging standard allowed for transmission of data to computers and for new ATV interactive services.

As of May 2003, 1,587 TV stations in the United States (94 percent) had been granted a DTV construction permit or license. Among those, 1,081 stations were actually broadcasting a DTV signal, and almost all were simulcasting their regular TV signal. According to the current schedule, all the stations are to cease broadcasting on their analog channel and completely switch to a digital signal by 2006.

High Definition Television (HDTV) provides high resolution in a 16:9 aspect ratio (see Figure 8-3). This aspect ratio allows the viewing of Cinemascope and Panavision movies. There is contention between the broadcast and computer industries about whether to use interlacing or progressive-scan technologies. The broadcast industry has promulgated an ultra-high-resolution, 1920×1080 interlaced format to become the cornerstone of a new generation of high-end entertainment centers, but the computer industry would like to settle on a 1280×720 progressive-scan system for HDTV. While the 1920×1080 format provides more pixels than the 1280×720 standard, the refresh rates are quite different. The higher-resolution interlaced format delivers only half the picture every 1/60 of a second, and because of the interlacing, on highly detailed images there is a great deal of screen flicker at 30 Hz. The computer people argue that the picture quality at 1280×720 is superior and steady. Both formats have been included in the HDTV standard by the **Advanced Television Systems Committee (ATSC)**, found at http://www.atsc.org.

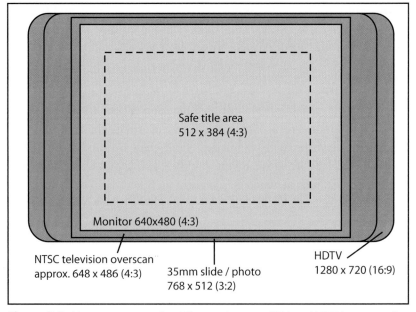

Safe title area
512 x 384 (4:3)

Monitor 640x480 (4:3)

NTSC television overscan
approx. 648 x 486 (4:3)

35mm slide / photo
768 x 512 (3:2)

HDTV
1280 x 720 (16:9)

Figure 8-3 Here you can see the difference between VGA and HDTV aspect ratios

WARNING *Today's multimedia monitors typically use a screen pixel ratio of 4:3 (800x600), but the new HDTV standard specifies a ratio of 16:9 (1280x720), which is much wider than it is tall (see Figure 8-3). There is no easy way to stretch and shrink existing graphic material to fit this new aspect ratio, so new multimedia design and interface principles will need to be developed for HDTV presentations.*

While more and more video is produced only for digital display platforms (for the Web, for a CD-ROM tour, or as an HDTV DVD presentation), analog television sets while still used, are rapidly being replaced by digital monitors that are becoming the most widely installed platforms for delivering and viewing video.

Digital Display Standards

- **Advanced Television System Committee (ATSC)** is the digital television standard for the United States, Canada, Mexico, Taiwan, and South Korea. It is being considered in other countries. It supports wide screen aspect ratio of 16:9 with images up to 1920×1080 pixels in size and a number of other image sizes, allowing up to six, standard-definition "virtual channels" to be broadcast on a single TV station using the existing 6 MHz channel. It boasts of "theater quality" because it uses Dolby Digital AC-3 format to provide 5.1 channel surround sound.

- **Digital Video Broadcasting (DVB)** is used mostly in Europe where the standards define the physical layer and data link layer of a distribution system.

- **Integrated Services Digital Broadcasting (ISDB)** is used in Japan to allow radio and television stations to convert to digital format.

Overscan and the Safe Title Area

As illustrated in Figure 8-3, it is common practice in the television industry to broadcast an image larger than will fit on a standard TV screen so that the "edge" of the image seen by a viewer is always bounded by the TV's physical frame, or bezel. This is called **overscan**. In contrast, computer monitors display a smaller image on the monitor's picture tube (**underscan**), leaving a black border inside the bezel. Consequently, when a digitized video image is displayed on an RGB screen, there is a border around the image; and, when a computer screen is converted to video, the outer edges of the image will not fit on a TV screen. Only about 360 of the 480 lines of the computer screen will be visible.

TIP *Avoid using the outer 15 percent of the screen when producing computer-generated graphics and titles for use in television video. The* **safe title area***, where your image will not be affected by overscanning, even in the worst conditions, is illustrated in Figure 8-3.*

Video Color

Color reproduction and display is different between televisions and computer monitors. Because computers use RGB component video (that is, they split colors into red, green, and blue signals), their colors are purer and more accurate than those seen on a television set that is using a composite input. Consequently, colors used in a graphic image created for computer video may display differently when that image is transformed into NTSC television video. If your monitor, scanner and printer are not calibrated and adjusted to conform to the specifications that an accepted color system like Pantone Color Systems represents, it will be impossible to calibrate your monitor to see what color you expect to be the end result of your labor on your video.

Indeed, NTSC television uses a limited color palette, restricted luminance (brightness) levels and black levels (the richness of the blacks). Some colors generated by your computer that display fine on an RGB monitor may be "illegal" for display on an NTSC television. These colors are particularly apparent in shades of red and white levels that, when uncalibrated, cause bleeding or noisy shimmering when displayed on a television. Most commercial broadcast facilities and TV studios will refuse to run video programs that include illegal colors. There are adjustments that can be made but, if these colors are overblown in the original product they will desaturate the other colors involved, along with the white level, making the end result of the video below the legal rate for transmission. Filters for converting illegal colors to legal colors are available in video and image-editing and processing applications to a point.

When producing a multimedia project, you should consider whether it will be played back on an RGB monitor and/or on a conventional television set. If your work is destined, for example, for a set-top player such as SEGA, Sony PlayStation, or Nintendo, choose your colors to meet the NTSC color specifications. There are many variables in providing perfect colors on a television. End users can control hue and balance (an adjustment not available on most RGB monitors), and it is not likely that many viewers of your project will have perfectly calibrated television sets. So this means that you are fighting an uphill battle from the beginning. It helps to do color corrections and editing on your computer, and then view the corrected image on a real television screen, not just the RGB monitor. For this, you will need a signal converter card or hardware on the motherboard that can provide NTSC output; video overlay cards usually offer this feature.

First Person

Captain's Log: We received some excellent design tips from Bernice T. Glenn:

As intermedia applications continue to proliferate, producers and designers need to know how to float between print and color pigment, digital color and RGB as viewed on a monitor, and analog color as viewed on a television screen. Color formulas for multimedia, especially when it is interactive, depend heavily on human factors.

Contrast—or the degree of tonal difference between one color and another—is often more important when working with color on a computer screen. A combination of pure yellow with pure violet, or blue and orange, for example, will vibrate when viewed in RGB. On video, disturbing flickers, extraneous colors, and other artifacts usually appear on the borders between pure complementary colors. On top of that, colors that look great on your computer monitor may not even show up when transferred to video.

Important elements can be emphasized by using fully saturated colors against a neutral background, whose color may complement as a grayed-down tint of the color.

When readability is important, contrast in color saturation and value between the type and its background really works, using almost any color combination.

Red or green may need to be avoided as cue colors [for menu buttons and icons] because 8 percent of the population is color blind to some extent and cannot see reds or greens in their true color value.

From "Ask the Captain," a monthly column written by Tay Vaughan for *NewMedia* magazine

---

TIP   *A useful trick is to grab a standard broadcast color test bar (if you are using an analog system), using a video frame grabber, and then save it as a PICT or TIFF image. When viewing the bar in Photoshop, for example, you can check the levels of each color by viewing red, green, and blue one at a time. The gradient of grays in the color bar should be smooth and even for each color channel. If possible, checking the signal output of your video is a better option, but not too many people have recourse to the sort of test generator needed. See Figure 8-4 for more information.*

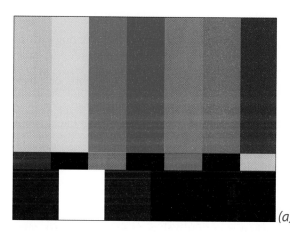

(a)

R: 204 G: 204 B: 204	R: 255 G: 255 B: 0	R: 0 G: 255 B: 255	R: 0 G: 255 B: 0	R: 255 G: 0 B: 255	R: 255 G: 0 B: 0	R: 0 G: 0 B: 255
R: 0 G: 0 B: 255	R: 19 G: 19 B: 19	R: 255 G: 0 B: 255	R: 19 G: 19 B: 19	R: 0 G: 255 B: 255	R: 19 G: 19 B: 19	R: 204 G: 204 B: 204

| R: 8 G: 62 B: 89 | R: 255 G: 255 B: 255 | R: 58 G: 0 B: 126 | R: 19 G: 19 B: 19 | 0 0 0 | 19 19 19 | 38 38 38 | R: 19 G: 19 B: 19 |

(b)

Figure 8-4   This SMPTE color bar pattern (*a*) can be used for calibration at the beginning of a videotape. The RGB values of each bar are included (*b*) so you can make your own screen using an image-editing application.

Interlacing Effects

In television, the electron beam actually makes two passes on the screen as it draws a single video frame, first laying down all the odd-numbered lines, then all the even-numbered lines, as they are interlaced. On an RGB monitor, lines are painted one-pixel thick and are not interlaced. Single-pixel lines displayed on an RGB monitor look fine; on a television, these thin lines flicker brightly because they only appear in every other field. To prevent this flicker, make sure your lines are greater than two pixels thick and that you avoid typefaces that are very thin or have elaborate serifs. If you are capturing images from a video signal, you can filter them through a de-interlacing filter provided by image-editing applications such as Photoshop or Fireworks. With typefaces, interlacing flicker can often be avoided by anti-aliasing the type to slightly blur the edges of the characters. The term "interlacing" has a different meaning on the Web, where it describes the progressive display of lines of pixels as image data is downloaded, giving the impression that the image is coming from blurry into focus as increasingly more data arrives (see Chapter 14).

Calibration

Too little emphasis is put upon calibration of video, light, monitors, sound and other equipment used for doing presentations. How many times have you recorded something at what you *thought* was the correct level, only to find out upon playback that it was a mumble or something that blew your hair out by the roots. In some devices you simply push in all the knobs to equalize the recording.

Text and Titles for Television

Titles for video productions can be created with an analog character generator, but your computer can do this digitally using video and image-editing software. Here are some suggestions for creating good titles:

■ Fonts for titles should be plain, sans serif, and bold enough to be easily read.

■ When you are laying text onto a dark background, use white or a light color for the text.

■ Use a drop shadow to help separate the text from the background image.

■ Never use black or colored text on a white background.

■ Do not kern your letters too tightly.

■ If you use underlining or drawn graphics, always make your lines at least two pixels wide. If you use a one-pixel-wide line (or a width measured in an odd number of pixels), the line will flicker when transferred to video due to interlacing.

- Use parallel lines, boxes, and tight concentric circles sparingly. When you use them, draw them large and with thick lines.

- Avoid colors that are too hot, because they will twinkle and buzz.

- Neighboring colors should be markedly different in intensity. For example, use a light blue and a dark red, but not a medium blue and a medium red.

- Keep your graphics and titles within the safe area of the screen. Remember that televisions tend to overscan computer output (see the earlier section "Overscan and the Safe Title Area").

- Bring titles on slowly, keep them on screen for a sufficient interval, and then fade them out.

- Avoid making busy title screens; use more pages instead.

Taking Care of Your Analog Tapes

WARNING   *Your original videotapes are irreplaceable, so always make a backup copy of these tapes before you begin editing—tapes can break, be erased, or be eaten up by machinery.*

- Always fast-forward new tapes to the end and then rewind them, a technique known as "packing," to make sure that tape tension is even from beginning to end. Unequal tape tension can cause timing and editing problems.

- Black-stripe your analog tape by running it through the recorder once with the lens cap on and without audio input. This way, only black and a uniform control track is recorded. Later, during editing, blank spots in your video program will be a quiet black instead of snowy noise. Also, try to put time-code on your tapes or video signal as it is input into whatever you are using to record your action. This will greatly aid you in choosing edit points later on, when you are combining video cuts on a nonlinear editing system.

- Before you begin editing, always remove the break-off tab on the back of your original video cassettes, in order to avoid accidental erasure or overwriting.

- Editing videotape on a tape-to-tape editor requires a lot of shuttling backward and forward, and this can deform the tape. For best results, do not reuse 8mm video cassettes.

- If you have **nonlinear editing (NLE)** software on your computer, digitize the shots you plan to use in your final product and then edit the digital footage. NLE allows you to piece together your final product from video, image, and audio elements stored in various files on your computer.

Digital Video

Full integration of digital video in cameras and on computers eliminates the analog television form of video, from both the multimedia production and the delivery platform. If your video camera generates a digital output signal, you can record your video direct-to-disk, where it is ready for editing. If a video clip is stored as data on a hard disk, CD-ROM, or other mass-storage device, that clip can be played back on a computer's monitor without special hardware.

Setting up a production environment for making digital video, however, *does* require hardware that meets minimum specifications for processing speed, data transfer, and storage. There are many considerations to keep in mind when setting up your production environment:

- Computer with FireWire (IEEE 1394 or i.Link) connection and cables
- Fast processor(s)
- Plenty of RAM
- Fast and big hard disk(s)for storing DV (digital video) data streams of raw video footage from a camera at DV's fixed transfer rate of 3.6 MBps. Your hard disk should support a transfer rate of about 8 MBps and have enough space free (about 108MB for 30 seconds of footage; 13GB for an hour). Then, multiply that times five to allow for editing! Removable media such as Zip and CD-RW will not work.
- Second display to allow for more real estate for your editing software
- Audio mixer to adjust sound output from the camcorder
- External speakers
- Television monitor to view your project (if it's for TV)
- Nonlinear editing (NLE) software

Digital Video Resolution

A video image is measured in pixels for digital video and scan lines for analog video. (HDTV) televisions are capable of 1920×1080p60, also known as 1920 pixels per scan line by 1080 scan lines, progressive at 60 frames per second.

Digital Video Architectures

A digital video architecture is made up of a format for encoding and playing back video files by a computer and includes a player that can recognize and play files created for that format. The major digital video architectures are Apple's QuickTime, Microsoft's Windows Media Format, and RealNetwork's RealMedia. Related video file formats are QuickTime movie (.mov), Audio Video Interleaved (.avi), and RealMedia (.rm). Some players recognize and play back more than one video file format.

Digital Video Compression

To digitize and store a 10-second clip of full-motion video in your computer requires transfer of an enormous amount of data in a very short amount of time. Reproducing just one frame of digital video component video at 24 bits requires almost 1MB of computer data; 30 seconds of full-screen, uncompressed video will fill a gigabyte hard disk. Full-size, full-motion video requires that the computer deliver data at about 30MB per second. This overwhelming technological bottleneck is overcome using digital video compression schemes or **codecs** (*co*ders/*dec*oders). A codec is the algorithm used to compress (code) a video for delivery and then decode it in real-time for fast playback. Different codecs are optimized for different methods of delivery (for example, from a hard drive, from a CD-ROM, or over the Web).

WARNING   *In order for your user to be able to view your digital video file, he or she must have both a player that is able to play the file format and software to decode the video based upon the codec you used when you compressed the file. A player will usually come with some standard codecs, licensed to be installed along with the player. If you use a codec that is not bundled with the player, your user will have to install a file that recognizes that codec in order to play your video.*

Real-time video compression algorithms such as MPEG, Indeo, JPEG, **Cinepak**, and **Sorenson** are available to compress digital video information at rates that range from 50:1 to 200:1. In addition to compressing video data, **streaming** technologies such as Adobe Flash, Microsoft Windows Media, QuickTime and RealPlayer are being implemented to provide reasonable quality low-bandwidth video on the Web. By starting playback of a video as soon as enough data has transferred to the user's computer to sustain this playback, users do not have to wait for an often very large file to download. Microsoft, RealNetworks, SHOUTcast, and Ogg/Vorbis are actively pursuing the commercialization of streaming technology on the Web.

MPEG

The **MPEG standards** were developed by the **Moving Picture Experts Group** (http://mpeg.telecomitalialab.com/), a working group convened by the International Standards Organization (ISO) and the International Electro-technical Commission (IEC), which created standards for the digital representation of moving pictures as well as associated audio and other data. Using **MPEG-1** (specifications released in 1992), you could deliver 1.2 Mbps (megabits per second) of video and 250 Kbps (kilobits per second) of two-channel stereo audio using CD-ROM technology. **MPEG-2** (specifications released in 1994), a completely different system from MPEG-1, required higher data rates (3 to 15 Mbps) but also delivered higher image resolution, picture quality, interlaced video formats, multiresolution scalability, and multichannel audio features. MPEG-2 was the video compression standard required for digital television (DTV) and making DVDs.

Some form of an MPEG standard is likely to become the method of choice for encoding motion images since MPEG standards have become widely accepted for both Internet and DVD-Video and are incorporated in the DTV specifications. However, different companies have implemented different variations on the MPEG standards, making it difficult to point to a single standard as the likely method of choice. For example, Microsoft uses MPEG-4 video as one of its video codecs, but it only supports the MPEG-4 video portion of the MPEG-4 specification.

The MPEG specifications since MPEG-2 include elements beyond just the encoding of the video. **MPEG-4** (specifications released in 1998 and 1999) provides a content-based method for assimilating multimedia elements. It offers indexing, hyperlinking, querying, browsing, uploading, downloading, and deleting functions, as well as "hybrid natural and synthetic data coding," which will enable harmonious integration of natural and synthetic audiovisual objects. With MPEG-4, multiple views, layers, and multiple sound tracks of a scene, as well as stereoscopic and 3-D views, are available, making virtual reality workable. MPEG-4 can adjust to varied download speeds, making it an attractive option for delivery of video on the Web. A group named the Internet Streaming Media Alliance (ISMA) released open specifications for Internet streaming based on MPEG-4 at the end of 2001.

MPEG-7, called the Multimedia Content Description Interface, went a step further by integrating information about the image, sound, or motion video elements being used in a composition. This information is carried already in the MPEG-4 standard. MPEG-7's descriptive elements can be used to describe simple features such as color or motion using Descriptors, or higher-level content such as facial expressions, personality characteristics, or any number of content-related variables using Description Schemes. One of the benefits of implementation of this standard will be the ability to quickly search through video archives looking for very specific types of video.

Digital Rights Management (DRM), a crucial issue to content creators, is being addressed in **MPEG-21**, which is under continuing development. It will provide a "Rights Expression Language" standard designed to communicate machine-readable license information and to do so in a secure manner. The idea here is that when you get what is called a Digital Item (or piece of content; for example, an image on the Web that you right-click to download), the file will let you know where to go to find who holds the rights to it.

http://www.mpeg.org
All about MPEG

Video Recording and Tape Formats

Given the explosion of videotape recording formats in the 1990s and the move to ATSC video standards in the 2000s, there is a confusing array of formats. The following sections will help you learn the categories of standards, and some of the basic technical differences between them, so that you can make an informed decision about the format that best suits your multimedia project.

Composite Analog Video

Composite video combines the luminance and chroma information from the video signal. As a result, it produces the lowest quality video and is most susceptible to **generation loss**, the loss of quality that occurs as you move from original footage to edit master to copy. This recording format was used for consumer analog video recording tape formats (such as Betamax and VHS) and was never adequate for most multimedia productions.

Component Analog Video

Component video separates the luminance and chroma information in order to improve the quality of the video and to decrease generation loss. This is the level for "prosumer"—industrial and professional video equipment. As mentioned earlier (in the section entitled "How Video Works"), there are different methods of separating the signals, producing different levels of quality within this category.

S-Video (Y/C)

In S-Video, color and luminance information are kept on two separate tracks: (Y/C). The result is a definite improvement in picture quality over composite video. This standard is used in **S-VHS** and Hi-8. Although basically oriented toward consumers, this format gained rapid acceptance in the "prosumer" and industrial markets (including much early multimedia production) because of the sharper image and slightly less generation loss from master to copy. It was inadequate for most professional and broadcast applications, however.

Three-Channel Component (Y/R-Y/B-Y, Y/U/V)

Professional quality requires further separation in the video signal, usually divided between luminance (Y) and two channels of chroma, but sometimes divided between the Red/Green/Blue primary additive colors (see the previous discussion in the section "How Video Works"). In the early

MPEG-21 is based on two essential concepts: the definition of a fundamental unit of distribution and transaction (the Digital Item) and the concept of Users interacting with Digital Items. The Digital Items can be considered the "what" of the Multimedia Framework (e.g., a video collection, a music album) and the Users can be considered the "who" of the Multimedia Framework.

The goal of MPEG-21 can thus be rephrased to: defining the technology needed to support Users to exchange, access, consume, trade and otherwise manipulate Digital Items in an efficient, transparent and interoperable way.

From Document ISO/IEC JTC1/SC29/WG11/N5231 (Coding of Moving Pictures and Audio, available at http://mpeg.telecomitalialab.com/standards/mpeg-21/mpeg-21.htm)

1980s, Sony began to experiment with a new portable, professional video format based on its consumer composite video format, Betamax. Called **Betacam**, it required speeding the tape up considerably (a 2-hour Betamax tape was used up in 20 minutes) and laying the signal on the tape in three component channels. The resulting format produced images that had none of the problems of traditional composite video, such as color shift and bleed or crawling edges on graphics. This evolved into Betacam SP, which features four channels of audio and is superior to 1-inch analog formats and even the D-2 composite digital format, in some cases. Though Panasonic developed their own standard based on a similar technology, called "MII," Betacam SP became the industry standard for professional analog video field recording. Betacam SP remained dominant until the switch to digital formats began in the mid- to late-1990s.

Composite Digital

Composite digital recording formats combine the luminance and chroma information, just as analog composite formats do, but they sample the incoming waveforms and encode the information in binary (0/1) digital code. While this method retains some of the image quality weaknesses of analog composite video, it also improves color and image resolution, and having the recording in a digital format eliminates generation loss when digital copies are made.

As is the case with so many of these formats, competing formats are being developed, primarily by Sony and its partners and Matsushita (Panasonic) and its partners (such as JVC and Philips). The D-2 format was developed primarily by Ampex and Sony, while the D-3 format was developed primarily by Panasonic. Their major advantage over a component digital format is the lower cost in equipment, although this equipment is expensive enough to find a market only at the professional level and has not been used much in multimedia production.

Component Digital

Most of the development since the mid-1990s has been in component digital formats, which adds the advantages of component signals to digital recording. Sony released the first equipment in this category with its D-1 format. It is an uncompressed format, so it has a very high quality image, but in order to save that much data, it uses a 19mm (¾-inch) tape. Because of its high quality, D-1 is at the pinnacle of NTSC video and is the mastering standard of choice among high-end editing facilities. However, this quality comes with an extremely high price tag. (A Quantel Harry editing system costs over $900,000 and can only work with 15 minutes of video.) The result is that this format really only fits super-high-end broadcast projects and not your standard multimedia title. It spawned several other digital component formats, including DCT (from Ampex), D-5 (from Panasonic), and Digital Betacam (from Sony, but using a ½-inch tape). Featuring four channels of CD-quality audio, Digital Betacam's video quality is almost equal to D-1 digital. It was a logical upgrade for professional videographers used to working in the Betacam product line, although another component digital format—the DV format—provided a quality level and price point that attracted many to that format.

The DV format is another component digital format, but it takes its samples at smaller bitdepths (typically 8 bits) and compresses the video, allowing for the use of smaller tape widths. The small tape size of the MiniDV tapes has pulled the consumer and some of the prosumer market away from VHS and S-VHS. Many professional videographers and the rest of the prosumers have moved to DVCPRO and DVCAM, professional formats that use the DV recording format, but provide professional features on the camcorders and tape decks.

ATSC Digital TV

It is also important not to confuse the digital formats using the NTSC standards with the new generation of all-digital DTV production equipment that conforms to standards developed by the Advanced Television Systems Committee (ATSC). These standards provide for both digital Standard TV (STV) and High Definition TV (HDTV) recordings that can be broadcast by digital TV transmitters to digital TV receivers. Since this video equipment has just been introduced, it is extremely expensive and is not of immediate interest to the multimedia producer. However, it will be important to remain current on DTV developments, since the ATSC standards also provide for Enhanced TV (ETV), potentially bringing the interactivity of multimedia and the Web to broadcast television. If you think about a combination of a TV series and its companion web site with the interactivity of a New Line Home Entertainment DVD using embedded infinifilm™ features and the real-time recording and playback features of TiVo or ReplayTV, you can begin to envision the possibilities of a new generation of multimedia delivered by DTV.

Comparing the Formats

Table 8-1 provides basic information about what was the most commonly used video recording formats. Formats are listed in the chronological order of their release as "industry standards."

Format (Year Introduced)	Analog/Digital	Tape Size	Video Standard for Input/Output	Description
NTSC Videotape				
Betamax (1975)	Analog	½ inch	Composite	This Sony format was the first consumer videotape format to find a market. The original format had a resolution of 260 lines. Although considered to be superior in quality to VHS, the format stalled in the marketplace when longer playing time and a price war among the many VHS competitors attracted more consumers. Nonetheless, machines recording in this format continued to be manufactured by Sony until 2002.
VHS (1976)	Analog	½ inch	Composite	Popular consumer format developed by Sony's competitor JVC, but unsuitable for video production because of low-quality image (250 lines of resolution) and quick generation loss. Also available in a compact cassette size, VHS-C.
Betacam (1982)	Analog	½ inch	Component	A professional version of Sony's consumer Betamax format. Only 300 lines of, but resolution maintained higher image quality through its use of true component I/O.
MII (1985)	Analog	½ inch	Component	Developed by Panasonic to compete with Sony's Betacam and Betacam SP. Provided 340 lines of resolution.
Betacam SP (1986)	Analog	½ inch	Component	An improvement of the original Betacam equipment, offering 340 lines of resolution. Became a broadcast industry standard for better than a decade, when digital alternatives began to take over.
D-2 (1986)	Digital	¾ inch (19mm)	Composite	Ampex uncompressed 8-bit, composite digital format. Since it is composite, it produces a lower quality signal than D-1, which is a component format.
D-1 (1987)	Digital	¾ inch (19mm)	Component	Sony-developed digital format providing uncompressed 8-bit 4:2:2 component video.
S-VHS (1988)	Analog	½ inch	S-Video (Y/C)	An improvement over VHS, since the video signal was divided into two parts and and resolution increased to 400 lines. Less generation loss than VHS, but still relatively low image quality.
Hi-8 (1989)	Analog	8mm	S-Video (Y/C)	Similar qualities as S-VHS, but smaller tape size. Resolution of 415 lines.
D-3 (1991)	Digital	½ inch	Composite	Panasonic 8-bit composite digital format developed to compete with D-2 and with about the same image quality. 450 lines of resolution.

Table 8-1 Recording Formats

Format (Year Introduced)	Analog/Digital	Tape Size	Video Standard for Input/Output	Description
NTSC Videotape Digital Betacam (1994)	Digital	½ inch	Component	Very high quality 10-bit 4:2:2 digital format with little compression (2:1). Continued Sony's commitment to the ½-inch Betamax-type cassette, while moving its popular Betacam line to digital recording.
D-5 (1994)	Digital	½ inch	Component	A high-quality, uncompressed 10-bit 4:2:2 component digital format developed by Panasonic. Provides a full 525 lines of resolution for NTSC and 625 for PAL.
DV (1995)	Digital	¼ inch	Component	First consumer digital format, providing 8-bit recording and 4:1:1 color sampling with 5:1 compression. Provides 500 lines of resolution. Created by a consortium of electronics companies, it is widely available in many consumer and prosumer models, replacing the analog S-VHS and Hi-8 formats. MiniDV is not a separate recording format; it uses the DV format and just uses a smaller cassette. The DV format is the basis for the professional DVCPRO and DVCAM lines of products, which add professional features to camcorders and VCRs.
D-7 (1995)	Digital	¼ inch	Component	Panasonic's DVCPRO format. A digital 8-bit 4:1:1 format, compressed at 5:1. It provides 525 lines of resolution for NTSC and 625 lines for PAL. Competes with Sony's DVCAM. (See note on use of the format under the DVCAM listing.)
D-9 (1995)	Digital	½ inch	Component	Uses 8-bit processing and 4:2:2 color sampling with 3.3:1 compression. Developed by JVC to compete with Sony's Digital Betacam, it is also called Digital-S and uses an S-VHS-type cassette. It provides 540 lines of resolution.
DVCAM (1996)	Digital	¼ inch	Component	Sony format to compete with Panasonic's DVCPRO. It uses 8-bit component digital recording and 4:1:1 color sampling. It provides 530 lines of resolution for NTSC. The high quality and low price of the DVCPRO and DVCAM lines have made them popular for industrial and prosumer video. They are also used as a "disposable" format for Electronic News Gathering (ENG) as, for example, in coverage of the 2003 war in Iraq.

Table 8-1 Recording Formats *(continued)*

Format (Year Introduced)	Analog/Digital	Tape Size	Video Standard for Input/Output	Description
NTSC Videotape				
Betacam SX (1996)	Digital	½ inch	Component	Records a compressed 8-bit, 4:2:2 component digital signal. Provides backward compatibility for analog Betamax formats. Its MPEG-2 compressed data provides fast transmission of data, a feature targeted to the ENG market.
DVCPRO 50 (1998)	Digital	¼ inch	Component	A variation of Panasonic's D-7 format, providing 4:2:2 sampling and only 3.3:1 compression.
DVCPRO P (1998)	Digital	¼ inch	Component	Another variation of the D-7 format, the "P" indicating it uses progressive scan with 4:2:0 sampling. Its resolution is 480 lines.
Digital 8 (1999)	Digital	8mm	Component	The DV format used by Sony, continuing its 8mm line. It is backward compatible with Sony's analog 8mm and Hi-8 tapes.
ATSC Videotape				
D-5 HD (1995)	Digital	½ inch	Component	Version of D-5 that provides either 1,080- or 720-line HDTV resolution.
D-11 (1997)	Digital	½ inch	Component	HDCAM format, providing compressed HDTV.
D-9 HD (2000)	Digital	½ inch	Component	Version of D-9 for HDTV, also using S-Video-type cassettes.
DVCPRO HD (2000)	Digital	¼ inch	Component	HDTV version of D-7 (DVCPRO), but backward compatible with NTSC DVCPRO, DV, and DVCAM tapes.

Table 8-1 Recording Formats *(continued)*

Note that some digital formats had been introduced by the late-1980s, but these were simply for digitally recording analog NTSC-standard signals. In 1995, Apple's FireWire technology was standardized as IEEE 1394, and Sony quickly adopted it for much of its digital camera line under the name i.Link. FireWire and i.Link connections allow a completely digital process, from the camera's CCD to the hard disk of a computer; and camcorders store the video and sound data on an onboard digital tape. The table differentiates between NTSC standard digital video formats and those for ATSC DTV.

The descriptions of the digital formats include information about bit-depth (usually 8 or 10 bits) and sampling ratio for color information. The sampling ratio is expressed as three values in the form 4:4:4 referring to the number of samples taken from each of the three channels of component video, Y/R-Y/B-Y, in that order. Professional formats tend to sample luminance and chroma at 4:2:2 and consumer formats at 4:1:1.

Shooting and Editing Video

To add full-screen, full-motion video to your multimedia project, you will need to invest in specialized hardware and software or purchase the services of a professional video production studio. In many cases, a professional studio will also provide editing tools and post-production capabilities that you cannot duplicate with your Macintosh or PC.

Expensive professional video equipment and services may not yield proportionately greater benefits than if you used consumer-grade equipment and nonlinear editors. As with audio equipment, you need to make balancing decisions using Vaughan's Law of Multimedia Minimums (see Chapter 5). Most likely, your goal is to expend resources without diminishing returns—in other words, to produce multimedia that is adequate and does its job, but doesn't break your bank. If you can, experiment with various combinations of video recording and playback devices hooked to your computer, and test the results using your multimedia-authoring platform. You can do a great deal of satisfactory work with consumer-grade video cameras and recording equipment if you understand the limitations of the technology.

Storyboarding

Preplanning is a factor that cannot be ignored without costing time loss, lots of unnecessary aggravation, and money that would be better spent elsewhere. Successful video production, of any sort, deserves the time it takes to make a plan to carry it out. It may take a little time at first, but you'll find it to be very helpful in the long run. Storyboards are like any sequential comic you read daily. Every day there are three or four panels showing a progression of story or information. Take the time to structure your production by writing it down and then engineer a sequential group of drawings showing camera and scene, shooting angles, lighting, action, special effects and how objects move through from start to finish. A storyboard can get everyone on one page quickly.

Shooting Platform

Never underestimate the value of a steady shooting platform. A classic symbol of amateur home movies is shaky camera work. Using a tripod or even placing the camera on a stable platform, such as a rolled-up sweater on the hood of a car, can improve a shot. With a little care, and careful adjustment of the lockdown screws, a sturdy conventional tripod can do wonders. If you must shoot handheld, try to use a camera with an electronic image stabilization feature for static shots, a "steady-cam" balancing attachment, or use camera moves and a moving subject to mask your lack of steadiness. Even using a rolling office chair and sitting facing the back with the camera balanced on the chair-back makes a convenient, stable dolly.

Lighting

Perhaps the greatest difference between professional camcorders and consumer camcorders is their ability to perform at low light levels. With proper lighting, however, it may be difficult for uninitiated viewers to differentiate between shots taken with an expensive studio-grade video camera and a Hi-8 camcorder. Using a simple floodlight kit, or even just being sure that daylight illuminates the room, can improve your image. Onboard battery lights for camcorders can be useful, but only in conditions where the light acts as a "fill light" to illuminate the details of a subject's face. As in photography, good lighting techniques separate amateurs from professionals in video shoots.

Illustrated in Figure 8-5 is a screen from The Lighting Lab. The standard lighting arrangement of a studio is displayed with fill, key, rim, and background lights. Changing any of these lights can make a dramatic difference in the shot. This project uses a QuickTime movie containing several hundred single-frame images of the model as she is lighted by every permutation of lamp and intensity; clicking a light switch instantly shows the effect of that combination. If you are not convinced that lighting is critical to the success of a photo or video shoot, it will become immediately clear with this exercise!

Figure 8-5 Good lighting is essential for quality video results.

Chroma Keys

Chroma keys allow you to choose a color or range of colors that become transparent, allowing the video image to be seen "through" the computer image. This is the technology used by a newscast's weather person, who is shot against a blue background that is made invisible when merged with the electronically generated image of the weather map. The weatherman controls the computer part of the display with a small handheld controller.

A useful tool easily implemented in most digital video editing applications is **blue screen**, **green screen**, **Ultimatte**, or chroma key editing. When Captain Picard of *Star Trek* fame walks on the surface of the moon, it is likely that he is actually walking on a studio set in front of a screen or wall painted blue. Actually placing Picard on the moon was, no doubt, beyond the budget of the shoot, but it could be faked using blue screen techniques. After shooting the video of Picard's walk against a blue background and shooting another video consisting of the desired background moonscape, the two videos were mixed together: wherever there was blue in the Picard shot, it was replaced by the background image, frame by frame.

Blue screen is a popular technique for making multimedia titles because expensive sets are not required. Incredible backgrounds can be generated using 3-D modeling and graphic software, and one or more actors, vehicles, or other objects can be neatly layered onto that background. Applications such as VideoShop, Premiere, Final Cut Pro, and iMovie provide this capability.

When you are shooting blue screen, be sure that the lighting of the screen is absolutely even; fluctuations in intensity will make this "key" appear choppy or broken. Shooting in daylight, and letting the sun illuminate the screen, will mitigate this problem. Also be careful about "color spill." If your actors stand too close to the screen, the colored light reflecting off the screen will spill onto them, and parts of their body will key out. While adjustments in most applications can compensate for this, the adjustments are limited. Beware of fine detail, such as hair or smoke, that wisps over the screen; this does not key well.

Figure 8-6 shows frames taken from a video of an actor shot against blue screen on a commercial stage. The blue background was removed from each frame, and the actor himself was turned into a photorealistic animation that walked, jumped, pointed, and ran from a dinosaur.

Composition

The general rules for shooting quality video for broadcast use also apply to multimedia.

When shooting video for playback from CD-ROM or the Web

> When I worked in live video at KCAL in Los Angeles, one of our anchor women wore a blouse that was the same chroma-key blue that we could program into our Ultimatte. Actually, the anchor should have known better. We, being the naughty guys we were, keyed a close-up of two big eyes from one of the other anchors onto her blouse and fed it into the stage floor monitor and waited to see how long it would take before she noticed it. It was a couple of minutes, while everyone was trying to keep a straight face, before she saw what we had done. She threw her script at us, and we all broke up laughing.
>
> Joe Silverthorn, Integrated Multimedia Professor, Olympic College

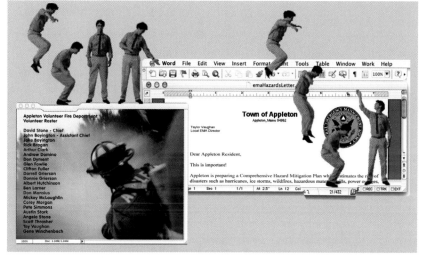

Figure 8-6 This walking, jumping, and pointing actor was videotaped against a blue screen.

in a small computer window, it is best to avoid wide panoramic shots. The effect of sweeping panoramas is lost in small windows. Use close-ups and medium shots, head-and-shoulders or even tighter. Depending upon the compression algorithm used (see the discussion on video compression earlier in the chapter), consider also the amount of motion in the shot: the more a scene changes from frame to frame, the more "delta" information needs to be transferred from the computer's memory to the screen, and the slower the playback speed will be. Keep the camera still instead of panning and zooming; let the subject add the motion to your shot, walking, turning, talking.

Optimizing Video Files for CD-ROM

CD-ROMs provide an excellent distribution medium for computer-based video, because they are inexpensive to mass produce, and they can store great quantities of information. CD-ROM players offer slow data transfer rates, but adequate video transfer can be achieved by taking care to properly prepare your digital video files. Without great care, these digital files may display poorly in low-bandwidth/high-compression environments:

- Limit the amount of synchronization required between the video and audio. With Microsoft's AVI files, the audio and video data are already interleaved, so this is not a necessity, but with QuickTime files, you should "flatten" your movie. **Flattening** means that you interleave the audio and video segments together.

- Use regularly spaced key frames, 10 to 15 frames apart, and temporal compression can correct for seek time delays. **Seek time** is how long it takes the CD-ROM player to locate specific data on the CD-ROM disc. Even fast 56x drives must spin up, causing some delay (and occasionally substantial noise).

- The size of the video window and the frame rate you specify dramatically affect performance. In QuickTime, 20 frames per second played in a 160×120-pixel window is equivalent to playing 10 frames per second in a 320×240 window. The more data that has to be decompressed and transferred from the CD-ROM to the screen, the slower the playback.

- Although interleaving CD-quality audio into your video production will theoretically yield the highest-quality sound, the volume of data required may be too great to transfer from the CD-ROM in real-time. Try a lower sampling rate and sample size to reduce the quantity of audio data.

- The software compression algorithm you specify will make a dramatic difference in performance. The Sorenson algorithm or codec, available within both AVI and QuickTime, is optimized for CD-ROM playback. But take care: it can take many hours of computation to compress just a few minutes of digital video.

■ Defragment your files before burning the master.

■ If you are working with QuickTime, consider using a specialized application such as Media Cleaner Pro to automatically optimize your digital video file for playback from CD-ROM.

DVD Recordable

DVD recordables are used for consumer audio and video recording. Three formats were developed: -R/RW (dash), +R/RW (plus), -RAM (random access memory). Dual Layer recording allows DVD-R and DVD+Rdiscs to store more data, up to 8.5GB per disc, compared with 4.7GB for single layer discs.

Chapter 8 Review

■ Chapter Summary

For your review, here's a summary of the important concepts discussed in this chapter.

Discuss important considerations in using digital video in multimedia

- Video places the highest performance demand on any computer system.
- Digital has replaced analog as the method of choice for making video for multimedia.
- Digital video gear produces excellent finished products at a fraction of the cost of analog.
- Digital video eliminates the image-degrading analog-to-digital conversion.
- There are many sources for digital video, but getting the rights can be difficult, time-consuming, and expensive.

Describe the basics of video recording and how they relate to multimedia production

- A charge-coupled device (CCD), converts the light that has been reflected from an object through the camera's lens.
- Four broadcast and video standards and recording formats are commonly in use around the world: NTSC, PAL, SECAM, and ATSC's HDTV.
- Computers generally require special hardware to capture video from a television signal.

List important considerations in converting from digital video to television

- Don't place critical information such as text in the outer 15 percent of the screen. Keep it within the safe title area.
- Colors on computer monitors are purer and more accurate than those seen on a television monitor, so select colors carefully and review them on a TV monitor.
- Avoid fine lines and harsh color contrasts.

List important considerations in shooting and editing video for use in multimedia

- Always import video and sound at the highest resolution and with the least amount of compression possible; reduce the resolution and compress the footage later according to your needs.
- Always shoot using a steady shooting platform.
- Good, even lighting is extremely important.
- Expensive sets are not required when using blue screen or matte techniques.
- Avoid wide panoramic shots and camera motion when shooting for a small computer window on CD-ROM or the Web.

Define popular video recording formats and discuss their strengths and weaknesses for use in multimedia

- S-VHS and Hi-8 provide adequate picture quality for most multimedia, but analog video is rapidly being replaced by digital recording standards.
- Multimedia producers are rapidly adopting digital recording formats, particularly the DV formats. Most editing is now being done on computers using nonlinear editing (NLE) software such as Premiere and Final Cut Pro.

Discuss some important considerations for preparing video for the Web and CD-ROM

- Codecs are digital video and audio compression schemes that compress a video for delivery and then decode it during playback.
- Streaming audio and video starts playback as soon as enough data has transferred to the user's computer to sustain this playback.

- The MPEG standards provide good media encoding abilities. MPEG-4 includes numerous multimedia capabilities and may become the preferred standard for video and audio in multimedia.

- CD-ROMs provide an excellent distribution medium for computer-based video.

- When preparing video for CD-ROM distribution, interleave the audio track(s) with the video track, use key frames every 10 to 15 frames, and keep the size of the video window small. The Sorenson codec is optimized for CD-ROM playback.

■ Key Terms

Advanced Television Systems Committee (ATSC) *(200)*
Betacam *(210)*
blue screen *(217)*
charge-coupled device (CCD) *(195)*
chroma keys *(216)*
Cinepak *(207)*
codecs *(207)*
component video *(209)*
composite video *(209)*
degaussing *(198)*
Digital Television (DTV) *(193)*
dubbing *(198)*
FireWire (IEEE 1394) *(194)*
flattening *(218)*
generation loss *(209)*

green screen *(217)*
helical scan *(195)*
High Definition Television (HDTV) *(200)*
interlacing *(199)*
Moving Picture Experts Group (MPEG) *(207)*
MPEG standards *(207)*
MPEG-1 *(207)*
MPEG-2 *(207)*
MPEG-4 *(208)*
MPEG-7 *(208)*
MPEG-21 *(208)*
National Television Standards Committee (NTSC) *(193)*
nonlinear editing (NLE) *(205)*

overscan *(201)*
Phase Alternate Line (PAL) *(199)*
progressive-scan *(199)*
RAID (Redundant Array of Independent Disks) *(192)*
RGB *(195)*
safe title area *(202)*
seek time *(218)*
Sequential Color and Memory (SECAM) *(199)*
Sorenson *(207)*
streaming *(207)*
S-VHS *(209)*
tracking *(196)*
Ultimatte *(217)*
underscan *(201)*

■ Key Term Quiz

1. A hard-disk system that will support high-speed data transfer rates is called a _____.

2. The television signal format used in the United States, Japan, and many other countries is known as _____.

3. Television screens use a process of building a single frame from two fields to help prevent flicker on television screens in a technique called _____.

4. When creating graphics for conversion to video, do not place any critical information such as text in the outside 15 percent of the image. Instead, keep it within the _____ (three words).

5. The technique in which playback of a video starts as soon as enough data has transferred to the user's computer to sustain this playback is called _____.

6. The television signal format used in France, Russia, and a few other countries is known as _____.

7. The digital video and audio compression schemes that compress a video for delivery and then decode it during playback are called _____.

8. QuickTime movies being prepared for a CD or web site should be processed so that the audio and video segments are interleaved together and all of the information is in one data file. This is called _____.

9. The length of time it takes the CD-ROM player to locate specific data on the CD-ROM disc is called
_____.

10. The codec that is within both AVI and QuickTime and is optimized for CD-ROM playback
is _____.

■ Multiple Choice Quiz

1. In a video camera, the sensor that picks up light is called a CCD. CCD stands for:
   a. color-coding data
   b. custom color descriptor
   c. chroma-calculation daemon
   d. charge-coupled device
   e. carbon crystal digitizer

2. A computer's output on the monitor is calibrated to display an image:
   a. smaller than the actual monitor's capability
   b. larger than the actual monitor's capability
   c. exactly the same size as the actual monitor's capability
   d. that adjusts automatically to the monitor's capability
   e. of a fixed size; whether it is larger or smaller than the monitor's capability depends on the monitor

3. Removing a residual magnetic field that distorts the colors on a television screen is called:
   a. tracking
   b. dubbing
   c. streaming
   d. flattening
   e. degaussing

4. A video signal transmitted with all the signals mixed together and carried on a single cable is called:
   a. RGB video
   b. composite video
   c. component video
   d. multiformat video
   e. chroma-key video

5. Which of the following is *not* a television signal format?
   a. MPEG
   b. NTSC
   c. PAL
   d. SECAM
   e. HDTV

6. Computer monitors draw the lines of an entire frame in a single pass; this technique is called:
   a. streaming
   b. progressive-scan
   c. packing
   d. flattening
   e. overscan

7. The video technique that allows you to choose a color or range of colors that become transparent, allowing the video image to be visible behind those colors in the overlying image, is known by all of the following *except:*
   a. blue screen
   b. Ultimatte
   c. chroma key
   d. interlacing
   e. All of the above are appropriate names.

8. Which of the following is a videotape format?
   a. GIF
   b. DVD-RW
   c. ComponentY
   d. Hi-8
   e. S-VHS

9. Red or green should be avoided as cue colors because:
   a. they represent negative ideas in some cultures
   b. they do not blend well with other colors
   c. color-blind individuals cannot see them correctly
   d. they are associated with "stop" and "go"
   e. they remind people of Christmas

10. Which of the following is *not* a good idea when creating titles (text) to be used in video?
   a. Fonts for titles should be plain, sans serif, and bold enough to be easily read.
   b. When you are laying text onto a dark background, use white or a light color for the text.
   c. Do not kern your letters too tightly.
   d. If you use underlining or drawn graphics, make sure your lines are only one pixel wide.
   e. Use a drop shadow to help separate the text from the background.

11. Which of the following is *not* a recommendation for caring for videotapes?
   a. Always fast-forward new tapes to the end and then rewind them to make sure that tape tension is even from beginning to end.
   b. Run your tape through the recorder once with the lens cap on and without audio input.
   c. Do not reuse 8mm video cassettes, as their small size makes them susceptible to stretch.
   d. Always make a backup copy of these tapes before you begin editing.

   e. Never remove the break-off tab on the back of your original video cassettes; doing so renders the tape unusable with some decks.

12. Which of the following is *not* a codec?
   a. MPEG
   b. DV
   c. NTSC
   d. Cinepak
   e. Sorenson

13. Generation loss occurs when:
   a. an analog tape is copied to another analog tape
   b. a digital tape is copied to another digital tape
   c. a digital file is copied to another hard drive
   d. a digital file is compressed with a lossy codec
   e. your teenage son gets his tongue pierced

14. MPEG stands for:
   a. Multiformat Processed-Event Graphics
   b. Multi-Phase Element Grid
   c. Meta-Program Environment Graph
   d. Moving Picture Experts Group
   e. Micro-Phase Electronic Guidance

15. Which of the following is *not* recommended for optimal video playback from CD-ROM?
   a. Use a large video window and a high frame rate.
   b. Interleave the audio and video segments together.
   c. Use regularly spaced key frames.
   d. Use the Sorenson codec.
   e. Defragment your files before burning the master.

■ Essay Quiz

1. List the steps involved in capturing video, compressing the video, and preparing it for CD-ROM. Briefly discuss the decisions you need to make with each step regarding compromises on image quality and other limiting factors.

2. Discuss how the computer monitor image differs from the television image. List the limitations in creating images on the computer destined for the television screen.

3. Discuss several considerations in shooting and editing video for multimedia. What techniques would you use to produce the best possible video, at a reasonable cost? Which of these techniques apply to *all* video, and which apply specifically to multimedia?

4. Briefly discuss what defines the quality of a video signal. What factors affect this quality? How do the various analog television signal formats differ in quality? How does the recording format affect this quality? What about digital format? How can you ensure that your video is of the best possible quality? If the end result is going to be a postage-stamp-sized streaming video clip at 10 frames per second, why would quality matter?

5. Define codec and list an example of a codec.

Lab Projects

■ Project 8.1

You have been tasked with planning a multimedia CD-ROM. You have 700MB to store 25 minutes of video. Discuss how you would go about deciding how to compress the video for the program. Be sure to include a discussion of the target platform.

■ Project 8.2

Go to a local electronics superstore. What kinds of video cameras are available? What capabilities do the "prosumer" DV cameras have? What features do they have that would be useful in multimedia? Document your findings.

■ Project 8.3

Locate three CD-ROMs that include video clips. Such clips, because of their file size, are usually stored externally to the actual executable. Search through the CD's folder structure to locate the clips. These clips can normally be opened in a media player such as QuickTime. To open clips in QuickTime, select Get Info, and note the clip's dimensions, file size, which codecs were used to compress the audio and video tracks, what the frame rate and data rate are for the clips.

■ Project 8.4

Locate three web sites that include streaming video clips. What format are they served in? Most sites that include links to video clips provide some identifying information to make their use easier; such as the dimensions, file size, and format. Make a note of your findings. Some clips are available in a streaming format and are not easily downloadable. Others can be downloaded. Download the clips you can and open them in QuickTime. Using QuickTime, select Get Info and list the codecs that were used to compress the clips.

■ Project 8.5

Prepare five graphic images using a paint or drawing program. Be sure to include a variety of colors and contrasts. Add text to the images. Use small text, large text, text with serifs, bold text, and text in contrasting and similar colors. Add drop shadows. Add boxes and other shapes to the images, in various weights.

Locate a computer with video-out capabilities, and view the images. Note your findings:

- Which color combinations worked well? Which did not?
- Were any colors distracting?
- What about the text and graphics? Which looked best?
- What about the safe title area? What percentage of the image was clipped? (Note that some computers have video outputs that underscan rather than overscan. Remember, such a setup does not accurately reflect the image size that would result from a computer-to-video conversion.)

Hardware

SELECTION of the proper platform for developing your multimedia project may be based on your personal preference of computer, your budget constraints, project delivery requirements, and the type of material and content in the project. Many developers believe that multimedia project development is smoother and easier on the Macintosh than in Windows, even though projects destined to run in Windows must then be ported across platforms. But hardware and authoring software tools for both Windows and Macintoshes have improved greatly. Hardware and software can easily be acquired and installed. Table 9-1 shows the penetration of operating systems as of 2006, and you can see that Apple has lost most of its market share (which at one time was 15 percent of all computer systems sold) to Windows-based platforms. As a practical consideration, it is easier to find multimedia hardware and software for Windows-driven PCs at Wal-Mart or Staples.

Windows	Mac OS	Other
95.06%	3.71%	1.23%

Table 9-1   Platform (Operating System) Penetration in 2006

Vaughan's Rule for Keeping Up

Upgrade to proven products that lie in the calm water, slightly behind the leading edge of the wave

1993

The rationale for trading in my workhorse Macintosh IIci for a Quadra 840AV in 1993 was that I would get at least three years of good use out of a computer that would remain at or near the top of the line long enough to justify its cost. Apple's RISC-based PowerMacs would begin shipping in 1994, and they would be more than twice as powerful as my Quadra. But that power will be available mainly to applications that have been written specifically for the PowerPC chip in native code. Indeed, it was rumored at the time that some applications, until

(continued)

Vaughan's Rule for Keeping Up *(continued)*

they were redesigned by their vendors, would actually run slower on the PowerPC than on my Quadra. You can capsize at the frothy, leading edge of technology, where the Surf Alligators live.

1996

By this point, my Quadra 840AV continued to perform just fine and was still well supported by software vendors. While writing the third edition of this book, however, Apple kindly loaned me a top-of-the-line Power Macintosh 9500 with all the bells and whistles, because some heavy-duty authoring packages now *require* the PowerMac's capabilities, and I wanted to test them. I let my assistant use the PowerMac; I knew that if I tried it and liked it, I wouldn't be able to go back (see Vaughan's One-Way Rule later in this chapter), and I also knew I could still get at least another year of good service out of my 840AV.

1998

Too many applications just wouldn't run on my Quadra 840AV, and I was too far behind the curve. I bought a 7500 Power-Mac, boosted the processor and cache, and added a second hard drive. It screamed, compared to the old Quadra, which was relegated to my 10-year-old's bedroom. But with the G3 Macintosh out on the market, and an entirely new operating system from Apple on the horizon, perhaps I have purchased only a year or two's grace before the leading edge of technology pinches again. However, I'm still safely behind what some call the "bleeding edge."

2001

Whoa, with the Mac 7500 I was way behind the edge! Too little RAM, no speed. G4s were out and OS X was shipping. When the new Photoshop 6 worked *slower* than Photoshop 5, I knew it was time, but I didn't have an extra $3,000 for fresh hardware. Instead of buying a new Mac, for about $500 I installed a Sonnet G4 Crescendo card and a stick of RAM into my old 7500. Bingo! In the game again. There are more than a few upgrade paths that will keep you going.

2003

It's been ten years. Keeping up has not only been exhausting, it has become annoying. Working with computers isn't like working with the tools of other trades: I have a cast iron plumber's wrench that continues to install kitchen sinks after more than a hundred years of duty. My expensive computer, though, can only do the job for a few years; then it dies, joining other computers and computer parts in a graveyard of relics in a corner of my barn. There is no longer "support" for my current machine, and the latest software won't even load. The industry's marketing argument is that this is a good thing, allowing for innovation and progress. My own practical argument, now that computers are "adequate" for making multimedia (see Vaughan's Law of Multimedia Minimums in Chapter 5), likens computers and operating systems to tungsten light bulbs designed to burn out every few months: if light bulbs never burned out, the manufacturers could sell you only one bulb, not many.

2006

Finally, I have a Power Mac G4 dual processor machine running at 1.25 GHz that will do all I need it to do, fast enough. With OS 10.4.7 (Tiger), the platform is stable. My disk storage measures hundreds of gigabytes, and I continue to back up important files regularly. A new wave of Intel-based Macs is selling well, but I have Windows XP running on a clone and no need for Boot Camp's easy switch between Mac and Windows on the same computer. Mac and Windows talk to each other over the network, anyway. In this calm water slightly behind the leading edge of the wave, my system never fails to boot, doesn't lock up in the middle of a file save, and is dependable. It even updates automatically with the latest software improvements so I am always current. It may be a long time before this setup becomes a graveyard relic.

Macintosh Versus Windows

Since its inception, the Macintosh has been, by definition, a multimedia computer: at the famous rollout of the Macintosh in January 1984 at Apple's annual shareholders' meeting, the new device actually introduced itself in a crudely synthesized voice:

> "Hello. I'm Macintosh. It sure is great
> to get out of that bag... Unaccustomed
> as I am to public speaking, I'd like to
> share with you a maxim I thought of
> the first time I met an IBM mainframe:
> Never trust a computer you can't lift!
> Obviously, I can talk, but right now I'd
> like to sit back and listen. So it is with
> considerable pride that I introduce the
> man who's been like a father to me,
> Steven Jobs."

Whereas the Macintosh had good built-in audio right from the start, in 1984 IBM personal computers could not process sound without very expensive add-on components. With its focus on business computing, the PC remained for many years able to provide only system beeps and limited sound effects on a tiny (and tinny) onboard speaker. That situation has changed, and today the Intel-based PC running Windows readily challenges the Macintosh in delivering excellent multimedia presentations.

The Macintosh Platform

All Macintoshes can record and play sound. Many include hardware and software for digitizing and editing video and producing DVD discs. High-quality graphics capability is available "out of the box." Unlike the Windows environment, where users can operate any application with keyboard input, the Macintosh *requires* a mouse.

There are significant variations in the ways you can set up your Macintosh hardware and software. The Macintosh computer you will need for developing a project depends entirely upon the project's delivery requirements, its content, and the tools you will need for production. Of course, the ideal production station is the newest, fastest, and most flexible computer you can get your hands on, but such a configuration may be beyond the scope of your budget. Thankfully, acceptable performance is not limited to the top-of-the-line configuration: all Macintosh models sold today are sufficient for multimedia development.

Apple introduced the first Power Macintosh computers based on reduced instruction-set computing (RISC) microprocessors during 1994. RISC technology was typically used in engineering workstations and commercial database servers designed for raw computational power, but in an alliance with IBM and Motorola, Apple designed and built this new line of RISC-based models. They supplanted earlier models based upon the Motorola 68000, 68030, and 68040 processors. In 1997, the G3 series was introduced with clock speeds greater than 233 MHz and offering higher performance than existing Pentium-based Windows machines. By 2003, the G4 computers offered gigahertz speeds and a dual processor arrangement with a 20-times performance increase over the G3, when running applications like Photoshop.

In 2006, Apple adopted Intel's processor architecture, an engineering decision that allows Macintoshes to run natively with any x86 operating system. Using the Intel Core, Intel Xeon 5100 series, and Intel Core 2 microprocessors, all models of Macintosh are pre-installed with the native version of the latest Mac OS. Using Boot Camp software, they can also run Windows XP.

When you upgrade from a 56 Kbps modem using plain old telephone lines to a wireless or cable connection to the Internet, you will experience the One-Way Rule firsthand as you slide into high bandwidth, and web pages download immediately to your monitor in complete and finished chunks. A while back,

Vaughan's One-Way Rule

Once you've tried it, you can't go back.

In 1987, a few weeks after HyperCard was released by Apple, I went to work there, designing and building the guided tour for an information management tool used in-house by Apple. I said I didn't know the software, but they said that's OK, nobody else does, either. They gave me a cubicle with my name on it, a Macintosh Plus with a 20MB hard disk, and I was up and running. The Macintosh II had been shipping for a short while, and every department at Apple was attempting to get this latest and hottest CPU—but most units were going to the retail channel. There were three Macintosh IIs among about 40 of us.

One afternoon, I sat at a Macintosh II, inserted my 800K disk, and ran my HyperCard stack. I couldn't believe it! The screen-to-screen dissolves and special effects I had carefully programmed on the Macintosh Plus went by so fast I couldn't see them. I had to reprogram everything, with a special test to check for CPU speed. If it was a fast machine, I programmed the visual effects to run slower; on a slow machine, faster. But the sad part was that I not only wanted this faster machine, I felt I needed it! I had had the same experience moving from a 300-baud modem to a 1200-baud modem and, later, from a 14-inch monitor to a 21-inch monitor.

tens of thousands of subscribers to a DSL provider in San Francisco went berserk when that company crashed into bankruptcy and pulled the high-bandwidth plug without warning—the chalkboard screech of those users going the wrong way was deafening!

The Windows Platform

Unlike the Macintosh computer, a Windows computer is not a computer per se, but rather a collection of parts that are tied together by the requirements of the Windows operating system. Power supplies, processors, hard disks, CD-ROM players, video and audio components, monitors, keyboards, and mice—it doesn't matter where they come from or who makes them. Made in Texas, Taiwan, Indonesia, India, Ireland, Mexico, or Malaysia by widely known or little-known manufacturers, these components are assembled and branded by Dell, IBM, Gateway, and others into computers that run Windows. If you are handy with a Phillips screwdriver and can read instructions, you can even order the parts and assemble your own computer "clone" to run Windows—at a considerable cost savings!

In the early days, Microsoft organized the major PC hardware manufacturers into the Multimedia PC Marketing Council, in order to develop a set of specifications that would allow Windows to deliver a dependable multimedia experience. (The fanfare rollout for this effort is described in a First Person in Chapter 7.) Since then, the multimedia PC, or **MPC** specification has evolved into "what a computer does." While Dell, HP, Gateway, IBM, and other vendors offer "managed PCs," which are business PCs without audio and are intended for networked use only, today, you might need to special order a retrograde computer that did not have audio, a CD-ROM drive, plenty of RAM and processor speed, and a high-resolution monitor.

Networking Macintosh and Windows Computers

If you are working in a multimedia development environment consisting of a mixture of Macintosh and Windows computers, you will want them to communicate with each other. You will also wish to share other resources among them, such as printers.

Local area networks (LANs) and **wide area networks (WANs)** can connect the members of a workgroup. In a LAN, workstations are usually located within a short distance of one another, on the same floor of a building, for example. WANs are communication systems spanning great distances, typically set up and managed by large corporations and institutions for their own use, or to share with other users.

First Person

In November 1985, during the COMDEX trade show in Las Vegas, members of the computer press were invited to the birthing party for a new Microsoft product called Windows. A crowd of journalists and friends of Microsoft had gathered in a small, low-ceilinged, hotel ballroom and were munching on hors d'oeuvres and sipping wine when the swinging doors to the pantry opened suddenly, and Bill Gates drove a golf cart onto the floor, towing a small trailer loaded down with hundreds of blue boxes filled with the new product. A cheer went up, and the boxes disappeared into waiting hands. It was a fun party held in the time before Gates had become the richest man in the world and necessarily employed a personal security force, before his personal income would skew by two dollars the difference between the mean and median income of all Americans. He chatted with a few of us and proudly autographed some User Guides. Mine says "I hope you like the product; thanks for coming, Tay."

Back in my office after the show, I loaded the software onto my XT from the five 5.25-inch floppy disks in the box and ran it. Windows was a dog. Indeed, during the ensuing days and months, Windows had a very hard time in the "operating environment" popularity contest and dropped to low-visibility status. But Gates seemed to have a vision, and while we didn't hear too much about Windows during the next years, Gates and Microsoft worked on the product steadily and didn't give up. Windows 3.0, released many years later, changed the world.

LANs allow direct communication and sharing of peripheral resources such as file servers, printers, scanners, and network modems. They use a variety of proprietary technologies, most commonly Ethernet, to perform the connections. They can usually be set up with twisted-pair telephone wire, but be sure to use at least "data-grade level 5" or **cat-5 cable**—it makes a real difference, even if it's a little more expensive! Bad wiring will give you a never-ending headache of intermittent and often untraceable crashes and failures.

WANs are expensive to install and maintain, but other methods for long-distance communication are available without a dedicated telephone or wireless network: dial-up connections to the Internet through an Internet Service Provider (ISP), such as America Online or MSN, allow messages and files to be uploaded to private electronic (e-mail) mailbox addresses and downloaded later by the recipient. You pay for a local telephone call and the length of time you are connected to the service (usually at a reasonable hourly rate). If you are working with people in various time zones (an artist in New York, a programmer in San Francisco, and a client in Singapore), all can communicate and share information with other locations at any time of day or night using intranets and/or extranets.

There are also, campus area networks (CANs) for educational or corporation applications and metropolitan area networks (MANs) that are used by utility, police and other related parties.

Personal area networks (PANs) connect personal communication devices such as telephones and personal digital assistants to themselves and to higher-level networks and the Internet. A wireless personal area network (WPAN) uses networking radio technologies such as Bluetooth and IrDA. A PAN of Bluetooth devices is also called a "piconet."

If you are operating a cross-platform multimedia development shop, you should install a local **Ethernet** system so that your PCs and Macintoshes can talk to each other and to your network printers as well. This is many times more efficient than carrying removable media among your machines. Macintoshes have Ethernet networking built in; your PCs will require inexpensive Ethernet cards, usually included in off-the-shelf machines. Ethernet is only a *method* for wiring up computers, so you still will need **client/server software** to enable the computers to speak with each other and pass files back and forth. Here you have two options: you can add software to your Macintosh to allow it to connect to a network of Windows PCs that use the Microsoft Client **TCP/IP** protocols, or you can add software to your Windows PC that allows it to connect to a network of Macintoshes using AppleTalk. Both require Ethernet as the connection method.

With DAVE from Thursby Systems (http://www.thursby.com), software is installed on the Macintosh so that it can connect to the Windows network (see Figure 9-1). To connect a PC to a network of Macintoshes, you can use PCMacLAN from Miramar (http://ca.miramar.com) for sharing the directories and files on all your computers, so that you do not have to install a dedicated server workstation.

Figure 9-1 Thursby Software Systems' DAVE provides easy, bi-directional file and printer sharing between Windows and Macintosh computers, and also allows multiple sharing and security options.

Connections

When you attend a conference where multimedia presentations are being shown, the human speakers usually sit facing the audience, which is treated to a view of the backside of the speakers' computers. Among the many devices—computers, monitors, disk drives, video projectors, light-valves, videodisc players, VCRs, mixers, sound speakers, and power strips—there are enough wires and connections to resemble the intensive-care ward of a hospital. Sometimes an attempt is made to drape these power and data hoses with a curtain.

The equipment required for developing your multimedia project will depend on the content of the project as well as its design. You will certainly need as fast a computer as you can lay your hands on, with lots of RAM and disk storage space. If you can find content such as sound effects, music, graphic art, clip animations, and QuickTime or AVI movies to use in your project, you may not need the extra tools for making your own. Typically, however, multimedia developers have separate equipment for digitizing sound from tapes or microphone, scanning photographs or other printed matter, and making digital still or movie images from videotape. Table 9-2 shows various connection methodologies and their data transfer rates.

Connection	Transfer Rate
Serial port	115 Kbit/s (.115 Mbit/s)
Standard parallel port	115 Kbit/s (.115 Mbit/s)
Original USB	12 Mbit/s (1.5 Mbit/s)
ECP/EPP parallel port	3 Mbit/s
IDE	3.3-16.7 Mbit/s
SCSI-1	5 Mbit/s
SCSI-2 (Fast SCSI, Fast Narrow SCSI)	10 Mbit/s
Fast Wide SCSI (Wide SCSI)	20 Mbit/s
Ultra SCSI (SCSI-3, Fast-20, Ultra Narrow)	20 Mbit/s
Ultra IDE	33 Mbit/s
Wide Ultra SCSI (Fast Wide 20)	40 Mbit/s
Ultra2 SCSI	40 Mbit/s
Hi-Speed USB	480 Mbit/s
IEEE-1394 (FireWire)	100-1600 Mbit/s
Wide Ultra2 SCSI	80 Mbit/s
Ultra3 SCSI	80 Mbit/s
Wide Ultra3 SCSI	160 Mbit/s
FC-AL Fiber Channel	100-400 Mbit/s

Table 9-2 Maximum Transfer Rates for Various Connections in megabits per second

SCSI

The **Small Computer System Interface (SCSI**—pronounced "scuzzy") was built into all models of the Macintosh, before Apple switched over to the less-expensive IDE bus starting with G3 Macs and iMacs. SCSI adds peripheral equipment such as disk drives, scanners, CD-ROM players, and other peripheral devices that conform to the SCSI standard. It was possible to connect as many as eight devices (ID numbers from 0 to 7) to a SCSI bus, but one of them must be the computer itself with ID 7, and one is usually the internal hard disk with ID 0. High-end Macintoshes (pre-G3) had two SCSI buses, internal and external, and so could hook up twice as many devices.

First Person

A few years ago I was on a flight from Dallas to Frankfurt and became involved in an unusual but gentlemanly competition. At Mach .75 and 40,000 above the sea, six of us contended for the two available 110-volt "Shavers Only" electrical outlets in the lavatories. Every hour or so we found we needed to recharge our laptop computers, and so, in the usual friendly manner of fellow travelers, we quietly negotiated a round-robin power schedule.

More recently, on an overnight flight across that same ocean aboard a brand-new aircraft, mine was the only seat showing its overhead light while I put the finishing touches on a multimedia presenta-tion. After a few hours, I needed to charge batteries, and with the small charger, power cord, and batteries in hand, I went forward to the lavatory. There was no 110-volt outlet. With increasing alarm, I checked the other lavatories. No outlets anywhere.

Behind the curtain of the galley, the flight attendants had gathered to chat while their passengers slept. No, there probably weren't any outlets on this plane, they responded ambivalently. I looked furtively around the galley; none there, either.

It would seem that 110-volt conveniences for passengers with shavers and laptops have gone to that same graveyard of services where you can find Channel 12 for listening to Air Traffic Control while en route, first-person televised views from the cockpit of takeoffs and landings, a catered piano bar and lounge aft, and (in the real old days) a tiny pack of four Winston cigarettes on your dinner tray next to a matchbook proudly emblazoned with the airline's logo.

No doubt there are safety, cost, and general reduction-of-hassle-from-passengers reasons, though airlines are beginning to install special low-voltage computer power outlets for laptops at business and first-class seats. I was, in the end, better off for the extra sleep.

SCSI cards could also be installed in PCs, and external peripheral devices such as hard disks, CD-ROM drives, tape drives, printers, scanners, rewritable cartridge drives, and magneto-optical drives could be connected to the installed card. When a SCSI device was connected to the interface card in a PC, it was mounted to the system as another drive letter. Thus, there were floppy disk drives mounted as drives A: and B:, a hard disk as drive C:, a CD-ROM drive as D:, and SCSI-based external devices as drives E:, F:, G:, and so on. While it was usually connected to a hard disk controller card in the PC, the internal disk drive C: could also be a SCSI device, connected to a SCSI card. With Ultra SCSI, it was possible to hook up as many as 32 devices to a computer. Serial SCSI allows for hot swapping, improved fault isolation, and faster data rates.

 CROSS PLATFORM   *In the past, not all PC SCSI cards and software drivers would recognize Macintosh-formatted, removable media such as Zip, Jaz, and Syquest cartridges or magneto-optical discs. The Macintosh, however, will usually recognize PC-formatted disks and devices; so many developers working in cross-platform environments use PC formatting for their removable media.*

You will need to set up your SCSI devices carefully, because SCSI cabling is sensitive to length and to resistance. Follow the instructions in your SCSI user's guide for proper termination and ID number assignment for SCSI devices. Having more than one external SCSI device can make your system "delicate," and even more will make it "fragile."

When your computer is not happy with your chain of SCSI peripherals, it is not forgiving and may refuse to boot up. Often you will need to adjust cable lengths and reconfigure terminating resistors, and then try again. Make sure that IDs assigned to peripherals are neither 0 nor 7, and that the same ID number is not assigned to two different devices. If you are likely to move different peripheral devices among several computers, it is good practice to put a sticker with that device's assigned SCSI ID on each and also label all devices connected to the computer. Always connect external devices with computer and device power off unless you are operating a system with a Serial SCSI that allows hot swapping. By clearly paying attention to the SCSI IDs of your peripherals, you can avoid dangerous ID conflicts (setting two devices to the same ID) when you boot up.

The hardware and the drivers for SCSI have improved over the years to provide faster data transfers across wider buses: SCSI-1 transfers data at a rate of 5MB/s and supports up to seven devices. The newer **SCSI-2** is divided into two classifications: **Fast SCSI** (10MB/s) and **Wide SCSI** (with an increased bus width to 16-bit). A composite of these two (**Fast/Wide SCSI**) can achieve data transfer rates of 20MB/s. The latest **SCSI-3 (Ultra SCSI)** can support up to 16,256 (128 per expander) devices and output 300 MB/s per direction; full duplex. Unlike the less-expensive IDE scheme, a SCSI controller does not demand CPU time, and because it can support many devices, it is often preferred for real-time video editing, network servers, and situations in which writing simultaneously to two or more disks (*mirroring*) is required.

SCSI devices may be installed (and interchanged) on both your PC and your Macintosh: until recently, with the advent of the Mac Intel chip, the PC would *not* read Macintosh-formatted hard disks and other data storage cartridges, but the Macintosh (usually) will read PC-formatted devices.

IDE, EIDE, Ultra IDE, ATA, and Ultra ATA

SCSI connections may connect both *internal* devices, which are inside the chassis of your computer and use the computer's power supply, and *external* devices, which are outside the chassis, use their own power supply, and are plugged into the computer by cable. **Integrated Drive Electronics (IDE)** connections, also known as **Advanced Technology Attachment (ATA)** connections, are typically only internal, and they connect hard disks, CD-ROM drives, and other peripherals mounted inside the PC.

If the label on the cable on the table at your house says you hook up the camera simple as a mouse, but the packets burn a pocket on a socket on the port, then get your receipt and call them to abort.

Tay Vaughan, inspired by *Why Computers Sometimes Crash!* by Dr. Seuss ☺

With IDE controllers, you can install a combination of hard disks, CD-ROM drives, or other devices in your PC. The circuitry for IDE is typically much less expensive than for SCSI, but comes with some limitations. For example, IDE requires time from the main processor chip, so only one drive in a master/slave pair can be active at once: this is called native command queueing. Because I/O loads are specifically designed to encounter almost no delays from seek time and rotational latency and because a master drive manages the operations of both drives attached to a controller, a failure of the master drive will disable both drives.

USB

A consortium of industry players including Compaq, Digital Equipment, IBM, Intel, Microsoft, NEC, and Northern Telecom was formed in 1995 to promote a Universal Serial Bus (USB) standard for connecting devices to a computer. These devices are automatically recognized ("plug-and-play") and installed without users needing to install special cards or turn the computer off and on when making the connection (allowing "hot-swapping"). USB technology has improved in performance since its introduction (see Table 9-2) and has become the connection method of choice for many peripheral devices, from cameras to keyboards to scanners and printers. USB uses a single cable to connect as many as 127 USB peripherals to a single personal computer. Hubs can be used to "daisy-chain" many devices. USBs are now common on video game consoles, cell phones, televisions, MP3 players, PDAs and portable memory devices. Wireless USB is the radio spectrum-based implementation that you may be enjoying in the daily use of your computer.

FireWire (IEEE 1394)

FireWire was introduced by Apple in the late 1980s, and in 1995 it became an industry standard (IEEE 1394) supporting high-bandwidth serial data transfer, particularly for digital video and mass storage. Like USB, the standard supports hot-swapping and plug-and-play, but it is faster, and while USB devices can only be attached to one computer at a time, FireWire can connect multiple computers and peripheral devices (peer-to-peer). Apple's operating systems and Microsoft's Windows XP both offer IEEE 1394 support. Because the standard has been endorsed by both the Electronics Industries Association and the Advanced Television Systems Committee (ATSC) it has become the most common method for connecting and interconnecting professional digital video gear, from cameras to recorders and edit suites. In fact, FireWire has replaced Parellel SCSI in many applications, because it's cheaper and because it has a simpler, adaptive cabling system.

Memory and Storage Devices

As you add more memory and storage space to your computer, you can expect your computing needs and habits to keep pace, filling the new capacity. So enjoy the weeks that follow a memory storage upgrade or the addition of a gigabyte hard disk; the honeymoon will eventually end.

To estimate the memory requirements of a multimedia project—the space required on a floppy disk, hard disk, or CD-ROM, not the **random access memory (RAM)** used while your computer is running—you must have a sense of the project's content and scope. Color images, text, sound bites, video clips, and the programming code that glues it all together require memory; if there are many of these elements, you will need even more. If you are *making* multimedia, you will also need to allocate memory for storing and archiving working files used during production, original audio and video clips, edited pieces, and final mixed pieces, production paperwork and correspondence, and at least one backup of your project files, with a second backup stored at another location.

> ## Vaughan's Law of Capacity
>
> ### You never have enough memory or disk space.
>
> Somewhere in my basement is an old drive that used 256K, 8-inch floppy disks. I often carried these big floppies from workplace to workplace in a sneaker network (by tennis shoe, that is, not wire or glass fiber). I was astounded and pleased when the new 5.25-inch disks came out, and then amazed by the high technology of 3.5-inch disks that fit in a shirt pocket. The higher-density floppies kept pace with the growing sizes of my project files, until I switched to color and began including sound and animation. For a while, segmenting and joining large files across several disks worked around the constraint, but it was tedious and inadequate for large digital video files. So I went to 44MB Syquest cartridges, then to 128MB magneto-optical disks and to Zip disks, then to 1–2GB Jaz cartridges. Now I burn a quick CD-R. My projects are measured in the hundreds of megabytes, and the blank CD-R costs only a few cents. Pretty soon, the cost of DVD blanks will come down, too, and large projects will measure in gigabytes.

It is said that when John von Neuman, often called "the father of the computer," was designing the ENIAC computer in 1945, there was an argument about how much memory this first computer should have. His colleagues appealed for more than the 2K Dr. von Neuman felt was sufficient. In the end, he capitulated and agreed to install 4K in the ENIAC, commenting "...but this is more memory than you will ever need."

Random Access Memory (RAM)

If you are faced with budget constraints, you can certainly produce a multimedia project on a slower or limited-memory computer. On the other hand, it is profoundly frustrating to face memory (RAM) shortages time after time, when you're attempting to keep multiple applications and files open simultaneously. It is also frustrating to wait the extra seconds required of each editing step when working with multimedia material on a slow processor.

In spite of all the marketing hype about processor speed, this speed is ineffective if not accompanied by sufficient RAM. A fast processor without enough RAM may waste processor cycles while it swaps needed portions of program code into and out of memory. In some cases, increasing available RAM may show more performance improvement on your system than upgrading the processor chip.

Read-Only Memory (ROM)

Unlike RAM, **read-only memory (ROM)** is not *volatile*. When you turn off the power to a ROM chip, it will not forget, or lose its memory. ROM is typically used in computers to hold the small BIOS program that initially boots up the computer, and it is used in printers to hold built-in fonts. **Programmable ROMs** (called **EPROMs**) allow changes to be made that are not forgotten. A new and inexpensive technology, **optical read-only memory (OROM)**, is provided in proprietary data cards using patented holographic storage. Like the CD recorders described later in the chapter, the cards are write-once. Typically, OROMs offer 128MB of storage, have no moving parts, and use only about 200 milliwatts of power, making them ideal for handheld, battery-operated devices.

Floppy and Hard Disks

Adequate storage space for your production environment can be provided by large-capacity hard disks; a server-mounted disk on a network; Zip, Jaz, or Syquest removable cartridges; optical media; CD-R (compact disc-recordable) discs; tape; floppy disks; banks of special memory devices; or any combination of the above.

Removable media (floppy disks, compact or optical discs, and cartridges) typically fit into a letter-sized mailer for overnight courier service. One or many disks or discs may be required for storage and archiving each project, and you should plan for backups kept off-site.

Floppy disks and hard disks are mass-storage devices for binary data—data that can be easily read by a computer. Hard disks can contain much more information than floppy disks and can operate at far greater data transfer rates. In the scale of things, floppies are, however, no longer "mass-storage" devices, and will soon be eliminated from the storage methods of choice.

A floppy disk is made of flexible Mylar plastic coated with a very thin layer of special magnetic material. A hard disk is actually a stack of hard metal platters coated with magnetically sensitive material, with a series of recording heads or sensors that hover a hairbreadth above the fast-spin-

Even though the processing performance of computers has increased considerably in the last several years, input/output (I/O) devices have not kept up with this trend. While processor speed gets roughly eight times faster every ten years, main memory access speed increases by only one-third in the same time period. As you realize, this widens the gap between I/O and processing times.

So our ability to efficiently use very fast computers depends on our ability to feed the processor with data sufficiently fast. This is called the *parallel I/O bottleneck*. The bad news is that this problem is expected to get worse.

From "Parallel Machines and Their Algorithms" by Takis Metaxas

ning surface, magnetizing or demagnetizing spots along formatted tracks using technology similar to that used by floppy disks and audio and video tape recording. Hard disks are the most common mass-storage device used on computers, and for making multimedia, you will need one or more large-capacity hard disk drives (see Vaughan's Law of Capacity earlier in the chapter).

As multimedia has reached consumer desktops, makers of hard disks have been challenged to build smaller-profile, larger-capacity, faster, and less-expensive hard disks. In 1994, hard disk manufacturers sold nearly 70 million units; in 1995, more than 80 million units. And prices have dropped a full order of magnitude in a matter of months. By 1998, street prices for 4GB drives (IDE) were less than $200. By 2001, 20GB drives cost less than $100. In 2003, an 80GB drive cost about $80 and a more common 120GB drive about $130. As network and Internet servers drive the demand for centralized data storage requiring terabytes (1 trillion bytes), hard disks will be configured into fail-proof redundant arrays offering built-in protection against crashes.

Zip, Jaz, Syquest, and Optical Storage Devices

For years, the **Syquest** 44MB removable cartridges were the most widely used portable medium among multimedia developers and professionals, but Iomega's inexpensive **Zip** drives with their likewise inexpensive 100MB, 250MB, and 750MB cartridges, built on floppy disk technology, significantly penetrated Syquest's market share for removable media. Iomega's **Jaz** cartridges, built based on hard disk drive technology, provided one or two gigabytes of removable storage media and have fast enough transfer rates for multimedia development. Pinnacle Micro, Yamaha, Sony, Philips, and others offer CD-R "burners" for making write-once compact discs, and some double as quad-speed players. As blank CD-R discs become available for less than a dollar each, this write-once media competes as a distribution vehicle. CD-R is described in greater detail a little later in the chapter.

Magneto-optical (MO) drives use a high-power laser to heat tiny spots on the metal oxide coating of the disk. While the spot is hot, a magnet aligns the oxides to provide a 0 or 1 (on or off) orientation. Like Syquest's and other hard disks, this is rewritable technology, because the spots can be repeatedly heated and aligned. Moreover, this media is normally not affected by stray magnetism (it needs both heat and magnetism to make changes), so these disks are particularly suitable for archiving data. The data transfer rate is, however, slow compared to Zip, Jaz, and Syquest technologies. One of the most popular formats uses a 128MB-capacity disk—about the size of a 3.5-inch floppy. Larger-format magneto-optical drives with 5.25-inch cartridges offering 650MB to 1.3GB of storage are also available.

Digital Versatile Disc (DVD)

In December 1995, nine major electronics companies (Toshiba, Matsushita, Sony, Philips, Time Warner, Pioneer, JVC, Hitachi, and Mitsubishi Electric) agreed to promote a new optical disc technology for distribution of multimedia and feature-length movies called **Digital Versatile Disc (DVD)** (see Table 9-3).

DVD Feature	DVD Specification
Disc diameter	120 mm (5 inches)
Disc thickness	1.2 mm (0.6 mm thick disc × 2)
Memory capacity	4.7 gigabytes/single side
Track pitch	0.74 micrometer
Wave length of laser diode	650 nanometer/635 nanometer
Numerical aperture (NA)	0.6
Error correction	RS-PC (Reed Solomon Product Code)
Signal modulation	8-16
Data transfer rate	Variable speed data transfer at an average rate of 4.69 Mbps for image and sound
Image compression	MPEG2 digital image compression
Audio	Dolby AC-3 (5.1 ch), LPCM for NTSC and MPEG Audio, LPCM for PAL/SECAM (a maximum of 8 audio channels and 32 subtitle channels can be stored)
Running time (movies)	133 minutes a side (at an average data rate of 4.69 Mbps for image and sound, including three audio channels and four subtitle channels)
File management structure	Micro UDF and ISO-9660

Table 9-3 DVD Main Specifications

With this new medium capable not only of gigabyte storage capacity but also full-motion video (MPEG2) and high-quality audio in surround sound, the bar has again risen for multimedia developers. Commercial multimedia projects will become more expensive to produce as consumers' performance expectations rise. There are three types of DVD, including DVD-Read Write, **DVD-Video** and **DVD-ROM**. These types reflect marketing channels, not the technology.

With **Dolby AC-3 Digital Surround Sound** as part of the specification, six discrete audio channels can be programmed for digital surround sound, and with a separate subwoofer channel, developers can program the low-frequency doom and gloom music popular with Hollywood. DVD also supports **Dolby Pro-Logic Surround Sound**, standard stereo, and mono audio. Users can randomly access any section of the disc and use the slow-motion and freeze-frame features during movies. Audio tracks can be programmed for as many as 8 different languages, with graphic subtitles in 32 languages. Some manufacturers such as Toshiba are already providing parental control features in their players. (Users select lockout ratings from G to NC-17.) True to marketing principles, DVD manufacturers express DVD capacities in billion byte quantities where "billion" or "Giga" means the vernacular 1000 x 1000 x 1000, not the more precise binary definition of 1024 x 1024 x 1024 bytes used by your computer. This makes the advertised capacity of a DVD disc sound about 7 percent bigger than it really is; you will not be able to record more than 4.37GB onto a blank disc!

There are three formats for manufacturing and writing DVDs: DVD-R/RW (with a dash), DVD+R/RW (with a plus sign), and DVD-RAM (random access memory). Dual Layer recording allows DVD-R and DVD+R discs to store more data, up to 8.5 Gigabytes per disc, compared with 4.7 Gigabytes for single-layer discs. DVD-R DL (dual layer) was developed for the DVD Forum by the Pioneer Corporation. DVD+R DL (double layer) was developed for the DVD+RW Alliance by Sony.

TIP   *The DVD-R specifications were released after the first-generation DVD-Video specifications, so some older DVD players may not be able to play discs burned to the newer DVD-R specs. If your project will fit on a 3.95GB DVD-R blank, try this media for compatibility with older players.*

Flash or Thumb Drives

These flash memory data storage devices are about the size of a thin cigarette lighter and can be integrated with USB or FireWire interfaces to store from 8 megabytes to several GB of data. They are available in every color of the rainbow, are extremely portable, and, because they have fewer moving parts, are more reliable than disk drives. If you are a student, you can dangle a flash drive on a lanyard around your neck; one for each class. Consisting of a small printed circuit board encased in a sturdy metal or plastic casing with a USB connector covered with a cap, the flash drive is usable, trendy as a status symbol, and convenient to use.

CD-ROM Players

Compact disc read-only memory (CD-ROM) players have become an integral part of the multimedia development workstation and are an important delivery vehicle for large, mass-produced projects. A wide variety of developer utilities, graphic backgrounds, stock photography and sounds, applications, games, reference texts, and educational software are available only on this medium.

CD-ROM players have typically been very slow to access and transmit data (150 KBps, which is the speed required of consumer Red Book Audio CDs), but developments have led to double-, triple-, quadruple-speed, 24x, 48x, and 56x drives designed specifically for computer (not Red Book Audio) use. These faster drives spool up like washing machines on the spin cycle and can be somewhat noisy, especially if the inserted compact disc is not evenly balanced.

CD Recorders

With a compact disc recorder, you can make your own CDs, using special CD-recordable (CD-R) blank optical discs to create a CD in most formats of CD-ROM and CD-Audio (see Chapter 18). Software, such as Roxio's Toast and Easy CD Creator, lets you organize files on your hard disk(s) into a "virtual" structure, and then writes them to the CD in that order. CD-R discs are made differently than normal CDs but can play in any CD-Audio or CD-ROM player. These write-once, enhanced CDs make excellent high-capacity file archives and are used extensively by multimedia developers for pre-mastering and testing CD-ROM projects and titles. Because they have become very inexpensive, they are also used for short-run distribution of finished multimedia projects.

CD-RW

A CD-RW recorder can rewrite 700MB of data to a CD-RW disc about 1000 times. Except for their capability of totally erasing a disc, CD-RWs act similar to CD-Rs and are subject to the same restrictions. Writing sessions must be closed before they can read in a CD-ROM drive or players, and though they can be extended, in most cases they cannot be overwritten. To reuse a CD-RW, you must first blank it.

Input Devices

A great variety of input devices—from the familiar keyboard and handy mouse to touchscreens and voice recognition setups—can be used for the development and delivery of a multimedia project. If you are designing your project for a public kiosk, use a touchscreen. If your project is for a lecturing professor who likes to wander about the classroom, use a remote handheld mouse. If you create a great deal of original computer-rendered art, consider a pressure-sensitive stylus and a drawing tablet.

Keyboards

A keyboard is the most common method of interaction with a computer. Keyboards provide various tactile responses (from firm to mushy) and have various layouts depending upon your computer system and keyboard model. Keyboards are typically rated for at least 50 million cycles (the number of times a key can be pressed before it might suffer breakdown).

The most common keyboard for PCs is the 101 style (which provides 101 keys), although many styles are available with more or fewer special keys, LEDs, and other features, such as a plastic membrane cover for industrial or food-service applications or flexible "ergonomic" styles. Macintosh keyboards connect to the USB port, which manages all forms of user input—from digitizing tablets to mice. Wireless keyboards use low-powered radio or light (infrared) waves to transmit data between devices.

Mice

A mouse is the standard tool for interacting with a graphical user interface (GUI). All Macintosh computers require a mouse; on PCs, mice are not required but recommended. Even though the Windows environment accepts keyboard entry in lieu of mouse point-and-click actions, your multimedia projects should typically be designed with the mouse or touchscreen in mind. The buttons on the mouse provide additional user input, such as pointing and double-clicking to open a document, or the click-and-drag operation, in which the mouse button is pressed and held down to drag (move) an object, or to move to and select an item on a pull-down menu, or to access context-sensitive help. The standard Apple mouse has one button; PC mice may have as many as three.

Trackballs

Trackballs are similar to mice, except that the cursor is moved by using one or more fingers to roll across the top of the ball. The trackball does not need the flat space required by a mouse, which is important in small confined environments and for portable laptop computers. Trackballs have at least two buttons: one for the user to click or double-click, and the other to provide the press-and-hold condition necessary for selecting from menus and dragging objects.

Touchscreens

Touchscreens are monitors that usually have a textured coating across the glass face. This coating is sensitive to pressure and registers the location of the user's finger when it touches the screen. The TouchMate system, which has no coating, actually measures the pitch, roll, and yaw rotation of the monitor when pressed by a finger, and determines how much force was exerted and the location where the force was applied. Other touchscreens use invisible beams of infrared light that crisscross the front of the monitor to calculate where a finger was pressed. Pressing twice on the screen in quick succession simulates the double-click action of a mouse. Touching the screen and dragging the finger, without lifting it, to another location simulates a mouse click-and-drag. A keyboard is sometimes simulated using an on-screen representation so users can input names, numbers, and other text by pressing "keys."

Touchscreens are not recommended for day-to-day computer work, but are excellent for multimedia applications in a kiosk, at a trade show, or in a museum delivery system—anything involving public input and simple tasks. When your project is designed to use a touchscreen, the monitor is the only input device required, so you can secure all other system hardware behind locked doors to prevent theft or tampering.

Magnetic Card Encoders and Readers

Magnetic (mag) card setups are useful when you need an interface for a database application or multimedia project that tracks users. You need both a card encoder and a card reader for this type of interface. The **magnetic card encoder** connects to the computer at a serial port and transfers information to a magnetic strip of tape on the back of the card. The **magnetic card reader** then reads the information encoded on the card. A visitor to a museum, for example, could slide an encoded card through a reader at any exhibit station and be rewarded with a personalized or customized response from an intelligent database or presentation system. French-speaking visitors to a Norwegian museum, for instance, could hear an exhibit described in French. This is a common method for reading credit card information and connecting it to your bank account.

TIP   *When you design a project to use mag cards or pen scanners, always provide immediate feedback to an action by the user, such as a beep response or a displayed message.*

Graphics Tablets

Flat-surface input devices are attached to the computer in the same way as a mouse or trackball. A special pen is used against the pressure-sensitive surface of the tablet to move the cursor. **Graphics tablets** provide substantial control for editing finely detailed graphic elements, a feature very useful to graphic artists and interface designers. Tablets can also be used as input devices for end users: you can design a printed graphic, place it on the surface of the tablet, and let users work with a pen directly on the input surface. On a floor plan, for instance, visitors might draw a track through the hallways and rooms they wish to see and then receive a printed list of things to note along the route. Some tablets are pressure sensitive and are good for drawing: the harder you press the stylus, for example, the wider or darker the line you draw. Graphic artists who try these usually fall prey to Vaughan's One-Way Rule and never return to drawing with a mouse.

Scanners

A scanner may be the most useful piece of equipment you will use in the course of producing a multimedia project. There are flat-bed, handheld, and drum scanners, though the most commonly available are color, flat-bed scanners that provide a resolution of 600 **dots per inch (dpi)** or better. Professional graphics houses may use even higher resolution drum scanners. Handheld scanners can be useful for scanning small images and columns of text, but they may prove inadequate for your multimedia development.

Be aware that scanned images, particularly those at high resolution and in color, demand an extremely large amount of storage space on your hard disk, no matter what instrument is used to do the scanning. Also remember that the final monitor display resolution for your multimedia project will probably be just 72 or 95 dpi—leave the very expensive ultra-high-resolution scanners for the desktop publishers. Most inexpensive flat-bed scanners offer at least 600 dpi resolution, and most allow you to set the scanning resolution.

Scans let you make clear electronic images of existing artwork such as photos, ads, pen drawings, and cartoons, and can save many hours when you are incorporating proprietary art into your application. Scans also can give you a starting point for your own creative diversions.

Optical Character Recognition (OCR) Devices

Scanners enable you to use **optical character recognition (OCR)** software, such as OmniPage from ScanSoft, a division of Nuance Communications (see Figure 9-2), or Recore from Maxsoft-Ocron, an ActiveX programming interface option that allows programmers to create custom applications including web-based OCR application. With OCR software and a scanner, you can convert paper documents into a word processing document on your computer without retyping or rekeying.

Barcode readers are probably the most familiar optical character recognition devices in use today—mostly at markets, shops, and other point-of-purchase locations. Using photo cells and laser beams, barcode readers recognize the numeric characters of the **Universal Product Code** (UPC) that are printed in a pattern of parallel black bars on merchandise labels. With OCR, or **barcoding**, retailers can efficiently process goods in and out of their stores and maintain better inventory control.

An OCR terminal can be of use to a multimedia developer because it recognizes not only printed characters but also handwriting. This facility may be beneficial at a kiosk or in a general education environment where user friendliness is a goal, because there is growing demand for a more personal and less technical interface to data and information.

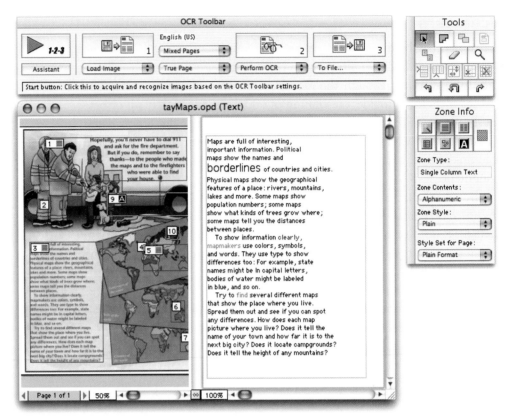

Figure 9-2 Working with a scanner, OCR software can save many hours of rekeying text.

Infrared Remotes

An infrared remote unit lets a user interact with your project while he or she is freely moving about. Remotes work like mice and trackballs, except they use infrared light to direct the cursor and require no cables to communicate. Remote mice work well for a lecture or other presentation in an auditorium or similar environment, when the speaker needs to move around the room.

Voice Recognition Systems

For hands-free interaction with your project, try **voice recognition systems**. These behavioral biometric systems usually provide a unidirectional cardioid, noise-canceling microphone that automatically filters out background noise and learn, to recognize voiceprints. Most voice recognition systems currently available can trigger common menu events such as Save, Open, Quit, and Print, and you can teach the system to recognize other commands that are more specific to your application. Systems available for the Macintosh and Windows environments typically must be taught to recognize individual voices and then be programmed with the appropriate responses to the recognized word or phrase. Dragon's Naturally Speaking takes dictation, translates text to speech, and does command-to-click, a serious aid for people unable to use their hands.

Digital Cameras

Digital cameras use the same CCD technology as video cameras, described in Chapter 8. They capture still images of a given number of pixels (resolution), and the images are stored in the camera's memory to be uploaded later to a computer. The resolution of a digital camera is determined by the number of pixels on the CCD chip, and the higher the Megapixel rating, the higher the resolution of the camera. Images are uploaded from the camera's memory using a serial, parallel, or USB cable, or, alternatively, the camera's memory card is inserted into a PCMCIA reader connected to the computer. Digital cameras are small enough to fit in a cell phone and, in a more complicated manner they can be used in a television studio or spy camera on an orbiting space craft.

Output Hardware

Presentation of the audio and visual components of your multimedia project requires hardware that may or may not be included with the computer itself, such as speakers, amplifiers, monitors, motion video devices, sound recorders and capable storage systems. It goes without saying that the better the equipment is, of course, the better the presentation. There is no greater test of the benefits of good output hardware than to feed the audio output of your computer into an external amplifier system: suddenly the bass sounds become deeper and richer, and even music sampled at low quality may sound acceptable.

TIP   *The quality of your audio recordings is greatly affected by the caliber of your microphone and cables. A unidirectional microphone helps filter out external noise, and good cables help reduce noise emitted from surrounding electronic equipment.*

Audio Devices

All Macintoshes are equipped with an internal speaker and a dedicated sound chip, and they are capable of audio output without additional hardware and/or software. To take advantage of built-in stereo sound, external speakers are required.

Digitizing sound on your Macintosh requires an external microphone and sound editing/recording software. The sound capabilities of both platforms and digitizing software are discussed in detail in Chapter 5.

TIP *Design your project to use many shorter-duration audio files rather than one long file. This simplifies the reaction of your project within your authoring system, and it may also improve performance because you will load shorter segments of sound into RAM at any one time.*

Amplifiers and Speakers

Often the speakers you use during a project's development will not be adequate for its presentation. Speakers with built-in amplifiers or attached to an external amplifier are important when your project will be presented to a large audience or in a noisy setting. Altec Lansing's three-piece amplified speaker system, for example, is designed for multimedia presentations and is small and portable. It includes its own digital signal processing (DSP) circuitry for concert hall effects; it has a mixer for two input sources (the computer's digital output and the CD-ROM player's audio output can be blended); and it uses a subwoofer sensitive to 35 Hz.

WARNING *Always use magnetically shielded speakers to prevent color distortion or damage to nearby monitors.*

Portable Media Players

The portable media player (PMP) is a hard disk- or flash memory-based electronic device that may be used for DVDs, CDs, audio (MP3, WAV, and Ogg Vorbis), video (MPEG, XviD, DivX), digital images (BMP, GIF, JPEG) and other media formats like Sony's PSP game consoles. IPod players by Macintosh are very prevalent among school age people and have become a status symbol. Companies that produce players of various sorts have come up with many "got-to-have" accessory items for each of their players. The downside of some players is that they are of a proprietary nature (controlling what music can be downloaded and played) and do not allow the user to stray from the line of choice they have made without great cost.

Monitors

The monitor you need for development of multimedia projects depends on the type of multimedia application you are creating, as well as what computer you're using. A wide variety of monitors is available for both Macintoshes and PCs. High-end, large-screen graphics monitors and LCD panels are available for both, and they are expensive.

Serious multimedia developers will often attach more than one monitor to their computers, using add-on graphics boards. This is because many authoring systems allow you to work with several open windows at a time, so you can dedicate one monitor to viewing the work you are creating or designing, and you can perform various editing tasks in windows on other monitors that do not block the view of your work. Figure 9-3 illustrates editing windows that overlap a work view when developing with Adobe's authoring environment, Director, on one monitor. Developing in Director is best with at least two monitors, one to view your work, the other to view the Score. A third monitor is often added by Director developers to display the Cast. See Chapter 11 for more about Director. For years, one of the advantages of the Macintosh for making multimedia was that it is very easy to attach multiple monitors for development work. Commencing with Windows 98, PCs can be configured for more than one monitor.

Figure 9-3 Without a second monitor, you will have difficulty editing your project and viewing it at the same time.

Video Devices

No other contemporary message medium has the visual impact of video. With a video digitizing board installed in your computer, you can display a television picture on your monitor. Some boards include a frame-grabber feature for capturing the image and turning it into a color bitmap, which can be saved as a PICT or TIFF file and then used as part of a graphic or a background in your project.

Display of video on any computer platform requires manipulation of an enormous amount of data. When used in conjunction with videodisc players, which give you precise control over the images being viewed, video

First Person

A bunch of us worked on a guided tour project destined for Sun SPARCstations. SPARCstations have large monitors with a screen resolution of 1024x768 pixels, but because we were most proficient with Macintosh graphics tools, we created most of the bitmapped artwork on Macintosh 13-inch, 640x480-pixel RGB monitors. Though the Macintosh software deftly managed the big image sizes, the process was very tiresome to the artists, because the 640x480 monitors provided only a window

onto the larger bitmap. We had to scroll the window back and forth over the larger image to see what we were doing. Dragging and dropping was a horror show.

Finally, we installed a 19-inch monitor and set up a Macintosh with a high-resolution video card. It was better, but there were not enough of them to go around. In the end, about 75 percent of the artwork was done in scrolling windows on the Macintosh, and it turned out great.

Large monitors do not necessarily increase the real estate available to

you for your graphics and information display: 35-inch monitors, or even the 50-foot projection displays common to auditoriums, may still provide just 640x480 pixels of resolution. The large monitors that do effectively increase the real estate also require higher-resolution boards in Macintosh or PC expansion slots. Again, these are expensive.

Always develop your project using the screen resolution of the destination platform.

cards let you place an image into a window on the computer monitor; a second television screen dedicated to video is not required. And video cards typically come with excellent special effects software.

There are many video cards available today. Most of these support various video-in-a-window sizes, identification of source video, setup of play sequences or segments, special effects, frame grabbing, digital moviemaking; and some have built-in television tuners so you can watch your favorite programs in a window while working on other things. Good video greatly enhances your project; poor video will ruin it.

Projectors

When you need to show your material to more viewers than can huddle around a computer monitor, you will need to project it onto a large screen or even a white-painted wall. **Cathode-ray tube (CRT) projectors**, liquid crystal display (LCD) panels, Digital Light Processing (DLP) projectors and Liquid crystal on silicon (LCOS) projectors and (for larger projects) Grating-Light-Valve (GLV) technologies are available. CRT projectors have been around for quite a while—they are the original "big-screen" televisions. They use three separate projection tubes and lenses (red, green, and blue), and the three color channels of light must "converge" accurately on the screen. Setup, focusing, and alignment are important for getting a clear and crisp picture. CRT projectors are compatible with the output of most computers as well as televisions.

LCD panels are portable devices that fit in a briefcase. The panel is placed on the glass surface of a standard overhead projector available in most schools, conference rooms, and meeting halls. While the overhead projector does the projection work, the panel is connected to the computer and provides the image, in thousands of colors and, with active-matrix technology, at speeds that allow full-motion video and animation. Because LCD panels are small, they are popular for on-the-road presentations, often connected to a laptop computer and using a locally available, overhead projector.

More complete LCD projection panels contain a projection lamp and lenses and do not require a separate overhead projector. They typically produce an image brighter and sharper than the simple panel model, but they are somewhat larger and cannot travel in a briefcase.

DLP projectors (it's done with mirrors) use a semiconductor chip arrayed with microscopic mirrors that are laid out in a matrix known as a Digital Micromirror Device (DMD), where each mirror represents one pixel in the projected image. Rapid repositioning of the mirrors reflects light out through the lens or to a heatsink (light dump).

Liquid crystal on silicon (LCOS or LCoS) is a micro-display technology mostly used for projection televisions. It is a reflective technology similar to DLP projectors but it uses liquid crystals instead of individual mirrors.

Grating-Light-Valves (GLVs) compete with high-end CRT projectors and use diffraction of laser (red, green and blue) light using an array of tiny movable ribbons mounted on a silicon base. The GLV uses six ribbons as the defraction gratings for each pixel. The alignment of the gratings is altered by electronic signals. This displacement controls the intensity of the diffracted light. These units are expensive, but the image from a light-valve projector is very bright and color-saturated and can be projected onto screens as wide as ten meters, at any aspect ratio.

Printers

With the advent of reasonably priced color printers, hard-copy output has entered the multimedia scene. From storyboards to presentations to production of collateral marketing material, color printers have become an important part of the multimedia development environment. Color helps clarify concepts, improve understanding and retention of information, and organize complex data. As multimedia designers already know, intelligent use of color is critical to the success of a project. Most printer manufacturers offer a color model—just as all computers once used monochrome monitors but are now color, most printers will become color printers.

The difficult decision when purchasing a printer is choosing between laser, solid ink, dye-sublimation, thermal, liquid inkjet, gel, or toner-based technology. While laser printers offer lower operating costs and higher print quality, they have a higher initial cost (from $300 to well over $1,000 versus inkjet printers at less than $100 to $800 or more). Laser printers are designed for higher volumes and offer larger ink (toner) capacity, providing a cost per page of about 3 cents. Inkjet pages may cost between 8 cents and 15 cents per page for black and white and 15 cents to 50 cents for color, with special paper costing an additional 2 cents to $1.50 per sheet. Some developers believe that a new $40 inkjet printer from e-Bay may not be such a good deal when they soon have to purchase refill ink cartridges for $39.95 each, adding that a drop of super mocha latte spilled on a client's laser printed (hot-fused) report brushes away without running the ink. The cost of color laser printers with on-board networking (see Figure 9-4) continues to fall, making them affordable for a start-up multimedia enterprise where cost-benefit is critical.

Figure 9-4 Ricoh offers specifications and information about its cost-effective color laser printers in a multimedia presentation at http://www.ricoh-usa.com.

Communication Devices

Many multimedia applications are developed in workgroups comprising instructional designers, writers, graphic artists, programmers, and musicians located in the same office space or building. The workgroup members' computers are typically connected on a local area network (LAN). The client's computers, however, may be thousands of miles distant, requiring other methods for good communication.

Communication among workgroup members and with the client is essential to the efficient and accurate completion of your project. Normal U.S. Postal Service mail delivery is too slow to keep pace with most projects; overnight express services are better. And when you need it immediately, an Internet connection is required. If your client and you are both connected to the Internet, a combination of communication by e-mail and by **FTP (File Transfer Protocol)** may be the most cost-effective and efficient solution for both creative development and project management.

In the workplace, use quality equipment and software for your communications setup. The cost—in both time and money—of stable and fast networking will be returned to you.

Modems

Modems can be connected to your computer externally at the serial port or internally as a separate board. Internal modems often include fax capability. Be sure you have a **Hayes compatible modem**. The **Hayes AT standard command set** (named for the ATTENTION command that precedes all other commands) allows you to work with most software communications packages.

Modem speed, measured in baud, is the most important consideration. Because the multimedia files that contain the graphics, audio resources, video samples, and progressive versions of your project are usually large, you need to move as much data as possible in as short a time as possible. Today's standards dictate at least a **V.90** 56 Kbps modem. Compression saves significant transmission time and money, especially over long distance. Today, tens of millions of people use a V.90 modem to connect to the Internet.

Modems modulate and de-modulate analog signals. According to the laws of physics, copper telephone lines and the switching equipment at the phone companies' central offices can handle modulated analog signals up to about 28,000 bps on "clean" lines, so 56 Kbps V.90 depends on hardware-based compression algorithms to crunch the data before sending it, decompressing it upon arrival at the receiving end. If you have already compressed your data into a .sit, .sea, .arc, or .zip file, you may not reap added benefit from the compression because it is difficult to compress an already-compressed file.

First Person

Around midnight, I got a phone call from a client in Europe. His investors were meeting later that day, and he needed the project now, not in two days by DHL courier. Compressed, the code was less than a megabyte. So I went to my office and cranked up the modem, dialed the overseas phone number, and connected. The modem software estimated a total transmission time of 73 minutes, and we started the XMODEM protocols. While the little packets of data were humming out across the continent and an ocean, I made a peanut butter sandwich and kept an eye on the Bytes Remaining counter as it worked its way down in ratchets of 1,024. It was hypnotic.

Annoying spikes and glitches in the phone system had always plagued my modem calls with intermittent transmission failures that required starting over. With about four minutes to go, I began suffering hot flashes and a pounding heart, and found myself riveted to the monitor with head in hands, cheering the system on. "Don't crash now! Just a little more... Pretty please with icing! Nice baby!" All the possible scenarios of disaster paraded in front of me: a shipping calamity in the English channel would cause the transatlantic cable to break at 30 fathoms; a street cleaning truck would take out the electric power pole on the street outside; mice would chew through the antenna leads of a lonely microwave station high in the Colorado Rockies... It all seemed suddenly so fragile. But it made it!

ISDN and DSL

For higher transmission speeds by telephone, you will need to use **Integrated Services Digital Network (ISDN)**, Switched-56, T1, T3, DSL, ATM, or another of the telephone companies' Digital Switched Network services.

ISDN lines offer a 128 Kbps data transfer rate—twice as fast as a 56 Kbps analog modem. ISDN lines (and the required ISDN hardware) are used for Internet access, networking, and audio and video conferencing. These dedicated telephone lines are more expensive than conventional analog or **POTS (plain old telephone service)** lines, so analyze your costs and benefits carefully before upgrading.

Newer and faster **Digital Subscriber Line (DSL)** technology using a dedicated copper line has overtaken ISDN in popularity. DSL uses signal frequencies higher than those used by voice or fax. When a DSL filter is connected to your phone jack, it splits the data (Internet) traffic from voice (phone) traffic, so voice traffic (talking on the phone and fax signals) goes to the phone or the fax machine while data traffic (surfing the Web, downloading large files or photos) goes to your computer. You can do both at the same time.

Cable Modems

In November 1995, a consortium of cable television industry leaders announced agreement with key equipment manufacturers for specifying some of the technical ways cable networks and data equipment talk with one another. 3COM, AT&T, COM21, General Instrument, Hewlett Packard, Hughes, Hybrid, IBM, Intel, LANCity, MicroUnity, Motorola, Nortel, Panasonic, Scientific Atlanta, Terrayon, Toshiba, and Zenith currently supply cable modem products. While the cable television networks cross 97 percent of property lines in North America, each local cable operator may use different equipment, wires, and software, and cable modems still remain somewhat experimental. This was a call for interoperability standards.

Cable modems operate at speeds 100 to 1,000 times faster than a telephone modem, receiving data at up to 10 Mbps and sending data at speeds between 2 Mbps and 10 Mbps. They can provide not only high-bandwidth Internet access but also streaming audio and video for television viewing. Most will connect to computers with 10BaseT Ethernet connectors.

Cable modems usually send and receive data asymmetrically—in that they receive more (faster) than they send (slower). In the downstream direction from provider to user, the data is modulated and placed on a common 6 MHz television carrier, somewhere between 42 MHz and 750 MHz. The upstream channel, or reverse path, from the user back to the provider is more difficult to engineer because cable is a noisy environment—with interference from HAM radio, CB radio, home appliances, loose connectors, and poor home installation. All this noise accumulates, and the overall noise increases as the signal travels upstream in the local cable network's branching tree structure, where signals from one home become mixed with the signals of hundreds, then thousands of other homes.

Fiber optic cable, a thin, transparent glass fiber that transmits light, is commonly used in telecommunication systems. It can sustain transmission distances of 80 to 140 km (50 to 87 miles) between regenerations of signal. Spreading optical pulses traveling over distance cause an effect known as dispersion that is effected by the bandwidth, quality of glass fiber, and length of travel. The signal (to convey quality to the end receptor) needs to be boosted along the way at intervals that correspond to the variables present.

Chapter 9 Review

■ Chapter Summary

For your review, here's a summary of the important concepts discussed in this chapter.

Define the two computer platforms most often used in multimedia and how their capabilities affect development and deployment choices

- Macintosh computers come ready to develop multimedia, with high-quality graphics and sound capabilities.

- A Windows computer is a collection of parts that are tied together by the requirements of the Windows operating system.

- The Multimedia PC Marketing Council was established to develop a set of specifications that would allow Windows to deliver a dependable multimedia experience.

Discuss how computers communicate and what protocols and tools are available to aid cross-platform communications

- Local area networks (LANs) connect nearby workstations, and allow direct communication and sharing of peripheral resources.

- Wide area networks (WANs) connect distant workstations and are expensive to install and maintain.

- Ethernet is a method for connecting computers. Client/server software enables the computers to speak with each other and pass files back and forth.

Describe how storage devices are connected to a computer, what storage choices are available, and the benefits and drawbacks of each type

- The Small Computer System Interface (SCSI) lets you add as many as 7 peripherals on one chain; Ultra SCSI allows up to 32 devices.

- Integrated Drive Electronics (IDE) connections, also called Advanced Technology Attachment (ATA) connections, connect up to four peripherals mounted inside the PC.

- Allocate enough storage for saving and archiving working files used during production; at least one backup of project files, and a second backup stored off-site.

- Install as much RAM as you can afford. A fast processor without enough RAM may waste processor cycles while it swaps needed portions of program code into and out of memory.

- DVD provides sharper and more detailed video resolution, Digital Surround Sound, six discrete audio channels, multiple audio and video tracks; discs provide random access, slow-motion, and freeze-frame capabilities.

- With a compact disc recorder, you can make your own CDs on blank optical discs in most formats of CD-ROM and CD-Audio.

Describe the various input devices available for personal computers and how they may be used in multimedia production and delivery

- Trackballs are useful in small confined environments and for portable laptop computers.

- Touchscreens have a pressure-sensitive textured coating that registers the location of the user's finger when it touches the screen, and are excellent for projects involving public input and simple tasks.

- Magnetic (mag) card readers are useful when you need an interface for a database application or multimedia project that tracks users.

- Graphics tablets use a special pen against the pressure-sensitive tablet surface to move the cursor.

- A scanner may be the most useful piece of equipment you will use in the course of producing a multimedia project. Scanners let you make electronic images of existing artwork, and can save many hours getting images into your application. When scanning, remember that your multimedia project will probably be displayed at 72 or 95 dpi.

- With OCR software and a scanner, you can convert paper documents into a word processing document on your computer, saving many hours of rekeying text. An OCR terminal can also recognize handwriting.

- An infrared remote mouse lets a user interact with your project while he or she is freely moving about.

- Voice recognition systems facilitate hands-free interaction with your project.

- Digital cameras capture still images of a given number of pixels (resolution), and the images are stored in the camera's memory to be uploaded later to a computer.

Describe the various output devices available for personal computers and how they may be used in multimedia production and delivery

- For best performance, design your project to use many shorter-duration audio files rather than one long file.

- Use a quality microphone and cables when recording.

- When your project will be presented to a large audience or in a noisy setting, use speakers with built-in amplifiers or attached to an external amplifier.

- Always use magnetically shielded speakers to prevent color distortion or damage to nearby monitors.

- Multiple monitors allow you to view the project on one while viewing various editing palettes on another. This has always been easy on the Macintosh, and has become available on PCs since Windows 98.

- With a video digitizing board installed in your computer, you can display a television picture on your monitor.

- Good video greatly enhances your project; poor video will ruin it.

- LCD panels are portable devices that fit in a briefcase. The panel is placed on the glass surface of a standard overhead projector available in most schools, conference rooms, and meeting halls.

- From storyboards to presentations to production of collateral marketing material, color printers have become an important part of the multimedia development environment.

Describe the various communications devices available for personal computers and how they may be used in multimedia production and delivery

- Communication among workgroup members and with the client is essential to the efficient and accurate completion of your project.

- Workgroup computers typically are connected on a local area network (LAN).

- Modems provide connectivity through standard phone lines, at up to 56 Kbps and more. Select a Hayes-compatible modem.

- ISDN lines, available for several years, provide 128 Kbps data transfer rate, and represent the low end of telephone companies' Digital Switched Network services.

- Cable modems provide Internet access at speeds faster than a telephone modem, over the same cable network that supplies the television signal; however, due to noise in the system, sending rates may be much slower than receiving rates.

Key Terms

Advanced Technology Attachment (ATA) *(235)*
barcoding *(245)*
cat-5 cable *(231)*
cathode-ray tube (CRT) projectors *(250)*
client/server software *(232)*
compact disc read-only memory (CD-ROM) *(241)*
Digital Subscriber Line (DSL) *(254)*
Digital Versatile Disc (DVD) *(240)*
Dolby AC-3 Digital Surround Sound *(240)*
Dolby Pro-Logic Surround Sound *(241)*
dots per inch (dpi) *(245)*
DVD-ROM *(240)*
DVD-Video *(240)*
Ethernet *(232)*
Fast SCSI *(235)*

Fast/Wide SCSI *(235)*
FTP (File Transfer Protocol) *(253)*
graphics tablet *(244)*
Hayes AT standard command set *(253)*
Hayes compatible modem *(253)*
Integrated Drive Electronics (IDE) *(235)*
Integrated Services Digital Network (ISDN) *(254)*
Jaz *(239)*
LCD (liquid crystal display) panels *(251)*
local area networks (LANs) *(230)*
magnetic card encoder *(244)*
magnetic card reader *(244)*
magneto-optical (MO) drive *(239)*
MPC *(230)*
optical character recognition (OCR) *(245)*
optical read-only memory (OROM) *(238)*

plain old telephone service (POTS) *(254)*
programmable ROM (EPROM) *(238)*
random access memory (RAM) *(237)*
read-only memory (ROM) *(238)*
SCSI-2 *(235)*
SCSI-3 (Ultra SCSI) *(235)*
Small Computer System Interface (SCSI) *(233)*
Syquest *(239)*
TCP/IP *(232)*
touchscreen *(243)*
trackball *(243)*
Universal Product Code *(245)*
V.90 *(253)*
voice recognition systems *(246)*
wide area network (WAN) *(230)*
Wide SCSI *(235)*
Zip *(239)*

Key Term Quiz

1. A network of workstations located within a short distance of one another that allows direct communication and sharing of peripheral resources such as file servers, printers, scanners, and network modems is called a(n) _____.

2. A network of workstations spanning great distances, typically set up and managed by large corporations and institutions for their own use, is known as a _____.

3. For the best network connections, be sure to use _____.

4. You can connect Windows and Macintosh computers using the _____ networking protocol.

5. To enable computers to speak with each other and pass files back and forth over a network, you will need to use _____ .

6. The interface system that came installed in all Macs was the _____.

7. The type of interface system that allows a computer to control a master/slave pair of drives is called _____.

8. The type of memory used by a computer to run several programs at the same time is called _____.

9. The type of memory that is not erased when power is shut off to it is called _____.

10. The type of memory that allows changes to be made that are not forgotten is called _____.

■ Multiple Choice Quiz

1. SCSI stands for:
   a. Server-Client Storage Interface
   b. Small Computer System Interface
   c. Serial Compression Schematic Interface
   d. Simple Communication Source Interface
   e. System-Centric Spanning Interface

2. How many IDE controllers can a PC motherboard support?
   a. 1
   b. 2
   c. 8
   d. 32
   e. unlimited

3. When you turn off the power to this type of storage, any data stored in it is lost.
   a. CD-ROM
   b. ROM
   c. OROM
   d. EPROM
   e. RAM

4. Which of these is *not* a type of removable storage medium?
   a. Zip
   b. Jaz
   c. Syquest
   d. ISDN
   e. magneto-optical

5. A hard disk is actually:
   a. a stack of optical platters read and written to by laser
   b. a static memory device; "disk" is a throwback to when they actually rotated
   c. a stack of hard metal platters coated with magnetically sensitive material
   d. a stack of flexible Mylar discs coated with a ferrous oxide magnetic coating
   e. a special type of Frisbee favored by programmers

6. DVD-Video differs from DVD-ROM in that:
   a. DVD-Video data is compressed at a much higher rate than DVD-ROM

   b. DVD-Video is playable only on set-top units; DVD-ROM only in computers
   c. DVD-Video is encrypted to prohibit piracy; DVD-ROM is not
   d. DVD-Video holds about half the data that DVD-ROM does
   e. there is no difference; they are just distinguished for marketing purposes

7. Which of these is *not* part of the DVD video specification?
   a. 720 pixels per horizontal line
   b. multiple audio tracks
   c. multiple text tracks
   d. set-top gaming support
   e. Dolby AC-3 Digital Surround Sound

8. If your working space is limited, or for laptop computers, consider using a:
   a. touchscreen
   b. graphics tablet
   c. trackball
   d. magnetic card reader
   e. barcode reader

9. A touchscreen is recommended for:
   a. pressure-sensitive drawing and painting
   b. projects that track users
   c. day-to-day computer work
   d. programs involving public input and simple tasks
   e. all of the above

10. A graphics tablet is recommended for:
    a. drawing and painting
    b. work requiring pressure-sensitive input
    c. projects requiring direct user input on a diagram
    d. graphic artists who want fine control over their tools
    e. all of the above

11. A barcode reader can:
    a. scan graphics into a computer
    b. read Universal Product Code patterns
    c. provide pressure-sensitive input

d. recognize spoken words when trained

e. all of the above

12. The "AT" in the Hayes AT standard command set was so named:

a. because a Hayes modem came standard with the "AT" PC computer specification

b. for the AppleTalk communications protocol that it uses

c. because the @ (at) symbol is the standard conjunction between the user ID and the domain (such as in most e-mail addresses)

d. because it established the Asynchronous Transfer mode

e. for the ATTENTION command that precedes all other commands

13. The maximum modulated analog signal that copper telephone lines and the switching equipment at the phone companies' central offices can handle is:

a. 28,000 bps

b. 56,000 bps

c. 128,000 bps

d. 256,000 bps

e. There is no theoretical maximum limit.

14. DSL stands for:

a. Data-Synchronous Link

b. Dynamic Streaming Language

c. Double-Sector Logic

d. Digital Subscriber Line

e. Domain Sampling List

15. A cable modem upstream channel's data rate is:

a. limited by FCC licensing requirements

b. slower than downstream because cable is a noisy environment

c. slower than downstream because most systems do not incorporate enough duplexing transponders

d. faster than downstream because the downstream traffic is much heavier

e. faster than downstream because the data is not mixed with video signals

■ Essay Quiz

1. Discuss the Macintosh and PC operating systems from the point of view of multimedia development and deployment. Why would you develop on one operating system when the majority of users might be using another system?

2. List the various protocols and settings for networking personal computers. Why is cross-platform communications important in a multimedia development environment?

3. List the types of fixed and removable storage devices available for multimedia, and discuss the strengths and weaknesses of each one.

4. You have been assigned to develop a complex multimedia kiosk for an auto club that will allow users with an account to enter a start point and an ending point, and have a map printed out. What input devices could be used to identify the user? What input devices could be used to enter start and end locations? Could one device do both functions? What about printing out the maps?

5. List the various methods of connecting a computer with the "world," and discuss the benefits and drawbacks of each.

Lab Projects

■ Project 9.1

Diagram a network of three workstations; designate one a scanning workstation, one a graphics development workstation, and one a testing workstation. Include at least two input devices and two storage devices for each one, making logical choices (for example, backups, testing, etc.). Add a server for backup, a printer, and a connection to the Internet to your diagram.

■ Project 9.2

Locate four separate computers in different environments. Diagram their components, including all input devices, output devices, and network/Internet connections. What devices do they all have in common? Is there a "standard" computer? Is there a "standard" for most computers today? Document your findings.

■ Project 9.3

Locate three DVD-Videos. If possible, select DVDs of something besides feature films, making sure they include "bonus" materials. What extra materials are included? What materials are only available on a PC? Why are these materials not available on the television? Document your findings.

■ Project 9.4

Most input and output devices have a certain resolution. Locate the specifications on the Web for a CRT monitor, a LCD monitor, a scanner, and a digital camera. Note the manufacturer, model, and resolution for each one. Document your findings.

CHAPTER 10

Basic Software Tools

THE basic tool set for building multimedia projects contains one or more authoring systems and various editing applications for text, images, sounds, and motion video. A few additional applications are also useful for capturing images from the screen, translating file formats, and moving files among computers when you are part of a team—these are tools for the housekeeping tasks that make your creative and production life easier. Special tools for delivering multimedia to the Internet and World Wide Web are discussed in Chapter 13.

The software in your multimedia toolkit—and your skill at using it—determines what kind of multimedia work you can do and how fine and fancy you can render it. Making good multimedia means picking a successful route through the software swamp. Alligators and learning curves can rise up out of this swamp to nip you in the knees.

Keep your tools sharp by upgrading them when new software and features become available, by thoroughly studying and learning each tool, by reading tips and tricks in the computer magazines and trade press, by keeping an eye on the conversations and **FAQs (Frequently Asked Questions)** files online and in Internet newsgroups, and by observing the practices and products of other multimedia developers. Remember, each new tool has a learning curve.

TIP *Always fill out the registration card for your new software and return it to the vendor, or register online. If the vendor pays attention to product marketing, you will frequently receive upgrade offers, special newsletters, and e-mails with helpful information.*

The tools used for creating and editing multimedia elements on both Windows and Macintosh platforms support the authoring systems described in Chapter 11. They do paint and image processing, image editing, drawing and illustration, 3-D and CAD, OCR and text editing, sound recording and editing, video and moviemaking, and various utilitarian housekeeping tasks.

In this chapter, you will learn how to:

- Understand common programs that are used to handle text in multimedia projects and determine when you should use them

- Determine which graphics programs to use in various multimedia projects, including draw, paint, and 3-D programs

- Understand how graphics and animation programs are used in multimedia projects and discuss their capabilities

- Select appropriate formats and architectures for integrating video on computers

- Identify tools used to handle video in multimedia projects and discuss their capabilities, as well as how they capture, process, and compress video

First Person

When I left graduate school, I joined the Carpenters Union and built highway bridges, apartment houses, and fine custom homes. The wholesale tool supply store that catered to the trade had one wall covered with more than a hundred different hammers—some for nailing big nails, some for tiny upholstery tacks, some for metal work, others with a hatchet on one side for shingles, or with a waffled striking head that would drive slick and wet nails under the roughest conditions. They all came in differ-

ent weights and handle lengths and shapes. I tested a few framing hammers and chose a 24-ounce waffle-head framing hammer that felt good. With it, I could drive big 16d nails in a single stroke. It had a wicked curved handle. It was a Vaughan hammer.

Next day at noon, the job boss took me aside and quietly told me that he limited hammer weight to 22 ounces, because the older guys on the crew couldn't keep up. My hammer was illegal, and if he saw it the next day, I'd be sent back to the hiring hall. "Sorry," I said, "jeez, I didn't know." He let me leave early so I could get to the tool store before it closed.

In producing multimedia, no tool is illegal. You should use the best tools that fit your talent, needs, and budget.

Text Editing and Word Processing Tools

A **word processor** is usually the first software tool computer users learn. From letters, invoices, and storyboards to project content, your word processor may also be your most often used tool, as you design and build a multimedia project. The better your **keyboarding** or typing skills, the easier and more efficient your multimedia day-to-day life will be.

Typically, an office or workgroup will choose a single word processor to share documents in a standard format. And most often, that word processor comes bundled in an **office suite** that might include spreadsheet, database, e-mail, web browser, and presentation applications.

Word processors such as Microsoft Word and WordPerfect are powerful applications that include spell checkers, table formatters, thesauruses, and prebuilt templates for letters, resumes, purchase orders, and other common documents. In many word processors, you can actually embed multimedia elements such as sounds, images, and video. Luckily, the population of single-finger typists is decreasing over time as children are taught keyboarding skills in conjunction with computer lab programs in their schools.

OCR Software

Often you will have printed matter and other text to incorporate into your project, but no electronic text file. With **optical character recognition (OCR)** software, a flat-bed scanner, and your computer, you can save many hours of rekeying printed words, and get the job done faster and more accurately than a roomful of typists.

OCR software turns bitmapped characters into electronically recognizable ASCII text. A scanner is typically used to create the bitmap. Then the software breaks the bitmap into chunks according to whether it contains text or graphics, by examining the texture and density of areas of the bitmap and by detecting edges. The text areas of the image are then converted to ASCII characters using probability and expert system algorithms. Most OCR applications claim about 99 percent accuracy when reading 8- to 36-point printed characters at 300 dpi and can reach processing speeds of about 150 characters per second. These programs do, however, have difficulty recognizing poor copies of originals where the edges of characters have bled; these and poorly received faxes in small print may yield more recognition errors than it is worthwhile to correct after the attempted recognition.

Figure 9-2 in Chapter 9 shows a magazine article in the process of bitmap-to-character conversion by OmniPage Pro from Caere. Notice the small box that displays an image of the actual section of the 300 dpi bitmap currently being analyzed. With this software, the formatting and layout of the original document can be recognized and imported into Microsoft Word with styles that maintain bolding and font size.

Painting and Drawing Tools

Painting and drawing tools, as well as 3-D modelers, are perhaps the most important items in your toolkit because, of all the multimedia elements, the graphical impact of your project will likely have the greatest influence on the end user. If your artwork is amateurish, or flat and uninteresting, both you and your users will be disappointed. Look in Chapters 14 and 16 for tips on designing effective graphical screens and in Chapter 6 for more about computer graphics.

Painting software, such as Photoshop, Fireworks, and Painter, is dedicated to producing crafted bitmap images. **Drawing software**, such as CorelDraw, FreeHand, Illustrator, Designer, and Canvas, is dedicated to producing vector-based line art easily printed to paper at high resolution.

Some software applications combine drawing and painting capabilities, but many authoring systems can import only bitmapped images. The differences between painting and drawing (that is, between bitmapped and drawn images) are described in Chapter 6. Typically, bitmapped images provide the greatest choice and power to the artist for rendering fine detail and effects, and today bitmaps are used in multimedia more often than drawn objects. Some vector-based packages such as Macromedia's Flash are aimed at reducing file download times on the Web, and may contain both bitmaps and drawn art.

Look for these features in a drawing or painting package:

- An intuitive graphical user interface with pull-down menus, status bars, palette control, and dialog boxes for quick, logical selection
- Scalable dimensions, so you can resize, stretch, and distort both large and small bitmaps
- Paint tools to create geometric shapes, from squares to circles and from curves to complex polygons
- Ability to pour a color, pattern, or gradient into any area
- Ability to paint with patterns and clip art
- Customizable pen and brush shapes and sizes
- Eyedropper tool that samples colors
- Autotrace tool that turns bitmap shapes into vector-based outlines
- Support for scalable text fonts and drop shadows
- Multiple undo capabilities, to let you try again
- History function for redoing effects, drawings, and text
- Property inspector
- Screen capture facility
- Painting features such as smoothing coarse-edged objects into the background with anti-aliasing (see illustration); airbrushing in variable sizes, shapes, densities, and patterns; washing colors in gradients; blending; and masking.

Not Anti-Aliased   Anti-Aliased

- Support for third-party special-effect plug-ins
- Object and layering capabilities that allow you to treat separate elements independently
- Zooming, for magnified pixel editing
- All common color depths: 1-, 4-, 8-, and 16-, 24-, or 32-bit color, and gray-scale
- Good color management and dithering capability among color depths using various color models such as RGB, HSB, and CMYK
- Good palette management when in 8-bit mode
- Good file importing and exporting capability for image formats such as PIC, GIF, TGA, TIF, PNG, WMF, JPG, PCX, EPS, PTN, and BMP

If you are new to multimedia and to these tools, you should take time to examine more than one graphics software package. Find someone who is already familiar with graphics applications. You will spend many days learning to use your painting and drawing software, and if it does not fit you and your needs, you will be unhappy. Many artists learn to use a single, powerful tool well.

First Person

During the early 1980s, I founded an accredited maritime school at Pier 66 in San Francisco, where we offered courses in everything from high-tech composite plastics and welding to Rules of the Road and celestial navigation. We also ran several marine trade certification programs. When I talked with Ford, General Motors, Cummins, and Caterpillar about setting up a course for marine diesel mechanics, I was surprised at their competitive interest in supporting the program. It turned out that a widely publicized survey had shown that a mechanic trained to work on a particular brand of engine would stick with it for life, loyally recommending and supporting that brand.

The same holds true for software. By the time you master an application, you have spent many hours on its learning curve. You will likely stay with that product and its upgrade path rather than change to another.

3-D Modeling and Animation Tools

3-D modeling software has increasingly entered the mainstream of graphic design as its ease of use improves. As a result, the graphic production values and expectations for multimedia projects have risen. With 3-D modeling software, objects rendered in perspective appear more realistic; you can create stunning scenes and wander through them, choosing just the right lighting and perspective for your final rendered image. Powerful modeling packages such as AutoDesk's Maya, Strata 3D, and Avid's SoftImage are also bundled with assortments of prerendered 3-D clip art objects such as people, furniture, buildings, cars, airplanes, trees, and plants. Specialized applications for creating and animating 3-D text are discussed in Chapter 7. Important for multimedia developers, many 3-D modeling applications also include export features enabling you to save a moving view or journey through your scene as a QuickTime or MPEG file. Figure 10-1 shows a simple architectural floor plan rendered to 3-D perspective by VectorWorks.

Each rendered 3-D image takes from a few seconds to a few hours to complete, depending upon the complexity of the drawing and the number of drawn objects included in it (see Chapter 7 for more about rendering). If you are making a complex walkthrough or flyby, plan to set aside many hours of rendering time on your computer.

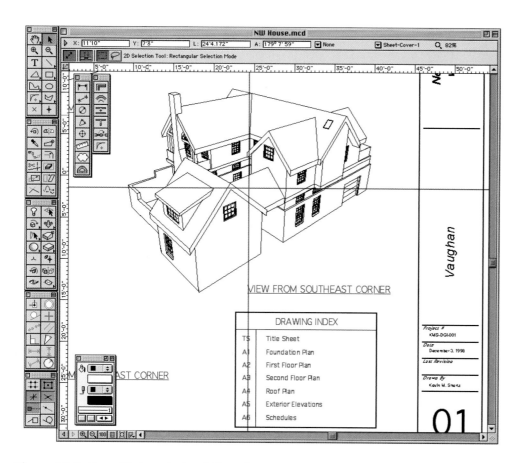

Figure 10-1 VectorWorks and other CAD applications can translate 2-D floor plans into 3-D perspective drawings with lighting and shadows

---

TIP *If there are small errors or things you would like to change in a rendered movie sequence, it may take less time to edit each frame of the affected sequence by hand, using an image-editing program, rather than re-rendering the corrected original.*

A good 3-D modeling tool should include the following features:

- Multiple windows that allow you to view your model in each dimension, from the camera's perspective, and in a rendered preview
- Ability to drag and drop primitive shapes into a scene
- Ability to create and sculpt organic objects from scratch
- Lathe and extrude features
- Color and texture mapping
- Ability to add realistic effects such as transparency, shadowing, and fog

- Ability to add spot, local, and global lights, to place them anywhere, and manipulate them for special lighting effects
- Unlimited cameras with focal length control
- Ability to draw spline-based paths for animation

WARNING *3-D imaging programs require speedy computers with lots of memory, and the learning curve is steep when you enter this world of nurbs, splines, and bump maps.*

Image-Editing Tools

Image-editing applications are specialized and powerful tools for enhancing and retouching existing bitmapped images. These applications also provide many of the features and tools of painting and drawing programs and can be used to create images from scratch as well as images digitized from scanners, video frame-grabbers, digital cameras, clip art files, or original artwork files created with a painting or drawing package.

TIP *If you want to print an image to a 300 dpi printer for collateral reports and attractive print-matter icons, work with the image in the image-editing application at 300 dpi (every pixel will be a very fine laser printer dot). Then, save your work as a PICT, TIFF, or BMP file and import it into your word processor. The printed result is a finely detailed image at a high resolution.*

Here are some features typical of image-editing applications and of interest to multimedia developers:

- Multiple windows that provide views of more than one image at a time
- Conversion of major image-data types and industry-standard file formats
- Direct inputs of images from scanner and video sources
- Employment of a virtual memory scheme that uses hard disk space as RAM for images that require large amounts of memory
- Capable selection tools, such as rectangles, lassos, and magic wands, for selecting portions of a bitmap
- Image and balance controls for brightness, contrast, and color balance
- Good masking features
- Multiple undo and restore features
- Anti-aliasing capability, and sharpening and smoothing controls
- Color-mapping controls for precise adjustment of color balance

- Tools for retouching, blurring, sharpening, lightening, darkening, smudging, and tinting

- Geometric transformations such as flip, skew, rotate, and distort, and perspective changes

- Ability to resample and resize an image

- 24-bit color, 8- or 4-bit indexed color, 8-bit gray-scale, black-and-white, and customizable color palettes

- Ability to create images from scratch, using line, rectangle, square, circle, ellipse, polygon, airbrush, paintbrush, pencil, and eraser tools, with customizable brush shapes and user-definable bucket and gradient fills

- Multiple typefaces, styles, and sizes, and type manipulation and masking routines

- **Filters** for special effects, such as crystallize, dry brush, emboss, facet, fresco, graphic pen, mosaic, pixelize, poster, ripple, smooth, splatter, stucco, twirl, watercolor, wave, and wind

- Support for third-party special-effect plug-ins

- Ability to design in layers that can be combined, hidden, and reordered

Plug-Ins

Image-editing programs usually support powerful **plug-ins** available from third-party developers that allow you to warp, twist, shadow, cut, diffuse, and otherwise "filter" your images for special visual effects. Vertigo's HotTEXT lets you turn text into 3-D objects. EyeCandy from AlienSkin Software offers a comprehensive set of filters. (Figure 10-2*a* shows a Corona filter from AlienSkin in action.) Kai's Power Tools (KPT) from Corel offers many special effects and has powerful built-in algorithms for making fractal images. In Figure 10-2*b* worms are added to an image using Gel.

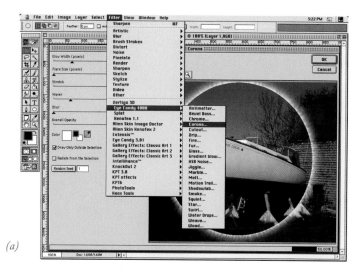

(a)

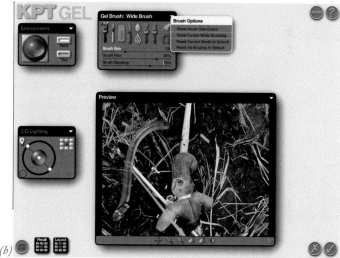

(b)

(c)

Figure 10-2 Cutouts, shadows, special brush effects, and a myriad of interesting visual changes are easy to do with plug-in filters

The PhotoTools suite from Extensis lets you quickly add drop shadows, bevels, glows, and embossing effects (see Figure 10-2c). The special effects available in plug-ins make image-editing fun!

Sound Editing Tools

Sound editing tools for both digitized and MIDI sound let you see music as well as hear it. By drawing a representation of a sound in fine increments, whether a score or a waveform, you can cut, copy, paste, and otherwise edit segments of it with great precision—something impossible to do in real-time (that is, with the music playing). The basics of computerized sound for both the Macintosh and Windows environments are discussed in Chapter 5.

System sounds are shipped with both Macintosh and Windows systems, and they are available as soon as you install the operating system. System sounds are the beeps used to indicate an error, warning, or special user activity. Using sound editing software, you can make your own sound effects and install them as system beeps, to the delight (or perhaps dismay) of colleagues and neighbors. You will need to install software for editing digital sounds.

Although you can usually incorporate MIDI sound files into your multimedia project without learning any special skills, using editing tools to make your own MIDI files requires that you understand the way music is sequenced, scored, and published. You need to know about tempos, clefs, notations, keys, and instruments. And you will need a MIDI synthesizer or device connected to your computer. Many MIDI applications provide both sequencing and notation capabilities, and some let you edit both digital audio and MIDI within the same application.

Animation, Video, and Digital Movie Tools

Animations and digital video movies are sequences of bitmapped graphic scenes (**frames**), rapidly played back. But animations can also be made within the authoring system by rapidly changing the location of objects, or **sprites**, to generate an appearance of motion. Most authoring tools adopt either a frame- or object-oriented approach to animation, but rarely both.

Moviemaking tools typically take advantage of QuickTime for Macintosh and Windows and **Microsoft Video for Windows**, also known as **Audio Video Interleaved (AVI)**, and let you create, edit, and present digitized motion video segments, usually in a small window in your project.

To make movies from video, you may need special hardware to convert the analog video signal to digital data. Macs and PCs with FireWire

(IEEE 1394) ports can import digital video directly from digital camcorders. Moviemaking tools such as Premiere, Final Cut Pro, VideoShop, and MediaStudio Pro let you edit and assemble video clips captured from camera, tape, other digitized movie segments, animations, scanned images, and from digitized audio or MIDI files. The completed clip, often with added transition and visual effects, can then be played back—either stand-alone or windowed within your project.

Video Formats

Formats and systems for storing and playing digitized video to and from disk files are available with QuickTime and AVI. Both systems depend on special algorithms that control the amount of information per video frame that is sent to the screen, as well as the rate at which new frames are displayed. Both provide a methodology for interleaving, or blending, audio data with video and other data so that sound remains synchronized with the video. And both technologies allow data to stream from disk into memory in a buffered and organized manner. **DVD (Digital Versatile Disc)** is a *hardware* format defining a very dense, two-layered disc that uses laser light and, in the case of recordable discs, heat to store and read digital information. The digital information or *software* on a DVD is typically **multiplexed** audio, image, text, and video data optimized for motion picture display using MPEG encoding.

QuickTime is an organizer of time-related data in many forms. Classic videotape involves a video track with two tracks of (stereo) audio; QuickTime is a multitrack recorder in which you can have an almost unlimited range of tracks. Digitized video, digitized sound, computer animations, MIDI data, external devices such as CD-ROM players and hard disks, and even the potential for interactive command systems are all supported by the QuickTime format. With QuickTime, you can have a movie with five different available languages, titles, MIDI cue tracks, or the potential for interactive commands.

QuickTime for Windows and Macintosh

The heart of QuickTime is a software-based **architecture** for seamlessly integrating sound, text, animation, and video (data that changes over time) on Macintosh and Windows platforms. QuickTime is also used to deliver multimedia to the World Wide Web as a plug-in for Netscape and Internet Explorer. On the Web, QuickTime can deliver 3-D animation, real-time special effects, virtual reality, and streaming video and audio. QuickTime is discussed in this chapter about software tools because, while it is not an "authoring tool," nor a video, image, sound, or text editor, its role as a powerful cross-platform integrator of multimedia objects and formats makes it a tool upon which multimedia developers depend.

QuickTime Building Blocks

Three elements make up QuickTime:

- QuickTime movie file format
- QuickTime Media Abstraction Layer
- QuickTime media services

The movie file format is a container that provides a standard method for storing video, audio, and even text descriptions about a media composition. The **Media Abstraction Layer** describes how your computer should access the media that is included in the QuickTime movie. The media services part of QuickTime not only has built-in support for over 35 media file formats, including most major video, still image, audio, animation, and MIDI formats, but also allows developers to plug in their own new or custom media formats. Remember, QuickTime is an architecture, a system for multimedia delivery, and is extensible.

QuickTime Pro is a necessary upgrade to the free QuickTime package so you can do more than simply play back movies. The upgrade contains two applications. **Movie Player** (see Figure 10-3) lets you import and combine over 30 different file formats. You can compress them into deliverable multimedia projects using the Sorenson Video and QDesign audio compressors so they will stream from any Internet-ready web server. With built-in filters in Movie Player, you can adjust colors, contrast, and brightness, and you can apply special effects to your composition, such as film noise and edge detection. The **Picture Viewer** application is used for viewing and converting still images among many standard image-file formats, including Photoshop's native format.

Figure 10-3 QuickTime's Movie Player and the Windows Media Player can play back video clips.

QuickTime includes built-in support for ten different media types (video, audio, text, timecode, music/MIDI, sprite/animation, tween, MPEG, VR, 3-D) and offers a comprehensive set of "services," such as:

- Timing and synchronization
- Audio and image data compression and decompression
- Image blitting, format conversion, scaling, composition, and transcoding
- Audio mixing, sample rate conversion, and format conversion
- Audio and video effects and transitions
- Synchronized storage read and write
- Media capture
- Media import and export
- Standard user interface elements, such as movie controllers, media pre-viewers, and media capture dialogs

QuickTime Embedded Commands for HTML

When delivering QuickTime projects on the World Wide Web, you can embed powerful commands into your HTML documents that control and fine-tune the display of your QuickTime file:

- **AUTOPLAY** starts a movie playing automatically.
- **BGCOLOR** sets a background color for the movie display.
- **CACHE** indicates whether the movie should be cached (Netscape Navigator 3.0 or later).
- **CONTROLLER** specifies whether to display the QuickTime movie controller bar.
- **HEIGHT** and **WIDTH** specify size of the movie in web pages.
- **HIDDEN** allows sound-only movies to play in the background without affecting the look of a web page.
- **HREF** indicates which URL to link to when the movie is clicked.
- **LOOP** loops movie playback automatically.
- **SCALE** scales the movie display automatically.
- **TARGET** provides a frame target for the URL specified in an HREF tag.
- **VOLUME** sets the default playback volume.

    In addition, QuickTime has the following VR commands:

- **CORRECTION** specifies an image correction mode.
- **FOV** sets the initial field-of-view angle.

- **NODE** sets the initial node.
- **PAN** sets the initial pan angle.
- **TILT** sets the initial tilt angle.

Microsoft Video for Windows

Audio/Video Interleaved (AVI) is a Microsoft-developed format for playing full-motion interleaved video and audio sequences in Windows, without specialized hardware. Video data is interleaved with audio data within the file that contains the motion sequence, so the audio portion of the movie remains synchronized to the video portion.

The AVI file format is not an extensible, "open" environment and lacks features needed for serious video editing environments. To improve this situation, a group of interested companies recently created the **OpenDML** file format to make AVI more useful for the professional market. But because QuickTime works with OpenDML files and delivers on both Macintosh and Windows platforms and across the Web, look for a growing number of neat multimedia projects housed in a QuickTime container.

Like Apple's QuickTime, AVI provides the following features:

- Playback from hard disk or CD-ROM
- Playback on computers with limited memory; data is streamed from the hard disk or CD-ROM player without using great amounts of memory
- Quick loading and playing, because only a few frames of video and a portion of audio are accessed at a time
- Video compression to boost the quality of your video sequences and reduce their size

Movie Editors

With the invention of QuickTime and Video for Windows, desktop video publishing (DVP) on Macintoshes and PCs became a digital process. Improved compression and decompression techniques allow quarter-, half-, and full-screen/full-motion movies instead of the small, 160x120-pixel-sized movies characteristic of earlier digital video experiments.

With desktop editing software and an appropriate video digitizing board, you can digitize video clips, edit the clip offline, add special effects and titles, mix sound tracks, and save the finished product as a digital file on magnetic or optical media.

Video digitizing boards for making Macintosh QuickTime movies from videotape are available from RasterOps, Radius, Fast, and others. The Targa board from TrueVision, VideoBlaster from Creative Labs, Super VideoWindows SL from New Media Graphics, and other boards are available for making AVI movies for Windows.

Specialized video editors have been designed around this technology for both the Macintosh and PC environments—for example, AVID's VideoShop, Media100, Fast's VideoMachine, Adobe's Premiere, and Apple's Final Cut Pro. These applications let you mix video clips, audio recordings, animation, still images, and graphics to create QuickTime or AVI movies. You arrange your clips linearly, cutting and pasting and layering them into transitions with special effects such as dissolves, page turns, spins, tinting, distorting, and replicating. A familiar push-button control panel is used for stop, rewind, play, fast-forward, record, and single-stop, and these applications display time references, frame counts, and audio and transparency levels.

Figure 10-4 shows a movie being edited in Final Cut Pro, with visual effects and sounds. Adobe's After Effects is a powerful addition to the video editing suite, with sophisticated tools for combining digital video, audio, and images into fully controlled time-based projects. Special video plug-ins for After Effects, which will make your movies look truly professional, are available from Alien Skin.

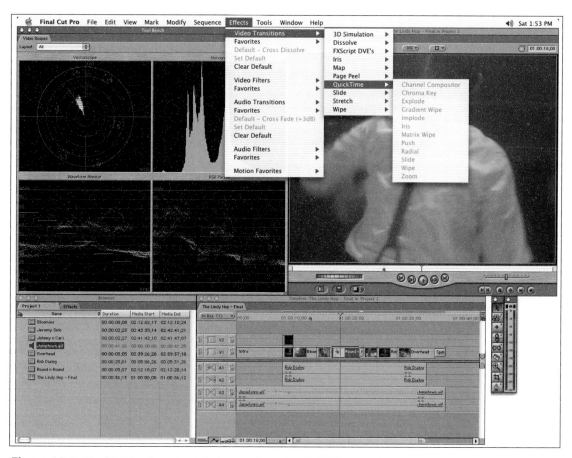

Figure 10-4 Final Cut Pro from Apple being used to edit a QuickTime movie

WARNING *Digital video editing and playback requires an immense amount of free disk space, even when the video files are compressed.*

TIP *Because digital movie data must stream rapidly and without interruption from your disk drive, be sure that you de-fragment and optimize your disk with a utility such as Norton's Speed Disk before recording and playing back your movie files. If your movie file is fragmented, the read head of the disk drive may need to pause sending data while it physically moves to wildly different locations on the disk; a de-fragmented file lets the head read sequentially from one adjoining sector to the next. Use disk optimizing utilities with caution, however: accidents have been known to happen, causing permanent data loss.*

Compressing Movie Files

Image compression algorithms are critical to the delivery of motion video and audio on both the Macintosh and PC platforms. Without compression, there is simply not enough bandwidth on the Macintosh or PC to transfer the massive amounts of data involved in displaying a new screen image every 1/30 of a second.

To understand compression, consider these three basic concepts:

- *Compression ratio*: The **compression ratio** represents the size of the original image divided by the size of the compressed image—that is, how much the data is actually compressed. Some compression schemes yield ratios that are dependent on the image content: a busy image of a field of multicolored tulips may yield a very small compression ratio, and an image of blue ocean and sky may yield a very high compression ratio. Video compression typically manages only the part of an image that changes from image to image (the *delta*).

- *Image quality*: Compression is either lossy or lossless. **Lossy** schemes ignore picture information that the viewer may not miss, but that means the picture information is in fact lost—even after decompression. And as more and more information is removed during compression, image quality decreases. **Lossless** schemes preserve the original data precisely—an important consideration in medical imaging, for example. The compression ratio typically affects picture quality because, usually, the higher the compression ratio, the lower the quality of the decompressed image.

- *Compression/decompression speed:* You will prefer a fast compression time while developing your project. Users, on the other hand, will appreciate a fast decompression time to increase display performance.

For compressing video frames, the MPEG format used for DVD employs three types of encoding: I-Frames (Intra), P-Frames (Predicted), and B-Frames (Bi-directional Predicted). Each type crams more or less information into the tiniest possible storage space. For example, B- and P-Frames only contain information that has changed from one frame to the next, so a sequence from a "talking head" interview might only contain data for the movement of lips (as long as the rest of the subject is still). B- and P-Frames cannot be played on their own, then, because they contain only the information about the lips that changed; the complete image is based on the data stored in the I-Frame. Sequences of these frame types are compiled into a GOP (Group of Pictures), and all the GOPs are stitched into a stream of images. The result is an MPEG video file.

Helpful Accessories

No multimedia toolkit is complete without a few indispensable utilities for performing some odd, but oft-repeated, tasks. These are the comfortable and well-worn accessories that make your computer life easier.

On both the Macintosh and in Windows, a screen-grabber is essential. Because bitmapped images are so common in multimedia, it is important to have a tool for grabbing all or part of the screen display so you can import it into your authoring system or copy it into an image-editing application. Screen-grabbing to the clipboard, for example, lets you move a bitmapped image from one application to another without the cumbersome steps of first exporting the image to a file and then importing it back into the destination application. In Windows, press the PRINT SCREEN key to place the contents of your screen onto the Clipboard. On the classic Macintosh, press the COMMAND key, CONTROL key, SHIFT key and the number 4 all at the same time, and then drag a rectangle across the screen. Whatever is in the rectangle is then placed on the clipboard, ready for pasting into an image-editing application. In Mac OSX, use the Grab utility to capture the screen.

Format converters are another indispensable tool for projects in which your source material may originate on Macintoshes, PCs, Unix workstations, or even mainframes. This is an issue particularly with image files, because there are many formats and many compression schemes.

Chapter 10 Review

■ Chapter Summary

For your review, here's a summary of the important concepts discussed in this chapter.

List several common programs that are used to handle text in multimedia projects, and discuss their uses

- A word processor is usually a regularly used tool in designing and building a multimedia project.
- Word processors are often bundled in an office suite that includes other general-purpose programs.
- Optical character recognition (OCR) software can import an image, analyze the image, and quickly convert it into editable text.

Discuss the factors affecting which graphics programs are used in multimedia

- The graphical impact of your project will likely have the greatest influence on the end user.
- Many authoring systems can import only bit-mapped images.
- Bitmapped images provide the greatest choice and power to the artist for rendering fine detail and effects.
- To master an application, you may have spent many hours learning it, and you will likely stay with that product rather than change to another.

List several common types of graphics and animation programs used in multimedia projects, and discuss their capabilities

- Select drawing and paint programs that have a wide range of capabilities.
- 3-D modeling software is easier to use than ever, and as a result has entered the mainstream, raising the bar for multimedia graphics.

- Image-editing applications can be used to enhance and retouch imported images and create them from scratch. They usually include features and tools found in painting and drawing programs. They often support third-party plug-ins.
- Animations and digital video movies are sequences of bitmapped graphic scenes or frames, rapidly played back.
- Animations can also be made within some authoring systems by moving objects or sprites to simulate motion.

Discuss the formats and architectures used to integrate video on computers

- Most video tools use QuickTime for Macintosh and Windows or Microsoft Video for Windows (AVI).
- QuickTime and AVI interleave audio data with video and other data and coordinate the streaming of data from disk to memory for smooth video and audio playback.
- QuickTime can store an almost unlimited range of tracks in over 35 media file formats, including most major video, still image, audio, animation, and MIDI formats.
- You can embed commands into your HTML documents that control and fine-tune the display of your QuickTime files in a browser.

List the tools used to handle video in multimedia projects, discuss their capabilities, and how they capture, process, and compress video

- With desktop editing software, you can digitize video, edit, add special effects and titles, mix sound tracks, and save the clip.

- When working with digital video, always de-fragment and optimize your disk before recording and playing back your movie files.
- Image compression algorithms enable delivery of motion video and audio on both the Macintosh and PC platforms.
- The compression ratio represents the size of the original image divided by the size of the compressed image.
- Lossy schemes ignore picture information the viewer may not miss.
- Lossless schemes preserve the original data precisely.
- Screen-grab and format conversion tools are useful in multimedia production.

■ Key Terms

3-D modeling software *(266)*
architecture *(271)*
Audio Video
  Interleaved (AVI) *(270)*
AUTOPLAY *(273)*
BGCOLOR *(273)*
CACHE *(273)*
compression ratio *(276)*
CONTROLLER *(273)*
CORRECTION *(273)*
Digital Versatile Disc
  (DVD) *(271)*
drawing software *(264)*
FAQs (Frequently Asked
  Questions) *(262)*
filters *(269)*
format converter *(277)*

FOV *(273)*
frames *(270)*
HEIGHT *(273)*
HIDDEN *(273)*
HREF *(273)*
image-editing
  application *(268)*
keyboarding *(263)*
LOOP *(273)*
lossless *(276)*
lossy *(276)*
Media Abstraction
  Layer *(272)*
Microsoft Video for
  Windows *(270)*
Movie Player *(272)*
multiplexed *(271)*

NODE *(274)*
office suite *(263)*
OpenDML *(274)*
optical character recognition
  (OCR) *(264)*
painting software *(264)*
PAN *(274)*
Picture Viewer *(272)*
plug-in *(269)*
SCALE *(273)*
sprites *(270)*
TARGET *(273)*
TILT *(274)*
VOLUME *(273)*
WIDTH *(273)*
word processor *(263)*

■ Key Term Quiz

1. FAQs stands for _____.

2. A package of software applications that might include a spreadsheet, database, e-mail, web browser, and presentation applications is called a(n) _____ (two words).

3. Software that turns bitmapped characters into electronically recognizable ASCII text is called _____.

4. Each graphic scene in an animation is referred to as a _____.

5. A graphic image on a screen that can be moved about to create animation is called a _____.

6. The Microsoft Video for Windows format is also known as _____.

7. The hardware format defining a very dense, two-layered disc read by laser is the _____.

8. When the audio, image, text, and video data is combined in one stream, it is said to be _____.

9. The size of the original image divided by the size of the compressed image is called the _____ (two words).

10. A program that changes an image from one type of graphics file to another is a _____ (two words).

■ Multiple Choice Quiz

1. As you design and build a multimedia project, your most often used tool may be your:
   a. word processor
   b. authoring system
   c. image processor
   d. drawing program
   e. format converter

2. Of all the multimedia elements in a project, the one that will likely have the greatest influence on the end user is the:
   a. video footage
   b. sound effects
   c. graphical impact
   d. packaging
   e. musical background

3. Painting software is dedicated to producing:
   a. vector images
   b. animations
   c. 3-D images
   d. bitmap images
   e. video clips

4. In a paint program, the eyedropper tool:
   a. fills an area with color
   b. erases an area around it
   c. removes (desaturates) the color in a region
   d. creates a gradient fill in an area
   e. samples colors

5. In a paint program, the autotrace tool:
   a. creates multisided polygon shapes
   b. turns bitmap shapes into vector-based outlines
   c. places text on a path
   d. fills an area with a pattern or background
   e. smoothes coarse-edged objects

6. Image-editing applications often include many of the features and tools of:
   a. animation programs
   b. 3-D programs
   c. video editing programs
   d. painting and drawing programs
   e. authoring systems

7. In an image-editing program, a virtual memory scheme:
   a. creates a 3-D model of an image
   b. uses hard disk space as RAM
   c. uses RAM to store disk images
   d. looks for patterns in an image
   e. allows two users to work on an image at the same time

8. In an image-editing program, look for a tool that uses _____ that can be combined, hidden, and reordered.
   a. styles
   b. formats
   c. frames
   d. cels
   e. layers

9. System sounds:
   a. are any sounds that your system is able to export
   b. are any sounds that are part of a larger sound composition
   c. are the sounds that are built into the authoring system
   d. are the beeps used to indicate an error, warning, or special user activity
   e. is the name of an industrial/bossa nova band from Dubuque, Illinois

10. Making your own MIDI files requires:
- a. knowledge of tempos, clefs, notations, and keys
- b. familiarity with musical instruments
- c. an understanding of how music is sequenced, scored, and published
- d. a MIDI synthesizer or device connected to your computer
- e. all of the above

11. Most authoring tools usually:
- a. use a frame-oriented approach to animation
- b. use an object-oriented approach to animation
- c. use both frame- and object-oriented approaches to animation
- d. use either a frame- or object-oriented approach to animation, but rarely both
- e. do not directly support animation, but allow animations to be imported in an appropriate format

12. Interleaving is:
- a. laying out tracks on a CD so that media that are close in sequence in the program are close on the CD
- b. creating an authoring sequence that follows a certain pattern; for example, image, video clip, text, and so on
- c. blending audio data with video and other data so that sound remains synchronized with the video
- d. a form of animation where one image changes into another
- e. a video transition where strips of one image slide across another image

13. DVD stands for:
- a. Dynamically-Variable Disc
- b. Distributed Video Disc
- c. Data-Vision Disc
- d. Double-Volume Disc
- e. Digital Versatile Disc

14. QuickTime is best defined as:
- a. an authoring tool
- b. a scripting language
- c. a digital video compression codec
- d. a software-based architecture
- e. a multimedia browser plug-in

15. You should defragment and optimize your disk with a utility before recording and playing back your movie files because:
- a. digital video is notorious for corrupting hard drives
- b. digital video recording is susceptible to residual magnetism from previous files
- c. digital video is stored in a low-level file format, and thus noncontiguous sectors can be "lost" if the file database is not accurate
- d. fragmented files often lose audio/video synchronization due to markers and cues being lost
- e. fragmented files require the drive head to jump around, which could affect performance

■ Essay Quiz

1. Why might a word processor be the most-used piece of software in a multimedia production? Think of all the project elements that a word processor might be used for, especially within project management and in content development.

2. List the various types of media used in a multimedia project. What types of tools are used to create these media? What types of tools are used to edit these media? What types of tools are used to convert these media among various formats?

3. Discuss what considerations you might take into account in selecting and using a graphics editing program. How would you determine whether the tool was capable in terms of your project's needs? What steps would you take to ensure that you got the most out of the software?

4. Define QuickTime and describe it in terms of its capabilities. What media can be included in it? Where and how can it be used? How does it stand alone? How can it be integrated into another format?

5. What are the two means of providing animation? How does each of them convey the idea of movement? How can object or sprite animation be controlled from within an authoring system? Discuss how frame-based animation relates to digital video formats.

Lab Projects

■ Project 10.1

Visit the web sites of three word processors, and locate a page that summarizes the capabilities of each. List the formats each is able to import from and export to. Do they support RTF? HTML? Can they import images, sounds, or video clips? What "container" do they use for these media? What features do they all have in common? What unique features does each one have? Document your findings.

■ Project 10.2

Find a page of text printed on a laser printer or better. Photocopy the page, and then photocopy the photocopy. Fax the page, and collect the fax.

Now scan the original, the third-generation photocopy, and the fax into an OCR program. How well did the program read the text? Document your findings in terms of the number of mistakes and the number of characters the program could not read.

■ Project 10.3

Visit the web sites of three image editors, and locate a page that summarizes the capabilities of each. List the formats each is able to import from and export to. Do they support layers? Do they allow users to "undo" actions? Do they support vector graphics, or just bitmap graphics? What plug-ins do they support? What features do they all have in common? What unique features does each one have? Document your findings.

■ Project 10.4

Visit the web sites of three 3-D programs, and locate a page that summarizes the capabilities of each. List the formats each is able to import from and export or output to. Do they include libraries of "primitives" (simple pre-made shapes)? Do they allow users to "undo" actions? How do they support features such as lights, cameras, bump maps, fog, etc.? What features do they all have in common? What unique features does each one have? Document your findings.

■ Project 10.5

Visit the web sites of three video editing programs, and locate a page that summarizes the capabilities of each. List the formats each is able to import from and export or output to. How do they handle clips? Is there an easy, intuitive, "drop and drag" interface? How many audio and video tracks are included? How are transitions and filters included? What features do all of them have in common? What unique features does each one have? Document your findings.

CHAPTER 11

Multimedia Authoring Tools

MULTIMEDIA authoring tools provide the important framework you need for organizing and editing the elements of your multimedia project, including graphics, sounds, animations, and video clips. Authoring tools are used for designing interactivity and the user interface, for presenting your project on screen, and for assembling diverse multimedia elements into a single, cohesive product.

Authoring software provides an integrated environment for binding together the content and functions of your project, and typically includes everything you need to create, edit, and import specific types of data; assemble raw data into a playback sequence or cue sheet; and provide a structured method or language for responding to user input. With multimedia authoring software, you can make

- Video productions
- Animations
- Games
- Interactive web sites
- Demo disks and guided tours
- Presentations
- Kiosk applications
- Interactive training
- Simulations, prototypes, and technical visualizations

Making Instant Multimedia

While this chapter discusses dedicated multimedia authoring systems, there is no reason to invest in such a package if your current software (or an inexpensive upgrade) can do the job. Indeed, not only can you save money by doing multimedia with tools that are familiar and already at hand, but you also save the time spent on the arduous and sometimes lengthy learning curves involved in mastering many of the dedicated authoring systems. Common desktop tools have become multimedia-powerful.

Some multimedia projects may be so simple that you can cram all the organizing, planning, rendering, and testing stages into a single effort, and make "instant" multimedia.

In this chapter, you will learn how to:

- Determine which of the different types of authoring systems is most appropriate for any given project
- Think about multimedia elements as objects and how they relate to and interact with each other and their environment, including programming tools
- Understand the metaphors that authoring programs use in their authoring environments
- Avoid the common pitfalls of cross-platform project development

Here is an example: The topic at your weekly sales meeting is sales force performance. You want to display your usual spreadsheet so the group can see real names and numbers for each member of the team, but then you want to add an animated, multicolored 3-D bar graph for visual impact. Preparing for your meeting, you annotate the cell containing the name of the most productive salesperson for the week, using sounds of applause taken from a public domain CD-ROM, or a recording of your CEO saying "Good job!" or a colleague's "Wait till next week, Pete!" At the appropriate time during the meeting, you click that cell and play the file. And that's it—you have just made and used instant multimedia.

WARNING *You need special multimedia tools for digitizing your sounds and for creating animations and movies before you can attach these objects to your Word, data, or presentation documents.*

Most personal computers sold today are able to produce at least the basic sound and animation elements of multimedia. Manufacturers of popular software for word processing, spreadsheets, database management, graphing, drawing, and presentation have added capabilities for sound, image, and animation to their products. You can use a voice annotation, picture, or QuickTime or MP2 movie from most word processing applications (see Figure 11-1). You can also click a cell in a spreadsheet to enhance its content with graphic images, sounds, and animations (see Figure 11-2). If you like, your database can include pictures, audio clips, and movies (see Figure 11-3), and your presentation software can generate interesting titles, visual effects,

Figure 11-1 With Microsoft Word documents, you can include various image formats, movies, and digitized sounds (including voice annotations).

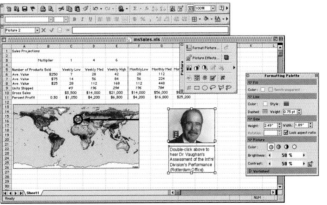

Figure 11-2 Spreadsheets can include embedded objects made with other applications.

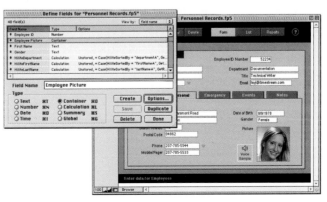

Figure 11-3 A FileMaker Pro employee database can include image and sound resources.

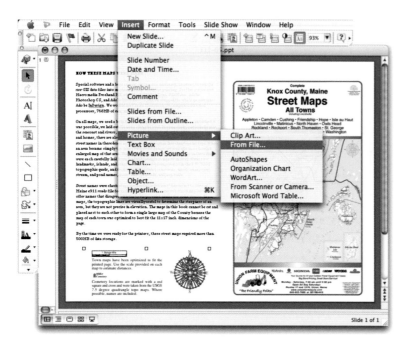

and animated illustrations for your product demo (see Figure 11-4). With these multimedia-enhanced software packages, you get many more ways to effectively convey your message than just a slide show.

Figure 11-4 Microsoft PowerPoint provides multimedia linking and embedding features.

First Person

Working draft of Chapter 4, revision 2, reads:

My father said that Mommy was still in a coma and my little brother was sleeping. We should go home now. So we went out the back way to the physician's parking lot—down the elevator and past the noisy kitchen with its racks of trays, white-uniformed cooks, piles of canned goods, and the steamy smells of institutional stew. The green screen door slammed indelibly into my five-year-old memory, and the attendant waved to my dad; he probably didn't know we were there on family business. It was all pretty serious.

We found Mommy's car behind the police station. I stayed in my seat while my father got out and walked very slowly around the twisted metal. He was calculating the impact forces, visualizing the accident in slow-motion freeze frames, and at one point, he leaned in through the broken glass and ran his hand across the dent in the steel glove compartment where my brother had smashed his face. He went around only the one time, then got back in. "She must have been doing about forty when she hit the pole," he offered as if I were an adult, and we drove out the narrow circular drive alongside the station house. It was a crisp, clear, football-and-pumpkins Saturday afternoon in October.

Editorial note to Sally: Per your comment last week, pick a good illustration from the file of images that I have attached. One of them should fit the bill... Thanks! See you next week.

Some Helpful Ways to Organize

Don't be overwhelmed when starting your multimedia project—there may be a lot of things to think about, but there are also a lot of things that have already been done for you. As the cliché goes, "There's no need to reinvent the wheel!" Consider the following tips for making your production work go smoothly:

- Use templates that people have already created to set up your production. These can include appropriate styles for all sorts of data, font sets, color arrangements, and particular page set-ups that will save you time.

- Use wizards when they are available—they may save you much time and pre-set-up work.

- Use named styles, because if you take the time to create your own it will really slow you down. Unless your client specifically requests a particular style, you will save a great deal of time using something already created, usable, and legal.

- Create tables, which you can build with a few keystrokes in many programs, and it makes the production look credible.

- Help readers find information with tables of contents, running headers and footers, and indexes.

- Improve document appearance with bulleted and numbered lists and symbols.

- Allow for a quick-change replacement using the global change feature.

- Reduce grammatical errors by using the grammar and spell checker provided with the software. Do not rely on that feature, though, to set all things right—you still need to proofread everything.

- Include identifying information in the file name so you can find the file later.

Types of Authoring Tools

This chapter arranges the various multimedia authoring tools into groups, based on the method used for sequencing or organizing multimedia elements and events:

- Card- or page-based tools
- Icon-based, event-driven tools
- Time-based tools

CARDS & PAGES

Card-based or **page-based** tools are authoring systems, wherein the elements are organized as pages of a book or a stack of cards. Thousands of pages or cards may be available in the book or stack. These tools are best used when the bulk of your content consists of elements that can be viewed individually, like the pages of a book or cards in a card file. The authoring system lets you link these pages or cards into organized sequences. You can jump, on command, to any page you wish in the structured navigation pattern. Card- or page-based authoring systems allow you to play sound elements and launch animations and digital video.

ICONS & OBJECTS

Icon- or object-based, event-driven tools are authoring systems, wherein multimedia elements and interaction cues (events) are organized as objects in a structural framework or process. Icon- or object-based, event-driven tools simplify the organization of your project and typically display flow diagrams of activities along branching paths. In complicated navigational structures, this charting is particularly useful during development.

TIME

Time-based tools are authoring systems, wherein elements and events are organized along a timeline, with resolutions as high as or higher than $\frac{1}{30}$ second. Time-based tools are best to use when you have a message with a beginning and an end. Sequentially organized graphic frames are played back at a speed that you can set. Other elements (such as audio events) are triggered at a given time or location in the sequence of events. The more powerful time-based tools let you program jumps to any location in a sequence, thereby adding navigation and interactive control.

Objects

In multimedia authoring systems, multimedia elements and events are often treated as **objects** that live in a hierarchical order of parent and child relationships. Messages passed among these objects order them to *do* things according to the **properties** or **modifiers** assigned to them. In this way, for example, Teen-child (a teenager object) may be programmed to take out the trash every Friday evening, and does so when they get a message from Dad. Spot, the puppy, may bark and jump up and down when the postman arrives, and is defined by barking and jumping modifiers. Objects typically take care of themselves. Send them a message and they do their thing without external procedures and programming. Objects are particularly useful for games, which contain many components with many "personalities," all for simulating real-life situations, events, and their constituent properties.

The Right Tool for the Job

Each multimedia project you undertake will have its own underlying structure and purpose and will require different features and functions. In the best case, you must be prepared to choose the tool that best fits the job; in the worst case, you must know which tools will at least "get the job done." Authoring tools are constantly being improved by their makers, who add new features and increase performance with upgrade development cycles of six months to a year. It is important that you study the software product reviews in computer trade journals, as well as talk with current users of these systems, before deciding on the best ones for your needs.

WARNING *Because multimedia-authoring systems are constantly being updated, make sure you purchase, learn, and use the latest version of software.*

Flash and PowerPoint are very convenient to use to get information out in a presentation over the Web. These programs (there are many others) have the capability for showing video, slide shows, and diagrams with sound and graphics.

E-learning modules such as those seen on PDAs, MP3 players, and intra-college networks may include web-based teaching materials, multimedia CD-ROMs or Web sites, discussion boards, collaborative software, wikis, simulations, games, electric voting systems, blogs, computer-aided assessment, simulations, animation, blogs, learning management software, and e-mail. This is also referred to as distance learning or blended learning, where online learning is mixed with face-to-face-learning.

Different Stages of Authoring

There are five distinct stages of multimedia authoring:

■ **Analysis**   What do you need to do and what do you use to do it?

■ **Design**   Create storyboards to tell the story of the project.

■ **Development**   Incorporate data and set it up as a prototype or model.

■ **Evaluation**   When the prototype application works the way you want it to, test it again, fine-tune it, make it sexy, and then review your work.

■ **Distribution**   When it is ready to go (after the evaluation phase), make it real. Package and distribute it.

Editing Features

The elements of multimedia—images, animations, text, digital audio and MIDI music, and video clips—need to be created, edited, and converted to standard file formats, using the specialized applications described in Chapters 4, 5, 6, 7, 8, and 10, which provide these capabilities. Also, editing tools for these elements, particularly text and still images, are often included in your authoring system. The more editors your authoring system has, the fewer specialized tools you may need. In many cases, however, the editors that come with an authoring system will offer only a subset of the substantial features found in dedicated tools. According to Vaughan's Law of Multimedia Minimums (see Chapter 5), these features may very well be sufficient for what you need to do; on the other hand, if editors you need are missing from your authoring system, or if you require more power, it's best to use one of the specialized, single-purpose tools.

Organizing Features

The organization, design, and production process for multimedia involves storyboarding and flowcharting. Some authoring tools provide a visual flowcharting system or overview facility for illustrating your project's structure at a macro level. Storyboards or navigation diagrams can also help organize a project and can help focus the over-all project scope for all involved. Because designing the interactivity and navigation flow of your project often requires a great deal of planning and programming effort, your storyboard should describe not just the graphics of each screen, but the interactive elements as well. Features that help organize your material are a plus. For example, planning ahead in an organized fashion may prevent countless moments of indecision, keep the client from changing her mind without periodic sign-offs on the materials included, and, in the long run save you money.

Programming Features

Multimedia authoring systems offer one or more of the following approaches, as explained in the following paragraphs:

- Visual programming with cues, icons, and objects
- Programming with a scripting language
- Programming with traditional languages, such as Basic or C
- Document development tools

Visual programming with icons or objects is perhaps the simplest and easiest authoring process. If you want to play a sound or put a picture into your project, just drag the element's icon into the playlist—or drag it away to delete it. Visual authoring tools such as Authorware and Adobe's Acrobat Direct are particularly useful for slide shows and presentations.

Authoring tools that offer a **very high level language (VHLL)** or interpreted scripting environment for navigation control and for enabling user inputs or goal-oriented programming languages—such as Adobe Acrobat Connect, Flash, Runtime Revolution's Runtime (a program that became the first RAD tool to create applications for the Intel Mac Platform), Tribework's iShell, and ToolBook—are more powerful by definition. The more commands and functions provided in the **scripting language**, the more powerful the authoring system. Once you learn a scripting language, you will be able to learn other scripting languages relatively quickly; the principles are the same, regardless of the command syntax and keywords used.

As with traditional programming tools, look for an authoring package with good debugging facilities, robust text editing, and online syntax reference. Other scripting augmentation facilities are advantageous, as well. In complex projects, you may need to program custom extensions of the scripting language for direct access to the computer's operating system.

A powerful document reference and delivery system is a key component of some projects. Some authoring tools offer direct importing of pre-formatted text, indexing facilities, complex text search mechanisms, and hypertext linkage tools. These authoring systems are useful for development of CD-ROM information products, online documentation and help systems, and sophisticated multimedia-enhanced publications.

With scripts, you can perform computational tasks; sense and respond to user input; create character, icon, and motion animations; launch other applications; and control external multimedia devices.

Interactivity Features

Interactivity empowers the end users of your project by letting them control the content and flow of information. Authoring tools should provide one or more levels of interactivity:

- **Simple branching**, which offers the ability to go to another section of the multimedia production (via an activity such as a keypress, mouse click, or expiration of a timer)
- **Conditional branching**, which supports a go-to based on the results of IF-THEN decisions or events
- A structured language that supports complex programming logic, such as nested IF-THENs, subroutines, event tracking, and message passing among objects and elements

Performance Tuning Features

Complex multimedia projects require exact synchronization of events— for example, the animation of an exploding balloon with its accompanying sound effect. Accomplishing synchronization is difficult because performance varies widely among the different computers used for multimedia development and delivery. Some authoring tools allow you to lock a production's playback speed to a specified computer platform, but others provide no ability whatsoever to control performance on various systems. In many cases, you will need to use the authoring tool's own scripting language or custom programming facility to specify timing and sequence on systems with different (faster or slower) processors. Be sure your authoring system allows precise timing of events.

Playback Features

As you build your multimedia project, you will be continually assembling elements and testing to see how the assembly looks and performs. Your authoring system should let you build a segment or part of your project and then quickly test it as if the user were actually using it. You should spend a great deal of time going back and forth between building and testing as you refine and smooth the content and timing of the project. You may even want to release the project to others who you trust to run it ragged and show you its weak points.

Delivery Features

Delivering your project may require building a run-time version of the project using the multimedia authoring software. A **run-time version** or **standalone** allows your project to play back without requiring the full authoring software and all its tools and editors. Often, the run-time version does not allow users to access or change the content, structure, and programming of the project. If you are going to distribute your project widely, you should distribute it in the run-time version. Make sure your authored project can be easily distributed.

Cross-Platform Features

It is also increasingly important to use tools that make transfer across platforms easy. For many developers, the Macintosh remains the multimedia authoring platform of choice, but 80 percent of that developer's target market may be Windows platforms. If you develop on a Macintosh, look for tools that provide a compatible authoring system for Windows or offer a run-time player for the other platform. iShell employs platform-independent XML (extensible Markup Language) to make compatibility a non-issue. Adobe Acrobat Connect allows you to create a project in almost any environment.

Internet Playability

Because the Web has become a significant delivery medium for multimedia, authoring systems typically provide a means to convert their output so that it can be delivered within the context of HTML or DHTML, either with special plug-ins or by embedding Java, JavaScript, or other code structures in the HTML document. Test your authoring software for Internet delivery before you build your project. Be sure it performs on the Web as you expect! Test it out for performance stability on as many platforms as you can.

Card- and Page-Based Authoring Tools

In the past card- and page-based authoring systems provided a simple and easily understood metaphor for organizing multimedia elements. Because graphic images typically formed the backbone of a project, both as navigation menus and as content, many developers first arranged their images into logical sequences or groupings similar to the chapters and pages of a book, or cards in a card catalog. Navigation routines became then, simply directives to go to a page or card that contained appropriate images and text, and associated sounds, animations, and video clips.

Page-based authoring systems contained media objects: the objects were the buttons, text fields, graphic objects, backgrounds, pages or cards, and even the project itself. The characteristics of objects were defined by properties (highlighted, bold, red, hidden, active, locked, and so on). Each object would have contained programming script, usually a property of that object, that was activated when an event (such as a mouse click) related to that object occurred. Events caused messages to pass along the hierarchy of objects in the project; for example, a mouse-clicked message could be sent from a button to the background, to the page, and then to the project itself. As the message traveled, it looked for handlers in the script of each object; if it found a matching **handler**, the authoring system then executed the task specified by that handler.

Most page-based authoring systems provided a facility for linking objects to pages or cards (by automatically programming branching go-to statements for navigation by mouse clicks), but having learned to write your own scripts and having understood the message-passing nature of these authoring tools was essential to making them perform well. Following are some typical messages that might have been passed along the object hierarchy of the HyperCard, Revolution, and ToolBook authoring systems:

HyperCard and Revolution Message	ToolBook Message
closeCard	leavePage
closeStack	leaveBook
idle	idle
mouseDown	buttonDown
mouseStillDown	buttonStillDown
mouseUp	buttonUp
newBackground	newBackground
openCard	enterPage
openStack	enterBook

Now let's look at specific examples. To go to the next card or page when a button was clicked, you would have placed a message handler into the script of that button. (In the languages demonstrated below, handlers began with "on" or "to handle.") An example in HyperTalk and MetaTalk would have been:

```
on mouseUp
  go next card
end mouseUp
```

An example in OpenScript (ToolBook) would look like:

```
to handle buttonUp
  go next page
end buttonUp
```

The handler, if placed in the script of the card or page, would have executed its commands when it received a "mouseUp" or "buttonUp" event message that occurred at any location on the card or page—not just while the cursor was within the bounds of a button.

Most card- or page-based authoring systems required a special intermediate file that also received scripted message handlers and acted as a repository for special routines and resources that were available to all projects being executed by the application. In HyperCard, this file was called Home; in ToolBook, you may have had one or more System Books.

Card- and page-based systems typically provided two separate layers on each card: a **background layer** that could be shared among many cards, and a foreground layer that was specific to a single card. Figure 11-5 demonstrates use of foreground and background layering by design: when the gray cover on the foreground layer was wiped away with an "eraser," the graphic image on the background layer was revealed. In this figure, an animated earth was made up of 18 characters and rotates underneath a marker to point out the habitat of the monkey species that is hidden below the cover. When enough of the cover is erased so the user can recognize the monkeys, the user released the mouse button and chose a name from a menu. If the name was incorrect, a sound played and a cat appeared and wagged its tail (the cat was a button icon), and the user could continue. If the user selected the correct monkey, an encyclopedia of information about that species was presented, and a pull-down menu (shown in Figure 11-5) provided access to a sound bite or video clip before going on. There were 25 monkeys, and the program kept score.

Figure 11-5 To the left, the peach cover in the foreground layer of a card is erased to reveal the image on the background layer beneath. At right, sound, animation, and video could be played in card- and page-based systems.

http://www.runrev.com (Revolution)

http://www.toolbook.com/index.php?src+sumthome (ToolBook)

Icon- and Object-Based Authoring Tools

Icon-based, event-driven tools provide a visual programming approach to organizing and presenting multimedia. First you build a structure or flowchart of events, tasks, and decisions, by dragging appropriate icons from a library. These icons can include menu choices, graphic images, sounds, and computations. The flowchart graphically depicts the project's logic. When the structure is built, you can add your content: text, graphics, animation, sounds, and video movies. Then, to refine your project, you edit your logical structure by rearranging and fine-tuning the icons and their properties.

With icon-based authoring tools, non-technical multimedia authors can build sophisticated applications without scripting. In Authorware from Adobe, by placing icons on a flow line, you can quickly sequence

Why is programming fun? What delights may its
practitioner expect as his reward?

First is the sheer joy of making things. As the child delights
in his mud pie, so the adult enjoys building things, especially things of
his own design. I think this delight must be an image of God's
delight in making things, a delight shown in the distinctiveness
of each leaf and each snowflake.

Second is the pleasure of making things that are useful to other
people. Deep within, we want others to use our work and to find it
helpful. In this respect the programming system is not essentially different from the child's first clay pencil holder "for Daddy's office."

Third is the fascination of fashioning complex puzzle-like
objects of interlocking moving parts and watching them work in
subtle cycles, playing out the consequences of principles built in from
the beginning. The programmed computer has all the fascination of
the pinball machine or the jukebox mechanism, carried to the ultimate.

Fourth is the joy of always learning, which springs from the
non-repeating nature of the task. In one way or another the problem
is ever new, and its solver learns something: sometimes practical,
sometimes theoretical, and sometimes both.

Finally, there is the delight of working in such a tractable medium.
The programmer, like the poet, works only slightly removed from pure
thought-stuff. He builds his castles in the air, from air, creating by ex-
ertion of the imagination. Few media of creation are so flexible, so easy
to polish and rework, so readily capable of realizing grand conceptual
structures. (As we shall see later, this tractability has its own problems.)

Yet the program construct, unlike the poet's words, is real in the sense
that it moves and works, producing visible outputs separately from
the construct itself. It prints results, draws pictures, produces sounds,
moves arms. The magic of myth and legend has come true in our time.
One types the correct incantation on a keyboard, and a display screen
comes to life, showing things that never were nor could be.

Programming then is fun because it gratifies creative
longings built deep within us and delights sensibilities we
have in common with all men.

From *The Mythical Man-Month: Essays in Software Engineering*
by Frederick P. Brooks, Jr., Kenan Professor of
Computer Science, University of North Carolina at Chapel Hill.

events and activities, including decisions and user interactions. These tools are useful for storyboarding, as you can change sequences, add options, and restructure interactions by simply dragging and dropping icons. You can print out your navigation map or flowchart, an annotated project index with or without associated icons, design and presentation windows, and a cross-reference table of variables. Like Authorware, Allen Communication's Quest is a visual design environment for organizing media objects with particular features that enhance courseware and training development. Figure 11-6 shows a project being authored in iShell from Tribeworks, which uses an outline to organize a project's many objects.

http://www.adobe.com

http://www.allencomm.com

http://www.tribeworks.com

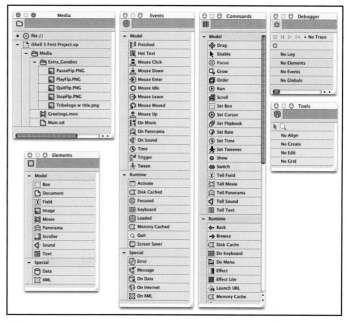

Figure 11-6 iShell's authoring interface allows for reuse of common multimedia elements in a drag-and-drop, object-oriented visual environment.

Time-Based Authoring Tools

Time-based systems are popular multimedia authoring tools. Each uses its own distinctive approach and user interface for managing events over time. Many use a visual timeline for sequencing the events of a multimedia presentation, often displaying layers of various media elements or events alongside the scale in increments as precise as one second. Others arrange long sequences of graphic frames and add the time component by adjusting each frame's duration of play.

Adobe Acrobat Connect

Adobe Acrobat Connect is a powerful and complex multimedia authoring tool from Adobe with a broad set of features to create multimedia presentations, animations, and blended learning experiences. It has a significant learning curve, but once mastered, it is among the most powerful multimedia development tools. In Connect, working with Adobe's Captivate, you assemble and sequence the elements of your project using myriad elements for presentation, including authoring, collaboration, meetings, events, web work, and training. Who knows—it just may wash dishes as well.

The following elements are contained within Adobe Acrobat Connect:

- **Presenter** has speedy content authoring, easy audio recording and editing, a rich viewing experience, and standards-compliant content.
- **Adobe Connect Training** with blended learning, interactive quizzes and surveys, and effortless curriculum management.
- **Adobe Connect Events** offers automated registration management, attendee qualification and notification, and detailed event tracking and reporting.
- **Adobe Connect Enterprise Server and Adobe Connect Enterprise Hosted** gives scalable deployment, flexible delivery management, single sign-on support, easy extensibility and failover support.

Flash

Flash is a time-based development environment. Flash, however, is also particularly focused on delivery of rich multimedia content to the Web. With the Flash Player plug-in, Flash delivers far more than simple static HTML pages. ActionScript, the proprietary, under-the-hood scripting language of Flash is based upon the international **ECMAScript** standard (http://www.ecma-international.org) derived from Netscape's original JavaScript.

Before Adobe purchased Macromedia in 2006, Macromedia claimed that 98.4 percent of web users can view Flash content—that was over 516 million users—using the Flash Player plug-in distributed with most browsers.

Director

Adobe's Director is a powerful and complex multimedia authoring tool with a broad set of features to create multimedia presentations, animations, and interactive multimedia applications. It requires a significant learning curve, but once mastered, it is among the most powerful of multimedia development tools. In Director, you assemble and sequence the elements of your project using a Cast and a Score.

Director movies are generally good for cross-platform delivery. To make run-time "projectors" for both platforms, however, you need to use a Mac version to make the Mac projector and a Windows version to make a Windows projector. This can be costly because you need a copy of Director on each platform. If you make a **Shockwave** projector, however, it will launch from both Mac and Windows platforms using the Shockwave Player.

Cast

The **Cast** is a multimedia database containing still images, sound files, text, palettes, QuickDraw shapes, programming scripts, QuickTime movies, Flash movies, and even other Director files. As shown in Figure 11-7, not only can you import a wide range of data types and multimedia element formats directly into this Cast, but you can also create multimedia elements from scratch using Director's own tools and editors.

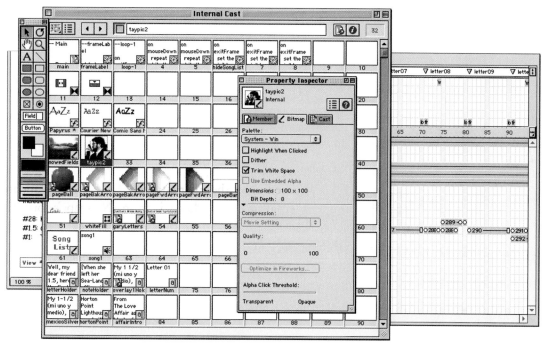

Figure 11-7 Director's Cast feature contains all the multimedia elements of your project.

A full-featured painting tool lets you create bitmapped artwork in any color depth. You can create gradients, tile patterns, and animated transformations (such as rotations and skews) of artwork. Other tools edit and create QuickDraw shapes, text, QuickTime movies, palettes, and scripts.

Score

Once you have imported or created the multimedia elements for your project and placed them into your Cast, you tie these Cast members together using the **Score** facility. Score is a sequencer for displaying, animating, and playing Cast members, and it is made up of frames that contain Cast members, tempo, a palette, timing, and sound information. Each frame is played back on a **stage** at a rate specified in the tempo channel. The Score provides elaborate and complex visual effects and transitions, adjustments of color palettes, and tempo control. In Figure 11-8, which shows a screen from the draft of an interactive multimedia novel, the frames are the vertical bands, and the channels are the numbered horizontal bands.

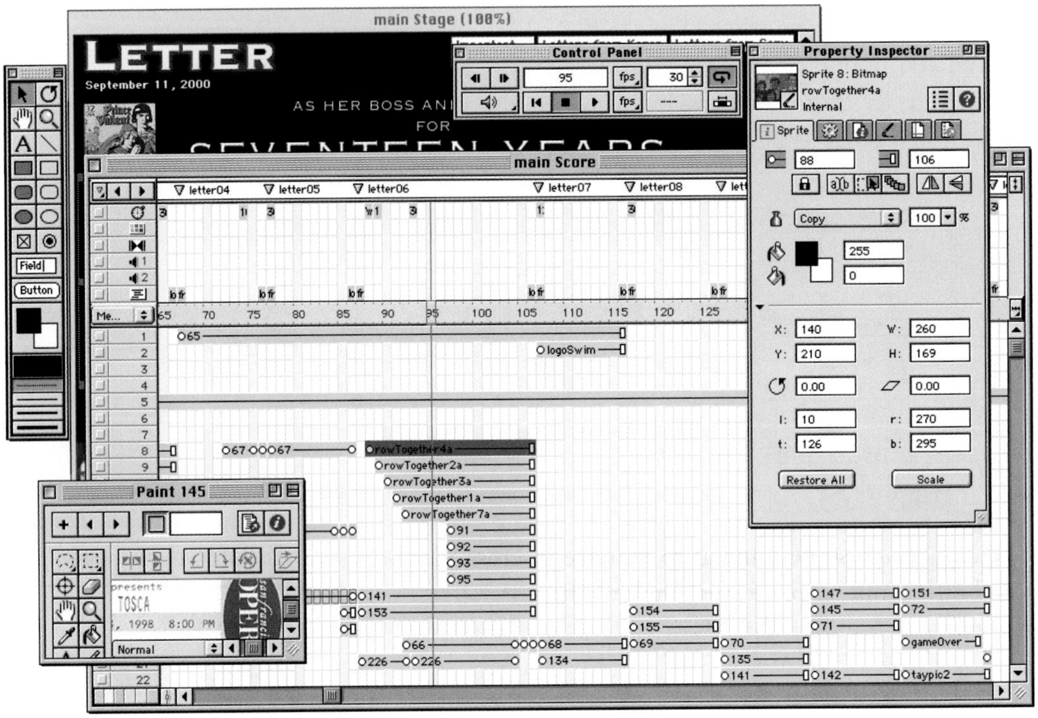

Figure 11-8 Director's Score features sequences and sets the tempo for playback.

Animations, for example, are made by placing a graphic, or **sprite**, onto the stage and changing its location slightly over several or more frames. When the frames are played back at tempo, the sprite moves. You can synchronize animations with sound effects by highlighting a range of frames and selecting the appropriate sound from your Cast.

Lingo

Director utilizes **Lingo**, a full-featured object-oriented scripting language, to enable interactivity and programmed control. A built-in script editor offers Lingo debugging facilities. Because you can attach scripts to individual elements of the Cast, you can copy and paste complete interactive sequences. Lingo also uses Xtras, which are special code segments used to control external sound and video devices. Several Xtras and extensive examples of their use are shipped with Director. With Lingo, you can also control operations on the Internet such as sending mail, reading documents and images, and building web pages on the fly.

Using Lingo scripts, you can chain together separate Director documents and call other files as subroutines. You can also import elements into your Cast using pointers to a file. This allows you to share the same elements among many Casts; when your Score calls for that element, it is loaded into RAM from the file. Chaining and sharing let you create Director projects as large or complex as your storage medium will accommodate.

Cross-Platform Authoring Notes

You face two major hurdles when you move multimedia projects across platforms. These hurdles have to do with the different schemes Macintosh and Windows computers have used to manage text and colors.

Here are some important tips for working with text in **cross-platform** applications:

- For text in boxes, center the text, leaving plenty of space or margin to avoid possible word-wrap on the other platform.

- TrueType, the most common format for fonts, is used on Mac OS X and Windows XP. Both platforms also, include native support for Adobe's Type 1 format and the Open Type format.

Colors can also be difficult to manage in cross-platform projects, because both computer platforms employ different palette-mapping systems. The colors you use on the Macintosh, for example, may not appear the same on the PC. When you convert a Macintosh 256-color graphics file to Windows, all colors are mapped to their nearest equivalents, so the results you get will depend on the color palettes used on each platform. Color palettes are discussed in detail in Chapter 6. The use of Pantone colors that have numbers and chip charts to identify them may help you get the color you seek.

TIP *If dithering a color image doesn't achieve the results you want (and your design allows it), try using a gray-scale image instead.*

Chapter 11 Review

■ Chapter Summary

For your review, here's a summary of the important concepts discussed in this chapter.

Define authoring systems, describe what they do, and list the three different types

- With authoring systems, you can create, edit, and import data; assemble raw data into a playback sequence or cue sheet; and provide a structured method or language for responding to user input.

- There are several types of authoring tools: icon-based, event-driven, and time-based.

List the main attributes, benefits, and drawbacks of the three types of authoring systems

- With icon-based, event-driven authoring systems, multimedia elements and interaction cues are organized as objects in a structural framework.

- The icon-based tool's ability to visually chart the project's structure is particularly useful during the development of complicated navigational structures.

- With time-based tools, elements and events are organized along a timeline.

- Time-based tools are best to use when you have a message with a beginning and an end.

- Some time-based tools let you program jumps to any location in a sequence, thereby adding navigation and interactive control.

Describe how authoring systems include multimedia elements, and how these elements interact with each other and their environment, including programming tools

- Multimedia elements and events are often treated as objects that live in a hierarchical order of parent and child relationships.

- Messages passed among these objects order them to do things according to the properties or modifiers assigned to them.

- These systems usually provide some way of programming the interaction.

List several advanced and/or desirable features of an authoring system

- Some authoring tools provide a visual flowcharting system or overview facility for illustrating your project's structure.

- Authoring tools should provide some means of interactivity, the ability to synchronize time-based events, the ability to quickly and easily test your project or a portion of it, a run-time player that can be easily distributed, work cross-platform and handle web playback.

- Some authoring tools offer direct importing of preformatted text, indexing facilities, complex text search mechanisms, and hypertext linkage tools.

Describe additional characteristics and capabilities of the mentioned types of authoring systems

- With icon-based, event-driven tools, you build a flowchart by dragging appropriate icons from a library, and then adding content.

- Because they use visual storyboard-sequence flowcharts, icon-based authoring tools allow non-technical authors to create sophisticated applications.

- Time-based systems generally use a visual timeline for sequencing the events in a presentation.

■ Key Term Quiz

background layer *(294)*
card-based *(288)*
Cast *(299)*
conditional branching *(291)*
cross-platform *(301)*
ECMAScript *(298)*
handler *(293)*
icon-based, event-driven
  tools *(295)*

Lingo *(300)*
modifiers *(288)*
objects *(288)*
page-based *(288)*
properties *(288)*
run-time version *(292)*
Score *(299)*
scripting language *(291)*

Shockwave *(298)*
simple branching *(291)*
sprite *(300)*
stage *(299)*
standalone *(292)*
time-based tools *(288)*
very high level language (VHLL) *(291)*
visual programming *(290)*

■ Key Terms

1. Elements are organized as pages of a book or a stack of cards in a(n) _____ (two words) authoring system.

2. Multimedia elements and interaction cues (events) are organized as objects in a structural framework or process in a(n) _____ (two words) authoring system.

3. Elements and events are organized along a timeline in a(n) _____ (two words) authoring system.

4. In multimedia authoring systems, multimedia elements and events are often treated as _____ that live in a hierarchical order of parent and child relationships.

5. Messages passed among these objects order them to do things according to the _____ or modifiers assigned to them.

6. Perhaps the simplest and easiest authoring process using icons or objects is called _____ (two words).

7. A version of an authoring system that allows your project to play back without requiring the full authoring software and all its tools and editors is called a _____ (two words) version.

8. A program or presentation that can be played on both the Mac and Windows operating systems is called _____ (two words).

9. When an authoring system controls branching based on the results of an IF-THEN decision, it is called _____ (two words).

10. A particular instance of a multimedia element in Director's score is called a _____.

■ Multiple Choice Quiz

1. A scripting language is considered:
   a. a very low level language (VLLL)
   b. an assembler language
   c. a subset of HTML
   d. a form of BASIC
   e. a very high level language (VHLL)

2. Scripting languages operate by processing small blocks of code when certain events occur. Such a block of code is called:
   a. a function
   b. a handler
   c. a process
   d. a script
   e. a protocol

3. To extend most scripting languages on the Windows operating system you would use:
   a. a Dynamic Link Library
   b. an external command or function
   c. a handler
   d. a protocol
   e. an environmental directive

4. For a project whose content consists of elements that can be viewed individually, this type of authoring system is particularly useful during development.
   a. card- or page-based tool
   b. icon-based, event-driven tool
   c. time-based tool
   d. scripting language
   e. All are equally useful.

5. In multimedia authoring systems, multimedia elements and events are often treated as objects that exist in a hierarchical relationship. This relationship is often called:
   a. servant and master
   b. host and client

   c. property and modifier
   d. creator and creature
   e. parent and child

6. Which of the following is *not* true regarding multimedia programming objects?
   a. They typically take care of themselves.
   b. They exist in a hierarchical system.
   c. They are useful for games.
   d. They pass messages among themselves.
   e. All of these statements are true.

7. Synchronization of media events is difficult because:
   a. there is no established standard for multimedia frame rates as there is for audio CDs
   b. users can adjust the playback rates on their computers
   c. performance varies widely among different development and delivery computers
   d. authoring systems do not provide any simple mechanism for determining when a media element begins and ends
   e. solar flares affect playback rates

8. Flash is best known as a multimedia tool used for:
   a. interactive automobile dashboards
   b. animating web sites
   c. foreign language testing
   d. database reconciliation
   e. financial planning

9. For a project that requires complicated navigational structures, the charting capabilities of this type of authoring system are particularly useful.
   a. card- or page-based tool
   b. icon-based, event-driven tool

c. time-based tool

d. scripting language

e. All are equally useful.

10. Director stores multimedia elements in its:

a. stage

b. Cast

c. Score

d. sprite

e. Lingo

11. For a project with a beginning and an end, this type of authoring system is particularly useful.

a. card- or page-based tool

b. icon-based, event-driven tool

c. time-based tool

d. scripting language

e. All are equally useful.

12. Director's timeline is called the:

a. Cast

b. stage

c. sprite

d. Lingo

e. Score

13. In Director you can animate an object by:

a. changing its location over several frames

b. creating an animation object in Director's Animation Editor

c. "tweening" the object within a frame

d. changing its location on separate subsequent cards

e. Animations can't be accomplished in Director, but must be imported from an animation program.

14. Most card-based programs have a layer that stays constant behind a layer above it that can be different on all other cards. This layer is called the:

a. master layer

b. system layer

c. prime layer

d. background layer

e. static layer

15. Which of these is *not* a problem you might encounter in porting a program from a Mac to the PC (or from the PC to Mac)?

a. Bitmapped images are larger on a PC.

b. Font sizes and shapes are slightly different.

c. Special characters are not the same.

d. Graphics with 256 colors have different colors.

e. All are potential problems.

■ Essay Quiz

1. List and describe the different types of authoring systems and discuss the strength of each one. Describe the type of project that might be particularly well suited for each of these types, and explain why you might face challenges using the other type.

2. Describe how authoring systems include multimedia elements. What is an object? Describe the process of bowling in terms of objects (the bowler, the ball, the pins, etc.) Discuss how these objects interact and how they might pass messages to each other. Include your thoughts about how you might include factors such as gravity or branching based on what happens to the objects.

3. List 15 events or interactions that might take place within a multimedia program. Consider events that are related to user interaction, such as with the mouse or keyboard, time-based events, system or Internet-related events, etc.

4. Describe Adobe Acrobat Connect (or another authoring package), and discuss the theatrical metaphors it uses in its authoring environment. How do these metaphors relate to the interactive and presentational aspects of multimedia creation?

5. Describe the problems you are likely to encounter in creating a cross-platform program, and list several ways to deal with these problems.

Lab Projects

■ Project 11.1

Visit the web sites of several authoring systems. Try to locate two that are icon-based/event-driven, and two that are time-based. Compare and contrast their capabilities. Classify each one regarding:

- Type (icon-based, or time-based)
- Cross-platform capabilities
- Web or browser abilities
- Programming language (if any)

Most sites will include example projects. Observe what kinds of projects they generally represent and document your findings.

■ Project 11.2

You have been assigned to manage a major training CD-ROM project. This project is to include a complex simulation of a workplace task and a reference database of images. Create a hypothetical flow diagram that illustrates the relationship between the simulation and the database. Discuss how you might design and produce this project.

■ Project 11.3

Contact a multimedia presentation company. What tools do they commonly use? Are these tools cross platform? Ask if they use any of the built-in editors to edit the data. What other tools were used? How do they test for cross-platform compatibility?

■ Project 11.4

Locate and view three interactive multimedia CD-ROMs. Classify the content. Is it a presentation? A reference? Training or education? Marketing? What authoring system was used to create each one? Was this a good choice for the content? Why or why not? Discuss your thoughts.

CHAPTER 12

The Internet and How It Works

THE material covered in this chapter is designed to give you an overview of the Internet while describing particular features that may be useful to you as a developer of multimedia for the World Wide Web. This chapter does *not* provide details about technology for connecting and using the Internet, about setting up servers and hosts, about installing and using applications, or what to do when you are warned of the following:

Embarrassing yourself on the stage of the civilized world can be avoided by education. Visit your local bookstore, where, along with the work you are now reading, you may discover as many as a hundred helpful volumes about all the simple and arcane aspects of the Internet. Buy one or two of these and dig in. Or, if you are already connected to the Internet, much of the documentation you may require can be found by surfing the Net itself. Use a search engine such as those listed below. Look particularly for documents called **FAQs (Frequently Asked Questions)**, because they contain answers.

AllTheWeb.com	*http://www.alltheweb.com*
AltaVista	*http://www.altavista.com*
AOL Search	*http://search.aol.com*
Ask	*http://www.ask.com*
Ask Jeeves	*http://www.askjeeves.com*
Dogpile	*http://www.dogpile.com*
Gigablast	*http://www.gigablast.com*
Google	*http://www.google.com*
HotBot	*http://www.hotbot.com*

In this chapter, you will learn how to:

- Discuss the origins of the Internet

- Define what a computer network is and how networks are conceptually structured

- Describe how the Domain Name System (DNS) manages the identities of computers connected to the Internet

- Define bandwidth and discuss how bandwidth limitations govern the delivery of multimedia over the Internet

- Define the most common protocols used on the Internet

- Define how protocols, MIME-types, and URLs are used to identify, serve, and deliver multimedia

- Discuss the World Wide Web, HTML, the limitations of HTML, and how various technologies are stretching the limitations of HTML

LookSmart	*http://www.looksmart.com*
Lycos	*http://www.lycos.com*
MSN Search	*http://search.msn.com*
Netscape Search	*http://search.netscape.com*
Open Directory	*http://dmoz.org/*
Yahoo	*http://www.yahoo.com*

Search engines on the World Wide Web

Internet History

The **Internet** began as a research network funded by the **Advanced Research Projects Agency (ARPA)** of the U.S. Defense Department, when the first node of the **ARPANET** was installed at the University of California at Los Angeles in September 1969. By the mid-1970s, the ARPANET "inter-network" embraced more than 30 universities, military sites, and government contractors, and its user base expanded to include the larger computer science research community. By 1983, the network still consisted of merely several hundred computers on only a few local area networks.

In 1985, the National Science Foundation (NSF) arranged with ARPA to support a collaboration of supercomputing centers and computer science researchers across the ARPANET. The NSF also funded a program for improving the backbone of the ARPANET, by increasing its bandwidth from 56 Kbps to T1 and then T3 (see "Connections" a little later in the chapter) and branching out with links to international sites in Europe and the Far East.

In 1989, responsibility and management for the ARPANET was officially passed from military interests to the academically oriented NSF, and research organizations and universities (professors and students alike) became increasingly heavy users of this ever-growing "Internet." Much of the Internet's etiquette and rules for behavior (such as for sending e-mail and posting to newsgroups) was established during this time.

More and more private companies and organizations linked up to the Internet, and by the mid-1990s, the Internet included connections to more than 60 countries and more than 2 million host computers with more than 15 million users worldwide. Commercial and business use of the Internet was not permitted until 1992, but businesses have since become its driving force. By 2001 there were 109,574,429 domain hosts and 407.1 million users of the Internet, representing 6.71 percent of the world's population. In 2006 (see Table 12-1), about one out of every 6 people around the world (15.7 percent) access the Internet, and more than 51 million domain names had been registered as "dot coms."

World Region	Population (2006 Est.)	Pop. Percentage of World	Internet Usage	Percentage of Penetration	Percentage of World
Africa	915,210,928	14.1 %	23,649,000	2.6%	2.3%
Asia	3,667,774,066	56.4 %	364,270,713	9.9%	35.6%
Europe	807,289,020	12.4 %	291,600,898	36.1%	28.5%
Middle East	190,084,161	2.9 %	18,203,500	9.6%	1.8%
North America	331,473,276	5.1 %	227,303,680	68.6%	22.2%
Latin America/Caribbean	553,908,632	8.5 %	79,962,809	14.4%	7.8%
Oceania / Australia	33,956,977	0.5 %	17,872,707	52.6%	1.7%
WORLD TOTAL	6,499,697,060	100.0 %	1,022,863,307	15.7%	100.0%

Table 12-1 World Internet Users and Population Stats (from www.internetworldstats.com, 2006)

First Person

When I was a kid, I took it for granted that you could see a million stars in the summer sky, and it wasn't until much later that I discovered the truth: only a paltry few thousand stars are actually visible to the naked eye from Earth. While "millions" is a perfect number for a ten-year-old's perception of an infinite universe, the term needs definition. For example, what does "133 million users on the Internet" really mean? The following exercise might help: Start counting to a million, incrementing by one every second: (One) (Two) (Three)... In a minute, you will have counted to 60; in an hour, to 3,600. In 277.77 hours, you will reach a million—that's 11.57 24-hour days of nonstop counting, no pizza, no beer. You could try for the Guinness Book of Records, but you won't stay awake long enough!

Internetworking

In its simplest form, a **network** is a cluster of computers, with one computer acting as a server to provide network services such as file transfer, e-mail, and document printing to the client computers of that network. Using gateways and routers, a **local area network (LAN)** can be connected to other LANs to form a **wide area network (WAN)**. These LANs and WANs can also be connected to the Internet through a server that provides both the necessary software for the Internet and the physical data connection (usually a high-bandwidth telephone line). Individual computers not permanently part of a network (such as a home computer or a laptop) can dial up to one of these Internet servers and, with proper identification and onboard client software, obtain an IP address on the Internet (see IP Addresses and Data Packets later in the chapter).

Internet Addresses

Let's say you get into a taxi at the train station in Trento, Italy, explain in English or Spanish or German or French that you wish to go to the Mozzi Hotel, and half an hour later you are let out of the car in a suburban wood—you have an address problem. You will quickly discover, as you return to the city in the back of a bricklayer's lorry to report your missing luggage and the cab driver, Mauro, who sped away in the rain, that you also have a serious language problem.

If you know how addresses work and understand the syntax or language of the Internet you will likely not get lost and will save much time and expense during your adventures. You will also be able to employ shortcuts and workarounds.

Top-Level Domains

When the original ARPANET protocols for communicating among computers were remade into the current scheme of TCP/IP (Transmission Control Protocol/Internet Protocol) in 1983, the **Domain Name System (DNS)** was developed to rationally assign names and addresses to computers linked to the Internet. **Top-level domains (TLDs)** were established as categories to accommodate all users of the Internet:

com	Commercial entities
edu	Degree-granting colleges and universities (other schools register in the country domain)
gov	U.S. federal government agencies (state and local agencies register in the country domain)
int	Organizations established by international treaties and international databases
mil	U.S. military
net	Computers belonging to network providers
org	Miscellaneous and non-government organizations
Two-letter country codes	More than 240 countries and territories

In late 1998, the Internet Corporation for Assigned Names and Numbers (ICANN) was set up to oversee the technical coordination of the Domain Name System, which allows Internet addresses to be found by easy-to-remember names instead of one of 4.3 billion individual IP numbers. In late 2000, ICANN approved seven additional TLDs:

aero	Air-transport industry
biz	Businesses
coop	Cooperatives
info	Unrestricted use
museum	Museums
name	For registration by individuals
pro	Accountants, lawyers, and physicians

Concerns about "rights" and "ownership" of domains are inappropriate. It is appropriate to be concerned about "responsibilities" and "service" to the community.

....

J. Postel, from the Network Working Group RFC 1591, March 1994

As a particular domain name is built up from the top-level domain, it consists of different levels separated by a period (spoken as "dot"). Since we read left to right, we tend to think first.second.third, left to right, but domain name levels are numbered right to left. Companies such as Microsoft, Apple, and IBM have second-level domain addresses that read microsoft.com, apple.com, and ibm.com—they are commercial (.com) operations with their second-level domain to the left of the top-level "com" domain. Government (.gov) agencies such as the Federal Bureau of Investigation, the Internal Revenue Service (a branch of the U.S. Treasury Department), and the White House have addresses that read fbi.gov, irs.ustreas.gov (note that the irs constitutes a third-level address), and whitehouse.gov.

NOTE   *The domain whitehouse.com was for many years a serious pornographic web site, quite an object lesson in the wonders of First Amendment rights and free speech, but likely very annoying to the residents at whitehouse.gov. Perhaps just as annoying, however, may be the domain's makeover as "America's Free Speech Forum," where anonymous tipsters can leave juicy news reports.*

Many second-level domains contain huge numbers of computers and user accounts representing local, regional, and even international branches as well as various internal business and management functions. So the Internet addressing scheme provides for sub-domains that can contain even more sub-domains. Like a finely carved Russian matryoshka doll, individual workstations live at the epicenter of a cluster of domains.

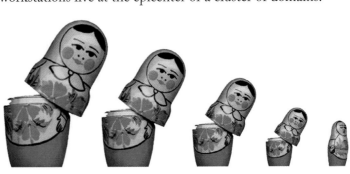

Within the education (.edu) domain containing hundreds of universities and colleges, for example, is a second-level domain for Yale University called yale. At that university are many schools and departments (medicine, engineering, law, business, computer science, and so on), and each of these entities in turn has departments and possibly sub-departments and many users. These departments operate one or even several servers for managing traffic to and from the many computers in their group and to the outside world. At Yale, the server for the Computing and Information Systems Department is named cis. It manages about 11,000 departmental accounts—so many accounts that a cluster of three subsidiary servers was installed to deal efficiently with the demand. These subsidiary servers are named minerva, morpheus, and mercury. Thus, minerva lives in the cis domain, which lives in the yale domain, which lives in the edu domain. Real people's computers are networked to minerva. Other real people are connected to the morpheus and mercury servers. To make things easy (exactly what computers are for), the mail system database at Yale maintains a master list of all of its people. So, as far as the outside world is concerned, a professor's e-mail address can be simply firstname.lastname@yale.edu; the database knows he or she is really connected to minerva so the mail is forwarded to that correct final address. In detailed e-mail headers, you may see the complete destination address listed as well as names of the computers through which your mail message may have been routed.

E-mail accounts are said to be "at" a domain (written with the @ sign). There are never any blank spaces in an Internet e-mail address, and while addresses on the Internet are normally case insensitive, conventional use dictates using all lowercase: the Internet will find tay@timestream.com, TAY@TIMESTREAM.COM, and Tay@Timestream.Com to be the same address.

The US Domain and Country Codes

The two-letter US domain is based on political boundaries and is used by federal, state, and local government agencies, high schools, technical/vocational schools, private schools, elementary schools, libraries, fire and police departments, and regular citizens. Any computer in the United States can be in the US domain. Some fictitious examples are as follows:

statue_liberty.nps.interior.fed.us	Federal agency
senate.fed.us	U.S. Senate
senate.state.pa.us	Pennsylvania state senate
assembly.state.ut.us	Utah state assembly
dmv.state.ca.us	California Department of Motor Vehicles

oakland.dmv.state.ca.us	Local office of DMV
police.ci.miami.fl.us	City department
fire.ci.weston.ma.us	City department
sheriff.co.alameda.ca.us	County department
ccsf.cc.ca.us	Public community college
lincoln-high.eh-parish.k12.la.us	Public school
appleton.lib.me.us	Public library
gda.pvt.k12.ma.us	Private school
chevron.richmond.ca.us	Business
lefigaro.portland.or.us	Restaurant
paddys.boston.ma.us	Bar

http://rfc.net/rfc1480.html

The Internet RFC 1480 describes the hierarchical rules for addresses in the US domain

Two-letter country codes, based on the International Standards Organization (ISO) document ISO-3166, are used in the addresses of all computers located outside the United States. Each country has an administrator who is responsible for organizing the naming hierarchy within that country's domain. Some countries use categories similar to com, edu, and org. Others base their naming hierarchies on political boundaries, as in the US country code.

schmidt@cage.rug.ac.be	Professor at University of Gent, Belgium
smythe@fiqus.unl.edu.ar	Student at L.C.S.A, Argentina
smith@iskratel.si	Commercial account, Slovenia
smith@laughs.co.uk	Commercial account, United Kingdom
smithe@idsc.gov.eg	Student at Cairo University, Egypt
smithy@udcf.gla.ac.uk	Researcher at University of Glasgow, Scotland
tsmith@library.usyd.edu.au	Scholar at University of Sydney, Australia

http://www.iana.org/cctld/cctld-whois.htm

List of two-letter country codes

IP Addresses and Data Packets

When a stream of data is sent over the Internet by your computer, it is first broken down into packets by the Transmission Control Protocol (TCP). Each packet includes the address of the receiving computer, a sequence number ("this is packet #5"), error correction information, and a small piece of your data. After a packet is created by TCP, the Internet Protocol (IP) then takes over and actually sends the packet to its destination along a route that may include many other computers acting as forwarders. **TCP/IP** is two important Internet protocols working in concert.

The 32-bit address included in a data packet, the **IP address**, is the "real" Internet address. It is made up of four numbers separated by periods, for example, 140.174.162.10. Some of these numbers are assigned by Internet authorities, and some may be dynamically assigned by an **Internet Service Provider (ISP)** when a computer logs on from a dial-up account. There are domain name servers throughout the Internet whose sole job is to quickly look up text-based domain name addresses in large distributed databases, convert them into real IP addresses, and then return them to you for insertion into your data packets. Every time you connect to http://www.google.com or send mail to president@whitehouse.gov, the domain name server is consulted and the destination address is converted to numbers.

TIP   *IP addresses and domain names can be used interchangeably. Thus, kona .midcoast.com is the same Internet address as 69.39.100.10. There are occasional problems with the Internet's DNS servers, and using the IP address, you may get connected immediately. With a Ping utility, or using the "whois" function in Unix, you can discover a domain's IP address.*

Connections

If your computer is connected to an existing network at an office or school, it is possible you are already connected to the Internet. Check with your system administrator about procedures for connecting to Internet services such as the World Wide Web; necessary browser software may already be installed on your machine. If you are an individual working from home, you will need a telephone dial-up account or broadband cable, Digital Subscriber Line (DSL), or wireless equipment to connect to your office network through an Internet Service Provider (ISP).

If you are connecting to the Internet through an online service such as America Online (AOL) or Microsoft Network (MSN) (see Figure 12-1), you will need special software provided by that service. AOL provides Web, FTP, and Gopher features (see Internet Services later in the chapter). MSN software is built into Windows and can be installed during Windows setup. Both act as ISPs to connect your computer to the *backbone* of the Internet—the ultra-high-bandwidth underlying network operated by MCI, AT&T, Sprint, and other telecommunications companies.

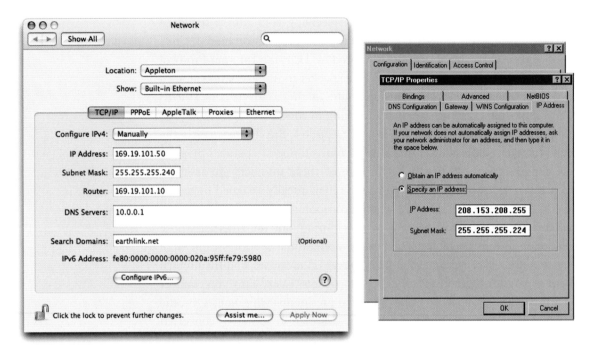

Figure 12-1 TCP/IP is used to connect to an Internet Service Provider.

For connecting to the Internet through an ISP, software typically consists of the **PPP (Point-to-Point Protocol)** application for dialing up and TCP/IP software for properly sending and receiving data once you are connected. ISPs usually provide one or more POPs (**Points of Presence**), which is a local telephone number for connecting to the ISP's server. (This should not be confused with another POP acronym, **Post Office Protocol**, which is used to retrieve e-mail from a mail server.) Figure 12-1 shows the PPP control panel for Macintosh and the Network Control Panel for Windows. Getting connected to the Internet can be a bit daunting, as there are many options to configure. However, most ISPs offer detailed instructions and kits to make this job easy.

The Bandwidth Bottleneck

Bandwidth is how much data, expressed in bits per second (bps), you can send from one computer to another in a given amount of time. The faster your transmissions (or the greater the bandwidth of your connection), the less time you will spend waiting for text, images, sounds, and animated illustrations to upload or download from computer to computer, and the more satisfaction you will have with your Internet experience. To think in bytes per second, divide the rate by eight. Table 12-2 lists the bandwidth of some common data transfer methods.

Type of Connection	Bandwidth (in bits per second) Without Compression	Comment
56K modem (Dial-Up)	56,000	Maximum analog modem speed for copper wires, data compressed using V91 standard. Actual is about 48 Kbps.
ISDN	56,000 to 128,000	Integrated Services Digital Network basic services (128,000 bps if no voice mixed in).
Frame relay	56,000 to 45,000,000	Dedicated service offered by long-distance phone companies.
Ethernet-10	10,000,000	Networking hardware and protocol, commonly uses two twisted pairs of copper wire.
T-1 (DS-1 in North America)	1,544,000	Equal to 24 leased lines at 56 Kbps.
E-1 (DS-1 in Europe	2,000,000	European equivalent of a T-1 connection.
DSL	1,500,000 to 9,000,000	Digital Subscriber Line service available in various technologies (HDSL, SDSL, ADSL, VDSL, and RDSL) with differing data rates, operating distances, and ratios between downstream and upstream speeds.
CableModem	3,000,000 upload; 7,000,000 download	Even though copper coaxial TV cable can be used in a bidirectional fashion, it was originally designed to carry limited signals in one direction.
Ethernet (Thin)	10,000,000	Older and slower Ethernet for two twisted pairs of copper wire.
Wireless (802.11)	3,000,000 to 54,000,000	Line-of-sight radio connection in the radio frequency (RF) bands of 2.4 Ghz (WiFi) or 5.8 Ghz.
T-3 (D-3 in North America)	45,000,000	Typical backbone speed of major ISPs in the United States (1996).
Fast SCSI III	80,000,000	Data transfer rate for Fast SCSI III or Ultra SCSI.
Fast Ethernet-100	100,000,000	Networking hardware and protocol, commonly uses two twisted pairs of copper wire.
OC-3	155,000,000	Upgrade for ISPs in the United States (1997).
OC-48	2,400,000,000 (2.4 gigabits per second)	Typical speed for intercity fiber-optic lines (called SONET or Synchronous Optical Network).
OC-48	2,400,000,000 (2.4 gigabits per second)	Typical speed for intercity fiber-optic lines (called SONET or Synchronous Optical Network).
ATM	In steps, from 45,000,000 to 145,000,000 to 2,400,000,000	Asynchronous Transfer Mode—protocol for sending and receiving voice and other data (53-byte cells, each with 5-byte headers and 48-byte content; cell headers waste about 10 percent of available bandwidth). The cell size was a compromisebetween U.S. and European members of the standards committee, one group wanting 48, the other group, more. The 53-byte compromise was based on the size needed for video without too much packet delay.
OC-255	13,210,000,000 (13.21 gigabits per second)	Really fast fiber-optic lines using SONET.

Table 12-2 Bandwidth of Typical Internet and Computer Connections /For more information visit www.cis.eku.edu/loy/cis300/bandwidth.html.

The bottleneck at a typical user's low-bandwidth modem connection is the most serious impediment to sending multimedia across the Internet. At low bandwidth, a page of text (3,000 bytes) can take less than a second to send, but an uncompressed 640×480, 8-bit/256-color image (about 300,000 bytes) can take a few minutes; an uncompressed 640×480, 24-bit/16 million-color image (about 900,000 bytes) can take many minutes to send.

To work within the constraints of this challenging bottleneck (until the bottleneck is cleared by the wide use of inexpensive, higher-speed cable modems and wireless connections—see Chapter 9 for more details), multimedia developers on the Internet have but a few options:

- Compress data as tightly as possible (into ZIP or SIT or TAR files) before transmitting.

- Require users to download data only once; then store the data in a local hard disk cache (this is automatically managed by most browsers).

- Design each multimedia element to be efficiently compact—don't use a greater color depth than is absolutely necessary or leave extra space around the edges.

- Design alternate low-bandwidth and high-bandwidth navigation paths to accommodate all users.

- Implement streaming methods that allow data to be transferred and displayed incrementally as it comes in (without waiting for the entire data file to arrive).

Internet Services

To many users, the Internet means the World Wide Web. But the Web is only the latest and most popular of services available today on the Internet. E-mail, file transfer, discussion groups and newsgroups, real-time chatting by text, voice, and video, and the ability to log into remote computers are common as well. Internet services are shown here.

Each Internet service is implemented on an Internet server by dedicated software known as a **daemon**. (Actually, daemons only exist on Unix/Linux systems—on other systems, such as Windows NT, the services may run as regular applications or background processes.)

Service	Purpose
http	For posting and reading documents (from the Hypertext Transfer Protocol used by the World Wide Web)
https	For posting and reading encrypted (secure) documents
pop	For receiving electronic mail (from Post Office Protocol)
ftp	For transferring files between computers; can be anonymous or password protected (from File Transfer Protocol)
gopher	For menus of material available on the Internet
usenet	For participating in discussion groups (from USErs NETwork)
telnet	For logging on and working from remote computers
irc	For real-time text messaging (from Internet Relay Chat)
smtp	For sending mail (Simple Mail Transport Protocol)
mud	For real-time game playing (from MultiUser Dimension)

FTP.ARL.MIL (Army Research Laboratory) Bandwidth Information

ARL has multiple high-speed connections to several significant networks, providing excellent performance for most document transfers:

- **DREN** This site is a primary node in the Defense Research and Engineering Network (DREN), which sports a variety of OC-12, OC-3, T-3 and T-1 communications links to other US Government facilities.

- **The Internet Backbone** This site is connected to the Internet "backbone" at strategic locations via a "cloud" of OC-12 ATM paths provisioned over AT&T's nationwide DISC ATM network:

  MAE-East in Washington DC
  FIX-West and MAE-West in San Francisco
  The Sprint NAP in Pensauken, NJ
  The NAP in Chicago, IL
  The "Giga-pop" in Washington state

- **NIPRNET (nee MILNET)** This site is gatewayed to a NIPRNET military Packet Switching Node that has multiple T-1 trunks.

  Moving 1 MByte of data over an OC-3 link takes about 0.1 seconds, if your end is up to it.

  Moving 1 MByte of data over a T-3 link takes about 1 second, if your end is up to it.

  Moving 1 MByte of data over a T-1 link takes about 8 seconds.

  Moving 1 MByte of data over a 56 Kbps link takes about 3 minutes.

  Moving 1 MByte of data over a 28.8 Kbps modem takes about 5 minutes.

  Naturally, no single file transfer ever gets the full bandwidth of these communications lines, as they are a shared resource. These figures should help you make a lower-bound estimate on how much time large file transfers might take.

  You are free to transfer large files from this site at any time.

  Information seekers from all domains are welcome to view this data. It is important that our guests understand that this is an official U.S. Government System for unclassified use only. Use of this system constitutes consent to security testing and monitoring.

....

webmaster@arl.army.mil

Daemons are agent programs that run in the background, waiting to act on requests from the outside. In the case of the Internet, daemons support protocols such as the **Hypertext Transfer Protocol (HTTP)** for the World Wide Web, the Post Office Protocol (POP) for e-mail, or the File Transfer Protocol (FTP) for exchanging files. You have probably noticed that the first few letters of a **URL (Uniform Resource Locator)**—for example, http://www.timestream.com/index.html—notify a server as to which daemon to bring into play to satisfy a request. In many cases, the daemon for the Web, mail, news, and FTP may run on completely different servers, each isolated by a security firewall from other servers on a network.

MIME-Types

To work with multimedia on the Internet, you must work within the requirements of the appropriate protocol, using recognizable documents and formats. A voice attachment to an e-mail message, for example, must be identified by the Post Office daemon for what it is, and then be transmitted with the correct coding to the receiving computer. The receiver must have the proper software (and hardware) for decoding the information and playing it back. To identify the nature of the data transmitted and, by inference, the purpose of that data, the Internet uses a standard list of file name extensions called **MIME-types (Multipurpose Internet Mail Extensions)**. Most browsers allow you to define MIME-types and map "helper apps" to the type for decoding and playing. For example, with Netscape Navigator you can define Adobe's Acrobat files (PDF files) as a MIME-type and select the Acrobat Reader as the player application.

These are not just used by the e-mail daemon but, by convention, by other Internet daemons, including the Web's HTTP daemon. Perhaps the most widely installed HTTP software for managing web pages is the open source application called Apache (http://www.apache.org). Table 12-3 shows a list of common MIME-types and their uses. (Note that many come from the Unix world, where the Internet was born.) You can also visit www.file-ext.com for more information.

Multimedia elements are typically saved and transmitted on the Internet in the appropriate MIME-type format and are named with the proper extension for that type. For example, Shockwave Flash animation files end in .swf; image files end in .jpg, .jpeg, .gif, or .png; sound files end in .au, .wav, .aif, .mp3, or another conforming format; QuickTime and other video clips end in .qt, .mov, or avi.

WARNING   *Because some MIME-types for multimedia data are new or experimental, not all servers may recognize them. If you have problems with a multimedia file, check with your Internet Service Provider to be sure your server can serve "experimental" MIME-types. Some ISPs will not install the requisite, and often costly, server software for high-bandwidth streaming MIME-types.*

Extension	Type	Use
ai	application/postscript	PostScript program
aif	audio/x-aiff	Audio
aifc	audio/x-aiff	Audio
AIFF	audio/x-aiff	Audio
aiff	audio/x-aiff	Audio
au	audio/basic	ULAW audio data
avi	video/x-msvideo	Microsoft video
bin	application/octet-stream	Binary executable
cpio	application/x-cpio	Unix CPIO archive
csh	application/x-csh	C shell program
dcr	application/director	Shockwave animation
dvi	application/x-dvi	TeX DVI data
eps	application/postscript	PostScript program
exe	application/octet-stream	Binary executable
fif	application/fractals	Fractal image format
gif	image/gif	CompuServe image format
gtar	application/x-gtar	GNU tape archive
gz	encoding/x-gzip	GNU zip compressed data
hqx	application/mac-binhex40	Macintosh BinHex archive
htm	text/html	Hypertext Markup Language
html	text/html	Hypertext Markup Language
ief	image/ief	Image
jpe	image/jpeg	JPEG image
jpeg	image/jpeg	JPEG image
jpg	image/jpeg	JPEG image
latex	application/x-latex	LaTeX document
man	application/x-troff-man	Unix manual page
me	application/x-troff-me	TROFF document
mov	video/quicktime	QuickTime video
movie	video/x-sgi-movie	SGI video
mpe	video/mpeg	MPEG video
mpeg	video/mpeg	MPEG video
mpg	video/mpeg	MPEG video
ms	application/x-troff-ms	TROFF document
pbm	image/x-portable-bitmap	PBM image
pgm	image/x-portable-graymap	PGM image
pnm	image/x-portable-anymap	PBM image

Table 12-3   Common MIME-Types Illustrate the Variety of Data Types and Formats Used on the Internet

Extension	Type	Use
ppm	image/x-portable-pixmap	PPM image
ps	application/postscript	PostScript program
qt	video/quicktime	QuickTime video
ra	audio/x-pn-realaudio	RealAudio sound
ram	audio/x-pn-realaudio	RealAudio sound
ras	image/x-cmu-raster	CMU raster image
rgb	image/x-rgb	RGB image
roff	application/x-troff	TROFF document
rtf	application/rtf	Rich Text Format
sh	application/x-sh	Bourne shell program
shar	application/x-shar	Unix shell archive
sit	application/x-stuffit	Macintosh archive
snd	audio/basic	ULAW audio data
t	application/x-troff	TROFF document
tar	application/x-tar	Unix tape archive
tcl	application/x-tcl	TCL program
tex	application/x-tex	TeX document
texi	application/x-texinfo	GNU TeXinfo document
texinfo	application/x-texinfo	GNU TeXinfo document
text	text/plain	Plain text
tif	image/tiff	TIFF image
tiff	image/tiff	TIFF image
tr	application/x-troff	TROFF document
txt	text/plain	Plain text
vox	audio	VoxWare
wav	audio/x-wav	WAV audio
xbm	image/x-xbitmap	X bitmap
xpm	image/x-xpixmap	X pixmap
xwd	image/x-xwindowdump	X Window dump image
Z	encoding/x-compress	Compressed data
zip	application/x-zip-compressed	Zip compressed data

Table 12-3 Common MIME-Types Illustrate the Variety of Data Types and Formats Used on the Internet *(continued)*

The World Wide Web and HTML

The World Wide Web (http://www.w3.org/) started in 1989 at the European Particle Physics Laboratory (CERN) as a "distributed collaborative hypermedia information system." It was designed by Tim Berners-Lee as a protocol for linking a multiplicity of documents located on computers anywhere within the Internet. This new Hypertext Transfer Protocol (HTTP) provided rules for a simple transaction between two computers on the Internet consisting of (1) establishing a connection, (2) requesting that a document be sent, (3) sending the document, and (4) closing the connection. It also required a simple document format called Hypertext Markup Language (HTML) for presenting structured text mixed with inline images.

An HTML document could contain hyperlinks or anchors (see Chapter 14) that referred to other similar documents. With browser software, users could then click on designated areas of hot text in one document and jump to another, which itself might have more hot text pointing to yet other documents. Users could surf from document to document across the Web, with HTML as the underlying buoyant framework.

Dynamic Web Pages and XML

HTML is fine for building and delivering uncomplicated *static* web pages. But you will need other tools and programming know-how to deliver *dynamic* pages that are built on the fly from text, graphics, animations, and information contained in databases or documents. JavaScript and programs written in Java may be inserted into HTML pages to perform special functions and tasks that go beyond the vanilla abilities of HTML—for mouse rollovers, window control, and custom animations.

Cold Fusion and PHP are applications running side by side, with a web server like Apache; they scan an outgoing web page for special commands and directives, usually imbedded in special tags. If they find a special tag in the page, the software will do what the tag tells it to do, like "get today's date and put it into that table cell" or "search this database for all customers with balances greater than $100 and, after alphabetizing, put that list into a table on the web page being served." Working hand-in-hand with these application servers, Oracle, Sybase, and mySQL offer software to manage **SQL (Structured Query Language)** databases that may contain not only text but also graphics and multimedia resources like sounds and video clips. In concert with HTML, these tools provide the power to do real work and perform real tasks within the context of the World Wide Web.

Flash animations and Director applications (see Chapter 11) can also be called from within HTML pages. These multimedia mini applications, often programmed by Web developers, use a browser plugin to display the action and perform tasks such as playing a sound, showing a video, or calculating a date. As with Cold Fusion and PHP, both use underlying programming languages (ActionScript and Lingo).

XML (eXtensible Markup Language) goes beyond HTML—it is the next evolutionary step in the development of the Internet for formatting and delivering web pages using styles. Unlike HTML, you can create your own tags in XML to describe exactly what the data means, and you can get that data from anywhere on the Web. In XML, you can build a set of tags like

```
<fruit>
<type>Tomato</type>
<source>California</source>
<price>$.64</price>
</fruit>
```

and your XML document, according to your instructions, will find the information to put into the proper place on the web page in the formatting style you assign. For example, with XML styles, you can declare that all items within the <price> tag will be displayed in boldface Helvetica type.

. . . .

http://www.xml.org

http://www.xml.com

More information about XML

. . . .

In development as a technique to deliver more pleasing web experiences, AJAX (Asynchronous JavaScript And XML) uses a combination of XML, CSS (cascading style sheets for marking up and styling information), and JavaScript to generate dynamic displays and allow user interaction within a web browser.

Multimedia on the Web

During the coming years, most multimedia experiences on the Internet will occur on the World Wide Web, programmed within the constraints of HTML, then stretched by the enhanced capabilities provided by XML, Java, JavaScript, AJAX, and special plug-ins like Flash and QuickTime to enable browsers to exceed their limits. To design and make effective multimedia for this environment, developers need to understand not only how to create and edit the elements of multimedia, but also how to deliver it for HTML browsers and plug-in/player vehicles. Well-crafted, professionally rendered sites on the Web include text, images, audio, and animation presented in a user-friendly interface that balances the bandwidth deficit against user patience. HTML, the plug-in tools, and players are discussed in Chapter 13. Techniques, tricks, and presentation styles for delivering multimedia on the Web are discussed in Chapter 14.

Inside the event horizon of the amazing World Wide Web explosion are many uncertainties and unsolved challenges. The bandwidth deficit will certainly be met with technology solutions that will be effectively marketed into homes and businesses. But the pressure of more and more users entering the Web will create a terrific need for high quality, compelling content; multimedia developers and entrepreneurs will fill this creative void.

The Web is becoming much more than a static library. Increasingly, users are accessing the Web for "web pages" that aren't actually on the shelves. Instead, the pages are generated dynamically from information available to the web server. That information can come from databases on the web server, from the site owner's enterprise databases, or even from other web sites.

. . . .

Charles Goldfarb, who invented SGML (the parent language of HTML and XML) and coined the term "markup language."

Chapter 12 Review

■ Chapter Summary

For your review, here is a summary of the important concepts discussed in this chapter.

Discuss the origins of the Internet

- The Internet began as a research network funded by the U.S. Defense Department in 1969.

- In 1989, the National Science Foundation took over its management, and research organizations and universities (professors and students alike) became increasingly heavy users of this ever-growing "Internet."

- Commercial and business use of the Internet was not permitted until 1992, but businesses have since become its driving force.

Define what a computer network is and how networks are conceptually structured

- A network is a cluster of computers, with one computer acting as a server to provide services such as file transfer, e-mail, and document printing to the client computers.

- Using gateways and routers, a local area network (LAN) can be connected to other LANs to form a wide area network (WAN).

- These LANs and WANs can also be connected to the Internet through a server that provides both the necessary software for the Internet and the physical data connection.

Describe what a computer network is and how the Domain Name System (DNS) manages the identities of computers connected to the Internet

- The Domain Name System (DNS) manages the names and addresses of computers linked to the Internet.

- Computers on the Internet manage names in sub-domains that are encapsulated so that visitors from outside the local network need not worry about the sub-domain names.

- When a stream of data is sent over the Internet by your computer, it is first broken down into packets by the Transmission Control Protocol (TCP).

- The IP (Internet Protocol) address is made up of four numbers between 0 and 255 separated by periods.

- Domain name servers throughout the Internet quickly look up domain name addresses and convert them into IP addresses.

- For connecting to the Internet through an ISP (Internet Service Provider), software typically uses a PPP (Point-to-Point Protocol) application for dialing up and TCP/IP software for properly sending and receiving data once you are connected.

Define bandwidth and discuss how bandwidth limitations govern the delivery of multimedia over the Internet

- Bandwidth is how much data, expressed in bits per second (bps), you can send from one computer to another in a given amount of time.

- The bottleneck at a typical user's low-bandwidth modem connection is the most serious impediment to sending multimedia across the Internet.

Define the most common protocols used on the Internet

- http and https for posting and reading documents (from the Hypertext Transfer Protocol used by the World Wide Web)

- POP for receiving electronic mail (from Post Office Protocol)

- ftp for transferring files between computers (from File Transfer Protocol)

- gopher, for menus of material available on the Internet

- usenet for participating in discussion groups (from USErs NETwork)
- telnet for logging on and working from remote computers
- irc for real-time text messaging (from Internet Relay Chat)
- smtp for sending mail (Simple Mail Transport Protocol)
- mud for real-time game playing (from MultiUser Dimension).

Define how protocols, MIME-types, and URLs are used to identify, serve, and deliver multimedia

- When a server receives a request, it is handled by a specific application called a daemon that responds to the request based on the protocol.
- The first part of the URL (Uniform Resource Locator) identifies the protocol to use to handle the request.
- Multimedia elements are typically saved and transmitted on the Internet in the appropriate MIME-type (for Multipurpose Internet Mail Extensions) format and are named with the proper extension for that type.

Discuss the World Wide Web, HTML, the limitations of HTML, and how various technologies are stretching the limitations of HTML

- The World Wide Web started in 1989 as a "distributed collaborative hypermedia information system" for linking documents located on computers anywhere within the Internet.
- Hypertext Transfer Protocol (HTTP) provides rules for contacting, requesting, and sending documents encoded with the Hypertext Markup Language (HTML).
- HTML includes structured text mixed with inline images.
- HTML's ability to handle multimedia is limited.
- JavaScript and Java applets can add interaction to a page.
- Cold Fusion and PHP can work with databases to create web pages on the fly.
- XML (eXtensible Markup Language) allows you to create your own tags and import data from anywhere on the Web.

■ Key Terms

Advanced Research Projects Agency (ARPA) *(309)*
ARPANET *(309)*
bandwidth *(316)*
daemon *(318)*
Domain Name System (DNS) *(311)*
FAQs (Frequently Asked Questions) *(308)*
Hypertext Transfer Protocol (HTTP) *(320)*
Internet *(309)*

Internet Service Provider (ISP) *(315)*
IP address *(315)*
local area network (LAN) *(310)*
MIME-types (Multipurpose Internet Mail Extensions) *(320)*
network *(310)*
Points of Presence *(316)*
Post Office Protocol *(316)*
PPP (Point-to-Point Protocol) *(316)*

Structured Query Language (SQL) *(323)*
TCP/IP *(315)*
top-level domain (TLD) *(311)*
Uniform Resource Locator (URL) *(320)*
wide area network (WAN) *(310)*
XML (eXtensible Markup Language) *(323)*

Key Term Quiz

1. The predecessor to the Internet, created by the Advanced Research Projects Agency, was known as the _____.

2. Many web sites include pages that have answers to common inquiries. These pages are known as _____.

3. A cluster of computers tied together to share files and communications is a(n) _____.

4 When a stream of data is sent over the Internet by your computer, it is first broken down into packets by the _____.

5. The set of four numbers separated by periods that points to a domain is a(n) _____.

6. PPP software is typically used to dial up to a(n) _____.

7. How much data, expressed in bits per second (bps), you can send from one computer to another in a given amount of time is called _____.

8. Each Internet service is implemented on an Internet server by dedicated software known as a _____.

9. To identify the nature of the data transmitted, the Internet uses a standard list of file name extensions called _____.

10. The tagging scheme that allows you to create your own tags and import data from anywhere on the Web is called _____.

Multiple Choice Quiz

1. A local area network (LAN) can be connected to other LANs to form:
   a. a wide area network
   b. a Transmission Control Protocol
   c. a MIME-type
   d. an Internet Service Provider
   e. a web hosting company

2. DNS stands for:
   a. Distributed Numbering System
   b. Device Nomenclature System
   c. Data Networking System
   d. Domain Name System
   e. Digital Neighborhood System

3. The levels of a domain name are separated by:
   a. a period
   b. the @ symbol
   c. forward slashes
   d. hyphens
   e. spaces

4. Commercial and business use of the Internet was not permitted until:
   a. 1969
   b. 1982
   c. 1989
   d. 1992
   e. 1998

5. Which of these is not a top-level domain?
   a. com
   b. edu
   c. gov
   d. mil
   e. cis

6. Which part of this URL "http://www.company.com/home.html" represents the second-level address?
   a. http
   b. www
   c. company

d. com

e. home.html

7. Which of the following is a valid IP address?

    a. 192.168.1.1

    b. www.apple.com

    c. activa@midcoast.com

    d. http://www.pages.net/index.html

    e. 12 Dreamcatcher Way, Hope, ME 04847

8. When a stream of data is sent over the Internet by your computer, it is first broken down into packets by the:

    a. Transmission Control Protocol

    b. Internet Protocol

    c. Post Office Protocol

    d. Simple Mail Transfer Protocol

    e. File Transfer Protocol

9. The protocol used for logging on and working from remote computers is:

    a. ftp

    b. gopher

    c. usenet

    d. telnet

    e. smtp

10. The MIME-type assigned to a data source depends on:

    a. the size of the data file

    b. the type of file being sent

    c. the end user's computer system

    d. the end user's browser

    e. the phase of the moon

11. Perhaps the most widely installed HTTP software for managing web pages is the open source application called:

    a. Apache

    b. Daemon

    c. ISP

    d. Acrobat

    e. Unix

12. Web pages are written in:

    a. MPEG

    b. HTML

    c. QuickTime

    d. TCP/IP

    e. MIME

13. One of the greatest benefits of XML is that:

    a. it allows you to create animated rollovers

    b. it compresses audio and video files, allowing larger files to be sent

    c. it connects local area networks with wide area networks

    d. it allows you to create your own tags for data

    e. it encapsulates data into packets for more reliable transmission

14. An IP address can be exchanged with a:

    a. MIME-type

    b. Point-to-Point Protocol

    c. domain name

    d. e-mail address

    e. usenet group

15. HTTP stands for:

    a. High-Technology Transmission Protocol

    b. Help Text Translation Protocol

    c. Hypertext Transfer Protocol

    d. Hardware Testing Tool Protocol

    e. How To Talk Protocol

■ Essay Quiz

1. List the most common web protocols and their uses.
2. Describe what the different parts of the URL http://www.secondLevel.topLevel/filename.filetype represent.
3. Briefly describe how a browser requests a URL, how the URL is handled, and how the server responds, in terms of the DNS system, encoding schemes, and data protocols.
4. Briefly describe the data rates of a 56K dial-up, ISDN, DSL, Cable Modem, and T1 connection. Roughly calculate how long it would take to download a web page consisting of a 5 kilobyte HTML page and 45 kilobytes of image files.
5. List the most common top-level domains, and describe what categories they are associated with.

Lab Projects

■ Project 12.1

The programs used to view or work with data served over the Internet are called "clients." Perhaps the most common client is the web browser. Write down your answers to the following questions:

What clients are available to handle http?

What clients are available to handle ftp?

What clients are available to handle pop and smtp?

Go to a shareware site, such as tucows.com, shareware.com, or some similar site, and identify three clients available for ftp, usenet, gopher, and telnet. Note your findings.

■ Project 12.2

You are given the task of developing a new web site for a cooking magazine. Think about the capabilities of XML to allow you to define your own data tags. What data types would you include? How might you format them? What would be the benefits in this case of being able to define your own tags? Create an outline of how you might structure the data included in a recipe.

■ Project 12.3

Open a web browser. Locate the "helper applications" preferences panel in the browser. (Note: this option varies among browsers and operating systems, and may not be available for some.)

Find the following MIME-types: audio/x-aiff; application/postscript; application/x-gtar; text/html; image/jpeg; video/mpeg; image/tiff; video/quicktime; audio/x-pn-realaudio. List an application commonly used to read or edit each type.

CHAPTER 13

Tools for the World Wide Web

T HIS chapter presents an overview of the many Internet tools that you that may wish to acquire for your multimedia toolbox as you are learning to make the Web stand up and dance. URLs and other pointers are also included here to lead you to information for obtaining, installing, and using these applications and utilities.

In the late 1990s, multimedia plug-ins and commercial tools aimed at the Web entered the marketplace at a furious pace, each competing for visibility and developer/user mind share in an increasingly noisy venue. In the few years since the birth of the first line-driven HTTP daemon in Switzerland, millions of web surfers had become hungry for "cool" enhancements to entertaining sites. Web site and page developers needed creative tools to feed the surfers, while surfers needed browsers and the plug-ins and players to make these cool multimedia enhancements work.

A combination of the explosion of these tools and user demand for performance is stressing the orderly development of the core HTML standard. Unable to evolve fast enough to satisfy the demand for features (there are committees, international meetings, rational debates, comment periods, and votes in the standards process), the HTML language is constantly being extended de facto by commercial interests. These companies regularly release new versions of web browsers containing **tags** (HTML formatting elements) and features not yet formally approved. By the time (measured in weeks!) millions of users have become dependent upon the features of new browser versions, the more carefully considered official specification has no choice but to incorporate them. By the time features are "official," of course—after more meetings, votes, and understated demonstrations of power—still newer browser versions have been released with yet newer, unofficial features.

What keeps this cycle from being chaotic are the natural selection forces of the marketplace: developers strive toward a successful product that works better and satisfies more users without mutating so far from the core standard that there are no sales and the company collapses. Developers also complain about the contention among browser vendors because they must program workarounds that compensate for the performance differences among them, and they must test the performance of their site on all or as many as possible.

Microsoft Internet Explorer, **Mozilla Firefox**, **Safari**, and other browsers contain many unofficial features and extensions for official HTML. Each provides a method for third-party developers to "plug in" special tools that take over certain computational and display activities. Navigator and Explorer also support the **Java** and **JavaScript** languages by which programmers can create Java **applets** and bits of programming code to extend and customize a browser's basic HTML capabilities, especially into the multimedia realm. Thus, while browsers provide the orchestrated foundation of HTML, third-party players and even nonprogrammers can create their own cadenzas to enhance browser performance or perform special tasks. It is often through the plug-ins and applets described in this chapter that multimedia reaches end users. Many of these tools are available as freeware and shareware; while others, particularly server software packages, are expensive, though most any tool can be downloaded from the Internet in a trial version. Try it. If you like it or use it, buy it. Be aware, however, as these heavily-used sites may harbor viruses.

The stunning growth of the Internet has caused many software developers to redirect their creative efforts toward providing solutions on the Web. This remains a new and lucrative frontier, and no developer wishes to be left behind.

Web Servers

As you learned in Chapter 12, the workings of the Web involve communication between two computers: a server and a client. The **server** delivers a file when a client asks for it. Because the playback or display performance of your multimedia content—particularly when it is a streaming MIME-type such as RealAudio or Shockwave/Flash or a QuickTime video—depends upon the speed and capabilities of the computer and software serving it (as well as the bandwidth and load factors of the Internet), you should know some basics.

A growing number of software vendors provide web servers of varying strength and capacity and for a variety of platforms, all of which meet the requirements of the Hypertext Transfer Protocol discussed in Chapter 12. A server is technically not the hardware, but the software—you should invest in server software that will stand up to your intended use and be supported by the vendor. Most vendors will also recommend hardware configurations. This combination of software and hardware is critical to your success and happiness if you wish to optimize response time (less than a second), your connections per second (as many as possible), and your throughput (plenty of room before your Internet connection is overwhelmed by traveling packets).

Web Browsers

Your computer's performance is as important as the bandwidth of your connection to the Web. Web **browsers** are applications that run on a user's personal computer (on the client side on the Internet) to provide the interactive graphical interface for searching, finding, and viewing text documents, sounds, animations, and other multimedia resources on the Web. In 1996, as many as 50 browsers competed for market share, each boasting special or unique features, performance, and cost. Rich Santalesa, editor of *NetGuide* magazine, predicted even then that "the browser wars are over—it's a battle between Microsoft and Netscape, and everyone else is going to dry up and blow away." Indeed, by mid-2001, only two serious competitors remained: Netscape and Microsoft, and Netscape, despite more than 40 million registered users, was beginning a chameleon act. Purchased by AOL, then alloyed by a merger with Time Warner, Netscape was repositioned as a "media hub," not a software company, giving the new Netscape a chance to sell advertising across its many media properties and experiment with subscriptions rather than just free services within the AOL-Time Warner media empire (which includes properties such as *Fortune* and *Time* magazines and the 24-hour cable news network CNN). By 2006, Netscape was dead. From Netscape's ashes arose Firefox as an open source competitor to Microsoft's Internet Explorer.

Despite the legal and financial seriousness of this competition, manifesting in very real congressional hearings and complicated multimillion-dollar antimonopoly lawsuits, some of those involved kept their sense of humor. Back in October 1997, late in the night after the gala announcement and rollout of Microsoft's new Explorer 4.0 in San Francisco, a group of Microsoft engineers drove 30 miles south to Netscape's headquarters and placed a truck-sized Explorer logo (the world-circling "e") on the front lawn of the competitor's headquarters, accented with a helium balloon saying "We Love You" and a greeting card with the message, "It's just not fair. Good people shouldn't have to feel bad. Best wishes, the IE team." By midmorning, Netscape's own engineers had crowned the Explorer logo with a giant dinosaur (their company mascot, named Mozilla), and nailed up a cardboard sign declaring, "Netscape 72, Microsoft 18" (the companies' market share at that time). Mozilla later spun out of Netscape in a free, open-source effort to standardize the browser's HTML engine.

Today, the majority of visitors to your web site will be using Microsoft's Internet Explorer, winner of the "browser wars" (see Table 13-1). In designing a web site, then, you should be certain that your documents and plug-ins work and look good using Internet Explorer.

Internet Explorer	Firefox	Safari	Opera	Unknown
85%	10%	2%	1%	2%

Table 13-1 Browser Market Penetration in 2006

• •

http://www.thecounter.com/

http://www.upsdell.com/BrowserNews/stat.htm

These URLs are for sites that report current statistics on web usage, including browsers being used to access sites. The Counter provides monthly statistics for those that have visited its own site. Browser News provides some general precautions about the reliability of statistics collected at web sites.

• •

Search Engines

You should become familiar with the operation of one or more search engines. They will ferret out information for you in seconds, information that would take months to find searching in a traditional library. Individualized personal search engines are available that can search the entire public Web, while enterprise search engines can search intranets, and mobile search engines can search PDAs and even cell phones.

Web Page Makers and Site Builders

To deliver multimedia on the Web today, you should know some HTML, meaning that you must place the proper tags and references into your documents to launch and control your multimedia. Many **HTML editors** and web page–making applications offer to shortcut your HTML learning curve and working effort. If you use one of these editors, enjoy its easing your work effort, but do not shy away from learning the syntax and tags of the language. Often these "helpers" generate extremely complicated HTML code (described by some programmers as "garbage") with the idea that if this code is hidden "under the hood," who cares? As you yourself become more informed and better at HTML coding, you might discover that you are the person who cares!

HTML documents are simple ASCII text files saved to disk without any formatting at all—no bolding, underlining, special fonts, margins, or tabs. Professional web page developers often use only a word processor like BBEdit for the Mac (see Figure 13-1) or WordPad in Windows rather than a souped-up, drag-and-drop, HTML page builder, and they insert text and tags into their documents manually or with personalized shortcut keys and helper scripts. HTML currently includes about 50 tags, and once you understand their properties and uses, coding, or **marking up**, a document and saving it to your web site can be a straightforward process. Plain HTML may not be enough to create dynamic sites on the fly, sites based upon user preferences or that display "live" information pulled from databases or spreadsheets. To build these kinds of pages, you should be familiar with programming environments such as Microsoft's Active Server Pages (.asp); Adobe's ColdFusion (.cfm), which uses ColdFusion Markup Language (CFML); or the open-source and readily available PHP. For other powerful options beyond plain HTML, knowledge of Dynamic HTML (DHTML), **eXtensible Markup Language (XML)**, and cascading style sheets (CSS) will enhance your skill set.

http://www.asp.net/

http://www.activeserverpage.org/

http://www.adobe.com/products/ coldfusion/

http://www.php.net/

Tools that add power to HTML pages.

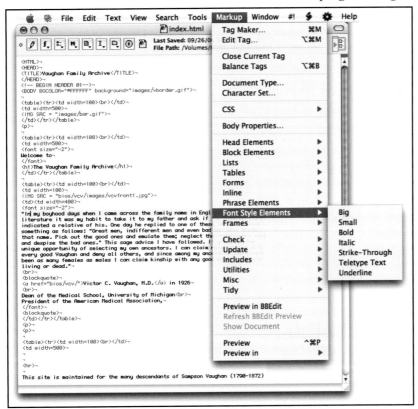

Figure 11-1 BBEdit is a professional programmer's text editor with dedicated features for web page development

HTML translators are built into many word processing programs, so you can export a word-processed document with its text styles and layout converted to HTML tags for headers, bolding, underlining, indenting, and so on. Some are more powerful than others. These work well for simple text documents but tend to choke on powerful HTML features such as tables, forms, frames, and other extensions. Dedicated editors are usually **WYSIWYG (What You See Is What You Get)** word processors, and they provide more power and more features specifically geared to exploiting HTML. Microsoft Word, for example, automatically opens web pages in a WYSIWYG view. On the downside, these "helpful" features may cause a page with many embedded graphics to load into the word processor very slowly while it interprets and lays out the page as a browser would, instead of just loading the text of the page's HTML code and letting you change a few tags or lines.

First Person

When I was 16, my grandmother loaned me $500 so I could buy my first car. It was a lovely, previously owned, British racing green 1950 MG-TD, happiest doing about 45 miles per hour on tree-lined summer roads in New England. When you hinged up the hood sideways, everything inside was simple and well defined; there was plenty of room to tweak the twin SU carburetors, adjust the distributor, and replace simple parts like the electric fuel pump. I even took the tiny four-cylinder engine entirely out and replaced the shell bearings on the crankshaft. A decade later, with my previously owned 1960 Ford

pickup, it was the same—replacing the radiator or changing the starter motor was a piece of cake, and there was plenty of room to work on the engine. But then automobiles got complicated. It started with elaborate emission control systems, then electronic ignitions, then air conditioning, and finally, computers. Opening the hood of a car today, most of us can only stare dumbly at the myriad hoses and wires and color-coded containers for special fluids; and it's so compact a fit, you can't slip a screwdriver between the engine and the fire wall. When the "check engine" light comes on, an expert needs to "pull" the computer

codes with a special, expensive reader to see what's wrong.

Writing HTML for the Web today is still simple. But unless you are an expert, you might be staring dumbly at the complex source code created by a new generation of high-powered, special web tools that will deliver mind-boggling multimedia pages built—no muss, no fuss—with simple drag and drop. But like my car today, which is happiest at 70 miles per hour and could cruise at twice that, you won't be doing much under the hood.

Among the many tools in this emerging marketplace, SharePoint Designer from Microsoft links to Microsoft Office and provides not only WYSIWYG support for many of the latest HTML formatting extensions, but also extensive web site management support through its extensions. InDesign from Adobe saves pages as HTML documents and as **Adobe Acrobat PDF** files. Corel's XMetal imports and converts files created in Word, WordPerfect, Ami PRO, and other word processors. It has a point-and-click interface for inserting valid HTML tags and elements and provides an enhanced URL editor to manage references and calls to other documents and files. **Adobe GoLive** is a WYSIWYG editor that lets you create and edit text pages, import images, and link to other documents, and offers enhanced integration with Acrobat PDF files. Dreamweaver MX from Adobe has become the most popular WYSIWYG HTML editor today.

Managing and maintaining a web site is a serious undertaking when the site contains many thousands of text documents, images, and other resources. Software and expert system tools for automated web page development, document management, and site activity analysis are becoming widely available. Combined with page builders and multimedia editors, these applications will evolve into the ubiquitous "word processors" of the new information age, essential to every home and office with outreach to the Web, and able to integrate and present all the elements of multimedia.

Plug-ins and Delivery Vehicles

Plug-ins add the power of multimedia to web browsers by allowing users to view and interact with new types of documents and images. **Helper applications**, or **players**, also provide multimedia power by displaying or running files downloaded from the Internet by your browser, but helpers are not seamlessly integrated into the operation of the browser itself. When an unrecognized embedded MIME-type that can't be displayed within your user's browser is called from an HTML document (sounds, movies, unusual text or image files), most browsers will automatically launch a helper application (if it is specified in the browser's preferences) to view or run it. However, this helper starts up and runs separately from the browser.

Many plug-ins are designed to perform special tasks not available without the plug-in installed. If you land on a web page containing embedded, compressed images, for example, and the proper plug-in to decompress those images is not installed, you will not be able to view the images.

Designers work around this problem by including hyperlinks in their pages, which direct the user to the site where the missing plug-in may be found. Users must then download and install the required plug-in, and then restart their browser. This is all a bit cumbersome. Until the marketplace determines which plug-ins will become de facto standards for the Web, however, developers have no alternative. Because downloading and installing plug-ins is perceived as a hassle for the end user, many tool developers use the Java and JavaScript capabilities already built into today's web browsers. To offer a plug-in's functionality to visitors at your own web site, you may need the addition of MIME-type information to a special setup file on your server that many plug-ins require. If you do not control or operate your own server, you should let your service provider know the MIME-types that you need to have supported. Setting up servers for some of the multimedia plug-ins is not a trivial task, and many Internet Service Providers will not support high-bandwidth data streams for fear of overwhelming their Internet connection by serving your streaming voice or video to the world. Indeed, while a plug-in or a player may be free and readily available to anyone who wishes it, the software to actually build, compress, manipulate, and serve the special data (such as for compressed images, compressed audio, streaming video, animations, and VRML worlds) may be difficult and expensive since the company makes money from the development tool, not the client software.

Text

Text and document plug-ins such as the popular **Adobe Acrobat Reader** get you past the display limitations of HTML and web browsers, where fonts are dependent on end users' preferences and page layout is primitive. In file formats provided by Adobe Acrobat, for example, special fonts and graphic images are embedded as data into the file and travel with it, so what you see when you view that file is precisely what the document's maker intended.

Images

Most browsers will read only bitmapped JPEG, GIF, and PNG image files. Vector files are a mathematical description of the lines, curves, fills, and patterns needed to draw a picture, and while they typically do not provide the rich detail found in bitmaps, they are smaller and can be scaled without image degradation. Plug-ins to enable viewing of vector formats (such as Flash) are useful, particularly when some provide high-octane compression schemes to dramatically shrink file size and shorten the time spent downloading and displaying them. File size and compression sound a recurring theme on the Internet, where data-rich images, movies, and sounds may take many seconds, minutes, or even longer to reach the end user.

Vaughan's Bandwidth Rule

$$\frac{Bandwidth}{File\ Size} = \text{Satisfaction}$$

Satisfaction with the Internet is a function of connection speed and the size of the data elements accessed.

Vector graphics are also **device-independent**, in that the image is always displayed at the correct size and with the maximum number of colors supported by the computer. Unlike bitmapped files, a single vector file can be downloaded, cached, and then displayed multiple times at different scaled sizes on the same or a different web page.

Sound

Sound over the Web is managed in a few different ways. Digitized sound files in various common formats such as MP3, WAV, AIF, or AU may be sent to your computer and then played, either as they are being received (**streaming** playback) or once they are fully downloaded (using a player). MIDI files may also be received and played; as discussed in Chapter 5, these files are more compact, but they depend upon your computer's MIDI setup for quality. Speech files can be specially encoded into a **token language** (a "shorthand" description of the speech components) and sent at great speed to another computer to be un-tokenized and played back in a variety of voices. Sound elements may also be embedded into projects made with Director, Authorware, PowerPoint, MetaCard, ToolBook, or other applications. And sounds may be embedded into QuickTime, Windows Media, AVI, and MPEG movie files. Some sounds can be **multicast** (using the multicast IP protocols for the Internet specified in RFC 1112), so multiple users can simultaneously listen to the same data streams without duplication of data across the Internet. Web-based telephones also transmit data packets containing sound information.

Animation, Video, and Presentation

The most data-intense multimedia elements to travel the Internet are **video streams** containing both images and synchronized sound, and commonly packaged as Apple's QuickTime, Microsoft's Video for Windows (AVI), and as MPEG files. Also data rich are the files for proprietary formats such as Keynote, **Microsoft PowerPoint**, and other presentation applications. In all cases, the trade-offs between bandwidth and quality are constantly in your face when designing, developing, and delivering animations or motion video for the Web.

Beyond HTML

When an ingot of pure silicon is "pulled" from a furnace, the process begins with a "seed crystal," around which the ingot forms. HTML is the seed crystal that is shaping and forming the nature of multimedia on the World Wide Web as it extrudes itself onto the Internet's data highway. Within the latticework of HTML servers and browsers, tags such as <OBJECT> (browser-specific for Internet Explorer) or <EMBED> (browser-specific for Firefox) enable text, sound, images, animations, and motion video across the Web. Hooks for powerful platform-independent Java applets and JavaScripts are built into most browsers, so you can design local interaction and activities without a lot of communication between client- and server-based **Common Gateway Interface (CGI)** programming. CGI is a standard for interfacing external applications with information servers, such as HTTP or web servers, and CGI programs can be written in C/C++, Fortran, PERL, TCL, a Unix shell, Visual Basic, or even AppleScript, as long as the language is supported by the server platform.

The following is an example of the combined <OBJECT> and <EMBED> tags used to display a Flash movie in both the Internet Explorer and Firefox browsers. A browser will only act on a tag it understands, ignoring tags it does not recognize. (See http://www.adobe.com/cfusion/knowledgebase/index.cfm?id=tn_4150)

```
<OBJECT classid="clsid:D27CDB6E-AE6D-11cf-96B8-444553540000"
codebase="http://download.macromedia.com/pub/shockwave/cabs/
flash/swflash.cab#version=6,0,40,0"
WIDTH="550" HEIGHT="400" id="myMovieName">
<PARAM NAME=movie VALUE="myFlashMovie.swf">
<PARAM NAME=quality VALUE=high>

<PARAM NAME=bgcolor VALUE=#FFFFFF>

<EMBED src="myFlashMovie.swf" quality=high bgcolor=#FFFFFF
WIDTH="550" HEIGHT="400"
NAME="myMovieName" ALIGN="" TYPE="application/x-shockwave-flash"
PLUGINSPAGE="http://www.macromedia.com/go/getflashplayer">
</EMBED>
```

3-D Worlds

Three-dimensional environments and experiences on the Web are now possible with Intel's Internet 3-D Graphics Software using **Adobe Director** for development and the Shockwave player for delivery. These have supplanted VRML (Virtual Reality Modeling Language) as an independent environment specifically designed to handle high-performance 3-D worlds containing 3-D text and images, textures, animations, morphs, multiple viewpoints, collision detection, gravity, sounds, and all the arcade elements associated with full-bore game action. With claims that well-executed interactive 3-D content can make nearly any web site more compelling and effective and can better attract, engage, and inform, Intel's algorithms and Adobe's delivery system allow 3-D content to be automatically scaled and tailored to each user's system and available bandwidth. Spinning off from a foundation of vector graphics and animation, 3-D renderings and creative whole worlds present only the latest of multimedia challenges and learning curves for web developers. As this 3-D technology becomes refined and end-user bandwidth increases during the first decade of the 21st century, the very shape of web pages will be altered forever.

....

http://www.adobe.com/products/director/3d/3dservices/
http://www.autodesk.com/
http://www.discreet.com
http://www.famous3d.com/
http://www.havok.com/
http://www.maxon.net/
http://www.newtek.com/
http://www.nvidia.com/
http://www.nxview.com/
http://www.righthemisphere.com/
http://www.softimage.com/

For more information about 3-D tools and technology

....

First Person

When I received a press release from Alternate Realities Corporation, a small startup company spun out of a large research effort in North Carolina, I was intrigued. ARC's president, David Bennett, claimed, "We are redefining Virtual Reality!" He went on to describe "a new generation virtual environment that is a 3-D, immersive, full-color, interactive system enclosed in a 16-foot dome or sphere that can be either portable (inflatable or interlocking) or permanent. The system includes a 360-degree projection system with a 180-degree field of view. Imagine a 16-foot helmet that fits over 15 people at the same time and is nonrestrictive! Larger units (in the 24-foot and up range) are in the early development stage."

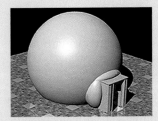

I knew I had to have one for my experiments with VRML! The 5-meter model, which fits in a 20×20-foot trade-show booth space, was available for $280,000, and the 7-meter model, perfect for my backyard, was only slightly more at $340,000.

Chapter 13 Review

■ Chapter Summary

For your review, here's a summary of the important concepts discussed in this chapter.

Discuss the current state of multimedia on the Internet

- The explosion of tools and user demand for performance is stressing the orderly development of the core HTML standard. The marketplace keeps this cycle from being too chaotic.

- Developers must program workarounds that compensate for the differences among Firefox, Explorer, and other browsers; they should test the performance of their site on all.

- Browsers contain many unofficial features to enable plug-ins and applets that help multimedia reach end users.

- The stunning growth of the Internet has caused many software developers to redirect their creative efforts toward providing solutions on the Web.

Define server and browser, and discuss their purposes, capabilities, and limitations

- Interactions on the Web involve communication between two computers: a server and a client. The server delivers a file when a client asks for it.

- Your site's server plays a big role in how well your site performs, so be sure that both your server and connection provide a sound plan for growth.

- Browsers are the apps that run on a user's personal computer to provide the interface for downloading and viewing documents and multimedia.

- Internet Explorer is the browser with the largest market share.

Discuss the uses and limitations of HTML, and the tools that are available to edit HTML pages

- To deliver multimedia on the Web today, you should know some HTML. HTML documents are simple ASCII text files. HTML currently includes about 50 tags.

- Professional web page developers often use only a word processor to edit their pages. Many HTML editors and web page-making applications offer to shortcut your HTML learning curve and working effort. Even if you use one of these editors, you should still understand the syntax and tags of the HTML language.

- Managing and maintaining a web site is a serious undertaking when the site contains many thousands of text documents, images, and other resources.

Describe how HTML can be extended through plug-ins and helper applications

- Plug-ins allow users to view and interact with new types of documents and images.

- Helper applications, or players, display or run files that your browser downloads, but run separately from the browser itself. Most browsers will automatically launch a helper when a file the browser can't handle is downloaded.

- Requiring visitors to download plug-ins can be cumbersome, and servers must be set up to correctly handle requests for special data types.

Define some of the more common media types, their uses, and how browsers or helper applications handle them

- Plug-ins to enable viewing of vector formats are useful, as they also allow much smaller file sizes.

- Digitized sound files in various common formats may be sent to your computer and then streamed (played as they are being received) or played by a player once they are fully downloaded. MIDI files are smaller, but they depend upon your computer's MIDI setup for quality.

- Sound elements may also be embedded into projects made with various authoring tools, or embedded into QuickTime, Windows Media, AVI, and MPEG movie files.

- The most data-intense multimedia elements are video streams containing both images and synchronized sound.
- In all cases, the trade-offs between bandwidth and quality are a constant consideration when designing, developing, and delivering animations or motion video for the Web.

Discuss other technologies gaining new ground on the Internet

- Conferencing and collaboration software with strong multimedia components is becoming available on the Internet.
- Many software tool companies are developing applications and design environments to work with Java.
- Web-enabled 3-D environments promise compelling and interactive multimedia experiences.

■ Key Terms

Adobe Acrobat PDF *(335)*
Adobe Acrobat Reader *(337)*
Adobe GoLive *(336)*
Adobe Director *(339)*
applets *(331)*
browsers *(332)*
Common Gateway Interface (CGI) *(339)*
device-independent *(338)*
eXtensible Markup Language (XML) *(334)*

helper applications/ players *(336)*
HTML editors *(333)*
HTML translators *(335)*
Java *(331)*
JavaScript *(331)*
marking up *(334)*
Microsoft Internet Explorer *(331)*
Microsoft PowerPoint *(338)*
Mozilla Firefox *(331)*

multicast *(338)*
plug-ins *(336)*
Safari *(331)*
server *(331)*
streaming *(338)*
tags *(330)*
token language *(338)*
video streams *(338)*
WYSIWYG (What You See Is What You Get) *(335)*

■ Key Term Quiz

1. HTML formatting elements in HTML-encoded pages are called _____.
2. Bits of Java programming code used to extend and customize a browser's basic HTML capabilities are called _____.
3. The software that sends information when a client requests it is the _____.
4. The applications that run on a user's personal computer and provide the interactive graphical interface for viewing web pages are called _____.
5. Adding HTML codes to a page is called _____.
6. Web page editors that visually show how a page looks as you are editing are often called _____ editors.
7. Programs that run within a browser and allow users to view and interact with files within the browser's window are called _____.
8. Programs that are triggered to run or display files that a browser downloads but cannot handle itself are called _____.
9. Media that is played as it is being received is said to be _____.
10. The standard programming interface for connecting external applications with information servers is called _____.

1. Perhaps the multimedia plug-in with the largest installed base is:
   a. SGV Viewer
   b. QuickTime
   c. Flash
   d. Mozilla
   e. HotJava

2. Which of these is *not* an issue related to the so-called browser wars?
   a. Developers must program workarounds to compensate for browser differences.
   b. Official HTML standards lag behind the browsers' capabilities.
   c. Browser developers are releasing new browser versions quickly, making it difficult for third-party developers to keep pace.
   d. Extending a particular browser's capabilities requires cumbersome plug-ins.
   e. Developers must test the performance of their site on different browsers.

3. The two most popular browsers in terms of number of users are Firefox and:
   a. Acrobat
   b. JavaScript
   c. Shockwave
   d. Internet Explorer
   e. Yahoo!

4. Which of these is *not* an issue you should consider when selecting an ISP?
   a. response time
   b. connections per second
   c. throughput
   d. MIME-type support
   e. All are factors to consider.

5. Helper applications run:
   a. on the client computer outside the browser
   b. on the client computer within the browser
   c. on the host computer outside the server
   d. on the host computer within the server
   e. on external devices such as an MP3 player or PDA

6. The helper application most commonly used to display documents with fonts and images embedded is:
   a. Adobe Acrobat
   b. Apple QuickTime
   c. Shockwave
   d. Microsoft FrontPage
   e. Microsoft PowerPoint

7. One criticism of visual page editors is that they:
   a. encrypt the code, making later editing impossible
   b. do not support features such as underlining and bold text
   c. use nonstandard HTML tags
   d. generate extremely complicated HTML code
   e. require the use of plug-ins

8. HTML documents are:
   a. encrypted and compressed data files
   b. simple ASCII text files
   c. complex Unicode-encoded files
   d. word processing files with intact text formatting
   e. streaming packet-data structures

9. A vector image that is displayed at the correct size and with the maximum number of colors supported by the computer is said to be:
   a. encrypted
   b. compressed
   c. device-independent
   d. an applet
   e. streaming

10. Which of these tags would most likely be used in HTML to view a multimedia element on the Web?
    a. <BLOCKQUOTE>
    b. <OBJECT>
    c. <OPEN>
    d. <MM>
    e. <FLASH>

11. Most browsers cannot directly display:
    a. JPEG images
    b. vector images
    c. GIF images
    d. PNG images
    e. Most browsers can display all of the above.

12. Speech files can be specially encoded into a _____ _____ and sent at great speed to another computer to be played back in a choice of voices.
    a. device-independent schema
    b. streaming protocol
    c. token language
    d. Java applet
    e. QuickTime movie

13. Which of the following is *not* a streaming media format?
    a. Adobe Acrobat
    b. Apple QuickTime
    c. Shockwave
    d. Microsoft Video for Windows (AVI)
    e. MPEG files

14. Which audio file type's sound quality is dependent on the client's computer setup?
    a. AIF
    b. AU
    c. MIDI
    d. Shockwave
    e. WAV

15. The technique that allows multiple users to simultaneously access the same data streams without duplication of data across the Internet is called:
    a. homing
    b. streaming
    c. packet-compression
    d. interleaving
    e. multicasting

■ Essay Quiz

1. Discuss the browser wars and the dynamics of browser development versus HTML standards. Why is it important to view your web pages on different browsers and platforms?

2. You have been assigned to select a server to host your company's web site. Discuss how you will make a selection, based on your target audience and the type of pages you will be serving. Are you serving an audience with state-of-the-art computers, or older PCs? Will you be streaming media files or sending static web pages? What is your company's growth projection? How will these factors affect the hosting package you choose?

3. You have been given the task of creating a new web site for your company. What tools will you use to create the pages? When might you use a word processor? When might you use a WYSIWYG tool? When might you use an HTML text editor? What are the strengths and weaknesses of each?

4. How have developers found ways around the limitations of HTML? Around browser limitations? Discuss the difference between plug-ins and helper applications, and how they are used to handle different files.

5. List several different advanced media types that are used on the Web. Discuss how these media are integrated on the Web today. Can the browser handle them? Can they be handled by plug-ins or helper applications?

Lab Projects

■ Project 13.1

Open a word processor that exports to HTML. Create a page of formatted text. Be sure to use different text styles, numerous colors, indenting, tables, and other options. Print the page out from the word processing program.

Export the page to HTML, and then open the HTML page in a Web browser. Print out the page from the browser. How does the browser-rendered page differ from the page in the word processor?

■ Project 13.2

View the source of the page you created in Project 13.1 in the browser. (Most browsers have a function that allows you to view the source HTML code of a web page.) Print out the source, either from the browser, or by copying the HTML code when you view the source, or by cutting and pasting. (Some browsers respond to the View Source command by automatically opening the HTML source in NotePad on the PC.)

Note how HTML treats various word processing features with its tags.

■ Project 13.3

Go to the web sites of the developers of Dreamweaver, Adobe GoLive, Bare Bones Software BBEdit, and Corel XMetal. Briefly summarize and compare the capabilities of each. How do they handle viewing source code? How do they handle inserting tags? How do they handle rendering the results? Can they forward the page to a browser for previewing? Can they forward to more than one browser?

■ Project 13.4

There is a large body of browser information available on the Web. A number of sites collect such data based on the fact that a browser identifies itself when it makes a request from a server.

Do a search on the Web for these statistics:

List the top five browsers by percentage and their market share.

1. Browser: Share (%):   4. Browser: Share (%):
2. Browser: Share (%):   5. Browser: Share (%):
3. Browser: Share (%):

What percentage of users have the following plug-ins installed, or capabilities turned on? (Some browsers include the option to turn certain functions such as Java, JavaScript, and others on or off.)

1. Java   4. Acrobat ReaderFlash
2. JavaScript   5. Shockwave
3. CSS   6. Apple QuickTime

■ Project 13.5

Go online and compare web hosting packages from three different Web hosts. Most hosting companies offer several options and prices. Select a basic, moderate, and advanced package from each host and describe that package's features and options. Do any of the host providers offer unique or unusual options?

Host _____ :

Package	Basic	Moderate	Advanced
Storage space:			
Bandwidth:			
Streaming capabilities:			
Cost			

Comments: _____

CHAPTER 14

Designing for the World Wide Web

Launched in 1989, the World Wide Web was not originally designed with multimedia in mind, but rather as a simple method for delivering text documents formatted in HTML, with occasional inline graphic illustrations and figures. By 1995, because it was operational, essentially free, and *good enough* to support traffic (see "Vaughan's Law of Multimedia Minimums" in Chapter 5), the Web had become a full-bore information highway of words and pictures with tens of millions of users cruising along it.

The Doppler back-draft of passing travelers has exposed the gristle of an overwhelming number of disappointing audio and visual experiences on the Web: "This is my home page; here is a list of my favorite places; this is me with my dog..." To fill this vacuum of content and presentation, inventive multimedia solutions and enhancements now compete for mind share, stretching the capabilities of HTML, web browsers, PCs, and the very fabric of the Internet in order to bring multimedia power to this environment. Plain text and pictures are no longer enough for this highway!

WARNING *Powerful multimedia tools can be used to create totally vacuous web pages.*

Working on the Web

This chapter investigates and illustrates some methods for developing and presenting the basic elements of multimedia within the constraints of HTML and the World Wide Web. This chapter is not intended to substitute for a more complete library of HTML, web design, and Internet how-to texts, but to present basic examples that will get you started. In 2001, there were more than 2,000 published books with the word "Internet" in their title. In 2003 there were more than 6,000. In 2006, there were more than 10,000 with the word "Internet" in their title!

BARNES&NOBLE.com
www.bn.com

| Title ▾ | Internet | SEARCH ❯ |

SEARCH RESULTS
We found **10,335** items for title: **Internet**.

The Workspace

Make your web pages look good on an 800×600 monitor in true color (millions). Working at 800×600, you will satisfy almost any viewer, according to a 2006 survey from TheCounter.com, a site where developers often gather web statistics:

Screen Resolution	Percentage of Users
640x480	0%
800x600	17%
1024x768	57%
Greater than 1024x768	19%
I have no idea.	3%

Depending upon the browser and preferences set by the user, the usable area of the screen will always be less than the monitor's display, and is not controllable by the designer. Browser toolbars and other "chrome" (shiny stuff around the edges) can be either hidden or shown by the user. If you want to maximize the browser active window size, in Internet Explorer press F11 (function key 11) and go back to regular mode by clicking the mouse; other browsers offer toggle switches in the "View" options. So design your web page for an 800-pixel-wide display by using tables and images that do not exceed 750 pixels across the page, and you will have room for browser scroll bars.

Nibbling

The principle you must always keep in mind when designing and making multimedia elements for the Web should be called "nibbling." At a serious metal-working supply store you can buy a power tool called a nibbler—it devours the edges of sheet metal in an ear-damaging staccato of rapid tiny bites. You must apply this concept, for example, to the elegant bitmapped logo you created in Photoshop when you trim it from 24- to 8- to 4-bit color depth and resize it from 96 pixels square to 64 pixels square. Nibble the audio clip of your client's theme song from 44.1 kHz to 11 kHz, and see if it's acceptable at an 8-bit sample size. Text as HTML is cheap: nibble your page design and throw away the pretty shadowed GIF graphic headers and image maps—re-create your text in HTML headers or emphasized text, and try coloring it. Put on your protective head gear—this compromising work is painful for you as the creator—and start nibbling, while constantly seeking a balance between quality and the patience of a user who is downloading your material at 56 Kbps from home. Every choice you make should be tempered by bandwidth worry.

> **WARNING**   *For every image file referenced in an HTML document, a separate Internet HTTP connection must be made between your computer and that image's server before the image itself is downloaded; so using many different tiny images (such as graphic images as bullets) may not be efficient. After a user has downloaded a file once, however, it should load more quickly from the user's local hard disk, where the browser stores them in a cache.*

HTML Is a Markup Language

You should have a basic understanding of HTML before you begin developing multimedia for the Web. HTML-coded documents, which are the fundamental vehicles for all types of information delivered on the World Wide Web, are explained in Chapters 4 and 13, but for this chapter you need to understand the basics of how HTML works.

HTML stands for Hypertext Markup Language. The "Markup Language" part of the name means that tags are used to do such things as format text and embed media. The tags are enclosed by angled brackets: < >. Some tags are bounding tags, requiring both an opening and closing tag. The closing tag is indicated by a leading forward slash inside the angled brackets. This example for bolded text illustrates the use of the two tags:

This text is bolded.

Other tags, such as the tag for inserting an inline image, stand by themselves:

<IMG src="grey_ball.gif">

Note that the tags may be written in either upper- or lowercase; some HTML editing programs have a switch allowing you to select the case in which you want the tags written in your document.

HTML and Multimedia

HTML provides tags for inserting media into HTML documents: the **<IMG> tag** for inline images; the **<EMBED>** and **<OBJECT>** tags for compound document embedding; and **<APPLET> tags** for code. (The <APPLET> and <EMBED> tags have been **deprecated** in HTML 4.0 in favor of the <OBJECT> tag.) A deprecated tag is not supported by the most recent HTML standard, yet its use remains supported by most browsers. The important <OBJECT> tag is used to insert a "nonstandard" item such as a Java applet, QuickTime movie, or Flash animation into an HTML document.

But it is not as simple as it seems. There is a difference between the way various versions of browsers handle multimedia elements and the plug-ins that play them. In playing a QuickTime movie, for example, the <OBJECT> tag is used by Internet Explorer on Windows platforms and requires the

QuickTime ActiveX control. The <EMBED> tag is used by older Netscape browsers, Internet Explorer for the Mac, and other browsers that support Netscape-style QuickTime plug-ins. The result is that browsers that understand the <OBJECT> tag ignore the <EMBED> tag, and browsers that cannot read the <OBJECT> tag need the <EMBED> tag.

So the <OBJECT> tag would include an <EMBED> tag to play a QuickTime movie on all browsers and platforms, and might look something like this:

```
<OBJECT CLASSID="clsid:02BF25D5-8C17-4B23-BC80-D3488ABDDC6B" WIDTH="160"
     HEIGHT="144" CODEBASE="http://www.apple.com/qtactivex/qtplugin.cab">
<PARAM name="SRC" VALUE="lizzie.mov">
<PARAM name="AUTOPLAY" VALUE="true">
<PARAM name="LOOP VALUE"="infinite">
<PARAM name="CONTROLLER" VALUE="false">
<EMBED SRC="lizzie.mov" WIDTH="160" HEIGHT="144" AUTOPLAY="true"
     CONTROLLER="false" PLUGINSPAGE="http://www.apple.com/quicktime/download/">
<IMG SRC="soccer.jpg" ALT="The Soccer Match">
</EMBED>
</OBJECT>
```

In the previous code, the browser plays the QuickTime movie named "lizzie," as long as it supports the .mov format and that MIME-type, and it will loop and play forever. If not supported, the browser will show a substituted JPEG image. Using the ALT attribute of the <IMG> tag here provides backward-compatibility with older browsers; if the browser has trouble with the JPEG image, it will display an alternate text label, in this case, "The Soccer Match."

TIP *If you develop multimedia for the Internet, budget time and effort for keeping current in this rapidly changing environment—staying at the leading edge takes effort. It will be some years before multimedia delivery tools and techniques for the Web stabilize.*

Text for the Web

Viewers of your web site may not be displaying the same "preferred" font that you used to design your page because user preferences in the browser may alter the way text in your document looks and flows. To make the best of this uncertainty, many developers design their documents in Times Roman for the proportional seriphed font, Verdana for proportional sans serif, and Courier as the mono-spaced font. These fonts readily move across platforms and are the default fonts users typically see if they do not set their own preferences. Although you can specify a font, and even alternate fonts, using the FACE attribute of the **<FONT> tag** (for example: <FONT FACE="Verdana, Arial, Helvetica">), that tag has been deprecated in the HTML 4.0 specification in favor of using cascading style sheets (CSS). Regardless of how you specify your fonts, browsers can only use a specified font if that font is installed on the end user's computer.

Great efforts are being made to define standard methods for displaying typefaces on the Web, but neither of the two rival camps, **TrueDoc** (from Bitstream) and **OpenType** (supported by Adobe, Microsoft, Agfa, and others), seem able to get their technology properly implemented and launched. The font problem will eventually be solved in one of two ways, or in a combination of both: either many more fonts will become readily and cheaply available and will be commonly installed by end users, or a method of embedding a font's character shapes into an HTML document will allow fonts to "ship" with the document. Both OpenType and TrueDoc embed font information in the HTML document—a more reassuring method for developers—but there are compatibility problems with embedded fonts and legal issues surrounding font foundry copyrights. Using an OpenDoc component called **WEFT (Web Embedding Font Tool)**, Microsoft already offers font-embedding capabilities. Refer to Chapter 4 for more details on formatting text in HTML documents.

If you are looking for some flexibility in font management at your web site, you can try using cascading style sheets (CSS), available in dynamic HTML (DHTML), for setting text styles across the pages of your site.

As with projects built for CD-ROM using a multimedia authoring tool, if you wish to absolutely control the look of text on your web page, you must use a graphic bitmap rather than text in your HTML document, but, as noted earlier, adding images in place of text increases the amount of time necessary to download your page. Embedding graphics into HTML documents is explained later in the chapter.

As you can see in Figure 14-1, you can tag text so that it is displayed as headers, boldface, italics, underlined, and in lists, but

Figure 14-1 Web browsers currently offer few methods for making pretty text in an HTML document.

the viewer's browser ultimately determines how these styles are displayed. You can try tags to control (somewhat) the attributes of displayed text: the **COLOR attribute**, <FONT COLOR="#0080FF">, will set the color of specific characters of text, and the **SIZE attribute**, <FONT SIZE="+2">, increases or decreases the size of the text displayed. You can also set the background color of individual cells in a table by using the **BGCOLOR attribute** in the cell's table data tag: <TD BGCOLOR="#0080FF">. This is useful for highlighting text information in complicated visual presentations.

Making Columns of Text

The most powerful feature of HTML may be found in the **<TABLE> tag**. Study this tag and its attributes! To the right, you'll see how to organize your text into two columns, so it displays more like a newspaper or a magazine, using a table (see Figure 14-2).

```
<HTML>
<HEAD>
<TITLE>The Explosion</TITLE>
</HEAD>
<BODY>
<DIV ALIGN="center">
<H2>The Explosion</H2>
</DIV>
<TABLE BORDER="0" CELLSPACING="20">
<TR VALIGN="TOP">
<TD WIDTH="40%">
... text for Column 1 goes here ...
</TD>
<TD WIDTH="40%">
... text for Column 2 goes here ...
</TD>
</TR>
</TABLE>
<HR>
</BODY>
</HTML>
```

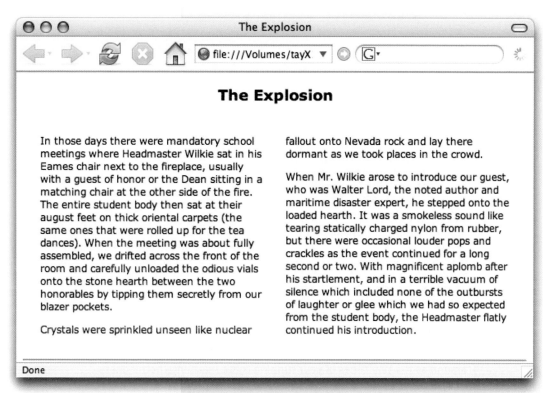

Figure 14-2 Using the <TABLE> tag, you can organize your text into columns.

Flowing Text Around Images

As you can see in Figure 14-3, it is possible (and easy) to "flow" text around an image using the **ALIGN attribute** of the <IMG> tag. This is a quick and simple method for mixing text and images in a pleasing layout. Add a <BR CLEAR=left> tag at the end of your text paragraph, so that if there is not enough text to fill the entire vertical height of the image, your next paragraph will begin on a new line, left-justified, and below the image. To add space around your image so it doesn't butt right up against the text, use the Horizontal Space (**HSPACE**) and Vertical Space (**VSPACE**) attributes of the <IMG> tag.

```
<HTML>
<HEAD>
<TITLE>Sailing</TITLE>
</HEAD>
<BODY>
<IMG SRC="gbsky.gif" ALIGN="left" HSPACE="15" VSPACE="5">
<H2>Departure</H2>
... text goes here ...
<BR CLEAR="left">
<hr>
</BODY>
</HTML>
```

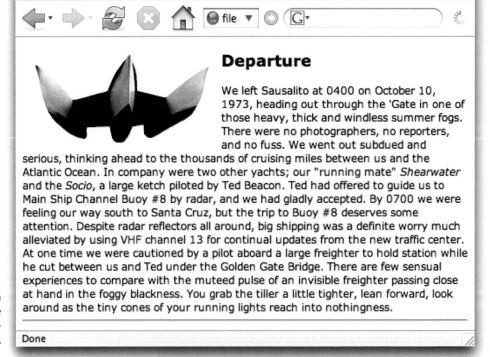

Figure 14-3 You can flow text around an image by using the ALIGN attribute of the <IMG> tag.

The following HTML code sets up a more complicated screen with flowing text (see Figure 14-4). It also includes a background image, a portrait image around which the text flows, and an image map that is used for navigation. (Background images and image maps are described later in this chapter.) This document also contains the foreign language special character ä, which is called out in the document using HTML's escape sequence for special characters, in this case, "&aumlaut;". An **escape sequence** begins with an ampersand and ends with a semicolon. Also, note the use of a <FONT size="6"> tag to make paragraphs begin with initial caps. A MIDI file is embedded in this page to provide background music.

```
<html>
<head>
<title>Annan lapsuus</title>
</head>
<body background="misc/annataus.gif">
<img src="misc/trans150.gif" width="20" align="left">
<img src="03/i03b.gif" hspace="10" width="264" height="342" align="left">
<h1>Annan lapsuus</h1>
<pre><i><b>
<font size="6">M</font>in&aumlaut; sain oman huoneen.
Sen sein&aumlaut;t on maalattu vihreiksi. Ja yhdelle
sein&aumlaut;lle on maalattu maisema. Mutta
joelle ei maalattu joutsenia, koska
min&aumlaut; en halunnut. Niihin voi kyll&aumlaut;sty&aumlaut;niin helposti.
<font size="6">I</font>si on tehnyt minulle kirjahyllyn.
Min&aumlaut; j&aumlaut;rjest&aumlaut;n siihen kaikki tavarat.
Kiiltokuva-albumit ja kirjan. Sen
nimi on "Tiina saa suukon". Vaikka
on minulla muitakin kirjoja, mutta
en min&aumlaut; en&aumlaut;&aumlaut; sellaisia lastenkirjoja lue.

"T&aumlaut;st&aumlaut; l&aumlaut;htien minun huoneeni on
aina hyv&aumlaut;ss&aumlaut; j&aumlaut;rjestyksess&aumlaut;", sanoin isille.

<img src="misc/komp4a5a.gif" align="left" border="0" usemap="#thispagemap">
</pre>
</i></b>
```

```
<map name="thispagemap">
<area shape="circle" coords="48,48,12" href="fhelp.htm">
<area shape="polygon" coords="50,50,0,0,100,0" href="fnavmap.htm">
<area shape="polygon" coords="50,50,0,100,100,100" href="f03.htm">
</map>

<EMBED SRC="03/pianobg.mid" width="0" height="2" autostart="true">
</body>
</html>
```

Figure 14-4 Images and text can be mixed in an HTML document. Note the use of escape sequences for special characters and the image map for navigation.

Images for the Web

Theoretically, the Web can support any graphics format the client and server have in common. Practically, even though web standards do not specify a graphics format you must use, all current releases of browsers recognize three image formats—GIF, PNG, and JPEG—without resorting to special plug-ins. These formats use built-in **compression** algorithms to reduce file size. (Graphic image formats are described in detail in Chapter 6.) For other graphics formats, such as CGM, CMX, DXF, and fractal- and wavelet-compressed images, special proprietary creation software and browser plug-ins may be required (see Chapter 13).

GIF and PNG Images

GIF images (Graphic Interchange File, also discussed in Chapter 6) are limited to 8 bits of color depth (256 colors). This is a commercial image format developed by CompuServe Information Services, an online company once owned by Unisys and presently folded into America Online. In late 1994, Unisys announced a patent fee charge to all software developers who use the GIF format. In an angry, industry-wide response, **PNG** (for Portable Network Graphics Specification) was developed as a new "open" format (not requiring fees) to replace GIF. Although the PNG format is in many ways an improvement on the GIF format it was intended to replace, concerns about backward-compatibility with older browsers slowed its acceptance. Most image creation programs now support the PNG format, and it is the native file format for Fireworks, a Macromedia product designed specifically for creating graphics for web pages.

First Person

A few years ago I somebody told me about an interesting web survey: how does the world pronounce GIF? The results turned out about 50/50 on the hard/soft question, my colleague claimed. Then I spent considerable time using that word (softly) in Europe before realizing everybody was being smirkingly polite about my outlandish pronunciation. In the San Francisco Bay Area, a world center for multimedia development, GIF has the soft "g" of "ginger," "gin," and "gybe." In New York, where little is soft, and in Europe, GIF has a more cutting, hard pronunciation, as in "giggling," "gingham," "girdled," "guilty," or "girls." The real question is whether the written word requires a prefixed dot.

JPEG Images

JPEG (Joint Photographic Experts Group) images may contain 24 bits of color depth (millions of colors). JPEG uses a powerful but **lossy** compression method that produces files as much as ten times more compressed than GIF. Lossy means that information in the original image is lost in the compression process and cannot be retrieved. A **lossless** compression method does not irretrievably discard the original data.

WARNING   *Do not edit and reedit files that are in JPEG format. Every time you open a JPEG image and edit it, then recompress and save it as a compressed JPEG, the image degrades. After a few editing/saving cycles, you will be very disappointed. Edit and archive your images in a 24-bit lossless graphic format (such as TIFF or BMP), then convert to JPEG (if you need to).*

TIP *If you download JPEG files from the Internet by FTP using Fetch, be sure to add ".jpg" and ".jpeg" to Fetch's list of binary file types (in the Customize/Suffix Mapping... menu). Otherwise Fetch will retrieve JPEG files in text mode and corrupt the data.*

The JPEG compression scheme compresses about 20:1 before visible image degradation occurs. Test the amount of compression acceptable for your JPEG image; stay inside the "threshold of visible error." To compress an image with JPEG, the image is divided into 8×8-pixel blocks, and the resulting 64 pixels (called a "search range") are mathematically described relative to the characteristic of the pixel in the upper-left corner. The binary description of this relationship requires far less than 64 pixels, so more information can be transmitted in less time. JPEG compresses slowly, about one to three seconds for a 1MB image depending upon computer speed, but JPEG can compress images as much as 75:1, with loss.

GIF or JPEG?

Use JPEG for photo-realistic images containing many colors, and avoid using it for images already forced into a 256-color palette or for line drawings or 1-bit black-and-white images. GIF compresses drawings and cartoons that have only a few colors in them much better than JPEG, which may introduce visible defects—sharp edges and lines that blur—especially with small-size text. Figures 14-5 and 14-6 show the "blocky" and "lossy" nature of the compressed JPEG images. For the Web, use the JPEG format for photorealistic images that are busy with color; use the GIF format for line art and drawings where there are large areas of the same color.

Figure 14-5 Both images at the top were saved in the JPEG format, which compresses image data and trades image quality for small file size. The resulting compressed images at the bottom show the "lossy" and "blocky" nature of compressed JPEGs. The photo at top left is 71K in size when saved as a GIF (not shown) and only 27K saved as a JPEG (bottom left). The drawing at top right is 17K when saved as a GIF (not shown) and 46K as a JPEG (bottom right).

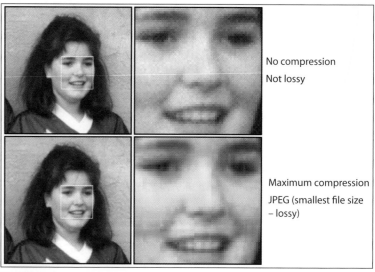

No compression
Not lossy

Maximum compression
JPEG (smallest file size – lossy)

Figure 14-6 Lossy compression schemes save disk space, but can also degrade an image. For the Web, line art is often better saved in GIF format than in JPEG.

Using Photoshop

Adobe's Photoshop is the "tool of choice" for most graphic artists, so it is worth taking some time to provide a few suggestions for creating GIF and JPEG images for use on the World Wide Web. If you use a different image-editing application, follow the same logic and use the commands appropriate for that application. Always work in native Photoshop format using PSD files—these images are typically in RGB mode and use the maximum color depth. They are larger, but they contain more information that can be usefully processed when resizing and dithering, and you will get better final results. PSD files also contain layers, a very useful application feature. When creating images for display on a web page, use 72 pixels per inch resolution, which is the resolution of most monitors. When you convert a 24-bit RGB image to an 8-bit image (change its mode), you lose huge amounts of color information that cannot be retrieved, meaning that the fine data is gone forever. So you should follow two practices in order to protect your original image. One is to save the original image in a 24-bit lossless image format (such as TIFF or BMP). The other is to do all of your image manipulation (such as resizing, sharpening, and hue adjustments) in RGB mode. Next, save this source image in RGB mode as a PSD file, before reducing the color palette by saving it as a GIF or using a lossy compression like JPEG. By saving the high-quality original and saving the manipulated image in the program's native format, you can return to them if you need to make changes later.

TIP   *When you scan an image, the scanner will often default to print resolution of 300 dpi. When displayed on a 72 dpi resolution monitor, the picture will be displayed over three times bigger than the original. Never fix this problem by changing the height and width attributes of the IMG tag. Even though this will display the image at the size you want, you still have a huge image file that will slow down the downloading and display of your page. Instead, use Photoshop or another image-editing program to resample the image at a 72 dpi resolution, and use the new image in your page.*

When you are satisfied with your image and ready to save it as a GIF, PNG, or JPEG file, archive it as described earlier. If you make any mistakes while converting modes or saving, you will still have the original, complete with any layers you might have used. To be very safe, duplicate the original file and open the copy before saving to other formats.

Saving as JPEG Files

To save your image as a JPEG file, you do not need to change Photoshop's mode from RGB, but if you are using layers, you will need to "flatten" the image, merging all layers into a single bitmap. Once an image is flattened and you have edited or saved it, its layers cannot be remade without a great deal of difficult cutting and pasting—so again, archive your original file! Photoshop will automatically ask if you wish to flatten when you select JPEG from the Save As... menu. You must name your file with the extension .jpg or .jpeg if you will use it on the Web. Then click on Save, and choose Maximum, High, Medium, or Low-quality compression in the dialog box that appears. Your file is ready for the Web.

Saving as GIF Files

To save a GIF file using Photoshop, you must first set the mode of your image to Indexed Color, converting it to the best 8-bit palette (256 colors) that will represent the image and be displayed well by web browsers. Note that the option of saving a Photoshop 24-bit RGB file in GIF format will not be available in Windows, and it will be grayed out on the Macintosh menu until you have converted your image to 8-bit mode: GIF is only for 8-bit images. Only one palette can be active at a time on an 8-bit monitor.

TIP *Use GIF files for line art and images that contain large areas of the same color (that can be easily compressed). Use JPEG for photorealistic images.*

Palettes When you change the mode to Indexed Color, you must specify the color depth of the converted image, the color palette to be used, and whether the colors of your image should be dithered (Diffusion or Pattern) or not (None). Figure 14-7 shows the mode changing dialog box from Photoshop, where the custom Netscape Navigator palette for Windows has been selected.

Figure 14-7 In Photoshop, changing the mode of your image from RGB Color to Indexed Color changes the color depth of your image.

Interlaced and Progressive Scans   Both GIF and JPEG images can be saved so that when your browser displays the image as it is being downloaded, you can immediately see a chunky approximation of the final image, with resolution improving as more and more data comes in. While in baseline, or normal configuration, image data is stored as a single top-to-bottom scan; in **interlaced** GIF and **progressive** JPEG files, the data is organized in a different sequence within the file. An interlaced GIF file, for example, is arranged into a series of four passes:

Pass 1 : Every 8th row, starting with row 0
Pass 2 : Every 8th row, starting with row 4
Pass 3 : Every 4th row, starting with row 2
Pass 4 : Every 2nd row, starting with row 1

Figure 14-8 shows Photoshop's **GIF89a** Export tool using Image Ready with its check box to enable saving an image as interlaced, and four increasingly resolved images.

One issue that seriously perplexed me when creating my first web site was choosing the right palette for photographic or continuous tone images. Because images have to be small, you have to dither them to 8 bits. Well, what 8-bit palette do you dither down to—Macintosh, Windows, Netscape, Mosaic, FireFox, MacWeb, etc., etc.?

Marlene Sinicki, Designer,
San Francisco

Figure 14-8 Interlacing and transparency settings when exporting a GIF89a file from Photoshop. With interlacing, the image incrementally improves its resolution as it downloads; transparency allows an image to "float" on a document background.

Transparency   The GIF89a specification allows for **transparency**: you can save your file with instructions to a browser to use the color that is in its own background for pixels that are your selected transparency color. In many cases, such as for company logos and inline illustrations, it is attractive to let an image float on top of the browser's background:

The background of the logo is white and would (without transparency) be displayed as a rectangle showing white to its edges. To make the white background of the GIF image transparent so that the tree and lettering float on the background, choose white as the transparency index color, and then save the file. Tools that provide a palette from which you can select the transparency index color are available for saving transparent GIF files.

You cannot make a JPEG file transparent.

Backgrounds

Most browsers allow you to specify an image or color to place in the background of your page. Text and images will float on top of this layer.

Background Coloring

You can colorize your documents by choosing background, text, and URL link colors. Color controls are attributes of the **<BODY> tag**, so you can only set the colors of an *entire* document's background; you cannot change coloring partway through. The BGCOLOR attribute of the <BODY> tag supported by Netscape Navigator lets you change the color of the background without having to specify a graphic image to load. The format Navigator understands is

```
<BODY BGCOLOR="#rrggbb">Document here</BODY>
```

where "#rrggbb" is a hexadecimal red-green-blue triplet used to specify the background color. (See Chapter 6 for an explanation of red-green-blue triplets.)

When you have chosen a background color, you will then want to set the color of your text and establish proper contrasts. Red on green shimmers, whereas black on black is invisible. So the four classes of text used in an HTML document are also attributes of Netscape's <BODY> tag.

The **TEXT attribute** of the <BODY> tag is used to control the color of all the normal text in a document—text that is not specially colored to indicate a link. The **LINK, VLINK,** and **ALINK attributes** let you control the coloring of link text. LINK text displays a URL that you have not visited, VLINK text shows a visited link, and ALINK is an active link. The default coloring of these in Netscape Navigator is TEXT = very light gray, LINK = blue, VLINK = purple, and ALINK = red. If you placed these default colors into a <BODY> tag using hexadecimal values, the tag would read

```
<BODY BGCOLOR="#CDCDCD" TEXT="#000000" LINK="#0000FF"
VLINK="#FF00FF" ALINK="#FF0000">
```

Background Images

You can specify a special background image for your document. Fifty-five textures are publicly available at Netscape's home server and can add polish with little effort. By using background images served directly from Netscape, it is possible that the image will already be in the cache on your user's hard disk and will load more rapidly.

Background images are automatically tiled, or repeated, across and down the page, so a randomly distributed "sandy" background image (see Figure 14-9) can easily be made up of a very small source image. None of your document can be displayed until the background image is loaded, so keep your background image small.

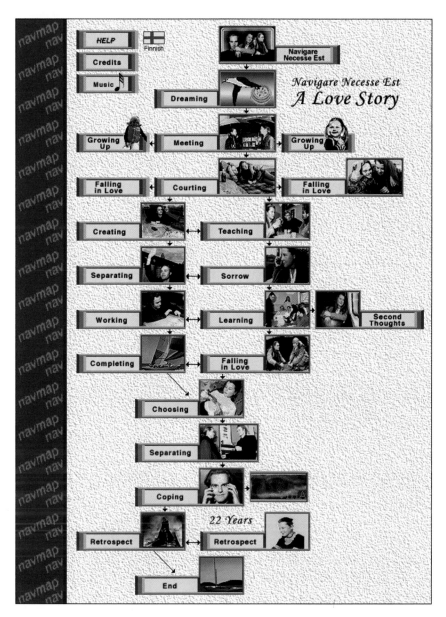

Figure 14-9 A simplified navigation map not only provides an overview of a multimedia project but also contains active links to documents using "hot" areas of the graphic. This is the navmap page from Navigare Necesse Est, a student-built love story. Clearly, the linking of information in such easy-to-make GUIs demonstrates the power of multimedia.

Load a background image into a document by specifying its URL (if it is available somewhere on the Web) or its file path (if it is on the same server as the page) in the BACKGROUND attribute of the <BODY> tag, for example:

```
<BODY BACKGROUND="http://home.netscape.com/home/bg/fabric/gray_fabric.gif">
```

TIP   *It is a good idea, often overlooked, to specify a background color (BGCOLOR="#rrggbb") similar to the prevailing color of the image in the <BODY> tag. If the user viewing your page has Image Loading turned off, or if your background image cannot be loaded for some reason, the page will still look close to the way you designed it. If the background image is not loaded for any reason by your browser, and a BGCOLOR was not also specified, then any of the foreground controlling attributes (TEXT, LINK, VLINK, and ALINK) will be ignored. If the image you specify as a background has transparent areas, the BGCOLOR will show through.*

Sidebars

In the navigation map shown in Figure 14-9, a commonly seen graphic layout was used: a vertical bar containing the word "navmap" is displayed at the left of the screen and in the background. When users scroll up or down, this bar remains stationary.

Assuming that most users will have a viewing window about 640 pixels wide, but some may be wider on higher-resolution monitors, make the graphic bar at the left as wide as you wish (say 75 pixels); then set the full width of your image to 1,000 pixels. Fill the space to the right of your bar with plain color or a texture. When this background image tiles, it will repeat itself only when the user widens the viewing window to more than 1,000 pixels; but the image will tile vertically in increments of its height. Here is the basic setup:

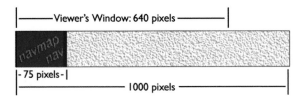

Clickable Buttons

To make a graphic image "clickable" so that it links to another document, simply include the image tag inside the bounding tags of an HTML anchor that points to that document's URL:

```
<A HREF="documentToGoTo.html">
<IMG SRC="imageDisplayed.gif" BORDER="0">
</A>
```

You can also use the <A> tag to provide a link to a larger graphic or even to a video clip from a small, thumbnail-sized image:

```
<A HREF="bigPicture.jpg"><IMG SRC="thumbnail.gif"></A>
<A HREF="videoClip.mpeg"><IMG SRC="thumbnail.gif"></A>
```

Be sure to include the **BORDER attribute** (BORDER="0") in the <IMG> tag if you wish to avoid showing a default border around the button image (usually two blue pixels wide).

Image Maps

Image maps are pictures with defined hot spots that link to other documents when a user clicks on them. Until recently, using image maps at a web site required a special **CGI (Common Gateway Interface)** program and a configuration or .map file containing the coordinates of the hot spots to be located on the server. It also required communication between client and server as well as processing time while the CGI program looked up the coordinates in the specified .map file on the server and associated them with a document. Depending upon Internet traffic and delays, performance could be sluggish. And setting up this kind of image map usually required help from a system administrator or the Internet Service Provider who owns the server. In this server-side system, the HTML <IMG> tag attribute, ISMAP, tells the server to launch the CGI program, look up the mouse coordinates in the referenced file, and deliver the specified document.

Browsers added support for client-side image maps so that mouse coordinates and their associated document URLs could be included in the client's own HTML document, thus avoiding the setup and communications hassles of the server-side system. This is managed by the **USEMAP attribute** of the <IMG> tag.

To make a client-side image map with USEMAP, you need three things: an image, a list of coordinates designating hot spots on the image, and the document URL associated with each hot spot. To program the image map into your HTML document, you use the USEMAP attribute of the <IMG> tag:

```
IMG src="compas.gif" hspace="5" vspace="50" border="0" usemap="#compass">
<MAP name="compass">
     <AREA shape="circle" coords="60,60,10" href="help.htm">
     <AREA shape="polygon" coords="60,60,0,0,120,0" href="back.htm">
     <AREA shape="polygon" coords="60,60,0,120,120,120" href="forward.htm">
     <AREA shape="polygon" coords="60,60,0,0,0,120" href="navmap.htm">
</MAP>
```

In the previous example, illustrated in Figure 14-10, "compas.gif" is the transparent image, the hspace="5" and vspace="50" attributes provide space between the image and the text around it, and the border="0" attribute makes the image borderless. The usemap="#compass" attribute points to the <map> extension tag that contains the coordinates and URLs. (The pound sign means the **<MAP> tag** is located in this same document.) A <MAP> segment may be placed anywhere in the body of the HTML document and is related to the correct image by the name="compass" attribute of the <MAP> tag. You can have more than one image map in an HTML document, but they must have different names.

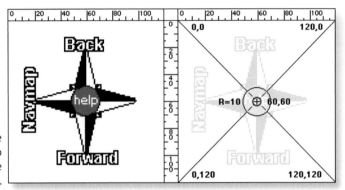

Figure 14-10 This enlarged image illustrates the coordinates used to define hot spots for image maps (the ruler is marked in pixels).

Within the <MAP> tag, the <AREA> tag defines the shape of the hot spot (as a circle, polygon, or rectangle) and anchors or links it to a URL. Areas are defined by x,y coordinates of the pixels in your bitmap: a circle by the x,y coordinates of its center location and radius (60,60,10), a polygon by a sequence of sets of x,y locations that close automatically (60,60,0,0,120,0 defines a triangle), or a rectangle (two x,y locations defining top left and bottom right).

Sound for the Web

In the beginning, when the Internet was primarily a collection of Unix machines, sound files were sent from machine to machine in **AU** format and, when downloaded, were played back using a sound application.

As the Web has developed, sound has become more important, and plug-ins currently allow embedding of sounds into documents. Browsers have become sound capable: Microsoft Internet Explorer offers the **<BGSOUND> tag** to play an AU, WAV, or MIDI sound track in a document background. Chapter 5 describes designing and making MIDI and digitized sound files in detail. Netscape and Internet Explorer offer the QuickTime plug-in for playing **AIFF**, **MIDI**, **WAV**, and AU formats. If your browser does not support the appropriate sound plug-in, your browser can still download the file and launch an external "viewer" or **helper application** to play it. These helper applications are usually chosen by you in the "File Helper Preferences" of your browser. **Streaming audio** is more useful for the Web, where a sound file can start playing as soon as data begins coming in. (Streaming information is provided by the LiveAudio and QuickTime plug-ins.) Plug-ins such as StreamWorks, VocalTec, and RealAudio (see Chapter 13) feature streaming capability and high compression/good fidelity, but they also require special software at the server. The QuickTime plug-in offers a fast-start feature to allow playing before a movie has been completely downloaded. (Even though a QuickTime file is called a movie, MIDI files and digitized sound embedded in a QuickTime movie will play even without video, text, or image tracks.) You can either embed HTML commands in a document to play a QuickTime movie automatically in the background, or you can display a controller providing stop, fast-forward, and rewind for the user.

> My eyes glaze over whenever someone rattles off a definition of multimedia. The glaze thickens when they focus on hardware speed or the merits of one platform or a multimedia, authoring tool. The key is to become well versed in a tool so you can make it perform whatever your content requires... it's more important to be creative.
>
> ....
>
> Alan Levine, Instructional Technologist, Maricopa Community Colleges, Arizona

```
With the Crescendo MIDI plug-in (which downloads and plays standard
MIDI files of MIME-type .mid or .midi), you can automatically launch
a background sound when a page opens by using the combined <OBJECT>
and <EMBED> tags:<OBJECT ID=Crescendo
    CLASSID="clsid:0FC6BF2B-E16A-11CF-AB2E-0080AD08A326"
    CODEBASE="http://activex.liveupdate.com/controls/cres.cab"
    HEIGHT="55" WIDTH="200" AUTOSTART="true">
<PARAM NAME="SONG" VALUE="theme.mid">
<EMBED TYPE="music/crescendo" SONG="theme.mid"
    PLUGINSPAGE="http://www.liveupdate.com/dl.html"
    HEIGHT="55" WIDTH="200" AUTOSTART="true">
</OBJECT>
```

Over time, sound will become more fully integrated into the way people use the World Wide Web, and it can be included in Shockwave, PowerPoint, Flash, and other presentation tools that use plug-ins and players.

Making sound for the Web requires the basic tools and techniques described in Chapter 5. Always nibble at your sound elements and reduce them to the lowest file sizes that will play acceptably. Remember, they will move across the Internet and may be downloaded or played on machines with low-bandwidth connections.

Animation for the Web

HTML makes no provision for animation, by itself delivering only a static page of text and graphics. Boring, many people said, and programmers went to work devising methods to liven up the view. Netscape 1.0 offered the (annoying) <BLINK> tag; Microsoft's Explorer offered the (annoying) <MARQUEE> tag to scroll text horizontally. JavaScript was applied to force (annoying) sliding text into the status bar. Arcane server-push/client-pull programming techniques refreshed images but loaded the network. Things were happening!

GIF89a

With Version 2.0 of Netscape Navigator, Netscape implemented a little-known animation feature of the final 1989 revision "a" of the GIF file format specification. It is possible to make simple animations by putting multiple images, or frames, into a single GIF89a file and display them with programmable delays (in 100ths of a second) between them.

When you use the <IMG> tag to embed a GIF89a multiframe image, Netscape Navigator downloads the file and stores it in the cache folder of your local hard disk. Once fully downloaded, the image plays each frame quickly and smoothly. Limit animated GIFs to small images, and use a more capable plug-in for animations over larger areas.

Plug-ins and Players

Prior to Adobe's acquisition, when Macromedia introduced Shockwave to allow the animation and interactivity of its flagship tool Directo to be embedded into pages viewed by Netscape Navigator, real animation and programmable power became available to web page developers. Later, they added Flash to their animation armory, which also uses Shockwave to create an .swf (Shockwave Flash) version of the native .fla file in order to make it displayable on a web page. **Players** and **plug-ins** were offered for other multimedia tools with animation capabilities, and the view came alive as long as the person viewing your page had installed the necessary file on his or her machine. Read Chapter 7 to learn the basics of animation. Pick a tool or method and start creating. Lokki, the Shockwaved seagull, was created by a beginner and was flying in just a few hours:

TIP *When embedding a Shockwave, Flash, PowerPoint, or other plug-in- or player-supported animation file into a web page, remember that cross-platform issues apply: if you use text fields, your fonts must properly map across platforms (see Chapter 4) unless you convert all text to bitmaps.*

The QuickTime movie format includes the ability to create Virtual Reality (VR) files, also displayed on a web page via a player. Flash and proprietary viewers can be used to present panoramas. Figure 14-11 shows a real estate sales panorama—when you drag the mouse across this player's window, the scene tracks and rotates in a 360-degree panorama. You can see adjacent rooms, too, by panning the image in a circle.

Animation software includes Swish (www. swishzone.com), Flash, Director, After Effects, DHTML, and animated GIF files built using shareware and freeware. Designers must be careful how they use animation though: too much motion and too many flashy colors can cheapen a web site. Subtle animation, however, enhances a site's content and messages.

Figure 14-11 Useful multimedia tools can enhance commercial web sites.

http://www.webstyleguide.com/multimedia/animation.html

http://www.needbeyond.com/animation/default.htm

http://www.members.aol.com/royalef/gifanim.htm

For animation styles and tips

Chapter 14 Review

■ Chapter Summary

For your review, here's a summary of the important concepts discussed in this chapter.

Describe the limitations of the World Wide Web for delivering multimedia

■ The World Wide Web was designed as a simple method for delivering text and graphics.

■ Make your web pages look good on minimal systems. The working space on a 640×480 monitor is actually about 600 pixels wide by 300 tall.

■ The overriding principle in designing web pages is to "nibble" away at the content in order to keep the size of the data as small as possible.

Discuss HTML, how it is structured, and how to use several of the most important tags for marking up a document

■ HTML provides tags for inserting media into HTML documents.

■ Use the <IMG> tag for inline images, the <INSERT> tag for multimedia objects, the <EMBED> tag for compound document embedding, and the <APP> and <APPLET> tags for code.

■ Specify a font, and even alternates for it, using the <FONT> tag, but remember: browsers can only use fonts already on their computer.

■ Use cascading style sheets (CSS) to set text styles across the pages of your web site.

■ Use a graphic bitmap if you wish to absolutely control the look of text in your HTML document.

■ The most powerful feature of HTML may be found in the <TABLE> tag.

Recognize important limitations for presenting good-looking images on the Web

■ The most commonly used image formats, GIF and JPEG, both use built-in compression algorithms to reduce file size.

■ GIF images are limited to 8 bits of color depth, or 256 colors.

■ GIF compresses drawings and cartoons that have only a few colors in them.

■ Use GIF files for line art and images that contain large areas of the same color. Use JPEG for photorealistic images.

■ The GIF89a specification allows for a selected transparency color. You cannot make a JPEG file transparent.

■ JPEG images may contain 24 bits of color depth.

■ JPEG uses a powerful but lossy compression method that produces files as much as ten times more compressed than GIF.

■ Use JPEG for photo-realistic images containing many colors.

■ Test the amount of compression acceptable for your JPEG image; stay inside the "threshold of visible error."

Lay out a web page using a background image

■ Most browsers allow you to specify an image or color to place in the background of your page in the <BODY> tag. Text and images will float on top of this layer.

■ The <TEXT> tag is used to control the color of all the non-link text in a document. The LINK, VLINK, and ALINK tags let you control the coloring of link text.

- Background images are automatically tiled, or repeated, across and down the page.

- Load a background image into a document by specifying its URL or file path in the BACK-GROUND attribute of the <BODY> tag.

Add interactivity to a web page by making images clickable

- Placing an image inside an HTML anchor tag makes the graphic image clickable.

- Image maps are pictures with defined hot spots that link to other documents when a user clicks on them.

- An image map has three parts: the image, a list of coordinates designating hot spots on the image, and a link associated with each hot spot.

Use the most common sound and animation functions

- Streaming audio, in which a sound file can start playing as soon as data begins coming in, is provided by several plug-ins.

- Always nibble at your sound elements and reduce them to the lowest file sizes that will play acceptably.

- HTML makes no provision for animation by itself.

- Limit animated GIFs to small images, and use a more capable plug-in for animations over larger areas.

- Shockwave, Flash, and QuickTime brought animation to the Web.

■ Key Terms

AIFF *(365)*
ALIGN attribute *(352)*
ALINK attributes *(360)*
<APPLET> tag *(348)*
AU *(364)*
BGCOLOR attribute *(351)*
<BGSOUND> tag *(364)*
<BODY> tag *(360)*
BORDER attribute *(363)*
COLOR attribute *(351)*
Common Gateway
  Interface (CGI) *(363)*
compression *(354)*
deprecated *(348)*
<EMBED> tag *(348)*
escape sequence *(353)*

<FONT> tag *(350)*
GIF *(355)*
GIF89a *(359)*
helper application *(365)*
HSPACE attribute *(352)*
<IMG> tag *(348)*
interlaced *(359)*
JPEG *(355)*
LINK attribute *(360)*
lossless *(355)*
lossy *(355)*
<MAP> tag *(364)*
MIDI *(365)*
<OBJECT> tag *(348)*
OpenType *(350)*
player *(366)*

plug-in *(366)*
PNG *(355)*
progressive scan *(359)*
SIZE attribute *(351)*
streaming audio *(365)*
<TABLE> tag *(351)*
TEXT attribute *(360)*
transparency *(359)*
TrueDoc *(350)*
USEMAP attribute *(363)*
VLINK attribute *(360)*
VSPACE attribute *(352)*
WAV *(365)*
Web Embedding Font Tool
  (WEFT) *(350)*

■ Key Term Quiz

1. The tag used for inline images is the _____.
2. The tag used for multimedia objects is the_____.
3. The tag used to specify a typeface is the_____.
4. Microsoft supports font-embedding capabilities in web pages through its _____.
5. Tags no longer included in the most current version of the HTML standard but still recognized by browsers have been _____.
6. Perhaps the most powerful feature of HTML may be found in the _____.
7. The color of visited link text is defined in the _____.
8. A new "open" format that was developed to replace GIF without requiring licensing fees is the _____.
9. The tag that defines hot spots on an image and the links associated with the hot spots is the _____.
10. The image specification that allows for both transparency and animation in a browser without a plug-in is _____.

■ Multiple Choice Quiz

1. The World Wide Web was originally designed to deliver:
   a. high-quality multimedia
   b. text documents with embedded graphics
   c. data in many formats, including file transfers, chat, and e-mail
   d. streaming media formats
   e. top-secret military information
2. The VGA standard of a 640x480-pixel monitor showing 256 colors is:
   a. the highest-resolution and color depth currently available
   b. the standard used by most browsers
   c. still used by a small number of users
   d. not used by a significant number of users
   e. no longer considered a viable standard
3. Which of these is the *only* way to ensure that text appears exactly the same across platforms?
   a. Create a bitmap image of the text.
   b. Use the <FONT> tag to include your specific font.

c. Include the font as a download on the server.
   d. Specify the font using cascading style sheets.
   e. Embed the font into the HTML code itself.
4. One of the most important tags, useful for creating columns of information, is:
   a. <BODY>
   b. <BACKGROUND>
   c. <EMBED>
   d. <HEAD>
   e. <TABLE>
5. Which of these statements about the GIF image specification is *false*?
   a. It can be used to embed animations.
   b. It can only include 256 colors.
   c. It is best used for drawings and cartoons that have only a few colors in them.
   d. It can be saved in an interlaced mode.
   e. It was developed by Microsoft in 1982.

6. The tag that includes attributes for text and link colors is:
   a. <BODY>
   b. <BACKGROUND>
   c. <EMBED>
   d. <HEAD>
   e. <TABLE>

7. Which of these is *not* an attribute of the <BODY> tag?
   a. TEXT
   b. LINK
   c. ALINK
   d. BLINK
   e. BGCOLOR

8. You make a graphic image "clickable" by including the image inside which tag?
   a. <A>
   b. <URL>
   c. <LINK>
   d. <CLICK>
   e. <GOTO>

9. CGI stands for:
   a. Computer Group Integration
   b. Common Gateway Interface
   c. Command Guide Interaction
   d. Complete Generation Interchange
   e. Complex Graphics Instruction

10. Which of these is *not* an image format supported by most browsers without a plug-in?
    a. GIF
    b. JPEG
    c. PNG
    d. CGM
    e. All are supported by most browsers.

11. When you change an image's mode to Indexed Color, which of these is *not* a specification that must be chosen?
    a. the color depth of the converted image
    b. the compression level to be used
    c. the color palette to be used

d. whether the colors of your image should be dithered or not
e. All of the above must be selected.

12. How many colors are in the Netscape Navigator palette?
    a. 16
    b. 40
    c. 216
    d. 254
    e. 256
    f. 512

13. When a background image is smaller than the browser window, the browser will:
    a. simply ignore the background
    b. display the background in the upper-left corner with the background color filling the rest of the window
    c. tile the background image to fill the window
    d. stretch the background image to fill the window
    e. crash

14. Which of the following is *not* part of the process of responding to server-side image map requests?
    a. The browser parses the image map coordinates to request the appropriate file.
    b. The server launches the CGI program in response to the browser's request.
    c. The server delivers the requested document.
    d. The browser displays the new document.
    e. All of the above are steps in this process.

15. When the browser downloads a file it cannot process itself, it can forward the file to an external application for processing. This external application is sometimes called:
    a. a plug-in
    b. a helper application
    c. a CGI script
    d. a JavaScript
    e. a Java applet

■ Essay Quiz

1. How is the World Wide Web used today? How do you use it? What types of sites do you visit? How has it changed in your personal experience?

2. Bandwidth limitations impose serious limitations on presenting multimedia over the web. What tools and strategies does a multimedia developer have to deal with the limitations of bandwidth?

3. HTML was never designed to include multimedia. What are the original design limitations of HTML? How has it been stretched to accommodate other media? How has the browser architecture been adapted to allow other media? What tools and strategies does a multimedia developer have to deal with these limitations?

4. List and describe the most important tags for multimedia in HTML.

5. What are the two most common graphics file formats in use on the Web today? Discuss what each is best suited for, its limitations, and its capabilities.

Lab Projects

■ Project 14.1

Select three different web pages, each from a different site and with differing layouts. Print out the web pages. Examine them carefully.

Draw lines on the printout where you think the various cells of the tables were used to construct the pages.

If possible, view the page on a Macintosh. Some browsers on the Macintosh allow you to "pull" images out of the page, enabling you to see how images are "sliced" and laid into a table.

■ Project 14.2

Again select three different web pages, each from a different site and with differing layouts. All browsers include the ability to view the source code of the web page. View the HTML source, and then print it out. Identify head, image, anchor (a), body, and table tags in the page by circling them.

(If you have access to a visual web page editor, import the source from the three pages in Lab Project 14.1 and note how the tables are laid out.)

■ Project 14.3

Select three different sites that present audio and three sites that present video, virtual reality, or animation. What data formats are used for the multimedia? Are different data rates offered? What plug-ins are required? Make a note of the URLs, media formats, data rates, and required plug-ins or helper applications.

■ Project 14.4

Again select three different web pages, each from a different site and with differing layouts, and try to find a monitor capable of at least 1024x768 pixels. Reduce the browser window. Does the layout contract past a certain point? Now widen the browser window. Does the layout expand beyond a certain point? Reduce the monitor's color depth to 256 colors. Note the appearance of the graphics. Is there any dithering? Make notes of your findings, including the site's URL.

■ Project 14.5

Locate a site that uses cascading style sheets. This will be visible either in the HTML code itself within the "style" tags, or may be referenced externally. If they are external, ask someone to help you access the file, if it is accessible. As in Project 14.4, print out the style sheet. Circle any fonts, colors, sizes, and other style information.

■ Project 14.6

Check the Web for current statistics on market penetration of browsers and the percentage of use of different monitor settings for viewing web pages. Compare those statistics with the text's numbers. How have things changed since this book was published?

CHAPTER 15

Planning and Costing

In this chapter, you will learn how to:

- Determine the scope of a multimedia project

- Recognize common obstacles to the successful completion of multimedia projects

- Identify tools and techniques to overcome project management problems

- Determine the cost, timeline, and tasks required to complete a project

- Discuss the process and elements of a multimedia project proposal

BEFORE you begin a multimedia project, you must first develop a sense of its **scope** and content, letting the project take shape in your head as you think through the various methods available to get your message across to your viewers. Then you must develop an organized outline and a plan that is rational in terms of the skills, time, budget, tools, and resources you have at hand. Proper project planning is as important as planning the layout and content. Your plans should be in place before you start to render graphics, sounds, and other components, and you should refer to them throughout the project's execution.

First Person

When I was nine, my father told me about China. He brought the big spinning globe into the kitchen and used a fork to point out where we were and where China was. He explained that if we dug a hole deep enough in the backyard, eventually we would come out in a place called Peking. After school the next day, I began, unannounced, trenching a pit into the rocky soil of our New England backyard. The first layer was tough sod, then there was some topsoil and loam, and then a thick stratum of moist pea gravel. I was

knee-deep into the next layer—hard-packed clay—when my father discovered my work site when he came home at the end of the day. He was pleased I had missed the septic tank by several feet and sternly suggested that more study would be required before I dug any further.

This was my first lesson in project planning, not to mention my first experience with project abandonment. Be sure you analyze the requirements of your multimedia project before you go to the tool shed.

The Process of Making Multimedia

Usually something will click in your mind or in the mind of a client that says, "Hey, wouldn't it be neat if we could…" Your visions of sound and music, flashy images, and perhaps a video will solve a business need, provide an attention-grabbing product demo, or yield a slick front end to an otherwise drab computer database. You might want to spark a little interest or a laugh in an otherwise dull meeting, build an interactive photo album for Christmas greetings to your family, or post your company's annual report in a new set of pages on the Web.

It is, of course, easiest to plan a project using the experience you have accumulated in similar past projects. Over time, you can maintain and improve your multimedia-planning format, just like a batch of sourdough starter. Just keep adding a little rye and water every time you do a project, and the starter for your next job gets a bit more potent as your estimates become tempered by experience.

Plan for the entire process: beginning with your first ideas and ending with completion and delivery of a finished product. Think in the overview. The stepwise process of making multimedia is illustrated in Figure 15-1.

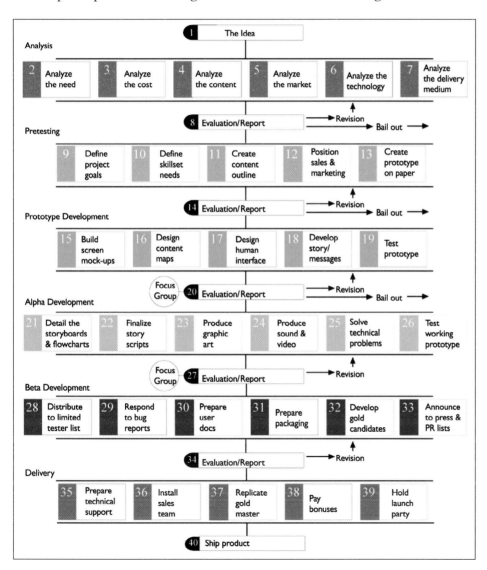

Figure 15-1 The process of making multimedia

Use this chart to help you get your arms around a new web site or CD-ROM production! Note the feedback loops for revisions based upon testing and experiment. Note also the constant presence of an "evaluation committee" (who could be simply a project manager) to oversee the whole.

Idea Analysis

The important thing to keep in mind when you are toying with an idea is balance. As you think through your idea, you must continually weigh your purpose or goal against the feasibility and cost of production and delivery.

Use whiteboard, notepaper, and scratch pads as you flesh out your idea, or use a note-taking or outlining program on your computer. Start with broad-brush strokes, and then think through each constituent multimedia element. Ultimately, you will generate a plan of action that will become your road map for production. Who needs this project? Is it worthwhile? Do you have the materials at hand to build it? Do you have the skills to build it? Your idea will be in balance if you have considered and weighed the proper elements:

- What is the essence of what you want to do? What is your purpose and message?

- Who is your intended audience? Who will be your end users? What do they already know about the subject? Will they understand industry terms (jargon), and what information do they need your project to communicate to them? What will their multimedia playback platforms be, and what are the minimal technical capabilities of those platforms?

- Is there a client, and what does the client want?

- How can you organize your project?

- What multimedia elements (text, sounds, and visuals) will best deliver your message?

- Do you already have content material with which you can leverage your project, such as videotape, music, documents, photographs, logos, advertisements, marketing packages, and other artwork?

- Will interactivity be required?

- Is your idea derived from an existing theme that can be enhanced with multimedia, or will you create something totally new?

- What hardware is available for development of your project? Is it enough?

- How much storage space do you have? How much do you need?

- What multimedia software is available to you?

- What are your capabilities and skills with both the software and the hardware?

- Can you do it alone? Who can help you?

- How much time do you have?

- How much money do you have?

- How will you distribute the final project?

- Will you need to update and/or support the final product?

You can maintain balance between purpose and feasibility by dynamically adding and subtracting multimedia elements as you stretch and shape your idea. You can start small and build from minimum capabilities toward a satisfactory result in an additive way. Or you can shoot the moon with a heavy list of features and desired multimedia results, and then discard items one by one because they are just not possible. Both additive and subtractive processes can work in concert. In the end, this process will yield very useful cost estimates and a production road map.

Consider the following scenario: You have videotape with four head-and-shoulders testimonials that will be perfect for illustrating your message. So add motion video to your list. You will need to purchase a video digitizing board and digitizing software, so add those items and their cost to your list as well. But you want to make your product available at a web site frequented by people without high-speed connections who will wait minutes for the video to play. Subtract motion video, but add tiny framed still images of the four talking heads (captured with your new video equipment) using short, one-sentence voice-overs of the speakers (recorded from the videotape). Subtract one of the four testimonials because you discover that particular executive is no longer with the firm and you don't have a signed release. Add animation instead. Subtract. Add. Subtract. In this manner, you will flesh out your idea, adding and subtracting elements within the constraints of the hardware, software, and your budget of cost and expertise.

The time you spend defining your project in this way—reality-testing it against technology and your abilities—might be your most valuable investment, even before you boot up a computer. At any point, you can decide to go forward or bail out.

TIP *Treat your multimedia idea like a business venture. As you visualize in your mind's eye what you want to accomplish, balance the project's profit potential against the investment of effort and resources required to make it happen.*

Hardware

The most common limiting factor for realizing a multimedia idea is hardware: no sound board, no sound effects; no synthesizer, no MIDI composed by you on-site; no high-resolution color display, no pretty pictures; no modem or network, no Internet. Begin by listing the hardware capabilities of the end user's computer platform (not necessarily the platform on which you will develop the project). If the capabilities are not enough, examine the cost of enhancing that delivery platform, and balance those results against your purpose and resources.

TIP *In the early days of multimedia development, most projects were designed for monitors set to a resolution of 640x480 pixels and 8-bit color depth (256 colors); this was the most common end-user hardware configuration. Today, designers commonly deliver projects, both on CD-ROM and for the Web, which require a minimum monitor resolution of 1024x768 pixels and "millions" of colors. Hardware improvements and cost drops have increased the assumed available "real estate" or "geography," and use of non-dithered high-color images has greatly improved the end-user experience.*

Idea Management Software

Software such as Microsoft Project, Designer's Edge (see Figure 15-2), outlining programs, and spreadsheets such as Excel can be useful for arranging your ideas and the many tasks, work items, employee resources, and costs required of your multimedia project. Project management tools provide the added benefit of built-in analysis to help you stay within your schedule and budget during the rendering of the project itself.

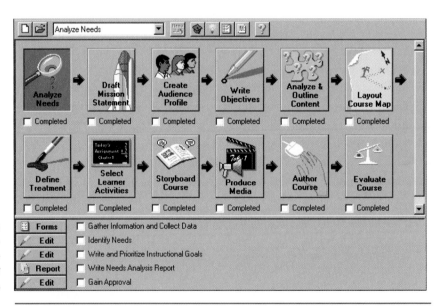

Figure 15-2 Designer's Edge, an integrated pre-authoring idea management tool from Allen Communication, generates helpful documents for instructional designers.

WARNING *Budget your time if you are new to project management software. It may be difficult to learn and to use effectively.*

Project management software typically provides **Critical Path Method (CPM)** scheduling functions to calculate the total duration of a project based upon each identified task, earmarking tasks that are critical and that if lengthened, will result in a delay in project completion. **Program Evaluation Review Technique (PERT) charts** provide graphic representations of task relationships, showing **prerequisites**, the tasks that must be completed before others can commence. **Gantt charts** depict all the tasks along a timeline.

The Paper Napkin

The very early idea of processing and preliminary planning sketched on the working-lunch paper napkin, shown in Figure 15-3, evolved into a complex multimedia project of many months duration.

First, we discussed, refined, and cultivated the idea as a preliminary project plan. Then we began by building a prototype, shown as the A-B portion of the napkin notes, which quite literally answered the question "How do we get from A to B with this idea?" The prototype was then carefully examined in terms of projected work effort and the technology required for implementing a full-blown version of the prototype. Based upon our experience, we then developed a more complete plan and cost estimate for full implementation, and the project was launched in earnest. Figure 15-4 shows a screen from the final product.

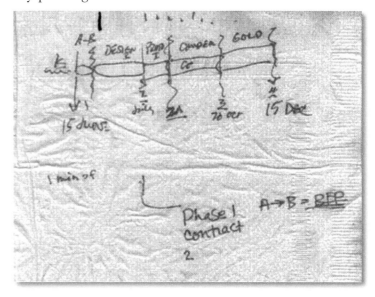

Figure 15-3 The ideas on this luncheon napkin evolved into an animated guided tour for Lotus's multimedia version of 1-2-3 in SmartSuite Millenium.

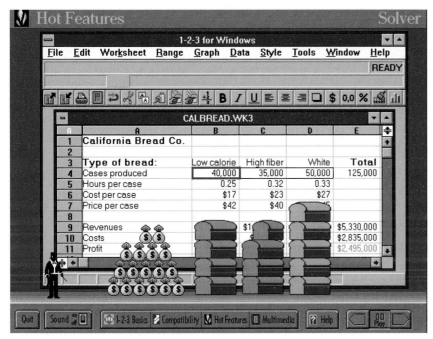

Figure 15-4 A screen from the guided tour for Lotus 1-2-3 for Windows with Multimedia SmartHelp

First Person

Last time I took the red-eye home, the fat guy behind me was pretty ill—sneezing and hawking incessantly over my headrest on the full, hot plane. My glasses blurred with misty droplets, and I wiped the fog away with the damp cocktail napkin under my Coke. That trip cost me four days sick in bed, and I promised I would never fly night coach again to make a meeting, no matter how important.

Then I broke my promise and, after a sleepless night on the plane,

found myself sitting in the muggy summer air on the bank of the Charles River, having lunch with Rob Lippincott and his multimedia team from Lotus. I pretended to be alert, but residual white noise from the plane ride beat in my ears, and my dry eyes wouldn't focus in the umbrella sunlight. Rob made intelligent notes with a ballpoint pen on a paper napkin while my own input to the creative process was reduced to grunts and short sentences. The smartest thing I did, though, was slip

the paper napkin with its notes into my briefcase as we left the table. After some sleep, I was able to retrieve the napkin and craft those luncheon thoughts into the backbone of a rational project proposal and action plan. We launched the venture, and about ten months later it went gold, shipping with Lotus's new Multimedia product, Lotus SmartSuite Millennium 9.8.

Pretesting

If you decide that your idea has merit, take it to the next step. Define your project goals in greater detail and spell out what it will take in terms of skills, content, and money to meet these goals. If you envision a commercial product, sketch out how you will sell it. Work up a prototype of the project on paper, with an explanation of how it will work. All of these steps help you organize your idea and test it against the real world.

Task Planning

There may be many tasks in your multimedia project. Here is a checklist of action items for which you should plan ahead as you think through your project:

- ❑ Design Instructional Framework
- ❑ Hold Creative Idea Session(s)
- ❑ Determine Delivery Platform
- ❑ Determine Authoring Platform
- ❑ Assay Available Content
- ❑ Draw Navigation Map
- ❑ Create Storyboards
- ❑ Design Interface
- ❑ Design Information Containers
- ❑ Research/Gather Content

- ❑ Assemble Team
- ❑ Build Prototype
- ❑ Conduct User Test
- ❑ Revise Design
- ❑ Create Graphics
- ❑ Create Animations
- ❑ Produce Audio
- ❑ Produce Video
- ❑ Digitize Audio and Video
- ❑ Take Still Photographs

- ❑ Program and Author
- ❑ Test Functionality
- ❑ Fix Bugs
- ❑ Conduct Beta Test
- ❑ Create Golden Master
- ❑ Replicate
- ❑ Prepare Package
- ❑ Deliver or Install at Web Site
- ❑ Award Bonuses
- ❑ Throw Party

In a white paper about producing educational software, Mentergy has allocated percentages of effort, as shown to the right.

Task	Percentage of Effort
Analyze need	3%
Draft mission statement	1%
Create audience profile	2%
Write objectives	2%
Analyze and outline content	6%
Lay out course map	2%
Define treatment	2%
Select learner activities	2%
Storyboard the course	19%
Author the course	28%
Evaluate the course	20%
Produce media	13%

Building a Team

Multimedia is an emerging technology requiring a set of skills so broad that multimedia itself remains poorly defined. Players in this technology come from all corners of the computer and art worlds as well as from a variety of other disciplines, so if you need to assemble a team, you need to know the people and skills it takes to make multimedia. (Refer to Chapter 3 for a description of the various skills and talents needed and how others have built successful teams.)

You should list the skills and software capabilities available to you. This list is not as limiting as your list of required hardware because you can always budget for new and more powerful software and for the learning curve (or consultant fees) required to make use of it. Indeed, authoring software is usually necessary only for development of the project, not its playback or delivery, and should be a cost or learning burden not directly passed to end users.

Building a matrix chart of required skills is often helpful to describe the makeup of your team. Figure 15-5 shows a skill matrix developed when four medium-sized multimedia development companies came together to bid on a single, large CD-ROM project. If you are building a complex web site, substitute Java/Perl programmer, HTML programmer, and Server Specialist into the proper row.

Staying at the leading edge is important. If you remain knowledgeable about what's new and expected, you will be more valuable to your own endeavors, your team, and to your employer or prospective clients. But be prepared for steep learning curves and difficult challenges in keeping your own skills (and those of your employees) current and in demand. And don't neglect team morale as hours grow long, deadlines slip, and tempers flare.

TIP *If you are looking for multimedia talent, try placing a Help Wanted ad in one of the job-hunting/help wanted sites on the Internet.*

In a business where success and failure often depends upon our ability to monitor and anticipate emerging technology, job recruiters see multimedia as very challenging. Not only does the fledgling multimedia industry incorporate some of the hottest computer technology tools, it draws on talent that comes from outside the traditional boundaries of data processing and MIS recruitment. The ill-defined but very technical skills needed for multimedia provide us, the industry recruiters, an exceptional opportunity for creativity. Our clients, too, need to be open-minded and flexible about the talent and skills required of multimedia developers.

Heinz Bartesch, Director of Sales and Marketing, The Search Firm (San Francisco)

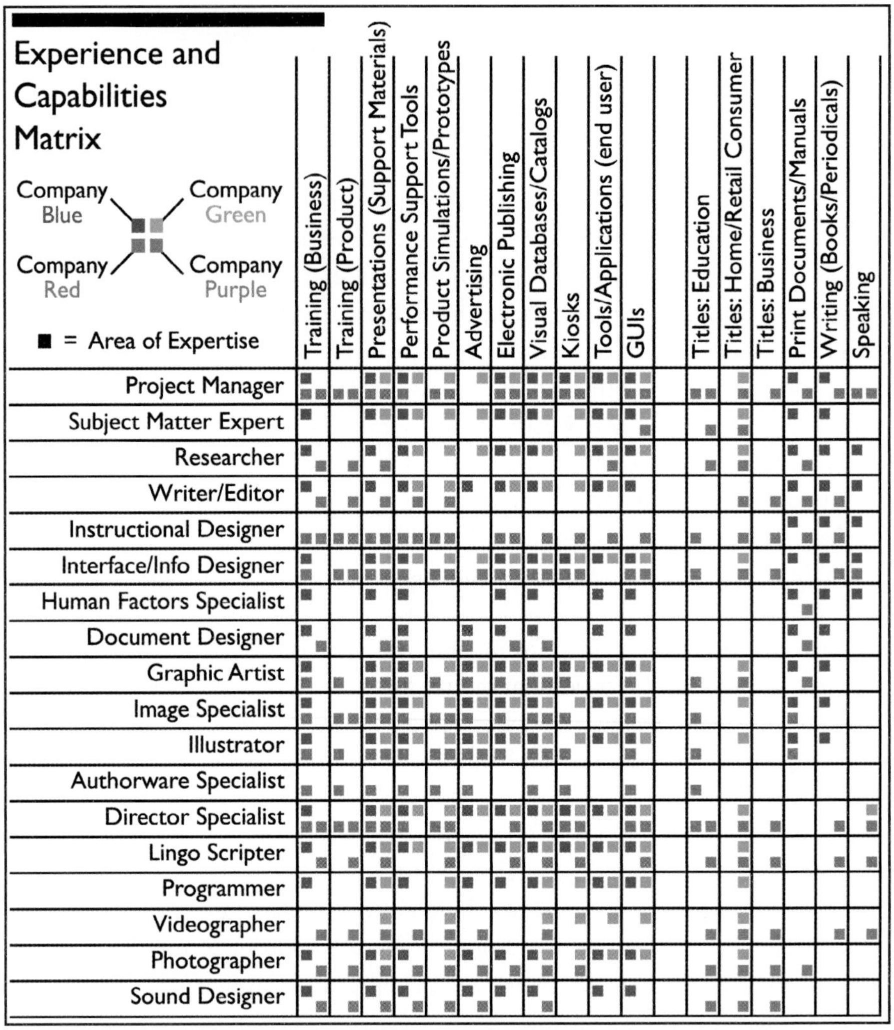

Experience and Capabilities Matrix

Company Blue — Company Green

Company Red — Company Purple

■ = Area of Expertise

Column headings:
- Training (Business)
- Training (Product)
- Presentations (Support Materials)
- Performance Support Tools
- Product Simulations/Prototypes
- Advertising
- Electronic Publishing
- Visual Databases/Catalogs
- Kiosks
- Tools/Applications (end user)
- GUIs
- Titles: Education
- Titles: Home/Retail Consumer
- Titles: Business
- Print Documents/Manuals
- Writing (Books/Periodicals)
- Speaking

Row labels:
- Project Manager
- Subject Matter Expert
- Researcher
- Writer/Editor
- Instructional Designer
- Interface/Info Designer
- Human Factors Specialist
- Document Designer
- Graphic Artist
- Image Specialist
- Illustrator
- Authorware Specialist
- Director Specialist
- Lingo Scripter
- Programmer
- Videographer
- Photographer
- Sound Designer

Figure 15-5 A matrix of available skills can assist you in planning for your project.

http://www.careerbuilder.com
http://lycos.oodle.com
http://www.monster.com
http://www.hotjobs.com
http://www.jobbankusa.com
http://www.dice.com
http://www.fedworld.gov/jobs/jobsearch.html
Web sites for job searching

Prototype Development

When you have decided that a project is worth doing, you should develop a working prototype. This is the point at which you begin serious work at the computer, building screen mock-ups and a human interface of menus and button clicks. Your messages and story lines will take shape as you explore ways of presenting them. For the prototype, sometimes called a **proof-of-concept** or **feasibility study**, you might select only a small portion of a large project and get that part working as it would in the final product. Indeed, after trying many different approaches in the course of prototyping, you may end up with several different approaches or candidates.

During this phase you can test ideas, mock up interfaces, exercise the hardware platform, and develop a sense about where the alligators live. These alligators are typically found in the swampy edges of your own expertise; in the dark recesses of software platforms that almost-but-not-quite perform as advertised and in your misjudgment of the effort required for various tasks. The alligators will appear unexpectedly behind you and nip at your knees, unless you explore the terrain a little before you start out.

Test your prototype along several fronts: technology (will it work on your proposed delivery platform or platforms?), cost (can you do this project within budget constraints?), market (can you sell it, or will it be properly used if it is an in-house project?), and human interface (is it intuitive and easy to use?). At this point you may wish to arrange a focus group, where you can watch potential end users experiment with your prototype and analyze their reactions. The purpose of any prototype is to test the initial implementation of your idea and improve on it based upon test results. So you should never feel committed or bound to any one option, and you should be ready and willing to change things!

Persuade the client to spend a small amount of money and effort up front to let you build a skeletal version of the project, including some artwork, interactive navigation, and performance checks. Indeed, there may be some very specific technology issues that need thorough examination and proof before you can provide a realistic estimate of the work and cost required. The focused experience of this proof will allow both you and the client to assess the project's goals and the means to achieve them.

Build in your experimental pilot as the first phase of your project. At the pilot's conclusion, prepare a milestone report and a functional demo. You will be paid for the work so far, and the client will get real demonstration material that can be shown to bosses and managers. If your demo is good, it will be a persuasive argument within the client's management hierarchy for completing the full-scale project. Figure 15-6 is excerpted from trial calculations that were the result of a prototype five-language CD-ROM project. In the prototyping, office staff read the voice-over script as a "scratch track," like using a stand-in for the real thing; later, professional talent was used in the recording studio. As a result of building a prototype, accurate estimates of required storage space on the disc were possible.

Calculation Sheet

CD-ROM Project

Allocation of Disc Space

Note 1: The following trial calculations are based upon the file sizes yielded by an early voice rendering of the project's English script.

Note 2: File sizes for low-resolution images (72dpi) of 640×480 and 768×512 pixel dimensions are estimated at 768KB each.

Note 3: File sizes for high-resolution images (300dpi) may range from 3.7MB to 4.5MB, depending upon image complexity and compression rates. The conservative figure of 4.5MB per high-resolution image is used in these estimates.

Note 4: More accurate real estate estimates will be available following finalization of the script and recording of the English version narration.

Note 5: Firm count of low-resolution images and their pixel dimensions will be calculated upon script freeze.

SUMMARY: There is adequate room on the disc for both sound and images if each language recording is limited to no more than 9 minutes.

Scratch Track File

(English)	Duration	(English)	Duration
SNDE01A	18.369	SNDE10A	5.658
SNDE01B	9.180	SNDE11A	23.856
SNDE01C	9.295	SNDE12A	14.314
SNDE02A	17.609	SNDE13A	14.193
SNDE03A	17.932	SNDE14A	7.487
SNDE04A	11.156	SNDE15A	16.172
SNDE05A	18.035	SNDE16A	19.450
SNDE06A	8.050	SNDE17A	5.830
SNDE07A	12.790	SNDE18A	21.443
SNDE08A	16.218	SNDE19A	12.295
SNDE09A	27.468	Total	306.800 Seconds
			5.113 Minutes
		plus Intro Fanfare (Shared by all languages)	30.0 Seconds

Figure 15-6 Trial calculations are possible after prototyping.

As part of your delivery at the end of the pilot phase, reassess your estimates of the tasks required as well as the cost. Prepare a written report and analysis of budgets and anticipated additional costs. This is also the proper time to develop a revised and detailed project plan for the client. It allows the client some flexibility and provides a reality check for you. At this point you can also finalize your budget and payment schedule for the continuation of the project, as well as ink a contract and determine overrun procedures.

Difficulties may arise if your client is disappointed in the quantity of material delivered or is otherwise not satisfied with your work. If you have kept good records of the time and effort spent during prototyping, you may be able to smooth the rough waters. Remember that developing multimedia is a "trying" experience—try this, try that, then try this again a bit differently—and the creative process soaks up a lot of hours and cost. Listen carefully to the client's reaction to your prototype, because many problems can be quickly fixed, and all constructive comments can certainly be woven into the next phase of development.

Alpha Development

As you go forward, you should continually define the tasks ahead, because just like navigating a supertanker, you should be aware of the reefs and passages that will appear along your course and prepare for them. With a prototype in hand and a commitment to proceed, the investment of effort will increase and, at the same time, become more focused. More people may become involved as you begin to flesh out the project as a whole.

Beta Development

By the time your idea reaches the **beta** stage of development, you will have committed serious time, energy, and money, and it is likely too late to bail out. You have gone past the point of no return and should see it through. But by now you have a project that is looking great! Most of the features are working, and you are distributing it to a wider arena of testers. In fact, you are on the downhill slope now, and your concern should be simply successfully steering the project to its well-defined goal.

Delivery

By the time you reach the delivery stage, you are **going gold**—producing the final product. Your worries slide toward the marketplace: how will your project be received by its intended audience? You must also deal with a great many practical details, such as who will answer the support hotline, or whether to co-locate a server or trust the current ISP to handle the predicted increased volume of hits. The alpha, beta, and final gold stages of project delivery for CD-ROM and the Web are discussed in Chapter 18.

First Person

Not every prototype segues naturally into a full-blown project. Sometimes a project is shut down at this milestone due to reality shock: the client chokes on cost-to-completion estimates. Sometimes it's the Reorg Alligator: new managers with new agendas axe the project. Sometimes the client just plain doesn't like your work. Then sometimes a project simply disappears like a dream forgotten by mid-morning.

We were invited to prepare the prototype for a large and intricate intranet site behind a corporate firewall—potentially a two-year involvement. We proposed a first phase, an analysis and definition of the company's structure and information-gathering and dissemination needs so we could lock down major content areas and the navigation design. We wanted to know how many buttons to put on the main menu and what they would say, before we spent long hours creating the bitmaps and animated GIFs of a neat interface. "No, no," they said, "our guys have put that together already."

So we negotiated for creation of artwork and HTML page styles that would provide a consistent look and feel throughout the site. We set a fixed price and provided a list of deliverables: (1) graphic style and GIF/JPEG elements for main home and subpages; (2) a complete site structure and map with navigationally functional "under construction" pages based on the organizational charts they would provide; and (3) working demo pages for two of the company's departments.

Then we had our first team meeting, and it soon became clear they needed hand-holding while their own MIS people transitioned from other tasks and got up to speed in their new jobs as in-house intranet team and webmasters. None had coded a page of HTML, although some had used editors and builders to get pages working. The database guy was stopped dead by an undefined Java error when accessing his massive SQL database. The server guy was still getting set up. The HTML guy was learning his authoring tools. There was neither a graphic artist nor a handy pool of company graphic

art from which our own contribution might spring. OK, we thought, so they're on the learning curve. We can start from scratch. We took the group leader aside and quietly suggested that she consider bringing on a full-time graphics person to support her team.

During the next weeks, we developed a classy look and feel and theme. After a couple of feedback/change loops, they loved it. We worked up the more detailed bits and pieces of our deliverable and tightened up the organization of their proposed navigation map. By prototype deadline, we had spent all the hours we had estimated for the job, and they had the site up and working in test mode. We had gotten their motor running.

The last time we saw the SQL database programmer was on the afternoon we picked up our milestone check—he was removing shrink-wrap from a new copy of Photoshop, and the HTML guy was deep into Cold Fusion. We never heard from them again.

Scheduling

Once you have worked up a plan that encompasses the phases, tasks, and work items you feel will be required to complete your project, you need to lay out these elements along a timeline. This will usually include **milestones** at which certain **deliverables** are to be done. If you are working for a client, these are work products that are delivered to the client for approval. To create this schedule, you must estimate the total time required for each task and then allocate this time among the number of persons who will be asynchronously working on the project (see, for example, Figure 15-7). Again, the notion of balance is important: if you can distribute the required hours to perform a task among several workers, completion should take proportionally less time.

PROJECT CALC SHEET						1				2	
C. 5 5	$112,000		MARCH				APRIL				MAY
	SALARY	1	2	3	4	5	6	7	8	9	10
1 CONTEN ORIGINATION FEE	5										
DIRECTOR	40	**0.1**	**0.1**	**0.1**	**0.1**	**0.1**	**0.1**	**0.1**	**0.1**	**0.1**	**0.1**
cost		0.22	0.22	0.22	0.22	0.22	0.22	0.22	0.22	0.22	0.22
EDITOR	20					**1**	**1**				
cost		0.00	0.00	0.00	0.00	1.12	1.12	0.00	0.00	0.00	0.00
WRITER A	40	**1**	**1**	**1**	**1**	**1**					
cost		2.24	2.24	2.24	2.24	2.24	0.00	0.00	0.00	0.00	0.00
RESEARCHER	16										
cost		0.00	0.00	0.00	0.00	0.00	0.00	0.00	0.00	0.00	0.00
subtotal number personnel		1.1	1.1	1.1	1.1	2.1	1.1	1.1	0.1	0.1	0.1
cost		2.46	2.46	2.46	2.46	3.58	1.34	0.22	0.22	0.22	0.22
2 ART											
DIRECTOR	35	**1**	**1**	**1**	**1**	**1**	**1**	**1**	**1**	**1**	**1**
cost		1.40	1.40	1.40	1.40	1.40	1.40	1.40	1.40	1.40	1.40
ART 1	18								**1**	**1**	**1**
cost		0.00	0.00	0.00	0.00	0.00	0.00	0.00	1.01	1.01	1.01
ART2	13										
cost		0.00	0.00	0.00	0.00	0.00	0.00	0.00	0.00	0.00	0.00
subtotal number personnel		1	1	1	1	1	1	1	2	2	2
cost		1.40	1.40	1.40	1.40	1.40	1.40	1.40	2.41	2.41	2.41
3 TECHNICAL											
DIRECTOR	35								**1**	**1**	**1**
cost		0.00	0.00	0.00	0.00	0.00	0.00	0.00	1.40	1.40	1.40

Figure 15-7 Portion of a spreadsheet used to schedule manpower and project costs

---

WARNING *Assigning twice as many people to work on a task may not cut the time for its completion precisely in half. Consider the administrative and management overhead of communication, networking, and necessary staff meetings required when additional staff is added.*

Scheduling can be difficult for multimedia projects because so much of the making of multimedia is artistic trial and error. A recorded sound will need to be edited and perhaps altered many times. Animations need to be run again and again and adjusted so that they are smooth and properly placed. A QuickTime or MPEG movie may require many hours of editing and tweaking before it works in sync with other screen activities.

Scheduling multimedia projects is also difficult because the technology of computer hardware and software is in constant flux, and upgrades while your project is under way may drive you to new installations and concomitant learning curves. The general rule of thumb when working with computers and new technology under a deadline is that everything will take longer to do than you think it will.

In scheduling for a project that is to be rendered for a client, remember that the client will need to approve or sign off on your work at various stages. This approval process can wreak havoc with your schedule since it takes time and depends upon factors beyond your control. Perhaps more importantly, the client feedback may also require revision of your work. In order to protect yourself from a capricious client, you need to have points during the project for **client sign-off** on the work, meaning that he or she has approved the work to that point. If the client changes his or her mind later in the process, then any revisions of the previously approved materials would require a **change order**, meaning that the client agrees to pay the additional costs for making the changes, rather than you having to eat that unbudgeted cost out of your profit margin.

First Person

Many times we have heard about the Feedback Alligator. Its mottled skin boasts an Escher-like pattern of lines and marks, showing apparently clear definition along the head and neck, but converging to a brown muddled wash at the tail. When the tail wags this alligator, all hell breaks loose, and multimedia contracts can be severely strained or lost altogether.

Feedback Alligators can appear when you throw a client into the mix of creative people... when necessary-for-client-satisfaction approval cycles can turn your project into an anorexic nightmare of continuing rework, change, and consequently diminished profit. These alligators typically slink out from the damps *after* you have locked down a contract and scope of work, when the creative guys are already being well paid to ply their craft.

For client protection, multimedia creative artists should be hired with a cap on budget and time. They should be highly skilled, efficient, and have a clear understanding of what a project's goals are, and they should be allowed to accomplish these goals with as much freedom as possible. But good multimedia artists should come close to the mark the first time.

They don't always. For example, you agree to compose background theme music to play whenever your client's logo shows on the screen. You master a sample cassette tape and pass it to the client. She doesn't quite like the sound but is not sure why. You go back to the MIDI sequencer and try again. The client still isn't sure that's it. Again, you make up a tape and pass it to her for review. No, maybe it needs a little more Sgt. Pepper... this is our logo, remember?

The process of client feedback can go on and on forever in a resonance of desire-to-please and creative uncertainty unless you have developed rules for limiting these cycles. While your client might always be right, you will still go broke working unlimited changes on a fixed budget.

So do two things to ward off the Feedback Alligator. First, make it clear up front (in your contract) that there will only be a certain number of review cycles before the client must pay for changes. Second, invite the client to the workstation or studio where the creative work is done. For sound, tickle the keyboard until the client says, "That's it!" Make 'em sign off on it. For artwork and animations, let the client spend an afternoon riding shotgun over the artist's shoulder, participating in color and design choices. Get the client involved.

If your client contact isn't empowered to make decisions but simply carries your work up to the bosses for "management approval," you are facing the unpleasant Son of Feedback Alligator. Demand a client contact who has budget and design authority.

TIP   *When you negotiate with your client, limit the number of revisions allowed (each revision costs time and money) before you rename the revisions as change orders and bill extra.*

Estimating

In production and manufacturing industries, it is a relatively simple matter to estimate costs and effort. To make chocolate chip cookies, for example, you need ingredients, such as flour and sugar, and equipment, such as mixers, ovens, and packaging machines. Once the process is running smoothly, you can turn out hundreds of cookies, each tasting the same and each made of the same stuff. You then control your costs by fine-tuning known expenses, like negotiating deals on flour and sugar in quantity, installing more efficient ovens, and hiring personnel at a more competitive wage. In contrast, making multimedia is not a repetitive manufacturing process. Rather, it is by nature a continuous research and development effort characterized by creative trial and error—a "trying" experience, as described previously. Each new project is somewhat different from the last, and each may require application of many different tools and solutions. Philosophers will counsel you that experience is something you get only after you need it!

In the area of professional services, let's consider some typical costs in the advertising community. Production of a storyboard for a 30-second commercial spot costs about $50,000. Postproduction editing time in a professional video studio runs upwards of $500 per hour. An hour of professional acting talent costs $350 or more at union scale. The emerging multimedia industry, on the other hand, does not have a track record long enough to have produced "going rates" for its services. A self-guided tour distributed with a software product, for example, may cost $15,000 for one client and $150,000 for another, depending upon the tour's length and polish. A short original musical clip may cost $50 or $500, based on the talent used and the nature of the music. A graphical menu screen might take 2 or 20 hours to develop, depending on its complexity and the graphic art talent applied. Without available going rates for segments of work or entire projects, you must estimate the costs of your multimedia project by analyzing the tasks that it comprises and the people who build it.

The first time you accomplish a multimedia task, it will demand great effort as you learn the software and hardware tools and the techniques required. The second time you do a similar task, you will already know where the tools are and how they work, and the task will require less effort. On the third take, you should be quite proficient.

TIP *To recoup learning-curve costs when you first perform a task, you must factor extra time into your budget; later you can increase your billing rate to reflect your improved skill level.*

Be sure you include the hidden costs of administration and management. It takes time to speak with clients on the telephone, to write progress reports, and to mail invoices. In addition, there may be many people in your workforce who represent specialized skills, for example, a graphic artist, musician, instructional designer, and writer. In this case, you'll need to include a little extra buffer of time and expense in your estimate to pay for these artists' participation in project meetings and creative sessions. Also, remember to include a line item in your budget for **contingencies**, as a little extra padding to cover the inevitable unexpected costs. Adding 10 percent to 15 percent of the total cost is a typical rule-of-thumb contingency amount.

As a general rule, there are three elements that can vary in project estimates: time, money, and people. As illustrated below, if you decrease any one of these elements, you'll generally need to increase one or both of the others. For example, if you have very little time to do a project (an aggressive schedule), it will cost more money in overtime and premium sweat, and it may take more people. If you have a good number of people, the project should take less time. By increasing the money spent, you can actually decrease the number of people required by purchasing efficient (but costly) experts; this may also reduce the time required.

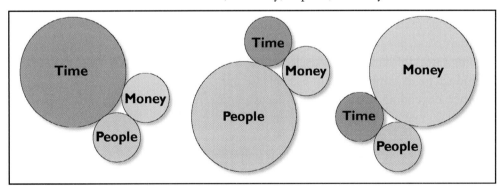

Do your best to estimate the amount of time it will take to perform each task in your plan. Multiply this estimate by your hourly billing rate. Sum the total costs for each task, and you now have an estimate of the project's total time and cost. Though this simple formula is easy, what is not so easy is diligently remaining within the budgeted time and money for each task. For this, you need good tracking and management oversight.

If you are working for an outside client, you will also need to determine a **payment schedule**. Payments are often divided into thirds: one-third up front upon the signing of a contract, one-third as work products are delivered and approved during the alpha and beta development phases, and one-third upon final approval of the completed production.

Billing Rates

Your billing rate should be set according to your cost of doing business plus a reasonable profit margin. Typical billing rates for multimedia production companies and web designers range from $60 to $150 an hour, depending upon the work being done and the person doing it. If consultants or specialists are employed on a project, the billing rate can go much higher. You can establish a rate that is the same for all tasks, or you can specify different rates according to the person assigned to a task. The Graphic Artists Guild (www.gag.org) provides its members a *Pricing & Ethical Guidelines* manual with pricing information based on real industry surveys. Pricing guides are also available at www.brennerbooks.com.

Everyone who contributes to a project should have two rates associated with their work: the employee's cost to the employer (including salary and benefits), and the employee's rate billed to the customer. The employee's cost, of course, is not included in your estimate, but you need to know this as part of your estimate—because your profit margin is the difference between the rate you charge the client and the cost to your company, less a proportion of overhead expenses (rental or leasing of space, utilities, phones, shared secretarial and administrative services, and so on). If your profit margin is negative, you should reconsider both your project plan and your long-term business plan.

Multimedia production companies and web site builders with high billing rates claim their skill-sets and experience allow them to accomplish more work in a given amount of time, expertly, thus saving money, time, and enhancing the finished quality and reliability of a project. This is particularly the case with larger-scale, complex projects. Smaller and leaner companies that offer lower billing rates may claim to be more streamlined, hungry, and willing to perform extra services. Lower rates do not necessarily mean lower-quality work, but rather imply that the company either supports fewer overheads or is satisfied with a reduced profit margin. The business of making multimedia is a "low entry barrier" enterprise because all you need to get started is some (relatively) inexpensive computer hardware and software, not a 70,000-square-foot factory or expensive tooling. You can make multimedia in a living room, basement, or garage. As more and more multimedia producers and web developers enter this marketplace, the competition is increasing and the free hand of supply and demand is driving prices (down).

Purchasers of multimedia services must, however, thoroughly examine the qualifications of a prospective contracting person or company to ensure that the work required can be accomplished on time and within budget. There is no more difficult business situation than a half-completed job and an exhausted budget.

First Person

We were asked by a large institution to complete a project that had fallen on the floor. It was really worse than that—the project had actually slipped through the cracks in that floor. The single known copy of work—representing about $30,000 in paid billings—had been copied to 19 high-density floppy disks and stored in a file cabinet. Here, they were discovered by the secretarial pool and formatted, to be used for WordPerfect documents. The secretaries remembered the whole thing because the stored backups contained protected files, so the disks were unusually difficult to erase! Luckily, bits and pieces of the project were unearthed on the hard disk of a computer that had been disconnected and stored in the basement. We were able to reconstruct much of the artwork, but not the interactive links.

As we studied the leavings of the embarrassed progenitors, we discovered a trail of missteps and errors. It became clear that the institution made a bad decision in hiring a well-qualified engineering firm at great expense (standard billing rates) to construct a difficult multimedia presentation. CAD/CAM drawings and finite element analysis were the forte of these engineers—not animated icons and colorful bitmaps with sound tracks. Furthermore, the engineering firm erred in selecting software that performed on the target hardware platform at about the speed of snails chasing a dog. Money had been spent, the product didn't work, and everyone involved was in gray limbo, slinking around, looking for a solution.

We determinedly pulled together the bits and pieces we could find, designed a snappy navigational structure we were proud of, and quickly fixed the big problem for a small fee (based upon our own standard billing rate). The institution, of course, was delighted and became a client of long standing.

Contractors and consultants can bring specialized skills such as graphic art, C and Java programming, database expertise, music composition, and video to your project. If you use these experts, be sure your billing rate is higher than theirs. Or, if you have a task the client has capped with a not-to-exceed cost, be sure your arrangement with the contractor is also capped. Contractors place no burden on your overhead and administration other than a few cups of coffee, and they should generate a generous profit margin for you during the course of your project. Be sure that contractors perform the majority of their work off-site, using their own equipment; otherwise, federal tax regulators may reclassify these freelancers as employees and require you to pay employee benefits. In 1998, in *Vizcaino v. Microsoft,* the U.S. Supreme Court required Microsoft Corporation to pay employee benefits to hundreds of workers that the court determined were regular employees rather than independent contractors. There are about 20 factors, according to the IRS, in determining whether a worker is an employee or an independent contractor for tax purposes, and companies may be liable for all employment benefits, including (as Microsoft discovered) stock option and stock sharing plans, if the work arrangement is not carefully constructed. However, when these outside workers are not classified as employees, then you run another risk—that they could retain ownership of the work they have created for you, limiting your right to use the material or restrict its use elsewhere. The best way to avoid this is to be sure that your contract with any outside workers clearly specifies the terms of ownership and rights of use of the product for which you are contracting. This "work for hire" issue is discussed in more detail in Chapter 17.

Example Cost Sheets

Figure 15-8 contains groups of expense categories for producing multimedia. If you use these in your own work, be sure to temper your guesses with experience; if you are new to multimedia production, get some qualified advice during this planning stage.

PROJECT DEVELOPMENT COSTS

Salaries
Client meetings
Acquisition of content
Communications
Travel
Research
Proposal & contract prep
Overhead

PRODUCTION COSTS

Management
     Salaries
     Communications
     Travel
     Consumables
Content Acquisition
     Salaries
     Research services
     Fees for licensing content
Content Creation
     All content categories
          Salaries
          Hardware/software
          Consumables
Graphics Production
     Fees for licensing images or animation clips
Audio Production
     Studio fees
     Talent fees
     Fees for licensing music rights
     Data storage

Video Production
     Studio fees
     Talent fees
     Fees for licensing stock footage
     Location fees
     Equipment rental
     Digital capture & editing
Authoring
     Salaries
     Hardware/software
     Consumables

TESTING COSTS

Salaries
Focus groups
     Facility rental
     Printing costs
     Food and incentives
     Coop fees (payment for participation)
Editing
Beta program

DISTRIBUTION COSTS

Salaries
Documentation
Packaging
Manufacturing
Marketing
Advertising
Shipping

Figure 15-8 There are many costs associated with producing multimedia.

First Person

I was downbound from Puget Sound to San Francisco, and the weather was up, with seas running heavy and winds gusting to 80 knots in our face. The Master and the First Mate were on the bridge, the old man sitting curled up in his upholstered high chair on the darkened starboard wing, the First pacing on the rubber mat behind the helmsman. The Third Mate was on watch, leaning over the radar screen and making fluorescent notes with a grease pencil. As I was a guest with no duties, I mostly hung out in the chart room while white water broke over the bows

and the shuddering propeller came out of the sea; wind screamed in the vents on the roof of the bridge. There wasn't much conversation that night, but the Master slowed us to five knots, concerned about the containers lashed to the forward deck.

When the young Third Mate came into the chart room, I asked, "Where are we?" and he took a sharp pencil, made a fine point on the chart, and drew a tiny circle around the point. Then he smiled, proud to have good radar bearings. The First Mate came in about a half hour later, and when I asked the same question, he circled an area about the size of a walnut.

As the Master left the bridge for his cabin, I asked him, too, where we were. He took his thumb and rubbed it on the chart in a rough oval about the diameter of his fist, saying, "Somewhere in here," and grinned at me as the ship heaved suddenly and we grabbed for the handholds.

The more experience these professionals had, the larger the circle they drew, and the less they relied upon pinpoint navigation. You should be prudent when costing a multimedia production; precision estimating can wreck your project.

RFPs and Bid Proposals

Often, potential clients don't have a clue about how to make multimedia, but they do have a vision or a mandate. You field a telephone call, a voice describes a need or a want, and you explain how you (and your company) can satisfy that need. Much of the talk may be instructional as you teach the client about the benefits and pitfalls of multimedia in all its forms. You seldom will glean enough information during this initial discussion to accurately estimate time or cost, so be prepared to answer these queries in vague terms while you present your available skill-sets and capabilities in the most favorable light. If the client is serious and your instruction well received, in short time you may be able to guide this client into good choices and reasonable decisions, working together to conceive and design an excellent product. Discussions will soon turn into design meetings. Somewhere along the way, you will sign a contract.

Occasionally you may encounter a more formal **Request for Proposal (RFP)**. These are typically detailed documents from large corporations that are "outsourcing" their multimedia development work. Figure 15-9 is an example of such a document that provides background information, scope of work, and information about the bidding process. Still, you should note that there is little "hard" information in this document; most bid proposals require contact with the client to fill in details prior to bidding.

Smythe Industries
Request for Proposal

Summary: The objective is to produce a family of materials which will develop a unique personality and visual image for the Smythe Campus in Vancouver, British Columbia, home of multiple Smythe subsidiaries and divisions.

As background, Smythe Industries was launched in 1995 following the acquisition of Wilson Aluminum Foundries, Ltd. (Canada) and Fenwick Rolling Mills, Inc. (U.S.A.) and is based in Vancouver. The site is also the headquarters for Global Aluminum Research, a research and development subsidiary. In addition, there are discussions concerning the establishment of a special alloy research institute at the Vancouver campus.

Each of the entities has unique personality traits, management structures, and business cultures which will need to be recognized and incorporated into the design process.

Audience & Message
Potential Employees - "employer of choice"
Business Development - "partner of choice"
   Metals Companies
   Academic Institutions
Government/Community officials - "good neighbor/citizen"
Smythe Employees - "credible/proud"
Scientific/Engineering Organizations - "credible research/scientifically advanced"

Tone and Manner:
Innovative, scientifically advanced, sophisticated, credible
Colorful: jewel colors/crisp/high contrast
Energetic, modern, innovative, cutting edge
Geometric lines & shapes (vs. free form)
A human element: photography, illustration, etc.
Personable, warm, intellectually inviting

Electronic Communications RFP

Multimedia Presentation Capabilities
Summary: The objective is to create a set of tools which will deliver key messages while positioning Smythe Vancouver as an innovative user of technology for communication. There will be two components to this project: a presentation format and a library of images. We would like to develop a library, including still imagery, audio, and QuickTime movies, that can be contained on a set of CDs. Note: all images should be created with the goal of repurposing across different mediums and projects.

The key purpose is to make core messages and the corporate personality come alive by utilizing sound and motion. These multimedia assets will be used for recruiting purposes at career centers, job fairs, and in-house for visiting recruits. They will also serve as presentation support material at scientific and engineering forums.

Smythe will work with the multimedia design firm to create and identify existing television clips, video, and other material which can serve to reinforce key messages.

External Web Site
Summary: As the most visible element of Smythe's Vancouver identity, the web site will set the stage for positioning the company in the research community as an employer of choice and a key player in esoteric alloy and metalurgical research. The web site will provide easy navigation for users to reach the areas of greatest interest to them, e.g. a particular business division, academic papers, employment opportunities, etc.

Figure 15-9 Some RFPs provide great detail.

The multimedia design firm will also be expected to create a library of images which can be utilized to update the site periodically. The design firm should also be prepared to provide input on ways to easily update and cost-effectively maintain the site. In addition, the web site should be created so that audio and live imagery can be incorporated and downloaded easily by users who have the appropriate equipment.

Internal Web Site
Summary: The internal web site is the primary medium for employee communication. It will be a useable, interesting tool for internal users and serve to reinforce corporate messages and the campus culture. Since the web site represents and includes different business entities on campus, this internal site will also introduce employees to activities in which other business units and groups are involved. The site will need to be designed with a template format so that it can be easily updated.

Production Elements for all Electronic Communications:
Icons: Develop an illustrative style for a family of icons shared across the CD-ROM, internal web site, and external web site.
Interface Design: Develop an interface design that provides design parameters and a personality for the internal web site and external web site. (Note: Internal and external web sites should carry a similar look and feel; however, it must be easy to distinguish between the two.)

Visual Image: Produce a library of visual images. This will require the additional production of video clips and sound clips.

Photography: A photo shoot schedule and plan will be developed with Smythe to most effectively maximize time and resources in shooting photos which can be used in print, in the Web sites, and in multimedia materials.

RFP Process

Quotations: Itemize quotes, e.g. project management, copy writing, editing, design, photography, illustrations, etc. Also provide 3 references.

Note: Smythe will write the HTML directives in-house and will also be posting to a server which is maintained in-house.

All quoutes should be submitted to:
Suzanne Petruski
Project Manager
Smythe Industries
65 Silver Foil
Vancouver, BC, CANADA

Figure 15-9 Some RFPs provide great detail. *(continued)*

A multimedia bid proposal will be passed through several levels of a company so that managers and directors can evaluate the project's quality and its price. The higher a bid proposal goes in the management hierarchy, the less chance it has of being read in detail. For this reason, you always want to provide an executive summary or overview as the first page of your proposal, briefly describing the project's goals, how the goals will be achieved, and the cost.

In the body of the proposal, include a section dealing with creative issues, and describe your method for conveying the client's message or meeting the graphic and interactive goals of the project. Also incorporate a discussion of technical issues, in which you clearly define the target hardware platform. If necessary, identify the members of your staff who will work on the project, and list their roles and qualifications.

The backbone of the proposal is the estimate and project plan that you have created up to this point. It describes the scope of the work. If the project is complicated, prepare a brief synopsis of both the plan and the timetable; include this in the overview. If there are many phases, you can present each phase as a separate section of the proposal.

Cost estimates for each phase or deliverable milestone, as well as payment schedules, should follow the description of the work. If this section is lengthy, it should also include a summary.

TIP *Make the proposal look good—it should be attractive and easy to read. You might also wish to provide an unbound copy so that it can be easily photocopied. Include separate, relevant literature about your company and qualifications. A list of clients and brief descriptions of projects you have successfully completed are also useful for demonstrating your capabilities.*

Finally, include a list of your terms. Contract terms may become a legally binding document, so have your terms reviewed by legal counsel. An example is shown in Figure 15-10. Terms should include the following:

- A description of your billing rates and invoicing policy (for example, what percentage is to be paid up front, how much at certain milestones, and how much upon delivery).

- Your policy on client sign-offs and change order costs.

- Your policy for billing out-of-pocket expenses for travel, telephone, courier services, and so forth.

- Your policy regarding third-party licensing fees for run-time modules and special drivers (the client pays).

- Specific statements of who owns what upon completion of the project. You may wish to retain the rights to show parts of the work for your own promotional purposes and to reuse in other projects segments of code and algorithms that you develop.

- An assurance to the client that you will not disclose proprietary information.

- Your right to display your credits appropriately within the work.

- Your unlimited right to work for other clients.

- A disclaimer for liability and damages arising out of the work.

Sample Terms:

We will undertake this assignment on a time-and-expenses basis at our current hourly rate of $___ per hour for __job title__, $___ per hour for __job title__, $___ per hour for __job title__, plus applicable taxes and reimbursement of authorized out-of-pocket expenses. Reasonable travel, express, freight, courier and telecommunication expenses incurred in relation to the project, will be considered pre-authorized. [Client] will be responsible for all licensing fees of third-party products incorporated (with [Client]'s knowledge and approval) into the final product. We will invoice [Client] either upon [Client]'s acceptance of the specified deliverables for each work phase specified above, or monthly, whichever is more often. [Client]'s authorization, either written or verbal, to commence a work phase will constitute acceptance of the previous phase's deliverables. Invoices are due and payable upon presentation. To commence work, we require a retainer in the amount of $_____, which will be deducted from the final invoice for the project.

Upon our receipt of final payment, [Client] shall own all rights, except those noted below, to the completed work delivered under this agreement, including graphics, written text, and program code. [Client] may at [Client]'s sole discretion copyright the work in [Client]'s name or assign rights to a third party. Ownership of material provided by third parties and incorporated in our work with [Client]'s knowledge and approval shall be as provided in any license or sale agreement governing said materials. We reserve the right to use in any of our future work for ourselves or any client all techniques, structures, designs and individual modules of program code we develop that are applicable to requirements outside those specified above. Further, our performance of this work for [Client] shall in no way limit us regarding assignments we may accept from any other clients now or at any time in the future.

We shall be allowed to show [Client]'s finished work, or any elements of it, to existing and prospective clients for demonstration purposes. If such demonstration showings would reveal information [Client] has identified to us as proprietary or confidential, we shall be allowed to create a special version for demonstrations which omits or disguises such information and/or [Client]'s identity as the client. We shall also be allowed to include a production credit display, e.g. "Produced by [Our Name]" or equivalent copy, on the closing screen or other mutually agreeable position in the finished work. Following [Client]'s acceptance of this proposal we shall also be allowed to identify [Client] as a client in our marketing communications materials.

In the event it is necessary in the course of this assignment for us to view or work with information of [Client]'s that [Client] identify to us as proprietary and confidential (possibly including customer lists, supplier data, financial figures and the like), we agree not to disclose it except to our principals, associates and contractors having confidentiality agreements with us.

We make no warranty regarding this work, or its fitness for a particular purpose, once [Client] accepts it following any testing procedures of [Client]'s choice. In any event, our liability for any damages arising out of this work, expressly including consequential damages, shall not exceed the total amount of fees paid for this work.

Figure 11-10 Sample contract terms adapted from language developed by the HyperMedia Group, Inc. (do not use without appropriate legal counsel)

It is a significant task to write a project proposal that creatively sells a multimedia concept, accurately estimates the scope of work, and provides realistic budget costs. The proposal often becomes a melting pot, in that you develop the elements of your idea during early conversations with a potential client and add the results of discussions on technique and approach with graphic artists and instructional designers. You blend what the client wants done with what you can actually do, given the client's budgetary constraints, and when the cauldron of compromise cools, your proposal is the result.

The Cover and Package

You have many options for designing the look and feel of your proposal. And though we are often warned to avoid judging a book by its cover, the reality is that it takes about two seconds for executives to assess the quality of the document they are holding. Sometimes, they decide before even touching it. Size up the people who will read your proposal and ferret out their expectancies; tailor your proposal to these expectancies.

If your client judges from the cover of your proposal that the document inside is amateurish rather than professional, you are already fighting an uphill battle. There are two strategies for avoiding this negative first impression:

1. Develop your own special style for a proposal cover and package, including custom fonts, cover art and graphics, illustrations and figures, unique section and paragraph styles, and a clean binding. Do your proposal first class.

2. Make the entire package plain and simple, yet businesslike. The plain part of the approach means not fussing with too many fonts and type styles. This austerity may be particularly successful for proposals to government agencies, where 10-point Courier Elite or 12-point Pica may be not just a de facto standard, but a required document format. For the simple part of the approach, a stapled sheaf of papers is adequate. Don't try to dress up your plain presentation with Pee-Chee folders or cheap plastic covers; keep it lean and mean.

Table of Contents

Busy executives want to anticipate a document and grasp its content in short order. A table of contents or index is a straightforward way to present the elements of your proposal in condensed overview. In some situations, you may also wish to include an **executive summary**—a prelude containing no more than a few paragraphs of pithy description and budget totals. The summary should be on the cover page or immediately following.

Needs Analysis and Description

In many proposals, it is useful to describe in some detail the reason the project is being put forward. This **needs analysis** and description is particularly common in proposals that must move through a company's executive hierarchy in search of approval and funding.

Target Audience

All multimedia proposals should include a section that describes the target audience and target platform. When the end user's multimedia capabilities have a broad and uncertain range, it is crucial to describe the hardware and software delivery platform you intend to provide. For instance, if your project requires a compact disc player but the end-user platform has none, you will need to adjust your multimedia strategy by revising the design or by requiring the end user to acquire a player. Some clients will clearly control the delivery platform, so you may not need to provide detail regarding system components.

Creative Strategy

A **creative strategy** section—a description of the look and feel of the project itself—can be important to your proposal, especially if the executives reviewing your proposal were not present for creative sessions or did not participate in preliminary discussions. If you have a library of completed projects that are similar to your proposed effort, it is helpful to include them with your proposal, pointing the client to techniques and presentation methods that may be relevant. If you have designed a prototype, describe it here, or create a separate heading and include graphics and diagrams.

Project Implementation

A proposal must describe the way a project will be organized and scheduled. Your estimate of costs and expenses will be based upon this description. The Project Implementation section of your proposal may contain a detailed calendar, PERT and Gantt project planning charts, and lists of specific tasks with associated completion dates, deliverables, and work hours. This information may be general or detailed, depending upon the demands of the client. The project implementation section is not just about how much work there is, but how the work will be managed and performed. You may not need to specify time estimates in work hours, but rather in the amount of calendar time required to complete each phase.

Budget

The budget relates directly to the scope of work you have laid out in the project implementation section. Distill your itemized costs from the project implementation description and consolidate the minute tasks of each project phase into categories of activity meaningful to the client.

Chapter 15 Review

■ Chapter Summary

For your review, here's a summary of the important concepts discussed in this chapter.

Determine the scope of a multimedia project

- Before beginning a project, develop a sense of its scope and content. Then develop an organized outline and a plan that considers the skills, time, budget, tools, and resources at hand.

- Tasks are the building blocks of project management. Allocate an estimated amount of time to each task, and place each one along a calendar-based timeline. The end of each phase is a natural place to set a milestone.

- Plan for the entire process, beginning with your first ideas and ending with completion and delivery of a finished product.

- Maintain balance between purpose and feasibility by dynamically adding and subtracting multimedia elements as you stretch and shape your idea.

Recognize common obstacles to the successful completion of multimedia projects

- Hardware is the most common limiting factor for realizing a multimedia idea. Consider the hardware capabilities of the end user's computer platform.

- Project management software can be useful for arranging ideas and tasks; additionally, the software may include built-in analysis to help stay within schedule and budget.

- Avoid the problem of cost run-ups by requiring clients to sign off at key stages in development and requiring change orders if a client changes specifications on you after signing off on them.

Identify tools and techniques to overcome project management problems

- Build a matrix chart of required skills to help describe the makeup of your team.

- Because there are few concrete standards for multimedia and developers are constantly "pushing the envelope," consider building a prototype to demonstrate that the idea is feasible and marketable.

- Lay out the phases, tasks, and work items along a timeline. Scheduling can be difficult to predict due to artistic trial and error and because the technology of computer hardware and software is in constant flux. Include client approval time. Negotiate the number of review cycles to avoid endless reviews.

Determine the cost, timeline, and tasks required to complete a project

- As a general rule, there are three elements that can vary in project estimates: time, money, and people.

- The budget is the total of estimated hours for each task times your hourly billing rate. There is no more difficult business situation than a half-completed job and an exhausted budget.

- Contractors and consultants can bring specialized skills to your project. Be sure they work off-site, using their own equipment, to avoid having them classified as employees.

Discuss the process and elements of a multimedia project proposal

- Many projects come about from a phone call or less formal contact.

- Occasionally you may receive a more formal detailed document called a Request for Proposal (RFP), generally from large corporations that are "outsourcing" their multimedia development work.

- A multimedia bid proposal should include an executive summary or overview, a section dealing with creative issues, a description of how the project's goals will be met, and a discussion of technical issues.

- The backbone of the proposal is the estimate and project plan, followed by cost estimates for each phase or deliverable milestone, as well as payment schedules. Finally, include a list of your terms reviewed by legal counsel. Make sure the proposal looks professional.

- All multimedia proposals should include a section that describes the target audience and target platform.

- Your estimate of costs and expenses will be based upon the detailed description of your project.

■ Key Terms

beta *(385)*
change order *(388)*
client sign-off *(388)*
contingencies *(390)*
creative strategy *(400)*
Critical Path Method (CPM) *(378)*
deliverables *(386)*

executive summary *(399)*
feasibility study *(383)*
Gantt charts *(379)*
going gold *(385)*
milestones *(386)*
needs analysis *(399)*
payment schedule *(390)*

prerequisites *(379)*
Program Evaluation Review Technique (PERT) charts *(378)*
proof-of-concept *(383)*
Request for Proposal (RFP) *(394)*
scope *(374)*

■ Key Term Quiz

1. A prototype is sometimes called a proof-of-concept or _____.
2. When a project reaches the delivery stage, it is said to be _____.
3. In constructing a project timeline it is important to identify _____, important tasks that must be completed before others begin.
4. A marker that delineates a significant point in a project's timeline—time to deliver work-in-progress, to invoice based upon real work done, to assess or test progress, and/or to solicit and receive constructive feedback—is called a _____.
5. A prototype in which most of the features are working, and you are distributing it to a wide arena of testers, is called a _____.
6. A project management strategy that calculates the total duration of a project based upon each identified task, earmarking tasks that are critical, is called the _____.
7. _____ provide graphic representations of task relationships, showing what tasks must be completed before others can commence.
8. _____ depict all the tasks along a timeline.
9. A(n) _____ is a detailed document, generally from large corporations who are outsourcing their multimedia development work, asking for companies to suggest projects in response to a defined need.
10. A proposal should begin with the _____, a prelude containing no more than a few paragraphs of pithy description and budget totals.

■ Multiple Choice Quiz

1. The building blocks of project management are:
   a. budgets
   b. tasks
   c. proposals
   d. milestones
   e. prerequisites

2. The best point to do focus group testing is with the:
   a. concept
   b. prototype
   c. beta
   d. gold master
   e. final version

3. Which of the following is not an area that would need to be tested in a prototype?
   a. technology (Will it work on your proposed delivery platform(s)?)
   b. cost (Can you do this project within budget constraints?)
   c. design (Will the colors and overall interface be attractive to potential users?)
   d. market (Can you sell it, or will it be properly used if it is an in-house project?)
   e. human interface (Is it intuitive and easy to use?)

4. In determining the feasibility of a project, the most common limiting technological factor is:
   a. the hardware on which the project is developed
   b. the network delivering the project
   c. the medium (CD-ROM, DVD, Internet) delivering the project
   d. the end user's hardware
   e. the telecommunications infrastructure

5. A proof-of-concept or pilot project should probably include all of these except:
   a. some artwork
   b. interface design
   c. packaging mock-ups
   d. interactive navigation
   e. performance checks

6. In the referenced report on producing educational software, the task requiring the greatest percentage of effort was authoring, at 28 percent. The second most demanding task was:
   a. analyze and outline content
   b. lay out course map
   c. select learner activities
   d. evaluate the course
   e. produce media

7. Which of the following is *not* a method typically used by project management software?
   a. Critical Path Method
   b. Feasibility Assessment Review Technique
   c. Program Evaluation Review Technique
   d. Gantt charts
   e. All of these are common methods.

8. Which of the following is *not* a reason why scheduling a multimedia project can be difficult?
   a. Much of the making of multimedia is artistic trial and error.
   b. Market forces may change the demand for the final product.
   c. The technology of computer hardware and software is in constant flux.
   d. Upgrades while your project is under way may add time to learn new hardware and software.
   e. Client feedback loops depend upon factors beyond your control.

9. When calculating the budget for a project, you should use two rates for each employee working on the project: the employee's rate billed to the customer, and:
   a. the employee's cost for tax purposes
   b. the employee's rate for discounted/special clients
   c. the employee's rate for rush/quick-turnaround projects
   d. the employee's cost to the employer
   e. the employee's rate for projects done on spec

10. Typical billing rates for multimedia production companies and web designers range from:
    a. $15 to $30 an hour
    b. $30 to $50 an hour
    c. $60 to $150 an hour
    d. $150 to $200 an hour

11. The business of making multimedia is a "low entry barrier" enterprise because:
    a. those with disabilities can create multimedia
    b. all you need to get started is some (relatively) inexpensive computer hardware and software
    c. there are free or low-cost web hosting solutions available
    d. lots of people can access web sites and CD-ROMs
    e. authoring systems make creating sophisticated projects fast and easy

12. Contractors and consultants should work off-site primarily because if they work on-site:
    a. they may compromise the company's confidential information

b. they increase the wear on company equipment

c. providing space for them adds to overhead.

d. they are generally less productive doing so

e. they may be legally considered employees

13. The first part of a proposal should be the:

a. executive summary

b. budget

c. timeline

d. project plan

e. terms and conditions

14. When the end user's multimedia capabilities have a broad and uncertain range, it is very important to describe:

a. the number of subcontractors working on the project

b. the authoring system that will be used on the project

c. the hardware and software platform intended for delivery.

d. the creative strategy that will be used to create the media

e. the colors and fonts to be used in the interface

15. If the executives reviewing your proposal were not present for creative sessions or did not participate in preliminary discussions, it may be important to include a description of the look and feel of the project itself, called a(n):

a. creative strategy

b. executive summary

c. terms and conditions

d. needs analysis

e. table of contents

■ Essay Quiz

1. You have been given the task of finding a new project for a fictional multimedia development company to produce on spec. The project is an instructional game designed to teach learners how to program in Java Script. Justify the project, discussing:

   a. the market for the product,

   b. the objectives of the project,

   c. technical limitations, if any, and

   d. a brief timeline.

2. List and briefly discuss the stages of a multimedia project. Be sure to define the milestones that mark the completion of the phase.

3. List at least ten primary tasks that go into producing a multimedia project. Place these steps in logical order. Comment on these steps with regard to whether they are critical to the timeline (which steps are dependent on the completion of an earlier step).

4. Discuss the factors that affect what a multimedia company might be able to charge for its work. Consider factors that affect overhead, factors related to experience and abilities, and factors related to the project itself.

5. Describe the various technical, management, and creative obstacles to accurately predict the time and resources needed to complete a multimedia project. How might the technical and creative problems be interrelated?

Lab Projects

Project 15.1

Select a project—perhaps an educational CD-ROM, a promotional DVD, a marketing web site, or a corporate intranet. Be creative, and specify the kind of organization you will be creating the project for. List the tasks required in developing the project. Specify how long each task will take.

Project 15.2

Based on the project specified in 15.1, create a team of at least three people for the project. Specify their titles, internal and external rates, and abilities. Write a one-paragraph bio explaining each team member's relevant experience and capabilities.

Project 15.3

Based on the project developed so far, assign the tasks to the team. Create a chart that clearly identifies the major tasks, which team member will be responsible for them, and when they will be done.

Project 15.4

Create a budget based on the task durations and rates for the project you have developed. Calculate both the internal cost (costs × hours) and the billing (rates × hours). Is the project profitable? Don't forget to include a reasonable amount for contingencies and overhead.

Project 15.5

Go online and locate an RFP for either a web site or multimedia CD-ROM. Suitable RFPs should be fairly large in scope, at least $25,000. Examine the RFP. How would you respond to it? Write an executive summary for an imaginary proposal you might write in response to the RFP.

Designing and Producing

DESIGNING and building multimedia projects go hand in hand. Indeed, design input to a project is never over until the product is actually frozen and shipped. The best products are often the result of continuing feedback and modifications implemented throughout the production process; projects that freeze a design too early become brittle in the production workplace, losing the chances for incremental improvement. But there is a danger: too much feedback and too many changes can kill a project, draining it of time and money. Always balance proposed changes against their cost to avoid the "creeping features" syndrome.

Just as the architect of a high-rise office tower must understand how to utilize the materials with which he or she works (lest the construction collapse on trusting clients), designers of multimedia projects must also understand the strengths and limitations of the elements that will go into their project. It makes no sense, for example, to design the audio elements of a multimedia project in memory-consuming 16-bit, 44.1 kHz stereo sound when the delivery medium will not have sufficient room for it; or to produce lengthy, full-screen, QuickTime movies to play at 30 frames per second over the Internet when targeted end users connect by modems; or to design lovely 1024×768 pixel graphics for elementary school laptops when that environment supports only 800×600 pixel screens. Architects don't design inner city parking garages with 14-foot ceilings and wide turning radii for 18-wheel big rigs, and they don't build them using wood or mud laid on a swampy foundation.

Designers must work closely with producers to ensure that their ideas can be properly realized, and producers need to confirm the results of their work with the designers. "These colors seem to work better—what do you think?" "It plays faster now, but I had to change the animation sequence..." "Doing the index with highlighted lines slows it down—can we eliminate this feature?" Feedback loops and good communication between the design and production effort are critical to the success of a project.

The idea processing (described in Chapter 15) of your multimedia project will have resulted in a detailed and balanced plan of action, a production schedule, and a timetable. Now it's time for implementation!

Designing

The design part of your project is where your knowledge and skill with computers, your talent in graphic arts, video, and music, and your ability to conceptualize logical pathways through information are all focused to create the real thing. Design is thinking, choosing, making, and doing. It is shaping, smoothing, reworking, polishing, testing, and editing. When you design your project, your ideas and concepts are moved one step closer to reality. Competence in the design phase is what separates amateurs from professionals in the making of multimedia.

TIP   *Never begin a multimedia project without first outlining its structure and content.*

Depending on the scope of your project and the size and style of your team, you can take two approaches to creating an original interactive multimedia design. You can spend great effort on the **storyboards**, or graphic outlines, describing the project in exact detail—using words and sketches for each and every screen image, sound, and navigational choice, right down to specific colors and shades, text content, attributes and fonts, button shapes, styles, responses, and voice inflections. This approach is particularly well suited for teams that can build prototypes quickly and then rapidly convert them into finished goods. Or you can use less-detailed storyboards as a rough schematic guide, allowing you to exert less design sweat up front and expend more effort actually rendering the product at a workstation.

The method you choose depends on whether the same people will do the whole thing (both designing and the implementing) or whether design and implementation are tasked to separate teams by other members, who of course need a more detailed specification (that is, detailed storyboard and sketches). Both approaches require the same thorough knowledge of the tools and capabilities of multimedia, and both demand a storyboard or a project outline. The first approach is often favored by clients who wish to tightly control the production process and labor costs. The second approach gets you more quickly into the nitty-gritty, hands-on tasks, but you may ultimately have to give back that time because more iterations and editing will be required to smooth the work in progress. In either case, the more planning on paper, the better and easier it will be to construct the project.

Designing the Structure

A multimedia project is no more than an arrangement of text, graphic, sound, and video elements (or *objects*). The way you compose these elements into interactive experiences is shaped by your purpose and messages.

How you organize your material for a project will have just as great an impact on the viewer as the content itself. With the explosive growth of the World Wide Web and proliferation of millions and millions of multimedia-capable HTML documents that can be linked to millions of other similar documents in the cyberspace of the Web, your designs and inventions may actually contribute to the new media revolution: other creators may discover your work and build upon your ideas and methods.

Navigation

Mapping the structure of your project is a task that should be started early in the planning phase, because navigation maps outline the connections or links among various areas of your content and help you organize your content and messages. A **navigation map** (or **site map**) provides you with a table of contents as well as a chart of the logical flow of the interactive interface. While at web sites a site map is typically a simple hierarchical table of contents with each heading linked to a page, as a more detailed design document your map may prove very useful to your project, listing your multimedia objects and describing what happens when the user interacts.

Just as eight story plots might account for 99 percent of all literature ever written (boy meets girl, protagonist versus antagonist, etc.), a few basic structures for multimedia projects will cover most cases: **linear**, **hierarchical**, **nonlinear**, and **composite**. Figure 16-1 illustrates the four fundamental organizing structures used in multimedia projects, often in combination:

- *Linear:* Users navigate sequentially, from one frame or bite of information to another.

- *Hierarchical:* Also called "linear with branching," since users navigate along the branches of a tree structure that is shaped by the natural logic of the content.

- *Nonlinear:* Users navigate freely through the content of the project, unbound by predetermined routes.

- *Composite:* Users may navigate freely (nonlinearly), but are occasionally constrained to linear presentations of movies or critical information and/or to data that is most logically organized in a hierarchy.

The method you provide to your viewers for navigating from one place to another in your project is part of the user interface. The success of the user interface depends not only upon its general design and graphic art implementations but also upon myriad engineering details—such as the position of interactive buttons or hot spots relative to the user's current activity, whether these buttons "light up," and whether you use standard Macintosh or Windows pull-down menus. A good user interface is critical to the overall success of your project.

Structural Depth Professor Judith Junger from the Open University of the Netherlands in Amsterdam suggests that when you design your multimedia product you should work with two types of structure: depth structure and surface structure. **Depth structure** represents the complete navigation map and describes all the links between all the components of your project (see Figure 16-1). **Surface structure**, on the other hand, represents the structures actually realized by a user while navigating the depth structure. Thus the following depth structure

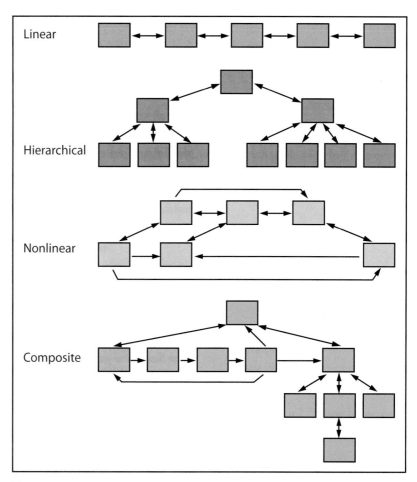

Figure 16-1 The four primary navigational structures used in multimedia

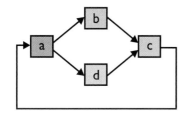

might be realized as the following surface structure:

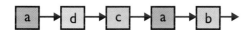

Some surface structures generated by users might look like this:

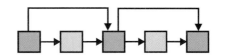

Sequential structure with optional paths

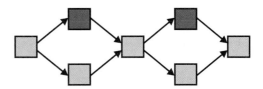

Sequential structure with alternative paths

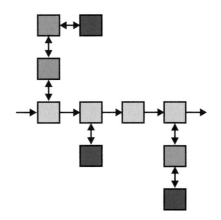

Sequential structure with sidesteps

The following depth structure for a quiz thus consists of three possible surface structures:

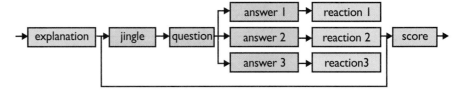

When you design your navigation map, it helps to think about surface structure—to view the product from a user's perspective. Surface structures are of particular interest to marketing firms in tracking users' routes through a web site to determine the effectiveness of the site's design and to profile a user's preferences. When a user's preferences are known, a custom web site experience can be dynamically tailored and delivered to that user. Acquisition and management of such profiling data is a hot topic, with privacy advocates claiming the personal information revealed in these surface structures is akin to a person's medical and health records.

First Person

Dear Tay,

With regard to the creation of interactive fiction, what kinds of software engineering strategies would you recommend for creating stories that maintain a strong sense of cumulative action (otherwise known as plot) while still offering the audience a high frequency of interaction? In other words, how do you constrain the combinatoric explosion of the narrative pathways, while still maintaining the Aristotelian sense of a unity of plot?

—Patrick Dillon, Atlanta, GA

One and one-half T-shirts to Patrick Dillon! Would have been two for your invocation of a famous Greek philosopher, but then I couldn't find "combinatoric" in Webster's. Aristotle himself would have been pleased by the harmonious balance of your reward: you have asked a really good question.

As multimedia and the power of computers begin to change our approach to literature and storytelling, new engineering strategies do need to be implemented.

When fiction becomes nonlinear, and users can choose among alternative plot lines, the permutations can become staggering. To an author, this means each new plot pathway chosen by user interaction requires its own development, and one story may actually become several hundred or more. To constrain this fearsome explosion of narrative pathways, yet retain a high frequency of interaction, try designing your fiction around a single core plot that provides the cumulative action, and use arrays of returning branches for detail and illustration. In this way you can entirely avoid the permutations of alternative universes and still offer the adventure of interactive exploration.

Dear Tay,

I just read your answer to Patrick Dillon's question about interactive fiction in your column. My response is difficult to contain: "Aaarrrrrgggghhhh!!!! You Ignorant Slut!" OK, perhaps I am overreacting, but you are refusing to let go of linearity. Why ever do you want to "constrain the combinatoric explosion of narrative pathways"? Good Lord, that's what makes the gametree bushy. This is exactly the kind of work that's well suited for a computer to perform—grinding out three billion story variations!

—Chris Crawford, San Jose, CA

Chris, I've been called a lot of things over the years (like Fay and Ray), and it's with a smile that I add your gift to my collection. Playing Jane Curtin to your Dan Aykroyd, I'll be happy to counter your counterpoint.

Your challenge represents a serious subject for multimedia designers today. I agree that interactive stories with too few branches are disappointingly flat and shallow. When a plot is broadly nonlinear, however, the permutations of events and possible outcomes become staggering, and the story as a whole becomes difficult to visualize and manage. Producing such work is also an intellectual challenge and costly in time and effort.

A truly open-ended "hypermedia" navigation system for consumer consumption risks death by shock caused by open arterial branches and loss of story pressure, where plot lines become too diffuse and users founder in trivia. Most users may, indeed, *prefer* a structured, organized, and well-defined story environment.

The argument for simplicity is voiced by Steven Levy, the author of *Hackers* and *Artificial Life*, who says, "There's really something to be said for documents with a beginning, middle, and end."

The shape of this new literature made possible by multimedia computers and wide-bandwidth cable and telephone delivery systems is being born in the working designs of developers. The final test for successful multimedia design is the marketplace, where consumers will decide.

Your interesting "algorithms for interpersonal behavior, personality models, artificial personality, languages of expression, and facial displays" represent, perhaps, a successful marriage of this computer power with literature containing malleable plots and seemingly endless variations. Indeed, your forthcoming epic game, *Le Morte D'Arthur,* will surely break new ground and quite possibly prove your point. Can't wait to get a copy!

From correspondence in "Ask the Captain," a monthly column by Tay Vaughan in *NewMedia* magazine.

> Because all forms of infor-
> mation—including text,
> numbers, photos, video,
> and sound—can exist in a
> common digital format, they
> can be used simultaneously
> as people browse through
> an information stream, just
> as people use their various
> senses simultaneously to
> perceive the real world.
>
> ....
>
> Bill Gates, Chairman,
> Microsoft Corporation

Many navigation maps are essentially nonlinear. In these navigational systems, viewers are always free to jump to an index, a glossary, various menus, Help or About... sections, or even to a rendering of the map itself. It is often important to give viewers the sense that free choice is available; this empowers them within the context of the subject matter. Nonetheless, you should still provide consistent clues regarding importance, emphasis, and direction by varying typeface size and look, colorizing, indenting, or using special icons.

The architectural drawings for your multimedia project are the storyboards and navigation maps. The storyboards are married to the navigation maps during the design process, and help to visualize the information architecture.

A simple navigation map is illustrated in Figure 16-2, where the subject matter of a small project to teach the basics of animation was organized schematically. The items in boxes are not only descriptions of content but also active buttons that can take users directly to that content. At any place in the project, users can call up this screen and then navigate directly to their chosen subject.

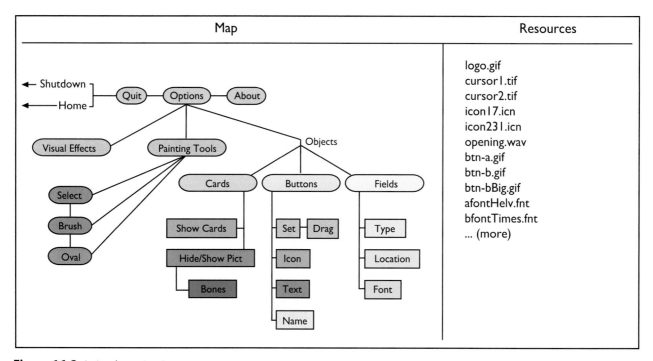

Figure 16-2 A simple navigation map

A storyboard for this same project, originally built for a small black-and-white low-resolution display, is organized sequentially, screen by screen, and each screen is sketched out with design notes and specifications before rendering. On the left, in Figure 16-3, are parts of the storyboard for this project; on the right are corresponding finished screens.

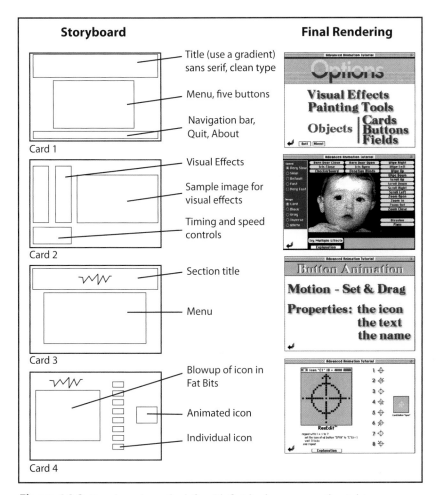

Figure 16-3 Storyboards on the left, with finished screens on the right

Multimedia provides great power for jumping about within your project's content. And though it is important to give users a sense of free choice, too much freedom can be disconcerting, and viewers may get lost. Try to keep your messages and content organized along a steady stream of the major subjects, letting users branch outward to explore details. Always provide a secure anchor, with buttons that lead to expected places, and build a familiar landscape to which users may return at any time.

Your content may not always be an assembly of discrete subjects as illustrated in Figure 16-2. If your material deals with a chronology of events occurring over time, for example, you may wish to design the structure as a linear sequence of events and then send users along that sequence, allowing them to jump directly to specific dates or time frames if desired

Really good software products should be simple, hot, and deep. People need to get into your software in about 20 seconds and get immediate positive feedback and reward; then they are smiling and having a good time and they want to go further. "Hot" means that you've got to be fully cooking the machine, with all its graphics and sound capabilities, conveying something dynamic and exciting that competes with what people are used to seeing in a movie or on TV. In terms of "deep," it's kind of like the ocean where there are people of all ages: some kids will just wade out in a foot of surf, other guys with scuba gear go way out and way deep. Make it possible for me to go as deep as I want, but don't force it on me. Just let the depth of your product unfold to me in a very natural way.

....

Trip Hawkins, Chairman & CEO, 3DO Company

(see Figure 16-4). A timeline will graphically show the positioning of your multimedia elements and can be helpful during the design phase: where there are overlapping events, you may wish to create cross-sectional paths or views for a "slice in time."

Even within a linear, time-based structure, you may still wish to sort events into categories regardless of when they occur. There is no reason you can't do this and offer more than one method of navigating through your content. Figure 16-5, for instance, illustrates a navigation map that accesses the same events from the timeline form of Figure 16-4, but arranged here instead into meaningful groups of events.

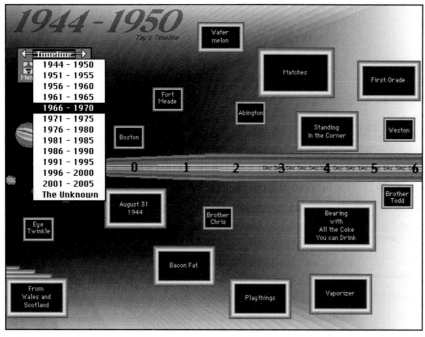

Figure 16-4   A chronological navigation map with active buttons

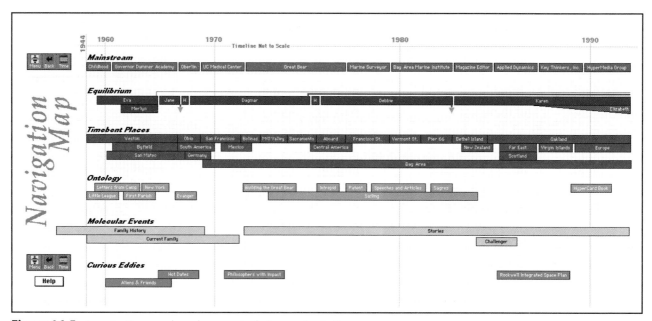

Figure 16-5   A navigation map based on events that are active buttons

Hot Spots, Hyperlinks, and Buttons

Most multimedia authoring systems allow you to make any part of the screen, or any object, into a **hot spot**. When users click a hot spot at that location, something happens, which makes multimedia not just interactive, but also exciting. Hot spots can be given more specific names based upon either their function or form. For example, if the hot spot connects the user to another part of the document or program or to a different program or web site, it is referred to as a **hyperlink**. If the hot spot is a graphic image designed to look like a push button or toggle switch, it is called a **button**, more formally defined as a meaningful graphic image that you click to make something happen. The term "tab" is used incorrectly by some as a synonym for button. Its use derives from the many dialog boxes in applications set up to look like the tabs of manila folders. The clickable tab labels at the top of the illustration below are hot spots, but are not buttons. The "real" buttons are along the bottom:

There are three general categories of hot spots based upon the form in which they appear: whether as text (which subdivides into hypertext and text buttons), graphic, or icon. Most authoring systems provide a tool for creating text buttons of various styles (radio buttons, check boxes, or labeled push buttons, for example), as well as graphic and icon buttons.

TIP   *Designing a good navigation system and creating original buttons appropriate for your project are not trivial artistic tasks. Be sure you budget sufficient time in your design process for many trials, so you'll be able to get your buttons looking and acting just right.*

CROSS PLATFORM *Windows does not manage icon resources in the same manner as Macintosh. Each Windows multimedia authoring tool allows for the construction and use of graphic buttons in its own way. If you are bringing Macintosh icons into a Windows tool, export them from the Macintosh as bitmaps, import them into your Windows authoring tool, and create appropriate mouse-clicking activities for highlighting and other effects.*

Text buttons and their fonts and styles are described in Chapter 4. Graphic buttons can contain graphic images or even parts of images—for example, a map of the world with each country color coded, and a mouse click on a country yields further information. **Icons** are graphic objects designed specifically to be meaningful buttons and are usually small (although size is, in theory, not a determining factor). Icons are fundamental graphic objects symbolic of an activity or concept:

Your navigation design must provide buttons that make sense, so their actions will be intuitively understood by means of their icon or graphic representation, or via text cues. Do not force your viewers to learn many new or special icons; keep the learning curve to a minimum. It's also important to include buttons that perform basic housekeeping tasks, such as quitting the project at any given point, or canceling an activity.

Once a style has been selected, you need to determine how your user will know that the button is active or is being selected. Highlighting a button or object, or changing its state, when the mouse cursor rolls over it or the button is clicked, is the most common method of distinguishing it as the object of interest. Highlighting is usually accomplished by reversing the object's colors: changing black to white or vice versa, or otherwise altering its colors. Drop shadows placed slightly below and to the right of a button can give it a 3-D look and, depending upon how you arrange the highlighting, can make a button appear out (not pressed) or in (pressed) as illustrated here:

Out   In

First Person

One day I launched an application named Disk Formatter on my Macintosh, just to see what it was about. Suddenly I was in a pretty scary user-interface predicament (Figure 16-6 is what I saw). I could tell from its name that the software erased and formatted hard disks and other media: my mounted hard disks were listed on the screen by SCSI number, and I was being prompted to select one of them. I looked over at the CPU and was pleased that the disk drive access light wasn't ticking away at sector-length intervals. I didn't know what the software was doing because I hadn't read the manual; I did know, however, what I wanted to do—back out and quit. Too much at stake to be fooling around here!

Well, there was no Cancel button and no Quit button, and OK was too risky with the radio button for my internal hard disk turned on. Did OK mean "OK, start formatting," or did it mean "OK, thanks for selecting that drive, now on to further options?" As a dialog box, the Disk Formatter application limited my choices to its own, and I didn't like any of them. I figured I would do an emergency power-down by pulling the plug on the CPU, and then I could restart. But before employing that ultimate solution for sticky-cursors, I found a key combination that happily quit the application. The screen went away and the application went into the trash.

I was pretty unhappy, though, about the application's design because there was no clear route to back out of the formatting activity, and OK implies going forward in most user interactions.

Hot Spots in Web Pages

HTML documents do not directly support interactive buttons that follow the rules of good interface design—by highlighting or otherwise confirming a mouse-down action. In most web browsers, you know you have clicked on a button only after the cursor changes while the browser seeks another document and loads it. But you *can* make plain and animated buttons for your HTML documents on the Web using plug-ins such as Flash and Shockwave, or JavaScripts. A simple JavaScript in an HTML document can be used to replace one image with another on mouseOver or hover. Other ways to make interesting buttons and interactive graphical interfaces on the World Wide Web are described more fully in Chapter 14.

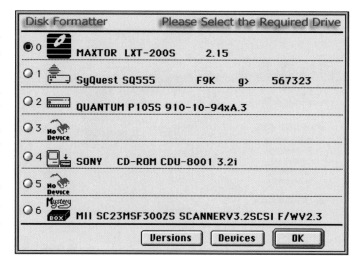

Figure 16-6 A user interface with no obvious Cancel or Quit provision

The simplest hot spots on the Web are the text anchors that link a document to other documents. This is because a browser usually indicates that some specific text is a hot link by coloring or underlining the text so it stands out from the body. Default colors for anchor text are a user-defined preference, though you can override the default in the <BODY> tag.

Other common buttons found on the Web consist of small JPEG or GIF graphic images that are themselves anchor links. Browsers indicate that an image is hot by drawing a border around it. (You can remove this border by placing "BORDER="0" into the <IMG> tag.) Larger images may be sectioned into hot areas with associated links; these are called **image maps**.

Figure 16-7 shows a graphic image of a village that has been programmed in HTML to have 32 hot spots with links (the document to open when clicked) and a JavaScript routine called "set" that will place an image into the frame at the left when the mouse rolls over that area. The code looks like this:

```
<AREA shape="rect" coords="180,85,230,135" href="../vendors/v25/index.html"
onmouseover="set('../vendors/v25/images/logomenu.gif');">
```

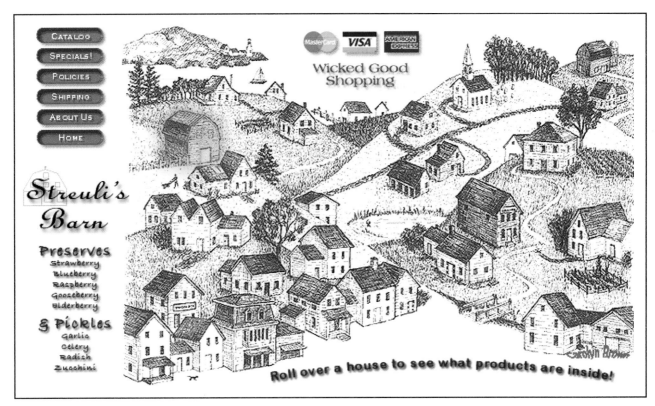

Figure 16-7 Using a large image map and JavaScript embedded in a normal HTML web page, when the mouse rolls over a house or barn, the content of that building is displayed as a separate graphic at the left. Users can actively explore this seaside village to discover what's hidden behind its doors.

Icons

On the Macintosh, icons have a special meaning, in that they constitute a suite of image resources that can be linked to the Finder and then used to identify an application or project. They are small (16×16 pixels) or large (32×32 pixels), may be colored, and usually have a text label attached:

> **TIP** *For a quick and simple way to change a Macintosh icon, highlight any file's icon by clicking on it once, open the Get Info... dialog (COMMAND-I), click once on the icon shown at the top left of the Get Info panel to highlight it, and paste any 32x32-pixel bitmap from the clipboard. The old icon is replaced with the new. You can also copy an icon to the clipboard from the Get Info panel (COMMAND-C). With this trick, you can customize the look of your desktop.*

In Windows XP, right-click on the existing icon you want to change and from the pop-up menu select Properties. If the Change Icon... button is active, left-click it. (If it is not active, the icon cannot be changed.) The Change Icon requester will display available icons for the program represented by the selected icon. To view others not included with the program, use the Browse... button to point to other icons. The new Browse requester (also named Change Icon) has Files of Type set to Icon files, so it is possible that any of the files listed contain at least one icon file (though many of them will not). You can use the Browse requester to point to the C:\WINDOWS\system32\shell32.dll file, which has the standard set of Windows XP icons (see Figure 16-8). If you are building a multimedia project in Windows, you can create custom icons and store them as .ico files. Visual Basic, for example, ships with a library of more than 450 icons ready to use in the following categories: arrows and pointers, communication, computers, drag and drop, elements, flags, industry and transportation, mail, miscellaneous, office, traffic signs, and writing. These icons are quite useful simply as clip art, but they are either small (32×32 pixels) or smaller (16×16 pixels). These smaller icons are primarily used as mouse pointers or cursors.

Icons (and .ico files that contain icons) are created using an icon editor such as IconDraw (freeware) or another editor utility. Icons in Windows, however, relate to the Windows operating system and to Program Manager (as do Finder icons on the Macintosh), and these icons are typically not

Designers will build screens where there are tiny little things going on all over it at different places, and everything has momentous significance. And then the user is supposed to be able to find these momentous things. So people just glaze over. If you want them to hit a button, put a big button right in the middle of the screen.
....
Trip Hawkins, Chairman & CEO, 3DO Company

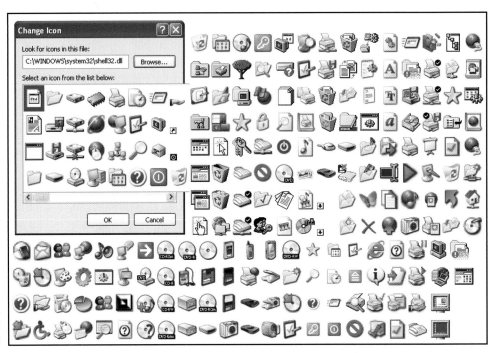

Figure 16-8 In Windows, many icons are installed with the system

available for easy use within an authoring tool. If you want to use a system icon, it is best to capture it off the screen and place the icon into your project as a bitmap. Use caution, however, because the design of some buttons (particularly those using corporate logos) may be protected by copyright or trademark.

Designing the User Interface

The **user interface** of your multimedia product is a blend of its graphic elements and its navigation system. If your messages and content are disorganized and difficult to find, or if users become disoriented or bored, your project may fail. Poor graphics can cause boredom. Poor navigational aids can make viewers feel lost and unconnected to the content; or, worse, viewers may sail right off the edge and just give up and quit the program.

Novice/Expert Modes

Be aware that there are two types of end users: those who are computer literate and those who are not. Creating a user interface that will satisfy both types has been a design dilemma since the invention of computers. The simplest solution for handling varied levels of user expertise is to provide a **modal interface**, where the viewer can simply click a Novice/Expert button and change the approach of the whole interface—to be either more or less detailed or complex. Modal interfaces are common on bulletin boards, for example, allowing novices to read menus and select desired activities, while experts can altogether eliminate the time-consuming download and display of menus and simply type an activity code directly into an executable command line. Both novices and experts alike may quickly learn to click the mouse and skip the annoying ragtime piece you chose for background music.

Unfortunately, in multimedia projects, modal interfaces are not a good answer. It's best to avoid designing modal interfaces because they tend to confuse the user. Typically, only a minority of users are expert, and so the majority are caught in between and frustrated. The solution is to build your multimedia project to contain plenty of navigational power, providing access to content and tasks for users at all levels, as well as a help system to provide some hand-holding and reassurance. Present all this power in easy-to-understand structures and concepts, and use clear textual cues. Above all, keep the interface simple! Even experts will balk at a complex screen full of tiny buttons and arcane switches, and will appreciate having neat and clean doorways into your project's content.

GUIs

The Macintosh and Windows graphical user interfaces (GUI, pronounced "gooey") are successful partly because their basic point-and-click style is simple, consistent, and quickly mastered. Both these GUIs offer built-in help systems, and both provide standard patterns of activity that produce standard expected results. The following actions, for example, are consistently performed by similar keystrokes when running most programs on the Macintosh or in Windows:

Action	Macintosh Keystroke	Windows Keystroke
New file	⌘-N	ALT-F-N or CTRL-N
Open file	⌘-O	ALT-F-O or CTRL-O
Save file	⌘-S	ALT-F-S or CTRL-S
Quit	⌘-Q	ALT-F-X or CTRL-Q
Undo	⌘-Z	ALT-E-U or CTRL-Z
Cut	⌘-X	ALT-E-T or CTRL-X
Copy	⌘-C	ALT-E-C or CTRL-C
Paste	⌘-V	ALT-E-R or CTRL-V

TIP *Since Cut, Copy, and Paste are used so often, this mnemonic device may help you to remember their keyboard shortcuts: X looks like scissors and is to Cut. C is straightforward; C is for Copy. Think of V as an upside-down insertion caret (used to insert text when copy editing) and you will remember that it is for Paste.*

Two readers didn't notice the screen had changed in different circumstances. This happened when the button they clicked on took them to a visually similar screen, and there was no visual effect as the screens changed. One reader was looking at the details of a hostel and clicked on the left-hand Next arrow. He arrived at a screen with details about another hostel, but did not notice he was looking at a different screen. He tried the right-hand Next arrow as well, and the screen changed back to the one he had been viewing initially, but again he did not notice the change and concluded the Next buttons did nothing. A visual effect or animation here would have provided a cue to make the screen changes more noticeable.

Lynda Hardman of the Scottish HCI Centre, after focus group testing the "Glasgow Online" hypertext system

For your multimedia interface to be successful, you, too, must be consistent in designing both the look and the behavior of your human interface. Multimedia authoring systems provide you with the tools to design and implement your own graphical user interface from scratch. Be prudent with all that flexibility, however. Unless your content and messages are bizarre or require special treatment, it's best to stick with accepted conventions for button design and grouping, visual and audio feedback, and navigation structure.

Vaughan's General Rule for Interface Design

The best user interface demands the least learning effort.

Stick with real-world metaphors that will be understood by the widest selection of potential users. For example, consider using the well-known trash can for deleting files, a hand cursor for dragging objects, and a clock or an hourglass for pauses. If your material is time-oriented, develop metaphors for past, present, and future. If it is topic-oriented, choose metaphors related to the topics themselves. If it is polar (the pros and cons of an issue, for example), choose relevant contrasting images.

TIP *Most multimedia authoring systems include tutorials and instructions for creating and using buttons and navigation aids. Typically, they also supply templates or examples of attractive backgrounds and distinctive buttons that serve as an excellent starting place. In a large project, you might want to use a different metaphor as the backbone of each major section, to provide a helpful cue for users to orient themselves within your content. For the Travel section, for example, you could use icons that are sailing ships with various riggings; for the Finance section, buttons that are coins of different denominations; and for the buttons of the International Business section, you could use colorful flags from various countries.*

Users like to be in control, so avoid hidden commands and unusual keystroke/mouse click combinations. Design your interface with the goal that no instruction manual or special training will be required to move through your project. Users do not like to have to remember keywords or special codes, so always make the full range of options easily available as interactive buttons or menu items. And finally, users do make mistakes, so allow them a chance to escape from inadvertent or dangerous predicaments ("Do you really want to delete? Delete/Escape"). Keep your interface simple and friendly.

Throw out your tried and true training or software development methodologies, and pretend that you're Spielberg or Lucas: think of what the viewer sees and hears and how the viewer interacts with the system you deliver. Create an "experience" for the viewer.

....

David A. Ludwig, Interactive Learning Designs

Computer graphics is more left- and right-brained— and not so spontaneous as doing it by hand. The ramp time is tedious; I am used to instant gratification with my fine artwork.

....

Cornelia Atchley, a fine artist creating multimedia art with computers, Washington, D.C.

Graphical Approaches

Designing excellent computer screens requires a special set of fine art skills, and not every programmer or graduate in fine arts may be suited to creating computer graphics. Like programmers who must keep up with current operating systems and languages, computer graphic artists must also stay informed about the rapidly changing canvas of new features, techniques, applications, and creative tools.

The artist must make broad design choices: cartoon stick figures for a children's game, rendered illustrations for a medical reference, scanned bitmaps for a travel tour of Europe. The graphic artwork must be appropriate not only for the subject matter, but for the user as well. Once the approach is decided, the artist has to put real pixels onto a computer screen and do the work. A multimedia graphic artist must always play the role of the end user during the design and rendering process, choosing colors that look good, specifying text fonts that "speak," and designing buttons that are clearly marked for what they do.

Things That Work Here are some graphical approaches that get good results:

- Neatly executed contrasts: big/small, heavy/light, bright/dark, thin/thick, cheap/dear (see Figure 16-9)

- Simple and clean screens with lots of **white space** (see Figure 16-10)

- Eye-grabbers such as Drop caps, or a single brightly colored object alone on a gray-scale screen

- Shadows and drop shadows in various shades

- Gradients

- Reversed graphics to emphasize important text or images

- Shaded objects and text in 2-D and 3-D

Figure 16-9 Contrasts attract the eye—Bud Knight, PGA Junior Champion at the turn of the century, was made thick by stretching him in an image-editing program.

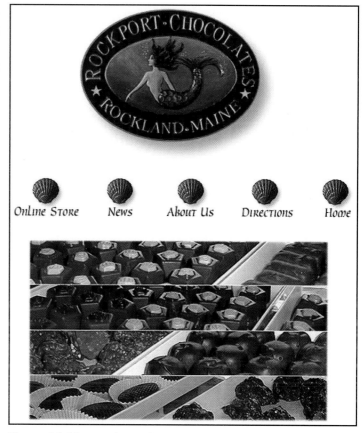

Figure 16-10 Use plenty of white space ("noninformation areas") in your screens.

Things to Avoid   Here are some mistakes you will want to avoid in creating computer graphics:

■ Clashes of color
■ **Busy screens** (too much stuff)
■ Using a picture with a lot of contrast in color or brightness as a background
■ Trite humor in oft-repeated animations
■ Clanging bells or squeaks when a button is clicked
■ Frilly pattern borders
■ Cute one-liners from famous movies
■ Requiring more than two button clicks to quit
■ Too many numbers (limit charts to about 25 numbers; if you can, just show totals)
■ Too many words (don't crowd them; split your information into bite-sized chunks)
■ Too many substantive elements presented too quickly

Most graphic artists will tell you that design is an "intuitive thing," but they will be hard-pressed to describe the rules they follow in their everyday work. They know when colors are not "working" and will change them again and again until they're right, but they usually won't be able to explain why the colors work or don't work. A project with a good navigation design, though it may have been developed with good planning and storyboarding, is indeed more often the result of many hours of crafty finagling with buttons and editors.

Audio Interfaces

A multimedia user interface may include important sound elements that reflect the rhythm of a project and may affect the attitude of your audience. Sounds can be background music, special effects for button clicks, voice-overs, effects synced to animation, or they may be buried in the audio track of a video clip. The tempo and style of background music can set the "tone" of a project. Vivaldi or Bach might be appropriate for a banking or investment annual report delivered on CD-ROM. Comic laughs and screeching effects might be appropriate for a clothing web site aimed at preteens. Choose music that fits the content and the atmosphere you wish to create. In all cases, use special effects sparingly. Always provide a toggle switch to disable sound. (Many AOL users prefer to disable the "You've Got Mail!" voice, for example.) And always test a project that contains sound with potential users.

http://www.tsworldofdesign.com/tutorial/interface.htm
Developing web site navigation interfaces around usability

http://www.digital-web.com/features/feature_2002-12b.shtml
Digital Web magazine, The Psychology of Navigation, Jan 2003

http://www.scottberkun.com/essays/essay09.htm
Fitts's UI Law applied to the Web

http://www.stcsig.org/usability/topics/articles/he-checklist.html
Heuristic evaluation: a system checklist (Xerox Corp.)

http://developer.apple.com/techpubs/mac/HIGOS8Guide/thig-2.html
Apple human interface guidelines

http://msdn.microsoft.com/library/default.asp?url=/library/en-us/dnwui/html/iuiguidelines.asp
Microsoft inductive user interface guidelines

http://www.useit.com/
Jakob Nielsen's guidelines for usability and Web design

http://www-3.ibm.com/ibm/easy/eou_ext.nsf/Publish/570
User-centered design

http://www.useit.com/alertbox/20000514.html
Eye-tracking study of Web readers

http://www.useit.com/alertbox/20020707.html
User empowerment and the fun factor

http://www.useit.com/alertbox/20020609.html
Reduce redundancy: decrease duplicated design decisions

http://www.useit.com/alertbox/20011209.html
DVD menu design: the failures of Web design re-created yet again

http://www.useit.com/alertbox/20010121.html
Usability metrics

http://desktoppub.about.com/cs/colorselection/p/index.htm
Color symbolism

http://desktoppub.about.com/od/howcolorworks/index.htm
Color basics and theory

http://www.webtechniques.com/archives/2001/02/kilian/
Effective Web writing

http://www.sun.com/980713/webwriting/
Writing for the Web (Sun Microsystems)

A Multimedia Design Case History

This section presents an example of the design process for a simple multimedia project about the construction and launch of a 31-foot ocean-going sailboat. This project was initially crafted in SuperCard (a Macintosh-only, page-based, authoring tool), but it was later ported to Adobe's Director (a time-based tool) so that it could be played on both Mac and Windows platforms (see Chapter 11 for details about authoring systems).

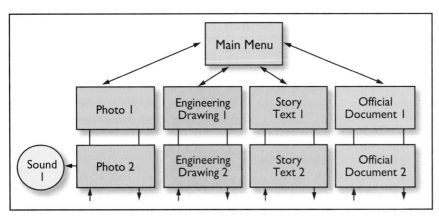

Figure 16-11 The first storyboard

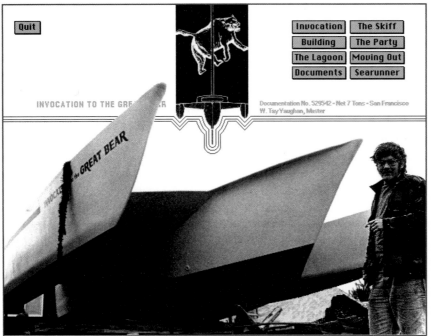

Figure 16-12 Main menu screen with relevant artwork as background

Storyboarding a Project

The source material (all that was available) practically sorted itself into logical groups: a pile of old photographs, a magazine article and newspaper clippings, engineering drawings, official documents, and some cassettes with recorded sounds. The first storyboard was a simple hierarchical structure with branches to each subject area, as shown in Figure 16-11.

Putting It Together

The most eye-catching photograph was chosen as a background for the main menu, and, as shown in Figure 16-12, the main menu was planned to contain clearly labeled buttons navigating to linear presentations of each topic area. From every screen in the project, users would be able to return to the main menu. Where sound bites were appropriate, clicking buttons on screens would play sounds. Adding a Quit button was necessary, also on the main menu, so that users would never be more than two button clicks from exiting the project (back to the main menu, and then quit).

The 50 or so 4×5 photographs were old color prints that offered poor contrast and faded colors (due to a saltwater dunking in a storm off the Central American coastline). Digitized on a flatbed scanner in gray-scale, however, they worked fine, and Photoshop was available to improve contrast. All the prints were scanned, cropped to the same dimension, optimized, and stored as bitmapped objects within Director. While at the scanner, merchant marine licenses and documents were also digitized, and the magazine article was scanned using OCR software to bring it into ASCII format. The story text was imported into the project.

After all the content was in Director's Cast (see Chapter 11), and work on the navigation system was under way, several issues emerged. First, it is terrifically boring to read a 3,000-word story by scrolling a long text field. Second, the photos were too small to be placed alone on a single screen. So it made sense to combine the story line with the images, even though they were not directly related; the story about launching the boat would progress from beginning to end as the boat was slowly built in the pictures. The storyboard changed to that shown in Figure 16-13.

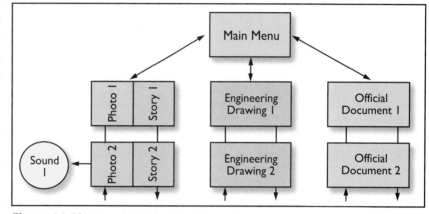

Figure 16-13 The second storyboard

The photo-essay-and-story combination worked out to 28 screens. The photos were placed into the score, and the text was cut and pasted into fields (see Figure 16-14). It became clear that users might want to scan rapidly through the photographs to watch the boat being built, ignoring the text of the story. So a special button was programmed to scan through the images until the mouse was clicked.

Figure 16-14 Snapshots are combined with text to form a 28-screen story line.

Images that did not fit into the photo essay about building the boat—for instance, the launching party with its roast pig, the long haul to the beach by trailer, and setting the mooring—were withdrawn from the pile of construction photographs; but because they were interesting, they were attached as separate branches accessible by button from the main menu. This was the third time the navigation changed, proving that you can continue to hang elements on a menu until the menu screen is too busy (and then you use submenus), or until you run out of material, as shown in Figure 16-15.

Next, the sound bites were recorded, digitized, and added to the project. Figure 16-16, the screen where the sounds were to play, shows the special button installed to play sound bites. It's simply a picture of a loudspeaker.

The documents for the project included engineering drawings, highway permits, and licenses. The highway permit, for example, was 8.5 by 11 inches (portrait); but after some experimentation, once it was scaled to

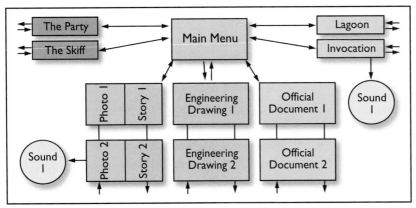

Figure 16-15 The third storyboard.

Figure 16-16 Sound is played when the loudspeaker icon is clicked.

480 pixels in height, it was (barely) readable and acceptable for this project. The licenses and drawings were in landscape orientation and fit more easily on a 640×480-pixel screen (see Figure 16-17).

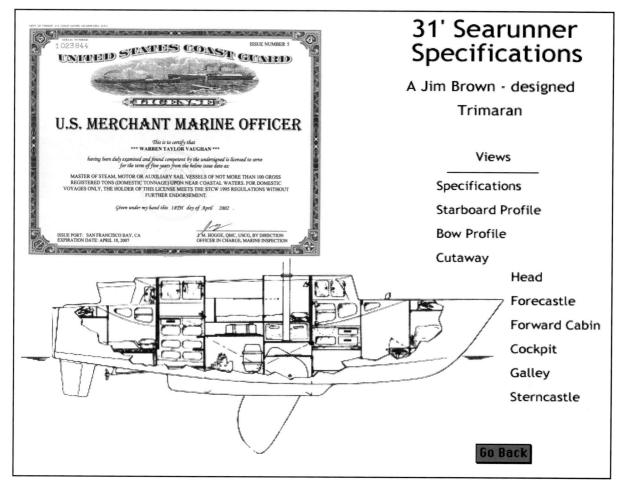

Figure 16-17 Larger fonts of some scanned documents can be read at 72 dpi resolution, and engineering drawings in landscape orientation can be resized to fit.

Reworking

The buttons on the main menu were the wrong color, so they were changed a few times until the color worked. Helvetica title text wasn't fancy enough, so it was reworked and a drop shadow was laid in. A special slider button was built and programmed to allow the construction sequence to go immediately to any of the pictures in the sequence. The backgrounds were tweaked a little, and the order of images changed somewhat. A small red car was animated to drive along the edge of the lagoon.

The project described here was simple and straightforward. With the exception of designing a few custom buttons for auto-scanning through some of the images and designing the animations, the entire project was a progression of screens of information, with links activated by clicking buttons.

Producing

By the time you reach the development phases of your multimedia project and you start building, you should already have taken care to prepare your plan and to get organized. The project plan (see Chapter 15) now becomes your step-by-step instruction manual for building the product. For many multimedia developers, following this plan and actually doing the construction work—being down in the trenches of hands-on creation and production—is the fun part of any project.

Production is the phase when your multimedia project is actually rendered. During this phase you will contend with important and continuous organizing tasks. There will be times in a complex project when graphics files seem to disappear from the server, when you forget to send or cannot produce milestone progress reports, when your voice talent gets lost on the way to the recording studio, or when your hard disk crashes. So it's important to start out on the right foot, with good organization, and to maintain detailed management oversight during the entire construction process. This rule applies to projects large and small, projects for you or for a client, and projects with 1 or 20 people on staff. Above all, provide a good time-accounting system for everyone working on the project. At the end of the week, it's hard to remember how much time you spent on the tasks you did on Monday.

> Developing multimedia can be like taking a joy ride in a washer/dryer. When it's all over you feel like you've been washed, rinsed, spun, and tumble-dried.
>
> Kevin McCarthy, Director of Business Development, Medius IV

TIP   *If your project is to be built by more than one person, establish a management structure in advance that includes specific milestones and the production expectations for each contributor.*

Starting Up

Before you begin your multimedia project, it's important to check your development hardware and software and review your organizational and administrative setup, even if you are working alone. This is a serious last-minute task. It prevents you from finding yourself halfway through the project with nowhere to put your graphics files and digitized movie segments when you're out of disk space, or stuck with an incompatible version of a critical software tool, or with a network that bogs down and quits every two days. Such incidents can take many days or weeks to resolve, so try to head off as many potential problems as you can before you begin. Here are some examples of things to think about.

- Desk and mind clear of obstructions?
- Fastest CPU and RAM you can afford?
- Time-accounting and management system in place?
- Biggest (or most) monitors you can afford?
- Sufficient disk storage space for all work files?
- System for regular backup of critical files?
- Conventions or protocols for naming your working files and managing source documents?
- Latest version of your primary authoring software?
- Latest versions of software tools and accessories?
- Communication pathways open with client?
- Breathing room for administrative tasks?
- Financial arrangements secure (retainer in the bank)?
- Expertise lined up for all stages of the project?
- Kick-off meeting completed?

First Person

At 18, I used to hang around with people who drove fast cars, and once volunteered to help an acquaintance prepare his Ferrari Berlinetta for a race at Watkins Glen. My job was to set the valves while my friend went over the suspension, brakes, and later, the carburetor. The car boasted 12 cylinders and 24 valves, and adjusting the clearance between tappet and rocker arm seemed to me akin to a jeweler's fine work. It required special wrenches and feeler gauges and an uncommon touch to rotate the high-compression engine so the cam was precisely at its highest point for each valve. I was blown away by the sheer quantity of moving parts under the Ferrari's long and shiny valve covers—my own fast car had only four cylinders and eight simple valves. It took me about seven exhausting hours (including double-checking) to get it right. As the sun came up, though, the engine sounded great!

Tuning up and preparing, I learned, is as important to the race as the race itself. My friend, however, learned a much tougher lesson: he spun out and rolled his Ferrari at the hairpin turn in the seventh lap. He crawled unhurt from the twisted wreckage, but all he was able to salvage from the car was the engine.

Working with Clients

Making multimedia for clients is a special case. Be sure that the organization of your project incorporates a system for good communication between you and the client as well as among the people actually building the project. Many projects have turned out unhappily because of communication breakdowns.

Client Approval Cycles

Provide good management oversight to avoid endless feedback loops—in this situation the client is somehow never quite happy, and you are forced to tweak and edit many times. Manage production so that your client is continually informed and formally approves by signing off on artwork and other elements as you build them. Develop a scheme that specifies the number and duration of client approval cycles, and then provide a mechanism for change orders when changes are requested after sign-off. For change orders, remember that the client should pay extra and the changes should be costly.

First Person

We made up two sample musical tracks to play in the background and sent them off by overnight courier to the client. Four days later, the client phoned to say that both were good, but they were wondering if we couldn't make it sound a little more like Windham Hill. So we redid the music and sent two more samples. Five days later, the client said the samples were great, but the

boss wanted something with a Sergeant Pepper feel. So we sent a fifth creation, this time with a note that they would have to either settle on one of the five styles submitted, supply the music themselves, or pay us more money to keep up the creative composition work. They chose the music the boss liked, but we wound up more than two weeks behind schedule and had spent significantly

more money and effort on this task than originally budgeted.

Several months later, in the next job requiring original music composition, we specified a maximum of two review/feedback cycles and added a clause for cost overrun beyond that. The first sound we submitted to this new client was approved, and we stayed ahead of schedule and budget.

Data Storage Media and Transportation

It's important that the client be able to easily review your work. Remember that either both you and the distant site need to have matching data transfer systems and media, or you need to provide a web or FTP site for your project. Organize your system before you begin work, as it may take some time for both you and the client to agree on an appropriate system and on the method of transportation.

Because multimedia files are large, your means of transporting the project to distant clients is particularly important. Typically, both you and the client will have access to the Internet at high bandwidth. If not, the most cost and time-effective method for transporting your files is on CD-R or DVD-ROM by an overnight courier service (FedEx, DHL, or U.S. Postal Service Express Mail). Material completed in time for an afternoon pickup will usually be at the client's site by the next morning.

If you use the Internet to deliver your multimedia to the client, be sure that you set up rules and conventions for naming files placed at an FTP site, and use codes in the subject headers of your e-mail to describe the content of the message. After a project has been under way for awhile, there will be many files and many communications, so these keywords and clues will make life easier. This is another place where planning ahead pays off!

Tracking

Organize a method for tracking the receipt of material that you will incorporate into your multimedia project. Even in small projects, you will be dealing with many digital bits and pieces.

Develop a **file-naming convention** specific to your project's structure. Store the files in directories or folders with logical names. If you are working across platforms, develop a file identification system that uses the DOS file-naming convention of eight characters plus a three-character extension. Use this convention on files for the Macintosh as well as the PC; otherwise, files transferred from the Macintosh to the PC may receive default names with strange characters and extensions that are difficult to interpret. You may also need to set up a database with file names as eight-character codes matched to lengthier descriptive names, so you know what the codes mean.

WARNING *Even if you are working in Windows, avoid using long file names with characters like spaces, periods, or colons. Those names may not map properly to other operating systems.*

Version control of your files (tracking editing changes) is critically important, too, especially in large projects. If more than one person is working on a group of files, be sure that you always know what version is the latest and who has the current version. If storage space allows, archive all file iterations, in case you change your mind about something and need to go back to a prior rendering.

Copyrights

Commonly used authoring platforms may allow access to the software programming code or script that drives a particular project. The source code of HTML pages on the Web may also be easily viewed.

In such an open-code environment, are you prepared to let others see your programming work? Is your code neat and commented? Perhaps your mother cautioned you to wear clean underclothing in case you were suddenly on a table among strangers in a hospital emergency room—well, apply this rule to your code. You can insert a copyright statement in your project that clearly (and legally) designates the code as your intellectual property (see Figure 16-18), but the code, tricks, and programming techniques remain accessible for study, learning, and tweaking by others.

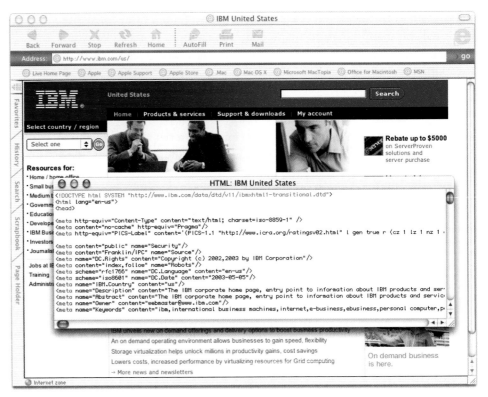

Figure 16-18 Typical copyright and ownership statements embedded in <meta> tags at the top of an HTML page

Hazards and Annoyances

Even experienced producers and developers commonly run into at least some light chop and turbulence during the course of a project's development. The experts, however, never crash when their vehicle shudders or loses some altitude. You can expect the going to get rough at any number of stages—from trying to design the perfect interface, to endless testing, to problems with client sign-off or payment. Expect problems beyond your control, and be prepared to accept them and solve them.

Small annoyances, too, can become serious distractions that are counterproductive. The production stage is a time of great creativity, dynamic intercourse among all contributors, and, above all, hard work. Be prepared to deal with some common irritants, for example:

- Creative coworkers who don't take (or give) criticism well
- Clients who cannot or are not authorized to make decisions
- More than two all-nighters in a row

- Too many custom-coded routines
- Instant coffee and microwaved corn dogs
- Too many meetings; off-site meetings
- Missed deadlines

If your project is a team effort, then it is critical that everyone works well together—or can at least tolerate one another's differences—especially when the going gets tough. Pay attention to the mental health of all personnel involved in your project, and be aware of the dynamics of the group and whether people are being adversely affected by individual personalities. If problems arise, deal with them before they become hazardous; the mix of special creative talents required for multimedia can be volatile. If you stay organized and flexible throughout, you will complete your project successfully. See Chapter 18 for how to deliver it!

First Person

In 1975, I was hired to deliver a 41-foot cruising sailboat from Fort Lauderdale to the British Virgin Islands for the charter trade. In three days I assembled a crew of strangers, provisioned the boat, and checked all the equipment. Then we took off across the Gulf Stream and into the Bermuda Triangle.

After two days it was clear that the cook was a bad apple. It wasn't just that she couldn't cook—she whined about everything: the stove wouldn't light, the boat heeled too much, her socks were wet, her sleeping bag tore on a cleat, her hair was tangled, she couldn't get her favorite radio station (now a few hundred miles astern). It was unending.

The whining began to envelop her in a smog-colored, onion-like layering, each new complaint accreting to the last one, like growing coral. By the fifth day, her unpleasant aura saturated the entire main cabin, and the rest of us had to seek sanctuary in the cockpit or the small aft cabin. Efforts were made to solve this bizarre situation, but by then, nobody could get near her (or wanted to).

When we pulled into tiny Caicos Island for water and fresh stores, I paid her off and arranged for a room at the quaint waterfront hotel, where she could wait three days for the weekly airplane back to Florida. Everyone felt bad about her disappointment and how it all turned out—for about an hour. The rest of the voyage was jubilant.

Chapter 16 Review

■ Chapter Summary

For your review, here's a summary of the important concepts discussed in this chapter.

Describe various strategies for creating interactive multimedia

- The best products are often the result of continuing feedback and modifications implemented throughout the production process.

- However, too much feedback and too many changes can kill a project; always balance proposed changes against their cost.

- You can either describe the project in great detail before the production, or you can use rough storyboards and refine the design as you produce it.

- If the design team is separate from the development team, it's best to produce a detailed design first.

Discuss different types of multimedia structures and how they might be organized

- How you organize your material for a project will have just as great an impact on the viewer as the content itself.

- Start mapping the structure of your project early in the planning phase.

- In a linear design, users navigate sequentially, from one frame or bite of information to another.

- In a hierarchical design, users navigate along the branches of a tree structure that is shaped by the natural logic of the content.

- In a nonlinear design, users navigate freely through the content.

- In a composite design, users may navigate nonlinearly but are occasionally constrained to linear presentations.

Cite concepts that affect the user interface, including structures and navigation maps

- The method you provide to your viewers for navigating from one place to another in your project is part of the user interface.

- Depth structure represents the complete navigation map and describes all the links between all the components of your project.

- Surface structure represents the structures actually realized by a user while navigating the depth structure.

- Too much navigational freedom can be disconcerting, and viewers may get lost.

Discuss hot spots, hyperlinks, and buttons and how they are typically used

- Hot spots can be text, graphic, and icon.

- Icons are fundamental graphic objects symbolic of an activity or concept.

- Most authoring systems provide a tool for creating buttons of all three types.

- Stick with accepted conventions for button design and grouping, visual and audio feedback, and navigation structure.

- Stick with real-world metaphors that will be understood by the widest selection of potential users.

- Avoid hidden commands and unusual keystroke/mouse click combinations.

Identify principles for successful project management of multimedia productions

- Production is the phase when your multimedia project is actually rendered.

- Provide a time-accounting system for everyone working on the project.

- Check your development hardware and software and review your organizational and administrative setup.

- Have a system for communication between you, the client, and the people actually building the project in place.

- Provide management oversight and control the client review process to avoid endless feedback loops.

- Establish a process in which your client is continually informed and formally approves the project as you develop it.

- Organize a method for tracking the receipt of material that you will incorporate into your multimedia project.

- Develop a file-naming convention specific to your project's structure.

- Version control of your files (tracking editing changes) is critically important, especially in large projects.

■ Key Terms

busy screens *(424)*
button *(415)*
composite navigation *(408)*
depth structure *(409)*
file-naming convention*(433)*
hierarchical navigation *(408)*
hot spot *(415)*

hyperlink *(415)*
icons *(416)*
image map *(418)*
linear navigation *(408)*
modal interface *(420)*
navigation map *(408)*
nonlinear navigation *(408)*

production *(430)*
site map *(408)*
storyboards *(407)*
surface structure *(409)*
user interface *(420)*
version control *(433)*
white space *(423)*

■ Key Term Quiz

1. The graphic outlines that describe each page of a project in exact detail are called _____.

2. A multimedia structure in which users navigate sequentially, from one frame or bite of information to another, could be called _____.

3. A multimedia structure in which users navigate along the branches of a tree structure that is shaped by the natural logic of the content could be called _____.

4. A multimedia structure in which users navigate freely through the content of the project, unbound by predetermined routes could be called _____.

5. A multimedia structure in which users may navigate freely, but are occasionally constrained to linear presentations, could be called _____.

6. The complete navigation map that describes all the links between all the components of your project is known as _____.

7. The structures actually realized by a user while navigating the project's content is known as _____.

8. Fundamental graphic objects that represent an activity or concept are called _____.

9. The standard that ensures that project files are given logical names and stored in folders with logical names is the _____.

10. Making sure that old files are archived and new versions are properly tracked is called _____.

■ Multiple Choice Quiz

1. Which of these is *not* an advantage of creating detailed storyboards before beginning production?
   a. It will be better and easier to construct the project.
   b. Less time is required in polishing the final product.
   c. Getting to the production stage is faster.
   d. It is better suited to separate design and production teams.
   e. Clients who like to tightly control the production process prefer it.

2. Which of these is *not* one of the listed types of organizational structures?
   a. linear
   b. hierarchical
   c. nonlinear
   d. composite
   e. recursive

3. The visual representation of a project that includes a table of contents as well as a chart of the logical flow of the interactive interface is often called:
   a. a storyboard
   b. a workflow diagram
   c. a prototype
   d. a navigation map
   e. a master layout

4. The method you provide to your viewers for navigating from one place to another in your project is part of the:
   a. script
   b. user interface
   c. storyboards
   d. depth structure
   e. surface structure

5. The generic term for any area of an image that can be clicked on is:
   a. a hot spot
   b. a storyboard
   c. an image map
   d. a rollover
   e. an icon

6. An interface in which a user can click a button and change the approach of the whole interface is called:
   a. a prototype
   b. a navigation map
   c. a modal interface
   d. a site map
   e. a transitional GUI

7. Having separate novice and expert interfaces for a multimedia program is generally not a good idea because:
   a. it tends to take up too much disk space or bandwidth
   b. novice users tend to get caught in the expert mode
   c. only a minority of users are expert; most users are caught in between and are frustrated
   d. most authoring systems are not capable of handling parallel structures
   e. it makes developing documentation awkward and unwieldy

8. GUI stands for:
   a. General/Universal/Individual
   b. General Utilization Instructions
   c. Global Usage Image
   d. Guidelines for Usability and Interaction
   e. Graphical User Interface

9. The Macintosh and Windows GUIs are successful partly because:
   a. they enable cross-platform file structures
   b. their basic point-and-click style is simple, consistent, and quickly mastered
   c. they are highly customizable, allowing programmers to use program-specific keyboard shortcuts
   d. they tend to make the computer run more efficiently
   e. slick marketing efforts tricked gullible consumers

10. Noninformation areas left intentionally free from visual clutter are often referred to as:
    a. negative space
    b. screen real estate
    c. advanced organizers
    d. white space
    e. depth structure

11. The standards that ensure that project files are given logical names and stored in folders with logical names are the:
    a. usability guidelines
    b. pattern-recognition algorithms
    c. file-naming conventions
    d. review-cycle management
    e. project tracking protocols

12. Perhaps the most significant problem with creating a multimedia program that gives users complete free reign is that:
    a. such freedom is difficult to program
    b. computers cannot yet process so many variables concurrently
    c. too much freedom can be disconcerting to users

    d. it is difficult to organize data into meaningful structures
    e. such interfaces tend to be cluttered and unwieldy

13. Default colors for anchor text are found in which HTML tag?
    a. <HEAD>
    b. <FRAME>
    c. <LINK>
    d. <COLOR>
    e. <BODY>

14. Which of these is probably *not* a good step to take before starting the production process for a multimedia project?
    a. Lock in the design so there are no further changes to delay production.
    b. Establish limits on client review cycles to reduce cost overruns.
    c. Set up an FTP site for sending and receiving production files.
    d. Establish clear file-naming and version control standards.
    e. Check the state of your hardware and software to ensure reliability and capability, and integrate any upgrades.

15. An image on a web page can be sectioned in HTML into areas that are clickable links. This is called:
    a. a sweet spot
    b. a site map
    c. a rollover
    d. a frameset
    e. an image map

■ Essay Quiz

1. You are given the task of managing a design and production team to complete a multimedia web site for your own company. The site is to use the latest plug-ins for interactive 3-D presentation. The design team consists of a writer and a designer, and the production team includes two programmers. Would you make sure the design and storyboards were "nailed down" before beginning production, or would you start and allow the design to be changed during the production process? How would factors such as the client, the technology, and the relationship between the design and production teams affect your approach?

2. List the four different types of multimedia structures. Next, describe four hypothetical projects, one that might be appropriate for each of the four types. For each of these four projects, comment on why the project is best suited to that structure and why each of the three structures is less appropriate for that project.

3. Discuss the relationship between a program's content, its interface, and its usability. What is the best way to make the content accessible to users without unnecessary complexity? Where are modal interfaces useful? What are their drawbacks? Where are navigation or site maps useful? How might you use "themes" to identify different areas of a program or different approaches to the content's structure?

4. What are the steps you would take in "gearing up" for the production phase of a multimedia project? Organize your thoughts according to the infrastructure (hardware, software, networks, web/FTP site), team management, and client interaction.

5. Describe the tracking process you might use to control the project development process. Be sure to include a discussion of version control, file-naming convention, client review cycles, and team management.

Lab Projects

■ Project 16.1

Locate three different web sites: a news site, a shopping site, and a hobby or special interest site. Print out the home page for each site (the home page should include the primary navigation; it should not be a "splash page" that includes little navigation). Circle all the buttons on the interface. Note any buttons that are common to each site. Compare the layout and structure of the sites, ignoring aesthetic considerations. List the buttons that are different. Comment on why the buttons are laid out and grouped as they are. Is the site accessible? How are icons used? How are menus used? Write a report documenting your observations, and include the printouts.

■ Project 16.2

Locate three different web sites that have similar content and that include site maps. Print out each site's map. How are the structures similar? How are they different? How are the differences related to their content? How are the differences related to a different way of structuring the information? Write a report documenting your observations, and include the printouts.

■ Project 16.3

Create a site map for a hypothetical multimedia CD project on the history of computers. Use the composite structure, and provide two means of navigating the content, one being a timeline. Be sure to include various options such as help, glossary, and so on. Trace the "surface" structures that three hypothetical users might take through the program: a novice user, an expert user, and someone looking for a particular fact about computer history. Explain why each user would take that particular path through the project.

■ Project 16.4

Using simple text blocks and icons, create a user interface for the project you developed in Project 16.3. Discuss what buttons are included, how they are logically grouped together, and why. What non-text interface elements might you include to provide navigational cues?

■ Project 16.5

Create five storyboards for the history of computers project. Storyboard a "splash screen," the main menu, a submenu, and two different content screens.

CHAPTER 17

Content and Talent

EVERY multimedia project includes **content**. It is the "stuff" from which you fashion your messages. It is also the information and material that forms the heart of your project, and it is that which defines what your project is about.

Practically, content can be any and all of the elements of multimedia. You might use your collection of wedding photographs and videotapes to create a special multimedia newsletter for family and relatives. Or you might edit portions of the audio track from these videotapes and capture still images to build a multimedia database of aunts, uncles, and cousins. This material is your project's content.

Content can have low and high **production value**. If you hire a team of professionals to shoot your wedding video, and then they digitize images and audio clips at broadcast quality, your content will have high production value. If you persuade Hillary Rodham Clinton to record the voice-over and Garry Trudeau, the "Doonesbury" artist, to retouch the images, it will have yet higher production value.

You must always balance the production value of your project against your budget and the desired result. For aerial photographs of the wedding reception, you would not likely commission the private launch of a spy satellite from Kennedy Space Center to achieve highest production value. Instead, you could rent a helicopter with paparazzi and still achieve good production value. Or you could photograph the wedding yourself from a neighboring rooftop and be satisfied with the lower production value. The production value of your project is a question of balance (see Vaughan's Law of Multimedia Minimums in Chapter 5).

Content has to come from somewhere—either you make it or you acquire it. Whether you make it, borrow it, or buy it depends upon your project's needs, your time constraints, and your pocketbook. Content that is destined for sale to the public is also wrapped up in numerous legal issues. Who owns the content? Do you have the proper rights to use it? Copyright laws, for example, establish rights for the creators or owners of literary works; musical works; dramatic works; pictorial, graphic, and sculptural works; motion pictures and other audiovisual works; and sound recordings. Do you have licenses for protected works and signed releases from anyone who appears in your project?

When the Vatican recently made a collection of artwork available on the World Wide Web, they made certain there was a digital "watermark" for each image; they would then know if the artwork was ripped off, without recourse to even higher laws. The Vatican is aware (as you should be) of the nature of the electronic revolution:

> In accordance with international regulations on Intellectual Property and Author's Rights, we inform our readers that the news items contained in the Vatican Information Service may be used in part or in their entirety, but only if the source (V.I.S., Vatican Information Service) is quoted. In the case of electronic retransmission (Internet, telematic networks, via PC-modem, fax, etc.), prior authorization from the Vatican Information Service is always required.

. . . .

http://www.vatican.va

http://www.christusrex.org

Collections of hundreds of classical images

. . . .

This chapter discusses some of the legal issues surrounding content and the use of talent in multimedia projects. It provides examples of contract terms and introduces you to sources and providers of content and talent. Needless to say, always consult an attorney versed in intellectual property law when you negotiate the rights and ownership of content.

Acquiring Content

Content acquisition can be one of the most expensive and time-consuming tasks in organizing a multimedia project. You must plan ahead, allocating sufficient time (and money) for this task.

■ If your project describes the use of a new piece of robotics machinery, for example, will you need to send a photographer to the factory for the pictures? Or can you digitize existing photographs?

> This is how you do things on a shoestring. Years ago, we created a basketball product starring Dr. J and Larry Bird. The first thing we knew we had to do was sign a contract with Dr. J. So we found a guy that knew his agent and we made a side deal with him to pay him to convince Julius to do it. And then we went to Julius and we made a deal where we gave him some stock in the company, rather than writing a huge check. And we convinced him of the educational value of what we were doing, instead of just trying to get it to be an arms-length financial deal. So we were able to sign him up with an advance of only $20,000. And he was quite easily the biggest name in basketball and one of the top two or three regarded professional athletes at the time. We got him for a royalty rate of 2 ½ percent (not what you hear today in a lot of cases), so you don't have to do things that have really high royalty rates and advances. By the way, he made a killing on the stock!
>
> Trip Hawkins, Chairman & CEO, 3DO Company

- Suppose you are working with 100 graphs and charts about the future of petroleum exploration. Will you begin by collecting the raw data from reports and memos, or start with an existing spreadsheet or database? Perhaps you have charts that have already been generated from the data and stored as TIFF or JPEG files?

- You are developing an interactive guide to the trails in a national park, complete with video clips of the wildlife that hikers might encounter on the trails. Will you need to shoot original video footage, or are there existing tapes for you to edit?

TIP Be sure to specify in your project plan the format and quality of content and data to be supplied to you by third parties. Format conversion and editing takes real time. Worse, if you have specified that images for a client's web site are to be 800x600 pixels, but the photo files you receive from your client's cousin are 320x240 pixels at 72 dpi, there will simply not be enough information in the image to enlarge it to the required resolution.

Using Content Created by Others

When a work is created, certain rights, such as for the work's public display or performance, its use in a broadcast, or its reproduction, are granted to its creator. Among the rights most relevant to a multimedia producer are **electronic rights**—the rights to publish a work in a computer-based storage and delivery medium such as a CD-ROM or on the Web. Since the late 1980s, investors in the multimedia marketplace have been quietly purchasing electronic rights (the right to reproduce works in electronic form) to the basic building blocks of content—including films, videos, photographic collections, and textual information bases—knowing that in the future these elements can and perhaps will be converted from their traditional form to computer-based storage and delivery. This is smart, but not easy; the many union-supported contract restrictions and performer and producer rights are not only complicated and difficult to trace but also very expensive to acquire.

WARNING   If you negotiate ownership or rights to someone else's content, be sure to get the advice of a skilled copyright and contracts attorney.

Obtaining the rights to content is not, however, a hopeless undertaking. For example, Amaze, Inc., acquired rights from several sources to produce a series of computer-based daily planners with a cartoon-a-day from Gary Larson's "The Far Side" or Cathy Guisewite's "Cathy," a word-a-day from Random House; or a question-a-day from the Trivial Pursuit game. Random House and Brøderbund's Living Books Division negotiated the rights to the Dr. Seuss books for multimedia use. Multimedia rights to Elvis Presley historical material, to the movie *Jurassic Park*, and to a myriad of other content have been acquired by multimedia developers and publishers.

Depending on the type and source of your content, the negotiations for usage rights can be simple and straightforward, or they may require complicated contracts and a stack of release forms. Each potential content provider you approach will likely have his or her own set of terms that you need to look at carefully, so that the terms are broad enough not to constrain the scope of your multimedia project.

Locating Preexisting Content

Preexisting content can come from a variety of sources, ranging from a trunk of old photographs in your neighbor's attic to a stock house or image bank offering hundreds of thousands of hours of film and video or still images, available for licensing for a fee.

If your needs are simple and fairly flexible, you may be able to use material from collections of **clip art**. Such collections of photographs, graphics, sounds, music, animation, and video are becoming widely available from many sources, for anywhere from fifty to several hundred dollars. Part of the value of many of these packages is that you are granted unlimited use, and you can be comfortable creating derivative versions tailored to your specific application. Carefully read the license agreement that comes with the collection before assuming you can use the material in any manner. In the six-point italicized type on the back of the agreement, you may discover that the licensor offers no guarantee that the contents of the collection are original works. Thus, the licensor bears no responsibility to indemnify you for inadvertently infringing on the copyrights of a third party. Even if the collection is described as allowing "free use," you may discover that the collection comes with severe restrictions on the way material can be used, or that a **royalty** is required for any use beyond wallpaper on your computer.

If your content needs are more specific or complex, a good place to start your search for material might be at a **still photo library**, a **sound library**, or a **stock footage** house. These resources may be public or private and may contain copyrighted works as well as materials that are in the public domain. **Public domain** means either that the work was never copyrighted in the first place or its copyright protection has expired over time and not been renewed; you can use public domain material without a license.

Mickey Mouse Goes to Washington

Unless you earn your living as an intellectual property lawyer, you probably don't know that the Supreme Court has granted certiorari in *Eldred v. Ashcroft*, a case that will test the limits of Congress's power to extend the term of copyrights. But while copyright may not seem inherently compelling to nonspecialists, the issues at stake in *Eldred* are vitally important to anyone who watches movies, listens to music, or reads books. If that includes you, read on.

Back in 1998, representatives of the Walt Disney Company came to Washington looking for help. Disney's copyright on Mickey Mouse, who made his screen debut in the 1928 cartoon short "Steamboat Willie," was due to expire in 2003, and Disney's rights to Pluto, Goofy, and Donald Duck were to expire a few years later.

Rather than allow Mickey and friends to enter the public domain, Disney and its friends—a group of Hollywood studios, music labels, and PACs representing content owners—told Congress that they wanted an extension bill passed.

Prompted perhaps by the Disney group's lavish donations of campaign cash— more than $6.3 million in 1997–98, according to the nonprofit Center for Responsive Politics—Congress passed, and President Clinton signed, the Sonny Bono Copyright Term Extension Act.

The CTEA extended the term of protection by 20 years for works copyrighted after January 1, 1923. Works copyrighted by individuals since 1978 got "life plus 70" rather than the existing "life plus 50." Works made by or for corporations (referred to as "works made for hire") got 95 years. Works copyrighted before 1978 were shielded for 95 years, regardless of how they were produced.

In all, tens of thousands of works that had been poised to enter the public domain were maintained under private ownership until at least 2019.

So far so good—as far as Disney and its friends were concerned, at least. In 1999, a group of plaintiffs led by Eric Eldred, whose Eldritch Press offers free online access to public domain works, filed a challenge to the statute. Eldred argues that the CTEA is unconstitutional on two grounds: first, because the statute exceeds Congress's power under the Copyright Clause; and, second, because the statute runs afoul of the First Amendment by substantially burdening speech without advancing any important governmental interest.

Eldred lost before the district court and the D.C. Circuit. However, there is good reason to believe that he may yet prevail in the Supreme Court.

....

Chris Sprigman, Counsel to the Antitrust Group in the Washington, D.C. office of King & Spalding.

(Contrary to many predictions, on January 15, 2003, the United States Supreme Court upheld the Act in a 7–2 decision.)

The National Archives in Washington D.C. is a rich source of content, both copyrighted and in the public domain. Other public sources include the Library of Congress, NASA, U.S. Information Agency, and the Smithsonian Institution, all in Washington D.C. You cannot, however, safely assume that all material acquired from a public source is in the public domain. You remain responsible for ensuring that you do not infringe on a copyright.

In addition to public sources, there are many other repositories of content material. Commercial stock houses offer millions of images, video and film clips, and sound clips, and they often own the works outright—so, when they grant you a license for use of their work, you don't have to worry about possible copyright infringement of the rights of third parties. Some stock sources also specialize in certain subjects. For example, if you want a video clip of a shark, you might contact a stock footage house that specializes in underwater videos.

Copyrights

Copyright protection applies to "original works of authorship fixed in any tangible medium of expression." The Copyright Act of 1976, as amended (17 U.S.C.A. §101 et. seq.) protects the legal rights of the creator of an original work. Consequently, before you can use someone else's work in your multimedia project, you must first obtain permission from the owner of the copyright. If you do not do this, you may find yourself being sued for **copyright infringement** (unauthorized use of copyrighted material).

Several changes in the law have created confusion over copyright protections. One change is that works now come under copyright protection as soon as they are created and presented in a fixed form. Prior to 1976, protection was only granted upon registration, but now works do not have to be registered with the U.S. Copyright Office to be protected. Because of this there is another crucial change: works no longer need a properly formatted statement of **copyright ownership** (for example, "Copyright © 2006 by Tay Vaughan") to be protected. Many people assume, because of the pre-1976 rules, that if there is not a copyright statement, the work is available to be used. While that may be true for older works, you should start with the assumption that a work *is* protected, unless there is a specific statement that it is in the public domain. There are **fair use** exceptions in which copyrighted material can be used without permission, but they are very limited and specific—primarily for educational and journalistic use and rarely for commercial use—so you should consult an attorney before assuming this exception applies to work you wish to use in a project.

Owning a copy of a work does not entitle you to reproduce the work, and you still need to obtain permission from the copyright owner to use it. If you buy a painting from an artist, the artist retains the copyright unless it is assigned to you. You do not have the right to reproduce the painting in any form, such as in postcards or a calendar, without permission.

. . . .

http://www.timestream.com/stuff/neatstuff/license.html

http://www.timestream.com/stuff/neatstuff/mmlaw.html

This white paper about licensing still images and an intellectual property law primer for multimedia developers by Dianne Brinson and Mark Radcliffe provide useful insights into complex legal issues

. . . .

For additional discussion about copyrights as they apply to original works created for a project, see "Using Content Created for a Project" later in this chapter, and visit the U.S. Copyright Office at http://www.copyright.gov/.

Digital Rights Management (DRM)

As rights and ownership are redefined for the information age, various rights management technologies are emerging and competing to become industry standard. Microsoft Windows Media Rights Manager (WMRM, Windows only) and the Windows Media 9 format incorporate extensive DRM capabilities. The Association of American Publishers is promoting DRM methodologies for protecting unauthorized copying of e-books. The Internet Streaming Media Alliance (ISMA) offers a content protection specification designed to provide a single, end-to-end encryption scheme for streaming media and file downloading that can be integrated with different key and rights management software and licensed content protection devices. A Digital Object Identifier (DOI), which has been proposed for identifying and exchanging intellectual property, provides a framework for managing intellectual content, for linking customers with content suppliers, for facilitating electronic commerce, and enabling automated copyright management for all types of media. The Digital Millenium Copyright Act of 1998 has set the rules. For an overview of this emerging battle, check out the URLs below.

. . . .

http://www.copyright.gov/laws/

http://www.webopedia.com/TERM/D/DMCA.html

http://www.isma.tv/

http://www.doi.org/

http://www.current.tv/make/

. . . .

Obtaining Rights

You should license the rights to use copyrighted material before you develop a project around it. You may be able to negotiate outright ownership of copyrighted material. If the owner does not wish to give up or sell ownership rights, however, you may still be able to **license** the rights to use that material. Keep in mind, however, that different rights for the same copyrighted work (for example, rights for public performance, broadcast use, or publication) may be assigned to different parties. When you are negotiating a license make sure that the party you are dealing with has ownership of the appropriate rights.

There are few guidelines for negotiating content rights for use in multimedia products. If you are dealing with content providers who are professionals familiar with electronic media, you may be given a standard **rate card** listing licensing fees for different uses, formats, and markets. Other content providers or owners may be less familiar with multimedia and electronic uses, and you will need to educate them.

Some **licensing agreements** may be as simple as a signed permission letter or release form describing how you may use the material. Other agreements will specify in minute detail how, where, when, and for what purpose the content may be used. Ideally, you would seek rights for **unlimited use**, which allows you to use the content anytime, anywhere, and in any way you choose; more likely, however, the final license would contain restrictions about how the material may be used. Try to retain the option to renegotiate terms in case you want to broaden the scope of use at a later date.

The following items are but a few of the issues you need to consider when negotiating for rights to use preexisting content:

- How will the content be delivered? If you limit yourself to CD-ROMs, for example, you may not be able to distribute your product over the Internet without renegotiation.

- Is the license for a set period of time?

- Is the license exclusive or nonexclusive? (In an exclusive use arrangement, no one else would be able to use the material in the manner stipulated.)

- Where will your product be distributed? There may be different rates for domestic and international distribution.

- Do you intend to use the material in its entirety, or just a portion of it?

- What rights do you need? You need to be sure you have the right to reproduce and distribute the material. In addition, you may wish to use the material in promotions for your product.

Explaining multimedia technology to people can be a challenge. Michelle, an eighth-grader, wanted to scan some 1920s photographs to use in the San Rafael Community Express, a multimedia magazine done for kids by kids. When Michelle asked the 80-year-old docent at the local museum if she could use the photographs for a computer project, the woman responded in horror that these were priceless pictures and that they couldn't be put in a computer—they'd be ruined. The team spent another 15 minutes explaining scanning to the woman by comparing a scanner to a copy machine and assuring her that the original photographs would be returned unharmed.

John MacLeod, Publisher and Chief Pizza Provider for the San Rafael Community Express, a HyperStudio-based interactive magazine created by seventh- and eighth-graders at Davidson Middle School, San Rafael, California

- What kind of credit line or end-credits might the content owner require you to display?

- Does the content owner have the authority to assign rights to you? It is important to ensure you will not be held liable if a third party later sues for copyright infringement.

- Do you need to obtain any additional rights to use the content? For example, if you use a clip from a movie, do you need to get separate releases from actors appearing in the clip or from the director or producer of the movie?

- Will the copyright owner receive remuneration for the license? If so, what form will it take? A one-time fee? Royalty? Or a simple credit attribution?

- In what format do you wish to receive the content? Specifying formats is particularly important with video dubbed from a master.

Derivative Works

Any text taken verbatim, or any image or music perfectly copied, clearly requires permission from its owner to incorporate it into your work. But there are some other, less clear-cut issues. For example, as a starter for your work, you may wish to incorporate but a tiny portion of an image owned by someone else, altering the image until the original is no longer recognizable. Is this legal? Indeed, how much of the original must you change before the product becomes yours or remains a **derivative work**? There are no simple answers to these tough questions.

Figure 17-1 shows an original photograph taken by Mark Newman, along with some artwork derived from it. Newman sold certain rights to 21st Century Media, which packages and sells assortments of stock photographs on CD-ROM to computer graphics and multimedia developers. The CD-ROM product contains these instructions:

> You may make copies of the digitized images contained on the Product for use in advertisements, public or private presentations, business communications, multimedia presentations, and other uses as long as the images are not used to create a product for sale. For example, you may not use the images to create calendars, posters, greeting cards, or books of image collections for sale. You may not use, in whole or in part, or alter a digitized image in any manner for pornographic use.

Suppose, however, that the image in Figure 17-1 were scanned from the pages of *National Geographic* or *Time*—what then? If you change 51 percent of the pixels, is the image yours? These questions of ownership will undoubtedly be resolved eventually in the courts.

Figure 17-1 The original photograph by Mark Newman was clipped and manipulated for use in a multimedia project. Who owns the resulting image?

> There is a serious issue facing multimedia developers. Now that they have tools to creatively modify things, how much of someone else's image, music, or video clip needs to be modified before ownership changes? This is up for grabs. There is a law called "fair use," which comes into play in a very limited way here. But I think there needs to be a law called "fair modification."
>
> Trip Hawkins, Chairman & CEO, 3DO Company

Use of images, sounds, and other resources from stock houses such as PhotoDisc or Index Stock Photography is perhaps the safest way to go, because ownership and your rights to use the material are clearly stated.

WARNING *Beware of clip media claiming to be public domain (where no copyrights apply) that include sounds from popular television shows or motion pictures.*

Permission must also be obtained to use copyrighted text. Figure 17-2 provides sample language for requesting permission to reprint copyrighted text material and sample terms that you might expect from the copyright owner.

Using Content Created for a Project

In the process of developing your multimedia project, interfaces will be designed, text written, lines of code programmed, and original artwork illustrated with photographs, animations, musical scores, sound effects, and video footage. Each of these elements is an original work. If you are creating a project single-handedly for yourself, you own the copyright outright. If other persons who are not your employees also contribute to the final product, they may own copyright of the element created by them or may share joint ownership of the product unless they assign or license their ownership rights to you. Never rely on a verbal agreement for assignment of rights. You should make it your practice in every project to get all assignments of rights or licensing terms in writing to protect everyone involved. You and your best friend may collaborate on a project today based on a

Typical request to a large publishing company:

Dear Sirs:

I am currently producing a computer-based multimedia presentation with a working title of (Title). My publisher is (Publisher, Publisher's Address). The anticipated completion date of the work is (Month/Year). It will be used for (Use).

This letter is to request your permission to incorporate into this work a brief passage from: (Title, Author, Edition, ISBN, Page).

The text I wish to reproduce is: (Text).

Please process this request at your earliest convenience and use this letter or your own form to return your approval by mail or fax to: (Your Name/Address).

The undersigned, having full authority, hereby grants permission to (Your Name) to copy and reproduce the referenced text for use in the work cited above.

Signed:_____

Typical terms from a large publishing company:

1. To give full credit in every copy printed, on the copyright page or as a footnote on the page on which the quotation begins, or if in a magazine or a newspaper, on the first page of each quotation covered by the permission, exactly as "Reprinted with the permission of (Publisher) from (Title) by (Author). Copyright (Year) by (Publisher)."

2. To pay on publication of the work, or within 24 months of the date of granting the permission, whichever is earlier, a fee of: $_____.

3. To forward one copy of the work and payment on publication to the Permissions Department of (Publisher).

4. To make no deletions from, additions to, or changes in the text, without the written approval of (Publisher).

5. That the permission hereby granted applies only to the edition of the work specified in this agreement.

6. That permission granted herein is nonexclusive and not transferable.

7. That this permission applies, unless otherwise stated, solely to publication of the above-cited work in the English language in the United States, its territories and dependencies and throughout the world. For translation rights, apply to the International Rights Department of (Publisher).

8. That unless the work is published within two years from the date of the applicant's signature (unless extended by written permission of (Publisher)) or, if published, it remains out of print for a period of six months, this permission shall automatically terminate.

9. This permission does not extend to any copyrighted material from other sources which may be incorporated in the books in question, nor to any illustrations or charts, nor to poetry, unless otherwise specified.

10. That the work containing our selection may be reproduced in Braille, large type, and sound recordings provided no charge is made to the visually handicapped.

11. That unless the agreement is signed and returned within six months from the date of issue, the permission shall automatically terminate.

Figure 17-2 Sample permission request and terms from a publisher for use of copyrighted text or images

handshake, but if there is a falling out that results in a dispute over ownership, having the terms in writing will save both of you from an expensive legal battle over who owns what.

The ownership of a project created by employees in the course of their employment belongs solely to the employer if the work fits the requirements of a "work made for hire." To meet the definition of a work made for hire, several factors must be weighed to determine whether the individual is legally an employee or an independent contractor. Among these factors are where the work is done, the relationship between the parties, and who provides the tools and equipment.

If the individual contributing to a project is not an employee, the commissioned work must fall within one of the following "work made for hire" categories: a contribution to a collective work, a work that is part of a motion picture or other audiovisual work, a translation, a supplementary work, a compilation, an instructional text, a test, answer material for a test, or an atlas (1976 Copyright Act, 17 U.S.C. § 201(b)). Even if the work falls within one of these categories, be sure to get an agreement in writing from every individual contributing to the work that it is being created as a work for hire. Figures 17-3 and 17-4 offer sample contracts with employees and contractors to precisely specify ownership issues.

The copyright ownership of works created in whole or in part by persons who fall under the definition of **independent contractor** may belong to that contractor unless the work is specially ordered or commissioned for use and qualifies as a work made for hire, in which case the copyright belongs to the entity commissioning the work.

In late April 1997, Bruce Lehman, Commissioner of Patents and Trademarks, publicly stated that the Proposed Guidelines negotiated by CONFU participants had failed to achieve consensus support. In May 1997, at its third "final" meeting in Washington, D.C., CONFU participants concurred. None of the Proposed Guidelines would survive the comment and endorsement process that ended in May.

[Ninety-three] organizations representing for-profit and nonprofit publishers, the software industry, government agencies, scholars and scholarly societies, authors, artists, photographers and musicians, the movie industry, public television, licensing collectives, libraries, museums, universities and colleges spent untold amounts of money and more than two and a half years of their time and their energy to find agreement on the scope of fair use in various electronic contexts. Now it seems that not enough of their constituents and in some cases, not even the participants themselves, agreed with the result to qualify the Proposed Guidelines as consensus documents. Forgive the overgeneralization, but users thought the Guidelines were over-restrictive, and copyright owners thought they were giving away too much.

From the web site of the Conference on Fair Use, an excellent resource and discussion area for gnarly copyright law issues: http://www.utsystem.edu/ogc/intellectualproperty/confu.htm

---

Partnerships often finish in quarrels; but I was happy in this, that mine were all carried on and ended amicably, owing, I think, a good deal to the precaution of having very explicitly settled, in our articles, everything to be done by or expected from each partner, so that there was nothing to dispute, which precaution I would therefore recommend to all who enter into partnerships; for whatever esteem partners may have for, and confidence in each other at the time of the contract, little jealousies and disgusts may arise, with ideas of inequality in the care and burden of the business, etc., which are attended often with breach of friendship and of the connection, perhaps with lawsuits and other disagreeable consequences.

From the Autobiography of Benjamin Franklin (circa 1784)

PROPRIETARY INFORMATION AND INVENTIONS AGREEMENT

NOTICE:

This agreement does not apply to an invention which qualifies fully under the provisions of Section 2870 of the Labor Code of California as an invention for which no equipment, supplies, facility, or trade secret information of (Company) was used and which was developed entirely on the employee's own time, and (a) which does not relate (1) to the business of (Company) or (2) to (Company's) actual or demonstrably anticipated research or development, or (b) which does not result from any work performed by the employee for (Company).

Employee's Name _____

Address _____

Date of Hire _____

In consideration of my employment by (Company) or any of its subsidiary or affiliated companies (all called "the Company") and the compensation paid me by the Company, I agree as follows:

1. I understand that my employment results in a confidential relationship between myself and the Company. It is expected that I will receive, during and for purposes of my employment, information about the Company's products, processes, business, plans, research programs, and like Company information (all called "the Company business"), which information is the property of the Company. I may also conceive of or develop ideas and inventions related to the Company business during or for purposes of my employment. The information received from the Company and information which I conceive or develop pertaining to the Company business are the sole property of the Company and are valuable trade secrets of the Company. I agree to preserve their value as Company property, by complying with the following requirements.

2. Except as required in the course of my employment, I shall not disclose to anyone or use at any time, either during or after my employment, any information about the Company business which is either received from the Company or conceived or developed by me, unless I have the prior written consent of the Company.

3. I agree to disclose promptly to the Company all inventions, ideas or conceptions, developments, and improvements (whether or not patentable or subject to copyright) which are made or conceived by me, either alone or together with others, during or as a result of my employment, provided that they pertain to the Company business. I will keep complete records of such matter and will and hereby do assign such matter to the Company, whether or not it has been tested or reduced to practice. Included are all data processing communications, computer software systems, programs, and procedures, which pertain to the Company business. All such records are and shall be the property of the Company alone.

4. Upon request of the Company, either during or after my employment, I will assist in applying for Letters Patent, or for copyright or Inventors Certificate or other appropriate legal form, on all such Inventions and Ideas, in this and in foreign countries, and will execute all papers necessary thereto, including assignments as may be requested by the Company, without further compensation to me. Such applications shall be filed at the expense of and under the control of the Company.

5. All unpublished data and information relating to the Company business, whether reduced to writing or not, are understood and agreed to be confidential and the sole property of the Company. This extends to all confidential information or data I may receive from or about any of the Company's licensees, customers, or others with whom the Company has a business relationship. I will maintain all such information in confidence and not use it other than as expressly requested by the Company, either during or after my employment with the Company, unless and until such information is published without fault on my part.

6. Upon termination of my employment, I will surrender all records and material relating to the Company business.

7. I am aware of no prior obligations which would prevent my compliance with the terms and spirit of this agreement.

8. This agreement shall be binding upon me and my heirs, executors, administrators, and assigns. The Company shall have the right to assign this agreement to any successor to the business in which I am employed.

Signed at _____ , on _____, 20__

Employee (Signature)

Witness (Signature)

(Address of Witness)

Figure 17-3
Sample employer/ employee agreement covering intellectual property and inventions; consult an attorney when preparing your own legal document.

Confidential

(Date)

(Name and Address of Consultant)

Dear (Consultant):

This document, when accepted and agreed to by you, will confirm our mutual understanding and agreement concerning your engagement as an independent contractor to render consulting services to (Employer Name).

You will be engaged as an independent contractor to provide such advice, consultation, and other assistance as may, from time to time, be requested by (Employer Name) in furtherance of (Employer Name)'s business in general and particularly for:

(General Statement of Scope of Work)

During the term of this Consulting Agreement, you agree to provide consulting services to (Employer Name), on the terms and conditions contained in Attachment A, "Description of Services and Reimbursement." Twice monthly you will submit a statement, in a form satisfactory to (Employer Name), setting forth the milestone reached and any authorized expenses incurred to be reimbursed by (Employer Name). Payment will be made according to the schedule in Attachment A.

The consulting services that you will provide are to be rendered at such times and at such places as are mutually agreed upon by (Employer Name) and you. You agree that (Employer Name) shall own all intellectual property rights, including but not limited to copyrights, patents, trade secrets, and trademarks in any and all products of your work within the scope of this Agreement. Said products will be copyrighted by (Employer Name) or in such other name as (Employer Name) may designate. You further agree that any work provided hereunder shall be considered "work made for hire" within the meaning of 17 U.S.C. 2201(b). However, (Employer Name) will give proper credit to you in a manner to be mutually agreed upon as appropriate to the creative direction of the work.

In the performance of the consulting services herein contemplated, you are, and shall be deemed to be for all purposes, an independent contractor (and not an employee or agent of (Employer Name)) under any and all laws, whether existing or future, including without limitation, Social Security laws, state unemployment insurance laws, withholding tax laws, and the payments and reports of any taxes and/or contributions under such laws. You will not be entitled to participate in any employee benefits accruing to employees of (Employer Name). You will not be authorized to make any material representation, contract, or commitment on behalf of (Employer Name).

You agree to comply with applicable laws, rules, and regulations in respect to self-employment, including without limitation, the payment of all taxes required, and you agree to furnish (Employer Name) evidence of the payment of such taxes if requested. In addition, you agree to defend, indemnify, and hold (Employer Name) harmless against all losses, liabilities, claims, demands, actions and/or proceedings, and all costs and expenses in connection therewith, including attorney's fees, arising out of your failure to comply with this paragraph.

The term of this Consulting Agreement shall be for the period of time described in Attachment A, subject to the following limitations:

Upon five (5) days written notice, either you or (Employer Name) may terminate this Consulting Agreement. Such termination shall be effective at the conclusion of said five-day period.

This Consulting Agreement shall terminate on your death.

Notwithstanding anything herein to the contrary, (Employer Name) may, without liability, terminate this Consulting Agreement for cause at any time, and without notice, and thereafter (Employer Name)'s obligations hereunder shall cease and terminate. The term "cause" shall mean, by way of example, but not by way of limitation:

Misappropriating funds or property of (Employer Name);

Attempting to obtain any personal profit from any transaction related to THIS consulting work which is adverse to the interest of (Employer Name);

Unreasonable neglect or refusal to perform the consulting services agreed to be performed by you under this Consulting Agreement;

Being convicted of a felony;

Being adjudicated a bankrupt; or

A breach of any of the other provisions of this Consulting Agreement.

Figure 17-4
Sample employer/consultant agreement in the form of a letter; hire an attorney when preparing your own legal documents.

Upon termination of this Consulting Agreement, for any reason, you will be paid your consulting fee on a pro rata basis, and you will be reimbursed for authorized expenses, to and including the effective date of such termination.

You agree to hold all Confidential Information in trust and confidence for (Employer Name), and except as may be authorized by (Employer Name) in writing, you shall not disclose to any person, and you shall take such reasonable precautions as may be necessary to prevent the disclosure of, any Confidential Information at all times during and after the term of this Consulting Agreement. For the purposes of this Consulting Agreement, "Confidential Information" shall mean all information obtained by you, or disclosed to you by (Employer Name), at any time before or during the term hereof, which relates to (Employer Name)'s or (Employer Name)'s clients' past, present, and future research, development, and business activities, and any other trade secrets, records, engineering notebooks, data, formulae, computer code, specifications, inventions, customer lists, and other proprietary information and data concerning (Employer Name) or any client, provided that Confidential Information shall not include information that becomes part of the public knowledge or literature (not as a result of any action or inaction on your part) either prior or subsequent to your receipt of such information.

Upon termination or expiration of this Consulting Agreement, you agree to return to (Employer Name) all written or descriptive matter, including but not limited to drawings, blueprints, descriptions, drafts, computer code, computer files, hardware, software, or other papers or documents that contain any Confidential Information.

(Employer Name) does not desire to receive information in confidence from you under this Consulting Agreement.

You represent and warrant that you are under no obligation or restriction nor will you assume any obligation or restriction which would in any way interfere or be inconsistent with the services to be furnished by you under this Consulting Agreement. In that regard, this Consulting Agreement will in no way restrict you from freely entering into other similar consulting agreements with other firms in the field as long as the provisions herein are honored.

(Employer Name) shall have sole discretion to make other consulting arrangements with other persons concerning any or all of the consulting services to be rendered by you under this Consulting Agreement.

(Employer Name) acknowledges and understands that he is the author of the work you are hired to consult on and that he is therefore responsible for its contents. In the event of a third party action against (Employer Name), (Employer Name) agrees to indemnify and hold you harmless if you are made a party to such action; provided however that (Employer Name) shall have no such responsibility to you if such suit arises due to your misconduct or gross negligence. You promise to provide (Employer Name) with all reasonable cooperation and assistance in any such action or proceedings.

If any action at law is necessary to enforce or interpret the terms of this Consulting Agreement, the prevailing party shall be entitled to reasonable attorneys' fees, costs, and necessary disbursements, in addition to any other relief to which such party shall be entitled.

This letter shall constitute the entire agreement between the parties hereto with respect to the subject matter hereof. In the event of any unresolved dispute in respect thereof, the matter shall be submitted to arbitration in accordance with the rules and regulations of the American Arbitration Association, and the decision of the arbitrator(s) shall be final and binding on both parties hereto.

The validity of this Consulting Agreement and any of its terms and conditions, as well as the rights and duties of the parties hereunder, shall be interpreted and construed pursuant to and in accordance with the laws of the State of California.

(Employer Name)

(Employer Signature)

Accepted and agreed to this _____ day of _____, 20__.

Consultant's Signature: _____

Consultant's Social Security Number or EIN: _____

Attachment A to the Consulting Agreement of (Date)

between (Employer Name) and (Consultant)

Description of Services and Reimbursement

Figure 17-4
Sample employer/consultant agreement in the form of a letter; hire an attorney when preparing your own legal documents. *(Continued)*

A copyright can belong to a single individual or entity, or it may be shared jointly by several entities. Make sure that copyright ownership issues have been resolved, in writing, before people contribute to your project.

Using Talent

After you have tested everybody you know and you still have vacant seats in your project, you may need to turn to professional talent. Getting the perfect actor, model, or narrator's voice is critical. You don't want to settle for a voice or an actor who is not quite polished or is ill suited to the part, or your whole project may have an amateurish feel.

Professional voice-over talents and actors in the United States usually belong to a union or guild, either **AFTRA (American Federation of Television and Radio Artists)** or **SAG (Screen Actors Guild)**. They are usually represented by a talent agent or agency that you can find in the yellow pages.

First Person

We put out a call for a multimedia acting job (male, mid-30s, credible voice, earnest smile), and 18 men showed up for tryouts at a local studio—17 were nonunion and 1 belonged to AFTRA. We videotaped each applicant as he read a prepared script, chatted with all of them, and asked them to walk around and jump up and down. The best choice by far, we thought at the end of a long day, was Dave Kazanjian, the union member.

"Oooh," we said to ourselves, "real union talent! This is going to cost us." So we got together with the client and ran tapes of half a dozen of the better actors trying out, without saying which one was our favorite. The client's choice was the same as ours, because Dave was very polished and professional and simply perfect for the part. Paying union-scale wages to the actor would double what we had estimated in our original budget, and we had naively assumed we could quickly and easily find the right talent from the nonunion pool. We ran the new numbers past the client, implying that the second-choice actor was more affordable, even if he wasn't quite perfect. Then we showed Dave's clip next to the other guy, and repeated it a few times, until the difference was really apparent. The comparison was persuasive, and in the end, the client supported the extra cost.

We all learned again that you get what you pay for: Dave did a terrific job. In future proposals, we used union scale in estimating cost, whether we hired a union actor or not.

Locating the Professionals You Need

Before you can safely put a professional in front of a camera or a microphone, you have to find the talent first and then deal with hiring and union contracts.

Begin by calling a **talent agency** and explain what you need. The agency will probably suggest several clients who might fit your needs and send you a collection of videotapes or cassettes as samples of the actors' work. After reviewing the tapes, you can arrange **auditions** of the best candidates, at your office or at a studio. You can also get in touch with several agencies and put out a **casting call** for screen or audio auditions. Furthermore, you are not limited to using union talent, and if your call is posted on bulletin boards in public places (in the theater department of a local university, for example), you may find yourself with many applicants, both union and nonunion, who are eager for the work.

If you run your own audition, be sure you are organized for it. You will need sign-up sheets for names and phone numbers, a sample script for applicants to read, a video camera or tape recorder, tracking sheets so you can coordinate actors' names with their video or audio clips, and hospitable coffee and donuts.

Working with Union Contracts

The two unions, AFTRA and SAG, have similar contracts and terms for minimum pay and benefits. AFTRA has approved an Interactive Media Agreement to cover on- and off-camera performers on all interactive media platforms. Figure 17-5 shows some AFTRA definitions related to interactive media.

DEFINITIONS

"Material": includes all products (audio or visual) derived from the recordation of the live-action performances of performers, whether or not such performances are incorporated into the final version of the fully-edited Interactive Program produced hereunder by Producer.

"Interactive": Interactive describes the attribute of products which enables the viewer to manipulate, affect or alter the presentation of the creative content of such product simultaneous with its use by the viewer.

"Interactive Media" means: any media on which interactive product operates and through which the user may interact with such product including but not limited to personal computers, games, machines, arcade games, all CD-interactive machines and any and all analogous, similar or dissimilar microprocessor-based units and the digitized, electronic or any other formats now known or hereinafter invented which may be utilized in connection therewith;

"Performers": Persons whose performances are used as on or off-camera, including those who speak, act, sing, or in any other manner perform as talent in material for Interactive Media.

Figure 17-5 From the AFTRA Interactive Media Agreement (reprinted courtesy of AFTRA, 260 Madison Avenue, New York, NY 10016)

The AFTRA and SAG contracts are lengthy and detailed. Both share language and job descriptions (such as principal, voice-over performer, extra, singer, and dancer). Also, both unions have approximately the same wage scales for these jobs. Table 17-1 shows the Screen Actors Guild categories for interactive media work and rates. Of course, an actor can always negotiate more than minimum wage.

	7/29/05	1/1/06	1/1/07	1/1/08
On-Camera Performers:				
Day Performers (including solo/duo singers)	$695.00	$716.00	$737.00	$759.00
	(+25%)	(+3%)	(+3%)	(+3%)
3-Day Performers (including solo/duo singers)	$1,757.00	$1,810.00	$1,864.00	$1,920.00
Weekly Performers (including solo/duo singers)	$2,411.00	$2,483.00	$2,557.00	$2,634.00
6 Day Overnight Location	$2,652.00	$2,731.00	$2,813.00	$2,897.00
Group Singers 3–8 (4-hour day)	$659.00	$679.00	$699.00	$720.00
Group Singers 9+ (4-hour day)	$575.00	$592.00	$610.00	$628.00
Dancers				
Rehearsal Days Only	$408.00	$420.00	$433.00	$446.00
Work Days (no rehearsal)				
Solo/Duo	$695.00	$716.00	$737.00	$759.00
Group 3–8	$609.00	$627.00	$646.00	$665.00
Group 9+	$532.00	$548.00	$564.00	$581.00
Weekly Option (includes rehearsals)				
Solo/Duo	$2,233.00	$2,300.00	$2,369.00	$2,440.00
Group 3-8	$2,047.00	$2,108.00	$2,171.00	$2,236.00
Group 9+	$1,861.00	$1,917.00	$1,975.00	$2,034.00
Off-Camera Performers:				
Day Performers (up to 3 voices/4-hour day)	$695.00	$716.00	$737.00	$759.00
Additional Voices (one-third of Day Performer rate for each voice)	$231.70	$238.70	$245.70	$253.00
Day Performer (1 voice/1 hour)	$347.50	$358.00	$368.50	$379.50
Engaged for 6 to 10 Voices for a 6-hour day	$1,390.00	$1,432.00	$1,474.00	$1,518.00
Singers (4-hour day)				
Solo/Duo	$695.00	$716.00	$737.00	$759.00
Hourly Rate	$347.50	$358.00	$368.50	$379.50
Group Singers 3–8	$368.00	$379.00	$391.00	$402.00
Group Singers 9+	$319.00	$329.00	$338.00	$349.00
Group Hourly Rate	$206.00	$212.00	$218.00	$225.00
Background Actor Rates:				
General Background Actor	$118.00	$122.00	$126.00	$130.00
Special Ability Actors and Stand-ins	$142.00	$146.00	$150.00	$163.00
SAG Pension and Health Contribution rate: 14.3%				

Table 17-1 From the Screen Actors Guild, Interactive Media Rates through 2008

If your talent needs are simple, you can usually get good contract advice directly from the union representative in your area or from the actors themselves. If your needs are elaborate or undefined, you may wish to consult an attorney or agent who specializes in this area and who can oversee the many required clauses and details of the contract.

Talent contracts are filled with quirky details and complicated formulas. Consider, for example, Article I.17.A.4(c)(i) of the AFTRA Interactive Media Agreement, which reads:

> If a solo or duo is called upon to step out of a group to sing up to fifteen (15) cumulative bars during a session, the solo/duo shall be paid an adjustment of fifty percent (50%) of the solo/duo rate in addition to the appropriate group rate for that day.

Although the concept of "stepping out" may be more in keeping with an MTV video project than with your own multimedia work, you need to keep an eye out for buried clauses that do apply to your project.

WARNING *If you create a multimedia product that incorporates union talent under contract, you will be restricted to using the material only for its initial primary use. Later, if you wish to spin off bits and pieces for other purposes (such as a commercial or as part of a product for sale to the public), you must then renegotiate with the talent and the union and pay for this expanded and supplemental use.*

Acquiring Releases

A union talent contract explicitly states what rights you have to the still and motion images and voices you make and use. If, however, your talent is non-union (a co-worker, perhaps, or a neighbor's child, student actor, waitress, or tugboat captain), be sure to require the person to sign a **release form**. This form grants to you certain permissions and specifies the terms under which you can use the material you make during a recording session.

Figure 17-6 is a sample release form that covers most situations in a multimedia project and provides nearly perfect rights to the producer. Because such forms are legal documents, always consult an attorney to be sure that the specific language of your own release document meets your requirements. For more about video and music releases and sample forms, check out http://www.current.tv/make/resources.

WARNING *Do not include any images or voices of people in your multimedia project—even if you yourself recorded and edited the material—unless you have their written consent to use it; it is in the public domain; you are reporting it as news, commentary, or parody (fair use); or it is work unarguably made for hire.*

Sometimes it is very difficult to do certain things because of previous rights that have been given out. For example, not too long ago I asked an executive from a media company if it would be possible to take some of his film footage and put it into a copyright library, to have something available for multimedia software developers to freely use in their interactive products? He said, "Well, we couldn't use a single frame of any film that was ever shot by a director who was a member of the Directors Guild of America." The bottom line is that there are so many rights attached to so many of these things, with so many different people involved, that it is very complicated even to figure out if you have the right to use it in any way, and again that's too bad because again, that is just going to slow us down.

Trip Hawkins, Chairman & CEO, 3DO Company

Release Form

This is a release and authorization to use the name, voice, sounds, image and likeness, and writings of the undersigned ("Model"), as obtained in the photography / filming / video / audio session / creative session taking place

_____ at, _____ ("the Session"), for commercial purposes by _____ and his respective successors and assigns (collectively, "Producer").

For valuable consideration, Model hereby authorizes the unlimited use in perpetuity by Producer of all recorded images, likenesses, voice and recorded sounds, and writings of Model obtained during the Session, and of Model's name in connection with such use. Model grants producer the rights to use such sounds, images, and likenesses in any and all media and forms now known or hereafter devised throughout the universe without limitation as to territory or term, including but not limited to advertising, literature, computer demonstrations, and packaging, whether in the form of photography, magnetic or electronic data storage, or any other form, both as obtained and as modified at Producer's sole discretion to suit business purposes of Producer. The compensation stated above shall be the sole compensation for all such use, and no further compensation, including but not limited to royalties, residuals, or use fees, shall be payable at any time.

Model further transfers and assigns all copyrights and all other rights in the recordings, sounds, images and likeness, and writings obtained at the Session to Producer. Producer shall have the right to register the copyright to these in the name of its choice and shall have the exclusive right to dispose of these in any manner whatsoever. This agreement constitutes the sole, complete, and exclusive agreement between Model and Producer.

Name:_____SIGNATURE: _____

Address:_____SOCIAL SECURITY NO.: _____

_____DATE: _____

Phone:_____

Figure 17-6 Sample release form; consult an attorney when preparing your own legal document

Chapter 17 Review

■ Chapter Summary

For your review, here's a summary of the important concepts discussed in this chapter.

Describe what content is, what production values are, and how to consider what a project's production values should be

■ Content is the information and material that forms the heart of your project—or what your project is about. Content can have both low and high production value. You must always balance the production value of your project against your budget and the desired result.

■ Content acquisition can be one of the most expensive and time-consuming tasks in organizing a multimedia project. Be sure to specify in your project plan the format and quality of content and data to be supplied to you by third parties. If you negotiate ownership or rights to someone else's content, be sure to get the advice of a skilled copyright and contracts attorney.

Identify the benefits and drawbacks of various sources of content such as clip art, stock libraries, and public domain sources

■ Preexisting content can come from a variety of sources. Clip art collections of photographs, graphics, sounds, music, animation, and video are relatively inexpensive, and you are generally granted unlimited use. If your content needs are more specific or complex, a still photo library, a sound library, or a stock footage house is a good choice.

Discuss the concepts of copyright, public domain, licensing, and derivative works

■ Some materials are in the public domain, meaning you can use the material without a license. But never *assume* a work is in the public domain, even if it bears no copyright notice.

■ Always make sure you have permission to use copyrighted material, or you may find yourself being sued for copyright infringement. Works come under copyright protection as soon as they are created and presented in a fixed form. Owning a copy of a work does not automatically entitle you to reproduce the work. If the owner does not wish to give up or sell ownership rights, however, you may still be able to license the rights to use that material.

Determine to whom a work is copyrighted, depending on who contracted the work and for what purpose

■ Negotiating rights to use preexisting content involves many factors. In some cases you can use materials "derived" from another work, but this is a gray area of copyright law.

■ In general, you own the copyright of works you create for yourself. You also own the copyright of works created by those whom you employ for the purpose of creating the work. If the contributor is not an employee, the work is not "work made for hire," and he or she has not assigned ownership to you, then that contributor holds the copyright for the work.

Discuss the process for identifying the appropriate talent for the production, including unions, contracts, and releases

■ Getting the perfect actor, model, or narrator's voice is critical. Professional talents and actors in the United States often belong to AFTRA or SAG and are represented by a talent agent or agency. The agency will probably suggest several clients who might fit your needs. Arrange auditions of the best candidates.

■ Check out talent contracts carefully, and think about any limitations on future use. If your talent is nonunion, be sure to have the person sign a release form.

Key Terms

AFTRA (American Federation of Television and Radio Artists) *(457)*

auditions *(458)*

casting call *(458)*

clip art *(445)*

content *(442)*

content acquisition *(443)*

copyright infringement *(447)*

copyright ownership *(447)*

copyright protection *(447)*

derivative work *(450)*

electronic rights *(444)*

fair use *(447)*

independent contractor *(453)*

license *(449)*

licensing agreements *(449)*

production value *(442)*

public domain *(445)*

rate card *(449)*

release form *(460)*

royalty *(445)*

SAG (Screen Actors Guild) *(457)*

sound library *(445)*

still photo library *(445)*

stock footage *(445)*

talent agency *(457)*

unlimited use *(449)*

Key Term Quiz

1. The information and material that forms the heart of your project—what your project is about—is _____.

2. Collections of media generally granted unlimited use are called _____.

3. If a work's copyright protection has expired and not been renewed, it is _____.

4. The term for unauthorized use of copyrighted material is _____.

5. Works come under _____ as soon as they are created and presented in a fixed form.

6. Even if the owner of a work does not wish to give up or sell ownership rights, you may still be able to _____ the rights to use that material.

7. A standard document that lists licensing fees for different uses, formats, and markets is called a _____.

8. If an artist takes another person's work and creates a new work based on the original, such a work is said to be _____.

9. Professional talents and actors in the United States are usually represented by a _____.

10. If your talent is nonunion, be sure to require the person to sign a _____.

Multiple Choice Quiz

1. Which of the following is not content?
    a. photographs
    b. animations
    c. video clips
    d. the graphical user interface
    e. the program's programming code

2. The responsibility for ensuring that content included in a product does not infringe on a copyright belongs to:
    a. the developer
    b. the original creator
    c. the product's purchaser
    d. the U.S. Copyright Office
    e. The Library of Congress

3. A source for free content in the public domain is:
    a. a clip art collection
    b. a stock photo/video library
    c. a government agency
    d. a publishing company
    e. a television network

4. The legal privilege to publish a work in a computer-based storage and delivery medium is often called:
    a. digital watermarks
    b. electronic rights
    c. computer publishing licenses
    d. new media contracts
    e. multimedia/Internet ownership

5. A disadvantage to using a clip art image from a stock library might be:
    a. it is available in high-resolution
    b. you are usually granted unlimited use
    c. you can alter the image for derivative works
    d. it is easily downloadable
    e. you do not have exclusive rights

6. If a work is in the public domain:
    a. you can secure a free license through the Public Domain Institute (PDI)
    b. you can license it with a $25 processing fee through the Library of Congress
    c. you can use the material without a license or permission
    d. you can use the material through the public domain contract, where some percentage of the profit is disbursed to nonprofit arts organizations
    e. it is publicly owned and thus cannot be reproduced for any purpose

7. Which of the following issues might you consider when negotiating for rights to use preexisting content?
    a. how the content will be delivered
    b. the license's period of time
    c. how the owner or artist will be credited
    d. whether the copyright owner will receive remuneration for the license
    e. all of the above

8. Works come under copyright protection:
    a. as soon as they have been submitted to the U.S. Copyright Office
    b. as soon as a notice is published in the legal notices of a local newspaper
    c. as soon as they are notarized by a notary public
    d. as soon as they are created and presented in a fixed form
    e. as soon as the original idea, concept, drawing, draft, or intent is communicated to someone else

9. Owning a work entitles you to reproduce that work if:
   a. you have purchased the work and possess a legal bill of sale
   b. you have the permission of the copyright owner
   c. the work is an original, unreproduced work that has not been previously copied
   d. the work's value is less than $100
   e. you have a *really* good lawyer

10. Which of the following are included in the guidelines for creating a work derived in part from another person's work?
    a. There are no clear-cut guidelines.
    b. Less than 10 percent of the original work was used.
    c. Using the work does not impact the sales or value of the original work.
    d. The derivative work is not clearly recognizable as the original work.
    e. The derivative work is in a different medium from the original.

11. In general, you may legally use a work in a project if:
    a. it has a digital approval code
    b. you paid someone to create it for you
    c. the work contains no copyright information
    d. it came from the school library
    e. you got it off the Internet

12. Which of the following unions deals with acting and talent?
    a. AFTRA
    b. IBEW
    c. AFL-CIO
    d. AFSCME
    e. CIA

13. In general, if you create a multimedia product that incorporates union talent under contract, you:
    a. will have unlimited rights across all media
    b. can use the material only in related media (such as Web/CD, newspaper/magazine, television/radio)
    c. will be required to pay royalties
    d. will have rights to the talent's firstborn children
    e. will be able to use the material only for its initial primary use

14. If you use nonunion talent, you:
    a. probably don't need to worry about getting a release
    b. should require the person to sign a release form
    c. need to notify the local union representative
    d. must state so plainly in the project's credits
    e. must pay a surcharge to the local union

15. You do not need to worry about having someone's written consent to use his or her image or voice in your production if:
    a. it was already used in the *National Enquirer*
    b. the subject is at least a first cousin
    c. it is work product made for hire
    d. the subject is younger than 18 years old
    e. you are recording a public event

■ Essay Quiz

1. List ten different kinds of content. Try to think of as many different variations as you can. List a high production value and low production value example of each.

2. You are assigned to create a CD-ROM on white-water rafting for a company in West Virginia. The product is going to be sent to subscribers of *Outside* magazine. This magazine's readership has a high level of disposable income. Discuss the creative process you might go through to determine the content you will use in this project. Where will you get it? Will you use clip art? Public domain content? Will you produce new materials? What will the production values be? How will you justify the expense? What are the production values on the project? What talent will you need for the project? Discuss how you will select the talent (on-screen versus voice-over, age, sex, ethnicity, etc.).

3. You are assigned to create a web site for a town's nonprofit historical society. Discuss the creative process you might go through to determine the content you will use in this project. Where will you get it? Will you use clip art? Public domain content? Will you produce new materials? What will the production values be? How will you justify the expense? What are the production values on the project?

4. List five issues related to the rights to license and use someone else's work. Discuss how these issues affect the scope of your project. Will they affect the number of units you may distribute or where, when, and how you may distribute your project? Discuss the advantages and problems associated with hiring union, non-union, and nonprofessional talent for a production. What factors would affect this decision?

Lab Projects

■ Project 17.1

Go online and locate three stock photo and video sources. Download comps of a photograph and a video clip from each of the sources. (Comps are small, low-resolution copies of the work that can be used for placement and testing.) Compare the cost, quality, and range of the offerings.

■ Project 17.2

Go online and locate three royalty-free music sources. Download two samples from each of the sources. Compare the cost, quality, and range of the offerings.

■ Project 17.3

Based on the research you did on the stock photo/video and royalty-free sources, estimate the total cost for content to develop a promotional presentation for a client. Assume you will use three 30-second video clips at about 320×240-pixel size, ten stock photographs at about 800×600 at 72 dpi resolution, and one approximately three-minute audio clip to loop as background music. What are the high and low ranges for these projects?

■ Project 17.4

Contact a creative services agency or talent agency and ask to see the sourcebook. Most large markets have at least one creative sourcebook. These sourcebooks, among other things, often include a number of head shots, or pages with the face and vital statistics for agency talent in the area. Such sourcebooks also include illustrators, photographers, and other creative artists. Select a person to act as a spokesperson, as well as an illustrator, for a CD-ROM project. Photocopy the pages you select from the sourcebook. Justify your decision.

■ Project 17.5

Look at the credits of three CD-ROMs. Copy the wording used in crediting various contributors. Look at several different web sites. Do they list credits? Why or why not?

Delivering

TEST IT—and then test it again; that's the unavoidable rule. You must test and review your project or web site to ensure that it is bug free, accurate, operationally and visually on target, and that the client's requirements have been met, even if that client is you.

Do this before the work is finalized and released for public or client consumption. A bad reputation earned by premature product release can destroy an otherwise excellent piece of work representing thousands of hours of effort. If you need to, delay the release of the work to be sure that it is as good as possible. It's critical that you take the time to thoroughly exercise your project and fix both big and little problems; in the end, you will save yourself a great deal of agony!

One of the major difficulties you face in testing the operation of your multimedia project is that its performance depends on specific hardware and system configurations and, in the case of the Internet, on end users' connection speeds. If you cannot control the end user's platform, or if the project is designed to be shown in many different environments, you must fully test your project on as many platforms as possible, including heavily loaded, complicated systems.

WARNING *Remember to budget for obtaining the hardware test platforms, as well as for the many hours of effort that testing will require.*

Few computer configurations are identical. Even identical hardware configurations may be running dissimilar software that can interact with your program in unexpected ways. The Macintosh environment is well known for its sensitivity to certain **extensions** (drivers and other parts of system software) that conflict with some software applications.

Windows uses its registry database to store configuration information and settings, and still uses the WIN.INI and SYS.INI files to hold custom information that may be different for each installation. If your project depends on the Windows Multimedia Extensions, you will discover a great variety of options and implementations. If your project depends on QuickTime and will be delivered for Windows platforms, you will need to be sure that the end user can install QuickTime from your CD or can download the QuickTime plug-in for use with a web browser.

TIP *If you are working for a client, clearly specify the intended delivery platform as well as its hardware and software configuration, and provide a clause in your agreement or contract that you will test only to that platform.*

Because any element of a computer's configuration may be the cause of a problem or a bug, you will spend a good portion of testing time configuring platforms, and additional time reproducing reported problems and curing them. It is not possible for even a well-equipped developer to test every possible configuration of computer, software, and third-party add-on boards. With this in mind, Apple Computer, for example, has an elaborate testing facility at its corporate offices in Cupertino, California, complete with all of Apple's computer models and most variations of hardware and software, which are made available to developers.

WARNING   *Not everyone can test software. It takes a special personality to slog through this process. Every feature and function must be exercised, every button clicked. Then the same tests must be repeated again and again with different hardware and under various conditions.*

Testing

The terms alpha and beta are used by software developers to describe levels of product development when testing is done and feedback is sought. **Alpha releases** are typically for internal circulation only and are passed among a select group of mock users—often just the team working on the project. These versions of a product are often the first working drafts of your project, and you can expect them to have problems or to be incomplete. **Beta releases**, on the other hand, are sent to a wider but still select audience with the same caveat: this software may contain errors, bugs, and unknown alligators that slither out of the swamp at day's end to bite startled designers from behind. Because your product is now being shown and used outside the privacy of its birth nest, its reputation will begin to take form during beta phase. Thankfully though, beta-level bugs are typically less virulent than alpha bugs.

Alpha Testing

You should remain flexible and amenable to changes in both the design and the behavior of your project as you review the comments of your alpha testers. Beware of alpha testing groups made up of kindly friends who can provide positive criticism. Rather, you need to include aggressive people who will attack all aspects of your work. The meaner and nastier they are, the more likely they will sweat out errors or uncertainties in your product's design or navigation system. In the testing arena, learn to skillfully utilize

From a letter with enclosed disk, delivered by overnight courier to 240 testers around the world:

We had a bit of a scare on this Beta. Here is the replacement copy for the infected B5 program disk. For your info, the virus that got past me was a strain of nVir. It was dormant and fooled Virus Detective, Virex, and Interferon. Virex 1.1 listed it as a harmless "Stub" that was left over from a previous cleanup. It wasn't until late yesterday that we discovered that it was real. I must apologize for letting this slip past me and thank the people in our tech support department for their help in calling all the members of the Beta test team and alerting them to this problem. If they didn't get hold of you, it was certainly not for lack of trying.

Ben Calica, letter author and a product manager who claims this product shortened his life span by two years.

friend and enemy alike. You will undoubtedly discover aspects of your work that, despite even the most insightful planning, you have overlooked.

Beta Testing

The beta testing group should be representative of real users and should not include persons who have been involved in the project's production. Beta testers must have no preconceived ideas. You want them to provide commentary and reports in exchange for getting to play with the latest software and for recognition as part of this "inside" process.

Managing beta test feedback is critical. If you ignore or overlook testers' comments, the testing effort is a waste. Ask your beta testers to include a detailed description of the hardware and software configuration at the time the problem occurred, and a step-by-step recounting of the problem, so that you can recreate it, analyze it, and repair it. You should also solicit general comments and suggestions. Figure 18-1 presents the search page from a web-based bug reporting system that is database driven and capable of managing thousands of reports about a complicated application in a meaningful way. (Apache is the most widely used HTTP daemon for serving web pages.)

Polishing to Gold

As you move through alpha and beta testing, and then through the debugging process toward a final release, you may want to use terms that indicate the current version status of your project. For example, **bronze** when you are close to being finished, gold when you have determined there is nothing left to change or correct and are ready to reproduce copies from your **golden master**. Some software developers also use the term **release candidate** (with a version number) as they continue to refine the product and approach a golden master. Going gold, or announcing that the job is finished, and then shipping, can be a scary thing. Indeed, if you examine the file creation time and date for many software programs, you will discover that many went gold at two o'clock in the morning.

Preparing for Delivery

If your completed multimedia project will be delivered to consumers or to a client who will install the project on many computers, you will need to prepare your files so they can be easily transferred from your media to the user's platform. Simply copying a project's files to the user's hard disk is often not enough for proper installation; frequently, you will also need to install special system and run-time files.

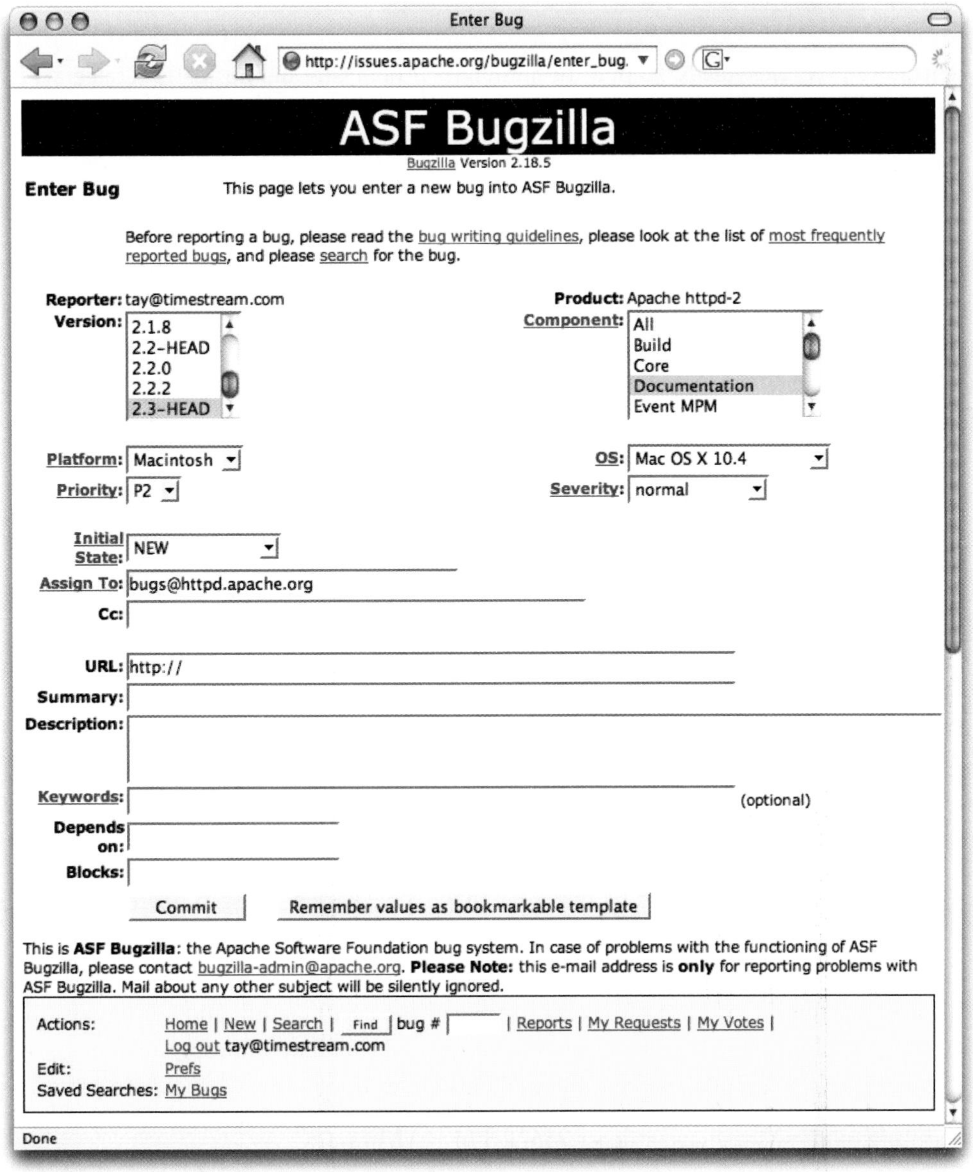

Figure 18-1 This page from a web-based bug reporting system seeks precise and reproducible descriptions of problems. In testing complex applications, thousands of bug reports may be received, and a dedicated quality control team may be tasked to deal with them.

So that end users can easily and automatically set up your project or application on their own computers, you may need to provide a single program that acts as an **installer**.

WARNING *The task of writing a proper installation routine is not a trivial one. Be sure you set aside adequate time in your schedule and money in your programming budget for writing and testing the installation program for your project platforms.*

First Person

We beat on the bronze version of the program right up to the last day, when we had to send a golden master to the duplicator by overnight courier. They were prepared to make 40,000 disks in a matter of hours and then hand-carry them directly to a trade show.

Like kids with sticks at a piñata birthday party, we did everything we could to make all the bugs tumble out of the program. Every time a bug appeared, we killed it. As we pounded and tested, fewer and fewer bugs fell out, until none appeared for about six hours straight, under every condition we could dream up. As the deadline for the courier's airport facility neared,

we were ready to apply the finishing touches to the product and stamp it gold. One of the guys waited in his car with engine running, ready for the sprint through commuter traffic to the airport.

We were saving the program every three minutes and nervously backing it up on different media about every ten minutes. We had built in a hidden software routine for debugging this project, and when the product manager clicked Save for the last time, he forgot to reset the program for normal use—we didn't know the master was flawed. Handling the disk like a uranium fuel rod traveling through heavy water, we packed it up and got it to the waiting car. An

hour later, our postpartum celebration was interrupted by a painful cry from down the hall—someone had discovered the flaw. By then the courier flight had departed.

We fixed it. Faced with the appalling possibility of 40,000 bad disks being invoiced to us instead of the client, we sent the exhausted product manager out on the midnight flight, without a chance even to go home and clean up. He had a golden master disk in his briefcase, one in his shirt pocket, one in his pants pocket, and one in a manila envelope that would never see an airport X-ray machine.

It is important to provide well-written documentation about the installation process so that users have a clear step-by-step procedure to follow. That documentation must include a discussion of potential problems and constraints related to the full range of your target platforms. Because you likely will not have control over the specification and configuration of the user's platform, it is critical that you include appropriate warnings in your installation document, like these examples:

- Must have at least 256MB of RAM
- Will not run unless QuickTime is installed
- 3MB available disk drive space
- Disable all screen savers before running
- Back up older versions before installing this update

Often a file named **README.TXT** or **ReadMeFirst** is a useful thing to include on the distribution disk of your project. This file can be a simple ASCII text file accessible by any text editor or word processing application. It should contain a description of changes or bugs reported since the documentation was printed and may also contain a detailed description of the installation process.

The clearer and more detailed your installation instructions are, the fewer frustrated queries you will receive from your project's users. If your project is designed for wide distribution, installation problems can cause you many headaches and a great deal of time and expense in providing answers and service over the telephone. Set up a product-related web site with pages for software registration, bug reporting, technical support, and program upgrades.

. . . .

From: Christopher Yavelow <Christopher@yav.com>

Subject: The case of the keyboardless kiosk

About ten days ago I posted an announcement to the list about our interactive kiosk installation at the new Netherlands Museum of Science and Technology (press release at: http://www.yav.com/docs/YMEMIMpr.html).

Now I've discovered that science museums at this level are the target of bands of teenage hackers that try to crash all the exhibits. Our exhibit fell prey to such a band last Friday.

Although the software is running inside of a kiosk built into a larger "The Music is the Message" exhibit housing AND the museum visitor has only a trackball and single push button to operate the exhibit AND there is *no* way to quit the software without issuing a command-Q from a keyboard which is double-locked inside the guts of the exhibit housing, some kids were able to get back to the desktop and delete the 60 MB of files associated with the exhibit... and they did so in such a way that Norton Utils (3.5) could not find them for un-erasing (I had to bring over a CD-ROM version and re-install the entire exhibit).

How did they do it? Is there a way to get back to the desktop in such a scenario: a (for all practical purposes) keyboardless kiosk with only a trackball and single button interface and no on-screen option to quit the application? There are no menus, the menubar is hidden, there are no quit buttons, AllowInterrupts is set to false, etc., etc.

Christopher Yavelow

YAV Interactive Media

Brederodestraat 47

2042 BB Zandvoort

The Netherlands

eMail: Christopher@yav.com

wSite: http://www.yav.com

Scary message found at an Internet newsgroup for multimedia programmers

. . . .

File Archives

Shareware and commercial utility programs for compressing and decompressing files have been in wide use in both the Macintosh and Windows environments for some time. These have been particularly popular with users of bulletin boards, the Internet, and online services such as America Online because compressed files take less time to transmit by modem than do uncompressed files. Most software that involves uploading and downloading online files automatically handles compression/decompression. Browsers often use "helper" applications to decompress documents downloaded from the Web:

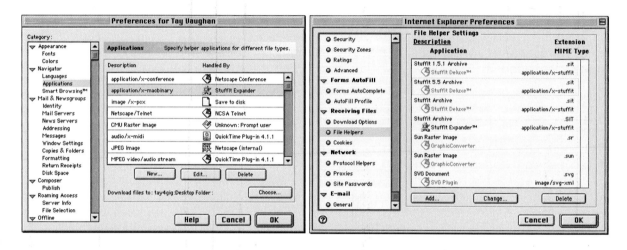

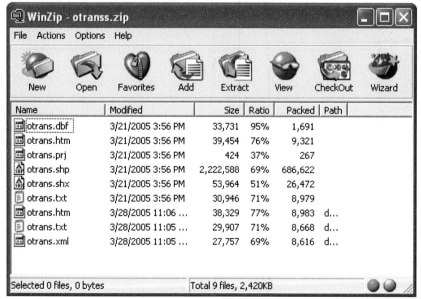

One or more of the files in your project can be compressed into a single file, called an **archive**. When that archive is then decompressed, or the files are expanded or extracted, each file in the archive is "reconstituted." Figure 18-2 shows the menu of a zipped archive. Archives are usually identified by file name extensions representing the compression software that was used, as shown in Table 18-1.

Figure 18-2 An archive can contain many compressed files.

Compression Software	Extension	Platform
PKZIP	.zip	Windows
ARC	.arc	Windows
PAK	.pak	Windows
Windows Install	.xx__	Windows
StuffIt	.sit	Macintosh
PackIt	.pit	Macintosh
DiskDoubler	.dd	Macintosh
CompactPro	.cpt	Macintosh
AppleLink	.pkg	Macintosh
Self-extracting	.sea	Macintosh
Self-extracting	.exe	Windows
BinHex	.hqx	Internet
Uuencode	.uu	Internet
Tar	.tar	Internet, Unix
Compress	.z	Internet, Unix
Gzip	.gz	Internet, Unix

Table 18-1 Common File Name Extensions for Compressed Files

Self-extracting archives are useful for delivering projects on disks in compressed form. On the Mac, these files typically carry the Windows-like file name extension .sea. On Windows platforms, these archives are executable files with an .exe file name extender. With self-extracting archives, the user simply runs the executable archive, and the compressed files are automatically decompressed and placed on the hard disk.

Some compression applications allow you to compress, split, and store large files on several floppy disks or Zip disks; the segments of these files are then automatically rejoined during installation.

Most compression utilities also provide an encryption or security feature, so that people who have access to disks containing private archive files cannot read them without authorization. This helps hide classified data.

Delivering on CD-ROM

The majority of multimedia products sold into retail and business channels are delivered on CD-ROM or DVD. While the very first users of CD-ROMs were owners of large databases like library catalogs, reference systems, and parts lists, today most computers are shipped with a CD-ROM or DVD drive, and software that is not downloadable from the Internet is often packaged on a disc.

Compact Disc Technology

A compact disc, or CD, is a thin wafer of clear polycarbonate plastic and metal measuring 4.75 inches (120mm) in diameter, with a small hole, or hub, in its center. The metal layer is usually pure aluminum, sputtered onto the polycarbonate surface in a thickness measurable in molecules. As the disc spins in the CD player, the metal reflects light from a tiny infrared laser into a light-sensitive receiver diode. These reflections are transformed into an electrical signal and then further converted to meaningful bits and bytes for use in digital equipment.

Pits on the CD, where the information is stored, are 1 to 3 microns long, about ½ micron wide, and ¹⁄₁₀ micron deep. (By comparison, a human hair is about 18 microns in diameter.) A CD can contain as many as three miles of these tiny pits wound in a spiral pattern from the hub to the edge. A layer of lacquer is applied to protect the surface, and artwork from the disc's author or publisher is usually silk-screened on the back side.

Compact discs are made in what is generally referred to as a **family process**. The glass master is made using the well-developed, photolithographic techniques created by the microchip industry: First an optically ground glass disc is coated with a layer of photo resistant material 1/10 micron thick. A laser then exposes (writes) a pattern of pits onto the surface of the chemical layer of material. The disc is developed (the exposed areas are washed away) and is silvered, resulting in the actual pit structure of the finished master disc. The master is then electroplated with layers of nickel one molecule thick, one layer at a time, until the desired thickness is reached. The nickel layer is separated from the glass disc and forms a metal negative, or **father**.

In cases where low runs of just a few discs are required, the father is used to make the actual discs. Most projects, though, require several **mothers**, or positives, to be made by plating the surface of the father.

In a third plating stage, **sons**, or **stampers**, are made from the mother, and these are the parts that are used in the injection molding machines. Plastic pellets are heated and injected into the mold or stamper, forming the disc with the pits in it. The plastic disc is coated with a thin aluminum layer for reflectance and lacquer for protection, given a silk-screened label for marketing, and packaged for delivery. Most of these activities occur in a particle-free clean room, because one speck of dust larger than a pit can ruin many hours of work. The mastering process alone takes around 12 hours.

CD-R

CD-R (compact disc-recordable) is an excellent method for distributing multimedia projects. CD-R writers and blank CD-R discs are inexpensive, and for short runs of a product, it is more cost effective to **burn** your work onto CD-Rs and custom label them with your own printer than to have the discs mastered and **pressed** using the expensive father and son method described previously. Many services with auto-loading equipment and 24-hour turnarounds can make short runs.

CD-R blanks that can hold as much as 84 minutes of Red Book sound (see the next section) or more than 700MB of data are made of a polycarbonate core coated with layers of reflective metals and special photosensitive organic dyes (see Figure 18-3). During the burning process, laser light hits the layer of dye, bakes it, and forms a pit. A 74-minute CD-R disc contains 333,000 sectors * 2048 bytes / sector for a capacity of 650.4MB. An 80 minute disc contains 360,000 sectors * 2048 bytes / sector for a data capacity of 703.1MB.

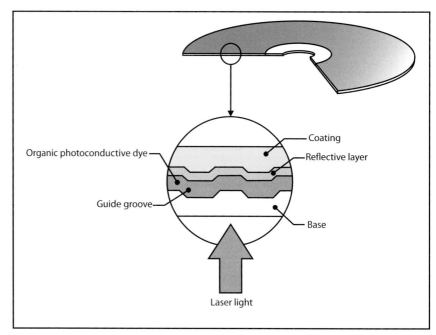

Figure 18-3 As a CD or DVD disc spins, laser light is beamed along a groove or track of lands (high points) and pits (low points). The difference in reflected light as the beam passes over these tiny spots is interpreted as binary data.

Compact Disc Standards

In 1979, Philips and Sony together launched CD technology as a digital method of delivering sound and music (audio) to consumers. This collaboration resulted in the **Red Book standard** (named for the color of the document's jacket), officially called the **Compact Disc Digital Audio Standard**. The Red Book standard defines the audio format for CDs available in music stores today; the Yellow Book is for CD-ROM; the Green Book is for **CD-I** (**Interactive**); the Orange Book is for write-once, read-only (WORM) CD-ROMs; and the **White Book** is for **Video CD** (**Karaoke CD**).

The Red, Yellow, Green, Orange, and White Books

Red Book remains the basis for standards that define more elaborate digital data formats for computers and other digital devices. Audio CDs can provide up to 80 minutes of playing time, which is enough for a slow-tempo rendition of Beethoven's Ninth Symphony. This was reported to be Philips and Sony's actual criterion during research and development for determining the size of sectors and ultimately the physical size of the CD itself.

A CD may contain one or more **tracks**. These are areas normally allocated for storing a single song in the Red Book format. CDs also contain lead-in information and a table of contents. Each track on the CD may use a different format; this allows you to create a mixed-mode disc that combines, for example, high-quality CD-Audio with Macintosh **Hierarchical File System (HFS)** CD-ROM or ISO 9660 data formats. Figure 18-4 illustrates the track layouts for Red Book, Yellow Book, Green Book, mixed mode, and for Kodak's **PhotoCD** Orange Book layout. Both Macintosh and Windows support commands to access both Red Book Audio and the data tracks on a CD, but you cannot access both at the same time.

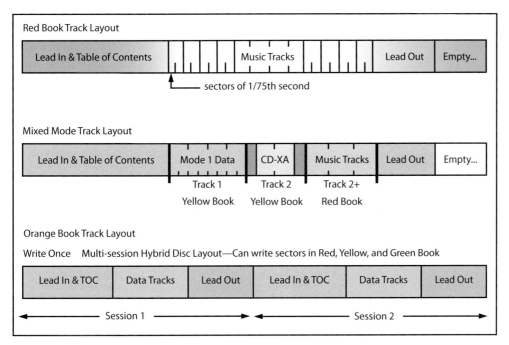

Figure 18-4 CD track layouts

Though a CD contains tracks, the primary logical unit for data storage on a CD is a **sector**, which is ⅟₇₅ second in length. Each sector of a CD contains 2,352 bytes of data. After every sector are another 882 bytes consisting of two layers of error-detecting and error-correcting information (EDC and ECC) and timing control data. A CD actually requires, then, 3,234 bytes to store 2,352 bytes of data. EDC and ECC allow a scratched or dirty data sector to be reconstructed by software fast enough to avoid dropout of music. Timing codes are used to display song-playing time on an audio CD player.

TIP   Because there is built-in error correction on CDs, small scratches may not affect playback, particularly when the scratch runs in a straight line from center to edge. To really wreck a CD, scratch it in an easy arc from the center to the rim; error correction won't keep up.

The disc spins at a constant linear velocity (CLV), so data can be read at a constant density and spacing. This means the rotational speed of the disc may vary from about 200 rpm when the read head is at the outer edge, to 530 rpm when it is reading near the hub. This translates to about 1.3 meters (51 inches) of travel along the data track each second. CD players use very sensitive motors so that no matter where the read head is on the disc, approximately the same amount of data is read in each second.

The CD's rotational speed and the density of the pits and lands on the CD allow data to be read at a sustained rate of 150 Kbps in a single-speed reader. This is sufficient for good audio, but it is very slow for large image files, motion video, and other multimedia resources, especially when compared to the high data-transfer rates of hard disk drives. New drives that spin many times faster when reading computer data, and slower for Red Book Audio, have been designed specifically for computers. In any case, CD access speed and transfer rate from CD-ROM is much slower than from a hard disk.

Philips and Sony developed the **Yellow Book** to provide an established standard for data storage and retrieval. Yellow Book adds yet another layer of error checking to accommodate the greater reliability required of computer data, and it provides two modes: one for computer data and the other for compressed audio and video/picture data.

The most common standard currently used for CD-ROM production evolved from the Yellow Book, with Microsoft joining the collaboration, and it was approved by the International Standards Organization as **ISO 9660**.

WARNING   *It is possible to damage your speakers if you play the digital track of a CD-ROM on your audio CD player. The digital data is decoded as full-volume noise by players that do not check for a data flag in the control field of the Q subchannel.*

Later, other standards were developed to deal with specific user requirements, such as synchronized interleaving of compressed audio and visual data in interactive digital movies (**Green Book**), and with formats for **write-once, read-only (WORM)** and magneto-optical CD technologies (**Orange Book**). A CD-R can have several separate images or **sessions** on it, each recorded at different times.

The Red, Yellow, Green, and Orange books describe the types of compact discs listed in Table 18-2.

Many multimedia developers place both Macintosh files and PC files on the same CD in a **hybrid format**, letting the user launch the proper applications for the appropriate platform. You can selectively hide the files of either platform when you create a hybrid so Windows users will not be confused by odd-looking Macintosh files in their directories, and vice versa. Graphics, text, and data files written in common formats such as DOC, TIF,

Name	Description	Comment
CD-Audio or CD-DA	Digital audio	Consumer audio discs
CD-ROM High Sierra	Read-only memory	Vestigial standard, seldom used
CD-ROM ISO 9660	Read-only memory	MS-DOS and Macintosh files
CD-ROM HFS	Read-only memory	Macintosh HFS files
CD-ROM/XA	Read-only memory	Extended Architecture
CD-I or CD-RTOS	Interactive	Philips Interactive motion video
CD-I Ready	Interactive/Ready	Audio CD with features for CD-I player
CD-Bridge	Bridge	Allows XA track to play on CD-I player
CD-MO	Magneto-optical	Premastered area readable on any CD player
CD-WO or CD-R	Write-once recordable	May use multiple sessions to fill disc
CD+G	Mixed mode	CD+Graphics - MTV on disc
CDTV	ISO 9660 variant	Commodore proprietary system
PhotoCD	Compressed images	Kodak multisession XA system
Video CD or Karaoke CD	Bridge	Karaoke full-motion MPEG video

Table 18-2 Compact Disc Formats

PIC, DBF, and WKS can be read from an ISO 9660 CD and imported into your application, whether the file was generated on a Macintosh or a PC.

DVD

Digital Versatile Discs (DVDs) employ a different (multi-layer, high-density) manufacturing process than audio and data CDs, and this technology provides as much as 15.9GB of storage on a single disc in the Double Sided, Dual-Layered format (DVD-18). More common and readily available are Single-Sided, Single-Layered discs offering 4.37GB of storage (DVD-5), often called "4.7GB Media."

In December 1995, nine major electronics companies (Toshiba, Matsushita, Sony, Philips, Time Warner, Pioneer, JVC, Hitachi, and Mitsubishi Electric) agreed to promote a new optical disc technology for distribution of multimedia and feature-length movies called DVD.

With this medium capable not only of gigabyte storage capacity but also full-motion video (MPEG2) and high-quality audio in surround sound, the bar was raised for multimedia developers: commercial multimedia projects become more expensive to produce as consumers' performance expectations rise.

There are three competing sets of standards for recording DVD: DVD-R/DVD-RW, DVD+R/DVD+RW, and DVD-RAM. The "R" and "RW" stand for recordable and rewritable respectively. DVD standards

Is DVD+R/+RW a real DVD format?

DVD+R/+RW recorders are the only DVD recorders that use just one operating mode, which always creates DVD-Video compatible discs. Whereas other formats have different physical disc types or different logical formats (methods used to record video on a disc) to offer the user a flexible recording experience, DVD+R/+RW offers the user flexibility and a rich feature set, without sacrificing compatibility. With DVD+R/+RW, there is no need to buy expensive dedicated players to allow playback of recorded discs, as the recordings can be played on the majority of the 100s of millions of DVD-Video players and DVD-ROM drives available today. Furthermore, also on a physical level DVD+RW and DVD+R are closer to the DVD format than competing formats, as they do not need special "pre-pits" on the disc that could affect compatibility. All in all, DVD+R/+RW is the most real recordable DVD format around.

...From a DVD+RW Alliance FAQ

Is +RW a DVD Format?

+RW is not the DVD Format created and authorized by the DVD Forum. Likewise, although strikingly similar in appearance to the DVD-RW, there is no DVD Format called DVD+RW or +RW among the Formats created and authorized by the DVD Forum. There is No Verification Process for +RW or DVD+RW products authorized by the DVD Forum. There is No Verification Laboratory authorized by the DVD Forum to test +RW or DVD+RW products. There are No Test Specifications for +RW or DVD+RW products authorized by the DVD Forum and available at DVD FLLC. Also, there is no guarantee for compatibility between the products employing the DVD Forum-approved Formats and the products employing the +RW or DVD+RW technology.

...From a DVD Format/Logo Licensing Corporation FAQ

are supported by the DVD Forum (www.dvdforum.com). DVD+ standards are supported by the DVD+RW Alliance (www.dvdrw.com). DVD-RAM has better recording features, but requires more specialized playback hardware.

DVD-R/DVD-RW and DVD+R/DVD+RW are similar and can be played back on most DVD players and drives.

With Dolby AC-3 Digital Surround Sound as part of the DVD specifications, six discrete audio channels can be programmed for digital surround sound, and with a separate subwoofer channel, developers can program the low-frequency doom and gloom music popular with Hollywood. DVD also supports Dolby Pro-Logic Surround Sound, standard stereo, and mono audio. Users can randomly access any section of the disc and use the slow-motion and freeze-frame features during movies. Audio tracks can be programmed for as many as 8 different languages, with graphic subtitles in 32 languages. Some manufacturers such as Toshiba are already providing parental control features in their players.

True to marketing principles, DVD manufacturers express DVD capacities in billion byte quantities where "billion" or "Giga" means the vernacular 1000 × 1000 × 1000, not the more precise binary definition of 1024 × 1024 × 1024 bytes used by your computer. This makes the advertised capacity of a DVD disc sound about seven percent bigger than it really is; you will not be able to record more than 4.37GB onto a blank disc!

TIP *The DVD-R specifications were released after the first-generation DVD-Video specifications, so some older DVD players may not be able to play discs burned to the newer DVD-R specs. If your project will fit on a 3.95GB DVD-R blank, try this media for compatibility with older players.*

Wrapping It Up

Packaging is an important area where sales and marketing issues extend the process of making multimedia into the real world of end users. Like the cover of a book, people will judge your work based upon the impression it makes.

If your project is for your own use, you may not need the pretty cover, cardboard box, and shrink-wrap that is required for over-the-counter software sold to consumers. If your project is for a client or for the Web, you may simply need to deliver it on any sufficient storage media or upload it to a server. But if your project is headed for wider distribution within a large company or organization or into retail channels, you will need to think about packaging.

If your project is destined to be sold into the consumer retail channel, then you have made a **title**. Software titles are most often distributed on CD-ROM. The software itself may, indeed, be only one item (the most important one) in a package that includes a user's manual, a registration card, quick reference guides, hardware adapters, and collateral marketing material from you or other parties with whom you have arrangements.

Retailers claim that consumers typically relate the finish of a package to quality and price of the product inside. The fancier, bigger, and heavier the package is, the higher its perceived value. Software manufacturers juggle the elements of this equation when they determine the cost of goods and shipping/freight add-ons and set the product's price point. Many big software boxes are shipped with plenty of sailboat fuel inside, and with cardboard or open-cell foam to hold the thin CD and manuals in place.

The art for your cover should reflect the content and function of the enclosed product; it should also follow normal rules for good design layout. Your company's logo should be prominent, and if this is one of a series of titles, the artwork should conform to the coordinated look or style you are using throughout that series or product line.

When your product reaches the retail channel, it may be displayed on shelves or racks, in kiosks, or it may be hung on brackets. You should be sure to put the name of your title on the front face and on the spine of the package. Use photo-quality images and high-caliber artwork for the front, because this is the most visible face of your package. Many packages are shrink-wrapped with thin plastic to protect them from fingerprints and pilferage at the retail outlet. Even after the shrink-wrap is on your package, there is room for additional artwork: bright stickers can be effective eye-catchers. And some vendors apply specially made holographic stickers to identify their product and to prevent unauthorized bootleg copies from reaching the marketplace.

Some vendors have developed unique or special solutions to make their product stand out. Authorware, for example, was once shipped in a custom-designed briefcase with carry handle. An expensive software package, this briefcase was easily absorbed in the purchase price. Fractal Design Painter was at one time shipped in a metal paint can with a colorful paper wrapper, and Eye Candy special effects for After Effects came in a metal movie reel case (see Figure 18-5). But package size and shape options are, more often than not, limited by the common constraints of the floor and shelf space found in retailing outlets and by the expense of fabricating a nonstandard container.

Most industrial cities boast more than one packaging specialist with whom you can consult. These outfits can supply cardboard and plastic boxes, printing, cutting, folding, and wrapping services. Environmentally responsible packaging, especially for compact discs, is becoming popular, and special sleeves and cardboard containers are available. Be sure to consider the weight and bulk of your package—an ounce of extra weight that pushes you over a zone or destination boundary might increase your shipping

Figure 18-5   Some software comes in interesting packages.

costs significantly. The outside wrap for shipping should be plain because pilferage, especially for international destinations and customs zones, can be a problem. Look for volume discounts and price breaks.

The current trend in software packaging is toward simplification. Indeed, as the information revolution takes hold, more software and documentation will be available for purchase and downloading directly from the Web, and today's boxes and bright packages will become quaint collector's items.

Delivering on the World Wide Web

Delivering multimedia projects built for the World Wide Web can be as simple as renaming a directory or transferring a group of files to a web server. Servers and networked systems are discussed in Chapters 9 and 13. On the face of it, the mechanics of actually putting a project on the Web are trivial, particularly because you have likely been designing, building, and testing within "web space" throughout the development of your project, anyway. But delivery of your project and **activation** of your pages by making them available to your intended audience on the Web, whether to the general public or to an intranet of select users behind a firewall, should be approached with caution. Here there are many technical considerations that, while outside the topic of multimedia per se, should be understood if you want your project to be a success.

A few years ago I taught a student of mine about HTML, just before she went off to a summer internship working on a traditional book publisher's web site. She returned to school three months later and demonstrated to me how one might use the Web to generate profits—at a time when many doubted it was easy to do. Working for the publisher, she was assigned the job of marketing a book for college students. She did her research and discovered how advertising in the search engines works: by "buying" the word "college" on a few of them, she was able to place an ad on search results that were related to colleges; visitors who clicked on her ad were linked to the publisher's web site, where they could purchase the book online. While explaining the process, she checked the online sales of her book: over 5,000 copies had been sold online within a month of publication—eight of them during the last hour!

Panagiotis Takis Metaxas,
Associate Professor
of Computer Science,
Wellesley College

If you own or host the delivery web server yourself, you will have better security control, better integration of your project into your internal LAN or intranet, and you can fine-tune the server's configuration parameters and specify and install any special software you need. On the other hand, you will likely need a full-time webmaster, and you will pay for a high-bandwidth connection directly to the Internet. When you have control of the server, you can provide secure commerce services for credit card transactions, encryption and passwords, special databases, and custom CGI programming. Server-side setup for plug-ins is discussed in Chapter 13. For multimedia projects requiring streaming technologies such as RealAudio or video conferencing, you can purchase and install the necessary software on the server.

If your project will reside at a site hosted by an Internet Service Provider (ISP) or a service such as America Online or MSN, you must discover during the planning phase of your project what your service's limitations might be and design your project within those limitations. It does no good to include PhotoCD image pacs, ToolVox meta voice files, or complex Java scripts in your web page, only to find that your ISP does not or will not support the MIME-type or purchase and install the necessary server software for you.

Internet directories like Yahoo, and search engines like Google, are important components of the Web's "how-to-find-it" functionality and power: using meta tags, be sure your project will register with the search engines and can be easily found.

http://www.allaboutyourownwebsite.com/web_site_promotion.php3

http://www.webpronews.com/wpn-4-20030318Getting-Listed-a-Search-Engine-Jump-Start.html

http://www.insideoutmarketing.com/index.php?p=pages&pid=4

http://office.microsoft.com/assistance/2002/articles/fpSearchRanking.aspx

Informative URLs for web site promotion and search engine submission

Chapter 18 Review

■ Chapter Summary

For your review, here's a summary of the important concepts discussed in this chapter.

Discuss important considerations in preparing your project for delivery in the marketplace

- A bad reputation earned by premature product release can destroy an otherwise excellent piece of work.

- Your product's performance will usually depend on specific hardware and system configurations and, in the case of the Internet, on end users' connection speeds. Online performance also depends on the amount of traffic to the site and the Internet route taken to the site.

- Fully test your project on as many platforms as possible, including heavily loaded, highly expanded systems.

- Budget for obtaining the hardware test platforms, as well as for the many hours of effort that testing will require.

- Your contract should clearly specify the intended delivery platform and its hardware and software configuration, and provide a clause that you will test only to that platform.

- If your project depends on QuickTime and will be delivered on Windows, be sure the end user can install QuickTime from your CD or can download the QuickTime plug-in.

List the steps a project should go through as part of the testing process, and describe their significance

- Any element of a computer's configuration may be the cause of a problem or a bug, so plan to spend lots of time configuring and testing various platforms and reproducing and fixing bugs.

- Alpha releases are typically circulated among a select group of mock internal users for testing.

- Beta releases are sent to a wider but still select audience with the understanding that the software may contain errors or bugs.

- Beta testers should include a detailed description of the hardware and software configuration and a step-by-step recounting of the problem so that you can re-create it.

List the considerations involved in preparing a product for distribution, including installation routines and compression

- You may need to provide a single program that acts as an installation routine, which is not a trivial task.

- Provide well-written documentation about the installation process so that users have a clear step-by-step procedure to follow.

- The clearer and more detailed your installation instructions are, the fewer frustrated users queries you will receive.

- Use a shareware or commercial compression utility for creating program archives that can then be decompressed and "reconstituted" into the original file structure.

- Self-extracting files allow the user to run the executable archive; compressed files are automatically decompressed and placed on the hard disk.

Discuss the CD-ROM standards as they apply to multimedia, including the various formats and file-naming conventions

- The majority of multimedia products sold into retail and business channels are delivered on CD-ROM.

- CD-R writers and blank CD-R discs are an inexpensive way to distribute multimedia projects.

- For short runs of a product, it is cheaper to burn your work onto CD-Rs and custom label them with your own printer.

- The Red Book standard defines the CD audio format; Yellow Book is for CD-ROM; Green Book is for CD-I (Interactive); Orange Book is for write-once, read-only (WORM) CD-ROMs; and White Book is for Video CD (Karaoke CD).

- A single-speed reader allows data to be read at a sustained rate of 150 Kbps, much slower than from a hard disk.

- The ISO 9660 standard is the most widely used digital data file format for CDs.

- ISO 9660 follows the MS-DOS file-naming conventions—directory names are limited to eight characters, and directories may not be nested more than eight deep.

List the considerations involved in selecting a CD-ROM file standard, in packaging, and in delivering projects

- Although you can access all files on the CD from either platform, a PC executable program will not run on a Macintosh, and vice versa.

- A hybrid format places both Macintosh files and PC files on the same CD, with both PC and Macintosh executable programs.

- Digital Versatile Disc (DVD) CDs are made with a multilayer, high-density manufacturing process that provides 4.7 gigabytes of storage.

- Packaging is an important consideration in marketing your project. Although users often equate quality with large boxes, high-caliber artwork, and fancy packaging, the current trend in software packaging is toward simplification.

- Delivering multimedia projects built for the World Wide Web can be as simple as renaming a directory or transferring a group of files to a Web server. On the other hand, hosting your own server for delivering your project means tackling a variety of issues, including security, server-side configuration, and access.

■ Key Terms

activation *(485)*
alpha release *(469)*
archive *(474)*
beta release *(469)*
bronze release *(470)*
burn *(477)*
CD-I (Interactive) *(478)*
CD-ROM/XA (Extended Architecture) *(481)*
Compact Disc Digital Audio Standard *(478)*
Digital Versatile Disc (DVD) *(481)*
extensions *(468)*
family process *(476)*
father *(477)*

golden master *(470)*
Green Book *(480)*
Hierarchical File System (HFS) *(479)*
hybrid format *(480)*
installer *(471)*
ISO 9660 *(480)*
Karaoke CD *(478)*
mother *(477)*
Orange Book *(480)*
PhotoCD *(479)*
pressed *(477)*
README.TXT, ReadMeFirst *(472)*
Red Book standard *(478)*

release candidate *(470)*
sector *(479)*
sessions *(480)*
self-extracting archive *(475)*
sons, stampers *(477)*
title *(483)*
tracks *(478)*
Video CD *(478)*
White Book *(478)*
write-once, read-only (WORM) *(480)*
Yellow Book *(480)*

■ Key Term Quiz

1. The test release of a product that is typically for internal circulation only and is passed among a select group of mock users is the _____ (two words).

2. The test release of a product that is sent to a select group of external users with the understanding that the software may contain errors and bugs is the _____ (two words).

3. The final release of a product when there is nothing left to change or correct and it is ready to be reproduced is the _____ (two words).

4. The test release of a product with a version number as the developers continue to refine the product and approach a final version is called a(n) _____ (two words).

5. A program that saves all necessary run-time files to the user's hard drive is called a(n) _____.

6. Many CD-ROM projects include a plain-text file containing a description of changes or bugs reported since the documentation was printed and a detailed description of the installation process. This file is often named _____.

7. When several files are compressed into a single file, it is usually called a(n) _____.

8. Compressed files can be saved with the ability to automatically decompress themselves and place the files on the built-in hard disk. Such files are called _____ (three words).

9. A CD-ROM that contains both Macintosh files and PC files on the same CD is a(n) _____.

10. A CD-R can have several separate images on it, each recorded at different times. Each of these is called a(n) _____.

■ Multiple Choice Quiz

1. When delivering a project, you should:
   a. not bother testing; it'll probably work
   b. test once on your development computer
   c. test on a couple of other computers
   d. test on several other computers at least once
   e. test on as many different computers as many times as you can

2. The pre-OS X Macintosh environment is well known for its sensitivity to certain drivers and other parts of system software that conflict with some software applications. These are known as:
   a. DLLs
   b. plug-ins
   c. sectors
   d. extensions
   e. headers

3. The files used by Windows to store configuration information and settings is called the:
   a. settings file
   b. parameters list
   c. registry database
   d. profile typesheet
   e. system configuration file

4. The beta testing group is best comprised of:
   a. the internal development team
   b. users typical of the target group for the software
   c. a cross-section of the computer-using public

   d. computer neophytes
   e. other programmers who are familiar with the authoring system used

5. Which of the following is an extension for a Macintosh file compressed as a self-extracting archive?
   a. .exe
   b. .hqx
   c. .zip
   d. .sea
   e. .sit

6. Which of the following is *not* an option for delivering a project?
   a. Burn CD-Rs of the project.
   b. Use a father disc to press CDs.
   c. Use a mother disc to press CDs.
   d. Use a son disc to press CDs.
   e. Deliver the project via the Web.

7. Compact discs are manufactured by etching a negative master, then pressing a positive imprint of that master, and then using a third-generation negative imprint from the positive to stamp out production discs. This process is called the:
   a. etching process
   b. stamper process
   c. milling process
   d. positive-negative process
   e. family process

8. Each sector of a CD contains 2,352 bytes of data. After every sector are another 882 bytes used for:
   a. copyright information
   b. encryption key storage
   c. file directory indexing and linking
   d. writing additional information
   e. error detection and correction

9. What is the maximum amount of data that a CD-R (compact disc-recordable) can hold?
   a. 44MB
   b. 128MB
   c. 256MB
   d. 700MB
   e. 4.7GB

10. The Compact Disc Digital Audio Standard used for consumer audio CDs available in music stores today is also known as:
    a. ISO 9660 standard
    b. Red Book standard
    c. Orange Book standard
    d. High Sierra standard
    e. CD-ROM/XA standard

11. The most widely used format for storing digital data in files on CDs is:
    a. ISO 9660 standard
    b. Yellow Book standard
    c. White Book standard
    d. CD-ROM/XA standard
    e. DVD-ROM standard

12. The compact disc standard that allows both computer data and compressed audio data and video/image information to be read and played back, apparently simultaneously, is called:

a. Red Book standard
b. Yellow Book standard
c. Green Book standard
d. DVD-ROM standard
e. CD-ROM/XA standard

13. The CD-I (Interactive) standard is proprietary to:
    a. Apple
    b. High Sierra
    c. JVC
    d. Kodak
    e. Philips

14. CD-ROM packages are shrink-wrapped with thin plastic:
    a. to prevent outgassing of harmful chemicals used in the manufacturing process
    b. to inhibit oxidation of the CD-ROM surface
    c. to protect them from fingerprints and pilferage at the retail outlet
    d. to reduce unauthorized bootleg copies
    e. for a more professional look

15. Which of the following is *not* a benefit of hosting your own web server for product delivery site on the Web?
    a. ability to specify and install any special software you need
    b. better security control
    c. ability to fine-tune the server's configuration parameters
    d. easy access to technical support
    e. ability to provide secure commerce services

■ Essay Quiz

1. List the testing stages involved in preparing a project for delivery. What type of testers should be part of each stage's testing team?

2. List the benefits and capabilities of file compression and archiving software.

3. Describe the two methods of copying CD-ROMs, and discuss the benefits and drawbacks of each method.

4. Cite the two primary methods for delivering a project, and discuss the benefits and drawbacks of each method.

5. List the various CD-ROM formats and summarize their purposes and capabilities.

Lab Projects

■ Project 18.1

Visit the web sites of three CD duplication companies. Do they all offer both duplication (mastering) and replication (burning CD-Rs)? What quantities are available? What options for labeling are available? What options for packaging are included? Document your findings by creating a table that briefly compares prices and options.

■ Project 18.2

Create a form that beta testers can return after testing, and be sure to include information regarding the conditions surrounding bugs.

■ Project 18.3

Use a shareware or freeware compression utility to compress five files—for example, a text file, a JPEG image, an executable file (an application). What percentage compression can you achieve? Repeat the compression, saving the files as self-extracting archives. Document your findings by creating a table that compares original size, compressed, and size compressed as self-extracting file.

■ Project 18.4

Locate five computer systems and compare their configurations. Document your findings by creating a table with the following information:

- What operating system and version is installed?
- What is the processor and what is its speed?
- How much RAM is installed?
- How much hard-drive space is available?
- Is QuickTime installed?
- What is the CD-ROM drive's speed?
- What is the video card/monitor's resolution and color depth?
- What are the system's sound capabilities?

■ Project 18.5

Locate five CD-ROMs or downloaded programs that include "readme" files. Read each of the files, and observe what each one includes. Document your findings by summarizing the contents of each one.

Glossary

The number in parentheses that follows each definition is the chapter in which the term is explained.

acoustics A branch of physics that studies sound. (5)

Acrobat PDF A widely used technique for integrating formatted text and graphics in a single file. (13)

Acrobat Reader An application for viewing Acrobat PDF files. (13)

activation Going gold in web space; making pages available to their intended audience on the Web. (18)

additive color Color created by combining colored light sources in three primary colors: red, green, and blue. (6)

Adobe GoLive A WYSIWYG editor for creating and editing web pages. (13)

Adobe PostScript A page description and outline font language. (4)

Advanced Research Projects Agency (ARPA) A branch of the Department of Defense which created a research network that was the beginning of the Internet. (12)

Advanced Technology Attachment (ATA) Also called Integrated Drive Electronics (IDE), this connects up to four peripherals mounted inside a PC. (9)

AIF Three-letter file extension for the AIFF file format used for storing sound data; preferred format for the Macintosh. (5)

AIFC File format for storing sound data. Similar to AIF, but with Macintosh compression schemes. (5)

AIFF File format for storing sound data; preferred format for the Macintosh. (5)

aLaw File format for storing sound data; European equivalent of uLaw. (5)

ALIGN attribute An attribute of the HTML <IMG> tag; specifies placement of the image, left, right, or centered. (14)

ALINK attribute Deprecated in favor of styles in HTML 4; this specifies the color of active links in a document. (14)

alpha release Test release of a product that is typically for internal circulation only and is passed among a select group of mock users. (18)

American Federation of Television and Radio Artists (AFTRA) Association of professional actors and voice-over talent. (17)

American Standard Code for Information Interchange (ASCII) Seven-bit character coding system most commonly used by computers. (4)

anchor A reference from one document to another document, image, sound, or file on the Web. (4)

animated GIF A collection of still images in a single file played back in a timed sequence to provide animation. (7)

animation Collection of images rapidly displayed to provide visual change over time. (7)

anti-aliasing Blends the colors along the edges of graphic objects and characters to create a soft transition between the letters/objects and the background. (4)

Apple Macintosh A brand of computer with unique operating system and user interface. (2)

applet A program written in Java that can be included in an HTML page. (13)

<APPLET> tag Calls a Java applet and includes it in an HTML page. (14)

archive A set of files compressed into a single file. The individual files are decompressed and reconstituted into the original, separate file. (18)

ARPANET Origin of the Internet, established at the University of California at Los Angeles in September 1969 for researchers working for the Advanced Research Projects Agency (ARPA) of the Department of Defense. (12)

assets Rendered graphics, sounds, and other components that are part of a multimedia project. (2)

attributes Text style characteristics, such as underlining and outlining; properties of an HTML tag. (4, 14)

.au Two-letter file extension for audio files based on the international telephone format of uLaw. (5)

audio specialist Designers and producers of music, voice-over narrations, and sound effects. (3)

Audio Video Interleaved (.avi)   Microsoft's format for interleaving digital video data with audio data. (5, 10)

auditions   Tryouts for talent roles or parts. (17)

authoring tools   Tools designed to manage and manipulate individual multimedia elements and provide user interaction. (1)

AUTOPLAY   QuickTime embedded HTML command, which starts a movie playing automatically. (10)

autotracing   A process that computes the boundaries of the shapes of colors within a bitmap image and then derives the polygon object that describes that image. (6)

background layer   A graphic layer behind other layers—often shared by multiple foreground layers. (11)

bandwidth   A description of the size or measurement of a pipeline through which data is sent, as well as how much data, expressed in bits per second (bps), you can send from one computer to another in a given amount of time. (1, 12)

barcoding   Printing or recognizing characters arranged in a pattern of parallel black bars. (9)

beta   Pre-release version of a project or application for testing. (15)

beta release   A test release of a product that is sent to a select group of external users with the understanding that the software may contain errors and bugs. (18)

Betacam SP   Industry standard for professional analog video recording. (8)

BGCOLOR   QuickTime embedded HTML command, which sets a background color for the movie display. (10)

BGCOLOR attribute   Deprecated in favor of styles in HTML 4; this specifies the background color of an HTML document or a table cell. (14)

<BGSOUND> tag   In some browsers, this plays a designated sound file when the page is loaded. (14)

binary compatible   Files that require no conversion when used on various computer platforms. (2)

bitdepth   Amount of data used to represent a digital sample. (5)

bitmap   A matrix of the individual pixels that form an image. (6)

blue screen   Shooting against a blue background, making that color transparent, and replacing it with other footage. (8)

BMP   A Windows bitmap image file format; designated with the .bmp file extension. (6)

<BODY> tag   This defines the body of a web page. (14)

BORDER attribute   Specifies border width around a table or (deprecated) an image. (14)

bronze release   Test release of a product when it's close to being finished. (18)

browser   An application such as Internet Explorer or Netscape Navigator for reading web pages. (1)

buffer   A place where data is stored temporarily. (5)

burn   Making a recordable CD-ROM or DVD disc. (18)

burners   Hardware devices used for reading and making CDs and DVDs. (1)

busy screen   A cluttered display. (16)

buttons   Graphic objects with or without text, which make things happen when they are clicked. (4, 16)

cache   Temporary storage of data; QuickTime-embedded HTML command; indicates whether the movie should be cached (Netscape Navigator 3.0 or later). (10)

card-based authoring system   In this system, elements are organized as a stack of cards or pages of a book. (11)

Cartesian coordinates   A pair of numbers that describe a point in two-dimensional space as the intersection of horizontal and vertical lines (the x and y axes). (6)

cascading style sheet (CSS)   A method of page layout in HTML offering detailed control of text and other styles; a separate file that defines the attributes of text displayed on a web page. (4, 14)

case insensitive   Both the uppercase and lowercase forms of a character are considered by the computer to be the same. (4)

case sensitive   Uppercase and lowercase letters are treated as distinct characters. (4)

Cast   A visual database of the multimedia elements of a project, used by Adobe's Director. (11)

casting call   Announcement for tryouts for talent roles or parts. (17)

cat-5 cable Twisted-pair telephone cable that is "data-grade level 5," and is used for network connections. (9)

cathode-ray tube (CRT) projectors Video projector that uses three separate projection tubes and lenses. The original "big-screen" TV, used for projecting computer output onto a large screen. (9)

CD-I (Interactive) Early CD format designed to play sound and pictures on a consumer-grade player connected to a television set. (18)

CD-quality Digitized sound at 44.1 kHz and 16 bits depth. (5)

CD-ROM (Compact disc read-only memory) A storage medium for computer data that may only be read by the computer; typically stores about 700MB of data or 80 minutes of full-screen video or sound. (1, 9)

CD-ROM/XA (Extended Architecture) A format for reading and writing CDs enabling several recording sessions to be written and read on a single CD-R (recordable) disc. (5)

cel Clear celluloid sheet used for drawing each frame in an animation. (7)

cel animation A method of overlaying layers of images and sequencing them into an animation. (7)

CGI (Common Gateway Interface) Server-based program scripts; a standard for interfacing external applications with information servers. (13)

change order Revision requested by a client. (15)

character entities The characters that make up an alphabet recognizable to web browsers according to ISO standards. They are indicated by a word or numbers prefixed by an ampersand and followed by a semicolon. (4)

character metrics General measurements applied to individual text characters. (4)

charge-coupled device (CCD) A sensor in a video camera that converts light to an electronic signal. (8)

chroma key Electronically making a color or range of colors transparent, allowing another image to be inserted in place of the color(s). (8)

Cinepak Compression algorithm for digital video data. (8)

client sign-off Approval from a client to go ahead with your project. (15)

client/server software Enables computers to speak with each other and pass files back and forth. (9)

clip art Art or other media elements obtained from collections. (17)

Clipboard An area of memory where data such as text and images is temporarily stored when you cut or copy. (6)

CMYK Subtractive color scheme consisting of cyan, magenta, yellow, and black, used in printing. (6)

codecs Digital video and audio compression schemes that code and compress data for delivery and then decode it for playback. (8)

COLOR attribute Deprecated in favor of styles in HTML 4; defines the color of text in a font element. (14)

color lookup table (CLUT) Table used to assign specified colors to a limited palette. (6)

color-cycling Rapidly altering the colors of an image according to a formula. (7)

Compact Disc Digital Audio Standard The Red Book standard for audio CDs. (18)

compact disc read-only memory See CD-ROM.

component video Video recording standard that separates the video signals for luminance and chroma information. (8)

composite A multimedia structure in which users may navigate freely, but are occasionally constrained to linear presentations. (16)

composite video Video recording standard in which all video signals are mixed together and carried on a single cable. (8)

compression Mathematical or systematic method of reducing the amount of data required in a file. (14)

condensed Text in which characters are squeezed together. (4)

conditional branching Navigation control based on the results of an IF-THEN decision. (11)

content The text, images, sounds, and video contained in a multimedia project. (1)

content acquisition Obtaining the text, images, sounds, and video contained in a multimedia project. (17)

contingencies Elements worked into planning and budgeting to allow for unexpected problems, expenses, and delays while developing a project. (15)

CONTROLLER QuickTime embedded HTML command; specifies whether to display the QuickTime movie controller. (10)

convergence A merger of two or more technologies. (1)

copyright infringement Using copyrighted material without permission. (17)

copyright ownership Ownership of the legal rights to use a copyrighted asset. (17)

copyright protection Legal rights belonging to the creator of an original work; wherein protection is automatically assigned to "original works of authorship fixed in any tangible medium of expression." (17)

CORRECTION QuickTime embedded HTML command; specifies an image correction mode. (10)

costing The stage in a multimedia project in which one estimates its cost. (2)

creative strategy Techniques and presentation methods relevant to a project when planning; description of the look and feel of a project. (15)

Critical Path Method (CPM) A scheduling function to calculate the total duration of a project based upon each identified task, earmarking tasks that are critical and that, if lengthened, will result in a delay in project completion. (15)

cross-platform Workable on more than one computer platform. (2)

daemon Agent programs that run in the background, waiting to act on requests from the outside. (12)

decibels (dB) A logarithmic measurement of the sound pressure level (loudness or volume) of a sound. (5)

degaussing Electronic process of readjusting the magnets that guide the electrons in a CRT. (8)

deliverables Work products that must be provided to the client. (15)

delivering The stage in a multimedia project when it is packaged and shipped to its intended audience. (2)

deprecated tag Not supported by the most recent HTML standard, yet its use remains supported by most browsers. (14)

depth structure The complete navigation map, which describes all of the links between all the components of a project. (16)

derivative work Material that is derived from another work. (17)

designing The stage in a multimedia project when the tasks needed for creating a finished project are planned. This creates the form and structure of a project. (2)

device dependent Results depend upon the device used, for example, playback of a sound. (5)

device independent Results are the same, regardless of the device used, for playback of a sound, for example. (5, 13)

DIB Device-independent bitmap; a common Windows image file format. (6)

digital audio Audio represented as a series of binary numbers. (5)

digital audio tape (DAT) Magnetic tape used for recording audio in a digital format. (5)

digital equalization (EQ) Modifying a recording's frequency content. (5)

digital manipulation Using a computer to edit photos, sounds, text, video, and other multimedia elements. (1)

digital signal processing (DSP) Processing a sound with reverberation, multitap delay, chorus, flange, and other special effects. (5)

Digital Subscriber Line (DSL) Dedicated copper telephone line for high-bandwidth connection to the Internet. (9)

Digital Versatile Disc See DVD.

digitized A varying quantity expressed as a sequence of numbers, usually in the binary system; the result when the original analog light waves of an image or sound waves of a sound are sampled and converted into binary digits. (2)

distributed resources Information and multimedia assets located at various places on the data highway. (1)

dithering Mathematical process used in reducing the number of colors in a palette, whereby the color value of a pixel is changed to the closest matching color value in a target palette; pixels of different colors are then intermixed to create the appearance of a color not in the new, limited palette. (4, 6)

Dolby AC-3 Digital Surround Sound   Process for encoding six discrete audio channels; included as part of the DVD specification. (9)

Dolby Pro-Logic Surround Sound   Enhanced audio available in the DVD specification. (9)

Domain Name System (DNS)   System developed to rationally assign names and addresses of computers linked to the Internet. (12)

dot pitch   Spacing (size) of the phosphorescing, colored-chemical dots found on the back of the glass face of a monitor. (6)

dots per inch (dpi)   Description of screen or printer resolution. (4)

downsampling   Reducing the number of samples of a sound. (5)

drawing software   For producing vector-based line art easily printed to paper at high resolution. (10)

Dreamweaver   A WYSIWYG, HTML editor that is part of the Adobe's suite of programs. (13)

dubbing   Copying a video recording from one tape or medium to another. (8)

DVD   Digital Versatile Disc; currently stores 4.7GB of data, including video data, for playback on consumer machines. (1, 9)

DVD-ROM   DVD-Read Only Memory; a DVD used for storing data that is to be read by a computer. (9)

DVD-Video   DVD used for recording video for playback. (9)

DXF   Proprietary format for exchanging architectural and engineering drawings across platforms. (6)

Dynamic HTML (DHTML)   A powerful extension of HTML used to improve control of page layouts and presentation. (4)

Dynamic Link Library (DLL)   Custom code used in Microsoft Windows to extend the features of an application. (11)

ECMAScript   International language standard derived from Netscape's original JavaScript. (11)

electronic rights   Rights to reproduce or use material in electronic form. (17)

<EMBED> tag   Deprecated in HTML 4; calls a multimedia element. (14)

environment   Conditions surrounding a multimedia project, including hardware, software, and people. (1)

escape sequence   Used in HTML to define special characters; begins with an ampersand, ends with a semicolon. (14)

Ethernet   Method of wiring computers to be part of a network. (9)

executive summary   The first part of a proposal: used to briefly describe the project's goals, how the goals will be achieved, and the project's cost. (15)

expanded   Text in which the characters are spaced apart from each other. (4)

eXtensible Markup Language (XML)   Allows creation of custom HTML tags and importing of data from anywhere on the Web. (12)

extensions   Drivers and other parts of system software that enable certain functions. (18)

extrude   Extends an object's shape some distance, either perpendicular to the shape's outline or along a defined path. (6)

fair use   Limited exceptions to copyright protection in which copyrighted material can be used without permission. (17)

family process   Process of pressing CDs from a glass master using fathers, mothers, and sons. (18)

FAQs   Frequently Asked Questions; these are lists of common questions and answers that provide useful information. (10)

Fast SCSI   A 10 MBps transfer rate within the SCSI-2 specification. (9)

father   A metal negative image of a glass master made of nickel. (18)

feasibility study   A test to see if a task is doable; often involves selecting only a small portion of a large project and getting that part working as it would in the final product. See prototype and proof-of-concept. (15)

File Transfer Protocol (FTP)   Method for exchanging files among computers connected to a network. (9)

file-naming convention   Agreed-upon rules for naming files. (16)

filters   Used by image-editing software for special effects. (10)

flare   Place(s) on an image where light is most intense. (6)

flattening   Interleaving the audio and video segments of a video clip together in a data file. (8)

font   A collection of characters of a single size and style belonging to a particular typeface family. (1, 4)

font mapping   Specifying an appropriate matching font when crossing platforms. (4)

font substitution   Substituting a font when the original font is unavailable on the target machine. (4)

<FONT> tag   Deprecated in HTML 4; sets characteristics of text elements. (14)

foundry   A place where typefaces are created. (4)

FOV   QuickTime embedded HTML command; sets the initial field-of-view angle. (10)

frame   In animation and digital video, one in a sequence of graphic images. (10)

Gantt chart   Planning chart that depicts tasks along a timeline. (15)

General MIDI   Method for creation and playback of digital music files that uses a numbering system ranging from 0 to 127 to identify musical instruments. (5)

generation loss   Loss of quality that occurs when you copy analog video from one tape to another. (8)

GIF   Graphic Interchange Format; a proprietary bitmap image format limited to a palette of 256 colors and widely used on the Web. (6)

GIF89a   A version of the GIF image file format specification that allows collection of still images into a single file to be played back in a timed sequence to provide animation. (14)

going gold   Finalizing and shipping a project. (15)

gold master   Final release of a product when there is nothing left to change or correct and it is ready to be reproduced. (18)

graphical user interface (GUI)   The collection of multimedia elements displayed on a computer screen for user interaction. (1)

graphics tablet   Input device that allows the user to move the cursor with a special pen on a pressure-sensitive surface. (9)

Green Book   Standard for CD-I format. (18)

handler   In a message-passing programming language, code that tells the application what to do when an event occurs. (11)

Hayes AT standard command set   Programming language used by modems. (9)

Hayes-compatible modem   Modem that uses the Hayes AT standard command set. (9)

HEIGHT   QuickTime embedded HTML command; one of the commands that specifies the size of a movie in web pages. (10)

helper applications   Applications that run files downloaded by a browser, but are not integrated into the browser itself. (13)

hexadecimal   Two-byte numbering system expressing 16 values from 0 to F; numbering system used for designating colors displayed by web browsers; rather than using values between 0 and 255, it uses a combination of two numbers or letters (1-9 and A-F). (6)

HIDDEN   QuickTime embedded HTML command; allows sound-only movies to play in the background without affecting the look of a web page. (10)

hierarchical   A multimedia structure in which users navigate along the branches of a tree structure that is shaped by the natural logic of the content. (16)

Hierarchical File System (HFS)   Macintosh file management system. (18)

High Definition Television (HDTV)   Digital TV with theater-quality pictures and CD-quality sound. (8)

hints (for Type 1 PostScript fonts)   Special instructions to help improve the resolution of text created with Type 1 PostScript fonts. (4)

hot spot   Clickable area on an image or screen. (16)

HREF   QuickTime embedded HTML command; indicates which URL to link to when the movie is clicked. (10)

HSPACE attribute   Deprecated in favor of styles in HTML 4; specifies white space on the left and right side of an image. (14)

HTML   Hypertext Markup Language; code used to create web pages. (1, 13)

HTML editors   Applications designed to make it easier to create HTML documents. (13)

HTML translator Programs built into word processing programs to allow you to export a document as an HTML document by automatically adding the necessary tags. (13)

hues Shades of color. (6)

hybrid format CD-ROM-playable on both Windows and Macintosh computers. (18)

hyperlink Connects the user to another part of the document or program or to a different program or web site. (16)

hypermedia A structure of linked elements through which users can navigate. (1)

hypertext Words keyed or indexed to associate them with other words and/or content. (4)

hypertext system Where keyed or indexed words allow rapid electronic retrieval of associated information. (4)

Hypertext Transfer Protocol (HTTP) Protocol providing rules for requesting, sending, and closing documents between two computers on the Internet. (12)

icon-based, event-driven authoring system A tool that provides a visual programming approach to organizing and presenting multimedia. (11)

icons Symbolic representations of objects and processes common to the graphical user interfaces of many computer operating systems. (4)

IGS Initial Graphics Exchange Standard; has largely replaced DXF as the format for exchanging architectural and engineering drawings among applications. (6)

image-editing applications Specialized and powerful tools for enhancing and retouching bitmapped images. (10)

<IMG> tag In HTML, places an image on a web page. (14)

independent contractor Worker who works for himself or herself and is hired for a particular task; unless provided otherwise in the contract for his or her services, ownership of any work created is retained by the independent contractor. (17)

information designer Designers who structure content, determine user pathways and feedback, and select presentation media. (3)

inks Special methods for computing color values, providing edge detection, and layering. (7)

installer Program that saves all necessary run-time files to the user's hard drive. (18)

instructional designer Designer who creates subject matter to be clear and properly presented for the intended audience. (3)

Integrated Drive Electronics (IDE) Hardware standard for connecting up to four input/output devices mounted inside a PC. Also called Advanced Technology Attachment (ATA). (9)

integrated multimedia The weaving part of the multimedia definition, where source documents such as montages, graphics, video cuts, and sounds merge into a final presentation. (1)

Integrated Services Digital Network (ISDN) Dedicated copper telephone line for data transfer at 128 Kbps. (9)

interactive multimedia The end user or viewer controls what and in what sequence the elements of multimedia are delivered. (1)

intercap An uppercase letter in the middle of a word. (4)

interface designer Designers who devise navigation pathways and content maps for user interaction. (3)

interlacing Process of building a single video frame from two fields to help prevent flicker; process of displaying a GIF image, line by line. (8)

Internet Worldwide network of linked computers. (12)

Internet Service Provider (ISP) Company or organization that provides connections to the Internet and other Internet-related services. (12)

inverse kinematics Linking objects, such as hands to arms, and defining their relationships and limits (for example, elbows cannot bend backwards). (7)

IP address Set of four numbers separated by periods defining the location of a device on the Internet. (12)

ISO 9660 Format for storing digital data in files on CDs. (18)

jaggies Ragged edges around the boundary of an object or text character. (4)

Java Object-oriented cross-platform programming language. (13)

Jaz   Brand of removable cartridge for storing data. (9)

JPEG   Joint Photographic Experts Group; designation for a bitmap image file format widely used on the Web for photo-realistic images; designated by the .jpg file extension. (6)

Karaoke CD   CD format allowing mix of video and audio. (18)

kerning   Controlling the space between individual character pairs in a line of text. (4)

keyboarding   Typing skills. (10)

keyframes   The first and last frame of an action. (7)

kinematics   Study of the movement and motion of structures that have joints. (7)

landscape   Wider-than-tall orientation for printing. (4)

lathe   Creating a 3-D object by rotating a profile of the shape around a defined axis. (6)

leading   Distance from one line of text to another. (4)

license   Legal document allowing use of copyrighted material. (17)

licensing agreements   Signed documents describing how copyrighted material may be used. (17)

linear   Starting at the beginning and running through to the end. (1)

linear multimedia   A multimedia structure in which users navigate sequentially, from one frame or bite of information to another. (16)

linear pulse code modulation   Sampling method used for consumer audio CDs. (5)

Lingo   Programming language of Adobe's Director. (11)

link   Navigational connection between conceptual elements. (4)

link anchor   In HTML, the clickable link to associated content. (4)

LINK attribute   Deprecated in favor of styles in HTML 4; specifies the color of unvisited links in a document. (14)

link end   Destination node linked to an anchor. (4)

liquid crystal display (LCD) panels   For displaying computer output; superseding CRT monitors. (9)

local area network (LAN)   Collection of computers connected together. (9)

localization   Translating or designing into a language or culture other than the one originally intended. (4)

look and feel   Combination of graphic screen elements and how they respond to user interaction. (2)

LOOP   QuickTime embedded HTML command; loops movie playback automatically. (10)

lossless   Compression method that does not lose data or quality. (14)

lossy   Compression method that loses image, audio, or video quality in favor of reducing file size. (14)

lowercase   Small letters. (4)

MACE compression   Method of compressing AIF sound files into AIFC files. (5)

magnetic card encoder   Device for programming the magnetic strip on a credit card or ID badge. (9)

magnetic card reader   Device for reading the magnetic strip on a credit card or ID badge. (9)

magneto-optical (MO) drive   Combines laser and magnetic techniques for read/write data storage. (9)

marking up   Specifying the look and presentation of a web page by adding tags to a document. (13)

media abstraction layer   Describes how a computer should access the media elements included in a QuickTime movie. (10)

Microsoft FrontPage   WYSIWYG editor for creating and editing web pages that also includes features for web site management through its FrontPage Extensions. (13)

Microsoft Internet Explorer   A web browser application. (13)

Microsoft PowerPoint   Presentation software. (13)

Microsoft Video for Windows   See Audio Video Interleaved.

Microsoft Windows   Brand of operating system that runs on a PC. (2)

MIDI   Musical Instrument Digital Interface; instruction-based system for creating music. (5)

MIDI keyboard   Keyboard used to generate MIDI instructions. (5)

milestone   Point in the development of a project that marks the end of a phase. (15)

MIME-type   Multipurpose Internet Mail Extensions; standard list of file name extensions used to identify the nature of data transmitted on the Internet. (12)

modal interface   Typically, where a viewer can click a Novice/Expert button and change the approach of the whole interface. (16)

modeling   Creating objects using a 3-D application. (6)

modifiers   Properties of objects that establish how objects should respond to messages. (11)

morphing   Smoothly blending two images so that one image seems to melt into the next. (6)

mother   A metal positive image of a glass master made of nickel. (18)

Movie Player   QuickTime tool for importing and combining different multimedia file formats. (10)

Moving Picture Experts Group (MPEG)   Organization tasked with developing standards for digital representation of moving pictures and associated audio and other data. (8)

MP3   File format for storing sound data that uses a compression scheme developed by the Motion Picture Experts Group (MPEG). (5)

MPC   Multimedia PC; early standards developed to integrate the multimedia capabilities of computers. (9)

MPEG   File format standards and compression specifications for video and audio data. (8)

MPEG-1   1992 specifications for the delivery of 1.2 Mbps of video and 250 Kbps of two-channel stereo audio using CD-ROM technology. (8)

MPEG-2   1994 specifications for 3 to 15 Mbps data rates for higher picture quality; the video compression standard required for digital television (DTV) and for making DVDs. (8)

MPEG-4   1998/9 specifications provide a content-based method for assimilating multimedia elements. (8)

MPEG-7   2002 specification, called the Multimedia Content Description Interface, integrates information about how the image, sound, or motion video elements are being used in a composition into a Description Scheme. (8)

MPEG-21   Audio/video specification providing an Intellectual Property Management and Protection (IPMP) system. (8)

multicast   Multiple users can simultaneously receive the same data streams without duplication of data across the Internet. (13)

multimedia   Any combination of text, art, sound, animation, and video delivered by computer or other electronic or digitally manipulated means. (1)

multimedia designer   Designers who examine the overall content of a project, create a structure, determine the design elements, and specify media. (3)

multimedia developers   People who weave multimedia into meaningful tapestries. (1)

multimedia elements   Text, graphics, animation, sound, and video. (1)

multimedia programmer   Programmers who integrate the elements of a project into a seamless whole using an authoring system or programming language. (3)

multimedia project   The software vehicle, messages, and the content presented on a computer or television screen; the process of making multimedia; its end result. (1)

multimedia skill set   Detailed knowledge of computers, text, graphic arts, sound, and video. (3)

multimedia title   A multimedia project shipped or sold to end users. (1, 18)

multiplexed   Combining audio, image, text, and video data into a single stream of data. (10)

navigation map   Structural representation of the entire content of a project. (16)

needs analysis   Early part of the planning process; determines the reason a project is being put forward. (15)

Netscape Navigator   A web browser application. (13)

network   A collection of computers connected together. (12)

node   Conceptual elements linked together in a hypertext system. (4)

NODE (command)   QuickTime-embedded HTML command; sets the initial node. (10)

nonlinear   Multimedia structure in which users navigate freely through the content of the project, unbound by predetermined routes. (1, 16)

nonlinear editing (NLE)   Allows assembly of a final video from video, image, and audio elements stored in various files on a computer. (8)

normalization   Adjusts the level of a number of tracks to bring them all to about the same sound level. (5)

NTSC   National Television Standards Committee; a television signal format used in the United States, Japan, and many other countries. (8)

<OBJECT> tag   This tag defines an embedded object such as a multimedia element. (14)

objects   A basic construction element of many multimedia authoring systems. (6, 11)

office suite   Software that typically includes spreadsheet, database, e-mail, web browser, and presentation applications. (10)

OpenDML   File format to make AVI more useful for the professional market. (10)

OpenType   Standard-driven method for displaying typefaces on the Web. (14)

operating system (OS)   The program code that runs a computer and its peripherals, as well as its user interface. (2)

optical character recognition (OCR)   Scanning printed text and converting that image to a word processing computer file. (9)

optical read-only memory (OROM)   A holographic storage medium with no moving parts. (9)

Orange Book   Standard for WORM (write-once, read-only) CD-ROMs. (18)

overscan   Broadcast of an image larger than will fit on a standard TV screen so that the "edge" of the image seen by a viewer is always bounded by the TV's physical frame, or bezel. (8)

page-based authoring system   Elements are organized as a stack of cards or pages of a book. (11)

painting software   Programs for producing crafted bitmap images. (10)

PAL   Phase Alternate Line; an analog broadcast video standard used in Europe, China, and other countries. (8)

palettes   Mathematical tables that define the color of a pixel displayed on a screen. (6)

PAN   QuickTime-embedded HTML command; sets the initial pan angle. (10)

path animation   Motion created by moving an object along a determined path. (7)

payment schedules   Contract elements that define when a client must make payments. (15)

PCX   One of the original bitmap image file formats; used in MS-DOS applications. (6)

pels   Picture elements or, more commonly, pixels; tiny dots that make up an image on a computer monitor. (6)

peripherals   Hardware attached to a computer, for example, printers, modems, and mice. (2)

persistence of vision   The chemical mapping that remains on the eye's retina for a brief time after viewing. (7)

phi   The human mind's need to conceptually complete a perceived action. (7)

PhotoCD   Kodak's format for storing high-resolution images on CD-ROMs. (18)

PICT   Image file format for Macintosh. (6)

Picture Viewer   Application in QuickTime Pro used for viewing and converting images among many standard image file formats. (10)

pixels   Picture elements; tiny dots that make up an image on a computer monitor. (4)

plain old telephone service (POTS)   Typical telephone installation at home or in a small business. (9)

planning   The first stage of building a multimedia project. (2)

platform   Hardware and operating system used to prepare or deliver multimedia. (1)

platform independent   Not limited to a single computer or operating system. (2)

player   Add-in to extend the capabilities of a web browser, allowing users to play programs or files downloaded from the Web that are not directly supported by the browser. (14)

plug-in   Add-in to extend the capabilities of a web browser, allowing users to view and interact with documents and images not directly supported by the browser. (13)

PNG   Portable Network Graphic; bitmap image file format created as a free alternative to the GIF format. (14)

point   Description of the vertical size of a text font, about 1/72nd of an inch. (4)

Point-to-Point Protocol (PPP)   Software protocol for dialing an Internet connection. (12)

Points of Presence (POP)   Connection point to the Internet provided by an ISP. (12)

portrait   Taller-than-wide orientation for printing. (4)

Post Office Protocol (POP)   Protocol for retrieving e-mail from a mail server. (12)

prerequisites   Tasks that must happen before other tasks. (15)

pressed   Making CDs using the family process. (18)

primitives   Geometric shapes such as blocks, cylinders, spheres, and cones used to create objects in 3-D applications. (6)

producer   A maker of multimedia; person with the overall responsibility for the production of a multimedia project. (3)

producing   Performing each of the planned tasks of a design to create a finished multimedia project. (2)

production   The stage in the development of a multimedia project when the plans are implemented and the project is created. (16)

production value   Value of the assets used in producing a project; the degree to which a media asset adds value and interest to a project. (17)

Program Evaluation Review Technique (PERT) chart   Graphic representation of task relationships, showing prerequisites—the tasks that must be completed before others can commence. (15)

Programmable ROM   EPROM; a microchip that allows changes to be made and to be retained when power is lost. (9)

progressive-scan   Drawing the lines of an entire video frame in a single pass on a CRT, without interlacing; method of storing and downloading a JPEG image so it displays more of the image as data becomes available. (8)

project manager   Person who organizes the production of multimedia, and a person responsible for the overall development and implementation of a project as well as for day-to-day operations. (3)

proof-of-concept   A prototype or working test of creative and engineering ideas for a project. (2)

properties   Characteristics of objects and elements such as shape, color, texture, shading, and location; characteristics that define the behavior of objects. (6, 11)

prototype   A working test of creative and engineering ideas. (2)

public domain   Material without copyright restrictions. (17)

quantization   Rounding off the value of each sound sample to the nearest integer. (5)

quantum theory   An explanation of how light is produced by atoms, developed by physicist Max Planck. (6)

QuickTimemovie (.mov)   A standard file format for displaying digitized motion video and other multimedia elements without special hardware. (5)

QuickTime VR (QTVR)   A method for viewing a single surrounding image as if you were inside the picture and able to look up or down, turn, or zoom in on features. (6)

random access memory (RAM)   Main memory chips in a computer; they lose their memory when power is lost. (9)

rate card   A list of licensing fees covering the different uses of media assets, different formats, and their use in different markets. (17)

read-only memory (ROM)   Chips that are made for a specific purpose; memory is never lost. (9)

ReadMeFirst   A plain-text file containing a description of changes or bugs reported since the documentation was printed. (18)

README.TXT   A plain-text file containing a description of changes or bugs reported since the documentation was printed. (18)

real estate   Viewing area on a display screen. (6)

Red Book   International standard, ISO 10149, for digitally encoding audio data on consumer music CDs. (5)

Redundant Array of Independent Disks (RAID)   A hard disk system that supports high-speed data transfer rates. (8)

release candidate   Test release of a product with a version number as the developers continue to refine the product and approach a final version. (18)

release form   Legal document transferring the rights to use images, sounds, or other copyrighted multimedia content to the producer of the project. (17)

rendering   Applying intricate algorithms and special effects to 3-D objects to create a final view. (6)

Request for Proposal (RFP)   Document that defines a client's need, requesting a proposed solution. (15)

resampling   Examining an existing digital recording and reducing the number of samples in it. See downsampling. (5)

RGB   Red, green, and blue; combined in the additive color method to create specific colors. (6)

RIFF   Resource Interchange File Format for multimedia development in Windows; designed to contain many types of files. (6)

royalty   Continuing payment for use of content or other materials. (17)

run-time version   A version of a project that allows it to play back without requiring the full authoring software and all its tools and editors. (11)

safe title   An area of a TV screen where title content will not be cut off due to overscan. (8)

sample   Digital information about a sound taken every nth fraction of a second. (5)

sample size   Number of binary digits used to represent the value of a sample. (5)

sampling rate   Frequency at which samples of a sound are taken. (5)

sans serif   A type style characterized by letters without a decoration at the end of the letter stroke. (4)

SCALE   QuickTime embedded HTML command; scales the movie display automatically. (10)

scene   Collection of objects arranged in a 3-D layout. (6)

scope of work   All the tasks and efforts required of a project. (15)

score   Sequencer for displaying, animating, and playing cast members in Director. (11)

Screen Actors Guild (SAG)   Association of professional actors and voice-over talent. (17)

screen capture   Snapshot of all or part of a screen, saved as a bitmap image. (6)

scripting   Outlining of the content of a project using words. (1)

scripting language   Programming language using natural-sounding phrases. (11)

scripts   Used by Unicode to describe the shared symbols of a language unified into a collection of symbols. (4)

scriptwriter   Person who creates character, action, and point of view through dialog and narration. (3)

SCSI-2 and SCSI-3   Data transfer specifications of SCSI. (9)

SDII   File format for storing sound data. (5)

SECAM   Sequential Color and Memory; an analog television signal format used in France, Russia, and a few other countries. (8)

sector   Storage block on a CD, 1/75 second in length, that contains 2,352 bytes of data. (18)

self-extracting archive   A program file that stores other compressed files that can be run to decompress and reconstitute the original files. (18)

sequencer software   Programs used to record and edit MIDI scores. (5)

serif   A type style characterized by letters with a decoration at the end of the letter stroke. (4)

server   Software that serves files and documents to a network; popular use also applies the term to the computer upon which the server software is running. (13)

session   One of several separate images on a CD-R disc, each recorded at different times. (18)

shading   Calculation by a 3-D program of the effect of light on an object within the scene, resulting in lit and shaded areas on the surface of objects. (6)

Shockwave   Tool from Adobe for launching and playing Director and Flash projects. (11)

simple branching   Simple navigation to another section of a multimedia project (via an activity such as a keypress, mouse click, or expiration of a timer). (11)

site map   Representation of the entire content of a web site, usually clickable. (16)

SIZE attribute   Deprecated in favor of styles in HTML 4; defines the size of text in the font element. (14)

Small Computer System Interface (SCSI)   System for adding peripheral devices to a computer. (9)

SND format   File format for storing sound data. (5)

software robots   Programs that visit millions of web pages and index the content of entire web sites. (4)

sons   Metal molds for mass-producing CDs. (18)

Sorenson   Real-time video compression codec available in both AVI and QuickTime that is optimized for CD-ROM. (8)

sound library   Collection of recorded sounds available for a project. (17)

sound synthesizer   Hardware that creates a sound from a mathematical representation. (5)

sprites   Graphic objects in a multimedia authoring system, often animated. (10)

stage   The visible screen in a Director project. (11)

stampers   Metal molds for mass-producing CDs. (18)

stand-alone   Version of a project that allows it to play back without requiring the full authoring software and all its tools and editors. (11)

still photo library   Collection of photos available for a project. (17)

stock footage   Video footage purchased or licensed for use from a library of video resources. (17)

storyboarding   Creating drawings or sketches to visualize the content of a project. (1)

storyboards   Graphic and text outlines that describe each part of a project in exact detail. (16)

streaming   A method of delivery of sound and video files over the Web; the computer begins playing the file as it continues to receive the rest of it, keeping ahead so playback does not pause or break up. (5)

streaming latency   The wait period before a streaming sound or video file begins to play. (5)

Structured Query Language (SQL)   Method for structuring and accessing data from a database. (12)

style   An attribute of a text character, such as boldface and italic. (4)

subject matter expert   Person with particular knowledge about the content of a project. (3)

subtractive color   Color created by combining colored media such as paints or ink that absorb (or subtract) some parts of the color spectrum of light and reflect the others back to the eye. (6)

surface structure   The structures actually realized by a user while navigating the project's content. (16)

Syquest   Brand of removable storage media. (9)

<TABLE> tag   This tag defines a table in HTML. (14)

tags   Codes that specify the visual display of web page content; used to mark up a document in HTML. (4, 13)

talent agency   Company that represents and solicits work for actors, voice-over artists, and other talent. (17)

TARGET   QuickTime embedded HTML command; provides a frame target for the URL specified in an HREF tag. (10)

TCP/IP   Transmission Control Protocol/Internet Protocol; rules for sending data to and receiving data from the Internet. (9, 12)

team building   Creating a group of talents for collaboration; activities that help a group and its members function at optimum levels of performance. (3)

testing   Stage in a multimedia project when it is determined whether or not a project meets its objectives, works properly on the intended delivery platform, and meets the needs of the client. (2)

TEXT attribute   In the <BODY> tag, used to control the default color of all the normal text in a document. (14)

texture   Color, patterns, and bitmap images applied to the surface of an object to make the object more realistic. (6)

3-D animation   Animation occurring in three axes, x, y, and z. (7)

3-D modeling software   Tools for creating 3-D images and animations. (10)

TIFF   Tagged Interchange File Format; a universal bitmapped image format. (6)

TILT   QuickTime embedded HTML command; sets the initial tilt angle. (10)

time stretching   Altering the length (in time) of a sound file without changing its pitch. (5)

time-based authoring system   A tool in which multimedia elements and events are organized along a timeline. (11)

token language   A shorthand description of speech. (13)

top-level domain (TLD)   Last dot-separated identity in a domain name, for example, .com, .edu. (12)

touchscreen   Touch-sensitive display. (9)

trackball   Pointing device used by rolling one or more fingers across the top of a ball to move the cursor. (9)

tracking   Adjusting the spacing among characters in a line of text. (4)

tracks   Areas normally allocated for storing a single song in the Red Book format. (18)

translate   Move from one location to another location. (7)

transparency   In the GIF89a specification, allows for a selected color to be transparent. (14)

TrueDoc   Standard-driven method for displaying typefaces on the Web. (14)

TrueType   An outline font methodology developed jointly by Apple and Microsoft. (4)

tweening   Drawing the series of frames in between the first and last frames in an action. (7)

2-D animation   Animation occurring on the flat Cartesian x and y axes. (7)

typeface   A family of graphic characters that usually includes many type sizes and styles. (4)

uLaw   Low-resolution file format for storing sound data based upon the international telephone format. (5)

Ultimatte   Process of shooting video against a blue or green background, making that color transparent, and replacing it with other footage. (8)

Ultra SCSI   A data transfer specification of SCSI. (9)

Unicode   Worldwide effort to include the characters from all known languages and alphabets in a standards-based methodology for display and printing. (4)

Uniform Resource Locator (URL)   Address of a document or file on the Internet. (12)

Universal Product Code (UPC)   International barcoding system used in tracking and selling consumer goods. (9)

unlimited use   Grant to use material, such as content for a project, everywhere, anytime, and in any medium. (17)

uppercase   Capital letters. (4)

USEMAP attribute   In an <IMG> tag, tells what map tag to use to specify hot spots in an image. (14)

user interface   Blend of a project's graphic elements and its navigation system. (16)

V.90   Protocols for transfer of data by modem. (9)

vector   A drawn line that is described by the location of its two endpoints. (6)

vector-drawn graphic   An image created from vector objects. (6)

version control   Making sure that old files are archived and new versions are properly tracked. (16)

very high level language (VHLL)   Programming facility offered by multimedia authoring systems to provide precise control of activities. (11)

VGA   Monitor resolution of 8 bits of color information per pixel. (6)

Video CD   CD format allowing mix of video and audio. (18)

video specialist   Person who shoots quality video, transfers video footage to a computer, and edits the footage into a usable product. (3)

video streams   A video file that streams into a computer in the background, keeping ahead of what has already been played so the playback doesn't pause or break up. (13)

visual programming   Authoring environment that uses drag-and-drop icons or objects. (11)

VLINK attribute   Deprecated in favor of styles in HTML 4; specifies the color of visited links in a document. (14)

voice recognition systems   Used with a microphone to recognize spoken words as input to a computer. (9)

VOLUME   QuickTime embedded HTML command; sets the default playback volume. (10)

VSPACE attribute   Deprecated in favor of styles in HTML 4; specifies white space above and below an image. (14)

wave format (WAV)   File format for storing sound data, native to the Windows operating system. (5)

Web Embedding Font Tool (WEFT)   Microsoft tool for font embedding. (14)

web site   A collection of pages and other multimedia assets on the Internet that are viewable/playable with a browser. (1)

White Book   Standard for Video CD (Karaoke CD). (18)

white space   Roomy blank areas in a screen or page layout. (4)

wide area networks (WANs)   Networks connecting groups of local networks. (9)

Wide SCSI   A 16 MBps transfer rate within the SCSI-2 specification. (9)

WIDTH   QuickTime embedded command in HTML; one of the commands that specifies the size of the movie on a web page. (10)

word processor   Tool for creating and editing formatted text documents. (10)

Write-Once, Read-Only (WORM)   A CD-ROM that cannot be overwritten or written to later, once writing has stopped. (18)

WYSIWYG   What You See Is What You Get. (4)

X-height   Height of the lowercase letter x. (4)

Yellow Book   Standard for CD-ROM format. (18)

Z dimension   Depth; the third axis of a 3-D coordinate system. (6)

Zip   Brand of removable storage media. (9)

Index

Numbers & Symbols

2-D animation, 172–173
3-D animation, 172–173
3-D modeling, 266–268
3-D rendering/drawing, 146–151
3-D worlds, 339–340
μLaw, 115

A

acoustics, 96–97
Acrobat Connect authoring tool, 297–298
Acrobat Reader, 337
activation, 485
additive color, 154
addresses, 311, 315
Advanced Research Projects Agency (ARPA), 309
Advanced Technology Attachment (ATA), 235–236
Advanced Television Systems Committee (ATSC) DTV, 199–201, 211
AFTRA (American Federation of Television and Radio Artists), 457
agreements, content use, 451–457
AIF format, 99, 112
AIFC format, 112
AIFF format, 112, 364
aLAW, 115
ALIGN attribute, 352
ALINK attribute, 360
alpha development, 385
alpha testing, 469–470
alphabets, text, 72–75
American Federation of Television and Radio Artists (AFTRA), 457
American National Standards Institute (ANSI), 74
amplifiers, 248
analog display standards, 198–201
analog tape care, 205
analog video format, 209–210
anchors, 57, 89
animated GIF, 180–183
animation, 170–191
    3-D drawing/rendering, 146–151
    3-D tools, 270–277
    bouncing ball, 180–183
    cel, 174
    computer, 172–173
    computer programs, 175–178
    editing software, 266–268
    file formats, 178–179
    motion, 170–171
    principles, 171–172
    rolling ball, 179–180
    scenes, 183–185
    summary, quiz, and projects, 186–191

text, 68
    Web design, 366–367
    Web tools, 338
ANSI (American National Standards Institute), 74
anti-aliased text, 56
Apple Macintosh. *See* Macintosh
APPLET tag, 348
applets, 331
approval cycles, 432
architecture, QuickTime, 271
archives, file, 474–475
ARPA (Advanced Research Projects Agency), 309
ARPANET, 309
art images. *See* images
ASCII (American Standard Code for Information Interchange), 73–74
assembly, editing sound, 104
assets, 23
associative thought, hypertext and, 85
ATA (Advanced Technology Attachment), 235–236
ATSC (Advanced Television Systems Committee) DTV, 199–201, 211
attributes, font, 51
AU format, web sound, 115, 364–365
audience, target, 400
audio. *See* sound
audio devices, 247–248
audio interfaces, 424–425
audio resolution, 101–102
audio specialists, 37–38
Audio Video Interleaved (AVI) files. *See* AVI (Audio Video Interleaved) files
auditions, 458
authoring tools, 284–307
    card- and page-based, 293–295
    cross-platform notes, 301
    defined, 2
    features, 290–293
    icon- and object-based, 295–297
    instant multimedia, 284–286
    organization, 287
    summary, quiz, and projects, 302–307
    time-based, 297–301
    types of, 287–289
AUTOPLAY command, 273
    autotracing, 146
AVI (Audio Video Interleaved) files, 117, 270, 274

B

backgrounds, 294, 360–362
ball, 179–180, 180–183
bandwidth, 2, 316–318
beta development, 385
beta testing, 470

Betacam format, 210
BGCOLOR, 273, 351
BGSOUND tag, 364
bid proposals, 394–400
billing rates, 391–393
binary compatible files, 20
binary, defined, 134
bit, defined, 134
bitdepth, 99
bitmaps. *See also* images
    capturing/editing images, 141–143
    clip art, 136–139
    converting between drawn images and, 145–146
    defined, 134
    overview, 134–136
    scanning images, 143–144
    software, 139–141
    vs. vector-drawn objects, 145
blue screens, 217
BMP files, 162
BODY tag, 360
BORDER attribute, 363
bouncing ball, 180–183
branching, simple/conditional, 291
bronze, 470
browsers, 2, 332–333
budget, 400
buffer, sound, 115
burners, CD-R, CD-ROM, DVD, 3, 477–478
business, multimedia in, 5–6
busy screens, 424
buttons
    choosing fonts, 57
    clickable, 362–363
    design, 414–417
    text in, 59–63

C

cable modems, 255
CACHE command, 273
calibration, digital display, 203
capturing images, 141–143
card-based authoring tools, 288, 293–295
Cartesian coordinates, 144–145
cascading style sheet (CSS) rules, 57, 66
case sensitivity, 53
cases, text, 53–54
Cast, 299
casting calls, 458
cat-5 cable, 231
cathode-ray tube (CRT) projectors, 250–251
CCD (charge-coupled device), 194–195
CD (compact disc), 119–120, 242, 476–483
CD-I, 478–481
CD-quality, 99
CD-R, 477–478